D1477211

Elements of
Computer Networking

An Integrated Approach

By

Narasimha Karumanchi

Dr. A. Damodaram

Dr. M. Sreenivasa Rao

☼ CONCEPTS   ☼ PROBLEMS   ☼ INTERVIEW QUESTIONS

Acknowledgements

Mother and *father*, it is impossible to thank you adequately for everything you have done, from loving me unconditionally to raising me in a stable household, where you persistent efforts traditional values and taught your children to celebrate and embrace life. I could not have asked for better parents or role-models. You showed me that anything is possible with faith, hard work and determination.

This book would not have been possible without the help of many people. I would like to thank them for their efforts in improving the end result. Before we do so, however, I should mention that I have done my best to correct the mistakes that the reviewers have pointed out and to accurately describe the protocols and mechanisms. I alone am responsible for any remaining errors.

First and foremost, I would like to express my gratitude to many people who saw me through this book, to all those who provided support, talked things over, read, wrote, offered comments, allowed me to quote their remarks and assisted in the editing, proofreading and design. In particular, I would like to thank the following individuals.

- *Navin Kumar Jaiswal*, Senior Consultant, Juniper Networks Pvt. Ltd.
- *A.Vamshi Krishna*, IIT Kanpur, Mentor Graphics Pvt. Ltd.
- *Kiran Kumar Pasupuleti*, IISc, Bangalore
- *Kota Veeraiah*, Head Master, Obulasuni Palle, Z. P. H. School
- *Potla Venkateswarlu*, Teacher, Kambhampadu, Z. P. H. School
- *Muralidhar*, Teacher, Durgi
- *Chaganti Siva Rama Krishna Prasad*, Founder, StockMonks Pvt. Ltd.
- *Naveen Valsakumar*, Co-Founder, NotionPress Pvt. Ltd.
- *Ramanaiah*, Lecturer, Nagarjuna Institute of Technology and Sciences, MLG
- *Hirak Chatterjee*, Yahoo Pvt. Ltd.
- *Swapnil Joshi*, Development Manager, IBM Software Labs
- *Suresh Kodati*, Development Manager, IBM Software Labs
- *Balakrishna Veerala, M-Tech., Factuly, GATE* Subjects.
- *Kondrakunta Murali Krishna,* B-Tech., Technical Lead, HCL

-Narasimha Karumanchi
M. Tech, *IIT Bombay*
Founder, *CareerMonk.com*

Other Titles by Narasimha Karumanchi

- Data Structures and Algorithms Made Easy
- Data Structures and Algorithms for GATE
- Data Structures and Algorithms Made Easy in Java
- Coding Interview Questions
- Peeling Design Patterns
- IT Interview Questions

Preface

Dear Reader,

Please Hold on! We know many people do not read the preface. But we would strongly recommend that you go through the preface of this book at least.

There are hundreds of books on computer networking already flooding the market. The reader may naturally wonder what the need of writing another book on computer networking is!

This book assumes you have basic knowledge about computer science. Main objective of the book is *not* to provide you the *catalog* of *computer networking protocols* and *their interview* questions. Before writing the book, we set ourselves the following *goals*:

- The book be written in *such a way* that readers without any background in computer networking should be able to understand it *easily* and *completely*.
- The book should present the concepts of *computer networking protocols* in *simple* and straightforward manner with a *clear − cut* explanation.
- The book should provide enough *realtime* examples so that readers get better understanding of the *computer networking* and also useful for the interviews. We mean, the book should cover *computer networking* interview questions.

Please remember, the books which are available in the market are lacking one or many of these goals. Based on my teaching and industrial experience, we thought of writing this book aiming at achieving these goals in a simple way. A 3-stage formula is used in writing this book, i.e.

Concepts + Problems + Interview Questions

We used very simple language such that a school going student can also understand the concepts easily. Once the concept is discussed, it is then interlaced into problems. The solutions of each and every problem are well explained.

Finally, interview questions with answers on every concept are covered. All the interview questions in this book are collected from various interviews conducted by top software development companies.

This book talks about networks in everyday terms. The language is friendly; you don't need a graduate education to go through it.

As a job seeker if you read complete book with good understanding, we are sure you will challenge the interviewers and that is the objective of this book.

This book is very much useful for the students of engineering degree and masters during their academic course. All the chapters of this book contain theory and their related problems. If you read as a student preparing for competition exams (e.g. GATE), content of this book covers all the required topics in full details.

It is *recommended* that, at least *one complete* reading of this book is required to get full understanding of all the topics. In the *subsequent* readings, you can directly go to any chapter and refer. Even though, enough readings were given for correcting the errors, due to human tendency there could be some minor typos in the book.

If any such typos found, they will be updated at *CareerMonk.com*. We request you to constantly monitor this site for any corrections, new problems and solutions. Also, please provide your valuable suggestions at: *Info@CareerMonk.com*.

Wish you all the best. We are sure that you will find this book useful.

Narasimha Karumanchi
M. Tech, *IIT Bombay*
Founder, *CareerMonk.com*

Dr. A. *Damodaram*
M.Tech. (C.S.E.), Ph.D. (C.S.E)
Director, School of IT

Dr. M. *Sreenivasa Rao*
Dean MSIT Programme,
M.Tech. (C.S.E.), Ph.D. (C.S.E)
Director, School of IT

Table of Contents

Organization of Chapters

1.1 Why Computer Networks are needed?

Computer networking is one of the most exciting and important technical fields of our time. Information and communication are two of the most important strategic issues for the success of every enterprise.

Necessity is the mother of invention, and whenever we really need something, humans will find a way to get it. Let us imagine we do not have computer networking in our lives now. People can communicate only with each other through phone (or fax). For example, sharing a printer between many computers will be difficult as printer cable must be attached to the computer which requires printing. Removable media such as diskettes or thumb drives must be used in order to share files or to transfer files from one machine to another machine.

Just imagine you need to transfer a file to one thousand computers. To *overcome* these problems, computer networks are *necessary*. Computer networks allow the user to access *remote programs* and *remote databases* either of the same organization or from other enterprises or public sources. Computer networks provide faster communication than other facilities. Many applications or software's are also developed for enhancing communication. Some examples are Email, Instance Messages, and internet phone.

1.2 What Is this Book About?

A unique feature of this book that is missing in most of the available books on computer networking is to offer a balance between theoretical, practical concepts, problems and interview questions.

Concepts + Problems + Interview Questions

This text provides academic researchers, graduate students in computer science, computer engineering, and electrical engineering, as well as practitioners in industry and research engineers with an understanding of the specific design challenges and solutions for computer networks.

- Covers architecture and communications protocols in detail with practical implementation examples and case studies.

- Provides an understanding of mutual relationships and dependencies between different protocols and architectural decisions.
- Offers an in-depth investigation of relevant protocol mechanisms.

The book offers a large number of questions to practice each exam objective and will help you assess your knowledge before you write the real exam. The detailed answers to every question will help reinforce your knowledge about different issues involving the design and configuration of networks.

1.3 Should I Take this Book?

This book is for a first course on computer networking. Although this book is more precise and analytical than many other introductory computer networking text books, it rarely uses any mathematical concepts that are not taught in high school.

I have made an effort to avoid using any advanced calculus, probability, or stochastic process concepts. The book is therefore appropriate for undergraduate courses, *GATE* preparation and for first-year graduate courses.

This book is for students who *want* to learn networking concepts and also for those who are preparing for competitive exams like GATE.

1.4 How to Use this book?

I would like to recommend at least two readings of this book. Upon first reading, you will start to *recognize protocols* being used in different networking enviroments.

In the second reading, you'll begin to see how these protocols can help you in your own network designs, and may also start to see new protocols not listed in the book.

One of the most valuable contributions of this book is that it is designed not merely to help you identify protocols, but to give you a sense of which protocols are appropriate in which contexts.

In the subsequent readings, you can directly go to any chapter and refer.

1.5 Organization of Chapters

The *second* chapter of this text book presents an overview of computer networking. This chapter introduces many key concepts and terminology and sets the stage for the rest of the book.

After completion of *second* chapter, I recommend reading remaining chapters in sequence. Each of these chapters leverages material from the preceding chapters. There are no major inter-dependencies among the chapters, so they can be read in any order.

The chapters are arranged in the following way:

3. *OSI and TCP/IP Models*: This chapter gives an introduction and necessary concepts of Open Systems Interconnection (OSI) and Transmission Control Protocol/Internet Protocol (TCP/IP) models which are used in all the remaining chapters. There are seven layers in the OSI Model, and four in the TCP/IP model. This is because TCP/IP assumes that applications will take care of everything beyond the Transport layer. It also compares both these models.
4. *Netwokring Devices*: This chapter provides detailed overview of networking devices such as hubs, bridges, switches, routers, gateways, firewalls etc...

Hubs, switches, routers, and access points are *used* to connect computers together on a network, but each of them has different capabilities. Each of these devices operates at different layers in OSI and TCP/IP models.

5. *LAN Technologies*: Local Area Network (LAN) in a data communications network is a technology used for connecting terminals, computers and printers within a building or other geographically limited areas. This chapter discusses medium access control techniques, random access techniques, static channelization techniques, LocalTalk, Ethernet, Token Ring and ends with error detection techniques at data link layer.

6. *ARP and RARP*: This chapter focuses on protocols which does the translation of IP addresses to MAC addresses and vice versa. ARP translates IP addresses into hardware addresses (MAC) and RARP translates machines addresses (MAC) into IP addresses.

7. *IP Addressing*: This chapter discusses about basics of IPv4 and IPv6 addressing. It provides *in-depth* analysis of classes of IP addressing, subnet masks, subnetting, supernetting, Classless Inter-Domain Routing [CIDR], Variable Length Subnet Mask [VLSM], and message formats of both IPv4 and IPv6.

8. *IP Routing*: This chapter presents different network routing protocols. It starts with overview of network routing and their classification. The protocols which were discussed in this chapter includes Flooding Routing Algorithm, Routing Information Protocol, Open Shortest Path First [OSPF], and Border Gateway Protocol.

9. *TCP and UDP*: In the earlier chapters, we discuss about the delivery of data in the following two ways:

    1. *Node-to-node delivery*: At the *data-link* level, delivery of frames take place between two nodes connected by a point-to-point link or a LAN, by using the data-link layers address, say MAC address.

    2. *Host-to-host delivery*: At the *network* level, delivery of datagrams can take place between two hosts by using IP address.

From user's point of view, the TCP/IP-based Internet can be considered as a set of application programs that use the Internet to carry out useful communication tasks. Most popular internet applications include Electronic mail (E-mail), File transfer, and Remote login. IP routing allows transfer of IP datagrams among a number of stations or hosts, where the datagram is routed through the Internet based on the IP address of the destination. But, in this case, several *application programs* (*processes*) running simultaneously on a source host has to communicate with the corresponding processes running on a remote destination host through the Internet. This requires an additional mechanism called *process-to-process* delivery, which is implemented with the help of a *transport-level* protocol.

The transport level protocol will require an additional address, called *port* number, to select a particular process among multiple processes running on the destination host. So, there is a requirement of the following third type of delivery system.

    3. Process-to-process delivery: At the transport level, communication can take place between processes or application programs by using port addresses

The additional mechanism needed to facilitate multiple application programs in different stations to communicate with each other simultaneously can be provided by a transport level protocol such as UDP or TCP, which is the topic of this chapter.

10. *TCP Error Control*: TCP is a reliable transport layer protocol. It allows the processes to deliver a stream of data (bytes) in order, without error, and without any part lost or duplicated. It provides mechanisms for detecting errors in:

- Duplicate segments
- Out-of-Order segments
- Lost or Missing segments
- Corrupted segments

Also, TCP provides a mechanism for error correction. In TCP, error detection and correction in TCP is achieved by:

1. Checksum
2. Acknowledgement
3. Timeout and retransmission

In this chapter, we discuss several error control algorithms such as Stop and Wait ARQ, Go Back N ARQ, Selective Reject ARQ etc...

11. *TCP Flow Control*: TCP provides a way for the receiver to control the amount of data sent by the sender. Nodes that send and receive TCP data segments can operate at different data rates because of differences in CPU and network bandwidth. As a result, it is possible for sender to send data at a faster rate than the receiver can handle.

If the receiver is slower than the sender, bytes will have to be dropped from the receiver's sliding window buffer. TCP deals with this issue using what is known as *flow control*.

As an example, consider a conversation with your friend. One of you listens while the other speaks. You might nod your head as you listen or you might interrupting the flow with a "Whoa, slow down, you are talking too fast!" This is actually flow control. Some of us are better at it than others, but we all do it to some degree. You nod to indicate you understood and are ready for the next statement of information or you tell your friend when they are going too fast. That's *flow* control.

This chapter focuses on such controlling algorithms for computer networks (*sliding window* mechanism, *segmentation* and *Nagling*).

12. *TCP Congestion Control*: In today's world, the *Transmission Control Protocol* (TCP) carries huge Internet traffic, so performance of the Internet depends to a great extent on how well TCP works. TCP provides a reliable transport service between two processes running on source and destination nodes.

In this chapter, we discuss another important component of TCP; *congestion control* mechanism. The important strategy of TCP is to send packets into the network and then to react to *observable events* that occur. TCP congestion control was introduced into the Internet in the late 1980s by *Van Jacobson*; roughly eight years after the TCP/IP protocol stack had become operational.

To address these issues, multiple mechanisms were implemented in TCP to govern the rate with which the data can be sent in both directions (*client to server* and *server to client*): *flow control*, *congestion control*, and *congestion avoidance*. These are the subject of this chapter.

13. *Session Layer*: The session layer resides above the transport layer, and provides value added services to the underlying transport layer services. The session layer (along with the presentation layer) adds services to the transport layer that are likely to be of use to applications, so that each application doesn't have to provide its own implementation. Layer 5 of the OSI reference model is

session layer. It does not add many communications features/functionality, and is thus termed a very thin layer. On many systems, the Layer 5 features are disabled, but you should nonetheless know what failures can be prevented by a session layer.

The session layer provides the following services:

    I.   Dialog management
    II.   Synchronization
    III.   Activity management
    IV.   Exception handling

This chapter ends with discussion on major session layer protocols such as AppleTalk Data Stream Protocol (ADSP), AppleTalk Session Protocol (ASP), Network Basic Input Output (NetBIOS), Password Authentication Protocol (PAP), Remote Procedure Call Protocol (RPC), and Secure Shell (SSH) Protocol

14. *Presentation Layer Protocols*: The presentation layer is the sixth layer of the OSI model. It responds to service requests from the application layer and issues service request to the session layer. The presentation layer performs certain functions that are requested sufficiently often to finding a general solution for users, rather than letting each user solve the problems. In particular, unlike all the lower layers, which are just interested in moving bits reliably from here to there, the presentation layer is concerned with the syntax and semantics of the information transmitted.

In this chapter we discuss about encryption and decryption concepts. Also, we look at an example encryption algorithm: *Huffman* coding algorithm.

15. *Network Security*: Network security refers to a set of activities and policies used by a network administrator to prevent and monitor unauthorized access of a computer network. These activities include protecting the usability, reliability, integrity, and safety of computer network and data.

This chapter starts with a history of network security instances followed by glossary of security terms. Then, we discuss about network security components such as:

- Authentication
- Authorization
- Data Integrity
- Confidentiality
- Availability
- Non-Repudiation

It also focuses on different types of network security attacks. This followed with discussion on cipher algorithms, in detailed analysis of encryption and decryption algorithms, message integrity, digital signatures, and Kerberos authentication system.

16. *Application Layer Protocols*: The application layer of the OSI model provides the first step of getting data onto the network. Application software is the software programs used by people to communicate over the network. Examples of application software are HTTP, FTP, email, and others. Although the TCP/IP protocol suite was developed prior to the definition of the OSI model, the functionality of the TCP/IP application layer protocols fits into the framework of the top three layers of the OSI model: application, presentation, and session.

In the OSI and TCP/IP models, information is passed from one layer to the next, starting at the application layer on the transmitting host and proceeding down the hierarchy to the physical layer, then passing over the communications channel (physical link) to the destination host, where the information proceeds back up the hierarchy, ending at the application layer. The application layer is built on the transport layer and provides network services to user applications. It provides the interface between the applications we use to communicate and the underlying network over which our messages are transmitted. Application layer protocols are used to exchange data between programs running on the source and destination hosts.

Application	Application Layer protocol	Underlying Transport protocol
E-Mail	SMTP	TCP
Remote terminal access	Telnet	TCP
Web	HTTP	TCP
File transfer	FTP	TCP
Streaming multimedia	HTTP (example: YouTube)	TCP or UDP
Internet telephony	RTP (example: Skype)	Typically UDP
Internet chat	IRC (Internet Relay Chat)	TCP
Host Configurations	DHCP (Dynamic Host Configuration Protocol)	UDP

The application layer is built on the transport layer and provides network services to user applications. It provides the interface between the applications we use to communicate and the underlying network over which our messages are transmitted. Application layer protocols are used to exchange data between programs running on the source and destination hosts. In this chapter, we discuss all the fore mentioned protocols in detail.

17. *Miscellaneous Concepts*: This chapter covers other important topics of computer networking (such as *Quality of Service* [QoS], *Ping* operation, *Wireless Networking* basics etc.) even though they are out of scope of this book.

At the end of each chapter, a set of problems/questions are provided for you to improve/check your understanding of the concepts. Wherever applicable, protocols are compared with other similar protocols.

The examples in this book are kept simple for easy understanding. The objective is to enhance the explanation of each concept with examples for a better understanding.

Introduction

2.1 What is a Computer Network?

A computer network is a group of computers that are connected together and communicate with one another. These computers can be connected by the telephone lines, co-axial cable, satellite links or some other communication techniques.

2.2 Basic Elements of Computer Networks

More and more, it is networks that connect us. People communicate online from everywhere. We focus on these aspects of the information network:

- Devices that make up the network (work stations, laptops, file servers, web servers, network printers, VoIP phones, security cameras, PDAs, etc..)
- Media that connect the devices
- Messages that are carried over the network
- Rules (protocols) and processes that control network communications
- Tools and commands for constructing and maintaining networks

Communication begins with a message that must be sent from one device to another. People exchange ideas using many different communication methods. All of these methods have *three* elements in common.

- The first of these elements is the *message source* (*sender*). Message sources are people, or electronic devices, that need to send a message to other individuals/devices.

- The second element of communication is the *destination(receiver)*, of the message. The destination receives the message and interprets it.
- A third element, called a *channel*, consists of the media that provides the pathway over which the message can travel from source to destination.

Important Question

From the choices below, select the best definition of a network.
    A. A collection of printers with no media.
    B. Devices interconnected by some common communication channel.
    C. A device that sends communication to the Internet.
    D. A shared folder stored on a server.

Answer: B.

2.3 What is an Internet?

Connecting two or more networks together is called an *Internet*. In other words, an Internet is a network of networks.

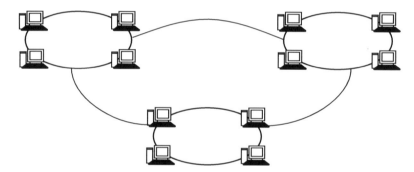

2.4 Fundamentals of Data and Signals

Data and *signals* are two of the basic elements of any computer network. A signal is the transmission of data. Both data and signals can be in either analog or digital form, which gives us *four* possible combinations:

1. Transmitting digital data using digital signals
2. Transmitting digital data using analog signals
3. Transmitting analog data using digital signals
4. Transmitting analog data using analog signals

2.4.1 Analog and Digital Data

Information that is stored within computer systems and transferred over a computer network can be divided into two categories: data and signals. Data are entities that convey meaning within a computer or computer system.

Data refers to information that conveys some meaning based on some mutually agreed up rules or conventions between a sender and a receiver and today it comes in a variety of forms such as text, graphics, audio, video and animation.

Data can be of two types:

- *Analog* data
- *Digital* data

Analog data take *continuous* values on some interval. Examples of analog data are voice and video. The data that are collected from the real world with the help of transducers are continuous-valued or analog in nature.

On the contrary, digital data take *discrete* values. Text or character strings can be considered as examples of digital data. Characters are represented by suitable codes, e.g. ASCII code, where each character is represented by a 7-bit code.

2.4.2 Analog and Digital Signals

If we want to transfer this data from one point to another, either by using a physical wire or by using radio waves, the data has to be converted into a signal. Signals are the electric or electromagnetic encoding of data and are used to transmit data.

Signals (electric signals) which run through conducting wires are divided into the following two categories. Also, a system used when transmitting signals is called a *transmission system*.

2.4.3 Analog Signals

Analog refers to physical quantities that vary continuously instead of discretely. Physical phenomena typically involve analog signals. Examples include temperature, speed, position, pressure, voltage, altitude, etc.

To say a signal is analog simply means that the signal is continuous in time and amplitude. Take, for example, your standard mercury glass thermometer. This device is analog because the temperature reading is updated constantly and changes at any time interval.

A new value of temperature can be obtained whether you look at the thermometer one second later, half a second later, or a millionth of a second later, assuming temperature can change that fast.

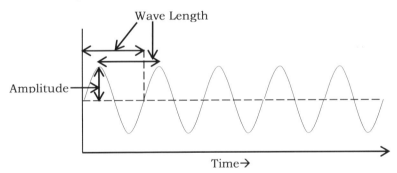

The readings from the thermometer are also continuous in amplitude. This means that assuming your eyes are sensitive enough to read the mercury level, readings of 37, 37.4, or 37.440183432°C are possible. In actuality, most cardiac signals of interest are analog by nature. For example, voltages recorded on the body surface and cardiac motion is continuous functions in time and amplitude.

In this, signals 0 and 1 are transmitted as electric waves. A system of transmitting analog signals is called *broadband* system.

2.4.4 Digital Signals

Digital signals consist of patterns of bits of information. These patterns can be generated in many ways, each producing a specific code. Modern digital computers store and process all kinds of information as binary patterns. All the pictures, text, sound and video stored in this computer are held and manipulated as patterns of binary values.

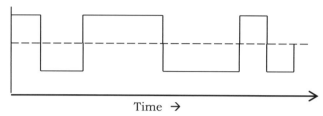

Time →

Basically, code 1 is transmitted when applying a specific voltage and code 0 is transmitted in the case of 0 V. A system of transmitting digital signals is called *baseband* system.

2.4.5 Converting Data into Signals

Like data, signals can be analog or digital. Typically, digital signals convey digital data, and analog signals convey analog data. However, we can use analog signals to convey digital data and digital signals to convey analog data. The choice of using either analog or digital signals often depends on the transmission equipment that is used and the environment in which the signals must travel.

2.4.6 Data Codes

One of the most common forms of data transmitted between a sender and a receiver is textual data. This textual information is transmitted as a sequence of characters. To distinguish one character from another, each character is represented by a unique binary pattern of 1s and 0s.

The set of all textual characters or symbols and their corresponding binary patterns is called a *data code*. Three important data codes are EBCDIC, ASCII, and Unicode.

2.4.7 Frequency

Frequency describes the number of waves that pass a fixed place in a given amount of time. So if the time it takes for a wave to pass is 1/2 second, the frequency is 2 per second. If it takes 1/100 of an hour, the frequency is 100 per hour.

High frequency waves
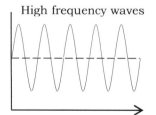

Low frequency waves
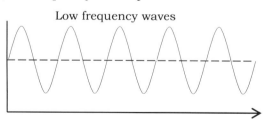

Usually frequency is measured in the *hertz* unit, named in honor of the 19th-century German physicist Heinrich Rudolf Hertz. The hertz measurement, abbreviated Hz, is the number of waves that pass by per second.

2.4.8 Bit Rate

Two new terms, bit interval (instead of period) and bit rate (instead of frequency) are used to describe digital signals. The bit interval is the time required to send one single bit. The bit rate is the number of bit interval per second. This mean that the bit rate is the number of bits send in one second, usually expressed in bits per second (*bps*) as shown in figure.

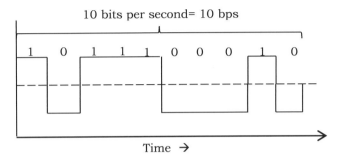

The speed of the data is expressed in bits per second (bits/s, bits per second or bps). The data rate R is a function of the duration of the bit or bit time:

$$R = \frac{1}{Bit\ Time}$$

Rate is also called *channel capacity* C. If the bit time is 10 *ns*, the data rate equals:

$$R = \frac{1}{10 \times 10^{-9}} = 10^8 \text{ bps or 100 million bits/sec}$$

This is usually expressed as 100 Mbits/s.

2.4.9 Baud Rate

The baud rate of a data communications system is the *number* of *symbols* per *second* transferred. A symbol may have more than two states, so it may represent more than one binary bit (a binary bit always represents exactly two states). Therefore the baud rate may not equal the bit rate, especially in the case of recent modems, which can have (for example) up to nine bits per symbol.

Baud rate is a technical term associated with modems, digital televisions, and other technical devices. It is also called as *symbol rate* and *modulation rate*. The term roughly means the speed that data is transmitted, and it is a derived value based on the number of symbols transmitted per second.

The units for this rate are either *symbols per second* or *pulses per second*. Baud can be determined by using the following formula:

$$Baud = \frac{Gross\ Bit\ Rate}{Number\ of\ Bits\ per\ Symbol}$$

This can be used to translate baud into a bit rate using the following formula:

$$Bit\ Rate = Bits\ per\ Symbol \times Symbol\ Rate$$

Baud can be abbreviated using the shortened form *Bd* when being used for technical purposes.

The significance of these formulas is that higher baud rates equate to greater amounts of data transmission, as long as the bits per symbol are the same. A system using 4800 baud modems that has 4 bits per symbol will send less data than a system using

9600 baud modems that also has 4 bits per symbol. So, all other things being equal, a higher rate is generally preferred.

2.4.10 Attenuation

Attenuation (also called *loss*) is a general term that refers to any reduction in the strength of a signal. Attenuation occurs with any type of signal, whether digital or analog. It usually occurs while transmitting analog or digital signals over long distances.

2.4.11 Signal to Noise Ratio

Signal to noise ratio measures the level of the audio signal compared to the level of noise present in the signal. Signal to noise ratio specifications are common in many components, including amplifiers, phonograph players, CD/DVD players, tape decks and others. Noise is described as hiss, as in tape deck, or simply general electronic background noise found in all components.

How is it expressed?

As the name suggests, signal to noise ratio is a comparison or ratio of the amount of signal to the amount of noise and is expressed in decibels. Signal to noise ratio is abbreviated *S/N Ratio* and higher numbers mean a better specification. A component with a signal to noise ratio of 100 dB means that the level of the audio signal is 100 dB higher than the level of the noise and is a better specification than a component with a S/N ratio of 90 dB.

Signal-to-noise ratio is defined as the power ratio between a signal and noise. It can be derived from the formula

$$\frac{S}{N} = \frac{P_{Signal}}{P_{Noise}} = \frac{\mu}{\sigma}$$

where μ is the signal mean or expected value
σ the standard deviation of the noise

2.5 Network Topologies

In a computer network, the way in which the devices are linked is called *topology*. Topology is the physical layout of computers, cables, and other components on a network. Following are few types of topologies which we will look at:

- Bus topology
- Star topology
- Mesh topology
- Ring topology

2.5.1 Bus Topology

A bus topology uses one cable (also called a *trunk*, a *backbone*, and a *segment*) to connect multiple systems. Most of the time, T-connectors (because they are shaped like the letter T) are used to connect to the cabled segment. Generally, coaxial cable is used in bus topologies.

Another key component of a bus topology is the need for *termination*. To prevent packets from bouncing up and down the cable, devices called *terminators* must be attached to both ends of the cable. A terminator absorbs an electronic signal and clears the cable so that other computers can send packets on the network. If there is no termination, the entire network fails.

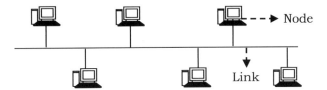

Only one computer at a time can transmit a packet on a bus topology. Systems in a bus topology listen to all traffic on the network but accept only the packets that are addressed to them. Broadcast packets are an exception because all computers on the network accept them. When a computer sends out a packet, it travels in both directions from the computer. This means that the network is occupied until the destination computer accepts the packet.

The number of computers on a bus topology network has a major influence on the performance of the network. A bus is a passive topology. The computers on a bus topology only listen or send data. They do not take data and send it on or regenerate it. So if one computer on the network fails, the network is still up.

Advantages

One advantage of a bus topology is *cost*. The bus topology uses less cable than other topologies. Another advantage is the ease of *installation*. With the bus topology, we simply connect the system to the cable segment. We need only the amount of cable to connect the workstations we have. The ease of working with a bus topology and the minimum amount of cable make this the most economical choice for a network topology. If a computer fails, the network stays up.

Disadvantages

The main disadvantage of the bus topology is the difficulty of *troubleshooting*. When the network goes down, usually it is from a break in the cable segment. With a large network this can be tough to isolate. A cable break between computers on a bus topology would take the entire network down. Another disadvantage of a bus topology is that the *heavier* the traffic, the *slower* the network.

Scalability is an important consideration with the dynamic world of networking. Being able to make changes easily within the size and layout of your network can be important in future productivity or downtime. The bus topology is not very scalable.

2.5.2 Star Topology

In star topology, all systems are connected through one central hub or switch, as shown in figure. This is a very common network scenario.

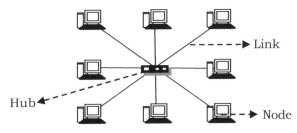

Advantages

One advantage of a start topology is the centralization of cabling. With a hub, if one link fails, the remaining systems are not affected like they are with other topologies, which we will look at in this chapter.

Centralizing network components can make an administrator's life much easier in the long run. Centralized management and monitoring of network traffic can be vital to network success. With this type of configuration, it is also easy to add or change configurations with all the connections coming to a central point.

Disadvantages

On the flip side to this is the fact that if the hub fails, the entire network, or a good portion of the network, comes down. This is, of course, an easier fix than trying to find a break in a cable in a bus topology.

Another disadvantage of a star topology is cost: to connect each system to a centralized hub, we have to use much more cable than we do in a bus topology.

2.5.3 Ring Topology

In ring topology each system is attached nearby systems on a point to point basis so that the entire system is in the form of a ring. Signals travel in one direction on a ring topology.

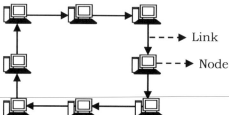

As shown in figure, the ring topology is a circle that has no start and no end. Terminators are not necessary in a ring topology. Signals travel in one direction on a ring while they are passed from one system to the next. Each system checks the packet for its destination and passes it on as a repeater would. If one of the systems fails, the entire ring network goes down.

Advantages

The nice thing about a ring topology is that each computer has equal access to communicate on the network. (With bus and star topologies, only one workstation can communicate on the network at a time.) The ring topology provides good performance for each system. This means that busier systems that send out a lot of information do not inhibit other systems from communicating. Another advantage of the ring topology is that signal degeneration is low.

Disadvantages

The biggest problem with a ring topology is that if one system fails or the cable link is broken the entire network could go down. With newer technology this isn't always the case. The concept of a ring topology is that the ring isn't broken and the signal hops from system to system, connection to connection.

Another disadvantage is that if we make a cabling change to the network or a system change, such as a move, the brief disconnection can interrupt or bring down the entire network.

2.5.4 Mesh Topology

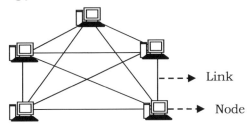

A mesh topology is not very common in computer networking. The mesh topology is more commonly seen with something like the national phone network. With the mesh topology, every system has a connection to every other component of the network.

Systems in a mesh topology are all connected to every other component of the network. If we have 4 systems, we must have six cables— three coming from each system to the other systems.

Two nodes are connected by dedicated point-point links between them. So the total number of links to connect n nodes would be

$$\frac{n(n-1)}{2} \text{ [Proportional to } n^2]$$

Advantages

The biggest advantage of a mesh topology is fault tolerance. If there is a break in a cable segment, traffic can be rerouted. This fault tolerance means that the network going down due to a cable fault is almost impossible.

Disadvantages

A mesh topology is very hard to administer and manage because of the numerous connections. Another disadvantage is cost. With a large network, the amount of cable needed to connect and the interfaces on the workstations would be very expensive.

2.5.5 Tree Topology

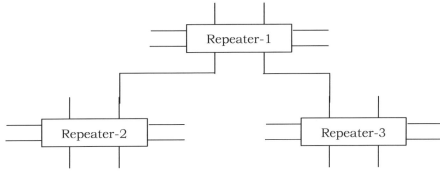

This topology can be considered as an extension to bus topology. It is commonly used in cascading equipment's. For example, we have a repeater box with 8-port, as far as we have eight stations, this can be used in a normal fashion. But if we need to add more stations then we can connect two or more repeaters in a hierarchical format (tree format) and can add more stations.

In the figure Repeater-1 refers to repeater one and so on and each repeater is considered to have 8-ports.

2.5.6 Unconstrained Topology

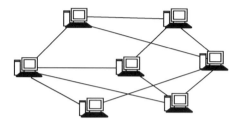

All the topologies discussed so far are symmetric and constrained by well-defined interconnection pattern. However, sometimes no definite pattern is followed and nodes are interconnected in an arbitrary manner using point-to-point links.

Unconstrained topology allows a lot of configuration flexibility but suffers from the complex routing problem. Complex routing involves unwanted overhead and delay.

2.6 Network Operating Systems

Network operating system NOS is an operating system that includes special functions for connecting computers and devices into a local area network (LAN).

Few standalone operating systems, such as Microsoft Windows NT, can also act as network operating systems. Some of the most well-known network operating systems include Microsoft Windows Server 2003, Microsoft Windows Server 2008, Linux and Mac OS X.

2.6.1 Peer-to-peer

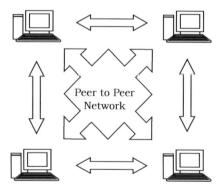

Peer − to − Peer networks are more commonly implemented where less than ten computers are involved and where strict security is not necessary. All computers have the same status, hence the term *peer*, and they communicate with each other on an equal footing. Files, such as word processing or spreadsheet documents, can be shared across the network and all the computers on the network can share devices, such as printers or scanners, which are connected to any one computer.

2.6.2 Client/server networks

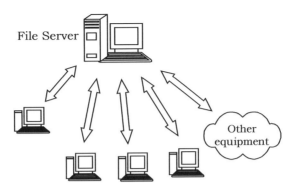

Client/Server networks are more suitable for larger networks. A central computer, or *server*, acts as the storage location for files and applications shared on the network. Usually the server is a higher than average performance computer.

The server also controls the network access of the other computers which are referred to as the 'client' computers. Typically, teachers and students in a school will use the client computers for their work and only the network administrator (usually a designated staff member) will have access rights to the server [figure on right side].

2.7 Transmission Medium

Communication across a network is carried on a *medium*. The medium provides the channel through which the data travels from source to destination. There are several types of media, and the selection of the right media depends on many factors such as cost of transmission media, efficiency of data transmission and the transfer rate. Different types of network media have different features and benefits.

2.7.1 Two wire open line

This is the simplest of all the transmission media. It consists of a simple pair of metallic wires made of copper or sometimes aluminums of between 0.4 and 1mm diameter, and each wire is insulated from the other. There are variations to this simplest form with several pairs of wire covered in a single protected cable called a *multi core cable* or molded in the form of a *flat ribbon*.

Example: Electric power transmission

This line consists of two wires that are generally spaced from 2 to 6 inches apart by insulating spacers. This type of line is most often used for power lines.

This type of media is used for communication within a short distance, up to about 50 Meters, and can achieve a transfer rate of up to 19200 bits per second.

2.7.2 Twisted Pair cable

As the name implies, the line consists of two insulated wires twisted together to form a flexible line without the use of spacers. It is not used for transmitting high frequency because of the high dielectric losses that occur in the rubber insulation. When the line is wet, the losses are high.

Twisted Pair cable is used for communication up a distance of 1 kilometer and can achieve a transfer rate of up to 1-2 Mbps. But as the speed increased the maximum transmission distances reduced, and may require repeaters.

Twisted pair cables are widely used in telephone network and are increasingly being used for data transmission.

2.7.3 Co-axial Cable

Coaxial cable is the kind of copper cable used by cable TV operators between the antenna and user homes. It is called *coaxial* because it includes one physical channel that carries the signal surrounded (after a layer of insulation) by another concentric physical channel, and both running along the same axis. The outer channel serves as a ground.

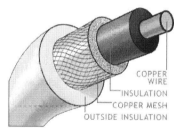

Larger the cable diameter, lower is the transmission loss, and higher transfer speeds can be achieved. A co-axial cable can be used over a distance of about 1 KM and can achieve a transfer rate of up to 100 Mbps.

2.7.4 Fiber Optic Cables

Fiber-based media use light transmissions instead of electronic pulses. Fiber is well suited for the transfer of data, video, and voice transmissions. Also, fiber-optic is the most secure of all cable media. Anyone trying to access data signals on a fiber-optic cable must physically tap into the media and this is a difficult task.

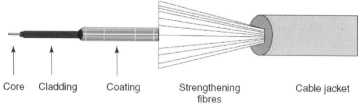

On the flip side, difficult installation and maintenance procedures of fiber require skilled technicians. Also, the cost of a fiber-based solution is more. Another drawback of implementing a fiber solution involves cost for fitting to existing network equipment/hardware. Fiber is incompatible with most electronic network equipment. That means, we have to purchase fiber-compatible network hardware.

Fiber-optic cable is made-up of a core glass fiber surrounded by cladding. An insulated covering then surrounds both of these within an outer protective sheath.

Since light waves give a much high bandwidth than electrical signals, this leads to high data transfer rate of about 1000 Mbps. This can be used for long and medium distance transmission links.

2.7.5 Radio, Microwaves and Satellite Channels

Radio, Microwaves and Satellite Channels use electromagnetic propagation in open space. The advantage of these channels depends on their capability to cove large geographical areas and being inexpensive than the wired installation.

The demarcation between radio, Microwave and satellite channels depends on the frequencies in which they operate. Frequencies below 1000 MHZ are radio frequencies and higher are the Microwave frequencies.

The radio frequency transmission may be below 30 MHZ or above 30 MHZ and thus the techniques of transmission are different. Above 30MHz propagation is on *line − of − sight* paths. Antennas are placed in between the line-of- sight paths to increase the distance.

Radio frequencies are prone to attenuation and, thus, they require repeaters along the path to enhance the signal. Radio frequencies can achieve data transfer rate of 100 Kbps to 400 Kbps.

Microwave links use *line − of − sight* transmission with repeaters placed every 100-200 KM. Microwave links can achieve data transfer rates of about 1000 Mbps.

Satellite links use microwave frequencies in the order of 4-12 GHz with the satellite as a repeater. They can achieve data transfer rates of about 1000 Mbps.

2.8 Types of Networks

2.8.1 Local Area Network [LAN]

A local area network (LAN) is a network confined to one location, one building or a group of buildings. LAN's are composed of various components like desktops, printers, servers and other storage devices. All hosts on a LAN have addresses that fall in a single continuous and contiguous range.

LANs usually do not contain routers. LANs have higher communication and data transfer rates. A LAN is usually administered by a single organization.

2.8.2 Metropolitan Area Network (MAN)

A metropolitan area network (MAN) is a large computer network that usually spans a city or a large campus. Usually a MAN interconnects a number of local area networks (LANs) using a high-capacity backbone technology (fibre-optical links). It is designed to extend over an entire city. That means it can be a single network (for example, cable television network) or connecting a number of LANs into a larger network.

A MAN may be fully owned and operated by a private company or be a service provided by a public company.

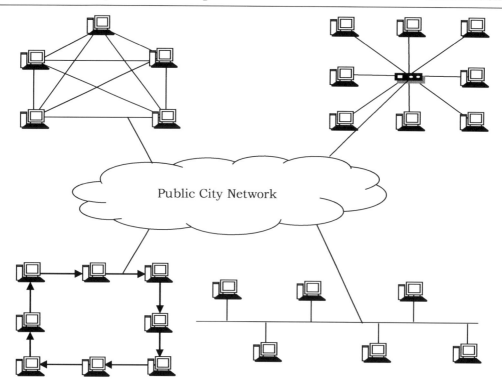

2.8.3 Wide Area Network [WAN]

A wide area network (WAN) provides long-distance transmission of data, voice, image and video information over large geographical areas that may comprise a country, or even the whole world. WANs may utilize public, leased, or private communication devices, usually in combinations, therefore span an unlimited number of miles.

A WAN that is wholly owned and used by a single company is often referred to as an enterprise network. Maintaining WAN is difficult because of its wider geographical coverage and higher maintenance costs. Internet is the best example of a WAN. WANs have a lower data transfer rate as compared to LANs.

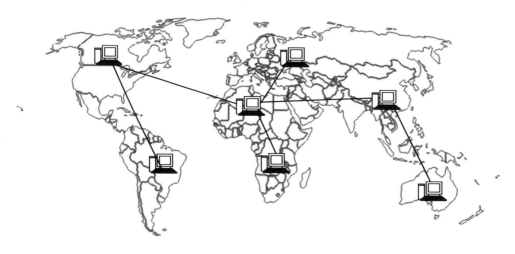

2.8.4 Personal Area Network

A personal area network (PAN) is a computer network organized around an individual person. PANs usually involve a computer, a cell phone and/or a handheld computing device such as a PDA.

We can use these networks to transfer files including email and calendar appointments, digital photos and music. Personal area networks can be constructed with cables [for example, USB] or be wireless [for example, Bluetooth].

Personal area networks generally cover a range of less than 10. PANs can be viewed as a special type LAN that supports one person instead of a group.

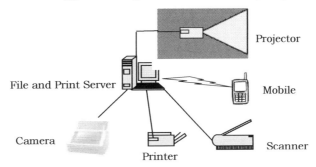

2.8.5 LAN vs. WAN

	LAN	WAN
Definition	LAN (Local Area Network) is a computer network covering a small geographic area, like a home, office, schools, or group of buildings.	WAN (Wide Area Network) is a computer network that covers a broad area (e.g., any network whose communications links cross metropolitan, regional, or national boundaries over a long distance
Maintenance costs	Because it covers a relatively small geographical area, LAN is easier to maintain at relatively low costs.	Maintaining WAN is difficult because of its wider geographical coverage and higher maintenance costs.
Fault Tolerance:	LANs tend to have fewer problems associated with them, as there are a smaller number of systems to deal with.	WANs tend to be fewer faults tolerant as it consists of a large number of systems there is a lower amount of fault tolerance.
Example	Network in an organization can be a LAN	Internet is the best example of a WAN
Geographical spread	LANs will have a small geographical range and do not need any leased telecommunication lines	WANs generally spread across boundaries and need leased telecommunication lines
Set-up costs	If there is a need to set-up a couple of extra devices on the	In this case since networks in remote areas have to be

	network, it is not very expensive to do that	connected hence the set-up costs are higher. However WANs using public networks can be setup very cheaply, just software (VPN etc.)
Ownership	Typically owned, controlled, and managed by a single person or organization	WANs (like the Internet) are not owned by any one organization but rather exist under collective or distributed ownership and management over long +distances
Components	Layer 2 devices like switches, bridges. layer1 devices like hubs , repeaters	Layers 3 devices Routers, Multi-layer Switches and Technology specific devices like ATM or Frame-relay Switches etc.
Data transfer rates	LANs have a high data transfer rate	WANs have a lower data transfer rate as compared to LANs
Technology	Tend to use certain connectivity technologies, primarily Ethernet and Token Ring	WANs tend to use technology like MPLS, ATM, Frame Relay and X.25 for connectivity over the longer distances
Connection	One LAN can be connected to other LANs over any distance via telephone lines and radio waves	Computers connected to a WAN are often connected through public networks, such as the telephone system. They can also be connected through leased lines or satellites
Speed	High speed(1000mbps)	Less speed(150mbps)

2.8.6 Wireless Networks

A wireless network is a computer network that uses a wireless network connection such as Wi-Fi. In wireless networks, can have the following types:

- Wireless PAN (WPAN): interconnect devices within a relatively small area that is generally within a person's reach.
- Wireless LAN (WLAN): interconnects two or more devices over a short distance using a wireless distribution method. IEEE 802.11 standard describes about WLAN.
- Wireless MAN (WMAN): connects multiple wireless LANs. IEEE 802.16 standard describes about WMAN.
- Wireless WAN (WWAN): covers large areas, such as between neighboring towns and cities, or city and suburb. The wireless connections between access points are usually point to point microwave links using parabolic dishes, instead of omnidirectional antennas used with smaller networks.

2.9 Connection-oriented and Connectionless services

There are two different techniques for transferring data in computer networks. Both have advantages and disadvantages. They are the connection-oriented method and the connectionless method:

2.9.1 Connection-oriented service

This requires a session connection be established before any data can be sent. This method is often called a reliable network service. It guarantees that data will arrive in the same order. Connection-oriented services set up virtual links between sender and receiver systems through a network. Transmission Control Protocol (TCP) is a connection-oriented protocol.

The most common example for the connection oriented service is the telephone system that we use every day. In connection oriented system such as the telephone system, a direct connection is established between you and the person at the other end.

Therefore, if you called from India to United States of America (USA) for 5 minutes, you are in reality actually the owner of that copper wire for the whole 5 minutes. This inefficiency however overcame by the multiple access techniques invented (refer *LAN Technologies* chapter).

Connection-oriented services set up *virtual* path between source and destination systems through a network. Connection-oriented service provides its services with the following three steps:
1. *Handshaking*: This is the process of establishing a connection to the desired destination prior to the transfer of data. During this hand-shaking process, the two end nodes decide the parameters for transferring data.
2. *Data Transfer*: During this step, the actual data is being sent in order. Connection oriented protocol is also known as *reliable* network service as it provides the service of delivering the stream of data in order. It ensures this as most of the connection oriented service tries to resend the lost data packets.
3. *Connection Termination*: This step is taken to release the end nodes and resources after the completion of data transfer.

2.9.2 Connectionless Service

Connectionless service does not require a session connection between sender and receiver. The sender simply starts sending packets (called *datagrams*) to the destination. This service does not have the reliability of the connection-oriented method, but it is useful for periodic burst transfers.

Neither system must maintain state information for the systems that they send transmission to or receive transmission from. A connectionless network provides minimal services. User Datagram Protocol (UDP) is a connectionless protocol.

Common features of a connectionless service are:
- Data (packets) do not need to arrive in a specific order
- Reassembly of any packet broken into fragments during transmission must be in proper order
- No time is used in creating a session
- No acknowledgement is required.

2.10 Segmentation and Multiplexing

In theory, a single communication, such as a music video or an e-mail message, could be sent across a network from a source to a destination as one massive continuous stream of bits. If messages were actually transmitted in this manner, it would mean that no other device would be able to send or receive messages on the same network while this data transfer was in progress.

These large streams of data would result in significant delays. Further, if a link in the interconnected network infrastructure failed during the transmission, the complete message would be lost and have to be retransmitted in full.

A better approach is to divide the data into smaller, more manageable pieces to send over the network. This division of the data stream into smaller pieces is called *segmentation*. Segmenting messages has two primary benefits.

First, by sending smaller individual pieces from source to destination, many different conversations can be interleaved on the network. The process used to interleave the pieces of separate conversations together on the network is called *multiplexing*.

Second, segmentation can increase the reliability of network communications. The separate pieces of each message need not travel the same pathway across the network from source to destination. If a particular path becomes congested with data traffic or fails, individual pieces of the message can still be directed to the destination using alternate pathways. If part of the message fails to make it to the destination, only the missing parts need to be retransmitted.

2.11 Network Performance

Network performance has been the subject of much research over the past decades. One important issue in networking is the performance of the network—how good is it? Internet data is packaged and transported in *small* pieces of data.

The flow of these small pieces of data directly affects a user's internet experience. When data packets arrive in a timely manner the user sees a continuous flow of data; if data packets arrive with *large delays* between packets the user's experience is *degraded*.

2.11.1 Round Trip Time

In TCP, when a host sends a segment (also called packet) into a TCP connection, it starts a timer. If the timer expires before the host receives an acknowledgment for the data in the segment, the host retransmits the segment. The time from when the timer is started until when it expires is called the *timeout* of the timer.

What should be the ideal *timeout* be? Clearly, the timeout should be larger than the connection's round-trip time, i.e., the time from when a segment is sent until it is acknowledged.

Otherwise, unnecessary retransmissions would be sent. But the timeout should not be much larger than the *round-trip time*; otherwise, when a segment is lost, TCP would not quickly retransmit the segment, thereby introducing significant data transfer delays into the application. Before discussing the timeout interval in more detail, let us take a closer look at the round-trip time (*RTT*).

The round trip time calculation algorithm is used to calculate the average time for data to be acknowledged. When a data packet is sent, the elapsed time for the acknowledgment to arrive is measured and the *Van Jacobean* mean deviation algorithm is applied. This time is used to determine the interval to retransmit data.

2.11.1.1 Estimating the Average Round Trip Time

The sample RTT, denoted with *SampleRTT*, for a segment is the time from when the segment is sent (i.e., passed to IP) until an acknowledgment for the segment is received. Each segment sent will have its own associated *SampleRTT*.

Obviously, the *SampleRTT* values will change from segment to segment due to congestion in the routers and to the varying load on the end systems. Because of this fluctuation, any given *SampleRTT* value may be atypical. In order to estimate a typical *RTT*, it is therefore natural to take some sort of average of the *SampleRTT* values.

TCP maintains an average of *SampleRTT* values, denoted with called *EstimatedRTT*. Upon receiving an acknowledgment and obtaining a new *SampleRTT*, TCP updates *EstimatedRTT* according to the following formula:

$$EstimatedRTT = (1-\alpha) * EstimatedRTT + \alpha * SampleRTT$$

The above formula is written in the form of a programming language statement - the new value of *EstimatedRTT* is a weighted combination of the previous value of *EstimatedRTT* and the new value for *SampleRTT*. A typical value of α is $\alpha = .1$, in which case the above formula becomes:

$$EstimatedRTT = .9 \ EstimatedRTT + .1 \ SampleRTT$$

Note that *EstimatedRTT* is a weighted average of the *SampleRTT* values. This weighted average puts more weight on recent samples than on old samples. This is natural, as the more recent samples better reflect the current congestion in the network. In statistics, such an average is called an *exponential weighted moving average* (*EWMA*). The word *exponential* appears in EWMA because the weight of a given *SampleRTT* decays exponentially fast as the updates proceed.

2.11.2 Causes for Latency?

Regardless of the speed of the processor or the efficiency of the software, it takes a finite amount of time to manipulate and present data. Whether the application is a web page showing the latest news or a live camera shot showing a traffic jam, there are many ways in which an application can be affected by latency. Four key causes of latency are: *propagation delay*, *serialization delay*, *routing* and *switching delay*, and *queuing* and *buffering delay*.

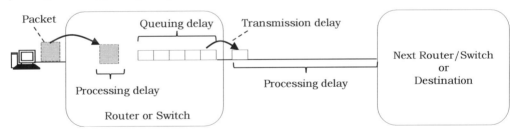

$$Latency = Propagation \ delay + Serialization \ delay + Queuing \ delay + Processing \ delay$$

2.11.2.1 Propagation Delay

Propagation delay is the primary source of latency. It is a function of how long it *takes* information to *travel* at the speed of light in the communications media from source to destination. In free space, the speed of light is approximately 3×10^5 km/sec. The speed of light is lower in other media such as copper wire or fiber optic cable. The amount of slowing caused by this type of transmission is called the *velocity factor* (VF).

Fiber optic cables typically measure around 70% of the speed of light whereas copper cable varies from 40% to 80% depending on the construct. Coaxial cable is commonly used and many types have a VF of 66%.

Satellite communication links use electromagnetic waves to propagate information through the atmosphere and space. The information is converted from electrical signals to radio signals by the transmitter and the antenna. Once these radio signals leave the antenna, they travel approximately at the speed of light for free space.

Let's calculate how long it will take an email to travel from Hyderabad to New York assuming that we are the only user on a private communications channel.

Ignoring the actual routes taken by undersea cables due to the ocean's floor, let's assume the path from Hyderabad to New York is the great circle distance of 5458 km.

$$Propagation\ delay = \frac{Distance\ (or\ length\ of\ physical\ link)}{Propagation\ speed}$$

The email sent using a copper link: $\frac{5458}{197863.022}$ = 23.58 ms

The email sent using a fiber-optic link: $\frac{5458}{209854.720}$ = 26.01 ms

The email sent using a radio link: $\frac{5458}{299792.458}$ = 18.21 ms

These are the latencies caused only by propagation delays in the transmission medium. If you were the only one sending one single data bit and you had unlimited bandwidth available, the speed of the packet would still be delayed by the propagation delay.

This delay happens without regard for the amount of data being transmitted, the transmission rate, the protocol being used or any link impairment.

2.11.2.2 Serialization Delay [Transmission Delay]

Serialization is the conversion of bytes (8 bits) of data stored in a computer's memory into a serial bit stream to be transmitted over the communications media. Serialization delay is also called *transmission delay* or *delay*. Serialization takes a finite amount of time and is calculated as follows:

$$Serialization\ delay = \frac{Packet\ size\ in\ bits}{Transmission\ rate\ in\ bits\ per\ second}$$

For example:

- Serialization of a 1500 byte packet used on a 56K modem link will take 214 milliseconds
- Serialization of the same 1500 byte packet on a 100 Mbps LAN will take 120 microseconds

Serialization can represent a significant delay on links that operate a lower transmission rates, but for most links this delay is a tiny fraction of the overall latency when compared to the other contributors.

Voice and video data streams generally use small packet sizes (~20 ms of data) to minimize the impact of serialization delay.

2.11.2.3 Processing Delay

In IP networks such as the Internet, IP packets are forwarded from source to destination through a series of IP routers or switches that continuously update their decision about which next router is the best one to get the packet to its destination. A router or circuit outage or congestion on a link along the path can change the routing path which in turn can affect the latency.

High performance IP routers and switches add approximately 200 microseconds of latency to the link due to *packet processing*. If we assume that the average IP backbone router spacing is 800 km, the 200 microseconds of routing/switching delay is equivalent to the amount of latency induced by 40km of fiber; routing/switching latency contributes to only 5% of the end to end delay for the average internet link.

2.11.2.4 Queuing and Buffer Management

Another issue which occurs within the transport layers is called *queuing latency*. This refers to the amount of time an IP packet spends sitting in a queue awaiting transmission due to over-utilization of the outgoing link after the routing/switching delay has been accounted for. This can add up to an additional 20 ms of latency.

2.11.3 Transmission Rate and Bandwidth

Transmission rate is a term used to describe the number of bits which can be extracted from the medium. Transmission rate is commonly measured as the number of bits measured over a period of one second.

The *maximum transmission rate* describes the fundamental limitation of a network medium:

If the medium is a copper Local Area Network, maximum transmission rates are commonly 10, 100, or 1000 Megabits per second. These rates are primarily limited by the properties of the copper wires and the capabilities of the network interface card are also a factor.

Fiber-optic the transmission rates range from around 50 Mbps up to 100 Gbps. Unlike copper networks, the primary factor limiting fiber-optic transmission rates is the electronics which operates at each end of the fiber. Wireless local area networks (LANs) and satellite links use modems (modulator/demodulator) to convert digital bits into an analog modulated waveform at the transmitter end of a link, and then at the receive end a demodulator will then convert the analog signal back into digital bits.

The limiting factor in transmitting information over radio-based channels is the bandwidth of the channel that is available to a particular signal and the noise that is present that will corrupt the signal waveform.

2.11.3.1 Radio Channel Bandwidth and Noise

Signals transmitted using radio waves occupy radio spectrum. Radio spectrum is not an unlimited resource and must be shared. To prevent radio interference between users the use of radio spectrum is controlled by nearly every government on the planet. The amount of radio spectrum occupied by any given radio signal is called its bandwidth.

The nature of radio spectrum use is beyond this paper but it's important to understand that generally the occupied radio spectrum of a modem signal will increase with the data rate:

- Higher modem data rates cause the modem to occupy more radio bandwidth
- Lower modem data rates will let the modem occupy less radio bandwidth

Since radio spectrum is a limited resource, the occupied radio bandwidth is an important limiting factor in wireless and satellite links.

Noise in the radio channel will perturb the analog signal waveform and can cause the demodulator at the receiver to change a digital one into a zero or vice versus. The effect of noise can be overcome by increasing the power level of the transmitted signal, or by adding a few extra error correcting bits to the data that is being transmitted. These error correcting bits help the receiver correct bit errors. However, the error correction bits increase the bandwidth that is required.

2.11.3.2 Data Bandwidth

In data transmission, the *data bandwidth* is synonymous to the transmission rate being used. Bandwidth is important because it defines the maximum capacity of a data link.

- A 10 Mbps copper LAN cannot sustain traffic flowing at a higher rate than 10 megabits every second.
- A satellite link using modems operating at a 600 Mbps rate cannot flow any more than 600 megabits every second.

It's very important to understand that data bandwidth is a maximum data flow obtainable over a given transportation segment over a given period of time.

2.11.4 Bandwidth × Delay Product

In data communications, bandwidth-delay product refers to the product of a data link's capacity (in bits per second) and its end-to-end delay (in seconds). The result, an amount of data measured in bits (or bytes), is equivalent to the maximum amount of data on the network circuit at any given time, i.e., data that has been transmitted but not yet acknowledged.

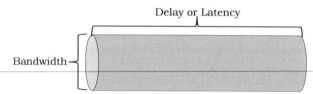

The Bandwidth × Delay Product, or BDP for short determines the amount of data that can be in transit in the network. It is the product of the availalbe bandwidth and the latency. Sometimes it is calculated as the data link's capacity multiplied by its round trip time (RTT). BDP is a very important concept in a Window based protocol such as TCP.

It plays an especially important role in high-speed / high-latency networks, such as most broadband internet connections. It is one of the most important factors of tweaking TCP in order to tune systems to the type of network used.

The BDP simply states that:

$$BDP \; (bits) \; = \; Total \; Available \; Bandwidth \; (bits/sec) \; \times \; Round \; Trip \; Time \; (sec)$$

2.11.5 Revisiting Queuing Delay

Queuing delay depends on the number and size of the other packets in the queue before it as well as the transmission rate of the interface. With queuing delays, below is the common question which arises frequently.

When is the queuing delay large and when is it insignificant?

The answer to this question depends on the rate at which traffic arrives at the queue, the transmission rate of the link, and the nature of the arriving traffic, that is, whether the traffic arrives occasionally or arrives in bursts. To get some insight here, let "*a*" denote the average rate at which packets arrive at the queue ("*a*" is in units of packets/sec). Also, assume that R is the transmission rate; that is, it is the rate (in bits/sec) at which bits are pushed out of the queue.

For simplicity, that all packets consist of L bits. Then the average rate at which bits arrive at the queue is La bits/sec. Finally, suppose that the queue is very big, so that it can hold basically an infinite number of bits. The ratio La/R, called the *traffic intensity*, often plays an important role in estimating the extent of the queuing delay.

$$Traffic\ Intensity = \frac{L \times a}{R}$$

Where, a is the average arrival rate of packets (e.g. packets/sec)
L is the average packet length (e.g. in bits), and
R is the transmission rate (e.g. bits/sec)

If $L \times a/R > 1$, then the average rate at which bits arrive at the queue exceeds the rate at which the bits can be transmitted from the queue. In this unfortunate situation, the queue will tend to increase without bound and the queuing delay will approach infinity. Therefore, one of the golden rules in traffic engineering is: Design your system so that the traffic intensity is no greater than 1.

Now think about the case $L \times a/R = 1$. Here, the nature of the arriving traffic impacts the queuing delay. For instance, if packets arrive periodically -that is, one packet arrives every L/R seconds - then every packet will arrive at an empty queue and there will be no queuing delay. On the other hand, if packets arrive in bursts but occasionally, there can be a considerable average queuing delay.

For instance, suppose n packets arrive simultaneously every $(L/R)n$ seconds. Then the first packet transmitted has no queuing delay; the second packet transmitted has a queuing delay of L/R seconds; and more commonly, the nth packet transmitted has a queuing delay of $(n-1) \times L/R$ seconds.

2.11.6 Throughput versus Bandwidth

Even though widely used in the field of networking, bandwidth and throughput are two commonly misunderstood concepts. When planning and building new networks, network administrators widely use these two concepts. Bandwidth is the maximum amount of data that can be transferred through a network for a specified period of time while throughput is the actual amount of data that can be transferred through a network during a specified time period.

Bandwidth can be defined as the amount of information that can flow through a network at a given period of time. Bandwidth actually gives the maximum amount of data that can be transmitted through a channel in theory. When you say that you have a 100 Mbps broadband line you are actually referring to the maximum amount of data that can travel through your line per second, which is the bandwidth.

Even though the basic measurement for bandwidth is bits per second (bps), since it is a relatively small measurement, we widely use kilobits per second (kbps), megabits bits per second (Mbps), and gigabits per second (Gbps).

Most of us know from experience that the actual network speed is much slower than what is specified. Throughput is the actual amount of data that could be transferred through the network. That is the actual amount of data that gets transmitted back and forth from your computer, through the Internet to the web server in a single unit of time.

When downloading a file you will see a window with a progress bar and a number. This number is actually the throughput and you must have noticed that it is not constant and almost always has a value lower than specified bandwidth for your connection.

Several factors like the number of users accessing the network, network topology, physical media and hardware capabilities can effect this reduction in the bandwidth. As you can imagine, throughput is also measured using the same units used to measure the bandwidth.

As you have seen, bandwidth and throughput seems to give a similar measurement about a network, at the first glance. They are also measured using the same units of measurement. Despite all these similarities they are actually different. We can simply say that the bandwidth is the maximum throughput you can ever achieve while the actual speed that we experience while surfing is the throughput.

To simplify further, you can think of the bandwidth as the width of a highway. As we increase the width of the highway more vehicles can move through a specified period of time. But when we consider the road conditions (craters or construction work in the highway) the number of vehicles that can actually pass through the specified period of time could be less than the above. This is actually analogous to the throughput. So it is clear that bandwidth and throughput gives two different measurements about a network.

2.11.7 Important Notes

Consider the following definitions:

R	Transmission rate (bits/second)
S	Signal speed (meters/second)
D	Distance between the sender and receiver (meters)
T	Time to create (build) one frame (microseconds)
F	Number of bits in a frame/packet
N	Number of data bits in a frame/packet
A	Number of bits in an acknowledgement
P	Percentage of time that bit are in the channel

1. Since R is the transmission rate, the amount of time required to transmit one bit is $\frac{1}{R}$.

2. Since there are F bits in a frame, time required to transmit the whole frame is $\frac{F}{R}$.

3. The bits must then travel the channel. Since D is the length of the channel and S is the speed of the signal, the time required to travel the channel is $\frac{D}{S}$.

   So, after the last bit is transmitted it requires $\frac{D}{S}$ time to get to the receiver.

4. Time required for a frame to be sent is: Time to create a frame + Time to transmit a whole frame + Time required by the last bit to travel = $T + \frac{F}{R} + \frac{D}{S}$.

5. Similarly the time required for an acknowledgement is $T + \frac{A}{R} + \frac{D}{S}$.

6. In the unrestricted protocol a new frame is built as soon as the last one is sent. So the time required to build a new frame is $T + \frac{F}{R}$.

7. For stop-and-wait, time required to build a new frame is $T + \frac{F}{R} + \frac{D}{S} + T + \frac{A}{R} + \frac{D}{S}$.

8. The time required to transmit a frame is $\frac{F}{R} + \frac{D}{S}$.

9. Let P be the percentage of time that bits are in the channel. With the unrestricted protocol we have: $P = \left(\frac{F}{R}\right) \times \frac{100}{\left(T+\frac{F}{R}\right)}$

With the stop and wait protocol we have: $P = \left(\frac{F}{R} + \frac{D}{S}\right) \times \frac{100}{\left(T+\frac{F}{R}+\frac{D}{S}+T+\frac{A}{R}+\frac{D}{S}\right)}$

10. *Effective data rate*: It is defined as the number of data bits sent per unit time. It is found by dividing the number of data bits by the elapsed time between sending two frames. For the unrestricted protocols the effective data rate is $\frac{N}{\left(T+\frac{F}{R}\right)}$. For the stop and wait protocol, it is $\frac{N}{\left(T+\frac{F}{R}+\frac{D}{S}+T+\frac{A}{R}+\frac{D}{S}\right)}$.

2.12 Network Switching

The purpose of a communication system is to exchange information between two or more devices. Such system can be optimized for voice, data, or both.

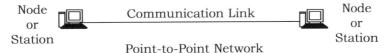

Point-to-Point Network

In its simplest form, a communication system can be established between two nodes (or stations) that are directly connected by some form of *point-to-point* transmission medium. A station may be a PC, telephone, fax machine, mainframe, or any other communicating device.

This may, however, be impractical, if there are many geographically dispersed nodes or the communication requires dynamic connection between different nodes at various times.

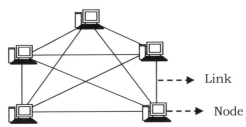

It is not efficient to build a physically separate path for each pair of communicating end systems. An alternative method to a *point-to-point* connection is *establishing* a *communication* network. In a communication network, each communicating *device* (or *station* or *node* or *host*) is connected to a network node.

The interconnected nodes are capable of transferring data between stations.

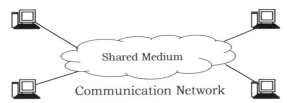

Communication Network

Depending on the architecture and techniques used to transfer data, two basic categories of communication networks are broadcast networks and switched networks.

- Broadcast Networks
- Switched Networks

2.12.1 Broadcast Networks

In *broadcast* networks, a single node transmits the information to all other nodes and hence, all stations will receive the data. A simple example of such network is a simple radio system, in which all users tuned to the same channel can communicate with each other. Other examples of broadcast networks are satellite networks and Ethernet-based local area networks, where transmission by any station will propagates through the network and all other stations will receive the information.

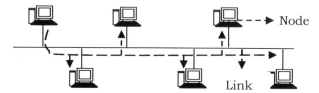

Broadcast is a method of sending a signal where multiple nodes may hear a single sender node. As an example, consider a conference room with full of people. In this conference room, a single person starts saying some information loudly.

During that time, some people may be sleeping, and may not hear what person is saying. Some people may not be sleeping, but not paying attention (they are able to hear the person, but choose to ignore). Another group of people may not only be awake, but be interested in what is being said. This last group is not only able to hear the person speaking, but is also listening to what is being said.

In this example, we can see that a single person is broadcasting a message to all others that may or may not be able to hear it, and if they are able to hear it, may choose to listen or not.

2.12.2 Switched Networks

A network is a series of connected devices. Whenever we have many devices, the interconnection between them becomes more difficult as the number of devices increases. Some of the conventional ways of interconnecting devices are

    a. Point to point connection between devices as in *mesh* topology.
    b. Connection between a central device and every other device as in *star* topology.
    c. Bus topology is not practical if the devices are at greater distances.

The solution to this interconnectivity problem is *switching*. A switched network consists of a series of interlinked nodes called *switches*. A switch is a device that creates temporary connections between two or more systems. Some of the switches are connected to end systems (computers and telephones) and others are used only for routing.

In a switched network, the transmitted data is not passed on to the entire medium. Instead, data are transferred from source to destination through a series of *intermediate* nodes, called *switchingnodes*. Such nodes are only concerned about how to move the data from one node to another until the data reaches its destination node.

Switched communication networks can be categorized into different types such as the following.

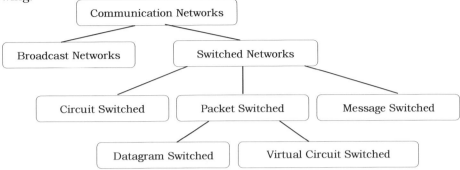

2.12.2.1 Circuit Switched Networks

The term circuit switching refers to a communication mechanism that establishes a path between a sender and receiver with guaranteed isolation from paths used by other pairs of senders and receivers. Circuit switching is usually associated with telephone technology because a telephone system provides a dedicated connection between two telephones. In fact, the term originated with early dialup telephone networks that used electromechanical switching devices to form a physical circuit.

In a circuit-switched network, also called *line-switched* network, a dedicated physical communication path is established between two stations through the switching nodes in the network. Hence, the end-to-end path from source to destination is a connected sequence of physical links between nodes and at each switching node the incoming data is switched to the appropriate outgoing link.

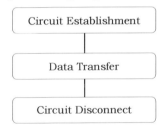

A circuit-switched communication system involves *three* phases: circuit establishment (setting up dedicated links between the source and destination); *data transfer* (transmitting the data between the source and destination); and *circuit disconnect* (removing the dedicated links). In circuit switching the connection path is established before data transmission begins (*on-demand*).

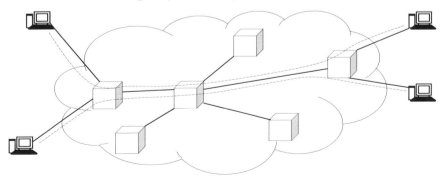

Therefore, the channel capacity must be reserved between the source and destination throughout the network and each node must have available internal switching capacity to handle the requested connection. Clearly, the switching nodes must have the intelligence to make proper allocations and to establish a route through the network.

The most common example of a circuit-switched network can be found in public telephone network supporting services such as POTS (plain old telephone systems) and long-distance calls.

2.12.2.2 Packet Switched Networks

The main alternative to circuit switching is packet switching which forms the basis for the Internet. A packet switching system uses statistical multiplexing in which communication from multiple sources competes for the use of shared media.

The main difference between packet switching and other forms of statistical multiplexing arises because a packet switching system requires a sender to divide each message into blocks of data that are known as packets. The size of a packet varies; each packet switching technology defines a maximum packet size.

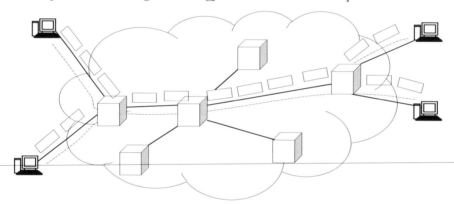

Three general properties define a packet switched paradigm:
1. Arbitrary, asynchronous communication
2. No set-up required before communication begins
3. Performance varies due to statistical multiplexing among packets

The first property means that packet switching can allow a sender to communicate with one recipient or multiple recipients, and a given recipient can receive messages from one sender or multiple senders. Furthermore, communication can occur at any time, and a sender can delay arbitrarily long between successive communications.

The second property means that, unlike a circuit switched system, a packet switched system remains ready to deliver a packet to any destination at any time. Thus, a sender does not need to perform initialization before communicating, and does not need to notify the underlying system when communication terminates.

The third property means that multiplexing occurs among packets rather than among bits or bytes. That is, once a sender gains access to the underlying channel, the sender transmits an entire packet, and then allows other senders to transmit a packet. When no other senders are ready to transmit a packet, a single sender can transmit repeatedly.

However, if n senders each have a packet to send, a given sender will transmit approximately $\frac{1}{n}$ of all packets.

In packet switching, packets can be handled in two ways:

1. Datagram
2. Virtual Circuit

2.12.2.2.1 Datagram Packet Switching

Datagram packet-switching is a *packet* switching technology. Each packet is routed independently through the network. Each packet can take any practical route to the desired destination. Therefore packets contain a header with the full information about the destination. The intermediate nodes examine the header of a packet and select an appropriate link to another node which is nearer to the destination. In this system, the packets do not follow a pre-established route, and the intermediate nodes do not require prior knowledge of the routes that will be used.

The packets may arrive out of order and they may go missing. The receiver will take care of re-ordering the packets and recover from missing packets.

In this technique, there is no need for setting up a connection. We just need to make sure each packet contains enough information to get it to destination. To give importance to critical packets, priorities can be attached to each packet.

The individual packets which form a data stream may follow different paths between the source and the destination. As a result, the packets may arrive at the destination out of order. When this occurs, the packets will have to be reassembled to form the original message. Because each packet is switched independently, there is no need for connection setup and no need to dedicate bandwidth in the form of a circuit.

Datagram packet switches use a variety of techniques to forward traffic; they are differentiated by how long it takes the packet to pass through the switch and their ability to filter out corrupted packets.

The most common datagram network is the Internet, which uses the IP network protocol. Applications which do not require more than a best effort service can be supported by direct use of packets in a datagram network, using the User Datagram Protocol (UDP) transport protocol. Applications like voice and video communications and notifying messages to alert a user that she/he has received new email are using UDP. Applications like e-mail, web browsing and file upload and download need reliable communications, such as guaranteed delivery, error control and sequence control. This reliability ensures that all the data is received in the correct order without errors. It is provided by a protocol such as the Transmission Control Protocol (TCP) or the File Transfer Protocol (FTP).

To forward the packets, each switch creates a table (maps destinations to output port). When a packet with a destination address in the table arrives, it pushes it out on the appropriate output port. When a packet with a destination address not in the table arrives, it will find the optimal route based on routing algorithms.

2.12.2.2.2 Virtual Circuit Packet Switching

Virtual circuit switching is a packet switching methodology whereby a path is established between the source and the final destination through which all the packets will be routed during a call. This path is called a virtual circuit because to the user, the connection appears to be a dedicated physical circuit. However, other communications may also be sharing the parts of the same path.

The idea of virtual circuit switching is to combine the advantages of circuit switching with the advantages of datagram switching. In virtual circuit packet switching, after a small connection setup phase only short (compared to full addresses) connection identifier are used per packet; this reduces the addressing overhead per packet.

Before the data transfer begins, the source and destination identify a suitable path for the virtual circuit. All intermediate nodes between the two points put an entry of the routing in their routing table for the call. Additional parameters, such as the maximum packet size, are also exchanged between the source and the destination during call setup. The virtual circuit is cleared after the data transfer is completed.

Virtual circuit packet switching is connection orientated. This is in contrast to datagram switching, which is a connection less packet switching methodology.

2.12.2.2.2.1 Advantages of Virtual Circuit Switching

Advantages of virtual circuit switching are:

- Packets are delivered in order, since they all take the same route;
- The overhead in the packets is smaller, since there is no need for each packet to contain the full address;
- The connection is more reliable, network resources are allocated at call setup so that even during times of congestion, provided that a call has been setup, the subsequent packets should get through;
- Billing is easier, since billing records need only be generated per call and not per packet.

2.12.2.2.2.2 Disadvantages of Virtual Circuit Switching

Disadvantages of a virtual circuit switched network are:

- The switching equipment needs to be more powerful, since each switch needs to store details of all the calls that are passing through it and to allocate capacity for any traffic that each call could generate;
- Resilience to the loss of a trunk is more difficult, since if there is a failure all the calls must be dynamically re-established over a different route.

2.12.2.3 Message Switched Networks

Prior to advances in packet switching, message switching was introduced as an effective alternative to circuit switching. In message switching, end-users communicate by sending each other a message, which contains the entire data being delivered from the source to destination node.

As a message is routed from its source to its destination, each intermediate switch within the network stores the entire message, providing a very reliable service. In fact, when congestion occurs or all network resources are occupied, rather than discarding the traffic, the message-switched network will store and delay the traffic until sufficient resources are available for successful delivery of the message.

The message storing capability can also lead to reducing the cost of transmission; for example, messages can be delivered at night when transmission costs are typically lower.

Message switching techniques were originally used in data communications. Early examples of message switching applications are Electronic mail (E-mail) and voice mail. Today, message switching is used in many networks, including adhoc sensor networks, satellite communications networks, and military networks.

Message-switched data networks are hop-by-hop systems that support two distinct characteristics: *store-and-forward* and *message delivery*.

In a message-switched network, there is no direct connection between the source and destination nodes. In such networks, the intermediary nodes (switches) have the responsibility of conveying the received message from one node to another in the network. Therefore, each intermediary node within the network must store all messages before retransmitting them one at a time as proper resources become available. This characteristic is called *store-and-forward*. In message switching systems (also called *store-and-forward* systems), the responsibility of the message delivery is on the next hop, as the message travels through the path toward its destination. Hence, to ensure proper delivery, each intermediate switch may maintain a copy of the message until its delivery to the next hop is guaranteed.

In case of message broadcasting, multiple copies may be stored for each individual destination node. The store-and-forward property of message-switched networks is different from queuing , in which messages are simply stored until their preceding messages are processed. With store-and-forward capability, a message will only be delivered if the next hop and the link connecting to it are both available. Otherwise, the message is stored indefinitely. For example, consider a mail server that is disconnected from the network and cannot receive the messages directed to it. In this case, the intermediary server must store all messages until the mail server is connected and receives the e-mails.

The store-and-forward technology is also different from admission control techniques implemented in packet-switched or circuit switched networks. Using admission control, the data transmission can temporarily be delayed to avoid overprovisioning the resources. Hence, a message-switched network can also implement an admission control mechanism to reduce network's peak load.

The message delivery in message-switched networks includes wrapping the entire information in a single message and transferring it from the source to the destination node. The message size has no upper bound; although some messages can be as small as a simple database query, others can be very large. For example, messages obtained from a meteorological database center can contain several million bytes of binary data. Practical limitations in storage devices and switches, however, can enforce limits on message length.

Each message must be delivered with a header. The header often contains the message routing information, including the source and destination, priority level, expiration time. It is worth mentioning that while a message is being stored at the source or any other intermediary node in the network, it can be bundled or aggregated with other messages going to the next node. This is called *message interleaving*. One important advantage of message interleaving is that it can reduce the amount of overhead generated in the network, resulting in higher link utilization.

Problems and Questions with Answers

Question 1: Suppose that a computer that is used as a switch can process 30,000 packets/second. Give a range of possible bit rates that traverse the I/O bus and main memory.

Answer: The 30,000 packets/second processing speed means 30,000 packets are going in and 30,000 packets are coming out of the switch every second. Therefore the I/O bus speed is 60,000 packets/second.

Minimum IP packet size = 64 bytes	Bit rate = 60,000×64×8 = 30.78 Mbps
Average IP packet size = 500 bytes	Bit rate = 60,000×500×8 = 240 Mbps
Maximum Ethernet frame size =1500 bytes	Bit rate = 60,000×1500×8 = 720 Mbps

Question 2:   Imagine the length of a cable is 2500 metres. If the speed of propagation in a thick co-axial cable is 60% of the speed of light, how long does it take for a bit to travel from the beginning to the end of the cable? Ignore any propagation delay in the equipment. (Speed of light c = 3 x 10^8 metres / sec)

Answer: Speed of propagation = 60% × c = 60 × 3 × 10^8 / 100 = 18 × 10^7 metres / sec. So it would take a bit 2500 / 18 × 10^7 = 13.9 μsecs.

Question 3:   Suppose that data are stored on 2.44 Mbyte floppy diskettes that weight 20 gm each. Suppose that an airliner carries 10^4 kg of these floppies at a speed of 2000 km/h over a distance of 8000 km. What is the data transmission rate in bits per second of this system?

Answer: Let us first calculate the time for which data was carried.

$$Speed = \frac{Distance}{Time}$$

So, Time = $\frac{Distance}{Speed} = \frac{8000\ km}{2000\ kmph}$ = 4 hrs.

Now 2.44 Mbytes = 2.44 × 10^6 × 8 bits = 19.52 × 10^6 bits.

Each floppy weighs 20 gm, and total load (of floppies) carried is 10^4 kg = 10^7gms. Hence, number of floppies carried = 10^7 gms / 20 gms = 500000.

Now each floppy contains 19.52 × 10^6 bits and so 500000 floppies will contain 19.52 × 10^6 × 500000 bits = 9760000 × 10^6 bits.

Now calculate data transmission speed:

$$Transmission\ speed\ = \frac{Data\ carried\ in\ bits}{Time} = \frac{9760000 \times 10^6\ bits}{(5\ hrs\ x\ 60\ mins\ x\ 60\ secs\ )}$$
$$= 542.2 \times 10^6\ bits/sec= 542.2\ Mbps.$$

Question 4:   A simple telephone system consists of two end offices and a single toll office to which each end office is connected by a 1-MHz full-duplex trunk. The average telephone is used to make four calls per 8-hour workday. The mean call duration is 6 min. Ten percent of the calls are long-distance (i.e., pass through the toll office). What is the maximum number of telephones an end office can support? Assume 4 kHz per circuit.

Answer: Each telephone makes 0.5 calls/hour at 6 minutes each. Thus, a telephone occupies a circuit for 3 min/hour. Twenty telephones can share a circuit. Since 10% of the calls are long distance, it takes 200 telephones to occupy a long-distance circuit full time. The interoffice trunk has $\frac{1000000}{4000}$=250 circuits multiplexed onto it. With 200 telephones per circuit, an end-office can support 200×250 = 50,000 telephones.

Question 5:   A channel has a bit rate of 4 kbps and a propagation delay of 20 msec. For what range of frame sizes does stop-and-wait give an efficiency of at least 50%?

Answer: Efficiency will be 50% when the time to transmit the frame equals the round trip propagation delay. At a transmission rate of 4 bits/ms, 160 bits takes 40 ms. For frame sizes above 160 bits, stop-and-wait is reasonably efficient.

Question 6: Suppose a 128 kbps peer-to-peer link is set up between earth and a rover on mars. The distance from the earth to mars (when they are the closest together) is approximately 55 Gm (Gigameter), and data travels over the link at the speed of light 3×10^8 meters/sec. Calculate the minimum RTT for the link.

Answer: Propagation delay of the link is $\frac{55 \times 10^9}{3 \times 10^8}$ = 184 secs. Thus, RTT = 368 secs.

Question 7: For the Question 6, calculate the *delay X bandwidth* product of the link.

Answer: The delay × bandwidth product for the link is the RTT × bandwidth = 23.5 Mb.

Question 8: For the Question 6, a camera on the rover takes pictures of its surroundings and sends these to the earth. How quickly can it reach Mission Control on Earth? Assume that each image is 5 Mb in size.

Answer: After a picture is taken, it must be transmitted on the link and completely propagated, before Mission Control can interpret it. Transmit delay for 5 Mb of data is 29 secs. Hence, total time = Transmit delay + Propagation delay = 223 secs.

Question 9: Calculate the latency (from first bit sent to the last bit received) for the following: 1 Gbps Ethernet with a single store and forward switch in the path, and a packet size of 5000 bits. Assume that each link introduces a propagation delay of 10 μs (micro second) and that the switch begins retransmitting immediately after it has finished receiving the packet.

Answer:

A) For each link it takes $\frac{1\ Gbps}{5000}$ = 5 μs to transmit the packet on the link, after which it takes an additional 10 μs for the last bit to propagate across the link. Thus for a LAN with only with only one switch that starts forwarding only after receiving the whole packet, the total transfer delay is the transmit delays + two propagation delays = 30 μs.

B) For 3 switched and thus 4 links, the total delay is 4 transmission delays + 4 propagation delays = 60 μs.

Question 10: Determine the maximum length of the cable (in km) for transmitting data at a rate of 500 Mbps in an Ethernet LAN with frames of size 10,000 bits. Assume the signal speed in the cable to be 2,00,000 km/s.
A) 1   B) 2   C) 2.5   D) 5

Answer: B

$$\frac{Frame\ Size}{Propagation\ time} = \frac{Length}{Signal\ Speed} + \frac{Length}{Signal\ Speed}$$

Propagation time = Transmission time + Collision signal time

$$\frac{Frame\ Size}{Propagation\ time} = \frac{2 \times Length}{Signal\ Speed}$$

$$\frac{10000\ bits}{500 \times 1000000\ bits/sec} = \frac{2 \times Length}{200000\ km/sec}$$

$$Length = 2\ km$$

Question 11: A packet switch receives a packet and determines the outbound link to which the packet should be forwarded. When the packet arrives, one other packet is halfway done being transmitted on this outbound link and four other packets are waiting to be transmitted. Packets are transmitted in order of arrival. Suppose all packets are 1,200 bytes and the link rate is 3 Mbps. What is the queuing delay for the packet? More generally, what is the queuing delay when all packets have length S, the transmission rate is T, X bits of the currently being transmitted packet have been transmitted, and n packets are already in the queue?

Solution: The arriving packet must first wait for the link to transmit 5,400 bytes or 43,200 bits. Since these bits are transmitted at 3 Mbps, the queuing delay is 14.3 msec. Generally, the queuing delay is $\frac{n \times S + (S-X)}{T}$.

Question 12: Suppose we would like to urgently deliver 60 Terabytes of data from *Hyderabad* to *London*. We have a 1000 Mbps dedicated link for data transfer available. Would you prefer to transmit the data via this link or instead use AirMail overnight delivery? Explain.

Answer: 60 Terabytes = $60 \times 10^{12} \times 8$ bits. So, if using the dedicated link, it will take $60 \times 10^{12} \times 8 / (1000 \times 10^6) = 480000$ seconds = 5.6 days. But with AirMail overnight delivery, we can guarantee the data arrives in one day, and it only costs us no more than USD 100.

Question 13: Two nodes, A and B, communicate through a store & forward network. Node A is connected to the network by a 10 Mbps link, while node B is connected by a 5 Mbps link. Node A sends two back-to-back packets of 1000 bits each. The difference between the arrival times of the two packets at B is 1 ms. What is the smallest capacity of a link along the path between A and B?

Note: Assume that there are no other packets in the network except the ones sent by A, and ignore the packet processing time. Assume both packets follow the same path, and they are not reordered. The arrival time of a packet at a node is defined as the time when the last bit of the packet has arrived at that node.

Answer: Since packets are sent back-to-back, the difference between the arrival times of the packets at B represents the transmission time of the second packet on the slowest link in the path. Thus, the capacity of the slowest link is 1000 bits/1 ms = 1 Mbps.

Question 14: Consider an infinite queue that can send data at 10 Kbps. Assume the following arrival traffic:

- During every odd second the queue receives an 1000 bit packet every 50 ms
- During every even second the queue receives no data.

Assume an interval I of 10 sec starting with an odd second (i.e., a second in which the queue receives data). At the beginning of interval I the queue is empty. What is the maximum queue size during interval I?

Answer: 10 packets. There are 20 packets arriving during the 1st second and 10 packets sent at the end of that second. Thus at the end of 1st second there are 10 packets in the queue. All the 10 packets will be sent at the end of 2nd second (since no new packets are received). Thus, at the end of 2nd second the queue size is 0. After that the process repeats.

(Note: The following alternate answers: 11 packets, 10 Kb, and 11 Kb all received maximum points. The 11 packets and 11 Kbps assume that at a time when a packet is received and another one is sent out, the received packet is already in the queue as the other packet is sent out.)

Question 15: For the Question 14, what is the average time (delay) a packet spends in the queue during interval I?

Answer:

- 1st packet arrives at time 0 and starts being transmitted immediately, at time 0.→ delay 0
- 2nd packet arrives at 0.05 s and starts being transmitted at 0.1 s (after the first packet) → delay 0.05 s
- 3rd packet arrives at 0.1 s and starts being transmitted at 0.2 s (after first two packets) → delay 0.1 s
- 4th packet arrives at 0.15 s and starts being transmitted at 0.3 s (after first three packets) → delay 0.15 s

...

- k^{th} packet arrives at $(k-1) \times 0.05$ s and starts being transmitted at (k-1)*0.1 s delay $(k-1) \times 0.05$ s

This process continues every 2 seconds.

Thus, the average delay of the first 20 packets is

$$\frac{(0 + 1 + 2 + \dots + 19) \times 0.05 \text{ s}}{20} = \frac{10 \times 19 \times 0.05 s}{20} = 0.475 \text{ s}$$

Alternate solution that approximates the average delay: We use Little's theorem: $avg\_delay = \frac{avg\_number\_of\_packets}{arrival\_rate}$. During an odd second the number of packets in the queue increases linearly from 0 to 10 and during the next second it decreases from 10 to 0. This means that the average number of packets in the queue is 5. Over an odd and an even second the average arrival rate is $\frac{20+0}{2} = 10$.

Then, $avg\_delay = \frac{avg\_number\_of\_packets}{arrival\_rate} = \frac{5}{10} = 0.5\text{sec}$.

(Note: The following answers also received maximum points: 0.575s and 0.5s.)

Question 16: Similar to Question 14 and Question 15, now assume that during odd seconds the queue receives 1000 bit packets every 25 ms (instead of every 50 ms), and during even seconds it still receives no data. For this traffic patterns answer the same questions. What is the maximum queue size during interval I?

Answer: 110 packets. In this case the queue is never empty. During the first 9 seconds of interval I there are 5 s×(1 s/25 ms) = 200 packets received and 90 packets sent out. Thus, at the end of the 9th second there are 110 packets in the queue.

(Note: The following answers also received the maximum number of points: 111 packets, 110 Kb, and 111 Kb.)

Question 17: For the Question 16, what is the average time (delay) a packet spends in the queue during interval I?

Answer: Packets received during first second

- 1st packet arrives at time 0 and starts being transmitted immediately, at time 0.→ delay 0
- 2nd packet arrives at 0.025 s and starts being transmitted at 0.1 s (after the first packet) → delay 0.075 s
- 3rd packet arrives at 0.05s and starts being transmitted at 0.2 s (after first two packets) → delay 0.15 s
- 4th packet arrives at 0.075 s and starts being transmitted at 0.3 s (after first three packets) → delay 0.225 s

...

- k^{th} packet arrives at $(k-1) \times 0.025$ s and starts being transmitted at $(k-1) \times 0.1$ s → delay $(k-1) \times 0.075$s

The average delay of the packets in the first two seconds is

$$\frac{(0 + 1 + \ldots + 39)*0.075s}{40} = \frac{20 \times 39 \times 0.075s}{40} = 1.4625 \text{ s}$$

Packets received during 3rd second: note that at the beginning of the 3rd second there are still 20 packets in the queue

- 1st packet arrives at time 0 and starts being transmitted immediately, at time 2s → delay 2
- 2nd packet arrives at 0.025s and starts being transmitted at 2+0.1 s → delay 2+0.075 s
- 3rd packet arrives at 0.05s and starts being transmitted at 2+0.2 s → delay 2+0.15 s
- 4th packet arrives at 0.075s and starts being transmitted at 2+0.3 s → delay 2+0.225 s

...

- k^{th} packet arrives at (k-1)*0.025s and starts being transmitted at 2+$(k-1) \times 0.1$ s → delay 2+$(k-1) \times 0.075$ s

The average delay of the packets in the first two seconds is

$$\frac{(0 + 1 + \ldots + 39) \times 0.075 \text{ s}}{40} = \frac{20 \times 39 \times 0.075s}{40} = 3.4625 \text{ s}$$

...

Packets received during 9th second: note that at the beginning of the 9th second there are still 80 packets in the queue

- 1st packet arrives at time 0 and starts being transmitted immediately, at time 8s → delay 2
- 2nd packet arrives at 0.025s and starts being transmitted at 8+0.1s → delay 8+0.075s
- 3rd packet arrives at 0.05s and starts being transmitted at 8+0.2s → delay 8+0.15s
- 4th packet arrives at 0.075s and starts being transmitted at 8+0.3s → delay 8+0.225s

...

- k^{th} packet arrives at (k-1) $\times$ 0.025s and starts being transmitted at 8+(k-1) $\times$ 0.1s → delay 8+(k-1) $\times$ 0.075s

The average delay of the packets in the first two seconds is

$$\frac{(0 + 1 + \ldots + 39) \times 0.075s}{40} = \frac{20 \times 39 \times 0.075s}{40} = 9.4625 \text{ s}$$

Thus, the average delay over 10 seconds is: $\frac{1.4625+3.4625+5.4625+7.4625+9.4625}{5} = 5.4625$

Alternate solution that approximates the average delay: The average arrival rate is 40 packets/2 sec = 20 packets/sec.

During the 1st sec the number of packets in the queue increases linearly from 0 to 30, thus the average number of packets in the queue in the 1st sec is 15. During 2nd second the queue decreases linearly from 30 to 20, thus the average number of packets in the queue is 25, and the average number of packets in the queue over the first two seconds is 20.

During 3rd and 4th seconds the process repeats with the difference that there are 20 packets in the queue at the beginning of the 3rd second. Thus, the average number of packets in the queue during the 3rd and 4th seconds is 20+20 = 40.

Similarly, the average number of packets during the 5th and 6th seconds is 40+20 = 60, during the 7th and 8th seconds 60+20=80, and during the 9th and 10th seconds is 80+20=100.

Thus the average number of packets over the entire interval I is $\frac{20+40+60+80+100}{5}$ = 60.

According to the Little's theorem avg_delay = $\frac{avg\_number\_of\_packets}{arrival\_rate}$ = $\frac{60}{10}$ = 6sec.

(Note: In general the average number of packets over the interval defined by the $2 \times k - 1$ and $2 \times k$ seconds is $k \times 20$, where $k >= 1$.)

Question 18: Suppose a CSMA/CD network is operating at 1 Gbps, and suppose there are no repeaters and the length of the cable is 1 km. Determine the minimum frame size if the signal propagation speed is 200 km/ms.

Answer: Since the length of the cable is 1 km, we have a one-way propagation time of p = $\frac{1 \text{ km}}{200 \text{ km/ms}}$ = 0.005 ms = 5 μs. So, $2 p$ = 10 μs.

If we have 1 Gbps, we can calculate the amount of bits transmitted in 10 μs.

Let L be the minimum frame size, then 10 μs = $\frac{L}{1 \text{ Gbps}}$ = $\frac{L}{1000 \text{ bits per μs}}$.
This gives the value of L. L = 10,000 bits.

So the minimum frame size should be 10,000 bits.

Question 19: A signal has a fundamental frequency of 1000 Hz. What is its period?

Answer: Period = $\frac{1}{Frequency}$ = 1 ms.

Question 20: A digital signaling system is required to operate at 9600 bps. If a symbol encodes a 4-bit word, what is the minimum required channel bandwidth?

Answer: The formula to use is

Maximum number of bits/sec=2×Channel bandwidth×Number of bits per sample

If number of different possible values of a sample is given, use the formula

Maximum number of bits/sec=2×Channel bandwidth× $log_2^{no \ of \ possible \ values \ of \ a \ sample}$

Note that $log_2^{no \ of \ possible \ values \ of \ a \ sample}$ gives us the number of bits needed to represent them or the number of bits/sample.

Based on above formula, 9600 = 2×h×4 or h = 1200 Hz.

Question 21: For the Question 20, what is the minimum bandwidth for 8-bit words?

Answer: 9600 = 2×h×8 or h = 600 Hz.

Question 22: A channel, whose bandwidth is 3 MHz, has an intended capacity of 20 Mbps, Assuming white thermal noise, what signal to noise ratio is required to achieve this capacity?

Answer: Use the formula:

$$\text{Maximum number of bits/sec = H} \times log_2^{1+\frac{S}{N}}$$

Substitute H = 3×10^6 and maximum no of bits/sec to 20×10^6 to get a $\frac{S}{N}$ of 100.6.

Question 23: Suppose that data is stored on 1.4 Mbyte floppy diskettes that weight 30 grams each. Suppose that an airliner carries 10^4 Kg of these floppies at a speed of

1000 Km/h over a distance of 5000 Km. What is the data transmission rate in bps of this system?

Answer: Each floppy measures 30 grams. We have the following

$$\text{Number of floppies} = 10^4 \times 10^3/30 = 333333.33$$

Total number of bits transported = Number of floppies $\times 1.4 \times 1024$ (not 1000!) $\times 1024 \times 8$

i.e., Number of bits/sec = Total number of bits transported/5*3600.

The answer is 217.4 Mbps.

Note: When we talk of computer momory, it is typically measured in powers of 2, thefore 1 Kb = 2^{10} bytes. When it comes to networks, we use clocks to send data, if a clock is 1 Khz, we transmit at the rate of 1 kilobits per sec, where the kilo is 1000, we are transmitting at the clock rate.

Question 24: Consider a 150 Mb/s link that is 800 km long, with a queue large enough to hold 5,000 packets. Assume that packets arrive at the queue with an average rate of 40,000 packets per second and that the average packet length is 3,000 bits. Approximately, what is the propagation delay for the link?

Answer: 800 km times 5 microseconds per km is 4,000 microseconds or 4 ms.

Question 25: For the Question 24:, what is the transmission time for an average length packet?

Answer: Link speed is 150 bits per microsecond, so a 3,000 bit packet can be sent in 20 microseconds.

Question 26: For the Question 24:, what is the traffic intensity?

Answer: Bit arrival rate is 40,000 times 3,000 or 120 Mb/s. Since the link rate is 150 Mb/s, I=0.8

Question 27: For the Question 24:, what is the average number of packets in the queue?

Answer: $\frac{I}{1-I}$ =4.

Question 28: What is the average number in the queue, if the average arrival rate is 80,000 packets per second?

Answer: In this case, the traffic intensity is 1.6, so the queue will be nearly full all the time. So, the average number is just under 5,000 packets.

Question 29: A user in Hyderabad, connected to the Internet via a 5 Mb/s connection retrieves a 50 KB (B=bytes) web page from a web server in New York, where the page references 4 images of 300 KB each. Assume that the one way propagation delay is 20 ms. Approximately how long does it take for the page (including images) to appear on the user's screen, assuming persistent HTTP?

Answer: Total time is 3RTT + Transmission time.

3RTT = 120 ms and Transmission time $=\frac{50\text{KB} + 1.2\text{MB}}{5 \text{ Mb/s}} = \frac{10 \text{ Mb}}{5 \text{ Mb/s}} = 2$ seconds

Total time = 2.12 seconds.

Question 30: For the Question 29, how long would it take using non-persistent HTTP (assume a single connection)?

$$2(1 + \text{number of objects in page})\text{RTT} + \text{Transmission time}$$
$$400 \text{ ms} + 2 \text{ seconds} = 2.4 \text{ seconds}$$

Question 31: Suppose a movie studio wants to distribute a new movie as a digital file to 1,000 movie theaters across country using peer-to-peer file distribution. Assume that the studio and all the theaters have DSL connections with an 8 Mb/s downstream rate and a 4 Mb/s upstream rate and that the file is 10 GB long. Approximately, how much time is needed to distribute the file to all the theaters under ideal conditions?

Answer: The total upstream bandwidth is about 4 Gb/s. Since the file must be delivered to 1,000 studios, we have 10 TB of data to be delivered. At 4 Gb/s, this takes 20,000 seconds, or roughly 6 hours.

Question 32: For the Question 24:, suppose the studio wanted to use the client-server method instead. What is the smallest link rate that is required at the studio that will allow the file to be distributed in under 40,000 seconds?

Answer: This time period is twice the time used for the first part, so the server's upstream bandwidth must be half as large as the upstream bandwidth of the peers in the first part. So, 2 Gb/s is enough.

Question 33: Suppose a file of 5,000 bytes is to be sent over a line at 2400 bps. Calculate the overhead in bits and time in using asynchronous communication. Assume one start bit and a stop element of length one bit, and 8 bits to send the byte itself for each character. The 8-bit character consists of all data bits, with no parity bit.

Answer: Each character has 25% overhead. For 10,000 characters, there are 20,000 extra bits. This would take an extra $\frac{5000}{2400}$ = 2.0833 seconds.

Question 34: Calculate the overhead in bits and time using synchronous communication. Assume that the data are sent in frames. Each frame consists of 1000 characters - 8000 bits and an overhead of 48 control bits per frame.

Answer: The file takes 10 frames or 480 additional bits. The transmission time for the additional bits is $\frac{480}{2400}$ = 0.2 seconds.

Question 35: What would the answers to Question 28 and Question 29 be for a file of 100,000 characters?

Answer: Ten times as many extra bits and ten times as long for both.

Question 36: What would the answers to Question 28 and Question 29 be for the original file of 10,000 characters except at a data rate of 9600 bps?

Answer: The number of overhead bits would be the same, and the time would be decreased by a factor of 4 = $\frac{9600}{2400}$.

Question 37: The loss of signal strength is called:
   A) Attenuation   B) Amplitude   C) Noise   D) Crosstalk

Answer: Attenuation

Question 38: Large networks that encompass parts of states, multiple states, countries and the world are called:
   A) MANs   B) LANs   C) PANs   D) WANs

Answer: D

Question 39: The __of a signal is the number of times a signal makes a complete cycle within a given time frame.

A) Bandwidth   C) Frequency   D) Amplitude   D) Spectrum

Answer: C

Question 40: In a ___ subnet, no unique dedicated physical path is established to transmit the data packets across the subnet?
A) Circuit-switched   B) Packet-switched   C) Large   D) Heavily loaded

Answer: B

Question 41: A dial-up telephone system uses which type of subnet?
A) Circuit-switched   B) Packet-switched   C) Broadcast   D) Logically switched

Answer: A

Question 42: A 2 km long broadcast LAN has 10^7 bps bandwidth and uses CSMA/CD. The signal travels along the wire at 2×10^8 m/s. What is the minimum packet size that can be used on this network?
A) 50 bytes   B) 100 bytes   C) 200 bytes   D) None of the above

Answer: C.

Total distance for RTT	=	4 Km
Transfer rate	=	2×10^8 m/s
Time to transfer	=	$\frac{4 \times 10^3}{2 \times 10^8} = 2 \times 10^{-5}$ s
Data rate	=	10^7 bps
Packet size	=	2×10^{-5}s $\times 10^7$ bps=200 bytes

Question 43: Station A uses 32 byte packets to transmit messages to Station B using a sliding window protocol. The round trip delay between A and B is 80 milliseconds and the bottleneck bandwidth on the path between A and B is 128 kbps. What is the optimal window size that A should use ?
A) 20   B) 40   C) 160   D) 320

Answer: B.

Path bandwidth	=	128 kbps
Time delay	=	80 ms
Total data	=	$80 \times 128 \times 10^3 \times 10^{-3}$ bits $= \frac{80 \times 128}{8} = 1280$ bytes
1 packet size	=	32 byte
Number of packets	=	$\frac{1280}{32} = 40$

CHAPTER

OSI and TCP/IP Models

3

3.1 Why OSI Model?

During the initial days of computer networks, they usually used proprietary solutions, i.e., technologies manufactured one company were used in the computer networks. And, that manufacturer was in-charge of all systems present on the network. There is no option to use equipment's from different vendors.

In order to help the interconnection of different networks, ISO (*InternationalStandards Organization*) developed a reference model called OSI (*Open Systems Interconnection*) and this allowed manufacturers to create protocols using this model. Some people get confused with these two acronyms, as they use the same letters. ISO is the name of the organization, while OSI is the name of the reference model for developing protocols.

> ISO is the organization; OSI is the model.

3.2 What is a Protocol-Stack?

Before understanding what a protocol is, let us take an example. In some cultures shaking head *up* and *down* means *yes*, in other cultures it means *no*. If we don't ensure correct communication, we will soon have a war on our hands! Protocols are the rules developed for communicating. In simple terms, a protocol is a standard set of rules and regulations that allow two electronic devices to connect to and exchange information with one another.

All of us are familiar with protocols for human communication. We have rules for speaking, appearance, listening and understanding. These rules govern different layers of communication. They help us in successful communication. Similarly, in computer networks, a protocol is a set of rules that govern communications between the computers.

A protocol stack is a complete *set* of network protocol layers that work together to provide *networking* capabilities. It is called a *stack* because it is typically designed as a hierarchy of layers, each supporting the one above it and using those below it.

The number of layers can vary between models. For example, TCP/IP (transmission control protocol/Internet protocol) has five layers (application, transport, network, data link and physical) and the OSI (open systems interconnect) model has seven layers (application, presentation, session, transport, network, data link and physical).

In order for two devices to communicate, they both must be using the same protocol stack. Each protocol in a stack on one device must communicate with its equivalent stack, or peer, on the other device. This allows computers running different operating systems to communicate with each other easily.

3.3 OSI Model

The OSI model divides the problem of moving data between computers into seven smaller tasks and they equate to the seven layers of the OSI reference model.
The OSI model deals with the following issues:

- How a device on a network sends its data, and how it knows when and where to send it.
- How a device on a network receives its data, and how to know where to look for it.
- How devices using different languages communicate with each other.
- How devices on a network are physically connected to each other.
- How protocols work with devices on a network to arrange data.

7	Application	**Network Processes to Applications** Provides network services to application processes (such as e-mail, file transfer [FTP], and web browsing)
6	Presentation	**Data Representation** This layer ensures data is readable by receiving system; formats data; negotiates data transfer syntax for application layer. *Examples*: ASCII, EBCDIC, Encryption, GIF, JPEG, PICT, and mp3.
5	Session	**Interhost Communication** This layer establishes, manages, and terminates sessions between applications. *Examples*: NFS, SQL, and X Windows.
4	Transport	**End-to-end connections** Deals with data transport issues between systems. It offers reliability, establishes virtual circuits, detects/recovers from errors, and provides flow control. *Examples*: TCP and UDP.
3	Network	**Addresses and Best Path Determination** Provides connectivity and path selection between two end systems. Routers live here. *Examples*: IP, IPX, RIP, IGRP, and OSPF.
2	Data link	**Access to Media** Provides reliable transfer of data across media. Responsible for physical addressing, network topology, error notification, and flow control. *Examples*: NIC, Ethernet, and IEEE 802.3.
1	Physical	**Binary Transmission** Uses signaling to transmit bits (0s and 1s). *Examples*: UTP, coaxial cable, fiber optic cable, hubs, and repeaters.

3.3.1 The Application Layer

The top layer of the OSI model is the Application layer. The first thing that we need to understand about the application layer is that it does not refer to the actual applications that users run. Instead, it provides the framework that the actual applications run on top of.

To understand what the application layer does, suppose for a moment that a user wanted to use *Google Chrome* to open an FTP session and transfer a file. In this particular case, the application layer would define the file transfer protocol. This protocol is not directly accessible to the end user.

The end user must still use an application that is designed to interact with the file transfer protocol. In this case, *Google Chrome* would be that application.

3.3.2 The Presentation Layer

The presentation layer does some rather complex things, but everything that the presentation layer does can be summed up in one sentence. The presentation layer takes the data that is provided by the application layer, and converts it into a standard format that the other below layers can understand.

Likewise, this layer converts the inbound data that is received from the session layer into something that the application layer can understand.

The reason why this layer is necessary is because applications handle data differently from one another. In order for network communications to function properly, the data needs to be structured in a standard way.

3.3.3 The Session Layer

Once the data has been put into the correct format, the sending host must establish a session with the receiving host. This is where the session layer comes into play. It is responsible for establishing, maintaining, and eventually terminating the session with the remote host.

The interesting thing about the session layer is that it is more closely related to the application layer than it is to the physical layer. It is easy to think of connecting a network session as being a hardware function, but in actuality, sessions are usually established between applications.

If a user is running multiple applications, several of those applications may have established sessions with remote resources at any time.

3.3.4 The Transport Layer

Transport layer is responsible for maintaining flow control. As you are no doubt aware, the Windows operating system allows users to run multiple applications simultaneously. It is therefore possible that multiple applications, and the operating system itself, may need to communicate over the network simultaneously. The Transport Layer takes the data from each application, and integrates it all into a single stream.

This layer is also responsible for providing error checking and performing data recovery when necessary. In essence, the Transport Layer is responsible for ensuring that all of the data makes it from the sending host to the receiving host.

3.3.5 The Network Layer

The Network Layer is responsible for determining how the data will reach the recipient. This layer handles things like addressing, routing, and logical protocols. Since this series is geared toward beginners, I do not want to get too technical, but The Network Layer creates logical paths, known as virtual circuits, between the source and destination hosts. This circuit provides the individual packets with a way to reach their destination. The Network Layer is also responsible for its own error handling, and for packet sequencing and congestion control.

Packet sequencing is necessary because each protocol limits the maximum size of a packet. The amount of data that must be transmitted often exceeds the maximum packet size. Therefore, the data is fragmented into multiple packets. When this happens, the Network Layer assigns each packet a sequence number.

When the data is received by the remote host, that device's Network layer examines the sequence numbers of the inbound packets, and uses the sequence number to reassemble the data and to figure out if any packets are missing.

If you are having trouble understanding this concept, then imagine that you need to mail a large document to a friend, but do not have a big enough envelope. You could put a few pages into several small envelopes, and then label the envelopes so that your friend knows what order the pages go in. This is exactly the same thing that the Network Layer does.

3.3.6 The Data Link Layer

The data link layer can be sub divided into two other layers; the Media Access Control (MAC) layer, and the Logical Link Control (LLC) layer. The MAC layer basically establishes the computer's identity on the network, via its MAC address. A MAC address is the address that is assigned to a network adapter at the hardware level. This is the address that is ultimately used when sending and receiving packets. The LLC layer controls frame synchronization and provides a degree of error checking.

3.3.7 The Physical Layer

The physical layer of the OSI model refers to the actual hardware specifications. The Physical Layer defines characteristics such as timing and voltage. The physical layer defines the hardware specifications used by network adapters and by the network cables (assuming that the connection is not wireless). To put it simply, the physical layer defines what it means to transmit and to receive data.

3.3.8 How OSI Model Works? [Communications between Stacks]

The OSI reference model is actually used to describe how data that is generated by a user, such as an email message, moves through a number of intermediary forms until it is converted into a stream of data that can actually be placed on the network media and sent out over the network. The model also describes how a communication session is established between two devices, such as two computers, on the network.

Since other types of devices, such as printers and routers, can be involved in network communication, devices (including computers) on the network are actually referred to as *nodes*. Therefore, a client computer on the network or a server on the network would each be *referred* to as a *node*.

While sending data over a network, it moves down through the OSI stack and is transmitted over the transmission media. When the data is received by a node, such as another computer on the network, it moves up through the OSI stack until it is again in a form that can be accessed by a user on that computer.

Each of the layers in the OSI model is responsible for certain aspects of getting user data into a format that can be transmitted on the network. Some layers are for establishing and maintaining the connection between the communicating nodes, and other layers are responsible for the addressing of the data so that it can be determined where the data originated (on which node) and where the data's destination is.

An important aspect of the OSI model is that each layer in the stack provides services to the layer directly above it. Only the *Application* layer, which is at the top of the stack, would not provide services to a higher-level layer.

The process of moving user data down the OSI stack on a sending node (again, such as a computer) is called *encapsulation*. The process of moving raw data received by a node up the OSI stack is referred to as *de-encapsulation*.

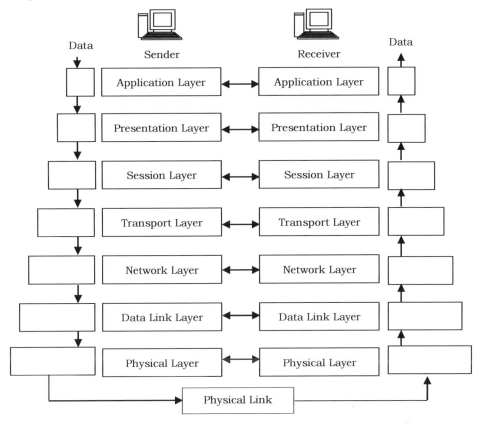

To encapsulate means to enclose or surround, and this is what happens to data that is created at the Application layer and then moves down through the other layers of the OSI model. A header, which is a segment of information affixed to the beginning of the data, is generated at each layer of the OSI model, except for the Physical layer.

This means that the data is encapsulated in a succession of headers—first the *Application* layer header, then the *Presentation* layer header, and so on. When the data reaches the *Physical* layer, it is like a candy bar that has been enclosed in several different wrappers.

When the data is transmitted to a receiving node, such as a computer, the data travels up the OSI stack and each header is stripped off of the data. First, the *Data Link* layer header is removed, then the *Network* layer header, and so on. Also, the headers are not just removed by the receiving computer; the header information is read and used to determine what the receiving computer should do with the received data at each layer of the OSI model.

In OSI model, the sending computer uses these headers to communicate with the receiving computer and provide the receiving computer with useful. As the data travels up the levels of the peer computer, each header is removed by its equivalent protocol.

These headers contain different information depending on the layer they receive the header from, but tell the peer layer important information, including packet size, frames, and datagrams.

Control is passed from one layer to the next, starting at the application layer in one station, and proceeding to the bottom layer, over the channel to the next station and back up the hierarchy.

Each layer's header and data are called *packages*. Although it may seem confusing, each layer has a different name for its service data unit. Here are the common names for service data units at each level of the OSI model.

Layer #	Name	Encapsulation Units	Devices	Keywords/Description
7	Application	data	PC	Network services for application processes, such as file, print, messaging, database services
6	Presentation	data		Standard interface to data for the application layer. MIME encoding, data encryption, conversion, formatting, compression
5	Session	data		Inter host communication. Establishes, manages and terminates connection between applications
4	Transport	segments		Provides end-to-end message delivery and error recovery (reliability). Segmentation/desegmentation of data in proper sequence (flow control).
3	Network	packets	router	Logical addressing and path determination. Routing. Reporting delivery errors
2	Data Link	frames	bridge, switch, NIC	Physical addressing and access to media. Two sublayers: Logical Link Control (LLC) and Media Access Control (MAC)
1	Physical	bits	repeater, hub, transceiver	Binary transmission signals and encoding. Layout of pins, voltages, cable specifications, modulation

3.4 TCP/IP Model

The TCP/IP model is a networking model with a set of communication protocols for the Internet and similar networks. It is commonly known as TCP/IP, because its *Transmission Control Protocol* (TCP) and *Internet Protocol* (IP) were the first networking protocols defined in this model.

The TCP/IP model, similar to the OSI model, has a set of layers. The OSI has seven layers and the TCP/IP model has *four* or *five* layers depending on different preferences. Some people use the Application, Transport, Internet and Network Access layers. Others split the *Network Access* layer into the Physical and Data Link components.

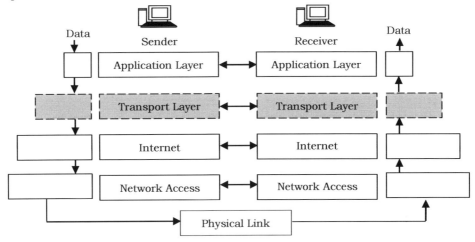

The OSI model and the TCP/IP models were both created independently. The TCP/IP network model represents reality in the world, whereas the OSI mode represents an ideal.

Layer #	Description	Protocols
Application	Defines TCP/IP application protocols and how host programs interface with transport layer services to use the network.	HTTP, Telnet, FTP, TFTP, SNMP, DNS, SMTP, X Windows, other application protocols
Transport	Provides communication session management between the nodes/computers. Defines the level of service and status of the connection used when transporting data.	TCP, UDP, RTP
Internet	Packages data into IP datagrams, which contain source and destination address information that is used to forward the datagrams between hosts and networks. Performs routing of IP datagrams.	IP, ICMP, ARP, RARP
Network Access	Specifies details of how data is physically sent through the network, including how bits are electrically signaled by hardware	Ethernet, Token Ring, FDDI, X.25, Frame Relay, RS-2

	devices that interface directly with a network medium, such as coaxial cable, optical fiber, or twisted-pair copper wire.	

3.4.1 Application Layer

Application layer is the top most layer of four layer TCP/IP model. Application layer is present on the top of the Transport layer. Application layer defines TCP/IP application protocols and how host programs interface with transport layer services to use the network.

This layer is comparable to the application, presentation, and session layers of the OSI model all combined into one.

Application layer includes all the higher-level protocols like DNS (Domain Naming System), HTTP (Hypertext Transfer Protocol), Telnet, FTP (File Transfer Protocol), SNMP (Simple Network Management Protocol), SMTP (Simple Mail Transfer Protocol), DHCP (Dynamic Host Configuration Protocol), RDP (Remote Desktop Protocol) etc.

3.4.2 Transport Layer

Transport Layer is the third layer of the four layer TCP/IP model. The position of the Transport layer is between Application layer and Internet layer.

Transport layer (also called *Host-to-Host* protocol) in the TCP/IP model provides more or less the same services with its equivalent Transport layer in the OSI model. This layer acts as the delivery service used by the application layer. Again the two protocols used are TCP and UDP. The choice is made based on the application's transmission reliability requirements.

It also ensures that data arrives at the application on the host for which it is targeted. Transport layer manages the flow of traffic between two hosts or devices. The transport layer also handles all error detection and recovery. It uses checksums, acknowledgements, and timeouts to control transmissions and end to end verification.

3.4.3 Internet Layer

Internet layer in TCP/IP model provides same services as the OSI model Network layer. Their purpose is to route packets to destination independent of the path taken.

The routing and delivery of data is the responsibility of this layer and is the key component of this architecture. It allows communication across networks of the same and different types, and performs translations to deal with dissimilar data addressing schemes. It injects packets into any network and delivers them to the destination independently to one another.

Since the path through the network is not predetermined, the packets may be received out of order. The upper layers are responsible for the reordering of the data. This layer can be compared to the network layer of the OSI model.

The main protocols included at Internet layer are IP (Internet Protocol), ICMP (Internet Control Message Protocol), ARP (Address Resolution Protocol), RARP (Reverse Address Resolution Protocol) and IGMP (Internet Group Management Protocol).

3.4.4 Network Access Layer

Network Access Layer is the first layer of the four layer TCP/IP model. Network Access layer defines details of how data is physically sent through the network. That means how bits are electrically or optically sent by hardware devices that interface directly with a network medium (such as coaxial cable, optical fiber, or twisted pair copper wire).

The protocols included in Network Access layer are Ethernet, Token Ring, FDDI, X.25, Frame Relay etc.

The most popular LAN architecture among those listed above is Ethernet. Ethernet uses an *access method* called *CSMA/CD* (Carrier Sense Multiple Access/Collision Detection) to access the media. An access method determines how a host will place data on the medium.

In CSMA/CD access method, every host has equal access to the medium and can place data on the wire when the wire is free from network traffic. When a host wants to place data on the wire, it will check the wire to find whether another host is already using the medium.

If there is traffic already in the medium, the host will wait and if there is no traffic, it will place the data in the medium. But, if two systems place data on the medium at the same instance, they will collide with each other, destroying the data. If the data is destroyed during transmission, the data will need to be retransmitted. After collision, each host will wait for a small interval of time and again the data will be retransmitted.

This is a combination of the Data Link and Physical layers of the OSI model which consists of the actual hardware.

3.5 Difference between OSI and TCP/IP models

The OSI model describes computer networking in seven layers. The TCP/IP model uses four layers to perform the functions of the seven-layer OSI model. The network access layer is functionally equal to a combination of OSI physical and data link layers.

The Internet layer performs the same functions as the OSI network layer. Things get a bit more complicated at the host-to-host layer of the TCP/IP model. If the host-to-host protocol is TCP, the matching functionality is found in the OSI transport and session layers.

Using UDP equates to the functions of only the transport layer of the OSI model. The TCP/IP process layer, when used with TCP, provides the functions of the OSI model's presentation and application layers. When the TCP/IP transport layer protocol is UDP, the process layer's functions are equivalent to OSI session, presentation, and application layers.

3.5.1 OSI comparison with TCP/IP Protocol Stack

The main differences between the two models are as follows:

- OSI is a reference model and TCP/IP is an implementation of OSI model.
- TCP/IP protocols are considered to be standards around which the internet has developed. The OSI model however is a *generic, protocol-independent* standard.

- TCP/IP combines the presentation and session layer issues into its application layer.
- TCP/IP combines the OSI data link and physical layers into the network access layer.
- TCP/IP appears to be a simpler model and this is mainly due to the fact that it has fewer layers.
- TCP/IP is considered to be a more credible model- This is mainly due to the fact because TCP/IP protocols are the standards around which the internet was developed therefore it mainly gains creditability due to this reason. Where as in contrast networks are not usually built around the OSI model as it is merely used as a guidance tool.
- The OSI model consists of 7 architectural layers whereas the TCP/IP only has 4 layers.

OSI #	OSI Layer Name	TCP/IP #	TCP/IP Layer Name	Encapsulation Units	TCP/IP Protocols
7	Application	4	Application	data	FTP, HTTP, POP3, IMAP, telnet, SMTP, DNS, TFTP
6	Presentation			data	
5	Session			data	
4	Transport	3	Transport	segments	TCP, UDP
3	Network	2	Internet	packets	IP
2	Data Link	1	Network Access	frames	
1	Physical			bits	

3.6 How does TCP/IP Model (Internet) work?

As we have seen, there are a set of protocols that support computer networks. Computers on the Internet communicate by exchanging packets of data, called Internet Protocol (IP) *packets*. IP is the network protocol used to send information from one computer to another over the Internet.

All computers on the Internet communicate using IP. IP moves information contained in IP packets. The IP packets are routed via special routing algorithms from a source to destination. The routing algorithms figure out the best way to send the packets from source to destination.

In order for IP to send packets from a source computer to a destination computer, it must have some way of identifying these computers. All computers on the Internet are identified using one or more IP addresses. A computer may have more than one IP address if it has more than one interface to computers that are connected to the Internet.

IP addresses are 32-bit numbers. They may be written in decimal, hexadecimal, or other formats, but the most common format is dotted decimal notation. This format breaks the 32-bit address up into four bytes and writes each byte of the address as unsigned decimal integers separated by dots. For example, one of *CareerMonk.com* IP addresses is $0xccD499C1$. Since, $0xcc$ = 204, $0xD4$ = 212, $0x99$ = 153, and $0xC1$ = 193, *CareerMonk.com* IP address in dotted decimal form is 204.212.153.193.

3.6.1 Domain Name System (DNS)

IP addresses are not easy to remember, even using dotted decimal notation. The Internet has adopted a mechanism, referred to as the *Domain Name System* (DNS), whereby computer names can be associated with IP addresses. These computer names are called *domain names*. The DNS has several rules that determine how domain names are constructed and how they relate to one another. The mapping of domain names to IP addresses is maintained by a system of *domain name servers*. These servers are able to look up the IP address corresponding to a domain name. They also provide the capability to look up the domain name associated with a particular IP address, if one exists.

3.6.2 TCP and UDP

Computers running on the Internet communicate to each other using either the Transmission Control Protocol (TCP) or the User Datagram Protocol (UDP). When we write *Java* programs that communicate over the network, we are programming at the application layer. Typically, we don't need to concern with the TCP and UDP layers. Instead, we can use the classes in the java.net package. These classes provide system-independent network communication. However, to decide which *Java* classes our programs should use, we do need to understand how TCP and UDP differ.

3.6.2.1 TCP [Transmission Control Protocol]

When two applications want to communicate to each other reliably, they establish a connection and send data back and forth over that connection. This is analogous to making a telephone call. If we want to speak to a person who is in another country, a connection is established when we dial the phone number and the other party answers.

We send data back and forth over the connection by speaking to one another over the phone lines. Like the phone company, TCP guarantees that data sent from one end of the connection actually gets to the other end and in the same order it was sent. Otherwise, an error is reported.

TCP provides a point-to-point channel for applications that require reliable communications. The Hypertext Transfer Protocol (HTTP), File Transfer Protocol (FTP), and Telnet are all examples of applications that require a reliable communication channel. The order in which the data is sent and received over the network is critical to the success of these applications. When HTTP is used to read from a URL, the data must be received in the order in which it was sent. Otherwise, we end up with a jumbled HTML file, a corrupt zip file, or some other invalid information.

Application: HTTP, ftp, telnet, SMTP,...
Transport: TCP, UDP,...
Network: IP,...
Link: Device driver,...

Definition: TCP is a connection-based protocol that provides a reliable flow of data between two computers.

Transport protocols are used to deliver information from one port to another and thereby enable communication between application programs. They use either a connection-oriented or connectionless method of communication. TCP is a connection-oriented protocol and UDP is a connectionless transport protocol.

The reliability of the communication between the source and destination programs is ensured through error-detection and error-correction mechanisms that are implemented within TCP. TCP implements the connection as a stream of bytes from source to destination. This feature allows the use of the stream I/O classes provided by java.io.

3.6.2.2 UDP [User Datagram Protocol]

The UDP protocol provides for communication that is not guaranteed between two applications on the network. UDP is not connection-based like TCP. But, it sends independent packets of data (called datagrams) from one application to another. Sending datagrams is much like sending a letter through the postal service: The order of delivery is not important and is not guaranteed, and each message is independent of any other.

Definition: UDP is a protocol that sends independent packets of data, called *datagrams*, from one computer to another with no guarantees about arrival. UDP is not connection-based.

For many applications, the guarantee of reliability is critical to the success of the transfer of information from one end of the connection to the other. However, other forms of communication don't require such strict standards. In fact, they may be slowed down by the extra overhead or the reliable connection may invalidate the service altogether.

Consider, for example, a clock server that sends the current time to its client when requested to do so. If the client misses a packet, it doesn't really make sense to resend it because the time will be incorrect when the client receives it on the second try. If the client makes two requests and receives packets from the server out of order, it doesn't really matter because the client can figure out that the packets are out of order and make another request. The reliability of TCP is unnecessary in this instance because it causes performance degradation and may hinder the usefulness of the service.

Another example of a service that doesn't need the guarantee of a reliable channel is the ping command. The purpose of the ping command is to test the communication between two programs over the network. In fact, ping needs to know about dropped or out-of-order packets to determine how good or bad the connection is. A reliable channel would invalidate this service altogether.

The UDP protocol provides for communication that is not guaranteed between two applications on the network. UDP is not connection-based like TCP. Rather, it sends independent packets of data from one application to another. Sending datagrams is much like sending a letter through the mail service: The order of delivery is not important and is not guaranteed, and each message is independent of any others.

The UDP connectionless protocol differs from the TCP connection-oriented protocol in that it does not establish a link for the duration of the connection. An example of a connectionless protocol is postal mail. To mail something, you just write down a destination address (and an optional return address) on the envelope of the item you're sending and drop it in a mailbox. When using UDP, an application program writes the destination port and IP address on a datagram and then sends the datagram to its destination. UDP is less reliable than TCP because there are no delivery-assurance or error-detection and error-correction mechanisms built into the protocol.

Application protocols such as FTP, SMTP, and HTTP use TCP to provide reliable, stream-based communication between client and server programs. Other protocols, such as the Time Protocol, use UDP because speed of delivery is more important than end-to-end reliability.

3.7 Understanding Ports

Generally speaking, a computer has a single physical connection to the network. All data destined for a particular computer arrives through that connection. However, the data may be intended for different applications running on the computer. So, how does the computer know to which application to forward the data? Through the use of ports.

Data transmitted over the Internet is accompanied by addressing information that identifies the computer and the port for which it is destined. The computer is identified by its 32-bit IP address, which IP uses to deliver data to the right computer on the network. Ports are identified by a 16-bit number, which TCP and UDP use to deliver the data to the right application.

In connection-based communication such as TCP, a server application binds a socket to a specific port number. This has the effect of registering the server with the system to receive all data destined for that port. A client can then rendezvous with the server at the server's port, as illustrated here:

Definition: The TCP and UDP protocols use ports to map incoming data to a particular process running on a computer.

In datagram-based communication such as UDP, the datagram packet contains the port number of its destination and UDP routes the packet to the appropriate application, as illustrated in this figure:

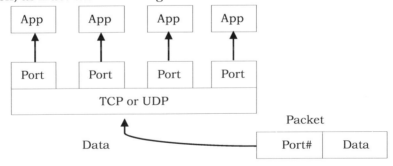

Port numbers range from 0 to 65,535 because ports are represented by 16-bit numbers. The port numbers ranging from 0 - 1023 are restricted; they are reserved for use by well-known services such as HTTP and FTP and other system services. These ports are called well – known ports. Your applications should not attempt to bind to them.

Port	Protocol
21	File Transfer Protocol
23	Telnet Protocol
25	Simple Mail Transfer Protocol
80	Hypertext Transfer Protocol

Problems and Questions with Answers

Question 1: A system has a n-layer protocol hierarchy. Applications generate messages of length M bytes. At each of the layers, an h-byte header is added. What fraction of the network bandwidth is filled headers?

Answer:
Given data:
- n-layered protocol.
- Each layer adds a h – byte header.

Hence, the total number of header bytes per message is hn.

So the relative space wasted on header is $\frac{hn}{M}$.

Question 2: Which answer correctly lists the OSI PDUs in order?
A) Data, Packet, Frame, Segment, Bit
B) Bit, Data, Packet, Segment, Frame
C) Data, Segment, Packet, Frame, Bit
D) Bit, Frame, Segment, Packet, Data

Answer: C

Question 3: Which of the following are true when comparing TCP/IP to the OSI Reference Model? (Choose two.)
A) The TCP/IP model has seven layers while the OSI model has only four layers.
B) The TCP/IP model has four layers while the OSI model has seven layers.
C) The TCP/IP Application layer maps to the Application, Session, and Presentation layers of the OSI Reference Model.
D) The TCP/IP Application layer is virtually identical to the OSI Application layer.

Answer: B and C

Question 4: In which layer of the TCP/IP stack is framing found?
A) Network   B) Data Link   C) Internet   D) Network Access

Answer: D

Question 5: Which OSI layer is concerned with reliable end-to-end delivery of data?
A) Application   B) Transport   C) Network   D) Data Link

Answer: B

Question 6: Logical addressing is found in the ___ layer, while physical addressing is found in the __ layer.
A) Physical, Network   B) Network, Physical
C) Data Link, Network   D) Network, Data Link

Answer: D

Question 7: The OSI Reference Model layers, in order from top to bottom, are:
A) Application, Physical, Session, Transport, Network, Data Link, Presentation
B) Application, Presentation, Network, Session, Transport, Data Link, Physical
C) Physical, Data Link, Network, Transport, Session, Presentation, Application
D) Application, Presentation, Session, Transport, Network, Data Link, Physical

Answer: D

Question 8: The process-to-process delivery of the entire message is the responsibility of the ___ layer.

A) Network   B) Transport   C) Application   D) Physical

Answer: B

Question 9: The ___ layer is the layer closest to the transmission medium.
A) Physical   B) Data link   C) Network   D) Transport

Answer: A

Question 10: Mail services are available to network users through the __ layer.
A) Data link   B) Physical   C) Transport   D) Application

Answer: D

Question 11: As the data packet moves from the lower to the upper layers, headers are

A) Added   B) Subtracted   C) Rearranged   D) Modified

Answer: B

Question 12: As the data packet moves from the upper to the lower layers, headers are

A) Added   B) Removed   C) Rearranged   D) Modified

Answer: A

Question 13: The __ layer lies between the network layer and the application layer.
A) Physical   B) Data link   C) Transport   D) None of the above

Answer: B

Question 14: Layer 2 lies between the physical layer and the __ layer.
A) Network   B) Data link   C) Transport   D) None of the above

Answer: A

Question 15: When data are transmitted from device A to device B, the header from A's layer 4 is read by B's __ layer.
A) Physical   B) Transport   C) Application   D) None of the above

Answer: B

Question 16: The ___ layer changes bits into electromagnetic signals.
A) Physical   B) Data link   C) Transport   D) None of the above

Answer: A

Question 17: The physical layer is concerned with the transmission of ___over the physical medium.
A) Programs   B) Dialogs   C) Protocols   D) Bits

Answer: D

Question 18: Which layer functions as a connection between user support layers and network support layers?
A) Network layer   B) Physical layer   C) Transport layer   D) Application layer

Answer: C

Question 19: What is the main function of the transport layer?
A) Node-to-node delivery   B) Process-to-process delivery
C) Synchronization   D) Updating and maintenance of routing tables

Answer: B

Question 20: Which of the following is an application layer service?
   A) Remote log-in   B) File transfer and access
   C) Mail service   D) All the above

Answer: D

Question 21: Best effort means packets are delivered to destinations as fast as possible. Is it true or false?

Answer: False. Best effort refers to no guarantees about performance of any kind, not high performance.

Question 22: In the OSI model, the transport layer can directly invoke (use) the data link layer. Is it true or false?

Answer: False. In the OSI model a layer can only use the service provided by the layer below it. In this case, the transport layer can only use the service provided by the networking layer.

Question 23: Data are transmitted over an internet in packets from a source system to a destination across a path involving a single network and routers. Is it true or false?

Answer: False

Question 24: In TCP/IP model, exactly one protocol data unit (PDU) in layer n is encapsulated in a PDU at layer $(n-1)$. It is also possible to break one n-level PDU into multiple $(n-1)$-level PDUs (segmentation) or to group multiple n-level PDUs into one $(n-1)$-level PDU (blocking). In the case of segmentation, is it necessary that each $(n-1)$-level segment contain a copy of the n-level header?

In the case of blocking, is it necessary that each n-level PDU retain its own header, or can the data be consolidated into a single n-level PDU with a single n-level header?

Answer: *No*. This would violate the principle of separation of layers. To layer $(n-1)$, the n-level PDU is simply data. The $(n-1)$ entity does not know about the internal format of the n-level PDU. It breaks that PDU into fragments and reassembles them in the proper order.

Question 25: For the Question 24, in the case of blocking, is it necessary that each n-level PDU retain its own header, or can the data be consolidated into a single n-level PDU with a single n -level header?

Answer: Each n -level PDU must retain its own header, for the same reason given in Question 24.

Question 26: A TCP segment consisting of 1500 bits of data and 20 bytes of header is sent to the IP layer, which appends another 20 bytes of header.This is then transmitted through two networks, each of which uses a 3-byte packet header. The destination network has a maximum packet size of 800 bits. How many bits, including headers, are delivered to the network layer protocol at the destination?

Answer: Data + Transport header + Internet (IP) header = 1820 bits. This data is delivered in a sequence of packets, each of which contains 24 bits of network header and up to 776 bits of higher-layer headers and/or data. Three network packets are needed. Total bits delivered = 1820 + 3 × 24 = 1892 bits.

Question 27: In the OSI model, the _____ layer is concerned with finding the best path for the data from one point to the next within the network.
   A) Data Link   B) Network   C) Physical   D) Application

Answer: B

Question 28: Error detection is performed at the __ layer of the OSI model?
    A) Data Link   B) Transport   C) Network   D) Both a and b

Answer: D

Question 29: ___ is a very powerful error detection technique and should be considered for all data transmission systems?
    A) Vertical redundancy check   B) Cyclic redundancy checksum
    C) Simple parity   D) Horizontal parity

Answer: B

Question 30: Which layer addresses do routers use to determine a packet's path?
    A) Data Link   B) Network   C) Physical   D) Application

Answer: B

Question 31: Why does the data communication industry use the layered OSI reference model?
1. It divides the network communication process into smaller and simpler components, thus aiding component development, design, and troubleshooting.
2. It enables equipment from different vendors to use the same electronic components, thus saving research and development funds.
3. It supports the evolution of multiple competing standards and thus provides business opportunities for equipment manufacturers.
4. It encourages industry standardization by defining what functions occur at each layer of the model.

A) 1 only   B) 1 and 4   C) 2 and 3   D) 3 only

Answer: B. The main advantage of a layered model is that it can allow application developers to change aspects of a program in just one layer of the layer model's specifications. Advantages of using the OSI layered model include, but are not limited to, the following:

- It divides the network communication process into smaller and simpler components, thus aiding compo- nent development, design, and troubleshooting
- It allows multiple-vendor development through standardization of network components
- It encourages industry standardization by defining what functions occur at each layer of the model
- It allows various types of network hardware and software to communicate

Question 32: Which of the following functionalities must be implemented by a transport protocol over and above the network protocol ?
A) Recovery from packet losses
B) Detection of duplicate packets
C) Packet delivery in the correct order
D) End to end connectivity

Answer: D. Transport protocols are mainly for providing end to end connections by making sockets. Recovery from packet loss & delivery in correct order, duplication is checked by Data link layer.

Question 33: Choose the best matching Group 1 and Group 2.

Group-1	Group-2
P. Data link layer	1. Ensures reliable transport of data over a physical point-to-point link
Q. Network layer	2. Encodes/ decodes data for physical transmission
R. Transport layer	3. Allowed-to-end communication between two processes

A) P-1, Q-4, R-3   B) P-2, Q-4, R-1
C) P-2, Q-3, R-1   D) P-1, Q-3, R-2

Answer: A.Transport layer is responsible for end to end communication, creation of sockets. Network layer routes the data from one node to other, till it reach to destination. Datalink layer ensures reliable data transfer by error correction, duplication check ordered delivery etc. P - 1, Q - 4, R - 3.

Question 34: Suppose we wanted to do a transaction from a remote client to a server as fast as possible. Would you use UDP or TCP? Why?

Answer: We would use UDP. With UDP, the transaction can be completed in one roundtrip time (RTT) - the client sends the transaction request into a UDP socket, and the server sends the reply back to the client's UDP socket. With TCP, a minimum of two RTTs are needed - one to set-up the TCP connection, and another for the client to send the request, and for the server to send back the reply.

Networking Devices

CHAPTER

4

4.1 Glossary

- *Bridge*: Network segments that typically use the same communication protocol use bridges to pass information from one network segment to the other.
- *Gateway*: When different communications protocols are used by networks, gateways are used to convert the data from the sender's
- *Hub*:Another name for a hub is a concentrator. Hubs reside in the core of the LAN cabling system. The hub connects workstations and sends every transmission to all the connected workstations.
- *Media Dependent Adapter*: A MDA is a plug-in module allowing selection among fiber-optic, twisted pair, and coaxial cable.
- *Media Filter*: When the electrical characteristics of various networks are different, media filter adapter connectors make the connections possible.
- *Multistation Access Unit*: MAUs are special concentrators or hubs for use in Token Ring networks instead of Ethernet networks.
- *Modems*: Modem is a device that *converts* digital signals to analog signals and analog signals to digital signals.
- *Network Interface Card*:NICs are printed circuit boards that are installed in computer workstations. They provide the physical connection and circuitry required to access the network.
- *Repeater*: Connectivity device used to regenerate and amplify weak signals, thus extending the length of the network. Repeaters perform no other action on the data.
- *Router*: Links two or more networks together, such as an Internet Protocol network. A router receives packets and selects the optimum path to forward the packets to other networks.
- *Switch*: A connection device in a network that functions much like a bridge, but directs transmissions to specific workstations rather than forwarding data to all workstations on the network.
- *Transceiver*: The name transceiver is derived from the combination of the words transmitter and receiver. It is a device that both transmits and receives signals and connects a computer to the network. A transceiver may be external or located internally on the NIC.

- *Firewall*: Firewall provides controlled data access. Firewalls can be hardware or software based and between networks. These are an essential part of a network's security strategy.

4.2 End Devices

In computer networks, the computers that we use on a daily basis are called *nodes* (also called *hosts* or end systems). They are called *hosts* because they host the application-level programs such as a Web browser or an electronic-mail program.

Sometimes, they are also called as *end systems* because they sit at the edge of the network connection. A node can be a computer or some other device, such as a printer. Every node has a unique network address, sometimes called a *Data Link Control* (DLC) address or *Media Access Control* (MAC) address.

An end device acts as the source (i.e., generates and sends messages) or as the destination (i.e., receives and consumes content) of the communication process.

In modern networks, a host can act as a client, a server, or both. Software installed on the host determines which role it plays on the network. Servers are hosts that have software installed that enables them to provide information and services, like e-mail or web pages, to other hosts on the network.

Some examples of end devices are:

- Computers, laptops, file servers, web servers.
- Network printers
- VoIP phones
- Security cameras
- Mobile handheld devices

4.3 Intermediary Devices

In addition to the end devices that people are familiar with, computer networks depends on intermediary devices to provide connectivity. These intermediary devices work behind the scenes to ensure that data flows across the network. Also, they connect the individual systems to the network and can connect multiple individual networks to form an *internetwork* (also called *Internet*). Examples of intermediary network devices are:

- Network Access Devices (hubs, switches, and wireless access points)
- Internetworking Devices (*routers*)
- Communication Servers and Modems
- Security Devices (*firewalls*)

The management of data as it flows through the network is also a role of the intermediary devices. These devices use the destination host address, along with information about the network interconnections, to determine the path that messages should take through the network. Processes running on the intermediary network devices perform these functions:

- Regenerate and retransmit data signals
- Maintain information about what pathways exist through the network and internetwork
- Notify other devices of errors and communication failures
- Direct data along alternate pathways when there is a link failure
- Classify and direct messages according to priorities

- Permit or deny the flow of data, based on security settings

The intermediate devices can be further classified by on their functionality as:

- *Connectivity Devices*: Connectivity devices are devices used to make physical network connections. They do *not make changes* to the data or transmission route. Connectivity devices operate at the physical layer of the OSI model.
- *Internetworking Devices*: Internetworking devices move data across a network. They *direct* data to specific locations within the network and/or *convert* data into alternative formats. Internetworking devices operate at OSI layers above the physical layer.

4.4 Connectivity Devices

4.4.1 Introduction

Connectivity devices are those devices used to make physical network connections. Connectivity devices operate at the physical layer of the Open Systems Interconnection Reference Model (OSI) model. The OSI model describes how computer services and procedures are standardized.

This standardization allows computers to share information and enables the interconnection of various networking connectivity devices regardless of vendor.

4.4.2 Network Interface Cards

A *network interface card* is a piece of computer hardware and its main functionality is to allow a computer to connect to a network. A network interface card is also called LAN *card*, *network adapter*, *network adapter boards, media access cards* or simply *NIC*.

Regardless of the name, they enable computers to communicate across a network. With this device, information packets can be transferred back and forth through a local area network (LAN). It acts a communication source for sending and receiving data on the network.

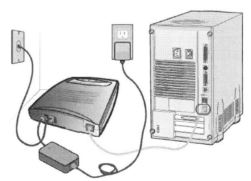

NIC provides physical access to a networking medium and often provides a low-level addressing system through the use of MAC addresses. It allows users to connect to each other either by using *cables* or *wirelessly*.

The network interface card (NIC) is an add-on component for a computer, much like a video card or sound card is. On most of the systems the NIC is integrated into the system board. On others it has to be installed into an expansion slot.

Most network interface cards have the *Ethernet* protocol as the language of the data that is being transferred back and forth. However, network interface cards do not all necessarily need physical Ethernet or other cables to be functional. Some have wireless capabilities through including a small *built-in antenna* that uses radio waves to transmit information.

The computer must have a software driver installed to enable it to interact with the NIC. These drivers enable the operating system and higher-level protocols to control the functions of the adapter.

Each NIC has a unique *media access control* (MAC) address to direct traffic. This unique MAC address ensures that information is only being sent to a specific computer name and not to multiple ones if not intended to. Circled in the picture below is an example of an integrated network interface card.

The MAC (Media Access Layer) address, or hardware address, is a 12-digit number consisting of digits 0-9 and letters A-F. It is basically a hexadecimal number assigned to the card. The MAC address consists of two pieces: the first signifies which vendor it comes from, the second is the serial number unique to that manufacturer.

Example MAC addresses:

00-B0-D0-86-BB-F7   01-23-45-67-89-AB   00-1C-B3-09-85-15

The NIC performs the following functions:

- It translates data from the parallel data bus to a serial bit stream for transmission across the network.
- It formats packets of data in accordance with protocol.
- It transmits and receives data based on the hardware address of the card.

4.4.3 Transceivers

The term *transceiver* does not necessarily describe a separate network device but rather embedded in devices such as network cards.

Transceiver is a short name for *transmitter-receiver*. It is a device that both transmits and receives analog or digital signals. The term transceiver is used most frequently to describe the component in local-area networks (LANs) that actually applies signals onto the network wire and detects signals passing through the wire. For many LANs, the transceiver is built into the network interface card (NIC). Older types of networks, however, require an external transceiver.

The transceiver does not make changes to information transmitted across the network; it adapts the signals so devices connected by varying media can interpret them. A transceiver operates at the physical layer of the OSI model.

Technically, on a LAN the transceiver is responsible to place signals onto the network media and also detecting incoming signals traveling through the same cable. Given the description of the function of a transceiver, it makes sense that that technology would be found with network cards (NICs).

4.4.4 Amplifiers and Repeaters

A repeater is an electronic device that receives a signal and retransmits it at a higher level or higher power, so that the signal can cover longer distances without degradation.

Transmitter sends a signal containing some information and after travelling some distance, usually, a signal get weakened (attenuated) due to energy loss in the medium. Therefore, it should be improved (or *amplified*). *Amplifier* is the circuit which magnifies the weak signal to a signal with more power.

Sometimes, this signal attenuation happens much before the arrival to the destination. In this case, signal is amplified and retransmitted with a power gain in one or more mid points. Those points are called *repeaters*. Therefore an amplifier is an essential part of a repeater.

Amplifier

Amplifier is an electronic circuit that increases the power of an input signal. There are many types of amplifiers ranging from voice amplifiers to optical amplifiers at different frequencies.

Repeater

The repeater is an electronic circuit that receives a signal and retransmits the same signal with a higher power. Therefore, a repeater consists of a signal receiver, an *amplifier* and a *transmitter*. Repeaters are often used in submarine communication cables as signal would be attenuated to just a random noise when travelling such a distance.

Different types of repeaters have different types of configurations depending on the transmission medium. If the medium is microwaves, repeater may consist of antennas and waveguides. If the medium is optical it may contain photo detectors and light emitters.

Difference between an Amplifier and a Repeater

1. Amplifier is used to magnify a signal, whereas repeater is used to receive and retransmit a signal with a power gain.
2. Repeater has an amplifier as a part of it.
3. Sometimes, amplifiers introduce some noise to the signal, whereas repeaters contain noise eliminating parts.

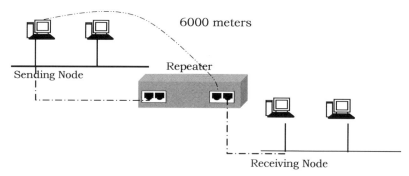

Thickwire can normally transmit a distance of 500 meters and this can be extended by introducing repeaters. *Thinwire* can normally transmit a distance of 185 meters, and can also be extended by using a repeater. This is the advantage to using a repeater. If a network layout exceeds the normal specifications of cable we can use repeaters to build network. This will allow for greater lengths when planning cabling scheme.

Repeaters *perform* no other action on the data. Repeaters were originally separate devices. Today a repeater may be a separate device or it may be incorporated into a hub. Repeaters operate at the physical layer of the OSI model.

4.4.5 Hubs

Hubs are commonly used to connect segments of a LAN. A hub contains multiple ports. When a packet arrives at one port, it is copied to the other ports so that all segments of the LAN can see all packets.

A *hub* contains multiple ports. When a packet arrives at one port, it is copied to all (broadcast) the ports of the hub. When the packets are copied, the destination address in the frame does not change to a *broadcast* address. It does this in a rudimentary way; it simply copies the data to all of the nodes connected to the hub.

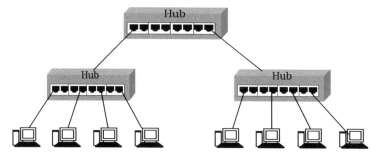

The main function of the hub is to broadcast signals to different workstations in a LAN. General speaking, the term hub is used instead of repeater when referring to the device that serves as the center of a network.

4.4.6 Modems

Modem is a device that *converts* digital signals to analog signals and analog signals to digital signals. The word modem stands for *modulation* and *demodulation*. The process of converting digital signals to analog signals is called *modulation*. The process of converting analog signals to digital signals is called *demodulation*. Modems are used with computers to transfer data from one computer to another computer through telephone lines.

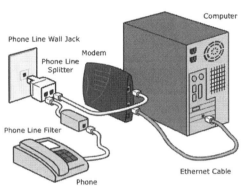

Types of Modem Connections

Modems have two types of connections and they are.
- Analog connection
- Digital connection

Analog Connection

The connection between the modem and the telephone line is called a *analog connection*. It converts digital signals from a computer to analogue signals that are then sent down the telephone line. A modem on the other end converts the analogue signal back to a digital signal the computer can understand. A workstation is connected to an analogue modem. The analogue modem is then connected to the telephone exchange analogue modem, which is then connected to the internet.

Digital Connection

The connection of modem to computer is called digital connection

Types of Modems

There are two types of modems:
- Internal modems
- External modems

Internal Modems

It fits into expansion slots inside the computer. It is directly linked to the telephone lines through the telephone jack. It is normally less inexpensive than external modem. Its transmission speed is also less external modem.

External Modems

It is the external unit of computer and is connected to the computer through serial port. It is also linked to the telephone line through a telephone jack. External modems are expensive and have more operation features and high transmission speed.

Advantages of Modems

- Inexpensive hardware and telephone lines
- Easy to setup and maintain

Disadvantage of Modems

- Very slow performance

4.4 Internetworking Devices

4.4.1 Bridges

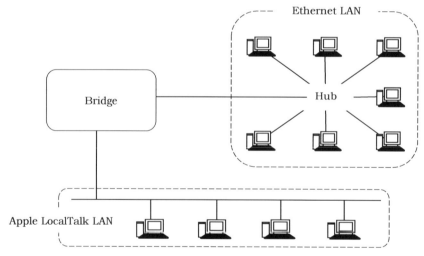

Bridge is a device which operates in both the physical and the data link layer of the OSI reference model. As a physical layer device, it *regenerates* the signal it receives. As a data link layer device, the bridge can check the physical (MAC) addresses (*source* and *destination*) contained in the frame.

Bridges can be used to divide a large network into *segments*. Bridges contain logic that allows them to keep the traffic for each *segment separate*. When a new frame enters to a bridge, the bridge not only regenerate the frame but it also checks the address of the destination and forwards the new copy only to the segment to which the destination address belongs.

A bridge device *filters* data traffic at a network boundary. Bridges reduce the amount of *traffic* on a LAN by dividing it into segments. Key features of a bridge are mentioned below:

- A bridge operates both in physical and data-link layer
- A bridge uses a table for *filtering/routing*
- A bridge does not *change* the physical (MAC) addresses in a *frame*

4.4.1.1 Why Use Bridges?

As an example, imagine for a moment that computers are people in a room. Everyone is glued to 1 spot and can't move around. If *Ram* wants to talk to *Mary*, he shouts out "*Hey Mary*" and *Mary* responds; and a conversation occur as a result.

On a small scale this works quite well. The Internet (as we know it today) is not just 2 or a few people talking directly to each other. The internet is literally billions of devices. If they were all placed into the same room (network-segment); imagine what would happen if *Ram* wanted to talk to *Mary*. *Ram* would yell "*Hey Mary!*" and Ram's voice would be lost in the crowd. Building a room to fit billions of people is equally ridiculous.

For this reason, networks are separated into smaller segments (smaller rooms) which allow devices who are in the same segment (room) to talk directly to each other's. But, for the devices outside the segment we need some sort of device (router) to pass messages from one room to the next room. But the vast number of segments (rooms) means we need some sort of addressing scheme so the various routers in the middle know how to get a message from *Ram* to *Mary*.

Segmenting a large network with an interconnect device (*bridge*) has many *advantages*. Among these are *reduced* collisions (in an Ethernet network), contained *bandwidth* utilization, and the ability to filter out unwanted packets. Bridges were created to allow network administrators to segment their networks transparently. What this means is that individual stations need not know whether there is a bridge separating them or not. It is up to the bridge to make sure that packets get properly forwarded to their destinations. This is the fundamental principle underlying all of the bridging behaviours we will discuss.

4.4.1.2 Types of Bridges

Several different types of bridges are available for internetworking LANs.

1. *Transparent Basic Bridge* [*Transparent Forwarding Bridge*]: Places incoming frame onto all outgoing ports *except* original incoming port.
2. *Transparent Learning Bridge*: Stores the origin of a frame (from which port) and later uses this information to place frames to that port.
3. *Transparent Spanning Bridge*: Uses a subset of the LAN topology for a loop-free operation.
4. *Source Routing Bridge*: Depends on routing information in frame to place the frame to an outgoing port.

4.4.1.2.1 Transparent Basic Bridges [Transparent Forwarding Bridge]

The simplest type of bridge is called the *transparent basic bridge*. It is called *transparent* because the nodes using a bridge are unaware of its presence. This bridge receives traffic coming in on each port and stores the traffic until it can be transmitted on the outgoing ports. It will not forward the traffic from the port from which it was received.

The bridge does not make any conversion of the traffic. The bridge forwards (*receive* and *subsequently transmit*) frames from one LAN to another. Obviously, the bridge forwards all frames like a *repeater*.

Transparent Bridge Forwarding

If the destination address is present in the forwarding database (table) already created, the packet is forwarded to the port number to which the destination host is attached. If it is not present, forwarding is done on all parts (*flooding*). This process is called *bridge forwarding*.

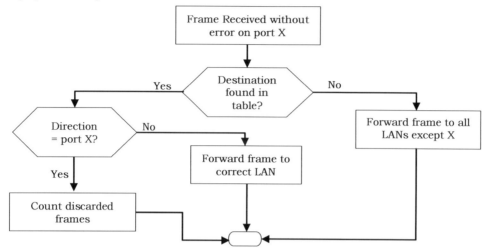

Bridge forwarding operation is explained with the help of flowchart.

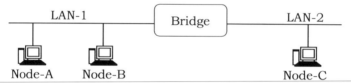

In the figure above, consider three nodes A, B, and C. Assume each node sends frames to all other nodes. The source addresses A, B are observed to be on network LAN-1, while the address of node C will be observed to be on network LAN-2.

Basic functions of the bridge forwarding are mentioned below.

1. If the source address is *not* present in the forwarding table, the bridge *adds* the source address and corresponding interface to the table. It then checks the destination address to determine if it is in the table.
2. If the destination address is listed in the table, it determines if the destination address is on the same LAN as the source address. If it is, then the bridge *discards* the frame since all the nodes have already received the frame.
3. If the destination address is listed in the table but is on a different LAN than the source address, then the frame is forwarded to that LAN.
4. If the destination address is not listed in the table, then the bridge forwards the frame to all the LANs except the one that which originally received the frame. This process is called *flooding*.

In some bridges, if the bridge has not accessed an address in the forwarding table over a period of time, the address is removed to free up memory space on the bridge. This process is referred to as *aging*.

Packets with a source A and destination B are received and discarded, since the node B is directly connected to the LAN-1, whereas packets from A with a destination C are forwarded to network LAN-2 by the bridge.

4.4.1.2.2 Transparent Bridge Learning

To learn which addresses are in use, and which ports (interfaces on the bridge) are closest to, the bridge observes the headers of received frames. By examining the MAC source address of each received frame, and recording the port on which it was received, the bridge may learn which addresses belong to the computers connected via each port. This is called *learning*.

The learned addresses are stored in the *interface address table* (*database*) associated with *each* port (*interface*). Once this table has been setup, the bridge examines the destination address of all received frames; it then scans the interface tables to see if a frame has been received from the same address (i.e. a packet with a source address matching the current destination address).

At the time of installation of a transparent bridge, the table is empty. When a packet is encountered, the bridge checks its source address and build up a table by associating a source address with a port address to which it is connected. The flowchart explains the learning process.

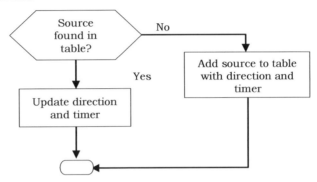

Table Building

The table building up operation is illustrated in figure. Initially the table is empty.

Address	Port

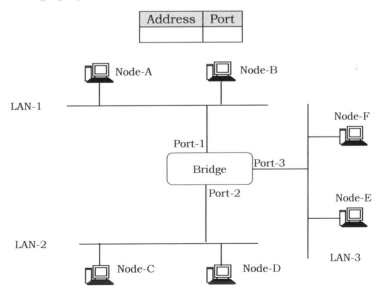

1. When node A sends a frame to node D, the bridge does not have any entry for either D or A. The frame goes out from all three ports. The frame floods the

network. However, by looking at the source address, the bridge learns that node A must be located on the LAN connected to port 1.

This means that frame destined for A (in future), must be sent out through port 1. The bridge adds this entry to its table. The table has its first entry now.

Address	Port
A	1

2. When node E sends a frame to node A, the bridge has an entry for A, so it forwards the frame only to port 1. There is no flooding. Also, it uses the source address of the frame (E in this case), to add a second entry to the table.

Address	Port
A	1
E	3

3. When node B sends a frame to C, the bridge has no entry for C, so once again it floods the network and adds one more entry to the table.

Address	Port
A	1
E	3
B	1

4. The process of learning continues as the bridge forwards frames.

Loop Problem

Forwarding and learning processes work without any problem as long as there is no redundant bridge in the system. On the other hand, redundancy is desirable from the viewpoint of reliability, so that the function of a failed bridge is taken over by a redundant bridge.

The existence of redundant bridges creates the so-called loop problem as shown figure. Assuming that after initialization tables in both the bridges are empty let us consider the following steps:

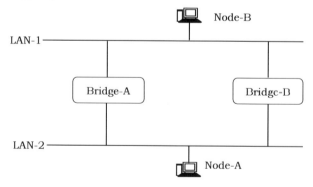

- *Step* 1: Node A sends a frame to node B. Both the bridges forward the frame to LAN 1 and update the table with the source address of A.
- *Step* 2: Now there are two copies of the frame on LAN-1. The copy sent by Bridge-A is received by Bridge-B and vice versa. As both the bridges have no information about node B, both will forward the frames to LAN-2.
- *Step* 3: Again both the bridges will forward the frames to LAN-1 because of the lack of information of the node B in their database and again Step-2 will be repeated, and so on.

So, the frame will continue to *loop* around the two LANs indefinitely.

4.4.1.2.3 Transparent Spanning Bridges

As seen in previous section, redundancy creates loop problem in the system and it is undesirable. To prevent loop problem, the IEEE (Institute of Electrical and Electronics Engineers) specification requires that the bridges use a special topology. Such a topology is known as *spanning tree* (a graph where there is no loop) topology.

The methodology for setting up a spanning tree is known as *spanning tree algorithm*. *Spanning tree algorithm* creates a tree out of a graph. Without changing the physical topology, a logical topology is created that overlay on the physical by using the following steps:

1. Select a bridge as *root-bridge*, which has the smallest ID.
2. Select root ports for all the bridges, except for the root bridge, which has least-cost path (say, minimum number of hops) to the root bridge.
3. Choose a *designated* bridge, which has least-cost path to the *root-bridge*, in each LAN.
4. Select a port as *designated port* that gives least-cost path from the *designated bridge* to the *root* bridge.
5. Mark the designated port and the root ports as *forwarding* ports and the remaining ones as *blocking* ports.

An Example

Let us walk through the below example for running the spanning tree algorithm on. Note that some of the LAN segments have a cost 3 times that of others. The following convention is used for the remaining discussion:

*   DC means designated cost for a LAN segment
*   Bridge-# means bridge number
*   A number around a bridge is a port number

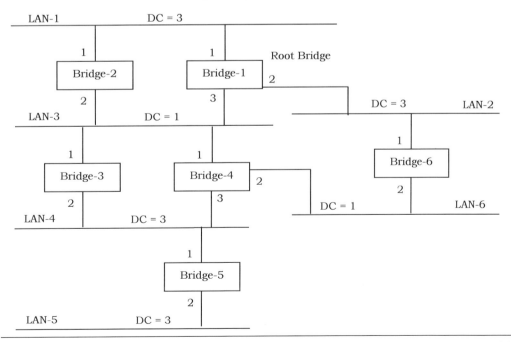

Step 1 of the algorithm is already shown in the first picture: Bridge 1 is chosen as the *root bridge* since all the bridges are assumed to have the same priority. The tie is broken by choosing the bridge with the smallest ID number.

Next, we determine the root path cost (RPC) for each port on each bridge *other than* the *root* bridge. Then each bridge other than the root chooses its port with the lowest RPC as the root port (RP). Ties are broken by choosing the *lowest-numbered* port. The root port is used for all control messages from the root bridge to this particular bridge.

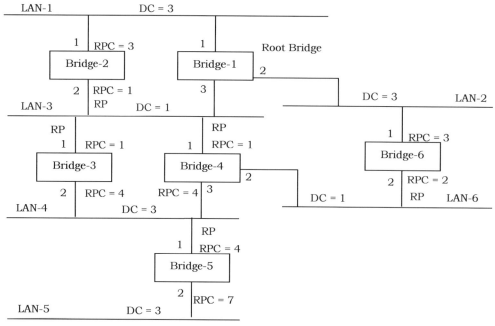

Sample RPC calculation: Consider port 1 of Bridge-5. Between it and root bridge we have to traverse at least LAN-3 and LAN-4, with costs 1 and 3 respectively. Total cost is 4. Thus RPC = 4 for port 1 of Bridge-5.

Next, step 3 of the algorithm is to select a designated bridge and a designated port on this bridge for each LAN segment. This is the bridge that gives the least cost (DPC, designated port cost) for getting between this LAN segment and the root bridge. The port on this bridge by which we attach this LAN segment is called the *designated port* (DP). If there is a tie for the lowest DPC, the bridge with the smallest ID number is chosen.

The root bridge is always the designated bridge for the LAN segments directly attached to it. The ports by which the root bridge attaches to the LAN segments are thus designated ports. We assume that no LAN segment attaches to the root bridge by more than 1 port. Since a root port cannot be chosen as a designated port, do not waste time even considering root ports as possible designated ports.

In the drawing on the next page, we see that LAN-1, LAN-2, and LAN-3 are directly attached to the root bridge via ports 1, 2, and 3 respectively on the root bridge. Thus we only need to consider LAN-4, LAN-5, and LAN-6. LAN-4 could use either port 2 on Bridge-3 or port 3 on Bridge-4 as its designated port. The DPC for each is 1 since anything sent from LAN-4 through such a port goes across LAN-3 to the root bridge and the cost of LAN-3 is just 1.

Since we have a tie for the DP we choose the one on the lowest number bridge. That means that Bridge-3 is the designated bridge and its port 2 is the designated port for LAN-3. For LAN-5 there is only one port that could be chosen, so the designated port for LAN-5 is port 2 on Bridge-5 and the designated bridge is Bridge-5. There is no choice for LAN-6 either as one port is a root port. Thus the designated port for S6 is the other one: port 2 on Bridge-4.

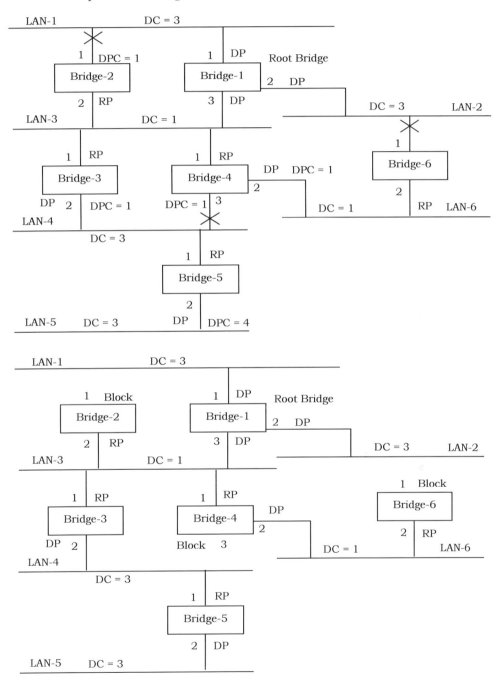

Finally, in step 4 each port that is not a root port or designated port is set to be in a blocking state so that no traffic can flow through it. The blocked ports are X-ed out above. This, then, produces our spanning tree (no loops). To better see the spanning tree, the picture can be redrawn as shown on the next page, with the root bridge as the root of the tree.

4.4.1.2.4 Translational Bridges

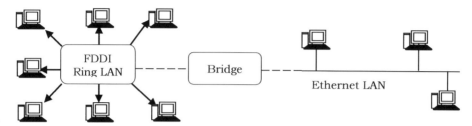

Translational bridges are a type of transparent bridge that connects LANs that use different protocols at the data link and physical layers, for example, FDDI (Fiber Distributed Data Interface) and Ethernet.

4.4.1.2.5 Source Routing Bridges

In source routing bridges, the routing operation is determined by the source host and the frame specifies which route the *frame* to follow. A host can discover a route by sending a *discovery* frame, which spreads through the entire network using all possible paths to the destination.

Each frame gradually gathers addresses as it goes. The destination responds to each frame and the source host chooses an appropriate route from these responses. For example, a route with minimum *hop-count* can be chosen. Whereas transparent bridges do not modify a frame, a source routing bridge adds a routing information field to the frame. Source routing approach provides a shortest path at the cost of extra burden on the network.

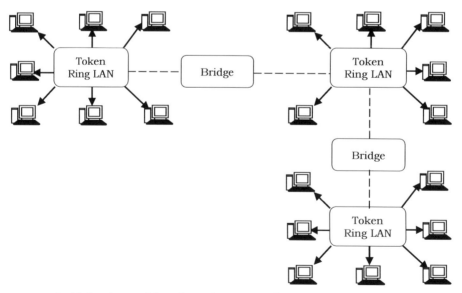

Source route bridging is used in token ring networks. A source route bridge links two or more rings together. There are fundamental characteristics in how a source route bridge transmits a frame between rings. A source route bridge does not create and maintain forwarding tables. The decision to forward or drop a frame is based on information provided in the frame.

The destination station is responsible for maintaining routing tables that define a route to all workstations on the network. The source workstation is responsible for determining the path of a frame to its destination. If no route information is available, then the source station has the ability to perform route discovery to learn the potential paths that can be taken.

4.4.2 Switches

Switch is a device that filters and forwards packets between LAN segments. Switch works at the layer 2 of the OSI model. The main purpose of the switch is to concentrate connectivity while making data transmission more efficient. Think of the switch as something that combines the connectivity of a hub with the traffic regulation of a bridge on each port. Switches makes decisions based on MAC addresses.

A switch is a device that performs switching. Specifically, it forwards and filters OSI layer 2 datagrams (chunk of data communication) between ports (connected cables) based on the MAC addresses in the packets.

As discussed earlier, a hub forwards data to all ports, regardless of whether the data is intended for the system connected to the port. This mechanism is inefficient; and switches tries to address this issue to some extent. This is different from a hub in that it only forwards the datagrams to the ports involved in the communications rather than all ports connected. Strictly speaking, a switch is not capable of routing traffic based on IP address (layer 3) which is necessary for communicating between network segments or within a large or complex LAN.

4.4.2.1 How a Switch works?

Rather than forwarding data to all the connected ports, a switch forwards data only to the port on which the destination system is connected. It looks at the Media Access Control (MAC) addresses of the devices connected to it to determine the correct port.

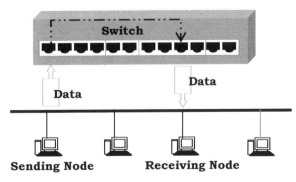

A MAC address is a unique number that is stamped into every NIC. By forwarding data only to the system to which the data is addressed, the switch decreases the amount of traffic on each network link dramatically.

4.4.2.2 Switching Methods

We can specify one of *four* possible forwarding methods for each port in a switch:

1. Cut-through
2. Fragment-free
3. Store-and-forward
4. Adaptive

4.4.2.2.1 Store and Forward Switching

In *store* and *forward* switching, Switch copies each of the complete Ethernet frame into the switch memory and computes a Cyclic Redundancy Check (CRC) for errors. If a Cyclic Redundancy Check (CRC) error is found, the Ethernet frame is dropped and if there is no Cyclic Redundancy Check (CRC) error, the switch forwards the Ethernet frame to the destination device. Store and Forward switching can cause delay in switching since Cyclic Redundancy Check (CRC) is calculated for each Ethernet frame.

4.4.2.2.2 Cut-through Switching

In *cut-through* switching, the switch copies into its memory only the destination MAC address (first 6 bytes of the frame) of the frame before making a switching decision. A switch operating in cut-through switching mode reduces delay because the switch starts to forward the Ethernet frame as soon as it reads the destination MAC address and determines the outgoing switch port. Problem related with cut-through switching is that the switch may forward bad frames.

4.4.2.2.3 Fragment-Free Switching

Fragment-free switching is an advanced form of cut-through switching. The switches operating in cut-through switching read only up to the destination MAC address field in the Ethernet frame before making a switching decision. The switches operating in fragment-free switching read at least 64 bytes of the Ethernet frame before switching it to avoid forwarding Ethernet runt frames (Ethernet frames smaller than 64 bytes).

4.4.2.2.4 Adaptive switching

Adaptive switching mode is a user-defined facility to maximize the efficiency of the switch. Adaptive switching starts in the default switch forwarding mode we have selected. Depending on the number of errors (say, CRC errors) at that port, the mode changes to the *best* of the other two switching modes.

4.4.3 Routers

4.4.3.1 What is Router?

Routers are *physical* devices that join multiple *networks* together. Technically, a router is a Layer 3 device, meaning that it connects two or more networks and that the router operates at the network layer of the OSI model.

Routers maintain a table (called *routing table*) of the available routes and their conditions and use this information along with distance and cost algorithms to determine the best route for a given packet. Typically, a packet may travel through a number of network points with routers before arriving at its destination.

The purpose of the router is to examine incoming packets (layer 3), chose the best path for them through the network, and then switches them to the proper outgoing port. Routers are the most important traffic controlling devices on large networks.

Routers are networking devices that forward data packets between networks using headers and *forwarding tables* to determine the best path to forward the packets. Routers also provide interconnectivity between *like* and *unlike* media (networks which use different protocols).

4.4.3.2 Understanding Concepts of Routers

As an example, assume that we want to send a postcard just based on person names (with minimum information). For example, *Bill Gates* [USA], *Sachin Tendulkar* [India] or *Albert Einstein* [USA] it would be routed to them due to their fame; no listing of the street address or the city name would be necessary. The postal system can do such routing to famous personalities, depending on the name alone.

In an Internet, a similar discussion is possible: *reach* any *website* anywhere in the world without knowing where the site is currently located. Not only that, it is possible to do so very efficiently, within a matter of a few seconds.

4.4.3.2.1 What is Network Routing?

How is this possible in a communication network, and how can it be done so quickly? The answer to this question is *Network routing*. *Network routing* is the ability to send a unit of information from source to destination by finding a path through the network, and by doing efficiently and quickly.

4.4.3.2.2 What is Addressing?

First, we start with a key and necessary factor, called *addressing*. In many ways, addressing in a network has similarities to postal addressing in the postal system. So, we will start with a brief discussion of the postal addressing system to relate them.

A typical postal address that we write on a postcard has several components—the name of the person, followed by the street address with the house number (*house address*), followed by the city, the state name, and the postal code. If we take the processing view to route the postcard to the right person, we essentially need to consider this address in the reverse order of listing, i.e., start with the postal code, then the city or the state name, then the house address, and finally the name of the person.

You may notice that we can reduce this information somewhat; that is, you can just use the postal code and leave out the name of the city or the name of the state, since this is redundant information. This means that the information needed in a postal address consists of three main parts: the postal code, the street address (with the house number), and the name.

A basic routing problem in the postal network is as follows:

1. The postcard is first routed to the city or the geographical region where the postal code is located.
2. Once the card reaches the postal code, the appropriate delivery post office for the address specified is identified and delivered to.
3. Next, the postman or postwoman delivers the postcard at the address, without giving much consideration to the name listed on the card.
4. Rather, once the card arrives at the destination address, the residents at this address take the responsibility of handing it to the person addressed.

The routing process in the postal system is broken down to three components:

- How to get the card to the specific postal code (and subsequently the post office),
- How the card is delivered to the destination address, and
- Finally, how it is delivered to the actual person at the address.

If we look at it in another way, the place where the postcard originated in fact does not need to know the detailed information of the street or the name to start with; the postal code is sufficient to determine to which geographical area or city to send the card. So, we can see that postal routing uses address hierarchy for routing decisions.

An advantage of this approach is the decoupling of the routing decision to multiple levels such as the postal code at the top, then the street address, and so on. An important requirement of this hierarchical view is that there must be a way to divide the complete address into multiple distinguishable parts to help with the routing decision.

Now, consider an electronic communication network; for example, a critical communication network of the modern age is the Internet. Naturally, the first question that arises is: how does addressing work for routing a unit of information from one point to another, and is there any relation to the postal addressing hierarchy that we have just discussed? Second, how is service delivery provided? In the next section, we address these questions.

4.4.3.2.3 Addressing and Internet Service: An Overview

In many ways, Internet addressing has similarities to the postal addressing system. The addressing in the Internet is referred to as *Internet Protocol* (IP) *addressing*. An IP address defines *two* parts: one part that is similar to the postal code and the other part that is similar to the house address; in Internet terminology, they are known as the *netid* and the *hostid*, to identify a network and a host address, respectively.

A host is the end point of communication in the Internet and where a communication starts. A host is a generic term used for indicating many different entities; the most common ones are a web-server, an email server, desktop, laptop, or any computer we use for accessing the Internet. A *netid* identifies a contiguous block of addresses.

4.4.3.2.4 Network Routing: An Overview

In the previous section, we provided a broad overview of addressing and transfer mechanisms for data in Internet communication services. Briefly, we can see that eventually packets are to be routed from a source to a destination. Such packets may need to traverse many cross-points, similar to traffic intersections in a road transportation network. Cross-points in the Internet are known as *routers*.

A router's functions are to read the destination address marked in an incoming IP packet, to consult its internal information to identify an outgoing link to which the packet is to be forwarded, and then to forward the packet. Similar to the number of lanes and the speed limit on a road, a network link that connects two routers is limited by how much data it can transfer per unit of time, commonly referred to as the band-width or capacity of a link; it is generally represented by a data rate, such as 1.54 megabits per second (Mbps). A network then carries traffic on its links and through its routers to the eventual destination; traffic in a network refers to packets generated by different applications, such as web or email.

Note: For more about IP Addressing and routing, refer *IP Addressing* and *Routing Protocols* chapters.

4.4.3.3 Types of Routers

Depending on the role that routers perform, routers can be classified in many different ways.

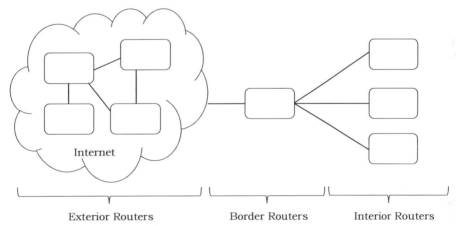

Exterior Routers   Border Routers   Interior Routers

4.4.3.3.1 Interior Routers

Interior routers work within networks. These routers handle packets travelling between nodes on the same Intra-network. An interior router is used to divide a large network into more easily manageable subnetworks. It can keep one part of a network secure from another and it can allow different technologies, for example, Ethernet and token ring, to be used in the same network.

4.4.3.3.2 Border Routers

Border routers exist on one network and their function is to connect that network with outside networks, including the Internet. They discover routes between the interior network and others and they handle incoming and outgoing traffic.

4.4.3.3.3 Exterior Routers

Exterior routers are most common on the Internet. They do not exist on a particular network but rather in the space between networks where data passes through on its way to its destination. Exterior routers do not store routes to particular hosts; but they store routes to other *routers*. Their primary role is to receive packets and then forward them in the direction of their destination.

4.4.4 Gateways

The term *gateway* is used in networking to describe the *gate* to the Internet. The *gateway* controls traffic that travels from the inside network to the Internet and provides security from traffic that wants to enter the inside network from the Internet.

A network gateway is an internetworking system which joins two networks that use different base protocols. A network gateway can be implemented completely in software, completely in hardware, or as a combination of both. Depending on the types of protocols they support, network gateways can operate at any level of the OSI model.

Since a gateway (by definition) appears at the edge of a network, related capabilities like firewalls tend to be integrated with it. On home networks, a router typically serves as the network gateway although ordinary computers can also be configured to perform equivalent functions.

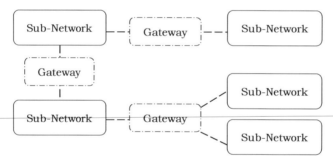

As mentioned earlier, the Internet is not a single network but a collection of networks that communicate with each other through gateways. A gateway is defined as a system that performs relay functions between networks, as shown in figure above. The different networks connected to each other through gateways are often called *subnetworks*, because they are a smaller part of the larger overall network.

With TCP/IP, all interconnections between physical networks are through gateways. An important point to remember for use later is that gateways route information packets based on their destination network name, not the destination machine. Gateways are completely transparent to the user.

4.4.1 Default Gateway

The default gateway is needed only for systems that are part of an internetwork (in the above figure, note that two subnetworks connected to same gateway). Data packets with a destination IP address not on the local subnet are forwarded to the default gateway. The default gateway is normally a computer system or router connected to the local subnet and other networks in the internetwork.

If the default gateway becomes unavailable, the system cannot communicate outside its own subnet, except for with systems that it had established connections with prior to the failure.

4.4.2 Multiple Gateways

If the default gateway becomes unavailable, data packets cannot reach their destination. *Multiple gateways* can be used to solve this problem.

4.4.3 Difference between Gateway and Router

4.4.3.1 Gateway

The *key difference* between gateway and router is, gateway it is defined as a network node that allows a network to interface with another network with different protocols. A router is a device that is capable of sending and receiving data packets between computer networks, also creating an overlay network.

Gateways and routers are two words are often confused due to their similarities. Both gateways and routers are used to regulate traffic into more separate networks. However, these are two different technologies and are used for different purposes.

The term gateway can be used to define two different technologies: gateway and default gateway. These two terms should not be confused. In terms of communications network, gateway it is defined as a network node that allows a network to interface with another network with different protocols. In simple terms, gateway allows two different networks to communicate with each other. It contains devices such as impedance protocol translators, rate converters, or signal translators to allow system interoperability.

A protocol translation/mapping gateway interconnects networks that have different network protocol technologies. Gateways acts as a network point that acts as an entrance to another network. The gateway can also allow the network to connect the computer to the internet. Many routers are available with the gateway technology, which knows where to direct the packet of data when it arrives at the gateway. Gateways are often associated with both routers and switches.

Default gateway is a computer or a computer program that is configured to perform the tasks of a traditional gateway. These are often used by ISP or computer servers that act as gateway between different systems. When getting an internet connection, an ISP usually provides a device that allows the user to connect to the Internet; these devices are called *modems*. In organizational systems a computer is used as a node to connect the internal networks to the external networks, such as the Internet.

4.4.3.2 Router

A router is a device that is capable of sending and receiving data packets between computer networks, also creating an overlay network. The router connects two or more data line, so when a packet comes in through one line, the router reads the address information on the packet and determines the right destination, it then uses the information in its routing table or routing policy to direct the packet to the next network. On the internet, routers perform *traffic directing* functions. Routers can also be wireless as well as wired.

The most common type of routers is small office or home routers. These are used for passing data from the computer to the owner's cable or DSL modem, which is connected to the internet. Other routers are huge enterprise types that connect large businesses to powerful routers that forward data to the Internet.

When connected in interconnected networks, the routers exchange data such as destination addresses by using a dynamic routing protocol. Each router is responsible for building up a table that lists the preferred routes between any two systems on the interconnected networks. Routers can also be used to connect two or more logical groups of computer devices known as subnets. Routers can offer multiple features such as a DHCP server, NAT, Static Routing, and Wireless Networking.

These days' routers are mostly available with built-in gateway systems make it easier for users with them not having to buy separate systems.

4.4.5 Firewalls

The term firewall was derived from *civil engineering* and intended to *prevent* the*spread* of fire from one *room* to another. From the computer security perspective, the Internet is an unsafe environment; therefore *firewall* is an excellent metaphor for network security.

A firewall is a system designed to prevent unauthorized access to or from a private network. Firewalls can be implemented in either hardware or software form, or a combination of both. Firewalls prevent unauthorized users from accessing private networks. A firewall sits between the two networks, usually a private network and a public network such as the Internet.

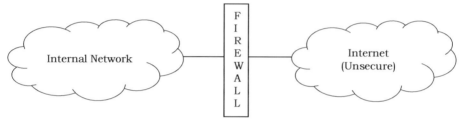

Connecting a computer or a network of computers may become targets for malicious software and hackers. A firewall can offer the security that makes a computer or a network less vulnerable.

Note: For more details, refer *Firewalls* section in *Network Security* chapter.

4.4.6 Differences between Hubs, Switches, and Routers

Today most routers have something combining the features and functionality of a router and switch/hub into a single unit. So conversations regarding these devices can be a bit misleading — especially to someone new to computer networking.

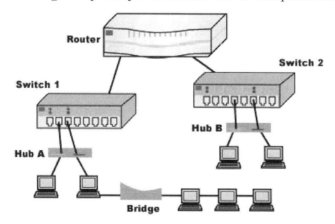

The functions of a router, hub and a switch are all quite different from one another, even if at times they are all integrated into a single device. Let's start with the hub and the switch since these two devices have similar roles on the network. Each serves as a central connection for all of your network equipment and handles a data type known as frames. Frames carry the data. When a frame is received, it is amplified and then transmitted on to the port of the destination PC. The big difference between these two devices is in the method in which frames are being delivered.

In a hub, a frame *broadcasts* to every one of its ports. It doesn't matter that the frame is only destined for one port. The hub cannot distinguish which port a frame should be sent to. Broadcasting it on every port ensures that it will reach its intended destination. This places a lot of traffic on the network and can lead to poor network response times.

Additionally, a 10/100Mbps hub must share its bandwidth with each and every one of its ports. So, when only one PC is broadcasting, it will have access to the maximum available bandwidth. If, however, multiple PCs are broadcasting, then that bandwidth will need to be divided among all of those systems, which will degrade performance.

A switch, however, keeps a record of the *MAC* addresses of all the devices connected to it. With this information, a switch can identify which system is sitting on which port. So, when a frame is received, it knows exactly which port to send it to, without significantly increasing network response times. And, unlike a hub, a 10/100Mbps switch will allocate a full 10/100Mbps to each of its ports. So regardless of the number of PCs transmitting, users will always have access to the maximum amount of bandwidth. It's for these reasons why a switch is considered to be a much better choice than a hub.

Routers are completely different devices. Where a hub or switch is concerned with transmitting frames, a router's job, as its name implies, is to route packets to other networks until that packet ultimately reaches its destination. One of the key features of a packet is that it not only contains data, but the destination address of where it's going.

A router is typically connected to at least two networks, commonly two Local Area Networks (LANs) or Wide Area Networks (WAN) or a LAN and its ISP's network, for example, your PC or workgroup and EarthLink. Routers are located at gateways, the places where two or more networks connect. Using headers and forwarding tables, routers determine the best path for forwarding the packets. Router use protocols such as ICMP to communicate with each other and configure the best route between any two hosts.

Problems and Questions with Answers

Question 1: In modern packet-switched networks, the source host segments long, application-layer messages (for example, an image or a music file) into smaller packets and sends the packets into the network. The receiver then reassembles the packets back into the original message. We refer to this process as *message segmentation*. Figure shows the end-to-end transport of a message with and without message segmentation. Consider a message that is 9.0106 bits long that is to be sent from source to destination in figure. Suppose each link in the figure is 1.5 Mbps. Ignore propagation, queuing, and processing delays.

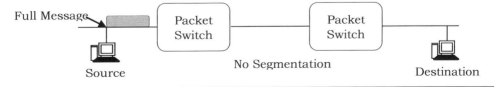

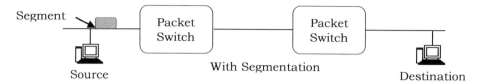

A) Consider sending the message from source to destination without message segmentation. How long does it take to move the message from the source host to the first packet switch? Keeping in mind that each switch uses store-and-forward packet switching, what is the total time to move the message from source host to destination host?

B) Now suppose that the message is segmented into 5,000 packets, with each packet being 1,500 bits long. How long does it take to move the first packet from source host to the first switch? When the first packet is being sent from the first switch to the second switch, the second packet is being sent from the source host to the first switch. At what time will the second packet be fully received at the first switch?

C) How long does it take to move the file from source host to destination host when message segmentation is used? Compare this result with your answer in part (A) and comment.

Answer:

A) Time to send message from source host to first packet switch $=\frac{9\times10^6}{1.5\times10^6}$sec = 6 sec. With store-and-forward switching, the total time to move message from source host to destination host = 6 sec × 3 hops = 18 sec.

B) Time to send 1st packet from source host to first packet switch = $\frac{1.5\times10^3}{1.5\times10^6}$ sec = 1 msec.

Time at which second packet is received at the first switch = 1.5×10^6 time at which first packet is received at the second switch = 2 × 1 msec = 2 msec.

C) Time at which 1st packet is received at the destination host = 1 msec × 3 hops = 3 msec . After this, every 1msec one packet will be received; thus time at which last (5000th) packet is received = 3 msec + 4999 × 1 msec = 5.002 sec.

It can be seen that delay in using message segmentation is significantly less (more than $\frac{1}{3}$rd).

Question 2:   For the following statement, indicate whether the statement is True or False.

Switches exhibit lower latency than routers.

Answer: True. No routing table look-up, no delays associated with storing data *queuing*, bits flow through the switch essentially as soon as they arrive.

Question 3:   Packet switches have queues while circuit switches do not. Is it true or false?

Answer: False. Routers have queues; switches do not, even though the packet switch must have more memory than a circuit switch to receive a full packet before it can forward it on.

Question 4:   Consider the arrangement of learning bridges shown in the following figure. Assuming all are initially empty, give the forwarding tables for each of the bridges B1-B4 after the following transmissions:

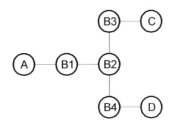

D sends to C; A sends to D; C sends to A

Answer: When D sends to C, all bridges see the packet and learn where D is. However, when A sends to D, the packet is routed directly to D and B3 does not learn where A is. Similarly, when C sends to A, the packet is routed by B2 towards B1 only, and B4 does not learn where C is.

The forwarding table for Bridge B1:

Destination	Next Hop
A	A-Interface
C	B2-Interface
D	B2-Interface

The forwarding table for Bridge B2:

Destination	Next Hop
A	B1-Interface
C	B3-Interface
D	B4-Interface

The forwarding table for Bridge B3:

Destination	Next Hop
C	C-Interface
D	B2-Interface

The forwarding table for Bridge B4:

Destination	Next Hop
A	B2-Interface
D	D-Interface

Question 5: Which type of bridge observes network traffic flow and uses this information to make future decisions regarding frame forwarding?
  A) Remote   B) Source routing   C) Transparent   D) Spanning tree

Answer: C

Question 6: Learning network addresses and converting frame formats are the function of which device?
  A) Switch   B) Hub   C) MAU   D) Bridge

Answer: D

Question 7: The device that can operate in place of a hub is a:
  A) Switch   B) Bridge   C) Router   D) Gateway

Answer: A

Question 8: Which of the following is NOT true with respective to a transparent bridge and a router?
  A) Both bridge and router selectively forward data packets

B) A bridge uses IP addresses while a router uses MAC addresses

C) A bridge builds up its routing table by inspecting incoming packets

D) A router can connect between a LAN and a WAN.

Answer: B. Bridge is the device which work at data link layer whereas router works at network layer. Both selectively forward packets, build routing table and connect between LAN and WAN but since bridge works at data link it uses MAC addresses to route whereas router uses IP addresses.

CHAPTER

LAN Technologies | 5

5.1 Introduction

The bottom two layers of the Open Systems Interconnection (OSI) model deal with the physical structure of the network and the means by which network devices can send information from one device on a network to another.

The data link layer controls how data packets are sent from one node to another.

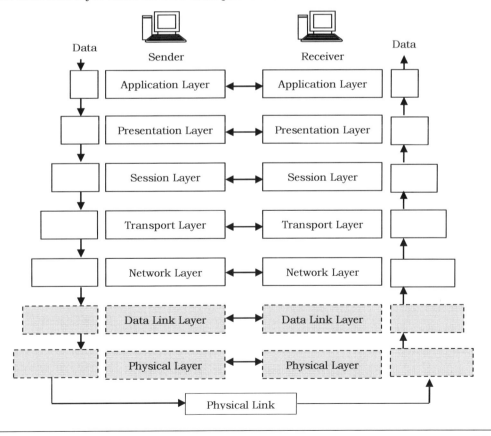

5.2 Types of Network Links

There are two types of network links: *point-to-point* links, and *broadcast* links.

5.2.1 Broadcasting Network Links

Broadcast is a method of sending a signal where multiple nodes may hear a single sender node. As an example, consider a conference room with full of people. In this conference room, a single person starts saying some information loudly.

During that time, some people may be sleeping, and may not hear what person is saying. Some people may not be sleeping, but not paying attention (they are able to hear the person, but choose to ignore). Another group of people may not only be awake, but be interested in what is being said. This last group is not only able to hear the person speaking, but is also listening to what is being said.

In this example, we can see that a single person is broadcasting a message to all others that may or may not be able to hear it, and if they are able to hear it, may choose to listen or not.

5.2.1.1 Simplex Broadcasting Network

Radio and TV stations are a good examples of everyday life *broadcast networks*. In this case the radio/TV stations are a type of communications called *Simplex*. In a simplex type of communication, data is only expected to flow in one direction.

5.2.1.2 Half-Duplex Broadcasting Network

Conference-room meetings are another everyday example of a broadcast network. In this example, everyone may speak to everyone else, but when more than one person speaks, interference (collision) from multiple conversations may make it impossible to listen to more than one conversation even though we can hear both conversations. In this conference-room example, we can see parties are able to share access to a common media (human voice as sound through the air.) They compete for access to speak, but for the most part, only one person speaks at a time for everyone to hear. This is an example of a type of communications called *half-duplex*.

5.2.1.3 Full-Duplex Broadcasting Network

Let us consider the singing competition where we can see a group of singers attempting to sing in Harmony. They can each speak separately on their own, but if they speak on different topics, the conveyed information for any of them may be lost by each other. This is an example of another type of communication called *full-duplex*.

This means that they are not only able to speak, but listen at the same time they are speaking. All of them will speak and listen at the same time. How is this possible? In order to sing in harmony, each singer must be able to hear the frequencies being used by the other singers, and strive to create a frequency with their voice that matches the desired frequency to create that harmony.

This feed-back of each singer to listen to the collective, and possibly key into a specific singer's voice is used by them as they sing to create the exact frequency needed, and ensure their timing is the same as the rest of the singers. All members are able to hear all other members, and speak at the same time. They are all acting as a *full-duplex* communications in a broadcast network.

5.2.2 Point-to-Point Network Links

Point-to-Point is a method of communication where one node speaks to another node. A woman in a restaurant whispers to her husband a message. Nobody else in the restaurant knows what was said. The conversation was only between them.

5.2.2.1 Simplex Point-to-Point Network

An example of a very simple *simplex* point-to-point network could be a doorbell (the circuit.) When the doorbell button is depressed at the front door, a signal is passed to bell which performs its functions to announce the button has been depressed. The bell does not send a message to button. The message travels only in one direction and takes place between the button and the bell.

5.2.2.2 Half-Duplex Point-to-Point Network

As an example, let us assume that we have a couple who are openly affectionate, sat on a bench in a park, and holding hands under a blanket.

Also, assume that this couple has their own code in holding hands for speaking to each other. For example, 3 squeezes maps to *I Love You* and 4 squeezes of the hand maps to *I Love You Too*. The wife squeezes her husband's hand 3 times. He gets this message, and smiles (acknowledging the receipt of the message) and then returns a new message of 4 squeezes. She smiles (acknowledging her receipt of the message she felt.) If both parties attempted to squeeze each other's hands at the same time, then the number of squeezes may be confused. So we can see each party may speak through squeezing each other's hands, but only one may speak at a time.

This conversation takes place only between these two people. Here we see point-to-point and *half-duplex*.

5.2.2.3 Full-Duplex Point-to-Point Network

Data can travel in both directions simultaneously. There is no need to switch from transmit to receive mode like in half duplex. Full-duplex network operates like a two-way, two-lane street. Traffic can travel in both directions at the same time.

5.3 Medium Access Control Techniques

As we have seen, networks can be divided into two types:

1) *Switched* communication network (also called *point-to-point*, *peer-to-peer*, and *switched*): *peer-to-peer* communication is performed with the help of transmission lines such as multiplexers and switches.
2) *Broadcast* communication network: In this we have a medium which is shared by a number of nodes. *Broadcast* is a method of sending a signal where multiple nodes may hear a single sender node.

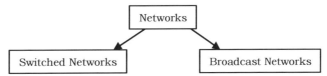

A point-to-point link consists of a single sender on one end of the link, and a single receiver at the other end of the link. Many link-layer protocols have been designed for point-to-point links; PPP (point-to-point protocol) and HDLC (High-level Data Link Control) are two such protocols.

Now, let us consider a different kind of scenario in which we have a medium which is shared by a number of users.

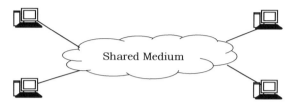

Any user can broadcast the data into the network. Now whenever it is broadcasted obviously there is a possibility that several users will try to broadcast simultaneously. This problem can be addressed with medium access control techniques.

Now question arises how different users will send through the shared media. It is necessary to have a protocol or technique to regulate the transmission from the users. That means, at a time only one user can send through the media and that has to be decided with the help of Medium Access Control (MAC) techniques. Medium access control techniques determines the next user to talk (i.e., transmit into the channel).

A good example is something we are familiar with - a classroom - where teacher(s) and student(s) share the same, single, broadcast medium. As humans, we have evolved a set of protocols for sharing the broadcast channel ("Give everyone a chance to speak." "Don't speak until you are spoken to." "Don't monopolize the conversation." "Raise your hand if you have question." "Don't interrupt when someone is speaking." "Don't fall asleep when someone else is talking.").

Similarly, computer networks have protocols called *multiple access* protocols. These protocols control the nodes data transmission onto the shared broadcast channel.

There are various ways to classify multiple access protocols. Multiple access protocols can be broadly divided into four types; random, round-robin, reservation and channelization. These four categories are needed in different situations. Among these four types, channelization technique is static in nature. We shall discuss each of them one by one.

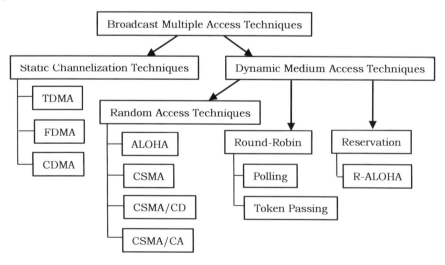

5.4 Random Access Techniques

Random access method is also called *contention-based* access. In this method, no station is assigned to control another. Random MAC techniques can be further divided into four different types; ALOHA, CSMA, CSMA/CD and CSMA/CA.

When each node has a fixed flow of information to transmit (for example, a data file transfer), reservation based access methods are useful as they make an efficient use of communication resources. If the information to be transmitted is bursty in nature, the reservation-based access methods are not useful as they waste communication resources.

Random-access methods are useful for transmitting short messages. The random access methods give freedom for each *node* to get access to the network whenever the user has information to send.

5.4.1 ALOHA

Aloha protocol was developed by *Abramson* at *University of Hawaii*. In the *Hawaiian* language, Aloha means *affection, peace*, and *compassion*. University of Hawaii consists of a number of islands and obviously they cannot setup wired network in these islands. In the University of Hawaii, there was a centralized computer and there were terminals distributed to different islands. It was necessary for the central computer to communicate with the terminals and for that purpose *Abramson* developed a protocol called *Aloha*.

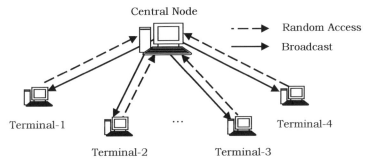

Central node and terminals (stations) communicate by using a wireless technique called *packet radio*. Each of these stations can transmit by using *uplink* frequency which is *random* access shared by all the terminals. After receiving the data, the central node retransmits by using a *downlink* frequency and that will be received by all terminals.

There are two different types of ALOHA:

1. Pure ALOHA
2. Slotted ALOHA

5.4.1.1 Pure Aloha

The first version of protocol given by *Amdrason* works like this:

1. If a node has data to send, send the data
2. If the message collides with another transmission, try resending later
3. In case of collision, sender waits random time before retrying

This simple version is also called *pure ALOHA*. Note that, in Pure ALOHA, sender does not check whether the channel is busy before transmitting.

5.4.1.1.1 Frames in Pure ALOHA

Pure ALOHA assumes all frames have the same length. A shared communication system like ALOHA requires a method for handling collisions. Collisions will occur when two or more systems try to send data at the same time. In the ALOHA system, a node transmits whenever data is available to send. If another node transmits at the same time, a collision occurs, and the frames that were transmitted are lost. However, a node can listen to broadcasts on the medium, even its own, and determine whether the frames were transmitted.

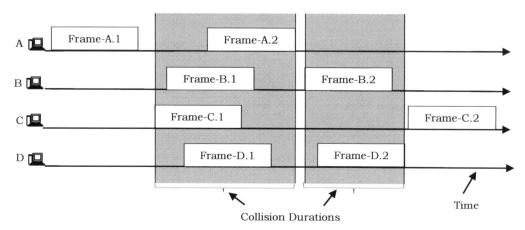

Collision Durations

As shown in diagram, whenever two frames try to occupy the channel at the same time, there will be a collision and both will be damaged. If first bit of a new frame overlaps with just the last bit of a frame almost finished, both frames will be totally destroyed and both will have to be retransmitted.

5.4.1.1.2 Pure ALOHA Protocol

Pure ALOHA uses two different frequencies for data transfers. The central node broadcasts packets to everyone on the outbound (also called *downlink*) channel, and the terminals sends data packets to the central node on the inbound (also called *uplink*) channel.

If data was received correctly at the central node, a short acknowledgment packet was sent to the terminal; if an acknowledgment was not received by a terminal after a short wait time, it would automatically retransmit the data packet after waiting a randomly selected time interval. This acknowledgment mechanism was used to detect and correct for collisions created when two terminals both attempted to send a packet at the same time.

- In pure ALOHA, the stations transmit frames whenever they have data to send.
- When two or more stations transmit at the same time, there will be a collision and the frames will get destroyed.
- In pure ALOHA, whenever any station transmits a frame, it expects the acknowledgement from the receiver.
- If acknowledgement is not received within specified time, the station assumes that the frame has been destroyed.

- If the frame is destroyed because of collision the station waits for a random amount of time and sends it again. This waiting time must be random otherwise same frames will collide again and again.
- Therefore pure ALOHA dictates that when time-out period passes, each station must wait for a random amount of time before resending its frame. This *randomness* will reduce collisions.

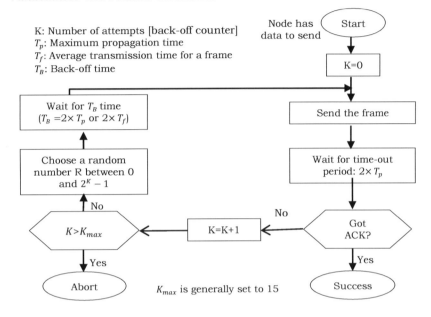

5.4.1.1.3 Pure ALOHA Vulnerable Time

We use the term vulnerable period to indicate the period of time that a packet can possibly collide with other packets. For the rest of discussion, assuming T_f is the average transmission time for a frame. In pure ALOHA, any node that has data to send will send it. We can see that the vulnerable period is $2 \times T_f$.

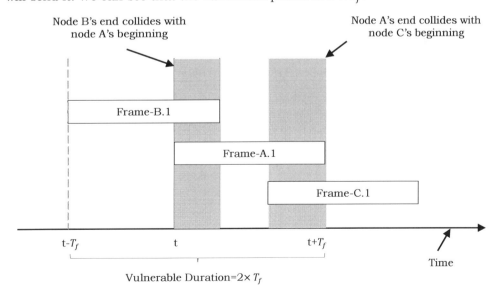

Packet transmitted within this range will overlap with other packets. As a result, collision will occur and the central node will send the garble packet to terminals.

When the garble packet is received by all terminals; they will know that packet has not been transmitted successfully and the terminals will perform retransmission. The retransmission technique is used here whenever there is a collision.

5.4.1.1.4 Throughput of Pure ALOHA

To assess Pure ALOHA, we need to predict its throughput (the rate of successful transmission of frames).

In the pure ALOHA, each station transmits information whenever the station has data to send. Stations send data in packets. After sending a packet, the station waits a length of time equal to the round-trip delay for an acknowledgment (ACK) of the packet from the receiver.

If no ACK is received, the packet is assumed to be lost in a collision and it is retransmitted with a randomly selected delay to avoid repeated collisions.

Let us assume that G is the average number of frames requested per frame-time and S is the throughput. Also assume that, stations are trying to send data follow Poisson distribution.

Poisson distribution expresses the probability of a given number of events occurring in a fixed interval of time and/or space; if these events occur with a known average rate and independently of the time since the last event.

The throughput for pure ALOHA is,

$$S = G \times e^{-2G}$$

From the above equation, we can see that the maximum throughput occurs at

$$G = 50\% \text{ (i.e. } \tfrac{1}{2}\text{) and is S} = 1/2e.$$

This is about 0.184. So, the best channel utilization with the pure ALOHA protocol is only 18.4%.

The probability of collision in pure ALOHA is,

$$1 - e^{-2GT}$$

Where T is the total time which is the sum of propagation and transmission times.

5.4.1.2 Slotted ALOHA

Slotted ALOHA is an improvement over the pure ALOHA. Slotted ALOHA was invented to improve the efficiency of pure ALOHA as chances of collision in pure ALOHA are very high.

In slotted ALOHA, the time of the shared channel is divided into discrete intervals called *slots*. The size of the slot is equal to the frame size.

5.4.1.2.1 Frames in Slotted ALOHA

In slotted ALOHA, the stations can send a frame only at the beginning of the slot and only one frame is sent in each slot. If any station is not able to place the frame onto the channel at the beginning of the slot i.e. it misses the time slot then the station has to wait until the beginning of the next time slot.

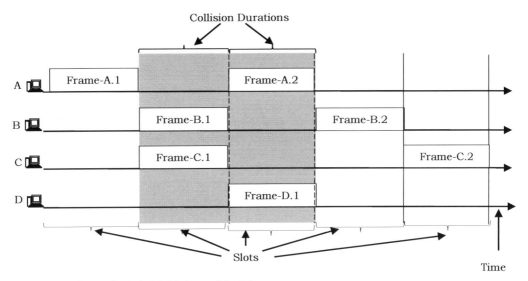

5.4.1.2.2 Slotted ALOHA Vulnerable Time

As seen above, for pure ALOHA the vulnerable time is two slots $(2 \times T_f)$. In slotted ALOHA, two packets either collide completely or do not overlap at all. The vulnerable period is reduced to one slot (T_f).

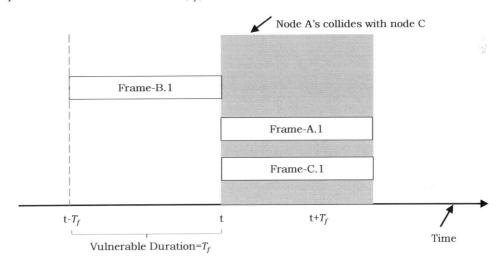

5.4.1.2.3 Throughput of Slotted ALOHA

In slotted ALOHA, there is still a possibility of collision if two stations try to send at the beginning of the same time slot as shown in figure. Slotted ALOHA still has an edge over pure ALOHA as chances of collision are reduced to one-half.

Let us assume that G is the average number of frames requested per frame-time and S is the throughput. The throughput for slotted ALOHA is,

$$S = G \times e^{-G}$$

From the above equation, we can see that the maximum throughput occurs at traffic load G = 100% (i.e. 1) and is S =1/e. This is about 0.368. So, the best channel utilization with the slotted ALOHA protocol is only 36.8%.

The probability of collision in slotted ALOHA is,

$$1 - e^{-2GT}$$

Where T is the total time which is the sum of propagation and transmission times.

5.4.2 Carrier Sense Multiple Access [CSMA]

The main problem with ALOHA protocols (both pure and slotted ALOHA) is that, when a node sends a packet other nodes does not know about that event. In case of pure and slotted ALOHA the medium was not checked before sending the packet. This problem is addressed in *carrier sense multiple access protocol* (CSMA).

The basic idea behind CSMA is, *listen before talk*. If someone else is speaking, wait until they are done. In networking terminology, this is called *carrier sensing*. That means, a node listens to the channel before transmitting. If a frame from another node is currently being transmitted into the channel, a node then waits (*backs off*) a random amount of time and then again senses the channel.

If the channel is sensed to be idle, the node then begins frame transmission. Otherwise, the node waits another random amount of time and repeats this process. CSMA reduces the possibility of collision, but cannot completely eliminate it. There are three different types of CSMA:

1. 1-Persistent CSMA
2. Non-Persistent CSMA
3. p-Persistent CSMA

5.4.2.1 1-Persistent CSMA

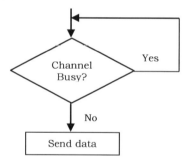

In this method, station that wants to transmit data senses the channel *continuously* to check whether the channel is idle or busy. If the channel is busy, the station waits until it becomes idle. When the station detects an idle-channel, it immediately transmits the frame with probability 1. Hence it is called 1-persistent CSMA. This method has the highest chance of collision because two or more nodes may find channel to be idle at the same time and transmit their frames. When the collision occurs, the nodes wait a random amount of time and start all over again.

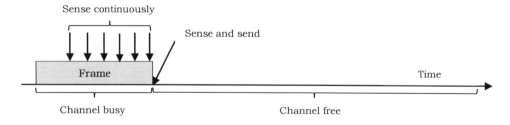

Disadvantage of 1-Persistent CSMA

The propagation delay greatly affects this protocol. As an example, just after the node-1 begins its transmission, node-2 also ready to send its data and senses the channel. If the node-1 signal has not yet reached node-2, node-2 will sense the channel to be idle and will begin its transmission. This will result in collision.

Even if propagation delay is zero, collision will still occur. If two nodes became ready in the middle of third node's transmission, both nodes will wait until the transmission of first node ends and then both will begin their transmission exactly simultaneously. This will also result in collision.

5.4.2.2 Non-Persistent CSMA

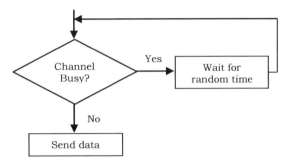

In non-persistent CSMA, a node senses the channel. If the channel is busy, then the node waits for a random amount of time and senses the channel again. After the wait time, if the channel is idle then it sends the packet immediately. If a collision occurs then the node waits for a random amount of time and start all over again.

In non-persistent CSMA, a node does not sense the channel continuously while it is busy. Instead, after sensing the busy condition, it waits for a randomly selected interval of time before sensing again.

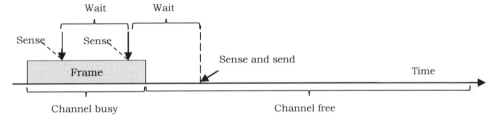

In this protocol, if a node wants to transmit a frame and if it finds that the channel is busy (some other node is using) then it will wait for random interval of time. After this wait time, it again checks the status of the channel and if the channel is free it will transmit.

In non-persistent CSMA the station does not continuously sense the channel for the purpose of capturing it.

Advantage of Non-Persistent CSMA

It reduces the chance of collision because the stations wait a random amount of time. It is unlikely that two or more stations will wait for same amount of time and will retransmit at the same time.

Disadvantage of Non-Persistent CSMA

It reduces the efficiency of network because the channel remains idle when there may be stations with frames to send. This is due to the fact that the stations wait a random amount of time after the collision.

5.4.2.3 p-Persistent CSMA

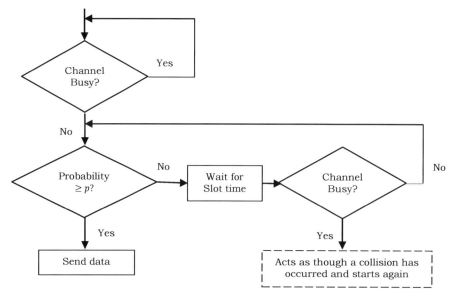

Whenever a station becomes ready to send, it senses the channel. If channel is busy, station waits until next slot. If channel is idle, it transmits with a probability p. With the probability $q = l - p$, the station then waits for the beginning of the next time slot. If the next slot is also idle, it either transmits or waits again with probabilities p and q.

This process is repeated till either frame has been transmitted or another station has begun transmitting. In case of the transmission by another station, the station acts as though a collision has occurred and it waits a random amount of time and starts again.

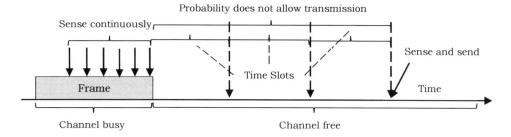

This method is used when channel has time slots such that the time slot duration is equal to or greater than the maximum propagation delay time.

Advantage of p-persistent CSMA

It reduces the chance of collision and improves the efficiency of the network.

5.4.3 CSMA with Collision Detection [CSMA/CD]

Several improvements have been done to the basic CSMA. A considerable performance improvement in the basic CSMA can be achieved with *collision detection* and that technique is called *Carrier Sense Multiple Access with Collision Detection* (CSMA/CD).

The CSMA/CD protocols are same as CSMA with addition of the collision-detection feature. Similar to CSMA protocols, there are 1-persistent, non-persistent, and p-persistent CSMA/CD protocols.

Similar to CSMA, CSMA/CD is a protocol in which the station senses the channel before sending frame. If the channel is busy, the station waits. Additional feature in CSMA/CD is that the stations can detect the collisions.

The stations abort their transmission as soon as they detect a collision. In CSMA this feature is not present. The stations continued their transmission even though they find that the collision has occurred. This leads to the wastage of channel time.

5.4.3.1 How it Works?

In CSMA/CD, a node *that* places data onto the channel after sensing the channel *continues* to sense the channel even after the data transmission. If two or more nodes sense the channel free at the same time, and begin transmitting at the same time, the *collision* is sure.

As soon as a collision is detected, the transmitting node releases a *jam* signal. *Jam* signal will alert the other nodes. As a result, transmitter's stops transmissions by random intervals. This reduces the probability of a collision after the first retry. The nodes are not supposed to transmit immediately after the collision has occurred. Otherwise there is a possibility that the same frames would collide again.

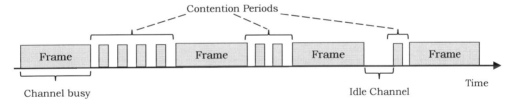

CSMA/CD uses the electric activity on the cable to find the status of the channel. A collision is detected by the *power* of the received pulse and then comparing it with the transmitted signal power.

After the collision is detected, the node stops transmitting and waits random amount of time (*back-off* time) and then sends its data again assuming that no other station is transmitting in this time. This time slot called *contention* slot. If the collision occurs again then the back-off delay time is *increased* progressively.

1. If the channel is idle, transmit; otherwise, go to Step 2.
2. If the channel is busy, continue sensing until the channel is idle, and then transmit immediately.
3. If a collision is detected during transmission, send a jam signal to other nodes sharing the medium saying that there has been a collision and then stop transmission.
4. After sending the jam signal, wait for a random amount of time, then try sending again.

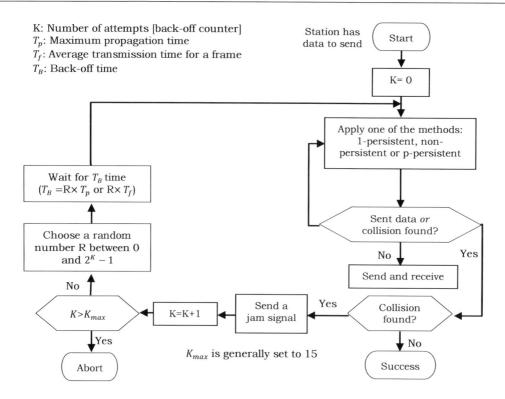

5.4.3.2 CSMA/CD Frame Format

IEEE 802.3 (Ethernet) is an example of CSMA/CD. It is an international standard. Refer *Ethernet* section for more details.

5.4.4 CSMA with Collision Avoidance [CSMA/CA]

Another improvement for CSMA is collision avoidance. It is used to improve the performance of the CSMA method. CSMA/CA (Carrier Sense Multiple Access/Collision Avoidance) is a protocol used in wireless networks (IEEE 802.11 networks) because they cannot detect the collision.

So, the only solution for wireless networks is collision avoidance. In the previous section, we have seen that CSMA/CD deals with transmissions after a collision has occurred. But, CSMA/CA acts to prevent collisions before they happen.

In CSMA/CA, a station will signal its intention to transmit before it actually transmits data. In this way, stations will sense when a collision might occur; this allows them to avoid transmission collisions.

Unfortunately, this broadcasting of the intention to transmit data increases the amount of traffic on the channel and slows down network performance.

CSMA/CA avoids the collisions using three basic concepts.

1. Inter-frame space (IFS)
2. Contention window
3. Acknowledgements

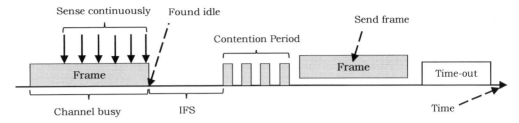

5.4.4.1 Inter-frame Space (IFS)

Whenever the channel is found idle, the station *does not* transmit immediately. It waits for a period of time called *inter-frame* space (IFS).

When channel idle, it may be possible that some distant station may have already started transmitting and the signal of that distant station has not yet reached other stations. The purpose of IFS time is to allow this transmitted signal to reach other stations.

If after this IFS time, the channel is still idle, the station can send, but it still needs to wait a time equal to contention time. IFS variable can also be used to define the priority of a station or a frame.

5.4.4.2 Contention Window

Contention window is an amount of time divided into slots. A station that is ready to send chooses a random number of slots as its wait time. The number of slots in the window changes according to the *binary exponential* back-off strategy. It means that; it is a set with one slot at the first time and then doubles each time the station cannot detect an idle channel after the IFS time.

This is very similar to the *p-persistent* method except that a random outcome defines the number of slots taken by the waiting station. In contention window, the station needs to sense the channel after each time slot. If the station finds the channel busy, it does not restart the process. It just stops the timer and restarts it when the channel is sensed as idle.

5.4.4.3 Acknowledgements

Despite all the precautions, collisions may occur and destroy the data. The positive acknowledgment and the time-out timer can help guarantee that receiver has received the frame.

5.4.4.4 How it works?

In CSMA/CA, as soon as a station receives a packet that is to be sent, it checks to be sure the channel is idle (no other node is transmitting at the time). If the channel is idle, then the packet is sent.

If the channel is not idle, the stations waits for a randomly chosen period of time, and then checks again to see if the channel is idle. This period of time is called the *back-off* factor, and is counted down by a *back-off* counter.

If the channel is idle when the *back-off* counter reaches *zero*, the node transmits the packet. If the channel is not idle when the *back-off* counter reaches *zero*, the *back-off* factor is set again, and the process is repeated.

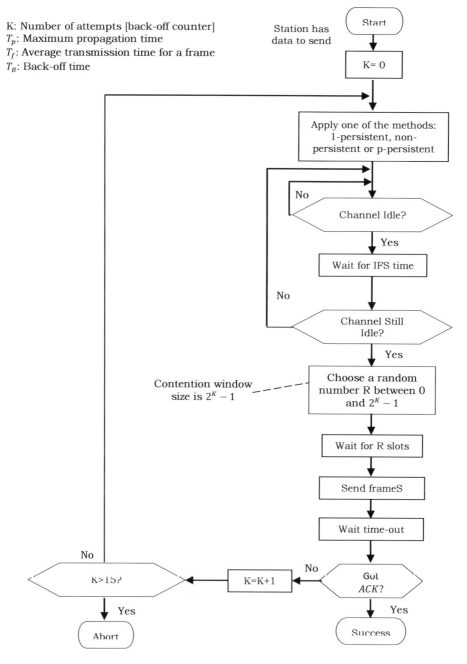

K: Number of attempts [back-off counter]
T_p: Maximum propagation time
T_f: Average transmission time for a frame
T_B: Back-off time

5.5 Static Channelization Techniques

In the previous sections we discussed about the medium access control protocols like ALOHA, CSMA and CSMA/CD. All these protocols were random in nature.

Channelization is a multiple access method in which the available bandwidth is shared in time, frequency or using code by a number of stations. It is similar to multiplexing. Basic idea of these approaches can be explained in simple terms using the cocktail party theory. In a cocktail party people talk to each other using one of the following modes:

- Frequency Division Multiple Access [FDMA]
- Time Division Multiple Access [TDMA]
- Code Division Multiple Access [CDMA

Suppose a cocktail party is going on in a big area. In this scenario, there are three possible alternatives.

In *one* case when all the people group in widely separated areas and talk within each group. That means in this case normally we have seen different people having different kinds of interest (let us say; old people) and groups in different locations where the cocktail party is going on, they talk among themselves and when all the people group in widely separated areas and talk within each group we call it *FDMA*. That means as if we have assigned different frequency bands to each of these groups and each of these groups are talking using different frequency bands.

Second alternative is when all the people are in the middle of the room but they take turn in speaking. Assume that some very important event is going on and all the people have gathered at a central place and each of them is taking turn in talking. So, in this case it is equivalent to. Here we have the basic approach, in terms of time the sharing is taking place.

Now the *final third* approach is interesting. When all the people are in a middle of the room but different pairs speak in different languages. As an example, consider an international conference. People from different countries will arrive there and obviously when they group together they may be speaking in different languages.

Let's assume that all of them have gathered near the central area but small groups are talking in different languages, a group is talking in English, a group is talking in French, a group is talking in German, another group is talking in may be Hindi. We can see that each of these groups will start talking simultaneously; and since they are speaking different languages the group talking in English although they are hearing the voices of people speak in Hindi or French or German will not interfere with their discussion. Here simultaneously all of them are talking but they are not interfering with each other because they are talking in different languages. This is equivalent to *CDMA*.

5.5.1 Frequency Division Multiple Access [FDMA] Technique

Frequency: The number of cycles per unit of time is called the frequency. For convenience, frequency is measured in cycles per second (cps) or Hertz (Hz). Hertz was named after the 19th century German physicist *h Hertz*.

Frequency tells the number of waves that pass a fixed place in a given amount of time. For example, if the time taken for a wave to pass is 1/3 second, the frequency is 3 per second. If it takes 1/200 of a second, the frequency is 200 per second.

Low Frequency Waves

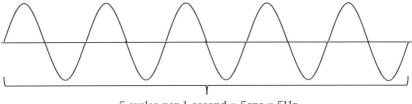

5 cycles per 1 second = 5cps = 5Hz

High Frequency Waves

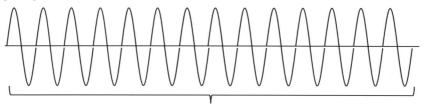

14 cycles per 1 second = 14cps = 14Hz

Now, let us focus on the concepts of *FDM* (Frequency Division Multiplexing) and *FDMA* (Frequency Division Multiple Access). FDM is a *physical* layer multiplexing technique. Using FDM to allow multiple users to utilize the same bandwidth is called FDMA. FDM uses a physical multiplexer. That means FDM works at the physical layer and allows multiple low bandwidth frequency signals to share the same high bandwidth frequency range.

5.5.1.1 Frequency Division Multiplexing

Frequency Division Multiplexing (FDM) divides the single high bandwidth (with bigger frequency range) channel into several smaller bandwidth channels (sub-channel). Each sub channel transmits data simultaneously using different frequency so that each sub-channel has its own frequency to use and is not affecting other sub-channels.

5.5.1.2 How does FDM works?

A radio is a good example to explain how FDM works. Note, that we are only using one bigger range of radio frequency and there are several radio stations broadcasting its service using different frequency. All we need to do is to adjust the radio to catch only certain radio broadcast on certain frequency.

FDM has drawback by dedicating such frequency to several smaller circuits even though the designated channel is not using it.

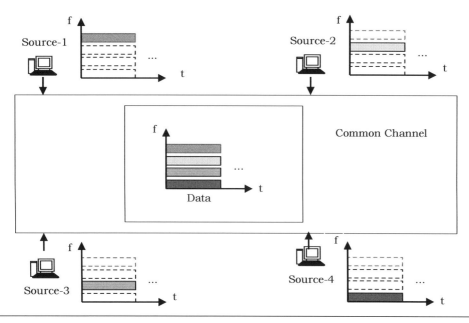

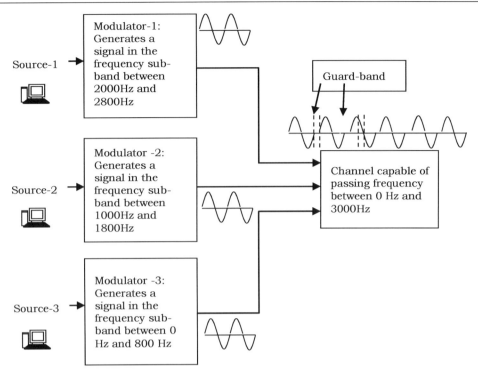

At the receiving end of the system, bandpass filters are used to pass the desired signal (the signal in the appropriate frequency sub-band) to the appropriate user and to block all the unwanted signals.

It is also appropriate to design an FDM system so that the bandwidth allocated to each sub-band is slightly larger than the bandwidth needed by each source. This extra bandwidth is called a *guard-band*.

As we can see in figure, FDM divides one channel (with frequency between 0 Hz and 3000 Hz) into several sub-channels including the Guard-band. Guard-band acts as a delimiter for each logical sub-channel so that the interference (crosstalk) from other sub-channel can be minimized.

For example, the multiplexed circuit is divided into 3 frequencies. Channel #1 (for Source-1) using 0-800 Hz for its data transfer and delimited by 200 Hz Guard-band. Channel #2 (for Source-2) using 1000-1800 Hz and delimited by 200 Hz too; and so on.

In regards to speed, we simply need to divide the main circuit amongst the available sub-channels. For example, if we have a 64 Kbps physical circuit and wanted to use 4 sub-channels, each sub-channel will have 16 Kbps.

However, Guard-band is also using this 64 Kbps physical circuit and therefore each channel will be using only 15 Kbps with 4 Guard-bands (1 Kbps per Guard-band). This calculation depends on the specification.

5.5.1.3 FDM and FDMA

We can see the signal sent by different channels have been shown in a three dimensional graph where the three dimensions are time, frequency and code. Also, we can see the signals coming from different channels are only varying in terms of frequency. However, in case of burst traffic (data that is transferred in short) the efficiency can be improved in FDMA by using a dynamic sharing technique to access a particular frequency band.

Now, normally for each of these channels a frequency is statically allocated but if the traffic is burst that means all the channels do not have data to send all the time. In such a case there can be under utilization of the channels because a channel is statically or permanently allocated to a particular station or user.

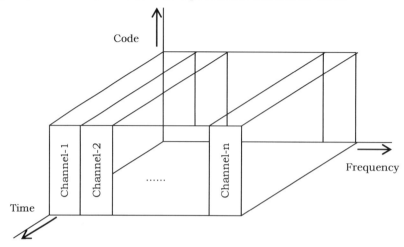

What can be done to improve the utilization? Solution would be, instead of statically allocating a channel to a station the channels can be assigned on demand.

That means depending on the requirement; channel can be allocated to different stations or users and that makes FDMA Frequency Division Multiple Access.

That means not only the overall bandwidth is divided into a number of channels but each channel can be allocated to a number of stations or users. If we have a number of channels, we can use the below equation to find the number of channels that can be used.

$$\text{Number of channels, } n = \frac{(Total\ available\ bandwidth - 2 \times Guard\ Bandwidth)}{Bandwidth\ allocated\ to\ each\ channel}$$

This is how we get the total number of channels that is possible in Frequency Division Multiplexing.

If we have n channels, since each channel can be shared by more than one user the total number of stations that can be provided a service can be greater than n. If it is statically allocated then the total number of number of stations that can be used in service is equal to n.

However, since this is allocated or assigned dynamically on demand the total number of stations can be larger than the number of channels. This is possible only when the traffic is bursty and if the traffic is streamed (continuously sent) then of course it cannot be done.

5.5.2 Time Division Multiple Access [TDMA] Technique

5.5.2.1 Time Division Multiplexing

The idea behind *Time Division Multiplexing* (TDM) is that if we have low-bit-rate streams (channels) then merge them into a single high-speed bit stream.

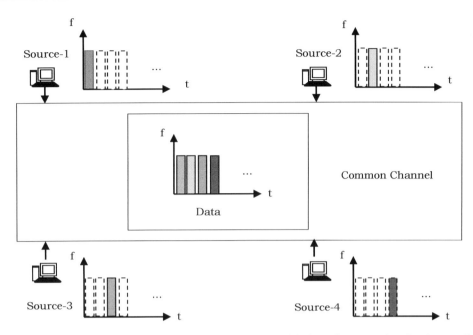

As an example, consider a channel with speed 192 kbit/sec from Hyderabad to Delhi. Suppose that three sources, all located in Hyderabad, each have 64 kbit/sec of data and they want to transmit to individual users in Delhi. As shown in Figure 7-2, the high-bit-rate channel can be divided into a series of *time slots*, and the time slots can be alternately used by the three sources.

The three sources are thus capable of sending all of their data across the single, shared channel. Clearly, at the other end of the channel (in this case, in Delhi), the process must be reversed (i.e., the system must divide the 192 kbit/sec multiplexed data stream back into the original three 64 kbit/sec data streams, which are then provided to three different users). This reverse process is called *demultiplexing*.

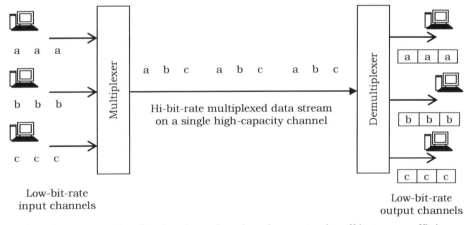

Choosing the proper size for the time slots involves a trade-off between efficiency and delay. If the time slots are too small (say, one bit long) then the multiplexer must be fast enough and powerful enough to be constantly switching between sources (and the demultiplexer must be fast enough and powerful enough to be constantly switching between users).

If the time slots are larger than one bit, data from each source must be stored (buffered) while other sources are using the channel. This storage will produce delay.

If the time slots are too large, then a significant delay will be introduced between each source and its user.

5.5.2.2 Synchronous TDM

In the above discussion, each stream has predefined slot positions in the combined stream, and the receiver must be aware which slots belong to which input stream. Both transmission ends, the transmitter and the receiver, must be perfectly synchronized to the slot period. For this reason, the technique is usually called *synhronous TDM*.

5.5.2.3 Statistical TDM [Asynchronous TDM]

There is another version of TDM, called *statistical TDM* (also called *Asynchronous TDM*). Statistical TDM is useful for applications in which the low-bit-rate streams have speeds that vary in time.

For example, a low-bit-rate stream to a single terminal in a computer network may fluctuate between 2 kbit/sec and 50 kbit/sec during an active connection session (for example, variable Internet connection speed).

If we assign the stream enough slots for its peak rate (that is, for 50 kbit/sec), then we will be wasting slots when the rate drops well below the peak value. This waste will be high if the system has many variable-speed low-bit-rate streams.

Statistical TDM works by calculating the average transmission rates of the streams to be combined, and then uses a high-speed multiplexing link with a transmission rate that is equal to (or slightly greater than) the statistical average of the combined streams. Since the transmission rates from each source are variable, we no longer assign a fixed number of time slots to each data stream.

Rather, we dynamically assign the appropriate number of slots to accommodate the current transmission rates from each stream. Since the combined rate of all the streams will also fluctuate in time between two extreme values, we need to buffer the output of the low-bit-rate streams when the combined rate exceeds the transmission rate of the high-speed link.

5.5.2.4 TDP and TDMA

We can see the signal sent by different channels have been shown in a three dimensional graph where the three dimensions are time, frequency and code. Also, we can see the signals coming from different channels are only varying in terms of time.

It is possible to assign the slots to different stations or users dynamically (similar to FDM). That means channel allocation can be done dynamically. If a particular channel is statically allocated to a single station or user in that case we call it Time Division Multiplexing.

If it is done dynamically based on demand then we call it time division multiple access. That means a particular channel can be shared by a number of stations or users. We are dividing into different time slots and each of these time slots can be shared by more than one station or user. That technique called TDMA or Time Division Multiple Access.

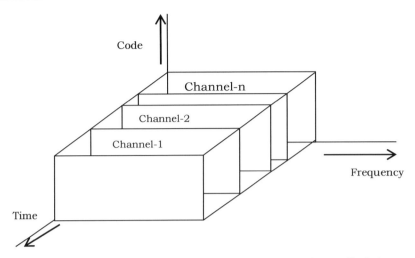

If we have a number of channels, we can use the below equation to find the number of channels that can be used.

$$\text{Number of channels, } n = \frac{\textit{number of bits for each station} \times (\textit{Total available bandwidth} - 2 \times \textit{Guard Bandwidth})}{\textit{Bandwidth allocated to each channel}}$$

This is how we get the total number of channels that is possible in Time Division Multiplexing.

5.5.2.5 Comparing FDM and TDM

FDM has both advantages and disadvantages relative to TDM. The main advantage is that unlike TDM, FDM is not sensitive to propagation delays. Disadvantages of FDM include the need for bandpass filters, which are relatively expensive. TDM, on the other hand, uses relatively simple and less costly digital logic circuits.

5.5.3 Code Division Multiple Access [CDMA] Technique

As seen in previous sections, in TDMA and FDMA, the transmissions from different stations are separated either in time or frequency. They are sent in different time slots or from different stations where different frequencies are used.

In CDMA, multiple users share the same frequency band simultaneously. Each user (station) has its own code words, which is approximately orthogonal to other code words. This feature makes the system bandwidth efficient and no interference among the stations. Because of unique assigned code station's; data is secured.

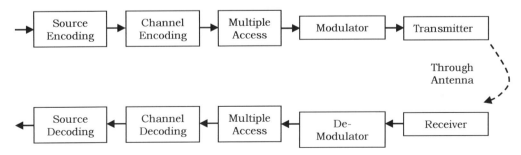

Block diagram of CDMA system is shown in figure. Since the human speech is in the analog signal, it has to be first converted into digital form. This function is performed by the source encoding module. After the source information is coded into a digital form, redundancy needs to be added to this digital message or data. This is done to improve performance of the communication system (due to noise).

5.5.3.1 Code Division Multiplexing

Code division multiplexing (CDM) takes signals from a set of sources at the same time and sends in the same frequency band. This is done by using orthogonal codes (also called *spreading code*, and *chip-sequence*) to spread each signal over a large frequency band. At the receiver, an appropriate orthogonal code is used again to recover the signal for a particular user.

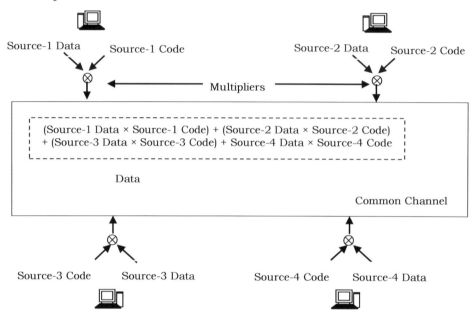

5.5.3.2 How does CDM works?

Let us walk through an example for understanding the working of CDM. Assume that binary data is coming from four different sources: Station-1 (S_1), Station-2 (S_2), Station-3 (S_3), and Station-4 (S_4). For simplicity, let us assume that 0 is represented by -1 and 1 is represented by $+1$. As shown in figure, 0 is coming from S_1, 1 is coming from S_2, 0 is coming from S_3, 1 is coming from S_4 and so on.

| Data Bit 0 → -1 | Data Bit 0 → -1 | No Data (Silence) → 0 |

Each of these stations is having an unique chip sequence (also called *spreading code* and *orthogonal code*). Chip sequence for S_1 is +1, +1, +1, +1 (essentially it is 1 1 1 1). On the other hand, for S_2 it is +1, -1, +1, -1 and it is different from the chip sequence of S_1 and then for S_3 the chip sequence is +1, +1, -1, -1 and again it is different either from S_1 and S_2. Finally, the chip sequence for S_4 is +1, -1, -1, +1. As we can see all these four chip sequences are unique. Each of them is different from the other three and binary input is multiplied with the chip sequences.

S_1	S_2	S_3	S_4
+1, +1, +1, +1	+1, -1, +1, -1	+1, +1, -1, -1	+1, -1, -1, +1

For S_1, multiplying the chip sequence +1, +1, +1, +1 with -1 becomes -1, -1 -1, -1. On the other hand, for S_2 multiplying +1 with +1, -1, +1 -1 becomes +1, -1, +1 -1. Then for

S_3, multiplying -1 with the chip sequence +1, +1, -1, -1 becomes -1, -1, +1, +1. For S_4, it is multiplied with +1. That means, multiplying +1 with the chip sequence +1, -1, -1, +1 becomes +1, -1, -1, +1.

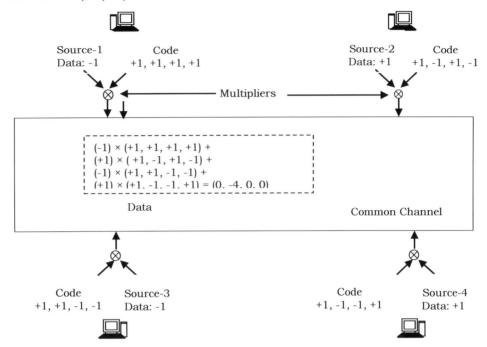

Now these are added bit by bit and for the first bit we can see that sum of +1, -1, +1, -1 becomes 0. For the second bit, -1, -1, -1, -1 becomes -4 (we have to add all the four). Similarly, for third bit -1, +1, +1, -1 it is 0 and for fourth bit −1, -1, +1, +1 it is 0.

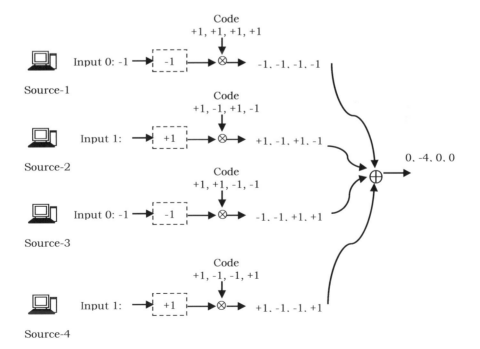

The final composite signal corresponds to 0, -4, 0, 0 and this can be sent over the medium. After it is received; the same chip sequences (which were used before transmission) are used for demultiplexing.

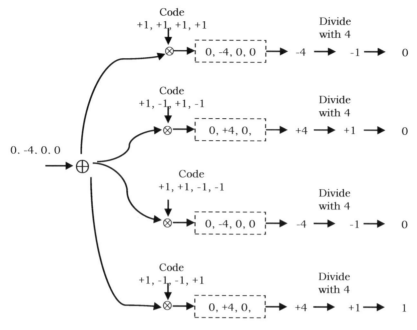

Therefore, multiplying 0, -4, 0, 0 with chip sequences gives:

- 0, -4, 0, 0 multiplying with +1, +1, +1, +1 becomes 0, -4, 0, 0
- 0, -4, 0, 0 multiplying with +1, -1, +1, -1 becomes 0, +4, 0, 0
- 0, -4, 0, 0 multiplying with +1, +1, -1, -1 becomes 0, -4, 0, 0
- 0, -4, 0, 0 multiplying with +1, -1, -1, +1 becomes 0, +4, 0, 0

Now, we have to perform the addition.

- Sum of all numbers in 0, -4, 0, 0 gives -4
- Sum of all numbers in 0, +4, 0, 0 gives +4
- Sum of all numbers in 0, -4, 0, 0 gives -4
- Sum of all numbers in 0, +4, 0, 0 gives +4

Then, we divide the resultants with 4 (since the total number of channels is 4).

- Dividing -4 with 4 gives -1
- Dividing +4 with 4 gives +1
- Dividing -4 with 4 gives -1
- Dividing +4 with 4 gives +1

The final result is -1, +1, -1, +1. Since -1 is nothing but 0, +1 is nothing but 1; the input transmitted data 0 1 0 1 is now recovered.

5.5.3.3 Selecting Spreading Code

If R is the bit rate of data (from a source station) then spreading factor is selected such that it occupies the entire frequency band of the medium. That means the number of bits in chip sequence is chosen such that it occupies the entire bandwidth of the channel. So it can be 8, it can be 16 or it can be 128 depending on the bandwidth of the medium. Therefore, the signal that comes out becomes m times; which are the number of bits in the chip sequence divided with the data rate of the source.

After multiplying, this is the signal that is being generated and now we can perform digital modulation (like QAM, QPSK kind of modulation) and then we can transmit by using an antenna. This is how the transmission is performed and as we can see the bandwidth here is at times the bandwidth of each of the channels.

At the receiving end; signals from all the transmitters are being received by antenna and then the composite signal is multiplied with the digital demodulator. After demodulation we get the composite signal and that is multiplied with unique pseudo random binary sequence. After multiplying with the same pseudo random sequence we get the original signal back. Of course it will have some noise because of interference and other problems but we get back the binary information.

5.5.3.4 Near-Far Problem

In the above discussion, we have assumed that the signals coming from different stations have equal strength. Essentially the *near-far* problem arises; because if there is a receiver which is receiving signal from a number of transmitters; depending on the distance if it is very near then the signal strength coming from that signal will be very high and the signal strength from the other signals will be low.

As a result, if the signal strength is very low then that will be ignored and will be considered as 0. Similarly, if the signal strengths are not equal then the noise will increase; that is, the interference will increase. In other words; the summation and the subsequent deduction is based on the assumption that they are of equal strength. That's why; some kind of power control mechanism is used at each of the transmitter to overcome the *near-far* problem as it is used in cellular telephone network.

5.5.3.5 Characteristics of Spreading Codes [Chip Sequences]

Let's now understand the pseudo-random chip sequence in detail. As discussed, each station is assigned with an unique m-bit code called *chip sequence*. This is done by using *linear feedback shift* register. You may recall that, in error detection using cyclic redundancy code (CRC), to generate cyclic redundancy code and also to check it; we used linear feedback shift register to generate a random sequence. That kind of linear feedback shift register can also be used here to generate those unique pseudo random binary sequences. These unique pseudo random sequences are used in transmitter as well as in receiver.

As mentioned earlier, we want each bit in the chip sequence to be *random*, *independent*, and *equiprobable* (to ensure equal number of 0's and 1's in chip sequence). These characteristics are achieved if the code exhibits the following three properties:

1. *Balance*: The difference between the number of 1's and 0's should be either zero or one.
2. *Run property*: Among the groups of 1's and 0's in the chip sequence, half the groups of each type should be one bit long, one fourth of the groups of each type should be two bits long, one eighth of the groups of each type should be three bits long, etc. The run property is an important indicator that the bits are random and independent.
3. *Correlation*: Consider a n-bit binary sequence $b_1 b_2 b_3 \ldots b_n$. We can write this binary sequence in matrix form as

$$[b] = [b_1 \quad b_2 \quad b_3 \quad b_4 \ldots \quad b_n]$$

Now consider a second n-bit sequence, say, $c_1 c_2 c_3 \ldots c_n$. Again, we can write this binary sequence in matrix form as

$$[c] = [c_1 \quad c_2 \quad c_3 \quad c_4 \ldots \quad c_n]$$

We can use matrix notation to signify a bit-by-bit $\oplus$ (exclusive-or operation) of the two sequences:

$$[b] \oplus [c] = [b_1 \oplus c_1 \quad b_2 \oplus c_2 \quad b_3 \oplus c_3 \quad b_4 \oplus c_4 \ldots \quad b_n \oplus c_n]$$

Let's consider one other operation—a cyclic shift. Let the notation $[b]^n$ indicates the sequence of bits $[b]$ cyclically shifted n places to the right. For example,

$$[b] = [b_1 \quad b_2 \quad b_3 \quad b_4 \ldots \quad b_n]$$
$$[b]^1 = [b_n \quad b_1 \quad b_2 \quad b_3 \ldots \quad b_{n-1}]$$
$$[b]^j = [b_{n-j+1} \quad b_{n-j+2} \quad b_{n-j+3} \quad b_n \quad b_1 \ldots \quad b_{n-j}]$$

The third desirable property of a chip sequence is that the n-bit sequence produced by $[b] \oplus [b]^j$ should exhibit balance for all non-zero values of j less than n (the number of 1's in $[b] \oplus [b]^j$ should differ from the number of 0's by no more than one for any value $1 \leq j \leq n - 1$).

Why does the *correlation* property help ensure *independence* and *randomness*?

Since $\oplus$ of two bits produces a *zero* if both bits are the same (if both bits are 0's or if both bits are 1's) and produces a *one* if the two bits are different (if one of the bits is 0 and the other is 1). If a sequence of bits is truly random and independent, then cyclically shifting the sequence by an arbitrary number of places; performing a bit-by-bit comparison of the original; and shifted sequences should produce the same number of agreements (the values of the two bits are the same) as disagreements (the values of the two bits are different). Of course, if the sequence contains an odd number of bits, the number of agreements and disagreements will have to differ by at least one.

5.5.3.6 Generating Chip Sequences

Chip sequences are not randomly chosen sequences. We do not generate them in an arbitrary manner. Generating them in an arbitrary manner will make the property of orthogonality not satisfied.

Let us use the symbol s_i to indicate the m-bit sequence code for station i and $\bar{s}_i$ is the complement of s_i. The chip sequences of all the stations are pair-wise orthogonal. That means; the normalized inner product of any two different codes will be 0. For example, s_1 is having the code +1, -1, +1, -1 and s_2's code is equal to +1, +1, -1, -1.

S_1 chip sequence	S_2 chip sequence
+1, -1, +1, -1	+1, +1, -1, -1

If we take the inner product of these two, which means multiplying +1 with +1 (first two bits) will give +1. Similarly, +1 with -1 will give -1, -1 with +1 gives -1, and -1 with -1 gives +1. Then, adding them will give us 0.

s_1	s_2	$s_1 \cdot s_2$
+1	+1	+1
-1	+1	-1
+1	-1	-1
-1	-1	+1
	Sum=0	

This is valid for any two distinct codes. That means;

$$s_1 \cdot s_2 = 0$$
$$s_1 \cdot s_3 = 0$$
$$s_1 \cdot s_4 = 0$$

On the other hand, multiplying the same code, say $s_1 \cdot s_1$, would give us 1.

s_1	s_1	$s_1 \cdot s_1$
+1	+1	+1
-1	-1	+1
+1	+1	+1
-1	-1	+1

Sum = 4
and 4/4 = 1

As shown above, adding them would give 4 and dividing the result with number of bits gives 1. So, we found that multiplying same chip sequences would give 1. Also, if we multiply with the complement then we get 0. That means;

$$s_i \cdot s_i = 1$$
$$s_i \cdot s_j = 0; \text{ if } i \neq j$$
$$s_i \cdot \overline{s_i} = 0$$

This is the *orthogonality* property that is to be satisfied by the chip sequences, only then the multiplexing and demultiplexing is possible. In other words transmission and subsequent recovery at the receiving end is possible only when this *orthogonal* property is satisfied.

5.5.3.6.1 Walsh Table

Now, let us concentrate on how the chip sequences are generated. What is the technique used to generate the chip sequences?

Chip sequences have to be pair-wise orthogonal. That can be done by using Walsh table in an interactive manner. That means, *Walsh* table can be used to generate orthogonal sequences in an interactive manner. Note that, number of sequences is always a power of two.

W_1 is +1 and is a one dimensional matrix; W_2 is a two dimensional matrix with four entries.

$$W_1 = [+1] \quad W_{2N} = \begin{bmatrix} W_N & W_N \\ W_N & \overline{W_N} \end{bmatrix}$$

From the above representation, we can compute W_{2N} from W_N.

For example, W_1 is +1 and to get W_2, we have substituted W_1, W_1, W_1 and $\overline{\overline{W_1}}$. That means, +1 +1 +1 and -1 then W_4, can be generated from W_2. This is how it is being done.

$$W_1 = [+1] \quad W_2 = \begin{bmatrix} +1 & +1 \\ +1 & -1 \end{bmatrix} \quad W_4 = \begin{bmatrix} +1 & +1 & +1 & +1 \\ +1 & -1 & +1 & -1 \\ +1 & +1 & -1 & -1 \\ +1 & -1 & -1 & +1 \end{bmatrix} \quad W_8 = \begin{bmatrix} W_4 & W_4 \\ W_4 & \overline{W_4} \end{bmatrix} = \begin{bmatrix} +1 +1 +1 +1 & +1 +1 +1 +1 \\ +1 -1 +1 -1 & +1 -1 +1 -1 \\ +1 +1 -1 -1 & +1 +1 -1 -1 \\ +1 -1 -1 +1 & +1 -1 -1 +1 \\ +1 +1 +1 +1 & -1 -1 -1 -1 \\ +1 -1 +1 -1 & -1 +1 -1 +1 \\ +1 +1 -1 -1 & -1 -1 +1 \mp 1 \\ +1 -1 -1 +1 & -1 +1 +1 -1 \end{bmatrix}$$

This way, we can generate the next bit sequences in an interactive manner. So, if the table for *N* sequences is known the table for *2N* sequences can be created and it can be proved that these sequences satisfy the orthogonal property.

5.6 LocalTalk

LocalTalk is a network protocol developed by *Apple* for *Macintosh* computers. Older computers can be connected through a serial port with special twisted pair cable and adapters. The main disadvantage of LocalTalk is the speed (230 Kbps).

Although LocalTalk networks are slow, they are popular because they are easy and inexpensive to install and maintain.

5.7 Ethernet

The most popular set of protocols for the Physical and Data Link layers is Ethernet. Ethernet operates at the first two layers of the OSI model: Physical and Data Link layers. Initially, Ethernet was given a name *Alto Aloha Network*. Ethernet was created by *Robert Metcalfe* (in 1973). Metcalfe thought the name *ether* suitable because the cable used to build a network is a passive medium that permits the propagation of data.

The cost of an Ethernet port on a node is very low compared to other technologies. Many vendors build Ethernet into the motherboard of the computer so that it is not necessary to purchase a separate NIC.

In Ethernet, both the data link and the physical layers are involved in the creation and transmission of frames. The physical layer is related to the type of LAN cabling and how the bits are transmitted and received on the cable. Ethernet divides the Data Link layer into two separate layers:

- Logical Link Control (LLC) layer
- Medium Access Control (MAC) layer

The MAC sublayer address is the physical hardware address of the source and destination computer. All devices on a LAN must be identified by a unique MAC address. This sublayer controls which computer devices send and receive the data and allows NICs to communicate with the physical layer. The next level of processing is the LLC sublayer. It is responsible for identifying and passing data to the network layer protocol.

5.7.1 How Ethernet Works?

Ethernet uses a protocol called CSMA/CD (Carrier Sense Multiple Access with Collision Detect). When one computer wanted to transmit, it would first check to see if any other machines were using the line. If the line was free, the sending computer tags the data it needed to send with a MAC (Media Access Control) address and loads it onto the network.

The MAC address identifies the intended recipient so that the machine possessing that unique MAC address would accept the data and all the other machines on the network would ignore it.

If the transmission line was busy, the computer would wait. If two machines try to send at the same time, each would react to the collision by waiting a random number of milliseconds before attempting to resend.

The process was simple, but it was also very limited. Multiple collisions could quickly reduce the performance of a large network. For example, it is easy to eavesdrop on the network's traffic with a fake MAC address. The network wasn't very robust. Damage to any cable in the network could cause the entire system down.

5.7.2 Ethernet and IEEE 802.3

Companies DEC, Intel, and Xerox created Version 2.0 of the Ethernet specification in 1982. Version 2.0 formed the basis for 802.3 standard. Although there are some minor differences between the two technologies, the terms Ethernet and 802.3 are generally used synonymously.

In reality, at the physical layer, 802.3 is the standard and at data link layer, both Ethernet Version 2.0 and 802.3 implementations are common.

Note: One important difference between Ethernet Version 2.0 and 802.3 is frame formats.

5.7.3 Ethernet Technology Choices

The following options for implementing Ethernet networks are available:

- Half- and full-duplex Ethernet
- 10-Mbps Ethernet
- 100-Mbps Ethernet
- 1000-Mbps (1-Gbps or Gigabit) Ethernet
- 10-Gbps Ethernet

OSI	*Ethernet*		
Data Link Layer	Logical Link Control (LLC)		
	Medium Access Control (MAC)		
Physical Layer	*Standard Ethernet*: 10Base5 10Base2 10BaseT 10BaseFX	*Fast Ethernet*: 100BaseT 100BaseFX 100BaseSX 100BaseBX	*Gigabit Ethernet*: 1000BaseT 1000BaseTX 1000BaseFX 1000BaseSX 1000BaseBX

For example, 10BaseT Ethernet protocol uses 10 for the speed of transmission at 10 megabits per second [Mbps], the *base* for *baseband* [means it has full control of the wire on a single frequency], and the *T* for *twisted pair* cable.

Fast Ethernet standards:

100BaseT	100 Mbps over Twisted-pair category 5
100BaseFX	100 Mbps over fiber optic cable
100BaseSX	100 Mbps over multimode fiber optic cable
100BaseBX	100 Mbps over single mode fiber cable

Gigabit Ethernet standards:

1000BaseT	1000 Mbps over 2-pair category 5
1000BaseTX	1000 Mbps over 2-pair category 6
1000BaseFX	1000 Mbps over fiber optic cable

1000BaseSX	1000 Mbps over multimode fiber cable
1000BaseBX	1000 Mbps over single mode fiber cable

The choice of an Ethernet technology depends on parameters like: location and size of user communities, bandwidth, and QoS requirements.

5.7.3.1 Half-Duplex and Full-Duplex Ethernet

The initial definition of Ethernet was for a shared medium with stations using the carrier sense multiple access/collision detection (CSMA/CD). CSMA/CD algorithm regulates the sending of frames, detects collisions when two nodes send at the same time.

With shared Ethernet, a station listens before it sends data. If the medium is already in use, the station defers its transmission until the medium is free. Shared Ethernet is *half duplex*, meaning that a station is either transmitting or receiving traffic, but not both at once.

A point-to-point Ethernet link which supports simultaneous transmitting and receiving is called *full-duplex Ethernet*. On a link between a switch port and a single station, for example, both the switch and the station can transmit at the same time.

This is beneficial if the station is a server that processes queries from many users. The switch can transmit the next query at the same time the server is sending a response to a previous query. The advantage of full-duplex Ethernet is that the transmission rate is theoretically double what it is on a half-duplex link.

Full-duplex operation requires the cabling to dedicate one wire pair for transmitting and another for receiving. Full-duplex operation does not work on cables with only one path (for example, coaxial cable).

5.7.3.2 10-Mbps Ethernet

Although 100-Mbps Ethernet is beginning to replace 10-Mbps Ethernet, 10-Mbps Ethernet can still play a role in your network design, particularly at the access layer. For some customers 10-Mbps capacity is sufficient. For customers who have low bandwidth needs and a small budget, 10-Mbps Ethernet is an appropriate solution if the network does not need to scale to 100-Mbps in the near future.

Many business applications do not benefit just with an upgrade to 100-Mbps Ethernet. Inefficient applications that send many small frames generate more collisions on 100-Mbps Ethernet and that decreases the throughput.

	10BASE5	10BASE2	10BASE-T
Topology	Bus	Bus	Star
Type of cabling	Thick coax	Thin coax	UTP
Maximum cable length (in meters)	500	185	100 from hub to station
Maximum number of attachments per cable	100	30	2 (hub and station or hub and hub)
Maximum collision domain (in meters)	2500	2500	2500
Maximum topology of a collision domain	5 segments, 4 repeaters, only 3 segments can have end systems	5 segments, 4 repeaters, only 3 segments can have end systems	5 segments, 4 repeaters, only 3 segments can have end systems

	10BASE-FP	10BASE-FB	10BASE-FL	Old FOIRL
Topology	Star	Backbone or repeater system	Repeater-repeater link	Repeater-repeater link
Maximum cable length (in meters)	500	2000	2000	1000
Allows end system connections?	Yes	No	No	No
Allows cascaded repeaters?	No	Yes	No	No
Maximum collision domain (in meters)	2500	2500	2500	2500

5.7.3.3 100-Mbps Ethernet

100-Mbps Ethernet (also called *Fast Ethernet* and 100BASE-T Ethernet), was initially standardized in IEEE 802.3u specification and is now merged into the 2002 edition of IEEE 802.3. It is very similar to 10-Mbps Ethernet. With some exceptions, 100-Mbps Ethernet is simply standard Ethernet, just 10 times faster.

In most cases, design parameters for 100-Mbps Ethernet are the same as 10-Mbps Ethernet, just multiplied or divided by 10.

5.7.3.4 Gigabit Ethernet

Gigabit Ethernet was initially defined in IEEE 802.3z specification and is now merged into the 2002 edition of IEEE 802.3. It operates essentially like 100-Mbps Ethernet, except that it is 10 times faster. It uses a standard 802.3 frame format and frame size.

5.7.3.5 10-Gbps Ethernet

One of the reasons that Ethernet is such a good choice for campus network designs is that it continues to grow with increasing bandwidth demands. In 2002, the IEEE standardized 10-Gbps Ethernet in the 802.3ae specification. The frame format of 10-Gbps Ethernet is same. This means that applications that use Ethernet do not need to change.

5.7.4 Ethernet Frames

As discussed earlier, in Ethernet, both the data link and the physical layers are involved in the creation and transmission of frames. The physical layer is related to the type of LAN cabling and how the bits are transmitted and received on the cable. The data link layer is divided into sublayers, the Logical Link Control (LLC) and the Media Access Control layers (MAC).

The MAC sublayer address is the physical hardware address of the source and destination computer. The next level of processing is the LLC sublayer. It is responsible for identifying and passing data to the network layer protocol.

Initially, companies DEC, Intel and XEROX created the DIX standard and defined DIX frame (also called Ethernet II). Later, Institute of Electrical and Electronics Engineers [IEEE] defined the IEEE 802.3 specification and defined IEEE 802.3 frames. There is a slight change in these two frame formats.

5.7.4.1 DIX Frame (Ethernet II) Format

Preamble	Destination Address	Source Address	Type	Data	Frame Check Sequence
Preamble	DA	SA	Type	Data	FCS
8	6	6	2	46-1500	4

Size in Bytes

Frame field	Description
Preamble	Indicates the start of a new frame and establishes synchronization conditions between devices. The last byte, or start frame delimiter, always has a 10101011-bit pattern. This byte indicates the start of a frame.
Destination Address (DA)	The Destination Address is the hardware (MAC) address of the receiving device.
Source Address (SA)	Specifies the hardware (MAC) address of the sending device.
Type	The Type field specifies the network layer protocol used to send the frame, for example TCP/IP.
Data	The Data field is for the actual data being transmitted from device to device. It also contains information used by the network layer and indicates the type of connection.
Frame Check Sequence	Contains CRC error-checking information.

5.7.4.2 IEEE 802.3 Frame Format

Preamble	Start Frame Delimiter	Destination Address	Source Address	Length	Data and Padding	Frame Check Sequence
Preamble	SFD	DA	SA	Length	Data/Pad	FCS
7	1	6	6	2	46-1500	4

Size in Bytes

Frame field	Description
Preamble	Indicates the start of a new frame and establishes synchronization conditions between devices. The last byte, or start frame delimiter, always has a 10101011-bit pattern. This byte indicates the start of a frame (same as DIX frame).
Start Frame Delimiter	The Start Frame Delimiter (SFD) has the same 10101011-bit sequence found at the end of the DIX preamble. Both formats use the same number of bytes to perform the synchronization of the signals.
Destination Address (DA)	The Destination address can be either 2 or 6 bytes. Whether 2 or 6 bytes are used, all devices within the same network must use the same format. IEEE protocols specify that a 10Mbs network must use 6 bytes. The 2 byte length is obsolete.
Source Address (SA)	Same as DA.
Length	The Length field indicates the number of bytes in the data field. If the data field is less than the required 46 bytes, a pad field is added to the data frame. The bytes added for padding purposes are usually zeros.

Data and Padding	The Data field is for the actual data being transmitted from device to device. It also contains information used by the network layer and indicates the type of connection.
Frame Check Sequence	Contains CRC error-checking information (same as DIX frame).

It should be noted that if one device uses an IEEE 802.3 NIC and the other device uses a DIX Ethernet NIC, they would not be able to communicate with one another. Devices must create the same Ethernet frame format in order to be compatible. One way to tell them apart is that the DIX frame has a *type* field, which defines the protocol used for the frame, and IEEE 802.3 has a *length* field in its place. IEEE 802.3 also has additional fields not used with the DIX format.

5.7.4.3 IEEE 802.2 LLC Format

In between the length field and the data/pad field, is the 802.2 LLC field.

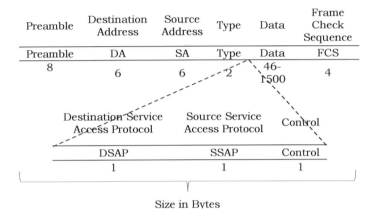

Size in Bytes

Frame field	Description
Destination Service Access Protocol	It is the protocol processing layer the data is to be sent to.
Source Service Access Protocol	It is the protocol used to encapsulate the data at the source.
Control	It is the field that defines the type of LLC frame this is.

5.7.4.4 SNAP Format of 802.2

SNAP (Sub-Network Access Protocol) was created by the IEEE to identify the Network layer protocol used. The original Ethernet version 2.0 *Type* field had been reused as a *Length* field by the IEEE when creating the IEEE 802.3 standard.

SNAP was defined to enable this Length field to remain while also allowing the vendor and protocol to be defined in the first 40 bits of the Data field. Together, these two fields (Organization and EtherType) are called *protocol ID*.

Destination Service Access Protocol	Source Service Access Protocol	Control	Organization	EtherType
DSAP (AA)	SSAP (AA)	Control	Organization	EtherType
1	1	1	3	2

Size in Bytes

Frame field	Description
Destination Service Access Protocol (AA)	AA in the DSAP fields indicates that the LLC field is using SNAP format.
Source Service Access Protocol (AA)	AA in the SSAP fields indicates that the LLC field is using SNAP format.
Control	It is the field that defines the type of LLC frame this is.
Organization	Organization is the field that indicates which organization created the protocol identified in the EtherType field, though generally this is coded as all zeros by most organizations.
EtherType	EtherType is a two-byte identifier for the protocol being used to encapsulate the data. For example, IP is indicated by the code 0x08-00 and ARP by 0x08-06.
Control	It is the field that defines the type of LLC frame this is.

5.7.4.5 Frame Types

There are three types of frames and each has a different purpose.

- Unicast frames
- Multicast frames
- Broadcast frames

If the first bit of the frame is 0, it is Unicast; if it is 1, it is multicast. Broadcast frames always have 1 as the second bit.

A *unicast* frame is addressed to a single network device. This means that the frame is to be read only by the device that matches the destination address. All other devices will receive a copy of the frame but will discard it because it does not match their destination address. The address used is the MAC of the network device.

A *multicast* frame is addressed to several but not all devices. All devices that are a part of the specified group may read the frame. A multicast address is a deviation from the normal hardware address. For example, a group of devices are assigned access to a particular server on the network. They are the only devices that receive frames announcing the availability of that server. Any device that does not belong to this group will ignore or discard these frames.

A *broadcast* frame is addressed for all network devices to read and process. A broadcast address is a unique address used only for broadcast frames. It is not a hardware address. Broadcast frames are transmitted across bridges and switches; but, routers will stop broadcast frames.

5.7.5 Physical Devices for an Ethernet network

There are three main pieces of Ethernet hardware:

1. Ethernet cards [also called Adapters, Network Interface cards]
2. Ethernet cables
3. Ethernet routers and hubs

A Network Interface Card (NIC) is a device that allows computers to be joined together in a LAN network. An Ethernet network interface card is installed in an available slot inside the computer, typically on the *motherboard*. The NIC assigns a unique Media Access Control (MAC) address to the machine, which is used to direct traffic between the computers on a network.

Ethernet cables have a number of styles [refer *Ethernet Technology Choices* section].

Ethernet hubs and Ethernet routers are like dispatchers in an Ethernet network because they direct data to the correct recipient. Hubs and routers can be connected to other devices, not only to computers and depending on the way they are connected, there are different Ethernet topologies.

5.8 Token Ring

Token ring local area network (LAN) technology is a local area network protocol and it resides at the data link layer (DLL) of the OSI model.

It was developed by IBM (in 19970s) and was a popular technology used in LANs (before Ethernet). Today it is difficult to find token ring based networks because the cost and flexibility of *Ethernet* came to dominate the market. The goal of Token Ring was to provide a simple wiring structure (say, using twisted-pair cable) that connects a computer to the network.

The related IEEE 802.5 specification is almost identical and completely compatible with IBM's Token Ring network implementations. The IEEE 802.5 specification was developed after IBM's Token Ring specification.

As its name indicates, nodes (computers) are arranged in a ring and single token is continuously passed from computer to computer.

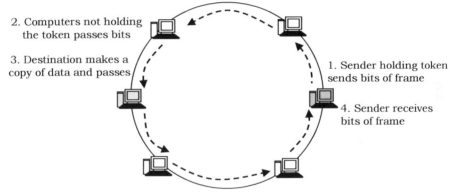

When a computer wants to send data to another computer, it waits for the token to come around and then attaches its data to it. The token is then passed to the next computer in the ring until it reaches the recipient computer. The recipient attaches two bits of data to the token to inform the sender that the data was received. Other computers can't send data until the ring is free again.

5.8.1 How it works?

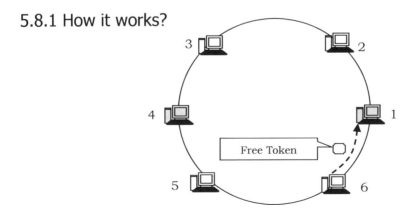

At the start, an empty information frames are continuously circulated on the ring. To use the network, a machine first has to capture the free Token and replace the data with its own message.

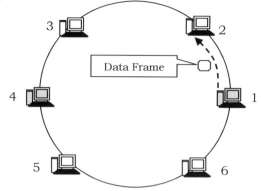

In the example above, machine 1 wants to send some data to machine 4, so it first has to capture the free Token. It then writes its data and the recipient's address onto the Token.

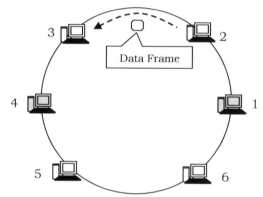

The packet of data is then sent to machine 2 who reads the address, realizes it is not its own, so passes it on to machine 3.

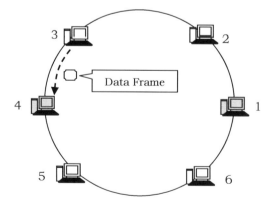

Machine 3 does the same and passes the Token on to machine 4.

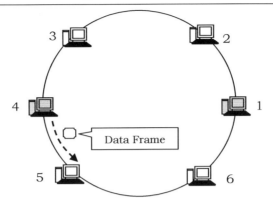

This time it is the correct address and so machine 4 reads the message. It cannot, however, release a free Token on to the ring; it must first send the frame back to machine 1 with an acknowledgement to say that it has received the data.

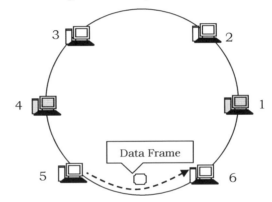

The receipt is then sent to machine 5 who checks the address, realizes that it is not its own and so forwards it on to the next machine in the ring, machine 6.

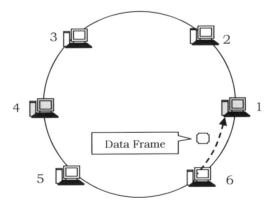

Machine 6 does the same and forwards the data to machine 1, who sent the original message.

Machine 1 recognizes the address, reads the acknowledgement from number 4 and then releases the free Token back on to the ring ready for the next machine to use

In summary, here is how it works:

1. Empty information frames are continuously circulated on the ring.

2. When a machine has a message to send, it inserts a token in an empty frame (this may consist of simply changing a 0 to a 1 in the token bit part of the frame) and inserts a message and a destination identifier in the frame.

3. The frame is then examined by each successive machine. If the workstation sees that it is the destination for the message, it copies the message from the frame and changes the token back to 0.

4. When the frame gets back to the originator, it sees that the token has been changed to 0 and that the message has been copied and received. It removes the message from the frame.

5. The frame continues to circulate as an *empty* frame, ready to be taken by a machine when it has a message to send.

5.8.2 Token Ring with Hub

The architecture of a typical Token Ring network begins with a physical ring but it is not compulsory. In IBM implementation, a star-wired ring, computers on the network are connected to a central hub. The logical ring represents the token's path between computers. The actual physical ring of cable is in the hub. Machines are part of a ring, but they connect to it through a hub.

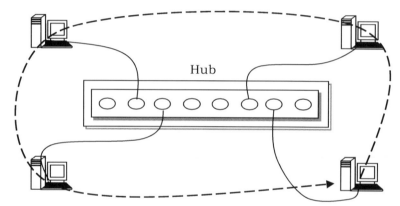

The Token still circulates around the network and is still controlled in the same manner. Using a hub or a switch greatly improves reliability because the hub can automatically bypass any ports that are disconnected or have a cabling fault.

5.8.3 Token and Data Frames

The basic transmission unit on Token-Ring is a frame. In simple terms, token frame in a token ring network is a 3-bit piece of data that constantly travels around the network. When a node (machine) indicates that it is ready to transmit data it converts the token frame to a data frame.

This data frame is then transmitted around the network until it reaches the receiving node, which once again converts it back into a token frame.

Token Ring and IEEE 802.5 support two basic frame types: tokens and data/command frames. Data/Command frames) vary in size, depending on the size of the Information field (which contains the data to be transmitted).

Data frames carry information for upper-layer protocols and command frames contain control information and have no data for upper-layer protocols.

5.8.3.1 Token Frame

Tokens are 3 bytes in length and consist of a start delimiter, an access control byte, and an end delimiter.

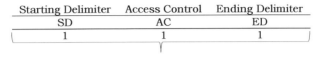

Starting Delimiter	Access Control	Ending Delimiter
SD	AC	ED
1	1	1

Size in Bytes

Frame field	Description
Start Delimiter	Indicates start of the frame.
Access Control	Indicates the frame's priority and whether it is a token or a data frame
End Delimiter	Indicates the end of the frame

Start Delimiter (SD) indicates the arrival of a frame or token. This field includes bits that are set to intentionally violate the Differential Manchester Code to distinguish this field as a delimiter. This byte is coded as JK0JK000, where the J and K bits are intentional Manchester encoding violations. These intentional violations delineate the token from normal traffic data. J is the encoding violation of a 1, and K is the encoding violation of a 0.

Access Control (AC) byte is coded as *PPPTMRRR*. The priority bits (PPP) provide eight levels of priority (000 through 111). The token indicator bit (T) of 0 determines that the following information is a token, a 1 designates the following information is a frame. The *Monitor* bit (M) is used to prevent frames from constantly circling the ring. The Priority Reservations bits (RRR) provide token reservation to ring stations.

Ending Delimiter (ED) byte is coded as JK1JK1IE, where the J and K bits are encoding violations and the I and E bits are the intermediate frame and error detection bits, respectively. The intermediate bit is set to 1 if there are more frames to transmit in this set. The error detection bit is set to 1 by a station that recognizes a CRC error in the frame so other stations downstream do not report the same error.

5.8.3.2 Data/Command Frame

Starting Delimiter	Access Control	Frame Control	Destination Address	Source Address	Data	Frame Check Sequence	Ending Delimiter	Frame Status
SD	AC	FC	DA	SA	Data	FCS	ED	FS
1	1	1	6	6	>=0	4	1	2

Size in Bytes

Frame field	Description
Start Delimiter	Indicates start of the frame
Access Control	Indicates the frame's priority and whether it is a token or a data frame
Frame Control	Contains either Media Access Control information for all computers or *end station* information for only one computer
Destination Address	Indicates the address of the computer to receive the frame
Source Address	Indicates the computer that sent the frame
Information, or data	Contains the data being sent
Frame Check Sequence	Contains CRC error-checking information
End Delimiter	Indicates the end of the frame

Frame Status	Tells whether the frame was recognized, copied, or whether the destination address was available

Starting Delimiter (SD) - Same as Token Frame.

Access Control (AC) - Same as Token Frame.

Frame Control (FC) field consists of eight bits, coded as TT00AAAA. The Frame Type bits (T) indicate the frame type. Bits 2 and 3 are reserved, and are always zero. Bits four through eight are Attention Codes which provide the token ring adapter of incoming MAC information that can be copied to a special Express Buffer in the token ring adapter.

Destination Address (DA) indicates the station which need to receive the frame. The Destination Address can be sent to a specific station, or a group of stations.

Source Address (SA): The Source Address is the MAC address of the sending station.

Data: A MAC frame *data* field contains token ring management information, and a non-MAC (LLC) data field contains user data.

Frame Check Sequence (FCS): A 32 bit Cyclical Redundancy Check (CRC) is performed on the frame data to provide an integrity check of the frame data. As each station copies the frame, the CRC is computed and compared with the value in the FCS frame to verify that the frame data is correct.

Ending Delimiter (ED) - Same as Token Frame.

Frame Status (FS) field provides information for the sending station regarding the status of the frame as it circulates the ring. The Frame Status field is coded as AF00AF00. The bits of the Frame Status field are duplicated, since this field does not fall under the CRC checking of the Frame Check Sequence bytes.

The Address Recognized Indicator (ARI) is set to 1 by the destination station if the destination station recognizes the frame. The Frame Copied Indicator (FCI) is set to 1 if the destination station was able to copy the frame into the local adapter buffer memory.

5.8.4 Token Ring Self Maintenance

When a Token Ring network starts up, the machines all take part in a negotiation to decide who will control the ring, or become the *active monitor* to give it its proper title. This is won by the machine with the highest MAC address who is participating in the contention procedure, and all other machines become *standby monitors*.

The job of the *active monitor* is to make sure that none of the machines are causing problems on the network, and to re-establish the ring after a break or an error has occurred. There can only be a single active monitor on a physical token ring. The *active monitor* performs ring *polling* every *seven* seconds and resets the ring when there appears to be a problem. The ring polling allows all machines on the network to find out who is participating in the ring and to learn the address of their *Nearest Active Upstream Neighbour* (NAUN).

Ring reset is performed after an interruption or loss of data is reported. Each machine knows the address of its NAUN. This is an important function in a Token Ring as it updates the information required to re-establish itself when machines enter or leave the ring.

When a machine enters the ring it performs a test to verify that its own connection is working properly, if it passes, it sends a voltage to the hub which operates a relay to insert it into the ring. If a problem occurs anywhere on the ring, the machine that is immediately after the fault will stop receiving signals. If this situation continues for a short period of time; it initiates a recovery procedure which assumes that its NAUN is at fault, the outcome of this procedure either removes its neighbor from the ring or it removes itself.

If the *active monitor* is removed from the ring or no longer performs the *active monitor* functions, one of the *standby monitors* on the ring will take over as *active monitor*.

5.8.5 Token Insertion Choices: Operational Modes

When a station has data to transmit, the station captures the token and produces a modified token as the header for the packet to indicate to other stations that the ring is no longer free. The amount of data in the packet can be arbitrary. The transmitting station is responsible for removing its packet from the ring and for generating a new free token when its transmission is over. There are several times when a new free token can be generated. The variations are: multiple-token, single-token, and single-packet operation.

5.8.5.1 Multiple-Token

In multiple-token mode, the transmitting machine generates a new free token and places it on the ring immediately following the last bit of transmitting data. This type of operation allows several busy tokens and one free token on the ring at the same time.

5.8.5.2 Single-Token

Single-token operation requires that a transmitting machine wait until it has cleared its own busy token before generating a new free token. If a packet is longer than the ring latency, however, the machine will receive (and erase) its busy token before it has finished transmitting data.

In this case, the machine must continue transmitting data and generate a new free token only after the last data bit has been transmitted. This is the same as multiple-token operation. Thus single-token and multiple-token operation differ only in cases for which the packet is shorted than the ring latency.

5.8.5.3 Single-Packet

For single-packet operation, a machine does not issue a new free token until after it has circulated completely around the ring and erased its entire transmitted packet. This type of operation is the most conservative of the three in ensuring that two transmissions do not interfere.

Both single-packet and single-token operation ensure that there is only a single token on the ring at any given time, but the difference is that single-packet operation requires that the complete packet be cleared before generating a new free token.

5.8.6 Physical devices for a Token Ring Network

Token ring connectivity needs three separate devices.

A Multistation Access Unit (MAU): A MAU is a hub-like device that connects to all token ring stations. Although the token ring stations are attached to the MAU in a physical star topology, a true ring is maintained inside the MAU.

Unlike an Ethernet hub, a MAU consists of physical or electronic relays which keep each station in a loopback state until a voltage is sent from the station to the MAU. Since this voltage does not affect data communications, it is called *phantom* voltage. Once this phantom voltage is received by the MAU, a relay is activated and that inserts the token ring station onto the ring.

A token ring lobe cable: A token ring lobe cable connects the token ring station to the MAU. This cable communicates over four wires; two for transmit and two for receive. The cable can be Shielded Twisted Pair (STP) or Unshielded Twisted Pair (UTP).

A token ring adapter card: A token ring adapter card is the physical interface that a station uses to connect to a token ring network. There are token ring adapter cards for almost every computer bus type.

5.8.7 Process for a Machine to Insert into the Token Ring

The process for a machine to insert into the Token Ring has following five phases:

- Phase 0—Lobe media check
- Phase 1—Physical insertion
- Phase 2—Address verification
- Phase 3—Participation in ring poll
- Phase 4—Request initialization

Phase 0—Lobe media check

The insertion process begins with a lobe test. This phase actually tests the transmitter and receiver of the Token Ring adapter and tests the cable between the adapter and the MAU. An MAU physically wraps the connection cables transmit wire back to its receive wire.

The effect is that the adapter can transmit media test MAC frames up the cable to the MAU (where it is wrapped) and back to itself. During this phase, the adapter sends lobe media test MAC frames to destination address 00-00-00-00-00-00 (with the source address of the adapter) and a Duplication Address Test (DAT) MAC frame (which contains the address of the adapter as both the source and destination) up the cable. If the lobe test passes, then phase one is complete.

Phase 1—Physical insertion

In phase two, a phantom current is sent to open the hub relay, once the hub relay opens the station and attaches itself to the ring. The station then checks to see if an active monitor (AM) is present by checking for any of these frames:

- Active monitor present (AMP) MAC frame
- Standby monitor present (SMP) MAC frame
- Ring purge MAC frames

If none of these frames are detected within 18 seconds, the station assumes that there is no active monitor present and it initiates the monitor contention process. Through the monitor contention process, the station with the highest MAC address becomes the active monitor. If contention is not completed within one second, the adapter fails to open. If the adapter becomes the AM and initiates a purge, and the purge process does not complete within one second, then the adapter fails to open. If the adapter receives a beacon MAC frame or a remove station MAC frame, then the adapter fails to open.

Phase 2—Address verification

As part of the duplicate address check phase, the station transmits a series of duplicate address MAC frames addressed to itself. If the station receives two frames back with the Address Recognized Indicator (ARI) and Frame Copied Indicator (FCI) set to 1, then it knows that this address is a duplicate on this ring, it detaches itself, and it reports a failure to open.

This is necessary because Token Ring allows Locally Administered Addresses (LAAs), and you could end up with two adapters with the same MAC address if this check is not done. If this phase does not complete within 18 seconds, the station reports a failure and detaches itself from the ring.

Note: If there is a duplicate MAC address on another ring, which is permissible in source-route bridged Token Ring networks, this will not be detected. The duplicate address check is only locally significant.

Phase 3—Participation in ring poll

In the ring poll phase, the station learns the address of its NAUN (Nearest Active Upstream Neighbor) and makes its address known to its nearest downstream neighbor. This process creates the ring map. The station must wait until it receives an AMP or SMP frame with the ARI and FCI bits set to 0. When it does, the station flips both bits (ARI and FCI) to 1, if enough resources are available, and queues an SMP frame for transmission.

If no such frames are received within 18 seconds, then the station reports a failure to open and de-inserts from the ring. If the station successfully participates in a ring poll, it proceeds into the final phase of insertion, request initialization.

Phase 4—Request initialization

In the request initialization phase, the station sends four request initialization MAC frames to the functional address of the Ring Parameter Server (RPS). If there is no RPS present on the ring, the adapter uses its own default values and reports successful completion of the insertion process. If the adapter receives one of its four request initialization MAC frames back with the ARI and FCI bits set to 1, it waits two seconds for a response. If there is no response, it retransmits up to four times. At this time, if there is no response, it reports a request initialization failure and de-inserts from the ring.

This is a list of the functional addresses:

C000.0000.0001	Active monitor
C000.0000.0002	Ring Parameter Server
C000.0000.0004	Network Server Heartbeat
C000.0000.0008	Ring Error Monitor
C000.0000.0010	Configuration Report Server
C000.0000.0020	Synchronous Bandwidth Manager
C000.0000.0040	Locate Directory Server
C000.0000.0080	NetBIOS
C000.0000.0100	Bridge
C000.0000.0200	IMPL Server
C000.0000.0400	Ring Authorization Server
C000.0000.0800	LAN Gateway

| C000.0000.1000 | Ring Wiring Concentrator |
| C000.0000.2000 | LAN Manager |

5.8.8 Efficiency of Token Ring Network

In a Token Ring Network, we don't have to worry about contention. We define the percent utilization as

$$U = 100 \times \frac{Time\ to\ send\ a\ frame}{Time\ to\ send\ a\ frame\ +\ Time\ to\ send\ a\ token}$$

Usually the time to send a token is small compared to the time to send a frame, so percent utilization is close to 100%.

5.9 Error Detection Techniques

A node's receiver can incorrectly decide that a bit in a frame is zero when it was transmitted as a one, and vice versa. Such bit errors are introduced by signal attenuation and electromagnetic noise. Because there is no need to forward a datagram that has an error, many link-layer protocols provide a mechanism to detect the presence of one or more errors. This is done by having the transmitting node set error-detection bits in the frame, and having the receiving node perform an error check. Error *detection* is a very common service among *data link-layer* protocols.

Errors can be *single –bit* or *multi-bit*. The term *single-bit* error means that only 1 bit of a given data unit (such as a byte, character, or packet) is changed from 1 to 0 or from 0 to 1.

In a single-bit error, only 1 bit in the data unit has changed.

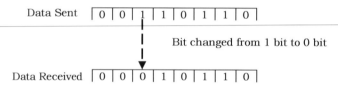

An example consider the figure above. It shows the effect of a single-bit error on a data unit. To understand the impact of the change, imagine that each group of 8 bits is an ASCII character with a 0 bit added to the left. In figure, 00110110 was sent but 00010110 was received.

The term *burst error* (or *multi-bit* error) means that 2 or more bits in the data unit have changed from 1 to 0 or from 0 to 1. Figure shows the effect of a burst error on a data unit.

A burst error means that 2 or more bits in the data unit have changed.

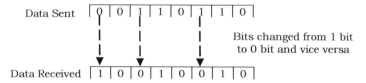

In this case, 00110110 was sent, but 10010010 was received. Note that a burst error does not necessarily mean that the errors occur in consecutive bits. The length of the burst is measured from the first corrupted bit to the last corrupted bit. Some bits in between may not have been corrupted.

5.9.1 Redundancy

The basic idea in detecting or correcting errors is redundancy. To be able to detect or correct errors, we need to send some extra bits with our data. These redundant bits are added by the sender and removed by the receiver. Their presence allows the receiver to detect or correct corrupted bits.

5.9.2 Detection Versus Correction

The correction of errors is more difficult than the detection. In error detection, we are looking only to see if any error has occurred. The answer is a simple yes or no. We are not even interested in the number of errors. A single-bit error is the same for us as a burst error. In error correction, we need to know the exact number of bits that are corrupted and more importantly, their location in the message.

The number of the errors and the size of the message are important factors. If we need to correct one single error in an 8-bit data unit, we need to consider eight possible error locations; if we need to correct two errors in a data unit of the same size, we need to consider 2^8 possibilities. You can imagine the receiver's difficulty in finding 10 errors in a data unit of 1000 bits.

5.9.3 Hamming Distance

The number of corresponding bits that differ between two codewords is the *Hamming distance* of those two codewords. For example, the Hamming distance between the codewords 1001 and 0101 is 2. The Hamming distance of two codewords can be calculated as the number of 1 bits in the bitwise exclusive-or of the two codewords: 1001 *xor* 0101 = 1100.

A code is the set of all codewords of a given length that are constructed by adding a specified number of check digits in a specified way to a specified number of data bits. The minimum Hamming distance of a code is the minimum of the Hamming distance between all possible pairs of codewords of that code. The following table indicates the Hamming distance between all pairs of a simple 4-bit binary code:

The Hamming distances between codewords of a simple 4-bit code.

	0000	0011	0101	0110	1001	1010	1100	1111
0000	-	2	2	2	2	2	2	4
0011	2	-	2	2	2	2	4	2
0101	2	2	-	2	2	4	2	2
0110	2	2	2	-	4	2	2	2
1001	2	2	2	4	-	2	2	2
1010	2	2	4	2	2	-	2	2
1100	2	4	2	2	2	2	-	2
1111	4	2	2	2	2	2	2	-

Because the minimum Hamming distance between any two codewords is 2, the Hamming distance of the code is 2.

5.9.4 Single Parity Checks

The simplest form of error detection is the use of a single parity bit. Suppose that the information to be sent, D has d bits. In an even parity scheme, the sender simply includes one additional bit and chooses its value such that the total number of 1s in the $d + 1$ bits (the original information plus a parity bit) is even. For odd parity schemes, the parity bit value is chosen such that there are an odd number of 1s.

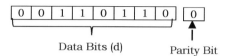

Data Bits (d)   Parity Bit

This parity check is thus computed as the modulo 2 sum of the data bits. If a single transmission error occurs, flipping one bit in the received frame, the modulo 2 sum of the bits in the frame will thus be 1, and the error is detected. In fact, the single parity check is sufficient to detect any odd number of transmission errors in the received frame.

5.9.5 Two-Dimensional Parity Checks

Another simple approach based on parity checks is to arrange the string of data bits into a two-dimensional array and append a parity bit to each row and column of data bits and an additional parity bit in the lower-right corner, as in figure.

For a sequence of $n = pq$ data bits, a total of $p + q + 1$ parity bits are appended. Similar to the single parity check, an odd number of errors in any row or column will be detected by the respective row or column parity check. In addition, an even number of errors in a single row or column will be detected by the respective column or row parity check. However, any pattern of four errors confined to two rows and two columns, as shown in figure, will go undetected.

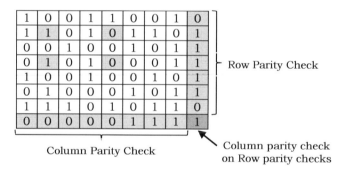

Column Parity Check   Column parity check
                             on Row parity checks

5.9.6 Checksums

A checksum is a value which is computed which allows you to check the validity of something. Checksums take on various forms, depending upon the nature of the transmission and the needed reliability. For example, the simplest checksum is to sum up all the bytes of a transmission, computing the sum in an 8-bit counter. This value is appended as the last byte of the transmission.

The idea is that upon receipt of n bytes, you sum up the first $n − 1$ bytes, and see if the answer is the same as the last byte. Since this is a bit awkward, a variant on this theme is to, on transmission, sum up all the bytes, the (treating the byte as a signed, 8-bit value) negate the checksum byte before transmitting it. This means that the sum of all n bytes should be 0.

These techniques are not terribly reliable; for example, if the packet is known to be 64 bits in length, and you receive 64 '\0' bytes, the sum is 0, so the result must be correct. Of course, if there is a hardware failure that simply fails to transmit the data bytes (particularly easy on synchronous transmission, where no "start bit" is involved), then the fact that you receive a packet of 64 0 bytes with a checksum result of 0 is misleading; you think you've received a valid packet and you've received nothing at all.

A solution to this is to do something like negate the checksum value computed, subtract 1 from it, and expect that the result of the receiver's checksum of the n bytes is 0xFF (-1, as a signed 8-bit value). This means that the 0-lossage problem got resolved.

As an another example, let's say the checksum of a packet is 1 byte long. A byte is made up of 8 bits, and each bit can be in one of two states, leading to a total of 256 (28) possible combinations. Since the first combination equals zero, a byte can have a maximum value of 255.

- If the sum of the other bytes in the packet is 255 or less, then the checksum contains that exact value.
- If the sum of the other bytes is more than 255, then the checksum is the remainder of the total value after it has been divided by 256.

Let's look at a checksum example:

$$\text{Bytes total} = 1151$$
$$\frac{1151}{256} = 4.496 \text{ (round to 4)}$$
$$4 \times 256 = 1024$$
$$1151 - 1024 = 127 \text{ checksum}$$

5.9.7 Cyclic Redundancy Check [CRC]

CRC is an international standard approach to error detection. It protects the data with a checksum or cyclic redundancy check. CRC was first developed by the CCITT (Comite Consultatif International Telegraphique et Telephonique) now called ITU – T (International Telecommunications Union - Telecommunications Standards Sector).

An error-detection technique used widely in today's computer networks is based on cyclic redundancy check (CRC) codes. CRC codes are also known as polynomial codes, since it is possible to view the bit string to be sent as a polynomial whose coefficients are the 0 and 1 values in the bit string, with operations on the bit string interpreted as polynomial arithmetic.

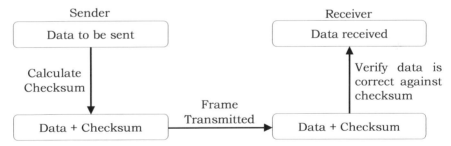

The Cyclic Redundancy Check is the most powerful of the redundancy checking techniques, the CRC is based on binary division. In CRC a sequence of redundant bits, called the *CRC* or the *CRC remainder* is appended to the end of a data stream. The resulting data becomes exactly divisible by a second, predetermined binary number.

At its destination, the incoming data is divided by the same number. The diagram below will show you the sequence of events that takes place when using CRC.

CRC technique is also applicable to data storage devices, such as a disk drive. In this situation each block on the disk would have check bits, and the hardware might automatically initiate a reread of the block when an error is detected, or it might report the error to software.

5.9.7.1 How it works?

One of the most popular methods of error detection for digital signals is the Cyclic Redundancy Check (CRC). CRC codes operate as follows. The basic idea behind CRCs is to treat the message string as a single binary word D (D for data), and divide it by a key word k that is known to both the transmitter and the receiver.

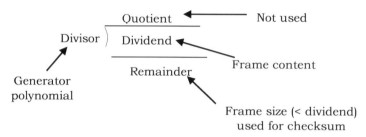

The remainder r left after dividing D by k constitutes the *check word* for the given message. The transmitter sends both the message string D and the check word r, and the receiver can then check the data by repeating the calculation, dividing D by the key word k, and verifying that the remainder is r. The only novel aspect of the CRC process is that it uses a simplified form of arithmetic, which we'll explain below, in order to perform the division.

By the way, this method of checking for errors is obviously not foolproof, because there are many different message strings that give a remainder of r when divided by k. In fact, about 1 out of every k randomly selected strings will give any specific remainder. Thus, if our message string is garbled in transmission, there is a chance (about $\frac{1}{k}$, assuming the corrupted message is random) that the garbled version would agree with the check word. In such a case the error would go undetected. Nevertheless, by making k large enough, the chances of a random error going undetected can be made extremely small. That's really all there is to it. The rest of our discussion will consist simply of refining this basic idea to improve its effectiveness.

When discussing CRCs it's customary to present the key word k in the form of a *generator polynomial* whose coefficients are the binary bits of the number k. For example, suppose we want our CRC to use the key $k - 37$. This number written in binary is 100101, and expressed as a polynomial it is $x^5 + x^2 + 1$.

In order to implement a CRC based on this polynomial, the transmitter and receiver must have agreed in advance that this is the key word they intend to use. So, for the sake of discussion, let's say we have agreed to use the generator polynomial 100101.

By the way, it's worth noting that that the remainder of any word divided by a 6-bit word will contain no more than 5 bits, so our CRC words based on the polynomial 100101 will always fit into 5 bits. Therefore, a CRC system based on this polynomial would be called a $5 - bit$ CRC. In general, a polynomial with k bits leads to a $k - 1\ bit$ CRC.

Now suppose I want to send you a message consisting of the string of bits $D = 0010$ 1100 0101 0111 0100 011, and I also want to send you some additional information that will allow you to check the received string for correctness.

Using our agreed key word $k = 100101$, I'll simply *divide D* by k to form the remainder r, which will constitute the CRC check word. However, we are going to use a simplified kind of division that is particularly well-suited to the binary form in which digital data is expressed. If we interpret k as an ordinary integer (37), it's binary representation, 100101, is really shorthand for

$$(1)2^5 + (0)\,2^4 + (0)\,2^3 + (1)\,2^2 + (0)\,2^1 + (1)\,2^0$$

Every integer can be expressed uniquely in this way, i.e., as a polynomial in the base 2 with coefficients that are either 0 or 1. This is a very powerful form of representation, but it's actually more powerful than we need for purposes of performing a data check.

Also, operations on numbers like this can be somewhat laborious, because they involve borrows and carries in order to ensure that the coefficients are always either 0 or 1. (The same is true for decimal arithmetic, except that all the digits are required to be in the range 0 to 9.)

To make things simpler, let's interpret our message D, key word k, and remainder r, not as actual integers, but as abstract polynomials in a dummy variable x (rather than a definite base like 2 for binary numbers or 10 for decimal numbers).

Also, we'll simplify even further by agreeing to pay attention only to the parity of the coefficients, i.e., if a coefficient is an odd number we will simply regard it as 1, and if it is an even number we will regard it as 0.

This is a tremendous simplification, because now we don't have to worry about borrows and carries when performing arithmetic. This is because every integer coefficient must obviously be either odd or even, so it's automatically either 0 or 1.

To give just a brief illustration, consider the two polynomials $x^2 + x + 1$ and $x^3 + x + 1$. If we multiply these together by the ordinary rules of algebra we get

$$(x^2 + x + 1)(x^3 + x + 1) = x^5 + x^4 + 2x^3 + 2x^2 + 2x + 1$$

but according to our simplification we are going to call every *even* coefficient 0, so the result of the multiplication is simply $x^5 + x^4 + 1$. You might wonder if this simplified way of doing things is really self-consistent.

For example, can we divide the product $x^5 + x^4 + 1$ by one of its factors, say, $x^2 + x + 1$, to give the other factor? The answer is yes, and it's much simpler than ordinary long division. To divide the polynomial 110001 by 111 (which is the shorthand way of expressing our polynomials) we simply apply the bit-wise exclusive-OR operation repeatedly as follows

```
        _____
1 1 1 ) 1 1 0 0 0 1
        1 1 1
        _____
          0 0 1 0
          0 0 0
          _____
            0 1 0 0
            1 1 1
            _____
              0 1 1 1
              1 1 1
              _____
                0 0 0
```

This is exactly like ordinary long division, only simpler, because at each stage we just need to check whether the leading bit of the current three bits is 0 or 1. If it's 0, we place a 0 in the quotient and *exclusively OR* the current bits with 000. If it's 1, we place a 1 in the quotient and *exclusively OR* the current bits with the divisor, which in this case is 111.

As can be seen, the result of dividing 110001 by 111 is 1011, which was our other factor, $x^3 + x + 1$, leaving a remainder of 000. (This kind of arithmetic is called the arithmetic of polynomials with coefficients from the field of integers modulo 2.)

So now let us concentrate on performing a CRC calculation with the message string D and key word k defined above. We simply need to divide D by k using our simplified polynomial arithmetic.

In fact, it's even simpler, because we don't really need to keep track of the quotient - all we really need is the remainder. So we simply need to perform a sequence of 6-bit *exclusive ORs* with our key word k, beginning from the left-most 1 *bit* of the message string, and at each stage thereafter bringing down enough bits from the message string to make a 6-bit word with leading 1. The entire computation is shown below:

```
00101 ) 0 0 1 0 1 1 0 0 0 1 0 1 0 1 1 1 0 1 0 0 0 1 1
        1 0 0 1 0 1
        _____

      0 0 1 0 0 1 0 1
          1 0 0 1 0 1
          _____

        0 0 0 0 0 0 0 1 0 1 1 1 0
                1 0 0 1 0 1
                _____

              0 0 1 0 1 1 1 0
                1 0 0 1 0 1
                _____

                0 0 1 0 1 1 0 0
                  1 0 0 1 0 1
                  _____

                  0 0 1 0 0 1 1 1
                    1 0 0 1 0 1
                    _____

                    0 0 0 0 1 0   remainder = CRC
```

Our CRC word is simply the remainder, i.e., the result of the last 6-bit exclusive OR operation. Of course, the leading bit of this result is always 0, so we really only need the last five bits. This is why a 6-bit key word leads to a 5-bit CRC. In this case, the CRC word for this message string is 00010, so when we transmit the message word D we will also send this corresponding CRC word.

When you receive them you can repeat the above calculation on D with our agreed generator polynomial k and verify that the resulting remainder agrees with the CRC word weincluded in our transmission.

What we've just done is a perfectly fine CRC calculation, and many actual implementations work exactly that way, but there is one potential drawback in our method. As you can see, the computation shown above totally ignores any number of "0"s ahead of the first 1 bit in the message. It so happens that many data strings in real applications are likely to begin with a long series of "0"s, so it's a little bothersome that the algorithm isn't working very hard in such cases.

To avoid this *problem*, we can agree in advance that before computing our n-bit CRC we will always begin by exclusive *ORing* the leading n bits of the message string with a string of n "1"s. With this convention (which of course must be agreed by the transmitter and the receiver in advance) our previous example would be evaluated as follows

```
0 0 1 0 1 1 0 0 0 1 0 1 0 1 1 1 0 1 0 0 0 1 1   ← Original message string
1 1 1 1 1                                       ← Fix the leading bits
─────────────────────────────────────────────
1 1 0 1 0 1 0 0 0 1 0 1 0 1 1 1 0 1 0 0 0 1 1   ← Fixed message string
1 0 0 1 0 1
─────────
0 1 0 0 0 0 0
  1 0 0 1 0 1
  ─────────
  0 0 0 1 0 1 0 0 1
        1 0 0 1 0 1
        ─────────
        0 0 1 1 0 0 0 1
            1 0 0 1 0 1
            ─────────
            0 1 0 1 0 0 0
              1 0 0 1 0 1
              ─────────
              0 0 1 1 0 1 1 1
                  1 0 0 1 0 1
                  ─────────
                  0 1 0 0 1 0 1
                    1 0 0 1 0 1
                    ─────────
                    0 0 0 0 0 0 0 1 0 0 0 1 1
                                  1 0 0 1 0 1
                                  ─────────
                                  0 0 0 1 1 0   remainder = CRC
```

So with the *leading zero fix* convention, the 5-bit CRC word for this message string based on the generator polynomial 100101 is 00110. That's really all there is to computing a CRC, and many commercial applications work exactly as we've described. People sometimes use various table-lookup routines to speed up the divisions, but that doesn't alter the basic computation or change the result. In addition, people sometimes agree to various non-standard conventions, such as interpreting the bits in reverse order, but the essential computation is still the same. (Of course, it's crucial for the transmitter and receiver to agree in advance on any unusual conventions they intend to observe.)

Now that we've seen how to compute CRC's for a given key polynomial, it's natural to wonder whether some key polynomials work better (i.e., give more robust *checks*) than others. From one point of view the answer is obviously yes, because the larger our key word, the less likely it is that corrupted data will go undetected. By appending an n-bit CRC to our message string we are increasing the total number of possible strings by a factor of 2^n, but we aren't increasing the degrees of freedom, since each message string has a unique CRC word. Therefore, we have established a situation in which only 1 out of 2^n total strings (*message + CRC*) is valid. Notice that if we append our CRC word to our message word, the result is a multiple of our generator polynomial. Thus, of all possible combined strings, only multiples of the generator polynomial are valid.

So, if we assume that any corruption of our data affects our string in a completely random way, i.e., such that the corrupted string is totally uncorrelated with the original string, then the probability of a corrupted string going undetected is $1/(2^n)$. This is the basis on which people say a 16-bit CRC has a probability of $1/(2^{16})$ = 1.5E-5 of failing to detect an error in the data, and a 32-bit CRC has a probability of $1/(2^{32})$, which is about 2.3E-10 (less than one in a billion).

Since most digital systems are designed around blocks of 8-bit words (called *bytes*), it's most common to find key words whose lengths are a multiple of 8 bits. The two most common lengths in practice are 16-bit and 32-bit CRCs (so the corresponding generator polynomials have 17 and 33 bits respectively). A few specific polynomials have come into widespread use. For 16-bit CRCs one of the most popular key words is 10001000000100001, and for 32-bit CRCs one of the most popular is 100000100110000010001110110110111. In the form of explicit polynomials these would be written as

$$x^{16} + x^{12} + x^5 + 1$$

and

$$x^{32} + x^{26} + x^{23} + x^{22} + x^{16} + x^{12} + x^{11} + x^{10} + x^8 + x^7 + x^5 + x^4 + x^2 + x + 1$$

The 16-bit polynomial is known as the *X25 standard*, and the 32-bit polynomial is the *Ethernet standard*, and both are widely used in all sorts of applications. (Another common 16-bit key polynomial familiar to many modem operators is 11000000000000101, which is the basis of the $CRC - 16$ protocol). These polynomials are certainly not unique in being suitable for CRC calculations, but it's probably a good idea to use one of the established standards, to take advantage of all the experience accumulated over many years of use.

Nevertheless, we may still be curious to know how these particular polynomials were chosen. It so happens that one could use just about ANY polynomial of a certain degree and achieve most of the error detection benefits of the standard polynomials. For example, *any n-bit CRC will certainly catch any single *burst* of m consecutive flipped bits* for any *m* less than *n*, basically because a smaller polynomial can't be a multiple of a larger polynomial. Also, we can ensure the detection of any odd number of bits simply by using a generator polynomial that is a multiple of the *parity polynomial*, which is $x + 1$. A polynomial of our simplified kind is a multiple of $x + 1$ if and only if it has an even number of terms.

It's interesting to note that the standard 16-bit polynomials both include this parity check, whereas the standard 32-bit CRC does not. It might seem that this represents a shortcoming of the 32-bit standard, but it really doesn't, because the inclusion of a parity check comes at the cost of some other desirable characteristics. In particular, much emphasis has been placed on the detection of two separated single-bit errors, and the standard CRC polynomials were basically chosen to be as robust as possible in detecting such double-errors. Notice that the basic *error word* E representing two erroneous bits separated by *j* bits is of the form $x^j + 1$ or, equivalently, $x^j - 1$. Also, an error *E* superimposed on the message *D* will be undetectable if and only if *E* is a multiple of the key polynomial *k*. Therefore, if we choose a key that is not a divisor of any polynomial of the form $x^t - 1$ for $t=1,2,...,m$, then we are assured of detecting any occurrence of precisely two erroneous bits that occur within *m* places of each other.

How would we find such a polynomial? For this purpose we can use a *primitive polynomial*. For example, suppose we want to ensure detection of two bits within 31 places of each other. Let's factor the error polynomial $x^{31} - 1$ into it's irreducible components (using our simplified arithmetic with coefficients reduced modulo 2). We find that it splits into the factors

$$x^{31} - 1 = (x+1) \times (x^5 + x^3 + x^2 + x + 1) \times (x^5 + x^4 + x^2 + x + 1) \times$$
$$(x^5 + x^4 + x^3 + x + 1) \times (x^5 + x^2 + 1) \times (x^5 + x^4 + x^3 + x^2 + 1) \times (x^5 + x^3 + 1)$$

Aside from the parity factor (x+1), these are all primitive polynomials, representing primitive roots of $x^{31} - 1$, so they cannot be divisors of any polynomial of the form $x^j - 1$ for any j less than 31. Notice that $x^5 + x^2 + 1$ is the generator polynomial 100101 for the 5-bit CRC in our first example.

Another way of looking at this is via recurrence formulas. For example, the polynomial $x^5 + x^2 + 1$ corresponds to the recurrence relation s[n] = (s[n − 3] + s[n − 5]) modulo 2. Beginning with the initial values 00001 this recurrence yields

```
                                                    |--> cycle repeats
0 0 0 0 1 0 0 1 0 1 1 0 0 1 1 1 1 1 0 0 0 1 1 0 1 1 1 0 1 0 1   0 0 0 0 1
```

Notice that the sequence repeats with a period of 31, which is another consequence of the fact that $x^5 + x^2 + 1$ is primitive. You can also see that the sets of five consecutive bits run through all the numbers from 1 to 31 before repeating. In contrast, the polynomial $x^5 + x + 1$ corresponds to the recurrence s[n] = (s[n − 4] + s[n − 5]) modulo 2, and gives the sequence

```
                                                    |--> cycle repeats
        0 0 0 0 1 0 0 0 1 1 0 0 1 0 1 0 1 1 1 1 1   0 0 0 0 1
```

Notice that this recurrence has a period of 21, which implies that the polynomial $x^5 + x + 1$ divides $x^{21} - 1$. Actually, $x^5 + x + 1$ can be factored as $(x^2 + x + 1)(x^3 + x^2 + 1)$, and both of those factors divide $x^{21} - 1$. Therefore, the polynomial $x^5 + x + 1$ may be considered to give a less robust CRC than $x^5 + x^2 + 1$, at least from the standpoint of maximizing the distance by which two erroneous bits must be separated in order to go undetected.

On the other hand, there are error patterns that would be detected by $x^5 + x + 1$ but would NOT be detected by $x^5 + x^2 + 1$. As noted previously, any n-bit CRC increases the space of all strings by a factor of 2^n, so a completely arbitrary error pattern really is no less likely to be detected by a *poor* polynomial than by a "good" one. The distinction between good and bad generators is based on the premise that the most likely error patterns in real life are NOT entirely random, but are most likely to consist of a very small number of bits (e.g., one or two) very close together. To protect against this kind of corruption, we want a generator that maximizes the number of bits that must be *flipped* to get from one formally valid string to another. We can certainly cover all 1-bit errors, and with a suitable choice of generators we can effectively cover virtually all 2-bit errors.

Problems and Questions with Answers

Question 1: What is early token release?

Answer: In normal token ring operation, a station sending information holds the token until the sending data circles the entire ring. After the sending station strips the data from the ring, it then issues a free token.

With Early Token Release (ETR), a token is released immediately after the sending station transmits its frame. This allows for improved performance, since there is no delay in the downstream neighbour waiting for the token. ETR is only available on 16 megabit rings.

Question 2: What is the difference between Ethernet and Token Ring networks?

Answer: Token Ring is single access, meaning there is only one token. So, at *any given time* only one station is able to use the LAN. Ethernet is a shared access medium, where all stations have equal access to the network at the *same* time.

Question 3: At what speeds does token ring run?

Answer: Token ring runs at speeds of 4 Mbps and 16 Mbps.

Question 4: What is a beacon frame?

Answer: A beacon frame is sent generated by a station or stations that do not detect a receive signal. A station or stations will broadcast these beacon MAC frames with until the receive signal is restored.

Question 5: Medium access methods can be categorized as random, maximized or minimized.

Answer: False

Question 6: ALOHA is an early multiple-random-access method that requires frame acknowledgment.

Answer: True

Question 7: In the carrier sense multiple-access (CSMA) method, a station must listen to the medium prior to the sending of data onto the line.

Answer: True

Question 8: In the carrier sense multiple-access (CSMA) method, the server will let a device know when it is time to transmit.

Answer: False

Question 9: Some examples of controlled-access methods are: reservation, polling and token passing.

Answer: True

Question 10: Carrier sense multiple access with collision avoidance (CSMA/CA) is CSMA with procedures added to correct after a collision has happened.

Answer: False

Question 11: Carrier sense multiple access with collision detection (CSMA/CD) is CSMA with a post collision procedure.

Answer: True

Question 12: FDMA, TDMA and CDMA are controlled-access methods.

Answer: False

Question 13: Channelization is a multiple-access method in which the available bandwidth of a link is shared in time, frequency, or through code, between stations on a network.

Answer: True

Question 14: In the reservation access method, a station reserves a slot for data by controlling transmissions to and from secondary stations.

Answer: False

Question 15: Multiple Access Protocols include:
  A. Random-Access Protocols   C. Channelization Protocols
  B. Controlled-Access Protocols   D. All of the above.

Answer: D

Question 16: ALOHA is an example of the earliest:
  A. Random-access method   C. Channelization protocols
  C. Controlled-access method   D. All of the above.

Answer: A

Question 17: Polling works with topologies in which one devise is designated as the ___station and the other devices are known as ___ devices.
            A. Secondary / primary   C. Permanent / switched
            B. Primary / secondary   D. Physical / virtual

Answer: B

Question 18: The select mode is used when:
 A. the sender has something to format.   C. the primary device has something to send.
 B. the receiver has something to receive.   D. the secondary device has something to send.

Answer: C

Question 19: The act of polling secondary devices is so that:
 A. The primary device can solicit transmissions from the secondary devices.
 B. The secondary devices can solicit transmissions from the primary devices.
 C. The secondary device wants to over-ride the primary device.
 D. The primary device is in flex mode.

Answer: A

Question 20: Polling is a type of:
            A. Random-access   C. channelization access
            B. Controlled-access   D. None of the above.

Answer: B

Question 21: In the reservation access method, a station needs to make a reservation before:
            A. Sending data   C. Both A and B.
            B. Receiving data D. None of the above.

Answer: A

Question 22: In a channelization access method, the available bandwidth of a link is shared:
            A. In time   C. via code
            B. In frequency D. All of the above.

Answer: D

Question 23: What is the advantage of controlled access over random access?

Answer: In a random access method, each station has the right to the medium without being controlled by any other station. However, if more than one station tries to send, there is an access conflict (collision) and the frames will be either destroyed or modified. To avoid access collisions or to resolve it when it happens, we need procedures to address the issues caused by collisions or to try to avoid them, if possible. Some examples of random access include ALOHA and CSMA.

In controlled access, the stations consult with one another to find which station has the right to send. A station cannot send unless it has been authorized by other stations. Three popular controlled access methods include: Reservation, polling and token-passing.

Question 24: Groups of n stations share a 64 *kbps* pure ALOHA channel. Each station outputs a 1000 bit frame on an average of once every 100 seconds. What is the maximum value of n (i.e. how many stations can be connected)?

Answer: The maximum throughput for pure Aloha is 18.4%.
Therefore the usable channel rate is equal to $0.184 * 56\ kbps = 11.77\ kbps$.

Bits per second outputted by each station $= \frac{1000\ bits}{100\ sec} = 10\ bps\ [bps = bits\ per\ second]$

n station outputs 10 bps on a channel which has the usable channel rate of 11.77 *kbps*.

$$\therefore n = \frac{11.77 \times 10^3}{10} = 1177 \text{ stations}$$

Question 25: Consider 2 stations at a distance of 2 *km* from each other. A station transmits frames of length 200 bits at the rate of 2 *Mbps*. Velocity of propagation is $3 \times 10^8\ m/s$. Assume that each station generates frames at an average rate of 10000 frames per second. What is the probability of collision for pure ALOHA?

Answer: Before solving the problem let us define the formulas for propagation and transmission times.

Transmission Time: The transmission time is the amount of time from the beginning until the end of a message transmission. In the case of a digital message, it is the time from the first bit until the last bit of a message has left the transmitting node. The packet transmission time in seconds can be obtained from the packet size in bit and the bit rate in bit/s as:

$$Packet\ Transmission\ Time = \frac{Packet\ size}{Bit\ rate}\ or\ \frac{Message\ Size}{Bandwidth}$$

For example, a 100 Mbit/s (or 10,000,000 bits per second) Ethernet and maximum packet size of 1526 bytes gives a maximum packet transmission time $= \frac{1526 * 8\ bit}{100\ 000\ 000} \approx 122$ μs.

Propagation Time: Propagation time is the amount of time it takes for the head of the signal to travel from the sender to the receiver. It can be computed as the ratio between the link length and the propagation speed over the specific medium.

$$Propagation\ time = \frac{Distance}{Propagation\ Speed}$$

From the problem statement we have the G value: 10^4 (10000 frames per second).

$Total\ time\ T = Transmission\ Time + Propagation\ time = \frac{2 \times 10^3}{3 \times 10^8} + \frac{200}{2 \times 10^6} = 66.67 \times 10^{-6}\ sec$

The probability of collision in pure ALOHA is:

$$= 1 - e^{-2GT}$$
$$= 1 - e^{-2 \times 10^4 \times 66.767 \times 10^{-6}}$$
$$= 1 - e^{-1.334}$$
$$= 1 - (2.718)^{-1.334} = 1 - 0.27 = 0.73$$

Question 26: Consider the delay of pure ALOHA versus slotted ALOHA at low load. Which one is less? Explain your answer.

Answer: Statistically pure ALOHA is supposed to be less efficient than slotted ALOHA (both at normal load or when collisions occur in a contention channel). However, if the load is low, then pure ALOHA is supposed to be as efficient as slotted ALOHA. But if we consider the delay of sending the packet in a slotted time as in the slotted ALOHA protocol, then we can say that slotted ALOHA's delay is more than the one in pure ALOHA protocol, which sends the packet immediately.

Question 27: The valid frame length must be at least 64 bytes long so as to prevent a station from completing the transmission of a short frame before the first bit has even reached the far end of the cable, where it may collide with another frame. How is the minimum frame length adjusted if the network speed goes up?

Answer: As the network speed goes up, the minimum frame length must go up or the maximum cable length must come down, proportionally so that the sender does not incorrectly conclude that the frame was successfully sent in case of collision.

Question 28: TDM with sources having different data rates: Consider the case of three streams with bit rates of 8 kbit/sec, 16 kbit/sec, and 24 kbit/sec, respectively. We want to combine these streams into a single high-speed stream using TDM.

Answer: The high-speed stream in this case must have a transmission rate of 48 kbit/sec, which is the sum of the bit rates of the three sources. To determine the number of time slots to be assigned to each source in the multiplexing process. We must reduce the ratio of the rates, 8:16:24, to the lowest possible form, which in this case is 1:2:3. T

he sum of the reduced ratio is 6, which will then represent the minimum length of the repetitive cycle of slot assignments in the multiplexing process. The solution is now readily obtained: In each cycle of six time slots we assign one slot to Source A (8 kbit/sec), two slots to Source B (16 kbit/sec), and three slots to Source: C (24 kbit/sec). Figure 7-4 illustrates this assignment, using "a" to indicate data from Source A, "b" to indicate data from Source B, and "c" to indicate data from Source C.

Question 29: Consider a system with four low-bit-rate sources of 20 kbit/sec, 30 kbit/sec, 40 kbit/sec, and 60 kbit/sec. Determine the slot assignments when the data streams are combined using TDM.

Answer: The rate ratio 20:30:40:60 reduces to 2:3:4:6. The length of the cycle is therefore 2 + 3 + 4 + 6 = 15 slots. Within each cycle of 15 slots, we assign two slots to the 10 kbit/sec source, three slots to the 15 kbit/sec source, four slots to the 20 kbit/sec source, and six slots to the 30 kbit/sec source.

Question 30: Explain why the hidden terminal problem can be solved by CSMA/CA protocol.

Answer: A hidden station problem occurs in a wireless LAN if we use CSMA access protocol. Suppose each station A, B, C and D aligns in a line from left to right. Assuming station A is transmitting from to B, however, station C cannot sense the transmission signal because it is out of range of A, it falsely assumes that it is safe to transmit to B. This will cause a collision at station B, which called a hidden station problem since the competitor is too far away to be detected.

The main reason to cause this problem is that the sender doesn't have a correct knowledge about the receiver's activity. CSMA can only tell whether there is an activity around. However, by using CSMA/CA protocol, the sender can get the receiver's status through the handshaking. For instance, station C can receive the stations B's CTS and know how long the station A will take to transmit data. It will stop its transmission request before station A completes.

Question 31: Given the following information, find the minimum bandwidth required for the path:
- FDM Multiplexing
- Five devices, each requiring 4000 Hz.
- 200 Hz guard band for each device.

Answer:
No. of devices = 5.
No. of guard bands required between these is 4.
Hence total bandwidth = (4000 × 5) + (200 × 4) = 20.8 KHz.

Question 32: A small Local Area Network (LAN) has four machines A, B, C and D connected in the following topology:

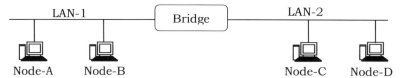

A) The node A sends a graphics file of size 10 MB simultaneously to nodes B, C, and D using Unicast packets constructed by the Universal Datagram Protocol (UDP). Calculate the utilization of LAN 1, given that each frame carries 1024 B of UDP payload data, and transmission is at 50 packets per second to each destination.
B) What is the utilization on LAN 2?

Answer: Refer *TCP and UDP* chapter.

Question 33: Consider a group of n stations sharing a 64 kbps pure (unslotted) aloha channel. Each station has one (NEW) packet arriving every 100 seconds and packets are 1000 bits long. What is the maximum value of n that the channel can accommodate?

Answer: The required data rate is n ×(1000 bits per packet)×(1 packet/100 seconds) = 10 n bps. Since, efficiency = 18%, with unslotted aloha, the available data rate is 0.18 * 64,000 bps = 11,520 bps.

$$
\begin{aligned}
\text{Rate required} &= \text{Rate available} \\
\rightarrow 10\,n &= 11 \\
\rightarrow 520\,n &\leq 1152 \text{ stations}
\end{aligned}
$$

Question 34: CSMA/CD: Suppose a CSMA/CD network is running at 10 Mbps over a 1-km cable with no repeaters. The signal speed in the cable is 200,000 km/sec. Compute the following.
A) End-to-end propagation delay   B) Worst-case collision detection time
C) Minimum frame size
D) Suppose we increase the bandwidth from 10 Mbps to 100 Mbps, how does it affect the above three values?

Question 35: For a peer-to-peer file-sharing application, do you agree with the statement, "There is no notion of client and server sides of a communication session"?

Answer: *No*. All communication sessions have a client side and a server side. In a *peer-to-peer* file-sharing application, the peer that is receiving a file is typically the client and the peer that is sending the file is typically the server.

Question 36: How does CSMA/CD react to collisions?

A) All systems jam the network, and then all begin transmitting again.

B) Hosts involved in a collision send an RTS signal indicating a time frame in which to retransmit.

C) Hosts involved in the collision send a jam signal, and then run an algorithm before retransmitting.

D) Collisions do not occur on CSMA/CD.

Answer: C.

Question 37: How is equal access to the wire managed in a collision-oriented environment such as Ethernet?

A) The hosts are given equal access based on the circulation of a token; hosts can only transmit when they hold the token.

B) Hosts are given prioritized access to the wire based on their MAC address.

C) Hosts are given equal access to the wire by being allowed to transmit at specified time intervals.

D) Hosts signal their desire to transmit by sending a contention alert.

E) Hosts check the wire for activity before attempting to send; if a collision happens, they wait a random time period before attempting to send again.

Answer: E.

Question 38: End-to-end packet delay of cut-through routers is smaller than of store & forward routers. Is it true or false?

Answer: True. With cut-though routers a packet starts being transmitted as soon as its header is processed; with store & forward routers a packet is first received in its entirety before being forwarded.

Question 39: Three users X, Y and Z use a shared link to connect to the Internet. Only one of X, Y or Z can use the link at a given time. The link has a capacity of 1Mbps. There are two possible strategies for accessing the shared link:

• TDMA: equal slots of 0.1 seconds.

• *Taking turns*: adds a latency of 0.05 seconds before taking the turn. The user can then use the link for as long as it has data to send. A user requests the link only when it has data to send.

In each of the following two cases, which strategy would you pick and why?

A) X, Y and Z send a 40 KBytes file every 1 sec.

B) X sends 80 KBytes files every 1sec, while Y and Z send 10 KBytes files every 1sec.

Answer:

A) TDMA. Why: Each of the users generate a load of 40 KB/s = 0.32 Mbps, which can be fully transmitted given the share of 0.33 Mbps available per user when partitioning the channel with TDMA. Taking turns on the other hand does not offer enough capacity for all the files to be transmitted: $3 \times 0.32 + 3 \times 0.05 = 1.11$ s > 1 s, and would incur extra overhead.

B) Taking Turns. Why? First, by using TDMA, X does not have enough capacity to transmit, 80 KB/s = 0.640 Mbps > 0.33 Mbps. Second, with TDMA, Y and Z waste 3 out of 4 slots. On the other hand, when taking turns, there is enough capacity to transmit all the data: $0.64 + 0.05 + 0.08 + 0.05 + 0.08 + 0.05 = 0.95$ s.

Question 40: Comparing pure ALOHA and slotted ALOHA, which one can lead to a shorter delay when the traffic load is very small? Why?

Answer: Pure ALOHA has shorter delay because it does not need to wait for the beginning for the next time slot.

Question 41: A variety of signal encoding techniques are used in the various LAN standards to achieve efficiency and to make the high data rates practical. Is it true or false?

Answer: True

Question 42: An algorithm is needed with CSMA to specify what a station should do if the medium is found busy. Is it true or false?

Answer: True

Question 43: The p-persistent algorithm with binary exponential backoff is efficient over a wide range of loads. Is it true or false?

Answer: False

Question 44: Ethernet has both a medium access control layer and a physical layer. Is it true or false?

Answer: True

Question 45: With full-duplex operation a station can transmit and receive simultaneously. Is it true or false?

Answer: True

Question 46: A technique known as slotted _____ organizes time on the channel into uniform slots whose size equals the frame transmission time. Transmission is permitted to begin only at a slot boundary.
A) Ethernet   B) ALOHA   C) boundary relay   D) CSMA

Answer: B

Question 47: Ethernet now encompasses data rates of _____.
A) 100 Mpbs, 1 Gbps, 10 Gbps, and 100 Gbps
B) 10 Mbps, 100 Mpbs, 1 Gbps, and 10 Gbps
C) 1 Gpbs, 10 Gbps, 100 Gbps, and 1000 Gbps
D) 10 Mbps, 100 Mbps, 1000 Mbps, and 10 Gbps

Answer: B

Question 48: A problem with _____ is that capacity is wasted because the medium will generally remain idle following the end of a transmission, even if there are one or more stations waiting to transmit.
A) 1-persistent CSMA   B) slotted ALOHA
C) p-persistent CSMA   D) nonpersistent CSMA

Answer: D

Question 49: One of the rules for CSMA/CD states, "after transmitting the jamming signal, wait a random amount of time, then attempt to transmit again". This random amount of time is referred to as the ___.
A) Precursor   B) Backoff   C) Backlog   D) carrier time

Answer: B

Question 50: Which of the following makes use of two optical fibre cables, one for transmission and one for reception, and utilizes a techniques known as intensity modulation.

A) 100BASE-T4   B) 10BASE-F   C) 100BASE-FX   D) 10BASE-T

Answer: C

Question 51: Why do 802.11 (wireless) networks use acknowledgements?

Answer: Unlike a wired Ethernet where collisions can be detected, it is difficult to detect a collision on a wireless network as the strength of the signal being transmitted is so much greater than the strength of the signal being received. Without being able to detect a collision, a sender is unsure if their transmitted data arrived intact, thus a mechanism for acknowledgements must be used.

Question 52: Why are the wires twisted in twisted-pair copper wire?

Answer: The twisting of the individual pairs reduces electromagnetic interference. For example, it reduces crosstalk between wire pairs bundled into a cable.

Question 53: Which type of Ethernet framing is used for TCP/IP and AppleTalk?
    A) Ethernet 802.3   B) Ethernet 802.2   C) Ethernet II   D) Ethernet SNAP

Answer: D. Ethernet 802.3 is used with NetWare versions 2 through 3.11, Ethernet 802.2 is used with NetWare 3.12 and later plus OSI routing, Ethernet II is used with TCP/IP and DECnet, and Ethernet SNAP is used with TCP/IP and AppleTalk.

Question 54: Ethernet is said to be non-deterministic because of which of the following?
    A) It is not possible to determine how long it will take to get a frame from one device to another.
    B) It is not possible to determine whether an error has occurred during the transmission of a frame.
    C) It is not possible to determine if another device wishes to transmit.
    D) It is not possible to determine the maximum time a device will have to wait to transmit.

Answer: D

Question 55: The multiplexer creates a frame that contains data only from those input sources that have something to send in __ multiplexing.
    A) Frequency Division   B) Statistical Time Division
    C) Synchronous Time Division   D) Dense Wavelength

Answer: B

Question 56: How many 8-bit characters can be transmitted per second over a 9600 baud serial communication link using asynchronous mode of transmission with one start bit, eight data bits, and one parity bit ?
    A) 600   B) 800   C) 876   D) 1200

Answer: B. Baud is the symbol which is sent over the link, baud = 9600 bits 18 bit character has baud size of 12 bits. So no. of characters = $\frac{9600}{12}$ = 800.

Question 57: A and B are the only two stations on an Ethernet. Each has a steady queue of frames to send. Both A and B attempt to transmit a frame, collide, and A wins the first backoff race, At the end of this successful transmission by A, both A and B attempt to transmit and collide. The probability that A wins the second backoff race is
    A) 0.5   B) 0.625   C) 0.75   D) 1.0

Answer: B. A wins the first back off race the conditions are (0,1). After that during second back off four conditions (0,1,2,3).

$$\text{Probability} = \frac{1}{2} \times \frac{3}{4} + \frac{1}{2} \times \frac{1}{2} = \frac{3}{8} + \frac{1}{4} = 0.625$$

Question 58: In a network of LANs connected by bridges, packets are set from one LAN to another through intermediate bridges. Since more than one path may exist between two LANs, packets may have to be routed through multiple bridges. Why is the spanning tree algorithm used for bridge-routing?
A) For shortest path routing between LANs
B) For avoiding loops in the routing paths
C) For fault tolerance   D) For minimizing collisions

Answer: B. Spanning tree algorithm for a graph is applied to find a tree free of cycles, so in this network we apply spanning tree algorithm to remove loops in routing paths.

CHAPTER

ARP and RARP

6

6.1 Address Resolution Protocol [ARP]

6.1.1 What is Address Resolution Protocol [ARP]?

Address Resolution Protocol [ARP] is a network layer protocol that is used to convert IP address into MAC address. Network interface cards (NICs) each have a hardware address or MAC address associated with them. Applications understand TCP/IP addressing, but network hardware devices (such as NICs) do not.

For example, when two Ethernet cards are communicating, they have no knowledge of the IP address being used. Instead, they use the MAC addresses assigned to each card to address data frames. The ARP was designed to provide a mapping from the logical 32-bit TCP/IP addresses to the physical 48-bit MAC addresses.

ARP resolves IP addresses used by TCP/IP-based software to media access control addresses used by LAN hardware.

6.1.2 Why do we need Address Resolution Protocol [ARP]?

An Internet is made of a combination of *physical* networks connected together by internetworking devices such as *routers* and *gateways*. A packet starting from a source host may pass through different physical networks before finally reaching the destination host.

The hosts and routers are recognized at the network level by their logical addresses. A *logical* address is an *Internetwork* address. A logical address is unique universally. It is called a logical address *because* it is usually implemented in software. Every protocol that deals with interconnecting networks requires logical addresses. The logical addresses in the TCP/IP protocol suite are called IP addresses and are 32 bits long.

However, packets pass through physical networks to reach these hosts and routers. At the physical level, the hosts and routers are recognized by their physical addresses. A physical address is a local address. Its scope is a local network. It should be unique locally, but not necessary universally. It is called a *physical address* because it is usually (not always) implemented in hardware. Examples of physical addresses are 48 bit MAC addresses in Ethernet and token ring protocols, which are imprinted on the NIC installed in the host or router.

The physical and logical addresses are two different identifiers. We need both of them because a physical network, such as an Ethernet can be used by two different protocols at the network layer such as IP and IPX (Novell) at the same time. Likewise, a packet at the network layer such as IP may pass through different physical networks such as Ethernet and LocalTalk.

This means that delivery of a packet to a host or a router requires two levels of addressing: logical and physical.

The main issue is that IP datagrams contain IP addresses, but the physical interface hardware on the host or router to which we want to send the datagram only understands the addressing scheme of that particular network.

6.1.3 Address Mapping and Resolution

We need to be able to map a logical address to its corresponding physical address and vice versa. These can be done using either *static* or *dynamic* mapping.

Static mapping means creating a table that associates a logical address with a physical address. This table is stored in each machine on the network. Each machine that knows, for example, the IP address of another machine but not its physical address, can look it up in the table. This has some limitations because physical addresses may change in the following ways:

A machine could change its NIC resulting in a new physical address. In some LANs, such as LocalTalk, the physical address changes every time the computer is turned on. A mobile computer can move from one physical network to another, resulting in a change in its physical address. To implement these changes, a static mapping table must be updated periodically. This creates a huge overhead on the network.

In *dynamic* mapping each time a machine knows one of the two addresses (logical or physical), it can use a protocol to find the other one.

Address resolution is the process of finding the address of a host within a network. In this case, the address is resolved by using a protocol to request information via a form of broadcast to locate a remote host. The remote host receives the packet and forwards it with the appropriate address information included. The address resolution process is complete once the original computer has received the address information.

Two protocols have been designed to perform dynamic mapping: Address Resolution Protocol (ARP) and Reverse Address Resolution Protocol (RARP). The first maps a logical address to a physical address; the second maps a physical address to a logical address.

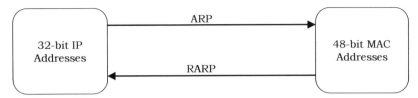

The goal of ARP is to enable each host on a network to build up a table of *mappings* between IP addresses and link-level addresses (MAC addresses). Since these mappings may change over time, the entries are *cleared out periodically* and *removed*. ARP takes advantage of the fact that many link-level network technologies (such as Ethernet and token ring) support broadcast. If a host wants to send an IP datagram to a host that it knows to be on the same network, it first checks for a mapping in the cache.

ARP maintains the protocol rules for making this translation and providing address conversion in both directions within the OSI layers, as shown in figure below. This utility is used to display and modify entries within the ARP table.

In summary, ARP translates IP addresses into MAC addresses and the Reverse Address Resolution Protocol (RARP) is used to find IP address from a MAC address.

6.1.4 Four Different Cases

Anytime a host, or a router, needs to find the physical address of another host or router on its network, it sends an ARP *query* packet. The packet includes the physical and IP addresses of the *sender* and the IP address of the *receiver*. Because the sender does not know the physical address of the receiver, the query is broadcast over the net-work.

Every host or router on the network receives and processes the ARP query packet, but only the intended recipient recognizes its IP address and sends back an ARP *response* packet. The response packet contains the *recipient's* IP and physical addresses. The packet is unicast directly to the sender using the physical address received in the query packet. Now sending system can send all the packets it has for this destination using the physical address received.

The following are *four* different cases in which the services of ARP can be used.

1. The sender is a host and wants to send a packet to another host on the *same* network. In this case, the logical address that must be mapped to a physical address is the destination IP address in the datagram header.
2. The sender is a host and wants to send a packet to another host on *another* network. In this case, the host looks at its routing table and finds the IP address of the next hop-router for this destination. If it does not have a routing table, it looks for IP address of the default router. The IP address of the router becomes the logical address that must be mapped to a physical address. Note that IP address is still the destination address but the physical address is the MAC address of the next hop-router for that destination.
3. The sender is a router that has received a datagram destined for a host on another network. It checks its routing table and finds the IP address of the next router. The IP address of the next router becomes the logical address that must be mapped to a physical address. Note that IP address is still the destination address but the physical address is the MAC address of the next router for that destination.

4. The sender is a router that has received a datagram destined for a host in the network. The destination IP address of the datagram becomes the logical address that must be mapped to a physical address.

6.1.5 How ARP resolves MAC addresses for Local Traffic

In this example, two TCP/IP nodes, nodes 1 and 2, are both located on the same physical network. Node 1 is assigned the IP address of 10.0.0.69 and Node 2 is assigned the IP address of 10.0.0.70.

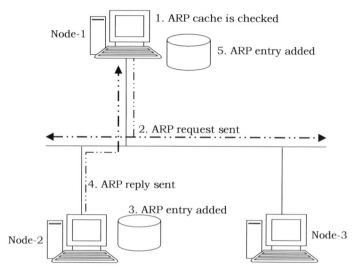

When Node 1 tries to communicate with Node 2, the following steps resolve Node 2's software-assigned address (10.0.0.70) to Node 2's hardware-assigned media access control address:

1. Based on the contents of the routing table on Node 1, IP determines that the forwarding IP address to be used to reach Node 2 is 10.0.0.70. Node 1 then checks its own local ARP cache for a matching hardware address for Node 2.
2. If Node 1 finds no mapping in the cache, it broadcasts an ARP request frame to all hosts on the local network with the question "What is the hardware address for 10.0.0.70?" Both hardware and software addresses for the source, Node 1, are included in the ARP request.
3. Each host on the local network receives the ARP request and checks for a match to its own IP address. If a host does not find a match, it discards the ARP request.
4. Node 2 determines that the IP address in the ARP request matches its own IP address and adds a hardware/software address mapping for Node 1 to its local ARP cache.
5. Node 2 sends an ARP reply message containing its hardware address directly back to Node 1.
6. When Node 1 receives the ARP reply message from Node 2, it updates its ARP cache with a hardware/software address mapping for Node 2.

Once the media access control address for Node 2 has been determined, Node 1 can send IP traffic to Node 2 by addressing it to Node 2's media access control address.

6.1.6 How ARP resolves MAC addresses for Remote Traffic

ARP is also used to forward IP datagrams to local routers for destinations that are *not* on the *local* network. In this situation, ARP resolves the media access control address of a router interface on the local network.

The following diagram shows how ARP resolves IP addresses to hardware addresses for two hosts on different physical networks connected by a common router.

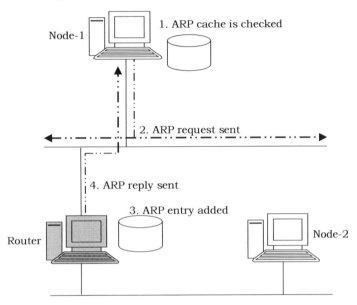

In this example, Node 1 is assigned an IP address of 10.0.0.69 and Node 2 uses an IP address of 192.168.0.69. Router interface 1 is on the same physical network as Node 1 and uses the IP address 10.0.0.1. Router interface 2 is on the same physical network as Node 2 and uses the IP address 192.168.0.1.

When Node 1 tries to communicate with Node 2, the following steps resolve Router interface 1's software-assigned address (10.0.0.1) to its hardware-assigned media access control address:

1. Based on the contents of the routing table on Node 1, IP determines that the forwarding IP address to be used to reach Node 2 is 10.0.0.1, the IP address of its default gateway. Node 1 then checks its own local ARP cache for a matching hardware address for 10.0.0.1.

2. If Node 1 finds no mapping in the cache, it broadcasts an ARP request frame to all hosts on the local network with the question "What is the hardware address for 10.0.0.1?" Both hardware and software addresses for the source, Node 1, are included in the ARP request.

   Each host on the local network receives the ARP request and checks for a match to its own IP address. If a host does not find a match, it discards the ARP request.

3. The router determines that the IP address in the ARP request matches its own IP address and adds a hardware/software address mapping for Node 1 to its local ARP cache.

4. The router then sends an ARP reply message containing its hardware address directly back to Node 1.

5. When Node 1 receives the ARP reply message from the router, it updates its ARP cache with a hardware/software address mapping for 10.0.0.1.

Once the media access control address for Router interface 1 has been determined, Node 1 can send IP traffic to Router interface 1 by addressing it to the Router interface 1 media access control address. The router then forwards the traffic to Node 2 through the same ARP process as discussed in this section.

6.1.7 ARP Cache

To minimize the number of broadcasts, ARP maintains a *cache* of IP address-to-media access control address mappings for future use. The ARP cache can contain both dynamic and static entries. Dynamic entries are added and removed automatically over time. Static entries remain in the cache until the computer is restarted.

Each dynamic ARP cache entry has a potential lifetime of 10 minutes. New entries added to the cache are *timestamped*. If an entry is not reused within 2 minutes of being added, it expires and is removed from the ARP cache. If an entry is used, it receives two more minutes of lifetime. If an entry keeps getting used, it receives an additional two minutes of lifetime up to a maximum lifetime of 10 minutes.

We can view the ARP cache by using the *arp* command. To view the ARP cache, type *arp − a* at a command prompt.

Sample output:

Interface: 192.168.1.2 --- 0xf

Internet Address	Physical Address	Type
192.168.1.1	00-08-5c-8d-4f-8f	dynamic
192.168.1.255	ff-ff-ff-ff-ff-ff	static
224.0.0.252	01-00-5e-00-00-fc	static
255.255.255.255	ff-ff-ff-ff-ff-ff	static

The ARP Cache is needed for improving efficiency on the operation of the ARP. The cache maintains the recent mappings from the Internet addresses to hardware addresses. The normal expiration time of an entry in the cache is 20 minutes from the time the entry was created.

6.1.8 Proxy ARP

Proxy ARP lets a router answer ARP requests on one of its networks for a host on another of its networks. This fools the sender of the ARP request into thinking that the router is the destination host, when in fact the destination host is *on the other side* of the router. The router is acting as a proxy agent for the destination host, relaying packets to it from other hosts.

6.2 Reverse Address Resolution Protocol [RARP]

6.2.1 What is Reverse Address Resolution Protocol (RARP)?

Reverse Address Resolution Protocol (RARP) is a network layer protocol used to convert an IP address from a given physical address. RARP is the complement of ARP.

As seen in previous section, ARP allows device a node to say *"I am Node 1 and I have Node 2's IP address, Node 2 please tell me your hardware address"*.

In contrast, RARP is used by Node 1 to say *"I am Node 1 and I am sending this broadcast using my hardware address, can someone please tell me my IP address?"*

The RARP packet format is almost identical to the ARP packet. An RARP request is broadcast, identifying the sender's hardware address, asking for anyone to respond with the sender's IP address. The reply is normally unicast.

6.2.2 Why do we need RARP?

When an IP machine happens to be a diskless machine, it has no way of initially knowing its IP address. But it does know its MAC address. RARP is used by many diskless systems to obtain their IP address when bootstrapped.

RARP enables diskless computers to obtain an IP address prior to loading any advanced operating system. Historically, it has been used for Unix-like diskless workstations (which also obtained the location of their boot image using this protocol) and also by corporations to roll out a pre-configured client (e.g. Windows) installation to newly purchased PCs.

6.2.3 RARP Server

RARP discovers the identity of the IP address for diskless machines by sending out a packet that includes its MAC address and a request for the IP address assigned to that MAC address. A designated machine, called a *RARP server*, responds with the answer.

The next question then is: who knows Node 1's IP address if Node 1 doesn't? The answer is that a special RARP server must be configured to listen for RARP requests and issue replies to them. Each physical network where RARP is in use must have RARP software running on at least one machine.

6.2.4 How RARP works?

RARP is used by Node 1 to say "I am Node 1 and I am sending this broadcast using my hardware address, can someone please tell me my IP address?" it is providing its own hardware address and asking for an IP address it can use.

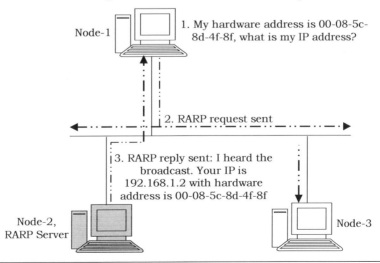

Any device on the network that is set up to act as an RARP server responds to the broadcast from the source. It generates an RARP reply.

Below are some key points in RARP process.

1. Sender generates RARP request message: The source node generates an RARP request message. It puts its own MAC address as both the sender MAC and also the destination MAC. It leaves both the sender IP Address and the destination IP Address blank, since it doesn't know either.
2. Sender broadcasts RARP request message: The source broadcasts the ARP request message on the local network.
3. Local nodes process RARP request message: The message is received by each node on the local network and processed. Nodes that are not configured to act as RARP servers ignore the message.
4. RARP server generates RARP reply message: Any node on the network that is set up to act as an RARP server responds to the broadcast from the source device. It generates an RARP reply. It sets the sender MAC address and sender IP address to its own hardware and IP address of course, since it is the sender of the reply. It then sets the destination MAC address to the hardware address of the original source device. It looks up in a table the hardware address of the source, determines that device's IP address assignment, and puts it into the destination IP address field.
5. RARP server sends RARP reply message: The RARP server sends the RARP reply message *unicast* to the device looking to be configured.
6. Source device processes RARP reply message: The source node processes the reply from the RARP server. It then configures itself using the IP address in the destination IP address supplied by the RARP server.

6.2.5 Issues with RARP

Problems with RARP include its use of a *broadcast*, *preventing* most routers from forwarding an RARP request and the minimal information returned (just the system's IP address).

While the RARP concept is simple, the implementation of an RARP server is *system dependent*. Hence not all TCP/IP implementations provide an RARP server.

These days, RARP has not been used. It has been over taken by BOOTP (Bootstrap Protocol) and DHCP (Dynamic Host Configuration Protocol). Both support a much greater feature set than RARP.

The primary limitations of RARP are that each MAC must be manually configured on a central server, and that the protocol only conveys an IP address. This leaves configuration of subnetting, gateways, and other information to other protocols or the user.

Another limitation of RARP compared to BOOTP or DHCP is that it is a non-IP protocol. This means that like ARP it can't be handled by the TCP/IP stack on the client, but is instead implemented separately.

In computing, BOOTP is a UDP network protocol used by a network client to obtain its IP address automatically. This is usually done in the bootstrap process of computers or operating systems running on them. The BOOTP servers assign the IP address from a pool of addresses to each client.

Note: For DHCP, refer *Application Layer Protocols* chapter.

Problems and Questions with Answers

Question 1: Assume the following Ethernet network exists:

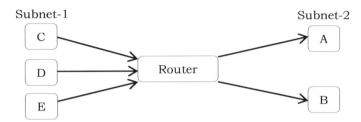

The IP and MAC addresses for each host and the router are as follows:

Host	IP Address	MAC Address
Router 1	125.100.15.10	e:f:g:h
Router 1	135.22.12.10	a:b:c:d
A	125.100.15.15	i:j:k:l
B	125.100.15.20	m:n:o:p
C	135.22.12.15	q:r:s:t
D	135.22.12.20	u:v:w:x
E	135.22.12.25	y:z:a:b

Assuming the ARP table is fully populated, list the ARP table for host E.

Answer: Host E only sees the other hosts on the 135.22.12.0/24 network (we are ignoring TTL values):

Host	IP Address	MAC Address
C	135.22.12.15	q:r:s:t
D	135.22.12.20	u:v:w:x
Router 1	125.100.15.10	e:f:g:h

Question 2: For the Question 1, if E transmits an Ethernet frame to C, what are the source and destination MAC and IP addresses?

Answer:

Host	IP Address	MAC Address
Source (E)	135.22.12.25	y:z:a:b
Destination (C)	135.22.12.15	q:r:s:t

Question 3: For the Question 1, if C transmits a frame to host B, what are the source and destination MAC and IP addresses when the frame leaves host C? When the frame arrives at host B?

Answer:

Leaving host C:

Host	IP Address	MAC Address
Source	135.22.12.15	q:r:s:t
Destination	125.100.15.20	a:b:c:d

Arriving at host B:

Host	IP Address	MAC Address
Source (E)	135.22.12.15	e:f:g:h
Destination (C)	125.100.15.20	m:n:o:p

Question 4: What is the primary purpose of ARP?

A) translate URLs to IP addresses
B) resolve IPv4 addresses to MAC addresses
C) provide dynamic IP configuration to network devices
D) convert internal private addresses to external public addresses

Answer: B

Question 5:   What is the difference between ARP and RARP?
Answer: ARP will resolve the MAC address of a device for which we know the IP address. RARP will resolve the IP address of the device for which we know the MAC address.

Question 6:   ARP is:
   A) A layer 3 protocol that is used by layer 3
   B) A layer 2 protocol that is used by layer 2
   C) A layer 3 protocol that is used by layer 2
   D) A layer 2 protocol that is used by layer 3
   E) A layer 2 protocol that is used by layer 1
   F) A layer 1 protocol that is used by layer 2
   G) A layer 1 protocol that is used by layer 1

Answer: D

CHAPTER

IP Addressing

7

7.1 Introduction

Let us start our discussion with a basic question: What is a *Protocol*? Well, a *protocol* is a set of communication rules used for connecting some computers in a network. As for example a man goes to some different land and wants to find his destination. Then there should be some standard pattern for such people to talk to each other or to communicate. These standard patterns are some set of rules with which we need to send our data to this distant land and talk to the person. Thus there is standard set of protocols without which our communication is impossible for the Internet. These *Protocols* are called *communication protocols*.

Communication between hosts can happen only if they can identify each other on the network. No doubt you have heard the term *IP address*. Unless you are a techie, though, you may not understanding of what an IP address actually is or how it works. Let's explore the concept with real world scenarios.

The Internet is a global network connecting billions of devices. Each device uses a *protocol* to communicate with other devices on the network. These protocols govern communication between all devices on the Internet.

In 1969, BBN Technologies started building the Interface Message Processors (IMPs) for the ARPANET and an important piece of the network was missing: the software that would govern how computers would communicate. Graduate students at various facilities funded by the US Department of Defense Advanced Research Projects Agency (ARPA) had been given the task in 1969 of developing the missing communication protocols. They formed an informal *network working group*. The students connected to ARPANET, who had been given the task in 1969 of developing the technical protocols, also began to establish the informal protocols that would influence interpersonal communications on the Internet in general.

From 1973 to 1974, *Cerf's* networking research group at *Stanford* worked out details of the idea, resulting in the first TCP specification. DARPA then contracted with BBN Technologies, Stanford University, and the University College London to develop operational versions of the protocol on different hardware platforms. Four versions were developed: TCP v1, TCP v2, TCP v3 and IP v3, and TCP/IP v4.

In 1975, a two-network TCP/IP communications test was performed between Stanford and University College London (UCL). In November, 1977, a three-network TCP/IP test was conducted between sites in the US, the UK, and Norway. Several other TCP/IP prototypes were developed at multiple research centers between 1978 and 1983.

Internet Protocol version 4 (IPv4), developed in 1981, currently controls the majority of intranet and Internet communication. It was the first viable protocol to handle distance computer communication. Predecessors had difficulty routing data over long distances with high reliably. Many questions were answered by IPv4 that were unknown at the time.

Over the next decade, the usefulness of IPv4 soon surfaced. IPv4's predecessors fell short of the requirements for large scale communication. IPv4 was developed by Internet Engineering Task Force (IETF) in September 1981. When IP was first standardized in September 1981, the specification required that each system attached to an IP-based internet be assigned a unique, 32-bit Internet address value.

7.2 What is an IP Address?

Just like your home has a mailing address in the same way any computer or device connected to the internet have a mailing address called the *Internet Protocol address*. IP address is short for Internet Protocol (IP) address. An IP address is an identifier for a computer or device on a TCP/IP network. Networks using the TCP/IP protocol route messages based on the IP address of the destination.

An IP address is a 32-bit number written in *dotted* decimal notation: four 8-bit fields (octets) converted from binary to decimal numbers, separated by dots.

Example IP addresses:

<blockquote>
122.169.236.244
78.125.0.209
216.27.61.137
</blockquote>

An IP address can either be *static* or *dynamic*. If it is static, then it will remain unchanged every time we connect a node to a network and if it is dynamic then a local DHCP (Dynamic Host Configuration Protocol) server grants a new IP address every time we connect a node to internet.

Note: For more details on DHCP, refer *Application Layer Protocols* chapter.

7.3 Understanding IP Address

As seen above, the 32 binary bits are divided into four octets (1 octet – 8 bits). Each octet is converted to decimal and separated by a period (dot). For this reason, an IP address is said to be expressed in dotted decimal format (for example, 172.16.81.100). The value in each octet ranges from 0 to 255 decimal, or 00000000 - 11111111 binary.

Here is how binary octets convert to decimal: The right most bit, or least significant bit, of an octet holds a value of 2^0. The bit just to the left of that holds a value of 2^1. This continues until the left-most bit, or most significant bit, which holds a value of 2^7.

x	2^x	2^x in Decimal
0	2^0	1
1	2^1	2
2	2^2	4
3	2^3	8

x	2^x	2^x in Decimal
4	2^4	16
5	2^5	32
6	2^6	64
7	2^7	128
8	2^8	256

So if all binary bits are a *one*, the decimal equivalent would be 255 as shown here:

1	1	1	1	1	1	1	1	
128	64	32	16	8	4	2	1	(128+64+32+16+8+4+2+1=255)

Here is a sample octet conversion when not all of the bits are set to 1.

0	1	0	0	1	0	0	1	
0	64	0	0	8	0	0	1	(0+64+0+0+8+0+0+1=73)

And this is sample shows an IP address represented in both binary and decimal.

10.	1.	22.	19	(decimal)
00001010.	00000001.	00010110.	00010011	(binary)

These octets are broken down to provide an addressing scheme that can accommodate large and small networks. There are five different classes of networks, A to E. This document focuses on addressing classes A to C, since classes D and E are reserved and discussion of them is beyond the scope of this document.

7.4 Why do we need IP addresses?

As an example, imagine for a moment that computers are people in a room. Everyone is glued to 1 spot and can't move around. If *Ram* wants to talk to *Mary*, he shouts out "Hey Mary" and Mary responds; and a conversation occur as a result. This looks great! right?

On a small scale this works quite well and is actually used regularly in some networking protocols between two (or a few) devices. The Internet (as we know it today) is not just 2 or a few people talking directly to each other. The internet is literally billions of devices. If they were all placed into the same room (network-segment); imagine what would happen if Ram wanted to talk to Mary. Ram would yell "Hey Mary!" and Ram's voice would be lost in the crowd. Building a room to fit billions of people is equally ridiculous.

For this reason, networks are separated into smaller *segments* (smaller rooms) which allow devices who are in the same segment (room) to talk directly to each other's. But, for the devices outside the segment we need some sort of router to pass messages from one room to the next room. But the vast number of segments (rooms) means we need some sort of addressing scheme so the various routers in the middle know how to get a message from Ram to Mary.

With the IP protocol, they assign a subnet to each segment (room), and the routers are told how to pass a message from one segment (room) to the next. For example, if Ram's address is 1.1.1.1, and Mary's address 2.2.2.2, and Ram's subnet is 1.1.1.0/24 (meaning the first 3 bytes of his address must match for it to be in his segment), Ram needs to pass his message to the router so it can be passed along to Mary's segment. Ram knows his router is 1.1.1.2, so he passes the message to the router, and the router passes it along to other routers in the middle until the message is passed to Mary's router at 2.2.2.1, which hands the message directly to Mary and Mary can send the reply back to Ram in the same way.

Note: For more details on subnets, refer *Subnetting* section.

Computers in the same subnet actually do communicate directly with each other using the MAC address. It actually starts by sending out an ARP request (ARP = Address Resolution Protocol) which means it shouts out "Who has the address X.X.X.X?" and whoever has that address replies and from that point on, they continue to talk to each other directly.

Note: For more details on ARP, refer *ARP and RARP* chapter.

7.5 IPv4 and IPv6

Two IP addressing standards are in use today. The IPv4 standard is most familiar to people and supported everywhere on the Internet, but the newer IPv6 standard is slowly replacing it. IPv4 addresses consist of four bytes (32 bits), while IPv6 addresses are 16 bytes (128 bits) long.

7.5.1 IPv4 Addressing Notation

This is what we discussed in previous few sections. An IPv4 address consists of four bytes (32 bits). These bytes are called *octets*. For readability, humans typically work with IP addresses in a notation called *dotted decimal*. This notation places *periods* (*dot* or "."*) between each of the four numbers (octets) that comprise an IP address. For example, an IP address that computer sees as

00001010 00000000 00000000 00000001

is written in dotted decimal as

10.0.0.1

7.5.2 IPv6 Addressing Notation

IP addresses change vastly with IPv6. IPv6 addresses are 16 bytes (128 bits) long rather than four bytes (32 bits). This larger size means that IPv6 supports more than 300,000,000,000,000,000,000,000,000,000,000,000,000 possible addresses! As an increasing number of cell phones and other consumer devices expand their networking capability and require own addresses. The smaller IPv4 address space will eventually run out and IPv6 become mandatory. IPv6 has significantly larger address space than IPv4.

IPv6 addresses are generally written in the following *hexadecimal* form:

hhhh:hhhh:hhhh:hhhh:hhhh:hhhh:hhhh:hhhh

In this full notation, pairs of IPv6 bytes are separated by a colon and each byte in turns is represented as a pair of hexadecimal numbers, like in the following example:

E3D7:0000:0000:0000:51F4:9BC8:C0A8:6420

As shown above, IPv6 addresses commonly contain many bytes with a zero value. Shorthand notation in IPv6 removes these values from the text representation (though the bytes are still present in the actual network address) as follows:

E3D7::51F4:9BC8:C0A8:6420

Finally, many IPv6 addresses are extensions of IPv4 addresses. In these cases, the rightmost four bytes of an IPv6 address (the rightmost two byte pairs) may be rewritten in the IPv4 notation. Converting the above example to mixed notation yields

E3D7::51F4:9BC8:**192.168.100.32**

IPv6 addresses may be written in any of the *full*, *shorthand* or *mixed* notation illustrated above.

7.5.3 What Happened to IPv5?

The version of Internet Protocol (IP) used on most computer networks today is four, typically called *IPv4*. The next version of IP expected to one day become the new worldwide standard is version six (*IPv6*). You might be curious to know what happened to the protocol version in-between, the IPv5.

Till date, Internet Protocol has been recognized has IPv4 only. Versions 0 to 3 were used while the protocol was itself under development and experimental process. So, we can assume lots of background activities remain active before putting a protocol into production.

Protocol version 5 was used while experimenting with stream protocol for internet. It is known to us as Internet Stream Protocol which used Internet Protocol number 5 to encapsulate its datagram. IP Version 5 (IPv5) was an IP-layer protocol that provides end-to-end guaranteed service across a network. That is, it was compatible with IP at the network layer but was built to provide a Quality of Service for streaming services.

In short, IPv5 never became an official protocol due to its overhead. Many years ago, Internet Stream Protocol (ST) was considered IP version five by industry researchers, but ST was abandoned before ever becoming a standard or widely known as IPv5. Work on ST and IPv5 is not expected to ever restart. Though it was never brought into public use, but it was already used.

7.6 Classful Addressing: IPv4 Address Classes

In order to provide the flexibility required to support *different size* networks, the designers decided that the IP address space should be divided into different address classes. The IPv4 address space can be subdivided into 5 classes - Class A, B, C, D and E. Each class consists of a *contiguous* subset of the overall IPv4 address range. This is called *classful* addressing because the address space is split into three predefined classes, groupings, or categories.

The 32 binary bits are divided into *four* octets (1 octet = 8 bits). These octets are broken down to provide an addressing scheme that can accommodate large and small networks. There are five different classes of networks, A to E. This document focuses on addressing classes A to C, since classes D and E are reserved and discussion of them is beyond the scope of this document.

The first part of an IP address identifies the network on which the host resides, while the second part identifies the particular host on the given network. The network number field is called the *network prefix, network number* or *network ID* (*Network Identifier*). The network-number field has been referred to as the network-prefix because the leading portion of each IP address identifies the network number.

Network ID	Host ID

or

Network Prefix	Host Number

or

Network Number	Host Number

All hosts on a given network share the same network-number but must have a unique host-number. Similarly, any two hosts on different networks must have different network-prefixes but may have the same host-number.

7.6.1 Class A Addresses

Each Class A network address has an 8-bit network ID with the highest order bit set to 0 and a seven-bit network number, followed by a 24-bit host-number. Class A networks are now referred to as /8 (pronounced *h eight*) since they have an 8-bit network-prefix.

0 1 2 3 4 5 6 7	0 1 2 3 4 5 6 7 0 1 2 3 4 5 6 7 0 1 2 3 4 5 6 7
0	
Network ID (8-Bits)	Host ID (24-Bits)

Because the highest number that 7 bits can represent in binary is 128, there are 128 possible Class A network addresses. Of the 128 possible network addresses, two are reserved for special cases. So, a maximum of 126 (2^7 -2)/8 networks can be defined.

The calculation requires that the 2 is subtracted because the /8 network 0.0.0.0 is reserved for use as the *default route* and the /8 network 127.0.0.0 (also written 127/8 or 127.0.0.0/8) has been reserved for the *loopback* function. Each /8 supports a maximum of 16,777,214 (2^{32}-2) hosts per network. The host calculation requires that 2 is subtracted because the all 0's (*this network*) and all 1's (*broadcast*) host-numbers may not be assigned to individual hosts.

Since the /8 address block contains 2^{31} (2,147,483,648) individual addresses and the IPv4 address space contains a maximum of 2^{32} (4,294,967,296) addresses, the /8 address space is 50% of the total IPv4 unicast address space.

7.6.2 Class B Addresses

Each Class B network address has a 16-bit network-ID with the two highest order bits set to 10 and a 14-bit network number, followed by a 16-bit host-number. Class B networks are now called /16 since they have a 16-bit network-ID.

0 1 2 3 4 5 6 7 0 1 2 3 4 5 6 7	0 1 2 3 4 5 6 7 0 1 2 3 4 5 6 7
1 0	
Network ID (16-Bits)	Host ID (16-Bits)

A maximum of 16,384 (2^{14})/16 networks can be defined with up to 65,534 (2^{16}-2) hosts per network. Since the entire /16 address block contains 2^{30} (1,073,741,824) addresses, it represents 25% of the total IPv4 unicast address space.

7.6.3 Class C Addresses

Each Class C network address has a 24-bit network-ID with the three highest order bits set to 110 and a 21-bit network number, followed by an 8-bit host-number. Class C networks are now referred to as /24 since they have a 24-bit network-ID.

0 1 2 3 4 5 6 7 0 1 2 3 4 5 6 7 0 1 2 3 4 5 6 7	0 1 2 3 4 5 6 7
1 1 0	
Network ID (24-Bits)	Host ID (8-Bits)

A maximum of 2,097,152 (2^{20})/24 networks can be defined with up to 254 (2^8-2) hosts per network. Since the entire /24 address block contains 2^{29} (536,870,912) addresses, it represents 12.5% (or 1/8th) of the total IPv4 unicast address space.

7.6.4 Class D Addresses

Class D addresses have their leading four-bits set to 1110 and are used to support IP *Multicasting*. The IPv4 networking standard defines Class D addresses as reserved for *multicast*.

Multicast is a mechanism for defining groups of nodes and sending IP messages to that group rather than to every node on the LAN (broadcast) or just one other node (unicast).

```
0 1 2 3 4 5 6 7 0 1 2 3 4 5 6 7 0 1 2 3 4 5 6 7 0 1 2 3 4 5 6 7
┌─┬─┬─┬─┬─┬─┬─┬─┬─┬─┬─┬─┬─┬─┬─┬─┬─┬─┬─┬─┬─┬─┬─┬─┬─┬─┬─┬─┬─┬─┬─┬─┐
│1│1│1│0│ │ │ │ │ │ │ │ │ │ │ │ │ │ │ │ │ │ │ │ │ │ │ │ │ │ │ │ │
├─┴─┴─┴─┴─┴─┴─┴─┴─┴─┴─┴─┴─┴─┴─┴─┴─┴─┴─┴─┴─┴─┴─┴─┴─┴─┴─┴─┴─┴─┴─┴─┤
│                   Multicast Group ID (28 bits)               │
└─────────────────────────────────────────────────────────────┘
```

Multicast is mainly used on research networks. As with Class E, Class D addresses should not be used by ordinary nodes on the Internet.

The first four bits of a Class D address must be 1110. Therefore, the first octet range for Class D addresses is 11100000 to 11101111, or 224 to 239. An IP address that starts with a value in the range of 224 to 239 in the first octet is a Class D address.

7.6.5 Class E Addresses

A Class E address has been defined. However, the IPv4 networking standard reserves these addresses for its own research. Therefore, no Class E addresses have been released for use in the Internet.

```
0 1 2 3 4 5 6 7 0 1 2 3 4 5 6 7 0 1 2 3 4 5 6 7 0 1 2 3 4 5 6 7
┌─┬─┬─┬─┬─┬─┬─┬─┬─┬─┬─┬─┬─┬─┬─┬─┬─┬─┬─┬─┬─┬─┬─┬─┬─┬─┬─┬─┬─┬─┬─┬─┐
│1│1│1│1│0│ │ │ │ │ │ │ │ │ │ │ │ │ │ │ │ │ │ │ │ │ │ │ │ │ │ │ │
├─┴─┴─┴─┴─┴─┴─┴─┴─┴─┴─┴─┴─┴─┴─┴─┴─┴─┴─┴─┴─┴─┴─┴─┴─┴─┴─┴─┴─┴─┴─┴─┤
│                 Reserved for future use (27 bits)            │
└─────────────────────────────────────────────────────────────┘
```

The first four bits of a Class E address are always set to 1s. Therefore, the first octet range for Class E addresses is 11110000 to 11111111, or 240 to 255.

7.6.6 Summary

IP Address Class	Number of bits for (Network ID/Host ID)	First Octet of IP Address	Number of Network ID Bits Used To Identify Class	Usable Number of Network ID Bits	Number of Possible Network IDs	Number of Host IDs Per Network ID
Class A	8/24	0xxx xxxx	1	8-1=7	2^7 -2 = 126	2^{24} -2 = 16, 277, 214
Class B	16/16	10xx xxxx	2	16-2=14	2^{14} -2 = 16,384	2^{16} -2 = 65,535
Class C	24/8	110x xxxx	3	24-3=21	2^{21} -2 = 2, 097, 152	2^8 -2 = 254

Note: For class D and class E we do not use the concept of Network-ID.

7.7 IPv4 Addressing Types

7.7.1 Unicast

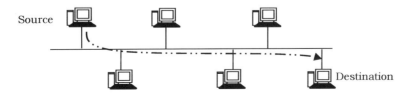

In this mode, data is sent only to one destined host. The destination address field contains 32-bit IP address of the destination host. Here source sends data to the targeted destination.

7.7.2 Broadcast

In this mode the packet is addressed to all hosts in a network segment. The destination address field contains special broadcast address i.e. 255.255.255.255. When a host sees this packet on the network, it is bound to process it. Here *source* sends packet, which is entertained by all the *nodes*.

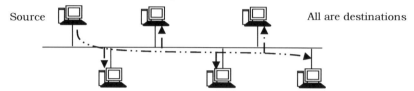

Broadcast signifies a one to all relation between the source and the destination. Broadcasts are mostly confined to the LAN and need special rules to travel beyond the router.

7.7.3 Multicast

This mode is a mix of previous two modes, i.e. the packet sent is neither destined to a single host nor all the hosts on the segment. In this packet, the destination address contains special address which starts with 224.x.x.x and can be entertained by more than one host.

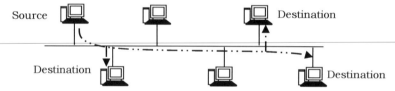

Here a *source* sends packets which are entertained by more than one nodes. Every network has one IP address reserved for network number which represents the network and one IP address reserved for broadcast address, which represents all the host in that network.

7.8 IPv4 Reserved Addresses

There are few reserved IPv4 address spaces which *cannot* be used on the *Internet*. These addresses serve special purpose and cannot be routed outside Local Area Network (LAN).

7.8.1 IP Loopback Address

127.0.0.1 is the loopback address in IP. Loopback is a test mechanism of network adapters. Messages sent to 127.0.0.1 do not get delivered to the network. Instead, the adapter intercepts all loopback messages and returns them to the sending application. IP applications often use this feature to test the behavior of their network interface.

As with broadcast, IP officially reserves the entire range from 127.0.0.0 through 127.255.255.255 for loopback purposes. Nodes should not use this range on the Internet, and it should not be considered part of the normal Class A range.

7.8.2 Zero Addresses

As with the loopback address range, the address range from 0.0.0.0 through 0.255.255.255 should not be considered part of the normal Class A range. 0.x.x.x addresses serve no particular function in IP, but nodes attempting to use them will be unable to communicate properly on the Internet.

7.8.3 Private Addresses

Private IP addresses are typically used on local networks including home, school and business LANs including airports and hotels. The IPv4 networking standard defines specific address ranges within Class A, Class B, and Class C reserved for use by private networks (intranets). The table below lists these reserved ranges of the IP address space.

Class	Private Start Address	Private Finish Address
A	10.0.0.0	10.255.255.255
B	172.16.0.0	172.31.255.255
C	192.168.0.0	192.168.255.255

IPv4 networking standard created private IP addressing to prevent a shortage of public IP addresses available to Internet service providers and subscribers. Devices with private IP addresses cannot connect directly to the Internet. Likewise, computers outside the local network cannot connect directly to a device with a private IP. Instead, access to such devices must be controlled by a router or similar device that supports Network Address Translation (NAT). NAT hides the private IP numbers but can selectively transfer messages to these devices, affording a layer of security to the local network.

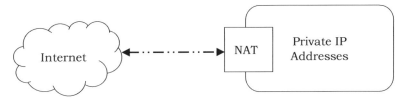

So, an IP address can be private (for use on a LAN) or public (for use on the Internet or WAN). IP addresses can be determined statically (assigned to a computer by a system administrator) or dynamically (assigned by another device on the network on demand).

An IP address is considered public if the IP number is valid and falls outside any of the IP address ranges reserved for private uses by IPv4 networking standard. Public IP addresses are used by Internet servers including those for Web sites and DNS servers), network routers or any computer connected directly to the Internet via a modem. Each public IP is assigned to a range or block of addresses. The Internet Assigned Numbers Authority (IANA) controls ownership of these IP ranges and assigns each block to organizations such as Internet Service Providers (ISPs) who in turn allocate individual IP addresses to customers.

Using a private IP address on a residential or business computer can improve network security and conserve public addressing space.

7.9 Packet Flow in an IPv4 Network

All the hosts in IPv4 environment are assigned unique logical IP addresses. When a host wants to send some data to another host on the local network (within LAN), it needs the physical (MAC) address of the destination host. To get the MAC address, the host broadcasts *ARP* message and asks to give the MAC address whoever is the owner of destination IP address.

All the hosts on that segment receives ARP packet but only the host which has its IP matching with the one in ARP message, replies with its MAC address. Once the sender receives the MAC address of receiving station, data is sent on the physical media.

In case, the IP does not belong to the local subnet (LAN); the data is sent to the destination by using Gateway of the subnet. To understand the packet flow we must first understand following components:

- *MAC Address*: Media Access Control Address is 48-bit factory hard coded physical address of network device which can uniquely be identified. This address is assigned by device manufacturers.
- *Address Resolution Protocol* [ARP]: ARP is used to acquire the MAC address of a host whose IP address is known. ARP broadcasts a packet which is received by all the hosts in the network segment. But only the host whose IP is mentioned in ARP responds to it by providing its MAC address.
- *Dynamic Host Control Protocol* [DHCP]: DHCP is a service by which a host is assigned IP address from a pre-defined address pool. DHCP server also provides necessary information such as Gateway IP, DNS Server Address, lease assigned with the IP etc. By using DHCP services network administrator can manage assignment of IP addresses at ease.
- *Domain Name System* [DNS]: This is very likely that a user does not know the IP address of a remote Server he/she wants to connect to. But he knows the name assigned to it for example, CareerMonk.com. When the user types in the name of remote server he wants to connect to the localhost behind the screens sends a DNS query. Domain Name System is a method to acquire the IP address of the host whose Domain Name is known.
- *Network Address Translation* [NAT]: Almost all devices in a computer network are assigned private IP addresses which are not routable on Internet. As soon as a router receives an IP packet with private IP address it drops it. In order to access Servers on public private address, computer networks use an address translation service, which translates between public and private addresses, called *Network Address Translation*. When a PC sends an IP packet out of a private network, NAT changes the private IP address with public IP address and vice versa.

We can now describe the packet flow. Assume that a user wants to access www.*CareerMonk*.com from her/his personal computer. She/he is having internet connection from her ISP. The following steps will be taken by the system to help her reach destination website.

Step: 1 – Acquiring an IP Address (DHCP)

When user's machine boots up, it searches for a DHCP server to get an IP address. For the same, machine sends a DHCPDISCOVER broadcast which is received by one or more DHCP servers on the subnet and they all respond with DHCPOFFER which includes all the necessary details like IP, subnet, Gateway, DNS etc. Machine sends DHCPREQUEST packet in order to request the offered IP address. Finally, DHCP sends DHCPACK packet to tell PC that it can keep the IP for some given amount of time aka IP lease.

Alternatively a machine can be assigned an IP address manually without taking any help from DHCP Server. When a PC is well configured with IP address details, it can now speak to other computers all over the IP enabled network.

Step: 2 – DNS query

When a user opens a web browser and types www.CareerMonk.com which is a domain name and a machine does not understand how to communicate with the server using domain names. Machine sends a DNS query out on the network in order to obtain the IP address pertaining to the domain name. The pre-configured DNS server responds the query with IP address of the domain name specified.

Step: 3 – ARP request

The machine finds that the destination IP address does not belong to its own IP address range and it has to forward the request to the Gateway. Gateway in this scenario can be a router or a Proxy Server. Though Gateway's IP address is known to the client machine but computers do not exchange data on IP addresses rather they need machine's hardware address which is Layer-2 factory coded MAC address.

To obtain the MAC address of the Gateway the client machine broadcasts an ARP request saying "Who owns this IP address?" The Gateway in response to the ARP query sends it MAC address. Upon receiving MAC address PC sends the packets to Gateway.

An IP packet has both source and destination addresses and this connects host with a remote host logically. Whereas MAC addresses helps systems on a single network segment to transfer actual data. This is important that source and destination MAC addresses change as they travel across the Internet (segment by segment) but source and destination IP address never changes.

7.10 IPv4 Datagram Header Format

An IP datagram consists of a header part and text part.

IP Header [20 Bytes]
Data [Variable Length]

The header has a 20 bytes fixed part and a variable length optional part. It is transmitted in big endian order (on little endian machines, software conversion is required).

00 To 03	04 To 07	08	09	10	11	12	13	14	15	16	17	18	19 To 31
Version	IHL	ToS				D	T	R	M	R0	Total Length		
IP Identification (IPID)										R0	DF	MF	Fragment Offset
Time-To-Live (TTL)		Protocol								Header Checksum			
Source IP Address													
Destination IP Address													
Options & padding (variable, usually none)													

Version: 4 bits

Identifies the version of IP used to generate the datagram. For IPv4, this is of course the number 4. The purpose of this field is to ensure *compatibility* between devices that may be running different versions of IP.

IHL: 4 bits

Internet Header Length (IHL) specifies the length of the IP header, in 32-bit words. This includes the length of any options fields and padding. The normal value of this field when no options are used is 5 (5 32-bit words = 5*4 = 20 bytes). Contrast to the longer *Total Length* field.

Type of Service: 8 bits

Type of Service (ToS) field is used carry information to provide quality of service (QoS) features, such as prioritized delivery, for IP datagrams. These parameters are to be used to guide the selection of the actual service parameters when transmitting a datagram through a particular network.

It contains a 3-bit precedence field (that is ignored today), 4 service bits, and 1 unused bit. The four service bits can be:

1000	Minimize Delay
0100	Maximize Throughput
0010	Maximize Reliability
0001	Minimize Monetary cost

This is a *hint* of what characteristics of the physical layer to use. The Type of service is not supported in most implementations. However, some implementations have extra fields in the routing table to indicate delay, throughput, reliability, and monetary cost.

Total Length: 16 bits

This field specifies the total length of the IP datagram, in bytes. Since this field is 16 bits wide, the maximum length of an IP datagram is 65,535 bytes, though most are much smaller.

Identification: 16 bits

This field uniquely identifies the datagram. It is usually incremented by 1 each time a datagram is sent. All fragments of a datagram contain the same identification value. This allows the destination host to determine which fragment belongs to which datagram.

It is an identification value assigned by the sender to help in assembling the fragments of a datagram. This field is used by the recipient to reassemble messages without accidentally mixing fragments from different messages. This is needed because fragments may arrive from multiple messages mixed together, since IP datagrams can be received out of order from any device.

Flags: 3 bits

It is used for fragmentation. DF means do not fragment. It is a request to routers not to fragment the datagram since the destination is incapable of putting the pieces back together.

MF means more fragments to follow. All fragments except the last one have this bit set. It is needed to know if all fragments of a datagram have arrived.

Fragment Offset: 13 bits

When fragmentation of a message occurs, this field specifies the offset, or position, in the overall message where the data in this fragment goes. It is specified in units of 8 bytes (64 bits). The first fragment has an offset of 0.

Time to Live: 8 bits

Specifies how long the datagram is allowed to *live* on the network, in terms of router hops. Each router decrements the value of the TTL field (reduces it by one) prior to transmitting it. If the TTL field drops to zero, the datagram is assumed to have taken too long a route and is *discarded*.

Protocol: 8 bits

This field tells IP where to send the datagram up to. Few commonly used protocols are:

Hex Value	Decimal Value	Protocol
00	0	Reserved
01	1	ICMP [Internet Control Message Protocol]
02	2	IGMP [Internet Group Management Protocol]
06	6	TCP [Transmission Control Protocol]
11	17	UDP [User Datagram Protocol]

Header Checksum: 16 bits

A checksum computed over the header to provide basic protection against corruption in transmission. This is not the more complex CRC code typically used by data link layer technologies such as Ethernet; it's just a 16-bit checksum. It is calculated by dividing the header bytes into words (a word is two bytes) and then adding them together.

The data is not check-summed, only the header. At each hop the device receiving the datagram does the same checksum calculation and on a mismatch, discards the datagram as damaged.

Source Address: 32 bits

It is the 32-bit IP address of the sender of the datagram. Note that even though intermediate devices such as routers may handle the datagram, they do not normally put their address into this field. It is always the device that originally sent the datagram.

Destination Address: 32 bits

It is the 32-bit IP address of the intended destination of the datagram. Again, even though devices such as routers may be the intermediate targets of the datagram, this field is always for the final destination.

Options: variable

The options may appear or not in datagrams. One or more of several types of options may be included after the standard headers in certain IP datagrams.

Padding: variable

If one or more options are included, and the number of bits used for them is not a multiple of 32, enough zero bits are added to *pad out* the header to a multiple of 32 bits (4 bytes).

7.11 IPv4 Fragmentation

Imagine a group of 100 friends wanting to go to a game, then we can easily see that not all can fit in one car. If we consider that a car can hold five people, we will need twenty cars to transport this entire group. The Internet transfer model also operates in this fashion. Suppose that a document that we want to download from a host (web-server) is 2 MB. Actually, it cannot be accommodated entirely into a single fundamental unit of IP, known as *packet* or *datagram*, due to a limitation imposed by the underlying transmission system. This limitation is called the Maximum Transmission Unit (MTU).

MTU is similar to the limitation on how many people can fit into a single car. In this manner, the document would need to be broken down (also called *fragmentation*) into smaller units that fit into packets. Each packet is then marked with both the destination and the source address, which is then routed through the Internet toward the destination. Since the IP delivery mechanism is assumed to be unreliable, any such packet can possibly get lost during transit, and thus would need to be retransmitted if the timer associated with this packet expires. Thus another important component is that content that has been broken down into smaller packets, once it arrives at the destination, needs to be reassembled (also called *de-fragmentation*) in the proper order before delivering the document.

The *total length* field in the IP header is 16 bits. That means the max size of of an IP datagram is 65535 bytes. But, the physical layer may not allow a packet size of that many bytes (for example, a max Ethernet packet is 1500 bytes). So, different network hardware can use different MTU. Due to this, IP must sometimes fragment (split) packets. When an IP datagram is fragmented, each fragment is treated as a separate datagram.

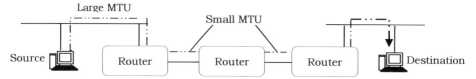

The fragments are sent separately and reassembled at the destination (not at a router). It does that because the router may have to fragment it again. Each fragment has its own header. The identification number is copied into each fragment. One bit in the *flags* field says *more fragments* are coming. If that bit is 0, then it indicates this is the last fragment. Fragment size is identified by their offset within the data packet.

7.11.1 An Example

Suppose we have a physical layer that can transmit a maximum of 660 bytes. And, suppose IP wants to send 1460 bytes of data. So, the IP datagram is a total of 1480 bytes, including the 20 byte IP header:

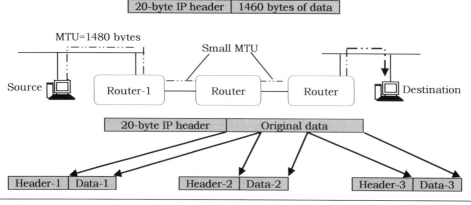

Here is what *Router* − 1 sends:

1. *First* packet: In that packet, *fragment flag* is 1, offset is 0.

20-byte IP header	640 bytes of data [MTU]

2. *Second* packet: In that packet, *fragment* flag is 1, offset is 80. The offset is 80 because (80 * 8) is 640, so the offset of that data is 640 byes into the packet. *Note*: all other fields of the IP header are identical to the first packet (except the checksum)!

20-byte IP header	640 bytes of data [MTU]

3. Third packet: In that packet, *fragment* flag is 0, offset is 160. The offset is 160 because (160 * 8) is 1280, so the offset of that data is 1280 byes into the packet. *Note*: all other fields of the IP header are identical to the first packet except the checksum.

20-byte IP header	180 bytes of data

The routers see 3 separate packets. The final destination reassembles the packet before passing the packet to the upper layers.

7.12 Limitations to IPv4 Classful Addressing

The designer of IP addressing never thought that the *Internet* would grow into what it has become today. Many of the problems that the Internet is facing today can be traced back to the early decisions that were made during its formative years.

- During the early days of the Internet, the seemingly unlimited address space allowed IP addresses to be allocated to an organization based on its request rather than its actual need. As a result, addresses were freely assigned to those who asked for them without concerns about the eventual depletion of the IP address space.
- The decision to standardize on a 32-bit address space meant that there were only 232 (4,294,967,296) IPv4 addresses available. A decision to support a slightly larger address space would have exponentially increased the number of addresses thus eliminating the current address shortage problem.
- The classful A, B, and C octet boundaries were easy to understand and implement. To promote the growth, they did not follow the efficient allocation of a finite address space.

The subsequent history of Internet addressing is focused on a series of steps that overcome these addressing issues and have supported the growth of the global Internet. The result of such steps is IPv6.

7.13 Subnet Masks and Subnetting

Before discussing the subnetting procedure, it is useful to become familiar with the basic concepts of *subnet masks*.

Since IP addressing operates at the *network layer* (Layer 3) of OSI, IP addresses must be able to identify *individual hosts* (such as a computer, printer, router, etc.) and *individual networks*. This can be achieved by dividing the 32-bit IP addresses into two parts: an initial *network ID* portion that identifies individual networks, followed by a *host ID* portion that identifies individual hosts on a given network. So, the IP addresses have following specification:

I.   A TCP/IP network is identified by the *network ID* portion of the IP address
II.   A *host* on *that network* is identified by the *host ID* portion of the IP address

7.13.1 Difference between MAC and IP Addresses

Let us start our discussion by understanding the difference between the MAC address at the Data-Link layer (Layer 2), and the IP address which operates at the Network layer (Layer 3). The MAC address uniquely identifies each network adapter (NIC or Network Interface Card) with a 48-bit binary number.

Each MAC address consists of *two* parts: the *first* part uniquely identifies the NIC *manufacturer*, and the *second* part uniquely identifies each NIC produced by a given manufacturer. A device attached to a TCP/IP network via a NIC is called a TCP/IP *host*. Note that the MAC addressing scheme does *not* provide a way to identify individual *networks*, only individual *hosts*.

7.13.2 Subnet Masks

With IP addressing, individual hosts can be uniquely identified, but in a different way. Hosts are identified by specifying *both*:

1.   The network on which the host resides (the network id), and
2.   A unique host number on that network (the host ID).

So, Layer 3 devices can work either with individual networks by using just the network ID, or with individual hosts by using both the network ID and host ID, i.e., the entire IP address.

Network layer (Layer 3) software and devices must be able to separate IP addresses into their network ID and host ID portions. This is achieved with the help of another 32-bit binary number called *subnet mask*. The use of the subnet mask is to tell which part of the IP address is the network ID, and which part is the host ID.

Since the network ID is always the leading part of an IP address and the host ID is always the trailing part, a simple *masking* scheme can be used. Class A, B, and C networks have *default masks*, also known as *natural masks*, as shown here:

IP Address Class	Default mask	Number of bits for Network ID	Number of bits for Host ID
Class A	255.0.0.0	8	24
Class B	255.255.0.0	16	16
Class C	255.255.255.0	24	8

Without subnetting:

A subnet mask always consists of a series of contiguous 1 bits followed by a series of contiguous 0 bits. These two portions of the subnet mask (all 1's and all 0's) correspond to the two parts of an IP address.

The 1 bits in the subnet mask match up with the network ID, and the 0 bits in the subnet mask match up with the Host ID in the IP address. By looking at the subnet mask, it is easy to tell which part of an IP address represents the network ID and which part represents the host ID.

With subnetting

Subnet Mask

An Address → Bitwise AND → Network
in the block   Operation   Address

The following example describes the use of a subnet mask to separate the network ID and host ID portions of an IP address for a Class B network (for Class B networks the first 2 octets of the IP address indicates the network ID and the last 2 octets indicates the host ID):

32-bit IP Address:	10010010 10101000 00000000 00000111
32-bit Subnet Mask:	**11111111 11111111** 00000000 00000000

Observe how the subnet mask consists of 2 octets of contiguous 1's (indicating the network ID part of the corresponding IP address), and 2 octets of contiguous 0's (indicating the host ID part of the corresponding IP address). Using the subnet mask, we can easily separate the IP address into its two parts:

Network ID:	10010010 10101000
Host ID:	00000000 00000111

Even though it is easy to understand the role of the subnet mask while working in binary, binary notation is in general too difficult and confusing for humans. Hence IP addresses and subnet masks are usually written in *dotted − decimal* notation, in which each octet is converted to its equivalent decimal number, and the four decimal numbers are separated with dots (i.e., periods). The IP address and subnet mask from the example above would appear in dotted-decimal as:

IP Address:	146.168.0.7
Subnet Mask:	255.255.0.0
Network ID:	146.168
Host ID:	0.7

Note that the network ID is usually seen written as 4 octets (which can be created by appending any necessary 0 octets to the end of the network ID as delimited by the subnet mask), and that leading 0 octets are usually dropped from the host ID, as in:

Network ID:	146.168.0.0
Host ID:	7

7.13.3 Subnetting

Finally, let us discuss the basic concepts of *subnetting*. Imagine that *CareerMonk* organization has obtained an official *public* network address from Internet Service Provider (ISP) to use on the *Internet*. They could equally well imagine that organization has chosen a *private* IP address to use for an internal TCP/IP network that will not be connected to the Public Internet (i.e., an *intranet*).

In either scenario, they have the same problem: Organization has enough hosts that they cannot coexist on the same TCP/IP network. The network must be broken up into separate subnetworks.

To segment the original network, we must devise an addressing scheme that is able to identify each *subnetwork* within the larger network. This will require the use of an additional *subnet ID* along with the original *network ID*. A given host will then be uniquely identified by the combination of:

1. A *network ID* that uniquely specifies the network on which the host resides (if the network is on the public Internet, this network ID is the address that will identify the network (including all its subnets) on the public Internet)
2. A *subnet ID* that uniquely specifies the subnetwork (within the original network) on which the host resides
3. A *host ID* that uniquely specifies the host on the subnetwork

An IP address already accommodates a network ID and a host ID, so all that is required is some way to create the subnet ID field. Since we can't expand the size of the IP address (32 bits for IPv4), we must *borrow* some bits from the existing address to use for the subnet ID. We can't borrow bits from the network ID part of the IP address because this has been pre-assigned by our ISP to uniquely identify our organization's network. Hence we are forced to borrow bits to create the subnet ID from the existing host ID field.

Network ID	Subnet ID [Bits borrowed from Host ID]	Host ID

The process of borrowing bits from the host ID field to form a new subnet ID field is called *subnetting*. The process is shown in table below:

Network ID	3 Bits Borrowed for Subnet ID	Host ID (3 bits Shorter)
10010010 10101000	000	00000 00000111

Observe that when we *borrow* bits from the host ID for the subnet ID, the original subnet mask is no longer correct. As shown in table below, the original subnet mask has binary 0's matching up with the bits in the new Subnet ID. Since binary 0's in the subnet mask indicate the Host ID field, the newly created *Subnet ID* field still appears to belong to the original Host ID field.

	Network ID	3 Bits Borrowed for Subnet ID	Host ID (3 Bits Shorter)
IP Address:	10010010 10101000	000	00000 00000111
Original Subnet Mask:	11111111 11111111	000 (0 bits here make subnet ID appear to be part of host ID)	00000 00000000

To eliminate confusion over what bits still belong to the original Host ID field and what bits belong to the new Subnet ID field, we must *extend* the binary 1's in the original *Subnet Mask* with enough 1 bits to match the size of the newly created *Subnet ID* field (and correspondingly *reduce* the number of 0's which originally identified the Host ID in the Subnet Mask by the same amount). The new subnet mask is called a *custom subnet mask*. After this adjustment, the total number of bits in the *custom subnet mask* will still be 32, but the number of binary 1's will have increased by the size of the subnet ID, and the number of binary 0's will have decreased accordingly. This operation is illustrated in table below:

	Network ID	Bits Borrowed for Subnet ID	Shortened Host ID
IP Address:	10010010 10101000	000	00000 00000111
Original Subnet Mask:	11111111 11111111	000	00000 00000000
Custom Subnet Mask	11111111 11111111	111 (1 bits here indicate field belongs to network ID)	00000 00000000

7.13.4 Subnetting Process

An important issue when *borrowing* bits from the host ID to create the subnet ID is to accurately determine the following information:

1. How many subnets are needed

2. How many bits must be *borrowed* from the host ID field for the new subnet ID field to accommodate the required number of subnets
3. What is the largest number of hosts that will ever be on a given subnet
4. How many bits must be retained in the host ID field to accommodate the maximum number of hosts needed

These queries make it clear that careful planning should be performed *before* the subnetting process. Once the pre-planning is over, the subnetting process involves the following steps:

1. Determine how many subnets are needed
2. Determine the maximum number of hosts that will be on any given subnet
3. Determine how many bits to borrow from the host ID field for the subnet ID field
4. Determine how many bits must remain in the host ID field (and therefore cannot be borrowed for the subnet ID)
5. Determine how many bits are in the original network ID and host ID fields
6. Check to ensure that the number of bits to be *borrowed* from the host ID does not exceed the number of bits to be retained for the host ID (i.e., check that the subnetting problem is solvable)
7. Set an optimal length for the subnet ID field, including room for future growth
8. Create a modified (*custom*) subnet mask for the network
9. Determine the valid subnet ID's for the network
10. Determine the valid ranges of IP addresses for each subnet on the network

7.13.5 An Example Subnetting Process

To get clear understanding of subnetting process, let us follow the *step-by-step* procedure.

1. Determine the required *number* of *subnets*

While estimating the number of subnets (let us denote it with S), it is required to consider not only current subnet needs, but also future growth. If there is any historical data available, use it as a guide to estimate how many subnets will be needed next year, two years from now, three, etc. In the subsequent steps, assume that $S = 5$.

2. Determine the maximum number of hosts that will be on any given subnet

In TCP/IP, a *host* is any device that attaches to the network via a network interface. The count should reflect the largest number of network interfaces that will ever be on a given subnet. Remember to include not only network interfaces for computers, but also any network interfaces in printers, routers, or any other networked devices. Some computers may have more than one NIC, in which case each NIC is counted separately. Let us denote it with H.

As with step 1, remember to plan for growth. Use historical data if available, but also look for upcoming changes that could lead to significant growth not reflected in the historical data. In the steps that follow, assume that $H = 50$.

3. Estimate how many bits to borrow from the host ID field for the subnet ID field

This step calculates the number of bits needed in the IP address for the subnet ID's. Let us denote it with s. That means, it finds the smallest integer s such that $2^s - 2 \geq S$.

As the following table describes, with s bits for the subnet ID, we can address 2^s different subnets. However, a subnet ID is not allowed to be either all 0's (which according to TCP/IP standards always means the *current subnet* and therefore cannot be used as a subnet ID for an actual subnet), or all 1's (which according to TCP/IP standards is always a *broadcast* address and therefore cannot be used as a subnet ID for an actual subnet). Hence with s bits for the subnet ID, the effective number of addressable subnets is $2^s - 2$, as shown in table below.

s = Number of bits for subnet ID	$2^s - 2$ = Number of addressable subnets	Valid subnet addresses (all 0's or all 1's are invalid and are shown crossed out)
1 (produces no valid addresses)	$2^1 - 2 = 2 - 2 = 0$	~~0~~ ~~1~~
2	$2^2 - 2 = 4 - 2 = 2$	~~00~~ 01 10 ~~11~~
3	$2^3 - 2 = 8 - 2 = 6$	~~000~~ 001 010 011 100 101 110 ~~111~~

Calculating *s* is easier if we rewrite the inequality $2^s - 2 \geq S$ as $2^s \geq S + 2$. If you are comfortable with the entries in table, you can quickly find the smallest s such that $2^s \geq S + 2$. For example, if S = 5, the value of s is 3. Similarly, with S = 7, the value of s is 4.

4. Determine how many bits must remain in the host ID field (and therefore cannot be borrowed for the subnet ID)

This step calculates the number of bits h needed in the IP address for the host ID's, and is similar to step 3. Let us denote that number with h. That means, it find the smallest integer h such that $2^h - 2 > H$.

In fact, the TCP/IP standards state that a host ID cannot be all 0's, since a 0 host ID always refers to the *current host* (and so can never be used as the address for a particular host), or all 1's, since all 1's indicates a *broadcast* address (and so can never be used for the address of a particular host). Hence the formula for finding the number of bits needed for the host ID's is exactly parallel to that used to calculate the number of bits needed for the subnet ID's. Similar to step 3, we look for the smallest integer h such that $2^h - 2 \geq H$. For example, if H = 50, the value of h is 6. Similarly, with H = 30, the value of h is 5.

5. Determine how many bits are in the original network ID and host ID fields

This step determines the total number of host ID bits in the *standard* subnet mask for assigned address class. Let us call the number of host ID bits with letter T. Table below shows the standard number of Host ID bits for each of the three major address classes, A, B, and C. To find the *address class* of a network ID, look at the first octet in dotted-decimal notation.

Once we know the address class, it is easy to determine the number of host ID bits from the table. For example, if we have been officially assigned a Class B address, T = 16; if we have been officially assigned a Class C address, T = 8; etc.

Address Class	Starting Octet for Network ID (in decimal)	Network ID Bits in Standard Subnet Mask	Host ID Bits in Standard Subnet Mask (T)
A	1 – 126	8	24
B	128 – 191	16	16

| C | 192 - 223 | 24 | 8 |

For example, assume the official network ID is 146.168.0.0. From the table, this is a Class B address (since 146 is between 128 and 191) and the number of host ID bits in the standard subnet mask is T = 16.

6. Check to ensure that the number of bits to be *borrowed* from the host ID does not exceed the number of bits to be retained for the host ID

If s + h > T, then we need more host ID bits than are available for official address class. We cannot meet subnetting requirements. That means the problem is not solvable using assigned address class. In this case; officially assigned Network ID requires so many bits in the IP address that there are not enough bits left over to satisfy your needs for subnet ID's and host ID's. In short, subnetting requirements S and H when taken together are too large for assigned address class.

We will either have to reduce the values of S and/or H, or apply for an official network ID that requires fewer network ID bits and leaves more host ID bits (i.e., change from class C to class B, or from class B to class A). If s + h > T, start over again at step 1 after changing requirements.

In our example, T = 16, s = 3, and h = 6. Hence s + h = 3 + 6 = 9, which is *not* greater than T = 16. Hence we can proceed to the next step.

7. Set an optimal length for the subnet ID field, including room for future growth

If s + h = T, skip the next step (step 8). We have exactly enough bits for the desired subnetting. Skip step 8 and go on to step 9. In our example, s + h = 3 + 6 = 9 and T = 16, so we must carry out step 8.

8. If s + h < T, then we have T – s – h extra bits to distribute between s and h in a manner that best provides for unanticipated future growth. Calculate r as r = T – s – h, the number of bits that we can deploy either for extra subnet ID bits and/or for extra host ID bits, then increase s and/or h accordingly.

We have r bits to distribute between s and h. Increase s and/or h until we have used up all r bits (at which point T = s + h, as in step 7).

Since we are more likely to run out of subnets before we run out of host ID's on any given subnet, it is probably safer to make sure that s is comfortably large before increasing h. Assume that at the beginning of step 8, T = 16, s = 7, and h = 6. We then have T – s – h = 16 – 7 – 6 = 3 bits to distribute between s and h. Since it is probably a safer hedge to increase s, you might give 2 of the 3 *extra* bits to s (making s = 9), and give 1 of the 3 extra bits to h (making h = 7). If done correctly, the new values of s and h will sum to T (9 + 7 = 16).

In the example we have been following from previous steps, r = T – s – h = 16 – 3 – 6 = 7 bits to distribute between s and h. We will increase s by 1 (making the new value of s = 4), and increase h by 6 (making the new value of h = 12). Since it is often more important to increase s than to increase h, we should carefully question our decision to increase s by only one. Let us assume that we have a very high degree of confidence in our original estimate for S, but are less sure of our original estimate for H. Hence we (perhaps atypically) decide to favor h over s in this step.

9. Determine the custom subnet mask for network

Start with the default (standard) subnet mask for your address class as shown in below: We will extend the network ID portion of the default subnet mask by replacing its leftmost zero octet (shown bolded in the table) with a new value.

Address Class	Default Subnet Mask	Leftmost Zero Octet
A	255.0.0.0	255.**0**.0.0
B	255.255.0.0	255.255.**0**.0
C	255.255.255.0	255.255.255.**0**

Calculate the new value for the leftmost zero octet in the standard subnet mask as:

$$256 - 2^{8-s}$$

For example, if the adjusted value of s is 4, we calculate $256 - 2^{8-4} = 256 - 2^4 = 256 - 16 = 240$. This value will replace the leftmost zero octet in the default subnet mask for our network class, thus forming the custom subnet mask. Since in Step 5 we determined that our network ID was Class B, our default subnet mask from table is 255.255.**0**.0. Replace the leftmost zero octet (shown in bold) with the value 240 to obtain the *custom subnet mask* 255.255.240.0.

10. Determine the Valid Network ID's for the New Subnets

The next step is to determine the network (and subnetwork) ID's for the new subnets. Start by identifying the leftmost 0 octet in the *original* network ID for network. This is the octet that corresponds to the leftmost 0 octet in the standard subnet mask (i.e., the octet shown bolded in table). For the original subnet mask in our example, it would be the *third* octet from the left (shown bolded): 146.168.0.0. For a Class A network, this will always be the second octet (as in 13.0.0.0), for a class B network, this will always be the third octet (as in 146.168.0.0), and for a Class C network, this will always be the fourth octet (as in 193.200.17.0).

Note this particular octet will always have all 0's in the extended subnet ID area (the area *borrowed* from the original host ID), and so is *not* a valid subnetwork ID (recall that a zero value is not permitted for either a network or subnetwork ID).

To obtain the first valid subnetwork ID, add 2^{8-s} to the leftmost 0 octet (as identified above) in the *original* network address. Now add 2^{8-s} to the same octet in the first subnetwork ID to get the second subnetwork ID, add 2^{8-s} to the same octet in the second to get the third, etc. Continue in this fashion until we have obtained $2^s - 2$ subnetwork ID's, or until we reach the value of your custom subnet mask. Note that the custom subnet mask value itself is not a valid network ID because the subnet ID is all 1's (the reserved broadcast address).

In our example, the original network ID is 146.168.**0**.0 (the leftmost zero octet is shown bolded), the updated value of s is 4, and $2^{8-s} = 2^{8-4} = 2^4 = 16$. We expect $2^s - 2 = 2^4 - 2 = 16 - 2 = 14$ subnets, which we find as follows:

The first network ID is obtained by adding 2^{8-s} (i.e., 16) to the leftmost 0 octet in the original network address, forming the first network ID, i.e., add 16 to the third octet (shown bolded) in 146.168.**0**.0 to yield

146.168.**16**.0 (first valid subnet ID)

The second subnet ID is obtained by adding 2^{8-s} (16) to the same octet in the first valid subnet ID (shown bolded above), i.e., add 16 to the third octet (shown bolded) in 146.168.**16**.0 to yield

146.168.**32**.0

To form the third network ID, again add 2^{8-s} (16) to the same octet in the second valid subnet ID (shown bolded above), i.e., add 16 to the bolded octet in 146.168.**32**.0 to yield

146.168.**48**.0

Repeat this procedure until you have obtained the expected 14 subnetwork addresses (or until you reach the custom subnet mask from Step 9). The results are shown in table below:

Original Network ID (Not a valid subnetwork address)	146.168.**0**.0
Network ID for Subnet 1	146.168.**16**.0
Network ID for Subnet 2	146.168.**32**.0
Network ID for Subnet 3	146.168.**48**.0
Network ID for Subnet 4	146.168.**64**.0
Network ID for Subnet 5	146.168.**80**.0
Network ID for Subnet 6	146.168.**96**.0
Network ID for Subnet 7	146.168.**112**.0
Network ID for Subnet 8	146.168.**128**.0
Network ID for Subnet 9	146.168.**144**.0
Network ID for Subnet 10	146.168.**160**.0
Network ID for Subnet 11	146.168.**176**.0
Network ID for Subnet 12	146.168.**192**.0
Network ID for Subnet 13	146.168.**208**.0
Network ID for Subnet 14	146.168.**224**.0
Custom Subnet Mask value (Not a valid subnetwork address)	146.168.**240**.0

11. Determine the Valid IP Addresses for Each Subnet

The final step in subnetting is to determine the valid IP addresses for each new subnetwork. To generate the valid IP addresses for a given subnetwork, start with that subnetworks network address. Add 1 to the rightmost octet in the subnet address to obtain the first valid IP address on that subnet. In our example:

Network ID of first subnet:	146.168.16.**0**
First valid IP address on that subnet:	146.168.16.**1**

Continue to add 1 to the rightmost octet until one of the following three conditions occurs:

1. The octet that you are incrementing reaches 255. When incrementing the value 255, instead of adding 1 (to get 256), roll the 255 back to 0 and add 1 to the next octet to the left. This operation is similar to a *carry* in ordinary decimal addition. For example, assume you have just added 1 to 146.168.16.**254** to obtain 146.168.16.**255**. The next step would *not* be to add 1 again to obtain 146.168.16.**256** (which is not a valid IP address). Instead, roll the 255 back to 0 and add 1 to the next octet to the left (the 16), yielding 146.168.**17.0**. From this point, continue to increment as before to obtain additional IP addresses for the current subnet.
2. While incrementing, you get to the point where another increment would reach one less than the network ID for the next subnet. In this case, you have listed all the valid IP addresses for the current subnet, and you must move on to the next subnet (by starting with its network ID and repeatedly incrementing the rightmost octet by 1).
3. We reach a total of $2^h - 2$ IP addresses for a given subnet. This is equivalent to condition 2 above, and in fact is just another way of looking at the same situation. As in condition 2, you have listed all the valid IP addresses for the current subnet. Move on to the next subnet by starting with its network ID and repeatedly incrementing by 1.

Repeat this process for all subnetworks to obtain a complete list of valid IP addresses for each subnet.

In our example, we start with 146.168.16.0, the network ID for the first subnet. Add 1 to the rightmost octet to obtain the first valid IP address for this subnet, namely 146.168.16.1. Again, add 1 to the rightmost octet to obtain the second valid IP address for this subnet, namely 146.168.16.2. Continue in this fashion until reaching 146.168.16.254, which after incrementing yields an IP address of 146.168.16.255. Note that this *is* a valid IP address on the subnet. The next valid IP address is found by rolling the 255 back to 0 and incrementing the next octet to the left, yielding 146.168.17.0.

Continue incrementing until reaching 146.168.17.255, which is followed by 146.168.18.0. Again, the process repeats until we hit 146.168.18.255, which is followed by 146.168.19.0. This process will continue all the way to 146.168.30.255, which is followed by 146.168.31.0. We continue to increment until reaching 146.168.31.254. We are now at the point where yet another increment would yield one less than the next subnet's network ID (i.e., if we were to carry out one more increment we would be at 146.168.31.255, which if it were itself incremented would yield the subnet ID for the next subnet, 146.168.32.0).

At this point we have a complete list of all valid IP addresses for the first subnet. We would then have to repeat the entire process for the second subnet, etc. table summarizes the IP addresses for the first subnet:

IP Addresses for Subnet 1 (Network Address 146.168.16.0)
146.168.16.1 to 146.168.16.255
146.168.17.0 to 146.168.17.255
146.168.18.0 to 146.168.18.255
146.168.19.0 to 146.168.19.255
146.168.20.0 to 146.168.20.255
146.168.21.0 to 146.168.21.255
...
146.168.30.0 to 146.168.30.255
146.168.31.0 to 146.168.31.254

Do not be confused by the fact that some valid IP addresses end in 0 or 255. This happens normally when subnetting, and the rules about not having network, subnetwork, or host ID's equal to all 0's or all 1's are not necessarily violated just because an *octet* is equal to all 0's or all 1's. The rules place restrictions on the values of network, subnetwork, and host ID's, *not* on the values of octets. To understand this, consider the IP address 146.168.17.0 from table and analyze it according to the custom subnet mask for our example network, 255.255.240.0.

	Standard Network ID Part of IP Address	Bits Borrowed from Host ID to form Subnet ID Part of IP Address	Shortened Host ID Part of IP Address
IP Address 146.168.17.0	10010010 10101000	0001	0001 00000000
Custom Subnet Mask 255.255.240.0	11111111 11111111	1111	0000 00000000

Notice that although the rightmost octet of the Host ID consists of all zero bits, the full Host ID is a total of 12 bits and is *not* all 0's (the sole one bit is shown bolded).

For a second example, consider the IP address 146.168.21.255 from table. Although the last octet is 255 (eight 1's in binary), the following analysis shows that the full host ID is *not* all 1 bits (the two zero bits in the host ID are shown bolded):

	Standard Network ID Part of IP Address	Bits Borrowed from Host ID to form Subnet ID Part of IP Address	Shortened Host ID Part of IP Address
IP Address	10010010	0001	**0101** 11111111

146.168.21.255	10101000		
Custom Subnet Mask 255.255.240.0	11111111 11111111	1111	0000 00000000

7.13.6 A Class C Example Subnetting Process

Suppose an ISP assigns a Class C network address of 193.200.35.0 to an organization (call it CareerMonk, Inc., or just *CMonk*). We will walk through the 11 steps presented above in order to subnet this Class C network.

1. Assume that CMonk currently needs 2 subnets, with practically no likelihood of adding other subnets in the future. Therefore, we set S at 2.
2. Also, assume that CMonk currently needs at most 25 hosts on any subnet. In the future, subnet size is not expected to pass 30 hosts. Hence, we set H at 30.
3. To find the smallest integer s such that $2^s - 2 \geq S$, we first rewrite the inequality as $2^s \geq S + 2$. Since S = 2, this becomes $2^s \geq 2 + 2$ or $2^s \geq 4$.
4. To find the smallest integer h such that $2^h - 2 \geq H$, we first rewrite the inequality as $2^h \geq H + 2$. Since H = 30, this becomes $2^h \geq 30 + 2$ or $2^h \geq 32$.
5. CMonk's assigned network address is 193.200.35.0, which begins with 193. Hence CMonk has a Class C network address for which T is 8.
6. Now we can calculate s + h = 2 + 5 = 7, which does not exceed the value of T (T = 8). Hence we have a solvable subnetting problem and can proceed to step 7.
7. Since s + h = 2 + 5 = 7 which is not equal to 8 (the value of T), we must carry out step 8.
8. Since s + h = 2 + 5 = 7 is less than T = 8, we have r = T – s – h = 8 – 2 – 5 = 1 bit left over to increase the value of either s or h. Since in general CMonk is more likely to run short of subnets rather than hosts on a subnet, we allocate the extra bit to s, incrementing s so that now s = 3. Note that now s + h = 3 + 5 = 8 = T.
9. To determine the custom subnet mask for CMonk's network, we start with the standard (default) subnet mask for Class C (CMonk's network class), which is 255.255.255.0. We will replace the leftmost zero octet in the original subnet mask (i.e., the 0 in 255.255.255.**0**), with a new octet that will extend the subnetwork ID into the host ID. Calculate the new value for the original leftmost zero octet as $256 - 2^{8-s}$, which is $256 - 2^{8-3}$ or $256 - 2^5$ or $256 - 32$ or 224. Hence the custom subnet mask for CMonk's network is 255.255.255.224.
10. Now we determine the valid network ID's for the new subnets by identifying the leftmost 0 octet in the original network ID assigned by the ISP. Since this network ID is 193.200.35.**0**, the leftmost 0 octet (the only 0 octet) is also the rightmost 0 octet (shown in bold). We now add $2^{8-s} = 2^{8-3} = 2^5 = 32$ to this 0 octet to get the new value for the octet in the first subnet ID: 32 + 0 = 32. Thus the network ID for the first subnet is

193.200.35.**32**

We continue adding 2^{8-s} to this octet until we either reach the value of the custom subnet mask (255.255.255.224) or until we have network addresses for $2^s - 2$ subnets (these two conditions are equivalent and so will occur at the same time). In our case, $2^s - 2 = 2^3 - 2 = 8 - 2 = 6$ subnets, so we continue adding 2^{8-s} five more times (for a total of six times) as shown below:

Original Network ID (not a valid subnet address since subnet ID is all 0's)	193.200.35.**0**
Address for subnet 1	193.200.35.**32**

Address for subnet 2	193.200.35.**64**
Address for subnet 3	193.200.35.**96**
Address for subnet 4	193.200.35.**128**
Address for subnet 5	193.200.35.**160**
Address for subnet 6	193.200.35.**192**
Custom Subnet Mask (not a valid subnet address since subnet ID is all 1's)	193.200.35.**224**

11. To determine the valid IP addresses for each subnet, we begin with the network ID for the subnet. Let us start with the first subnet whose address is 193.200.35.32. To find the first IP address on the subnet, we add 1 to the rightmost octet of the subnet address: 32 + 1 = 33. Thus the first IP address on subnet 1 is

> **193.200.35.33**

We will continue incrementing until we reach 255, or until the next increment would reach two less than the next subnet address, or until we have generated 2^h – 2 IP addresses (these last two conditions are equivalent and will always occur at the same time). Since in our case h = 5, we can expect $2^5 - 2 = 32 - 2 = 30$ IP addresses per subnet. The valid IP addresses for subnet 1 are shown in the following table:

Subnet 1 Address #	IP Address
1	193.200.35.33
2	193.200.35.34
3	193.200.35.35
4	193.200.35.36
5	193.200.35.37
6	193.200.35.38
7	193.200.35.39
8	193.200.35.40
9	193.200.35.41
10	193.200.35.42
11	193.200.35.43
12	193.200.35.44
13	193.200.35.45
14	193.200.35.46
15	193.200.35.47
16	193.200.35.48
17	193.200.35.49
18	193.200.35.50
19	193.200.35.51
20	193.200.35.52
21	193.200.35.53
22	193.200.35.54
23	193.200.35.55
24	193.200.35.56
25	193.200.35.57
26	193.200.35.58
27	193.200.35.59
28	193.200.35.60
29	193.200.35.61
30	193.200.35.62

Note that if we increment the last octet of the 30th IP address (table), we get 63, which is one less than the network ID for the next subnet. Hence 193.200.35.62 is indeed the final IP address on subnet 1. The IP addresses for the remaining 5 subnets can be found in a similar manner.

7.14 Supernetting and Classless Inter-Domain Routing [CIDR]

As the Internet evolved and become more familiar to people it become clear that Internet would face several serious scaling problems. These included:

1. *Exhaustion* of *class* B *addresses*: The problem of class B exhaustion has occurred simply because the class B address space is too large for many middle-sized organizations and the class C address space is rarely enough to fulfil networking requirements. By the time problems started only the half of the total number of 16384 class B addresses are available. There is a total of about 2 million class C addresses and a small number of them were already allocated by service providers. A class B network would consist of a maximum of 65534 hosts and a class C network consist with a maximum of only 254 hosts. The classification of internet networks is not practicable since very few organizations have tens of thousands of hosts, but almost all organizations have lots more hosts than 254.

2. *Routing information overload*: The routing tables in the Internet have been growing as fast as the Internet and the router technology specifically and computer technology in general has not been able to keep pace. In December 1990 there were 2190 routes and 2 years later there were over 8500 routes. In July 1995 there were over 29,000 routes, which require approximately 10 MB in a router with a single peer.

3. *Eventual exhaustion of IP addresses*

7.14.1 What is Classless Inter-Domain Routing [CIDR]?

Classless Inter-Domain Routing (CIDR) attempts to solve first two problems by defining a method to slow the growth of routing tables and reduce the need to allocate new IP network numbers. It does not attempt to solve the *third* problem. CIDR was developed in the 1990s as an alternative scheme for routing network traffic across the Internet.

CIDR *removes* concept of class A, B, C, network addresses (hence the name *classless*) and uses the concept of network-prefix. It uses network-prefix instead of 3 bits of IP address to determine the dividing point between network-ID and host-ID. CIDR supports arbitrary sized networks (dashed line between network ID and host ID indicates that it will be varying) instead of standard 8, 16, or 24 bit network numbers.

Network ID	Host ID

CIDR is also called *supernetting* as it allows multiple subnets to be grouped together for network routing.

Supernetting is the term used when multiple network addresses of the same Class are combined into blocks. The process of creating *supernets* is called as *route aggregation*. If the IP networks are *contiguous*, we may be able to use a *supernet*. If the IP networks are *not contiguous*, we may not be able to use a *supernet*.

When *subnetting*, we borrowed bits from the host ID portion, which increases the number of bits used for the network ID portion. With *ssupernetting* we do exactly the opposite, meaning we take the bits from the network ID portion and give them to the host ID portion.

Network ID	Supernet ID [Bits borrowed from Network ID]	Host ID

Supernetting concept is most often used to combine class C addresses. To combine two class C networks, the third octet of the first address must be evenly divisible by 2. If we would like to supernet 8 networks, the mask would be 255.255.248.0 and the third octet of the first address needs to be evenly divisible by 8.

For example, 198.41.15.0 and 198.41.16.0 could not be combined into a supernet, but we would be able to combine 198.41.18.0 and 198.41.19.0 into a supernet.

The subnet mask for a class C IP network is normally 255.255.255.0. To use a supernet, the number of bits used for the subnet mask is *reduced*. For example, by using a 23 bit mask (255.255.254.0 -- 23 bits for the network ID of the IP network, and 9 bits for the host ID), we effectively create a single IP network with 512 addresses.

7.14.2 Classful vs. Classless Subnetting

To subnet an IP address for a network; we have two options: classful and classless.

7.14.2.1 Classful subnetting

Classful subnetting is the simplest method. It tends to be the most wasteful because it uses more addresses than are necessary. In classful subnetting we use the same subnet mask (default) for each subnet, and all the subnets have the same number of addresses in them. Classless addressing allows us to use different subnet masks and create subnets tailored to the number of users in each group.

In classful addressing, all IP addresses have a network and host portion. In classful addressing, the network portion ends on one of the separating dots in the address (on an octet boundary). Classful addressing divides an IP address into the *network* and *host* portions along octet boundaries.

In the classful addressing system all the IP addresses that are available are divided into the five classes A,B,C,D and E, in which class A,B and C address are frequently used because class D is for Multicast and is rarely used and class E is reserved and is not currently used.

Class A:

```
0 1 2 3 4 5 6 7 0 1 2 3 4 5 6 7 0 1 2 3 4 5 6 7 0 1 2 3 4 5 6 7
┌─┬─────────────────────────┬───────────────────────────────────┐
│0│                         │                                   │
└─┴─────────────────────────┴───────────────────────────────────┘
     Network ID                         IIost ID
     (8-Bits)                           (24-Bits)
```

Class B:

```
0 1 2 3 4 5 6 7 0 1 2 3 4 5 6 7 0 1 2 3 4 5 6 7 0 1 2 3 4 5 6 7
┌─┬─┬─────────────────────────────┬───────────────────────────────┐
│1│0│                             │                               │
└─┴─┴─────────────────────────────┴───────────────────────────────┘
         Network ID                         Host ID
         (16-Bits)                          (16-Bits)
```

Class C:

```
0 1 2 3 4 5 6 7 0 1 2 3 4 5 6 7 0 1 2 3 4 5 6 7 0 1 2 3 4 5 6 7
┌─┬─┬─┬───────────────────────────────────────────┬───────────────┐
│1│1│0│                                           │               │
└─┴─┴─┴───────────────────────────────────────────┴───────────────┘
              Network ID                               Host ID
              (24-Bits)                                (8-Bits)
```

Class D:

| 0 | 1 | 2 | 3 | 4 | 5 | 6 | 7 | 0 | 1 | 2 | 3 | 4 | 5 | 6 | 7 | 0 | 1 | 2 | 3 | 4 | 5 | 6 | 7 | 0 | 1 | 2 | 3 | 4 | 5 | 6 | 7 |

| 1 | 1 | 1 | 0 | | | | | | | | | | | | | | | | | | | | | | | | | | | | |

Multicast Group ID (28 bits)

Class E:

| 0 | 1 | 2 | 3 | 4 | 5 | 6 | 7 | 0 | 1 | 2 | 3 | 4 | 5 | 6 | 7 | 0 | 1 | 2 | 3 | 4 | 5 | 6 | 7 | 0 | 1 | 2 | 3 | 4 | 5 | 6 | 7 |

| 1 | 1 | 1 | 1 | 0 | | | | | | | | | | | | | | | | | | | | | | | | | | | |

Reserved for future use (27 bits)

Each of the IP address belongs to a particular class that's why they are *classful* addresses. Earlier this addressing system did not have any name, but when classless addressing system came into existence then it is named as *classful* addressing system. The main disadvantage of classful addressing is that it limited the flexibility and number of addresses that can be assigned to any device.

7.14.2.2 Classless subnetting

Classless addressing uses a variable number of bits for the network and host portions of the address.

It treats the IP address as a 32 bit stream of ones and zeroes, where the boundary between network and host portions can fall anywhere between bit 0 and bit 31. Classless addressing system is also called CIDR (Classless Inter-Domain Routing). Classless addressing is a way to allocate and specify the Internet addresses used in inter-domain routing more flexibly than with the original system of Internet Protocol (IP) address classes.

Below are the example routing protocols being in use.

Classful Routing Protocols	Classless Routing Protocols
RIP Version 1	RIP Version 2
[Routing Information Protocol Version-1]	[Routing Information Protocol Version-2]
IGRP [Interior Gateway Routing Protocol]	EIGRP [Enhanced Interior Gateway Routing Protocol]
EGP [Exterior Gateway Protocol]	OSPF [Open Shortest Path First]
BGP3 [Border Gateway Protocol 3]	IS-IS [Intermediate System to Intermediate System]
	BGP4 [Border Gateway Protocol 4]

Note: For details on these protocols, refer IP Routing chapter.

7.14.3 Why Use CIDR?

Before CIDR technology was developed, Internet routers managed network traffic based on the class of IP addresses. In this system, the value of an IP address determines its subnetwork for the purposes of routing. CIDR is an *alternative* to traditional IP subnetting that organizes IP addresses into subnetworks independent of the value of the addresses themselves.

7.14.4 CIDR Notation

CIDR specifies an IP address range using a combination of an IP address and its associated network mask. CIDR notation uses the following format:

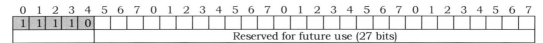

$$xxx.xxx.xxx.xxx/n$$

where *n* is the number of (leftmost) 1 bits in the network mask.

The above notation is called *CIDR block* or *CIDR mask*. For example, 192.168.12.0/23 applies the network mask 255.255.254.0 to the 192.168 network, starting at 192.168.12.0. This notation represents the address range 192.168.12.0 to 192.168.13.255.

Compared to traditional class-based networking, 192.168.12.0/23 represents an *aggregation* of the two Class C subnets 192.168.12.0 and 192.168.13.0 each having a subnet mask of 255.255.255.0. That means,

$$192.168.12.0/23 = 192.168.12.0/24 + 192.168.13.0/24$$

Additionally, CIDR supports Internet address allocation and message routing independent of the traditional class of a given IP address range. For example, 10.4.12.0/22 represents the address range 10.4.12.0 to 10.4.15.255 (network mask 255.255.252.0). This allocates the equivalent of four Class C networks within the much larger Class A space.

7.14.5 Examples of Supernetting Process

Let's take a look at a typical networking problem for a medium-size organization. In this example, CareerMonk needs IP addresses for 1,000 hosts. There are no class A or class B addresses available, so CareerMonk applies for and receives a block of four class C addresses. CareerMonk can now employ these addresses using one of the following three options:

- The address block may be used to create four separate class C networks.
- The addresses may be subnetted to create more than four subnetworks.
- The addresses may be combined to create one supernetwork.

Figure shows IP addresses within the following class C subnetworks:

1. 192.168.64.0
2. 192.168.65.0
3. 192.168.66.0
4. 192.168.67.0

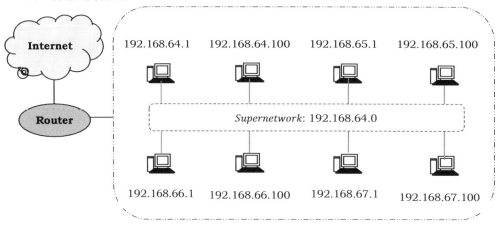

The addresses pass the prerequisites. They are consecutive and the third octet of the first address is divisible by 2 (64 mod 2 = 0). These four smaller networks have been combined to create the 192.168.64.0 supernetwork. Class C supernetworks will usually assume the address of the subnetwork with the lowest IP address, in this case, 192.168.64.0.

7.14.5.1 Creating the Supernetwork Mask

Before we discuss creating a supernetwork mask, we should cover some points about the regular class C subnet mask. The default subnet mask for class C networks is 255.255.255.0. In binary format, this is written as:

11111111.11111111.11111111.00000000

The 1's in the mask represent the network ID of the address, and the 0's represent the host ID. When a subnetwork is created, we first create the subnet mask by changing some of the 0's in the host ID section to 1's.

For example, to create four separate subnetworks from one class C network, we would simply add two bits ($2^2 = 4$) to the default subnet mask. Example below shows how this is done.

Original subnet mask:

Network ID	Host ID
11111111.11111111.11111111.	00000000

New subnet mask:

Network ID	Host ID
11111111.11111111.11111111.11	000000

With this new subnet mask, the network has been transformed from one class C network with up to 254 hosts to four separate subnetworks, each with 64 ($2^6 = 64$) hosts. However, because the IP with all host bits set to 0 and the IP address with all bits set to 1 are both reserved, there is actually a limit of 62 hosts for each subnetwork.

To create a *supernetwork*, we reverse the procedure. Remember, what we are trying to do here is create room to combine networks by creating space for a larger number of hosts. To achieve this, we start with the default subnet mask of 255.255.255.0 (for Class C) and use some of the bits reserved for the network ID to identify the host ID. Example below shows we would create a new supernetwork by combining four separate subnetworks.

New supernet mask:

11111111.11111111.11111100.00000000

Original subnet mask:

11111111.11111111.11111111.00000000

This new supernetwork can now accommodate 2^{10}, or 1024 hosts. If the first network ID is 192.168.64.0, the next three network IDs will be 192.168.65.0, 192.168.66.0, and 192.168.67.0.

7.14.5.2 Processing of Incoming Packets

Now, when the router for the new supernet receives an incoming packet, the new supernet mask is applied to the destination IP address, and a bitwise AND operation is performed. If the result of this bitwise AND operation and the lowest network IP address are the same, the router knows that the packet must be routed to a host on the supernet.

A bitwise AND operation compares an IP address to a subnet mask to discover which network an IP packet will be routed to.

7.14.5.3 Bitwise AND operations

The principle behind bitwise AND operation is simple: If the first operand has a value of 1 (true) and the second operand has a value of 1 (true), then the value returned is true. In all other cases, the value returned is false (0).

Let's look at an example of this procedure. If a packet arrives at the router with the destination address 192.168.64.48, the supernet mask 255.255.252.0 is applied to the destination address.

```
          11000000.10101000.01000000.00110000   (Destination IP address)
   AND    11111111.11111111.11111100.00000000   (Supernet mask)
 Returns  11000000.10101000.01000000.00000000
```

In this example, the value returned by the bitwise AND operation is 192.168.64.0. This is the lowest available IP address on the supernet. This router then uses this information to forward the incoming packet to a host on the newly created supernetwork.

Let us walk through *another example* of supernetting: Two class C network numbers of 198.41.78.0 and 198.41.79.0. The addresses pass the prerequisites. They are consecutive and the third octet of the first address is divisible by 2 (78 mod 2 = 0). To further understand what is being done, let's look at the addresses in binary.

The third octet of the first address (78) is 01001110. The second (79) is 01001111. The binaries are the same except for the last bit of the address (the 24th bit of the IP address). The 78 network is supernet 0 and the 79 network is supernet 1.

The subnet mask for this example supernet is 23 bits, or 255.255.254.0. All devices on the network must be using this subnet mask. Any device that is not using this subnet mask would be unreachable.

The broadcast address for all devices on the example supernet is 198.41.79.255. Most modern devices don't require us to fill out the broadcast address, as it can be deduced from the IP address and the subnet mask. The broadcast address is used as a special destination signifying all hosts on the network.

As with any IP network, the first number in the range (.0 in a class C) has special significance, and can't be assigned to any hosts on the network. The first number in the range is called network ID. Conversely, the last or highest number in the range (.255 in a class C) is called the *broadcast* address, and also can't be used by any host on the network.

Because of these unique addresses, it would probably be wise not to use the 198.41.78.255 and 198.41.79.0 addresses (in the above example), even though these should be perfectly legal addresses for hosts when using a supernet.

7.15 Variable Length Subnet Mask [VLSM]

Using *classical subnetting* the subnets are of *same size*. Using *VLSM* the subnets can be of *variable* size. Using this concept, we can subnet an already subnetted network into multiple subnets with variable subnet masks and then allocate them within original network.

VLSM allows an organization to use more than one subnet mask within the same network address space. Implementing VLSM is often called *subnetting a subnet*. It can be used to maximize addressing efficiency.

7.15.1 VLSM Allocation Strategy

The following procedure shows how VLSM can be used in to allocate IP addresses.

1. Sort the subnet requirements by size with largest subnet first.
2. For each required subnet, allocate address space out of the smallest available subnet.

7.15.2 Examples of VLSM Process

As an example, assume that an administrator have 192.168.1.0/24 network. The suffix /24 (pronounced as *slash* 24) indicates the number of bits used for network ID.

Also, assume that organization is having three different departments with different number of hosts. *Technical* department has 100 computers, *Sales* department has 50 computers, *Accounts* has 25 computers and *HR* (Human Resources) has 5 computers. In CIDR, the subnets are of fixed size. Using the same methodology the administrator cannot fulfill all the requirements of the network.

The following procedure shows how VLSM can be used in order to allocate department-wise IP addresses as mentioned in the example.

1. Make a list of Subnets possible.

Subnet Mask	Slash Notation	Hosts per Subnet
2.55.255.255.0	/24	254
2.55.255.255.128	/25	126
2.55.255.255.192	/26	62
2.55.255.255.224	/27	30
2.55.255.255.240	/28	14
2.55.255.255.248	/29	6
2.55.255.255.252	/20	2

2. Sort the requirements of IPs in descending order (Highest to Lowest).

Technical	100
Sales	50
Accounts	25
HR (Human Resources)	5

3. Allocate the highest range of IPs to the highest requirement, so let us assign 192.168.1.0/25 (255.255.255.128) to Technical department. This IP subnet with network ID 192.168.1.0 has 126 valid host IP addresses which satisfy the requirement of Technical department. The *subnet mask* used for this subnet has 10000000 as the last octet.

4. Allocate the next highest range, so let's assign 192.168.1.128 /26 (255.255.255.192) to Sales department. This IP subnet with network ID 192.168.1.128 has 62 valid host IP Addresses which can be easily assigned to all Sales departments' PCs. The subnet mask used has 11000000 in the last octet.

5. Allocate the next highest range, i.e. Accounts. The requirement of 25 IPs can be fulfilled with 192.168.1.192/27 (255.255.255.224) IP subnet, which contains 30 valid host IPs. The network number of Accounts department will be 192.168.1.192. The last octet of subnet mask is 11100000.

6. Allocate next highest range to HR department. The HR department contains only 5 computers. The subnet 192.168.1.224/29 with mask 255.255.255.248 has exactly 6 valid host IP addresses. So this can be assigned to HR department. The last octet of subnet mask will contain 11111000.

By using VLSM, the administrators can subnet the IP subnet such a way that least number of IP addresses is wasted. Even after assigning IPs to every department, the administrator, in this example, still left with plenty of IP addresses which was not possible if he/she has used CIDR.

7.16 IPv6 [Internet Protocol Version 6]

Around 1992, the IETF (Internet Engineering Task Force) became aware of a global shortage of IPv4 addresses, and technical problems in deploying new protocols due to limitations imposed by IPv4.

7.16.1 What is IPv6?

IPv6 stands for Internet Protocol version 6. Similar to IPv4, it works on Network Layer (Layer-3). IPv6 is the *next generation* protocol designed by the IETF to replace the current version IPv4.

Most of today's Internet uses IPv4, which is now nearly twenty years old. Due to the enormous growth there is shortage of IPv4 addresses, which are needed by all new machines added to the Internet.

IPv6 fixes a number of problems in IPv4, such as the limited number of available IPv4 addresses. It also adds many improvements to IPv4 in areas such as routing and network auto configuration. IPv6 is expected to gradually replace IPv4.

7.16.2 Why new IP Version?

IPv4 was designed in early 80's and did not get any major change afterward. At the time of its design, Internet was limited only to a few Universities for their research and to Department of Defense, USA. IPv4 is 32 bits long which offers around 4,294,967,296 (2^{32}) addresses. This address space was considered more than enough that time. Given below are major points which played key role in birth of IPv6:

- Internet has grown exponentially and the address space allowed by IPv4 is saturating. There is a need of protocol which can satisfy the need of future Internet addresses which are expected to grow in an unexpected manner.
- IPv4 on its own does not provide any *security* feature which is vulnerable as data on Internet, which is a public domain, is never safe. Data has to be encrypted with some other security application before being sent on Internet.
- Quality of service (QoS): Quality of Service (QoS) is available in IPv4 and it depends on the 8 bits of the IPv4 Type of Service (TOS) field and the identification of the payload. IPv4 Type of Service (TOS) field has limited functionality and payload identification (uses a TCP or UDP port) is not possible when the IPv4 datagram packet payload is encrypted.

7.17 IPv6 Features

The new IP addressing is not designed to be backward compatible with IPv4. IPv6 is redesigned entirely. It has the following features.

7.17.1 Vast Address Space

In contrast to IPv4, IPv6 uses 4 times more bits (128 bits) to address a device on the Internet. This can provide 300,000,000,000,000,000,000,000,000,000,000,000,000 (approximately 3.4×1038) different combinations of addresses.

This address can accumulate the aggressive requirement of address allotment for almost everything in this world. According to a research estimate, 1564 addresses can be allocated to every square meter of this earth.

7.17.2 Simplified Header

IPv6's header has been simplified by moving all unnecessary information and options (which are present in IPv4 header) to the end of the IPv6 header. IPv6 header is only twice as bigger than IPv4 providing the fact the IPv6 address is four times longer.

7.17.3 End-to-end Connectivity

Every system now has unique IP address and can traverse through the internet without using NAT (Network Address Translation). After IPv6 is fully implemented, every host can directly reach other host on the Internet.

7.17.4 Auto-configuration

IPv6 supports both stateful and stateless auto configuration mode of its host devices. This way absence of a DHCP server does not put stop inter segment communication.

7.17.5 Faster Forwarding/Routing

IPv6's simplified header puts all unnecessary information at the end of the header. All information in first part of the header is enough for a *router* to take routing decision. This makes routing decision as quickly as looking at the mandatory header.

7.17.6 IPSec [IP Security]

Network security is integrated into the design of the IPv6 architecture. Internet Protocol Security (IPsec) was originally developed for IPv6, but found optional deployment first in IPv4 (into which it was back-engineered).

The IPv6 specifications mandate IPsec implementation as a fundamental interoperability requirement.

7.17.7 No Broadcast

IPv6 does not have any Broadcast support. It uses multicast to communicate with multiple hosts.

7.17.8 Anycast Support

This is another characteristic of IPv6. IPv6 has introduced Anycast mode of packet routing. In this mode, multiple interfaces over the Internet are assigned same *anycast* IP address. Routers, while routing, sends the packet to the nearest destination.

7.17.9 Mobility

IPv6 was designed keeping mobility feature in mind. This feature enables hosts (such as mobile phone) to roam around in different geographical area and remain connected with same IP address.

IPv6 mobility feature takes advantage of auto IP configuration and Extension headers.

7.17.10 Enhanced Priority support

Where IPv4 used 6 bits DSCP (Differential Service Code Point) and 2 bits ECN (Explicit Congestion Notification) to provide Quality of Service (QoS) but it could only be used if the end-to-end devices support it, that is, the source and destination device and underlying network must support it.

In IPv6, *Traffic* class and *Flow* label are used to tell underlying routers how to efficiently process the packet and route it.

7.17.11 Smooth Transition

Large IP address scheme in IPv6 enables to allocate devices with globally unique IP addresses. This assures that mechanism to save IP addresses such as NAT is not required. So devices can send/receive data between each other, for example VoIP and/or any streaming media can be used much efficiently. Other fact is, the header is less loaded so routers can make forwarding decision and forward them as quickly as they arrive.

7.17.12 Extensibility

One of the major advantages of IPv6 header is that it is extensible to add more information in the option part. IPv4 provides only 40-bytes for options whereas options in IPv6 can be as much as the size of IPv6 packet itself.

7.18 Hexadecimal Number System

Before introducing IPv6 address format, we shall look into Hexadecimal Number System. The hexadecimal (base 16) number system operates the same way as the decimal (base 10) number system, except it is *based* on sixteen instead of ten. There are 16 *Hexadecimal* digits. They are the same as the decimal digits up to 9, but then there are the letters A, B, C, D, E and F in place of the decimal numbers 10 to 15:

Hex	Binary	Octal	Decimal
0	0	0	0
1	1	1	1
2	10	2	2
3	11	3	3
4	100	4	4
5	101	5	5
6	110	6	6
7	111	7	7
8	1000	10	8
9	1001	11	9
A	1010	12	10
B	1011	13	11
C	1100	14	12
D	1101	15	13
E	1110	16	14
F	1111	17	15

7.19 IPv6 Addressing Notation [IPv6 Address Structure]

The most dramatic change from IPv4 to IPv6 is the length of network addresses. There are three ways to represent IPv6 addresses in text strings.

1. IPv6 addresses are 128 bits long but are normally written as eight groups of 4 hexadecimal digits each. For example, below is a valid IPv6 address.

> 3ffe:6a88:85a3:08d3:1319:8a2e:0370:7344
> ABCD:EF01:2345:6789:ABCD:EF01:2345:6789
> 2001:DB8:0:0:8:800:200C:417A

2. Some types of addresses contain long sequences of zeros. To further simplify the representation of IPv6 addresses, a contiguous sequence of 16-bit blocks set to 0 in the colon hexadecimal format can be compressed to ::, called *double-colon*. That means if a 4 digit group is 0000, it may be omitted.

For example,

> 3ffe:6a88:85a3:0000:1319:8a2e:0370:7344

can be written as:

> 3ffe:6a88:85a3::1319:8a2e:0370:7344

Following this rule, if more than two consecutive colons result from this omission, they may be reduced to two colons, as long as there is only one group of more than two consecutive colons. The below list of IPv6 addresses are valid.

> 2001:2353:0000:0000:0000:0000:1428:57ab
> 2001:2353:0000:0000:0000::1428:57ab
> 2001:2353:0:0:0:0:1428:57ab
> 2001:2353:0::0:1428:57ab
> 2001:2353::1428:57ab

Similarly, the address FE80:0:0:0:2AA:FF:FE9A:4CA2 can be compressed to FE80::2AA:FF:FE9A:4CA2 and the address FF02:0:0:0:0:0:0:2 can be compressed to FF02::2.

Examples:

IPv6 Address	Compressed Representation
2001:DB8:0:0:8:800:200C:417A	2001:DB8::8:800:200C:417A
FF01:0:0:0:0:0:0:101	FF01::101
0:0:0:0:0:0:0:1	::1
0:0:0:0:0:0:0:0	::

Zero compression can only be used to compress a single contiguous series of 16-bit blocks expressed in colon hexadecimal notation. We cannot use zero compression to include part of a 16-bit block. For example, we cannot express FF02:30:0:0:0:0:0:5 as FF02:3::5. The correct representation is FF02:30::5.

To determine how many 0 bits are represented by the ::, we can count the number of blocks in the compressed address, subtract this number from 8, and then multiply the result by 16. For example, in the address FF02::2, there are two blocks (the *FF02* block and the 2 block.) The number of bits expressed by the :: is 96 (96 = (8 − 2)×16). Zero compression can only be used once in a given address. Otherwise, we could not determine the number of 0 bits represented by each instance of ::.

Also leading zeros in all groups can be omitted, thus

> 2001:2353:02de::0e13

is the same thing as

> 2001:2353:2de::e13

3. An alternative form that is sometimes more convenient when dealing with a mixed environment of IPv4 and IPv6 nodes is x:x:x:x:x:x:d.d.d.d, where the x's are the hexadecimal values of the six high-order 16-bit pieces of the address, and the d's are the decimal values of the four low-order 8-bit pieces of the address (standard IPv4 representation). Examples:

> 0:0:0:0:0:0:13.1.68.3
> 0:0:0:0:0:FFFF:129.144.52.38

or in compressed form:

> ::13.1.68.3
> ::FFFF:129.144.52.38

7.19.1 IPv6 Alternative Formats

7.19.1.1 IPv4–mapped IPv6 Address

These addresses are used to embed IPv4 addresses in an IPv6 address. This type of address is used to represent IPv4 nodes as IPv6 addresses. It allows IPv6 applications to communicate directly with IPv4 applications. For example, 0:0:0:0:0:ffff:192.1.56.10 and ::ffff:192.1.56.10/96 (shortened format).

7.19.1.2 IPv4–compatible IPv6 Address

This type of address is used for *tunnelling*. It allows IPv6 nodes to communicate across an IPv4 infrastructure. For example, 0:0:0:0:0:0:192.1.56.10 and ::192.1.56.10/96 (shortened format). The following figure shows the configuration of two nodes on separate subnets using IPv4-compatible addresses to communicate across an IPv4 router.

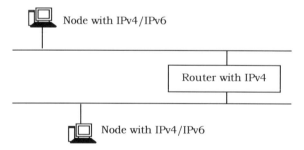

IPv4-compatible addresses, derived from IPv4 public addresses, provide a method for connecting IPv6 hosts or sites over the existing IPv4 Internet infrastructure. IPv6 traffic, when used with IPv4-compatible addresses, does not require the addition of IPv6 routers. Its traffic is encapsulated with an IPv4 header.

7.20 IPv6 Prefixes

The prefix is the part of the address that indicates the bits that have fixed values or are the bits of the network identifier. The high-order bits of an IPv6 address specify the network and the rest specify particular addresses in that network. So, all the addresses in a network have the same first n bits. Those first n bits are called the *prefix*. We use /n to denote a prefix n bits long. For example, this is how we write down the network containing all addresses that begin with the 32 bits 2001:0db8:

> 2001:db8::/32

We use this notation whenever we are talking about a whole network, and don't care about the individual addresses in it. The above can also be read as 'all addresses where the first 32 bits are 00100000000000010000110110111000'. But hex is easier to read. If we are talking about a specific address, the prefix sometimes doesn't matter, because we have specified every bit in the address. So this is an address – no need to specify a prefix:

> 2001:db8::6:1

However, addresses are often written with their proper prefix included, like this:

> 2001:db8::6:1/64

The /64 tells us that this is an address with a 64 bit prefix. Writing addresses this way can result in confusion, so always make sure it is clear from the context if you have written an address with a prefix length.

Note: IPv4 implementations commonly use a dotted decimal representation of the network prefix known as the subnet mask. A subnet mask is not used for IPv6. Only the prefix length notation is supported.

7.21 IPv6 Subnets

We can divide any network up into smaller networks (called subnets) by defining more bits after the prefix. For example, 2001:db8::/32 is a /32 network again, and a /48 subnet of it:

> 2001:db8::/32 is a /32 network
> 2001:db8:0001::/48 is /48 network

Note that the difference is that a further 16 bits have been specified (remember each hex digit represents 4 bits). The original 32 plus the additional 16 make 48 in all. 16 bits can express 65536 different values, so there are 65536 distinct /48 networks in any /32 network:

> 2001:db8:0000::/48
> 2001:db8:0001::/48
> [...]
> 2001:db8:FFFE::/48
> 2001:db8:FFFF::/48

7.21.1 Subnets and networks

The difference between a network and a subnet is really one of convenience and usage; there is no technical difference. An ISP's /32 network is a subnet of some larger network, just as all those /48 networks are subnets of a /32.

Having bigger the prefix means the smaller is the network (contains fewer hosts). A /96 is a network the size of the entire existing IPv4 Internet, because it has 32 bits' worth of host addresses in it (96 + 32 = 128). A /120 has only 8 bits left for hosts, so it's the same size as an IPv4 class C subnet: 256 addresses.

7.21.2 Calculating subnets

How many /64 subnets are there in a /48? To work this out, just deduct the size of the network (in bits) from the size of the subnet, and raise 2 to that power. 64 - 48 = 16, and 2^{16} is 65536, so there are 65536 /64 subnets in a /48 network.

How many /64 networks are there in a /60? Again, deduct the size of the network from the size of the subnet. 64 - 60 = 4, and 2^3 is 16, so there are 16 /64 subnets in a /60.

It works for any size prefix and subnet. How many /93 subnets are there in a /91 network? 93 - 91 = 2, so there are four subnets. How many /12 subnets in a /9 network? 12 - 9 = 3, so there are eight subnets. And so on.

7.22 IPv6 Addressing Types

In IPv4, we have the unicast, broadcast and multicast addresses. In IPv6, we have unicast, multicast and anycast. With IPv6 the broadcast addresses are not used anymore, because they are replaced with multicast addressing.

7.22.1 Unicast

The unicast Network topology involves one to one association with the source and destination.

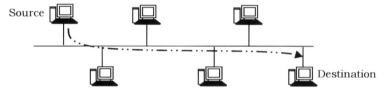

A unicast address identifies a single interface within the scope of the type of unicast address. With the appropriate unicast routing topology, packets addressed to a unicast address are delivered to a single interface. To accommodate load-balancing systems, RFC 2373 allows for multiple interfaces to use the same address as long as they appear as a single interface to the IPv6 implementation on the host.

7.22.2 Multicast

A multicast address identifies multiple interfaces. With the appropriate multicast routing topology, packets addressed to a multicast address are delivered to all interfaces that are identified by the address.

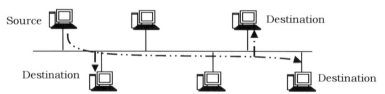

In multicast there is a one to many associations between the source and the destination.

7.22.3 Anycast

Anycast is a type of network topology just like its predecessors, unicast, multicast and broadcast.

Anycast is the new player on the block. Anycast is based on IPv6 and the communication typically happens between a single sender and several nearest receivers in a group. Anycast technology is a system that increases both the speed and security of the Internet naming system and, consequently, the entire Internet by creating many copies of the some data in multiple locations across the world.

An anycast address identifies multiple interfaces. With the appropriate routing topology, packets addressed to an anycast address are delivered to a single interface, the nearest interface that is identified by the address. The *nearest* interface is defined as being closest in terms of routing distance. A multicast address is used for *one-to-many* communication, with delivery to multiple interfaces. An anycast address is used for *one-to-one-of-many* communication, with delivery to a single interface.

The routing tables on the router are updated using IPv6 to give the packets the path to the nearest destination, making the transfer much faster. IPv6 determines automatically as to which destination end points are closest, and sends them the packets like a Unicast. The destination then carries on relays the packets to its nearest hosts until all destinations are addressed.

Many of the content delivery networks (CDNs) use this feature to increase the speed.

7.23 Unicast IPv6 addresses

This is similar to the unicast address in IPv4 – a single address identifying a single interface. The following types of addresses are unicast IPv6 addresses:

1. Aggregatable global unicast addresses
2. Link-local addresses
3. Site-local addresses
4. Special addresses

7.23.1 Aggregatable global unicast addresses

Aggregate global IPv6 addresses are the equivalent of *public* IPv4 addresses. Aggregate global addresses can be routed publicly on the Internet. Any device or site that wishes to traverse the Internet must be uniquely identified with an aggregate global address.

7.23.2 Link-local addresses

Link-local IPv6 addresses are used only on a single link (subnet). Any packet that contains a link-local source or destination address is never routed to another link. Every IPv6-enabled interface on a host (or router) is assigned a link-local address. This address can be manually assigned, or auto-configured.

7.23.3 Site-local addresses

Site-local IPv6 addresses are the equivalent of *private* IPv4 addresses. Site-local addresses can be routed within a site or organization, but cannot be globally routed on the Internet. Multiple private subnets within a *site* are allowed.

7.23.4 Special addresses

The first field of a reserved or special IPv6 address will always begin 00xx. 1/256th of the available IPv6 address space is reserved. Various reserved addresses exist, including the following.

7.23.4.1 Unspecified Address

The unspecified address (0:0:0:0:0:0:0:0 or ::) is used only to indicate the absence of an address. It is equivalent to the IPv4 unspecified address of 0.0.0.0. The unspecified address is typically used as a source address for packets that are attempting to verify the uniqueness of a tentative address. The unspecified address is never assigned to an interface or used as a destination address.

7.23.4.2 Loopback address

The loopback address (0:0:0:0:0:0:0:1 or ::1) is used to identify a loopback interface. Similar to IPv4, it enables a node to send packets to itself. It is equivalent to the IPv4 loopback address of 127.0.0.1. Packets addressed to the loopback address are never sent on a link or forwarded by an IPv6 router.

7.24 Multicast IPv6 addresses

Multicast IPv6 addresses are the equivalent of IPv4 multicast addresses. Interfaces can belong to one or more multicast groups. Interfaces will accept a multicast packet only if they belong to that group. Multicasting provides a much more efficient mechanism than broadcasting, which requires that every host on a link accept and process each broadcast packet.

7.25 Anycast IPv6 addresses

Anycast addresses identify a group of interfaces on multiple hosts. So, multiple hosts are configured with an identical address. Packets sent to an anycast address are sent to the nearest (i.e., least number of hops) host. Anycasts are indistinguishable from any other IPv6 unicast address.

Practical applications of anycast addressing are a bit difficult to see through clearly. One possible application would be a server farm providing an identical service or function, in which case anycast addressing would allow clients to connect to the *nearest* server.

7.26 IPv6 Datagram Header Format

IPv6 has a much simpler packet header compared with IPv4. It by includes only the information needed for forwarding the IP datagram. IPv4 has a fixed length header of size 40 bytes. Fixed length IPv6 header allows the routers to process the IPv6 datagram packets more efficiently.

7.26.1 IPv6 Datagram Packet Structure

The following figure shows the structure of IPv6 datagram packet.

IPv6 Header	Extension Header	Upper Layer Protocol Data

IPv6 datagram packet header can be divided in to three parts:

1) IPv6 datagram packet header
2) Extension Header
3) Upper Layer Protocol Data

IPv6 datagram packet has also extension headers of varying lengths. If extension headers are present in IPv6 datagram packet, a *Next Header* field in the IPv6 header points the first extension header. Each extension header contains another Next Header field, pointing the next extension header. The last IPv6 datagram packet extension header points the upper layer protocol header (Transmission Control Protocol (TCP), User Datagram Protocol (UDP), or Internet Control Message Protocol

(ICMPv6)). There is no *options* field in IPv6 datagram packet header, which was present in IPv4 header.

7.26.2 IPv6 Datagram Packet Header

00 To 03	04 To 07	08 to 15	16 to 23	24 To 31
Version	Priority		Flow Label	
Payload Length			Next Header	Hop Limit
Source IPv6 Address				
Destination IPv6 Address				

7.26.2.1 Version

The size of the *Version* field is 4 bits. The Version field shows the version of IP and is set to 6 for IPv6.

7.26.2.2 Traffic Class

The size of *Traffic Class* field is 8 bits. Traffic Class field is similar to the IPv4 Type of Service (ToS) field. The Traffic Class field indicates the IPv6 packet's class or priority.

7.26.2.3 Flow Label

The size of *Flow Label* field is 20 bits. The *Flow Label* field provide additional support for real-time datagram delivery and quality of service features. The purpose of Flow Label field is to indicate that this packet belongs to a specific sequence of packets between a source and destination and can be used to prioritized delivery of packets for services like voice.

7.26.2.4 Payload Length

The size of the *Payload Length* field is 16 bits. The Payload Length field shows the length of the IPv6 payload, including the extension headers and the upper layer protocol data

7.26.2.5 Next Header

The size of the *Next Header* field is 8 bits. The Next Header field shows either the type of the first extension (if any extension header is available) or the protocol in the upper layer such as TCP, UDP, or ICMPv6.

7.26.2.6 Hop Limit

The size of the *Hop Limit* field is 8 bits The Hop Limit field shows the maximum number of routers the IPv6 packet can travel. This Hop Limit field is similar to IPv4 Time to Live (TTL) field.

This field is typically used by distance vector routing protocols, like Routing Information Protocol (RIP) to prevent layer 3 loops (routing loops).

7.26.2.7 Source Address

The size of the *Source Address* field is 128 bits. The Source Address field shows the IPv6 address of the source of the packet.

7.26.2.8 Destination Address

The size of the *Destination Address* field is 128 bits. The Destination Address field shows the IPv6 address of the destination of the packet.

Problems and Questions with Answers

Question 1:   An IP packet has arrived with the first 8 bits as shown:

0100 0010

The destination discards the packet. Can you guess the reason?

Answer: There is an error in this packet. The 4 left-most bits (0100) show the version, which is correct. The next 4 bits (0010) show the header length, which means ($2 \times 4 = 8$), which is wrong. The minimum number of bytes in the header must be 20. The packet has been corrupted in transmission.

An IP packet has arrived with the first few hexadecimal digits as shown below:

4 5 00 0028 00010000 01 02..........

Question 2:   How many hops can this packet travel before being dropped? The data belong to what upper layer protocol?

Answer: To find the time-to-live field, we should skip 8 bytes (16 hexadecimal digits). The time-to-live field is the *ninth* byte, which is 01. This means the packet can travel only one hop. The protocol field is the next byte (02), which means that the upper layer protocol is IGMP.

Question 3:   Suppose an IP datagram containing 256 bytes of data is divided into two fragments, each containing 128 bytes of data. Fill in the table for the header fields for the two fragments. The header length is measured in units of 4 bytes.

Header field	Datagram	Fragment 1	Fragment 2
Header length	5		
Total length	276		
Identification	3		
MF	0		
Fragment offset	0		

Answer: An IP datagram of 256 bytes of data is divided into two fragments, each containing 128 bytes of data. The header length is 20 bytes but measured in units of 4 bytes. Total length is the sum of header and data bytes. Identification number is the same in all fragments to indicate that they belong to the same original datagram.

MF flag is always 1 for all fragments except for the last fragment. Fragment offset indicates where the fragment's data belongs in the original datagram measured in units of 8 bytes.

Header field	Datagram	Fragment 1	Fragment 2
Header length	5	5	5
Total length	276	148	148
Identification	3	3	3
MF	0	1	0
Fragment offset	0	0	16

Question 4:   When the destination router receives an IP fragment, it keeps the fragment in a buffer until the other fragments are 1 received. Does the router know how much buffer space to allocate for the reassembly of the IP datagram?

Answer: Usually the destination host does not know the required amount of buffers when an IP fragment arrives, unless it is the last fragment (identified by MF=0).

Question 5: Suppose that the destination router receives 3 out of 4 fragments, but the reassembly timer expires and the router discards these fragments. Sometime later, the last fourth fragment arrives. How does the router treat this fragment?

Answer: When the reassembly timer expires, the router will discard the 3 fragments received so far. When the last fourth fragment arrives, the router will treat the fragment as a new datagram and start another reassembly timer. When this timer expires later, this fourth fragment will be discarded also.

Question 6: Why is the IP header checksum recalculated at every router?

Answer: The IP header checksum is recalculated at every router because some of the IP header fields will change, such as the TTL and (if fragmentation occurs) total length, MF flag, and fragment offset.

Question 7: Suppose a TCP message that contains 2048 bytes of data and 20 bytes of TCP header is passed to IP for delivery across two networks of the Internet. The first network uses 14 byte headers and has a MTU of 1024 bytes; the second uses 8-byte headers with an MTU of 512 bytes. Each network's MTU gives the size of the largest IP datagram that can be carried in a link-layer frame. Give the sizes and offsets of the sequence of fragments delivered to the network layer at the destination host. Assume all IP headers are 20 bytes. Note: the IP requires that fragmentation should always happen on 8-byte boundaries.

Answer: Consider the first network. Packets have room for 1024 - 20 = 1004 bytes of IP-level data; because 1004 is not a multiple of 8 each fragment can contain at most 8× $\lfloor 1004/8 \rfloor$ = 1000 bytes. We need to transfer 2048 + 20 = 2068 bytes of such data. This would be fragmented into fragments of size 1000, 1000, and 68.

Fragment	Size	Offset
1	1000	0
2	1000	1000
3	68	2000

Over the second network, the 68-byte packet would be unfragmented but the 1000-data-byte packet would be fragmented as follows. The IP header is 20 bytes, leaving 512-20 = 492 bytes for IP-level data. Again rounding down to the nearest multiple of 8, each fragment could contain 488 bytes of IP-level data. 1000 bytes of such data would become fragments with data sizes 488, 488, and 24.

Fragment	Size	Offset
1	488	0
2	488	488
3	24	976
4	488	1000
5	488	1488
6	24	1976
7	68	2000

Question 8: An organization has a class C network 196.10.10 and wants to form subnets for five departments, which host as follows:

1. 55 hosts
2. 50 hosts
3. 45 hosts

4.   25 hosts
5.   20 hosts

There are 195 hosts in all. Design a possible arrangement of subnets to make each department in a different subnet. For each subnet, give subnet mask and range of IP addresses.

Answer: Class C network: 196.10.10

Department	Subnet Mask	Subnet ID	Range of Address
1: 55 Hosts	255.255.255.192	196.10.10.0	196.10.10.0 – 196.10.10.63
2: 50 Hosts	255.255.255.192	196.10.10.64	196.10.10.64 – 196.10.10.127
3: 45 Hosts	255.255.255.192	196.10.10.128	196.10.10.128 – 196.10.10.191
4: 25 Hosts	255.255.255.224	196.10.10.192	196.10.10.192 – 196.10.10.223
5: 20 Hosts	255.255.255.224	196.10.10.224	196.10.10.224 – 196.10.10.255

Question 9:   Node A needs to send a payload (data) size of 1400 bytes (octets) to node B across the networks as shown below. Data needs to be fragmented because the payload is too big to fit the smallest MTU size (620 bytes) in one of the network.

Show the Data Length, More Flag, and Fragment Offset values in each of the resulting fragments.

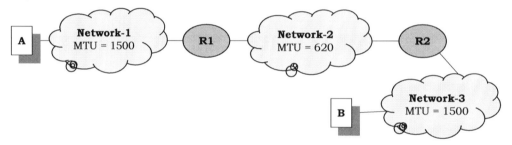

Answer:
1.   Determine that actual data size for transmission: The dada needs to be transmitted is 1400 octets. We will assume that the size of the IP header is 20 octets.

$$
\begin{aligned}
\text{MTU Frame} &= \text{Header} + \text{Data} \\
620 &= 20 + \text{Data} \\
\text{Data} &= 620\text{-}20 = 600
\end{aligned}
$$

So, each frame can carry an IP datagram with a 20-octet header and **600** data octets. Note the 600 is divisible by 8. If not, we need to take the nearest multiple of 8 in the Data part of the MTU frame. The reason is that the fragment offset must be a multiple of 8-byte.

2.   The number of fragments needed to transmit 1400 data octets:

Define
n = number of fragments
d = total number of data to be transmitted at the network layer = IP data = 1400
m = maximum data size for the network = 600

$$
n = \left\lceil \frac{d}{m} \right\rceil = \left\lceil \frac{1400}{600} \right\rceil = \lceil 2.33 \rceil = 3
$$

So, we need 3 fragments, 2 fragments of 600 octets and the last one is (1400 – 2 × 600) = 200 octets.

Please note that the fragment offset is in 8-byte unit.

Fragment Number	Data Length	Fragment Offset (8-byte)	More Flag
1	600	0	1
2	600	600/8 = 75	1
3	200	75+75 = 150	0

Both *Fragment Offset* and *More Flag* are used for reassembly of fragments. The *More Flag* is one except for the last fragment. The *More Flag* for the last fragment is 0 to indicate no more fragments.

Question 10: Convert the IP address whose hexadecimal representation is C0A8000D.

Answer: 11000000.10101000.00000000.00001101 = 192.168.0.13.

Question 11: What does this address tell you about its location?

Answer: This is a private IP address and the host is located in a private network. ie, it is not directly reachable from the public internet.

Question 12: An IP datagram reassembly algorithm uses a timer to avoid having a lost fragment tie up buffers indefinitely. Suppose that a datagram was fragmented into three fragments, and the first two arrive, but the timer goes off before the last fragment arrives. The algorithm has discarded the first two fragments, now it has – finally – the missing third fragment. What does it do with it?

Answer: As far as the receiver is concerned, this is a part of a new datagram, since no other parts of it are known. It will therefore be queued up until the rest show up. If they do not, this third fragment will time out too.

Question 13: In the IPv4 addressing format, the number of networks allowed under Class C addresses is
A) 2^{14} B) 2^7 C) 2^{21} D) 2^{24}

Answer: C. For class C address, size of network field is 24 bits. But first 3 bits are fixed as 110; hence total number of networks possible is 2^{21}.

Question 14: In an IPv4 datagram, the M bit is 0, the value of HLEN is 10, the value of total length is 400 and the fragment offset value is 300. The position of the datagram, the sequence numbers of the first and the last bytes of the payload, respectively are
A) Last fragment, 2400 and 2789   B) First fragment, 2400 and 2759
C) Last fragment, 2400 and 2759   D) Middle fragment, 300 and 689

Answer: C. Since M bit is 0, so there is no fragment after this fragment. Hence this fragment is the last fragment.

Now, HLEN defines the length of header in datagram. Since Hlen is 10, the size of header is 10 × 4 = 40 B.

Length of data = Total length – Header length = 400 – 40 = 360 B

Now, fragment offset of data in original datagram is measured in units of 8 B.

To find first Byte of this fragment,

$$\frac{First\ byte}{8} = fragment\ offset$$
$$First\ byte = 300 \times 8 = 2400\ B$$

And since length of data is 360 B. So, last byte on this datagram will be 2759.

Question 15: Suppose a company has obtained a block of IP space, in the form of 128.119.152.0/21. How many IP addresses have been allocated to this company? Now this company wants to build 4 subnets, each subnet having the same amount of IP addresses, and 4 subnets use up all allocated IP addresses. What are the 4 subnet address space? What is the subnet mask for each subnet?

Answer: The company has been allocated with 2^{32-21}= 2048 IP addresses.

The four subnets are: 128.119.152.0/23, 128.119.154.0/23, 128.119.156.0/23, 128.119.158.0/23. Each subnet contains 512 IP addresses. The subnet mask for each subnet is 255.255.254.0.

Question 16: Consider sending a 2400-byte datagram into a link that has an MTU of 700 bytes. Suppose the original datagram is stamped with the identification number 422. How many fragments are generated? What are the values in the various fields in the IP datagram(s) generated related to fragmentation?

Answer: The maximum size of data field in each fragment = 680 (because there are 20 bytes IP header). Thus the number of required fragments

$$\left\lceil \frac{2400 - 20}{680} \right\rceil = 4$$

Each fragment will have Identification number 422. Each fragment except the last one will be of size 700 bytes (including IP header). The last datagram will be of size 360 bytes (including IP header). The offsets of the 4 fragments will be 0, 85, 170, 255. Each of the first 3 fragments will have flag=1; the last fragment will have flag=0.

Question 17: Look at the 40byte dump of an IP packet containing a TCP segment below.

45 20 03 c5 78 06 00 00 34 06 ca 1f d1 55 ad 71 c0 a8 01 7e

00 50 9a 03 3e 64 e5 58 df d0 08 b3 80 18 00 de 00 02 00 00

Identify all the fields of the IP and TCP header.

Answer: IP header: IP version 4, Header Length: 20 bytes, ToS = 20, Total Length = 0x03c5 = 965 bytes, Identification = 0x7806, Flags = 0, Fragment offset = 0, TTL = 0x34 = 52, Proto = TCP, Header Checksum = 0xca1f, Source IP address = 209.85.173.113, Destination IP address = 192.168.1.126.

TCP header: src port = 80, destination port = 39427, sequence number =0x3e64e558, ack number = 0xdfd008b3, header length = 8*4 = 32bytes, unused = 0, flags : URG = 0, ACK = 1, PSH =1, RST =0, SYN = 0, FIN = 0, receive window = 0x000de, Internet checksum = 0x0002, urgent data pointer = 0.

Question 18: Consider a router that interconnects three subnets: Subnet 1, Subnet 2, and Subnet 3. Suppose all of the interfaces in each of these three subnets are required to have the prefix 223.1.17/24. Also suppose that Subnet 1 is required to support up to 63 interfaces, Subnet 2 is to support up to 95 interfaces, and Subnet 3 is to support up to 16 interfaces. Provide three network addresses (of the form a.b.c.d/x) that satisfy these constraints.

Answer: 223.1.17.0/26   223.1.17.128/25   223.1.17.192/28.

Question 19: Consider a subnet with prefix 128.119.40.128/26. Give an example of one IP address (of form xxx.xxx.xxx.xxx) that can be assigned to this network. Suppose an ISP owns the block of addresses of the form 128.119.40.64/26. Suppose it wants to create four subnets from this block, with each block having the same number of IP addresses. What are the prefixes (of form a.b.c.d/x) for the four subnets?

Answer: Any IP address in range 128.119.40.128 to 128.119.40.191.

Four equal size subnets: 128.119.40.64/28, 128.119.40.80/28, 128.119.40.96/28, 128.119.40.112/28.

Question 20: CareerMonk Inc., is assigned 4 blocks of 256 addresses from ISP, 207.16.204.[0-255], 207.16.205.[0-255],
207.16.206.[0-255] and 207.16.207.[0-255].
A) In class-based addressing, what is the class name for these addresses? What would be the subnet mask?
B) In this case, what corresponding network prefix(es) appear to routers outside of the ISP?
C) If instead your ISP uses classless interdomain-routing (CIDR) to assign addresses to Bears Inc., what are the masks and corresponding network prefix(es) that appear to routers outside of the ISP?

Answer:

A) It is using Class C addressing. Subnet Mask: 11111111 11111111 11111111 00000000.

B) 207.16.204.0/24, 207.16.205.0/24, 207.16.206.0/24, 207.16.207.0/24.

C) Mask: 11111111 11111111 11111100 00000000 (207.16.204.0/22).

Question 21: CIDR allocates IP addresses less efficiently than Classful Addressing. Is it true or false?

Answer: False. CIDR enables finer grain address allocation, thus improving address allocation efficiency over Classful Addressing.

Question 22: IP does not guarantee that all data will be delivered or that the data that are delivered will arrive in the proper order. Is it true or false?

Answer: True

Question 23: In IPv6 fragmentation may only be performed by routers along a packet's delivery path. Is it true or false?

Answer: False

Question 24: The principal feature of __ is that it can encrypt and/or authenticate all traffic at the IP level.
A) Datagram   B) Layer   C) Packet   D) subnet

Answer: A

Question 25: A next generation IP, known as __ , provides longer address fields and more functionality than the current IP.
A) IPv3   B) IPv4   C) IPv5   D) IPv6

Answer: D

Question 26: For virtually all protocols data are transferred in blocks called __ .
A) Datagrams   B) PDUs   C) Segments   D) NSAPs

Answer: B

Question 27: Which of the following is NOT an enhancement of IPv6 over IPv4?
A) Improved error recovery   B) Expanded address space
C) Address auto configuration   D) Support for resource allocation

Answer: A

Question 28: A network has been the address 160.10.184.0/21. How many hosts are available for this network?

Answer: 32 - 21 = 11 bits left for the host address where 2^{11} = 2048 (In fact it is 2046 as we cannot have a host with all zeroes or all ones.)

Question 29: For the previous question, what is an example IP address of a host on this network?

Answer: Lots of answers, one address could be 160.10.184.3.

Question 30: A host has been assigned the address 140.16.79.19/21. What is the netmask?

Answer: The netmask will mask off the leftmost 21 bits: 255.255.248.0

Question 31: For the previous question, what is the IP address of the network?

Answer: We AND the netmask of 255.255.248.0 with the IP address 140.16.79.19 which yields 140.16.72.0/21.

Question 32: Consider a router that connects three subnets: sub1, sub2 and sub3. Suppose all of the interfaces in each of these three subnets are required to have the prefix 223.1.17.0/24, and each subnet is required to support up to 60 interfaces. Provide three network addresses of the form $a.b.c.d/x$ (where 24 < x ≤ 32) that satisfies these constraints.

Answer: Use the leftmost 2 bits of the 4th octet for the network. The three networks could be (1) 223.1.17.64/26, (2) 223.1.17.128/26, and (3) 223.1.17.192/26. This leaves the right-most 6 bits for a host on the network where 26 > 60.

Question 33: Take a look at the figure representing the IPv4 header from the chapter. Why must the checksum for an IP header be recalculated at every hop?

Answer: Whenever a packet arrives at a router, the TTL (time-to-live) must be decremented. Because the header is altered, the checksum must be recalculated. Also, check traceroute section from Miscellaneous chapter.

Question 34: Take a look at the figure representing the IPv6 header from the chapter. Notice this does not include a checksum. Why does IPv6 choose not to have a checksum?

Answer: The primary reason had to do with performance: calculating and verifying a checksum takes computation time and thus can slow down the processing of a router. IPv6 chose to eliminate this field for these performance reasons.

However, IPv6 felt it could do so because checksums are also being determined both above at the transport layer as well as below at the link-layer (i.e. local area networks.)

Question 35: An organization has a class C network 196.10.10 and wants to form subnets for five departments, which host as follows:

Class A--55 hosts
Class B--50 hosts
Class C--45 hosts
Class D--25 hosts
Class E--20 hosts

There are 195 hosts in all. Design a possible arrangement of subnets to make each department in a different subnet. For each subnet, give subnet mask and range of IP addresses.

Answer: Class C network: 196.10.10

Department	Subnet Mask	Subnet ID	Range of Address
A: 55 Hosts	255.255.255.192	196.10.10.0	196.10.10.0 – 196.10.10.63
B: 50 Hosts	255.255.255.192	196.10.10.64	196.10.10.64 – 196.10.10.127
C: 45 Hosts	255.255.255.192	196.10.10.128	196.10.10.128 – 196.10.10.191
D: 25 Hosts	255.255.255.224	196.10.10.192	196.10.10.192 – 196.10.10.223
E: 20 Hosts	255.255.255.224	196.10.10.224	196.10.10.224 – 196.10.10.255

Question 36: We are given the assignment of setting subnet addresses for 4 buildings of a company. The number of Internet connected PCs in each building is given in the following table. Assume that the 131.155.192.0/19 address block is given to us for this purpose. Use the following table to show the addresses of the four subnets that we created.

Building	# of PCs	Subnet address (CIDR format)
1	2200	
2	1620	
3	550	
4	500	

Answer:

Building	# of PCs	Subnet address (CIDR format)
1	2200	131.155.192.0/20
2	1620	131.155.208.0/21
3	550	131.155.216.0/22
4	500	131.155.220.0/23

Question 37: The following is a forwarding table at router R, which uses Classless Interdomain Routing (CIDR).

Destination Network	Next Hop
139.179.222.0/25	R1
139.179.128.0/17	R2
139.179.120.0/21	R3
139.179.216.0/21	R4
139.179.0.0/16	R5

Suppose packets with the following destination IP addresses arrive at router R. Determine to what next hop each of these packets will be delivered (Give only one answer for each destination.)

I.   139.179.60.1
II.   139.179.226.4
III. 139.179.124.55
IV.   139.179.223.18
V.   139.179.127.222

Answer:

I.   139.179.60.1 → R5
II.   139.179.226.4 → R2
III. 139.179.124.55 → R3
IV.   139.179.223.18 → R4
V.   139.179.127.222 → R3

Question 38: Divide the network with CIDR prefix 139.179.0.0/17 into /20 subnetworks. Show each subnetwork in CIDR format.

Answer: Since we need to form /20 subnets from /17 network, it gives us 8 (20 − 17=3 bits and $2^3 = 8$) such /20 subnetworks.

$$
\left.\begin{array}{l}
139.179.0.0/20 \\
139.179.16.0/20 \\
139.179.32.0/20 \\
139.179.48.0/20 \\
139.179.64.0/20 \\
139.179.80.0/20 \\
139.179.96.0/20 \\
139.179.112.0/20
\end{array}\right\} 139.179.0.0/17
$$

Question 39: Suppose the following four subnetworks are aggregated into a single subnetwork: 139.179.192.0/20, 139.179.208.0/20, 139.179.224.0/20, 139.179.240.0/20. Find the CIDR prefix that should be used in order to advertise this aggregated subnetwork.

Answer:

$$
\left.\begin{array}{l}
139.179.192.0/20 \\
139.179.208.0/20 \\
139.179.224.0/20 \\
139.179.240.0/20
\end{array}\right\} 139.179.192.0/18
$$

Question 40: Which addresses are valid host addresses?
   A) 201.222.5.17   B) 201.222.5.18   C) 201.222.5.16
      D) 201.222.5.19   E) 201.222.5.31

Answer: A,B, and D. Subnet addresses in this situation are all in multiples of 8. In this example, 201.222.5.16 is the subnet, 201.22.5.31 is the broadcast address. The rest are valid host IDs on subnet 201.222.5.16.

Question 41: You are a network administrator and have been assigned the IP address of 201.222.5.0. You need to have 20 subnets with 5 hosts per subnet. What subnet mask will you use?
   A) 255.255.255.248   B) 255.255.255.128
   C) 255.255.255.192   D) 255.255.255.240

Answer: A. By borrowing 5 bits from the last octet, we can have 30 subnets. If we borrow 4 bits we could only have 14 subnets. The formula is $2^n - 2$. By borrowing 4 bits, we have $2^4 - 2 = 14$. By borrowing 5 bits, you have $2^5 - 2 = 30$. To get 20 subnets, we would need to borrow 5 bits and the subnet mask would be 255.255.255.248.

Question 42: You are given the IP address of 172.16.2.160 with a subnet mask of 255.255.0.0. What is the network address in binary?
   A) 10101100 00010000   B) 00000010 10100000
   C) 10101100 00000000   D) 11100000 11110000

Answer: A. To find the network address, convert the IP address to binary--10101100 00010000 00000010 10100000 and then AND it with the subnet mask 11111111 11111111 00000000 00000000.

The rest is 10101100 00010000 00000000 00000000, which is 172.16.0.0 in decimal. The first octet rule states that the class of an address can be determined by the numerical value of the first octet.

Question 43: Which addresses are incorrectly paired with their class?
   A) 128 to 191, Class B   B) 192 to 223 Class B
   C) 128 to 191, Class C   D) 192 to 223, Class C

Answer: B and C. Address classes are: 1 to 126, Class A; 128 to 191, Class B, 192 to 223, Class C; 224 to 239, Class D; and 240 to 255, Class E) The first octet rule states that the class of an address can be determined by the numerical value of the first octet.

Question 44: Which addresses are incorrectly paired with their class?

    A) 1 to 126, Class A   B) 128 to 191, Class A
    C) 1 to 126, Class B   D) 128 to 191, Class B

Answer: B and C.

Class A	1 to 126
Class B	128 to 191
Class C	192 to 223
Class D	224 to 239
Class E	240 to 255

The first octet rule states that the class of an address can be determined by the numerical value of the first octet.

Question 45: Which addresses are incorrectly paired with their class?

    A) 240 - 255, Class D   B) 240 - 255, Class E
    C) 224 - 239, Class D   D) 224 - 239, Class E

Answer: A and D.

Address classes are:

Class A	1 to 126
Class B	128 to 191
Class C	192 to 223
Class D	224 to 239
Class E	240 to 255

Question 46: Which IP Address Class is incorrectly paired with its range of network numbers?

    A) Class A addresses include 192.0.0.0 through 223.255.255.0
    B) Class A addresses include 1.0.0.0 through 126.0.0.0
    C) Class B addresses include 128.0.0.0 through 191.255.0.0
    D) Class C addresses include 192.0.0.0 through 223.255.255.0
    E) Class D addresses include 224.0.0.0 through 239.255.255.0

Answer: A

Class A addresses include 1.0.0.0 through 126.0.0.0
Class B addresses include 128.0.0.0 through 191.255.0.0
Class C addresses include 192.0.0.0 through 223.255.255.0
Class D addresses include 224.0.0.0 through 239.255.255.0

Question 47: Which IP Address Class can have 16 million subnets but support 254 hosts?

    A) Class C   B) Class A   C) Class B   D) Class D

Answer: A.

IP Address Class	Possible Subnets	Possible Hosts
A	254	16M
B	64K	64K
C	16M	254

Question 48: Which IP Address Class can have 64,000 subnets with 64,000 hosts per subnet?

    A) Class B   B) Class A   C) Class C   D) Class D

Answer: A.

IP Address Class	Possible Subnets	Possible Hosts
A	254	16M
B	64K	64K
C	16M	254

Question 49: Given the address 172.16.2.120 and the subnet mask of 255.255.255.0. How many hosts are available?
   A) 254   B) 510   C) 126   D) 16,372

Answer: A. 172.16.2 120 is a standard Class B address with a subnet mask that allows 254 hosts. You are a network administrator and have been assigned the IP address of 201.222.5.0. You need to have 20 subnets with 5 hosts per subnet. The subnet mask is 255.255.255.248.

Question 50: Which IP address can be assigned to an Internet interface?
   A) 10.180.48.224   B) 9.255.255.10
   C) 192.168.20.223   D) 172.16.200.18

Answer: B. The IP address which can be assigned to an Internet interface is a public IP address. Private IP address are found in the following ranges:

   • From 10.0.0.0 to 10.255.255.255
   • From 172.16.0.0 to 172.31.255.255
   • From 192.168.0.0 to 192.168.255.255

Also some special IP addresses (like the local loopback address 127.0.0.1, multicast addresses) can't be assigned to an Internet interface. In this question only answer B doesn't belong to the range of private IP address.

Question 51: What will happen if a private IP address is assigned to a public interface connected to an ISP?

   A) Addresses in a private range will be not routed on the Internet backbone.
   B) Only the ISP router will have the capability to access the public network.
   C) The NAT process will be used to translate this address in a valid IP address.
   D) Several automated methods will be necessary on the private network.
   E) A conflict of IP addresses happens, because other public routers can use the same range.

Answer: A

Question 52: When is it necessary to use a public IP address on a routing interface?

   A) Connect a router on a local network.
   B) Connect a router to another router.
   C) Allow distribution of routes between networks.
   D) Translate a private IP address.
   E) Connect a network to the Internet.

Answer: E

Question 53: Given the address 192.168.10.19/28, which of the following are valid host addresses on this subnet? (Choose two)
   A) 192.168.10.29   B) 192.168.10.16
   C) 192.168.10.17   D) 192.168.10.31
   E) 192.168.10.0

Answer: A and C. 192.168.10.19/28 belongs to 192.168.10.16 network with mask of 255.255.255.240. This offers 14 usable ip address range from 192.168.10.17 – 30. Use the cram table above if you are confused.

Question 54: Convert the following decimal IP address to binary.

130.85.65.38

Answer: 10000010.01010101.01000001 .00100110

Question 55: Given 130.85.0.0/20 as the IP address, answer the following questions. How many usable IP address do you have per subnet?

Answer: 4094

Question 56: For the Question 55, what is the total number of subnets you have?

Answer: 16

Question 57: For the Question 55, what is the broadcast address?

Answer: 130.85.15.255

Question 58: Given 130.85.0.0/23 as the IP address, answer the following questions. How many usable IP address do you have per subnet?

Answer: 510

Question 59: For the Question 58, what is the total number of subnets you have?

Answer: 128

Question 60: For the Question 58, what is the last usable address in this subnet?

Answer: 130.85.1.254

Question 61: Given 130.85.8.0/22 as the IP address, answer the following questions. How many usable IP address do you have per subnet?

Answer: 1022

Question 62: For the Question 61, what is the total number of subnets you have?

Answer: 64

Question 63: For the Question 61, what is the subnet mask?

Answer: 255.255.252.0

Question 64: For the Question 61, is IP address 130.85.12.231 in this subnet?

Answer: No

Question 65: Given 65.20.0.0/14 as the IP address, answer the following questions. How many usable IP address do you have per subnet?

Answer: 262142

Question 66: For the Question 65, what is the first usable address in this subnet?

Answer: 65.20.0.1

Question 67: For the Question 65, what is the broadcast address for this subnet?

Answer: 65.23.255.255

Question 68: For the Question 65, what is the subnet mask?

Answer: 255.252.0.0

Question 69: Given 130.85.28.32/27 as the IP address, answer the following questions. How many usable IP address do you have per subnet?

Answer: 30

Question 70: For the Question 69, what is the first usable address in this subnet?

Answer: 130.85.28.33

Question 71: For the Question 69, what is the broadcast address?

Answer: 130.85.28.63

Question 72: For the Question 69, is IP address 130.85.28.65 in this subnet?

Answer: No

Question 73: Given 68.32.20.8/29 as the IP address, answer the following questions. How many usable IP address do you have per subnet?

Answer: 6

Question 74: For the Question 73, what is the first usable address in this subnet?

Answer: 68.32.20.9

Question 75: For the Question 73, what is the subnet mask?

Answer: 255.255.255.248

Question 76: For the Question 73, what is the broadcast address?

Answer: 68.32.20.15

Question 77: For the Question 73, is IP address 68.32.20.13.16 in this subnet?

Answer: No

Question 78: Given 130.85.33.177/26 as the IP address, answer the following questions. What is the Network ID for this subnet?

Answer: 130.85.33.128

Question 79: For the Question 78, what is the first usable address in this subnet?

Answer: 130.85.33.129

Question 80: For the Question 78, what is the subnet mask?

Answer: 255.255.255.192

Question 81: For the Question 78, what is the broadcast address?

Answer: 130.85.33.191

Question 82: Given 130.85.68.33/18 as the IP address, answer the following questions. What is the Network ID for this subnet?

Answer: 130.85.64.0

Question 83: For the Question 82, what is the first usable address in this subnet?

Answer: 130.85.64.1

Question 84: For the Question 82, what is the subnet mask?

Answer: 255.255.192.0

Question 85: For the Question 82, what is the broadcast address?

Answer: 130.85.127.255

Question 86: Given 68.120.54.12/12 as the IP address, answer the following questions. What is the Network ID for this subnet?

Answer: 68.112.0.0

Question 87: For the Question 86, what is the first usable address in this subnet?

Answer: 68.112.0.1

Question 88: For the Question 86, what is the subnet mask?

Answer: 255.240.0.0

Question 89: For the Question 86, what is the broadcast address?

Answer: 68.127.255.255

Question 90: Address 192.5.48.3 belongs to
    A) class A   B) class B   C) class C   D) class D

Answer: C. Address 192.5.48.3 belongs to class C.

Question 91: Unlike Ipv4, Ipv6 does not include the following field in the base header
    A) Next Header field   B) Field for Fragmentation information
    C) Flow Label   D) Kind field

Answer: B. Unlike Ipv4, Ipv6 does not include the field for Fragmentation information in the base header.

Question 92: 127.0.0.1 is a
    A) Limited broadcast address   B) Direct broadcast address
    C) Multicast address   D) Loop-back address

Answer: D. 127.0.0.1 is a loop-back address.

Question 93: Network address prefixed by 1110 is a
    A) Class A address   B) Multicast address
    C) Class B address   D) Reserve address

Answer: B. Network address prefixed by 1110 is a multicast address.

Question 94: One of the header fields in an IP datagram is the Time to Live (TTL) field. Which of the following statements best explains the need for this field?
    A) It can be used to prioritize packets
    B) It can be used to reduce delays
    C) It can be used to optimize throughput
    D) It can be used to prevent packet looping

Answer: D. Whenever Time to live field reaches zero we discard the packet,so that we can prevent it from looping.

CHAPTER

IP Routing

8

8.1 Introduction

The purpose of the router is to examine incoming packets, chose the best path for them through the network; and then switches them to the proper outgoing port. Routers are the most important traffic-regulating devices on large networks.

Routers are networking devices that forward data packets between networks using *headers* and *forwarding tables* to determine the best path to forward the packets. Routers work at the network layer of the TCP/IP model *or* layer 3 of the OSI model.

As an example, assume that we want to send a postcard just based on person names (with minimum information). For example, *Bill Gate*s [USA], *Sachin Tendulkar* [India] or *Albert Einstein* [USA] it would be routed to them due to their fame; no listing of the street address or the city name would be necessary. The postal system can do such routing to famous personalities, depending on the name alone.

In an Internet, a similar discussion is possible: *reach* any *website* anywhere in the world without knowing where the site is currently located. Not only that, it is possible to do so very efficiently, within a matter of a few seconds. This is the problem which *network routing protocols* solve.

8.1.1 What is Network Routing?

How is this possible in a communication network, and how can it be done so quickly? The answer to this question is *Network routing*. *Network routing* is the ability to send a unit of information from source to destination by finding a path through the network, and by doing *efficiently* and *quickly*.

8.1.2 What is Addressing?

First, we start with a key and necessary factor called *addressing*. In many ways, addressing in a network has similarities to postal addressing in the postal system. So, we will start with a brief discussion of the postal addressing system to relate them.

A typical postal address that we write on a postcard has several components—the name of the person, followed by the street address with the house number (*house address*), followed by the city, the state name, and the postal code.

If we take the processing view to route the postcard to the right person, we essentially need to consider this address in the reverse order of listing, i.e., start with the postal code, then the city or the state name, then the house address, and finally the name of the person.

You may notice that we can reduce this information somewhat; that is, you can just use the postal code and leave out the name of the city or the name of the state, since this is redundant information. This means that the information needed in a postal address consists of three main parts: the postal code, the street address (with the house number), and the name.

A basic routing problem in the postal network is as follows:

1. The postcard is first routed to the city or the geographical region where the postal code is located.
2. Once the card reaches the postal code, the appropriate delivery post office for the address specified is identified and delivered to.
3. Next, the postman or postwoman delivers the postcard at the address, without giving much consideration to the name listed on the card.
4. Rather, once the card arrives at the destination address, the residents at this address take the responsibility of handing it to the person addressed.

The routing process in the postal system is broken down to three components:

- How to get the card to the specific postal code (and subsequently the post office),
- How the card is delivered to the destination address, and
- Finally, how it is delivered to the actual person at the address.

If we look at it in another way, the place where the postcard originated in fact does not need to know the detailed information of the street or the name to start with; the postal code is sufficient to determine to which geographical area or city to send the card. So, we can see that postal routing uses address hierarchy for routing decisions.

An advantage of this approach is the decoupling of the routing decision to multiple levels such as the postal code at the top, then the street address, and so on. An important requirement of this hierarchical view is that there must be a way to divide the complete address into multiple distinguishable parts to help with the routing decision.

Now consider an electronic communication network; for example, a critical communication network of the modern age is the Internet. Naturally, the first question that arises is: how does addressing work for routing a unit of information from one point to another, and is there any relation to the postal addressing hierarchy that we have just discussed? Second, how is service delivery provided? In the next section, we address these questions.

8.1.3 Addressing and Internet Service: An Overview

The addressing in the Internet is referred to as *Internet Protocol* (IP) *addressing*. An IP address defines *two* parts: one part that is similar to the postal code and the other part that is similar to the house address; in Internet terminology, they are known as the *network ID* (*netid*) and the *host ID* (*hostid*), to identify a network and a host address, respectively. A host is the end point of communication in the Internet and where a communication starts (for example, a web-server, an email server, desktop, laptop, or any computer we use for accessing the Internet). A *netid* identifies a contiguous block of addresses.

Network ID	Host ID

Note: For more details on addressing, refer *IP Addressing* chapter.

Like any service delivery system, we also need a delivery model for the Internet. For example, in the postal system, one can request guaranteed delivery for an additional fee. The Internet's conceptual framework (called TCP/IP-Transmission Control Protocol/Internet Protocol), depends on a delivery model in which TCP is in charge of the reliable delivery of information and IP is in charge of routing.

IP protocol does not worry about whether the information is reliably delivered to the address or is lost during transit. This is somewhat similar to saying that the postal system will route a postcard to the house address, while residents at this address (not the postal authority) are responsible for ensuring that the person named on the card receives it. While this may seem odd at first, this paradigm has been found to work well in practice, as the success of the Internet shows.

A key difference in the Internet compared to the postal system is that the sending host first sends a *test signal* (*beacon*) to the destination address (host) to see if it is reachable, and waits for an acknowledgment before sending the actual message. Since the beacon also uses the same transmission mechanism, i.e., IP, it is possible that it may not reach the destination. In order to allow for this uncertainty to be factored in, another mechanism known as a *timer* is used. That is, the sending host sends the beacon, and then waits for a certain amount of time to see if it receives any response.

If it does not hear back, it tries to send the beacon a few more times, waiting for a certain amount of time before each attempt, until it stops trying after reaching the limit on the maximum number of attempts. The basic idea, then, requires that the receiving host should also know the address of the sender so that it can acknowledge the receipt of the beacon. As you can see, this means that when the sending host sends its beacon, it must also include its source IP address.

Once the connectivity is established through the beacon process, the actual transmission of the content transpires. This is where a good analogy is not available in the postal system; rather, the road transportation network is a better fit to describe an analogy. If we imagine a group of 100 friends wanting to go to a game, then we can easily see that not all can fit in one car. If we consider that a car can hold five people, we will need twenty cars to transport this entire group. The Internet transfer model also operates in this fashion.

Suppose that a document that we want to download from a host (web-server) is 2 MB. Actually, it cannot be accommodated entirely into a single fundamental unit of IP, known as packet or datagram, due to a limitation imposed by the underlying transmission system. This limitation is known as the Maximum Transmission Unit (MTU). MTU is similar to the limitation on how many people can fit into a single car.

Thus, the document would need to be broken down into smaller units that fit into packets.

Each packet is then labeled with both the destination and the source address, which is then routed through the Internet toward the destination. Since the IP delivery mechanism is assumed to be unreliable, any such packet can possibly get lost during transit, and thus would need to be retransmitted if the timer associated with this packet expires. Thus another important component is that content that has been broken down into smaller packets, once it arrives at the destination, needs to be reassembled in the proper order before delivering the document.

Note: For more details on *fragmentation*, refer *IP Addressing* chapter.

8.1.4 Network Routing: An Overview

In the previous section, we have got broad overview of *addressing* and transfer mechanisms for data in Internet communication services. Briefly, we can see that eventually packets are to be routed from a source to a destination. Such packets may need to traverse many cross-points, similar to traffic intersections in a road transportation network. Cross-points in the Internet are called *routers*.

A *router* reads the destination address in an incoming IP packet, checks its internal information to identify an outgoing link to which the packet is to be forwarded, and then to forward the packet. Similar to the number of lanes and the speed limit on a road, a network link that connects two routers is limited by how much data it can transfer per unit of time, commonly referred to as the *bandwidth*; it is generally represented by a data rate, such as 1.54 megabits per second (Mbps). A network then carries traffic on its links and through its routers to the eventual destination; traffic in a network refers to packets generated by different applications, such as web or email.

Suppose that traffic suddenly increases, for example, because of many users trying to download from the same website; then, packets that are generated can possibly be queued at routers or even dropped. Since a router maintains a finite amount of space (called *buffer*), to temporarily store backlogged packets, it is possible to reach the buffer limit.

Since the basic principle of TCP/IP allows the possibility of an IP packet not being delivered, the finite buffer at a router is not a problem. On the other hand, from an efficient delivery point of view, it is desirable not to have any packet loss during transit. This is because the reliable delivery notion works on the principle of retransmission and acknowledgment and any drop would mean an increase in delay due to the need for retransmission.

In addition, during transit, it is also possible that the content enclosed in a data packet is possibly corrupted due to, for example, an electrical signalling problem on a communication link. This then results in garbling of a packet. From an end-to-end communication point of view, a garbled packet is the same as a lost packet.

Thus, for efficient delivery of packets, there are several key factors to consider:

1. Routers with a reasonable amount of buffer space,
2. Links with adequate bandwidth,
3. Actual transmission with minimal error, and
4. The routers' efficiency in switching a packet to the appropriate outgoing link.

We have already briefly discussed why the first two factors are important. The third factor is error-free transmission system is an enormous subject by itself. Thus, we next move to the fourth factor.

Why is the fourth factor important? A packet is to be routed based on the IP address of the destination host. But, like street address information in a postal address, there are far too many possible hosts; it is impossible and impractical to store all host addresses at any router. For example, for a 32-bit address, theoretically a maximum of 2^{32} hosts are possible. Rather, a router needs to consider a coarser level of address information, i.e., the *netid* associated with a host, so that an outgoing link can be identified quickly just by looking up the netid. Recall that a netid is very much like a postal code. There is, however, a key difference—netids do not have any geographical proximity association as with postal codes. For example, postal codes in the United States are five digits long and are known as ZIP (Zonal Improvement Plan) codes. Consider now Kansas City, Missouri, where a ZIP code starts with 64 such as 64101, 64102, and so on. Thus, a postcard can be routed to Kansas City, MO ("64") which in turn then can take care of routing to the specific ZIP code. This idea is not possible with IP addressing since netids do not have any geographical proximity. In fact, an IP netid address such 134.193.0.0 can be geographically far away from the immediately preceding IP netid address 134.192.0.0. Thus, at the netid level, IP addressing is fiat; there is no hierarchy.

You might be wondering why IP address numbering is not geographic. To give a short answer, an advantage of a nongeographic address is that an organization that has been assigned an IP address block can keep its address block even if it moves to a different location or if it wants to use a different provider for connectivity to the Internet. A geographically based address system usually has limitations in regard to providing location-independent flexibility.

In order to provide the flexibility those two netids that appear close in terms of their actual numbering can be geographically far away, core routers in the Internet need to maintain an explicit list of all valid netids along with an identified outgoing link so that when a packet arrives the router knows which way to direct the packet. The list of valid netids is quite large, currently at 196,000 entries. Thus, to minimize switching time at a router, efficient mechanisms are needed that can look up an address, identify the appropriate outgoing link (direction), and process the packet quickly so that the processing delay can be as minimal as possible.

There is, however, another important phase that works in tandem with the lookup process at a router. This is the updating of a table in the router, known as the routing table that contains the identifier for the next router, known as the next hop, for a given destination netid. The routing table is in fact updated ahead of time. In order to update such a table, the router would need to store all netids it has learned about so far; second, if a link downstream is down or congested or a netid is not reachable for some reason, it needs to know so that an alternate path can be determined as soon as possible. This means that a mechanism is required for communicating congestion or a failure of a link or non-reachability of a netid. This mechanism is known as the routing protocol mechanism. The information learned through a routing protocol is used for generating the routing table ahead of time.

If new information is learned about the status of links or nodes, or the reachability of a netid through a routing protocol, a routing algorithm is then invoked at a router to determine the best possible next hop for each destination netid in order to update the routing table. For efficient packet processing, another table, known as the forwarding table, is derived from the routing table that identifies the outgoing link interfaces. The forwarding table is also known as the Forwarding Information Base (FIB). We will use the terms forwarding table and FIB interchangeably.

It should be noted that a routing algorithm may need to take into account one or more factors about a link, such as the delay incurred to traverse the link, or its available bandwidth, in order to determine the best possible path among a number of possible paths. If a link along a path does not have adequate bandwidth, congestion or delay might occur. To minimize delay, an important function, called traffic engineering, is performed. Traffic engineering is concerned with ways to improve the operational performance of a network and identifies procedures or controls to be put in place ahead of time to obtain good network performance.

Finally, there is another important term associated with networking in general and net-work routing in particular, labeled as architecture. There are two broad ways the term architecture from the architecture of a building is applicable here: (1) a floor inside a building may be organized so that it can be partitioned efficiently for creating office spaces of different sizes by putting in flexible partitions without having to tear down any concrete walls, (2) it provides standardized interfaces, such as electrical sockets, so that equipment that requires power can be easily connected using a standardized socket without requiring modification to the building or the floor or the equipment.

Similarly, there are several ways we use the term architecting a network: for example, from the protocol point of view, various functions are divided so that each function can be done separately, and one function can depend on another through a well-defined relationship. From a router's perspective, architecting a net-work refers to how it is organized internally for a variety of functions, from routing protocol handling to packet processing. From a network perspective, this means how the network topology architecture should be organized, where routers are to be located and bandwidth of links determined for efficient traffic engineering, and so on. Later, we will elaborate more on architectures.

To summarize, we can say that the broad scope of network routing is to address routing algorithms, routing protocols, and architectures, with architectures encompassing several different aspects for efficient routing.

8.2 What are Routing Algorithms?

The main function of the network layer is routing packets from source to destination. The algorithms that choose the routes and the data structures that they use are major area of network layer design.

The routing algorithm is that part of the network layer software responsible for deciding which output line an incoming packet should be transmitted on. If the subnet uses datagrams internally, this decision must be made for every arriving data packet since the best route may have changed since last time. In the subnet using virtual circuits such decision is made ones per session.

8.3 Classification of Routing Algorithms

Routing algorithms can be classified based on the following criteria:

1. Static versus Dynamic (Non-adaptive versus Adaptive)
2. Single-path versus Multi-Path
3. Intra-domain versus Inter-Domain
4. Flat versus Hierarchical
5. Link-state versus Distance Vector
6. Host-intelligent versus Router-Intelligent

8.3.1 Static versus Dynamic Routing Algorithms

This category is based on how and when the routing tables are set-up and modified. Adaptive routing is also called *dynamic* routing and Non-adaptive is also called *static* routing.

Static routing algorithms do not base their routing decisions on measurements or estimates of the current traffic and topology. The selection of the route from source to destination is computed in advance (offline) and downloaded to the routers when the network is booted.

Static routing systems cannot react to network changes, they generally are considered unsuitable for today's large, constantly changing networks. Most of the dominant routing algorithms today are dynamic routing algorithms.

Dynamic routing algorithms adjust to changing network circumstances by analyzing incoming routing update messages. If the message indicates that a network change has occurred, the routing software recalculates routes and sends out new routing update messages.

8.3.1.1 Difference between Static and Dynamic Routing

- Static routing *manually* sets up the optimal paths between the source and the destination computers. On the other hand, the dynamic routing uses dynamic protocols to *update* the routing table and to find the optimal path between the source and the destination computers.
- The routers that use the static routing algorithm do not have any controlling mechanism if any faults in the routing paths. These routers do not sense the faulty computers encountered while finding the path between two computers or routers in a network.

  The dynamic routing algorithms are used in the dynamic routers and these routers can sense a faulty router in the network. Also, the dynamic router eliminates the faulty router and finds out another possible optimal path from the source to the destination. If any router is down or faulty due to certain reasons, this fault is circulated in the entire network.
- The static routing is suitable for very *small* networks and they cannot be used in large networks. As against this, dynamic routing is used for *larger* networks. The manual routing has no specific routing algorithm.
- The static routing is the *simplest* way of routing the data packets from a source to a destination in a network. The dynamic routing uses *complex* algorithms for routing the data packets.
- The static routing has the advantage that it requires minimal memory. Dynamic router, however, have quite a few memory overheads, depending on the routing algorithms used.

8.3.2 Single-path versus Multi-path

In a single-path routing, only a *single path* exists between any two networks. These protocols are incapable of load balancing traffic. An example of a single-path protocol is standard Border Gateway Protocol (BGP). Single-path routing is simple to configure. In single path algorithms, only a single path is stored in the routing table.

In a multipath routing infrastructure, multiple paths exist between networks. These protocols are better for performing load balancing. Multipath routing is more complex to configure. In multi-path algorithms, multiple paths are stored in the routing table.

8.3.3 Intra-domain versus Inter-domain

Intra-domain routing protocols work only within domains. Examples of intra-domain protocols are RIP and OSPF.

Inter-domain routing protocols work within and between domains. An example of an inter-domain protocol is BGP.

8.3.4 Flat versus Hierarchical

In a flat routing, each network ID is represented individually in the routing table. The network IDs have no network/subnet structure and cannot be summarized.

In a hierarchical routing, groups of network IDs can be represented as a single routing table entry through route summarization. The network IDs in a hierarchical internetwork has a network/subnet/sub-subnet structure. A routing table entry for the highest level (the network) is *also* the route used for the subnets and sub-subnets of the network.

Hierarchical routing simplify routing tables and lower the amount of routing information that is exchanged, but they require more planning. IP implements hierarchical network addressing, and IP internetworks can have a hierarchical routing structure.

In hierarchical routing, the internetwork can be divided into routing domains (also called *regions* or *areas*). A routing domain is a collection of contiguous networks connected by routers that share the routing information for the routes within the domain.

Routing domains are connected by a common routing domain called the *backbone*. Intra-domain routing is performed by the routers within the domain. Inter-domain routing is performed by domain routers connected to the backbone.

8.3.5 Link-state versus Distance Vector

Distance vector routing is so named because it involves two factors: the *distance* (*metric*) of a destination, and the *vector* (*direction*) to take to get there. Routing information is only exchanged between directly connected neighbours.

This means a router knows from which neighbour a route was learned, but it does not know where that neighbour learned the route; a router can't see beyond its own neighbours. This aspect of distance vector routing is sometimes called *routing by rumor*.

Link-state routing requires that all routers know about the paths reachable by all other routers in the network. Link-state information is *flooded* throughout the link-state domain to ensure all routers contain a synchronized copy of the area's link-state database.

From this common database, each router constructs its own relative shortest-path tree, with itself as the root, for all known routes.

8.3.6 Host-intelligent versus Router-intelligent

This classification is based on whether the source knows about the entire route or just about the next-hop where to forward the packet. Some routing algorithms assume that the source end node will determine the entire route. This is usually called *source routing*. In source-routing systems, routers act as store-and-forward devices.

They just send the packet to the next stop. These algorithms are also called *Host-Intelligent Routing*, as entire route is specified by the *source* node. In this type, the hosts have the routing intelligence.

Other algorithms assume that hosts know *nothing* about routes. In these algorithms, routers determine the path through the internet based on their own own strategy. In this type, the routers have the *routing intelligence*.

8.4 Routing Algorithm Metrics

Routing tables contain information used by switching software to select the best route. In this section we will discuss the different nature of information they contain, and the way they determine that one route is preferable to others?

Routing algorithms have used many different metrics to determine the best route. Efficient routing algorithms select route based on multiple metrics. All the following metrics have been used:

8.4.1 Path length

Path length is the most common routing metric. Some routing protocols allow network administrators to assign arbitrary costs to each network link. In this case, path length is the sum of the costs associated with each link traversed.

Other routing protocols define *hop count*. *Hop-count* is a metric that specifies the number of passes through internetworking products, such as routers, that a packet must pass through in a route from a source to a destination.

8.4.2 Delay

Routing *delay* is the time required to move a packet from source to destination. Delay depends on many factors, including the bandwidth of intermediate network links, the port queues (receive and transmit queues that are there in the routers) at each router along the way, network congestion on all intermediate network links, and the physical distance to be traveled.

8.4.3 Bandwidth

Bandwidth is the available traffic capacity of a link. Although bandwidth is a rating of the maximum attainable throughput on a link, routes through links with greater bandwidth do not necessarily provide better routes than routes through slower links. For example, if a faster link is busier, the actual time required to send a packet to the destination could be greater.

8.4.4 Load

Load refers to the degree to which a network resource, such as a router, is busy. Load can be calculated in a variety of ways, including CPU utilization and packets processed per second.

8.4.5 Communication cost

Communication cost is another important metric, especially because some companies may not care about performance as much as they care about operating expenditures. Although line delay may be longer, they will send packets over their own lines rather than through the public lines that cost money for usage time.

8.4.6 Reliability

Reliability in routing algorithms is the dependability (usually described in terms of the *bit-error* rate) of each network link. Some network links might go down more often than others. After a network fails, certain network links might be repaired more easily or more quickly than other links.

Any reliability factor can be taken into account in the assignment of the reliability ratings, which are arbitrary numeric values, usually assigned to network links by network administrators.

8.5 Flooding Routing Algorithm

Flood routing is a very simple routing strategy involving less hardware setup. The basic idea of this routing algorithm is that a packet received from a node is copied and transmitted on all outgoing links of that node except for the link that the packet arrived from.

After the first transmission, all the routers within one hop receive the packet. After the second transmission, all the routers within two hops receive the packet, and so on. Unless a mechanism stops the transmission, the process continues; as a result, the volume of traffic increases with time.

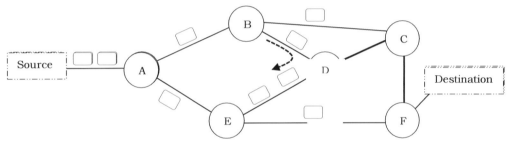

In this figure, two packets arrive at node A from a source. The first packet is copied to both nodes B and E. At nodes B and C, the copies of the packet are copied to their neighbouring nodes.

In flooding, all possible routes between source and destination are tried. A packet will always get through if a path exists. As all routes are tried, at least one packet will pass through the shortest route. All nodes, directly or indirectly connected, are visited. Main limitation flooding is that it generates vast number of duplicate packets.

It is necessary to use suitable mechanism to overcome this limitation. One simple is to use hop-count; a hop counter may be contained in the packet header, which is decremented at each hop, with the packet being discarded when the counter becomes zero. The sender initializes the hop counter. If no estimate is known, it is set to the full diameter of the subnet.

Another approach is keep track of packets, which are responsible for flooding using a sequence number and avoid sending them out a second time. A variation, which is slightly more practical, is selective flooding. The routers do not send every incoming packet out on every line, only on those lines that go in approximately in the direction of destination. Some of the important utilities of flooding are:

- Flooding is highly robust, and could be used to send emergency messages.
- Flooding always chooses the shortest path, since it explores every possible path in parallel.

- Can be useful for the dissemination of important information to all nodes (e.g., routing information).

8.6 Internet architecture

The Internet is a collection of different autonomous systems connected together by the core network as shown in figure.

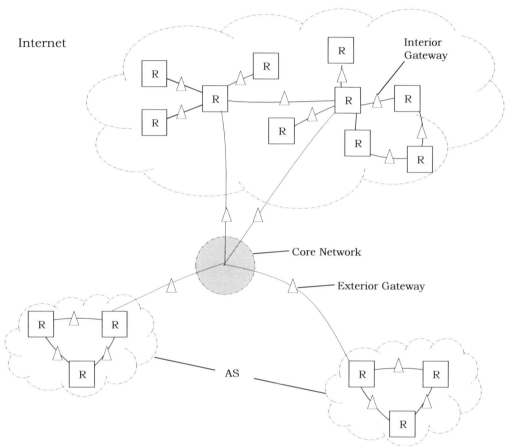

8.6.1 Autonomous system

As internet is a network of networks that spans the entire world and since it is not under the control of a single organization or body, one cannot think of forcing a single policy for routing over it. Thus, comes the concept of autonomous system.

An autonomous system (AS) is a collection of networks and subnetworks. One AS is independent of another AS. An AS can have its own routing algorithm and it can be managed independently. Within AS, one network is connected to another network by a gateway called the *interior gateway*.

The protocol an interior gateway uses to route a packet inside an autonomous system is called *Interior Gateway Protocol* (IGP). The IGP used in one autonomous system can be different than that in another autonomous system. In telecommunications domain an autonomous system is often called an access network.

8.6.2 Core network

The autonomous systems are connected together in a form of a network called the *core network* or *backbone network*. The gateways that connect all the autonomous systems to the core network are called exterior gateways and the routing protocol these exterior gateways use is called the *Exterior Gateway Protocol* (EGP).

Unlike IGPs the EGP cannot be different on different exterior gateways and it must be an Internet standard.

8.7 Routing protocols

In Internet, routers need to exchange routing information. The Internet is an interconnection of networks, often called domains (also called AS), that are under different responsibilities. An AS can be a small enterprise that manages a few routers in a single building, a larger enterprise with a hundred routers at multiple locations, or a large Internet Service Provider (ISP) managing thousands of routers.

Two classes of routing protocols are used to allow these domains to efficiently exchange routing information:

1. Interior Gateway Protocol [IGP] or Intra-Domain Routing Protocols
2. Exterior Gateway Protocol [EGP] or Inter-Domain Routing Protocols

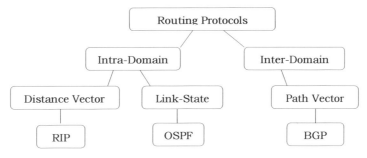

8.7.1 IGP

In small and slowly changing network the network administrator can establish or modify routes manually. Administrator keeps a table of networks and updates the table whenever a network is added or deleted from the autonomous system. The disadvantage of the manual system is obvious; such systems are neither scalable nor adaptable to changes.

Automated methods must be used to improve reliability and response to failure. To automate the task this task, interior router (within an autonomous system) usually communicate with one another, exchanging network routing information from which reachability can be deduced. These routing methods are called Interior gateway Protocols (IGP) [also called *Intra-Domain* Routing Protocols].

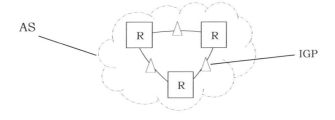

One of the most widely used IGPs is Routing Information Protocol (RIP). This protocol uses a technique called Distance Vector Algorithm. Link State (LS) and Open Shortest Path First (OSPF) are other examples of commonly available interior gateway protocols.

8.7.2 EGP and BGP

To make the network that is hidden behind the autonomous systems reachable throughout the internet each autonomous system agrees to advertise network reachability information to other Autonomous systems.

An autonomous system shares routing information with other autonomous systems using the Border Gateway Protocol (BGP) [also called *Inter-Domain* Routing Protocols]. Previously, the Exterior Gateway Protocol (EGP) was used.

BGP is used in modern TCP/IP. BGP is very important since it is used on the current Internet and other larger internetworks. EGP is an *obsolete* protocol that was used for communication between non-core routers and the router core in the *early* Internet.

Current BGP, BGP4, is capable of carrying routing information only for IPv4. Some extensions have been added to this protocol so that it can be used for other network layer protocols such as IPv6. And, this new protocol is called BGP4+.

8.8 Routing Information Protocol [RIP]

Routing Information Protocol (RIP) is a distance-vector routing protocol. It uses hop count as a metric to determine the best path to the destination.

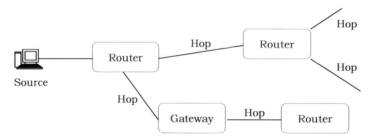

RIP is not good when we have an alternative path with the same number of routers, but with a faster bandwidth. RIP doesn't understand that as it's a distance vector and not a link state protocol. A link state can calculate the fastest link not depending on the *hop count*, and its limit is 15 hops.

RIP was designed for exchanging information within a limited size network, such as a network of 250 routes or a maximum of 15 hops. A RIP router maintains a routing table and periodically sends announcements to inform other RIP routers of the networks it can reach.

RIP also announces when it can no longer reach previously reachable networks. RIP version 1 uses IP *broadcast* packets for its announcements. A later enhancement, RIP version 2, also allows IP *multicast* packets for its announcements.

8.8.1 Routing Updates

RIP sends routing-update messages at regular intervals and when the network topology changes. When a router receives a routing update that includes changes to an entry, it updates its routing table to redirect the new route. The metric value for the path is increased by one, and the *sender* is indicated as the *next hop*.

RIP routers maintain only the best route (the route with the lowest metric value) to a destination. After updating its routing table, the router immediately begins transmitting routing updates to inform other network routers of the change.

These updates are sent independently of the regularly scheduled updates that RIP routers send.

8.8.2 Routing Metric

RIP determines the number of hops between the destination and the router, where *one hop* is *one link*. This hop count is called RIP *metric*. Given a choice of routes, RIP uses the route with the lowest metric, and therefore the route that takes the lowest number of hops.

If multiple routes have the same metric, RIP chooses the first route it finds. RIP is limited to routes of 15 hops or less. If a network is more than 15 hops away, RIP does not put its route into the router's routing table.

RIP suits star topologies very well. It is less suited to a meshed (multiply connected) network, because in meshed networks it learns multiple copies of routes, with different metrics.

8.8.3 Neighbours

To maintain its table of RIP routes, the RIP router periodically receives broadcasts of routing information from neighbouring routers, called RIP *neighbours*. Similarly, the router periodically broadcasts its routing information to its neighbours. The router removes routes from the table if the neighbouring routers do not keep them up to date (refresh them).

Each router interface's RIP neighbours must be in the same subnet as the interface.

8.8.4 RIP Timers

RIP uses number of timers to regulate its performance. These include a routing-update timer, a route timeout, and a route-flush timer. The routing-update timer clocks the interval between periodic routing updates.

Generally, it is set to 30 seconds; with a small random number of seconds added each time the timer is reset to prevent collisions.

Each routing-table entry has a route-timeout timer associated with it. When the route-timeout timer expires, the route is marked invalid but is retained in the table until the route-flush timer expires.

8.8.5 RIP Stability Features

RIP specifies a number of features designed to adjust for rapid network-topology changes. For example, RIP implements *split-horizon* and *hold-down* mechanisms to prevent incorrect routing information from being propagated.

In addition, the RIP hop-count limit prevents routing loops from continuing indefinitely. Typical features of RIP are: hop-count limit, hold-downs, split horizons, and poison reverse updates.

8.8.5.1 Hop-Count Limit

RIP permits a maximum hop count of 15. Any destination greater than 15 hops away is tagged as unreachable. RIP's maximum hop count greatly restricts its use in large internetworks, but prevents a problem called *count to infinity* from causing endless network routing loops.

Count to Infinity Problem

The classic distance vector convergence problem is known as the count-to-infinity problem and is a direct result of the asynchronous announcement scheme.

When RIP for IP routers add routes to their routing table, based on routes advertised by other routers, they keep only the best route in the routing table and they update a lower cost route with a higher cost route only if is being announced by the same source as the current lower cost route.

In certain situations, as shown in figures below, this causes the *count-to-infinity* problem.

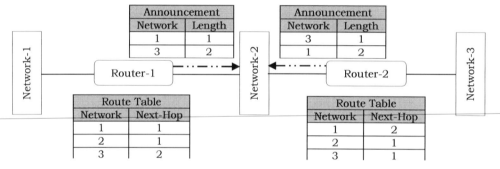

Assume that the inter-network in figure has converged. For simplicity, assume that the announcements sent by Router 1 on Network 1 and Router 2 on Network 3 are not included.

Now assume that the link from Router 2 to Network 3 fails and is sensed by Router 2. As shown in figure, Router 2 changes the hop count for the route to Network 3 to indicate that it is unreachable, an infinite distance away.

For RIP for IP, infinity is 16.

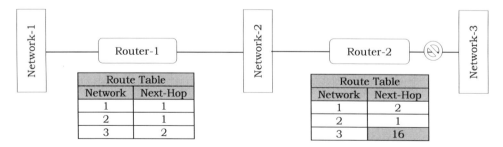

However, before Router 2 can advertise the new hop count to Network 3 in a scheduled announcement, it receives an announcement from Router 1.

The Router 1 announcement contains a route to Network 3 which is two hops away.

Because two hops away is a better route than 16 hops, Router 2 updates its routing table entry for Network 3, changing it from 16 hops to three hops, as shown in figure.

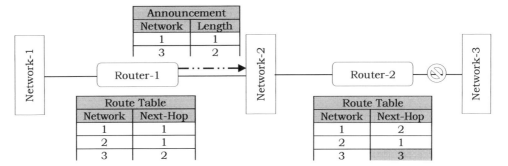

When Router 2 announces its new routes, Router 1 notes that Network 3 is available three hops away through Router 2.

Because the route to Network 3 on Router 1 was originally learned from Router 2, Router 1 updates its route to Network 3 to four hops.

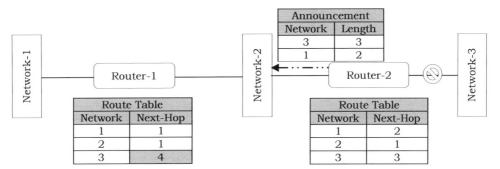

When Router 1 announces its new routes, Router 2 notes that Network 3 is available four hops away through Router 1.

Because the route to Network 3 on Router 2 was originally learned from Router 1, Router 2 updates its route to Network 3 to five hops.

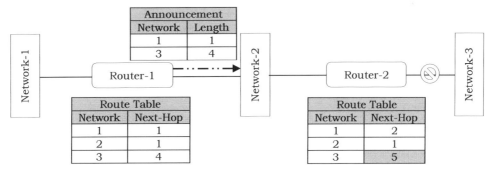

The two routers continue to announce routes to Network 3 with higher and higher hop counts until infinity (16) is reached. Then, Network 3 is considered unreachable and the route to Network 3 is eventually timed out of the routing table. This is known as the count-to-infinity problem.

The count-to-infinity problem is one of the reasons why the maximum hop count of RIP for IP internetworks is set to 15 (16 for unreachable). Higher maximum hop count values would make the convergence time longer when count-to-infinity occurs.

Also note that during the count-to-infinity in the previous example, the route from Router 1 to Network 3 is through Router 2. The route from Router 2 to Network 3 is through Router 1. A routing loop exists between Router 1 and Router 2 for Network 3 for the duration of the count-to-infinity problem.

8.8.5.2 Hold-Downs

Hold-downs are used to prevent regular update messages from inappropriately reinstating a route that has gone bad. When a route goes down, neighbouring routers will detect this. These routers then calculate new routes and send out routing update messages to inform their neighbours of the route change. This activity begins a wave of routing updates that filter through the network.

Triggered updates do not instantly arrive at every network device. It is therefore possible that a device that has yet to be informed of a network failure may send a regular update message (indicating that a route that has just gone down is still good) to a device that has just been notified of the network failure. In this case, the latter device now contains incorrect routing information.

Hold-downs tell routers to hold down any changes that might affect recently removed routes for some period of time. The hold-down period is usually calculated to be just greater than the period of time necessary to update the entire network with a routing change. Hold-down prevents the count-to-infinity problem.

8.8.5.3 Split Horizons

Split horizon helps reduce convergence time by not allowing routers to advertise networks in the direction from which those networks were learned. The only information sent in RIP announcements are for those networks that are beyond the neighbouring router in the opposite direction. Networks learned from the neighbouring router are not included.

Split horizon eliminates count-to-infinity and routing loops during convergence in single-path internetworks and reduces the chances of count-to-infinity in multi-path internetworks. Figure shows how split horizon keeps the RIP router from advertising routes in the direction from which they were learned.

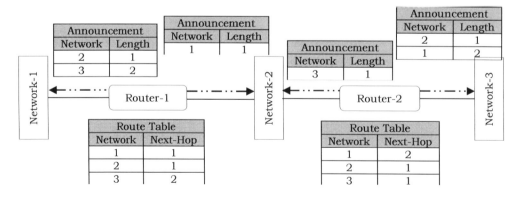

8.8.5.4 Split Horizon with Poison Reverse

Split horizon with poison reverse differs from simple split horizon because it announces all networks. However, those networks learned in a given direction are announced with a hop count of 16, indicating that the network is unreachable. In a single-path internetwork, split horizon with poison reverse has no benefit beyond split horizon.

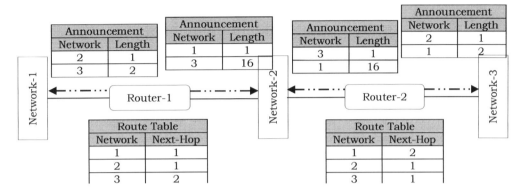

However, in a multipath internetwork, split horizon with poison reverse greatly reduces count-to-infinity and routing loops. Count-to-infinity can still occur in a multipath internetwork because routes to networks can be learned from multiple sources.

In figure, split horizon with poison reverse advertises learned routes as unreachable in the direction from which they are learned. Split horizon with poison reverse does have the disadvantage of additional RIP message overhead because all networks are advertised.

8.8.6 Routing Table Format

Each entry in a RIP routing table provides a variety of information, including the ultimate destination, the next hop on the way to that destination, and a metric. The metric indicates the distance in number of hops to the destination. Other information can also be present in the routing table, including various timers associated with the route. A typical RIP routing table is shown in figure.

Destination Network	Hop-Count	Distance	Timers	Flags
Network-1	Router-3	3	t_1, t_2, t_3	x, y
Network-2	Router-5	6	t_1, t_2, t_3	x, y
Network-3	Router-1	2	t_1, t_2, t_3	x, y
...	...	...	...	...

RIP maintains only the best route to a destination. When new information provides a better route, this information replaces old route information. Network topology changes can provoke changes to routes, causing, for example, a new route to become the best route to a particular destination.

When network topology changes occur, they are reflected in routing update messages. For example, when a router detects a link failure or a router failure, it recalculates its routes and sends routing update messages. Each router receiving a routing update message that includes a change updates its tables and propagates the change.

8.8.7 RIP Packet Formats

8.8.7.1 RIP v1 Message Format

The following section focuses on the RIP packet format. RIP messages can be broadly classified into two types: routing information messages and messages used to request information. Both uses same format, which consists of fixed header information followed by optional list of network and distance pairs. Following figure illustrates the RIP v1 message format.

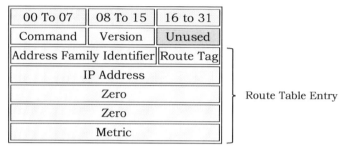

The fields of the RIP v1 packet are as follows:

Command

Command field indicates that the packet is a request or a response. The request command requests the responding system to send all or part of its routing table. Destinations for which a response is requested are listed later in the packet. The response command represents a reply to a request or, more frequently, an unsolicited regular routing update.

In the response packet, a responding system includes all or part of its routing table. Regular routing update messages include the entire routing table. It is a 1-byte field containing either 0x01 or 0x02. 0x01 indicates a RIP request for all or part of the routing tables of neighbouring routers. 0x02 indicates a RIP response consisting of all or part of a neighbouring router's routing table.

Version number

Version number field specifies the RIP version being implemented. With the potential for many RIP implementations in an internetwork, this field can be used to signal different, potentially incompatible, implementations.

It is a 1-byte field set to the value of 0x01 for RIP v1.

Address family identifier

Address family identifier field follows a 16-bit field of all zeros and specifies the particular address family being used.

On the Internet (a large, international network connecting research institutions, government institutions, universities, and private businesses), this address family is typically IP (value = 2), but other network types may also be represented.

It is a 2-byte field identifying the protocol family. This is set to the value of 0x00-02 to indicate the IP protocol family.

Address

Address follows another 16-bit field of zeros. In Internet RIP implementations, this field typically contains an IP address.

Zero

Not used.

Metric

Metric field follows two more 32-bit fields of zeros and specifies the hop count. The hop count indicates how many internetwork hops (routers) must be traversed before the destination can be reached.

It is a 4-byte field for the number of hops to the IP network that must be a value from 1 to 16. The metric is set to 16 in a General RIP Request or to indicate that the network is unreachable in a RIP response (announcement).

8.8.7.2 RIP v2 Message Format

Most of the slow convergence problems are handled by split horizon, poison reverse, and triggered updates. However, RIP cannot increase network diameter or disseminate network bit masks needed to properly interpret routes thus it is a poor choice for modern network. An updated version of RIP, known as RIPv2, solves this problem.

RIP Version 2 (RIPv2) RIP Version 2 adds a *network mask* and *next hop address* field to the original RIP packet while remaining completely compatible with RIP. Thus RIPv2 routers can coexist with RIP routers without any problems.

The *subnet mask* field contains the network bit mask associated with the destination; it also allows the implementation of CIDR addressing.

This will allow RIP to function in different environments, which may implement variable subnet masks on a network.

The *next hop address* field provides the address of the gateway thus allowing optimization of routes in an environment which uses multiple routing protocols thus having to ability to understand other routing protocol which may provide a better route path to a destination.

Following figure illustrates the RIP v2 message format.

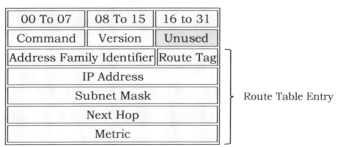

The fields of the RIP v2 packet are as follows:

Command

Command field indicates that the packet is a request or a response. The request command requests the responding system to send all or part of its routing table.

Destinations for which a response is requested are listed later in the packet. The response command represents a reply to a request or, more frequently, an unsolicited regular routing update.

In the response packet, a responding system includes all or part of its routing table. Regular routing update messages include the entire routing table.

It is a 1-byte field containing either 0x01 or 0x02. 0x01 indicates a RIP request for all or part of the routing tables of neighbouring routers.

0x02 indicates a RIP response consisting of all or part of a neighbouring router's routing table.

Version number

Version number field specifies the RIP version being implemented. With the potential for many RIP implementations in an internetwork, this field can be used to signal different, potentially incompatible, implementations.

It is a 1-byte field set to the value of 0x01 for RIP v1.

Address family identifier

Address family identifier field follows a 16-bit field of all zeros and specifies the particular address family being used.

On the Internet (a large, international network connecting research institutions, government institutions, universities, and private businesses), this address family is typically IP (value = 2), but other network types may also be represented.

It is a 2-byte field identifying the protocol family. This is set to the value of 0x00-02 to indicate the IP protocol family.

Address

Address follows another 16-bit field of zeros. In Internet RIP implementations, this field typically contains an IP address.

Subnet mask

Subnet mask contains the subnet mask for the entry. If this field is zero, no subnet mask has been specified for the entry.

Next hop

Next hop field indicates the IP address of the next hop to which packets for the entry should be forwarded.

Metric

Metric field follows two more 32-bit fields of zeros and specifies the hop count. The hop count indicates how many internetwork hops (routers) must be traversed before the destination can be reached.

It is a 4-byte field for the number of hops to the IP network that must be a value from 1 to 16. The metric is set to 16 in a General RIP Request or to indicate that the network is unreachable in a RIP response (announcement).

8.9 Open Shortest Path First [OSPF]

Open Shortest Path First (OSPF) is a link-state routing protocol. OSPF is another Interior Gateway Protocol. It is designed to be run as an Interior Gateway Protocol (IGP) to a single Autonomous System (AS).

The Internet Engineering Task Force (IETF) group was formed in 1988 to design an IGP based on the Shortest Path First (SPF) algorithm for use in the Internet. OSPF was created because in the mid-1980s, the Routing Information Protocol (RIP) was not capable of serving large, heterogeneous internetworks. OSPF being a SPF algorithm scales better than RIP.

As a link state routing protocol, OSPF contrasts with RIP and IGRP, which are distance vector routing protocols. Routers running the distance vector algorithm send all or a portion of their routing tables in routing update messages, but only to their neighbours.

8.9.1 OSPF Terminology

Neighbour

A neighbour is an adjacent router that is running a process with the adjacent interface assigned to the same area.

Adjacency

It is a logical connection between a router and the Designated Router (DR) and Backup Designated Router (BDR).

Link

A network or router interface assigned to any network. In algorithm, OSPF Link is the same as the interface.

Interface

An interface is a physical interface on a router. If the link is up the interface is up.

State

It is the functional level of an interface that determines whether or not full adjacencies are allowed to form over the interface.

Link State (LS)

It is the description of router interface (= link). It contains the following data.

- A single IP interface address and interface mask (unless the network is an unnumbered point-to-point network)
- Output cost(s): cost of sending data packet on the interface, expressed in the linkstate metric (advertised as the interface link cost). The cost of an interface must be greater than zero.
- List of neighbouring routers: other routers attached through this link.

Link State Advertisement [LSA]

The LSA is an OSPF data packet containing link-state and routing information which is shared with the other routers.

Link State PDU

- It is a unit of data describing the local state of router's interfaces and adjacencies.
- Each LS PDU is flooded throughout the *routing domain*.
- The collected LS advertisements of all routers and networks forms the LSDB.

Link State Database (LSDB)

- Each router will have a logically separated LSDB for each area the router is connected to.
- Two routers interfacing the same area must have (for that area) identical LSDBs.
- LSDB is a collection of all LS PDUs originated from the area's routers. Each router advertises directly connected networks via LS PDU. Every router has its own view of the network – it builds topologic database.

Shortest Path Computation

It is performed on the link state database in order to produce a router's routing table. Each router has an identical LSDB, leading to an identical representation of the network topology graph.

Each router generates its routing table from this graph by computing a tree of shortest paths with the local router as root of this tree.

Shortest Path Tree (SPT)

Shortest Path Tree is derived from the collected LS PDUs using the Dijkstra algorithm. Shortest path tree with local router as root, gives the shortest path to any IP destination network or host (only the next hop to the destination is used in the forwarding process).

Routing table

Routing table is derived from the Shortest Path Tree. Each entry of this table is *indexed* by a destination, and contains the destination's cost and a *set* of paths (described by its type and next hop) to use in forwarding packets to the destination.

Designated Router [DR]

The Designated Router (DR) is used only when the OSPF router is connected to a broadcast (Multi-Access) domain. It is used to minimize the number of adjacencies formed. The DR is chosen to push / receive routing information to / from the other routers.

Backup Designated Router [BDR]

The Backup Designated Router (BDR) is used as a hot standby for the DR. The BDR still receives all of the routing updates but does not flood LSAs.

OSPF Areas

These are similar to EIGRP Autonomous Systems (ASes). OSPF areas are used to establish a hierarchical network.

Area Border Router

An Area Border Router (ABR) is a router that has interfaces assigned to more than one area. An interface can only be assigned to one area but a router may have multiple interfaces. If the interfaces are assigned to different areas then the router is considered an ABR.

Autonomous System Boundary Router

An Autonomous System Boundary Router (ASBR) is a router with interface(s) connected to an external network or different AS. An example would be an interface connected to an EIGRP Autonomous Network. The ASBR is responsible for taking the routes learned from the EIGRP network and injecting them into the OSPF routing Protocol.

Non-Broadcast Multi-Access

NBMA are networks like Frame Relay, X.25 and ATM. While these networks allow for multiple-access they do not have any broadcast capabilities like Ethernet. Special consideration is required when configuring an NBMA network with OSPF.

Broadcast (multi-access)

Ethernet allows for broadcast and multi-access. It requires the election of a Designated Router and a Backup Designated Router.

Point to Point

This configuration eliminates the need for DR and BDR.

Router ID

The Router ID is the highest IP address of all configured Loopback interfaces. It is then used to represent the router. If there are no loopback interfaces configured the Router ID will use the highest IP address of any of its configured interfaces.

OSPF Features

OSPF has the following features:

- This protocol is *open*, which means that its specification is in the public domain. That means, anyone can implement it without paying license fees.
- OSPF is based on the *SPF* algorithm (also called *Dijkstra's* algorithm, named after the person credited with its creation).
- *Fast Convergence*: OSPF can detect and propagate topology changes faster than RIP. Count-to-infinity does not occur with OSPF.
- OSPF is a link-state routing protocol that calls for the sending of link-state advertisements (LSAs) to all other routers within the same hierarchical area. Information on attached interfaces, metrics used, and other variables are included in OSPF LSAs. As a link-state routing protocol, OSPF contrasts with RIP, which are distance-vector routing protocols. Routers running the distance-vector algorithm send all or a portion of their routing tables in routing-update messages only to their neighbors.

- Support for Authentication: OSPF specifies that all the exchanges between routers must be *authenticated*. It allows a number of authentication methods. Different areas can choose different authentication methods. The idea behind authentication is that only authorized router are allowed to advertise routing information.
- OSPF include *Type of Service* routing. It can calculate separate routes for each Type of Service (TOS), for example it can maintain separate routes to a single destination based on *hop-count* and *high throughput*.
- OSPF provides *load balancing*. When several equal-cost routes to a destination exist, traffic is distributed equally among them.
- OSPF uses different message formats to distinguish the information acquired from within the network (internal sources) with that which is acquired from a router outside (external sources).
- *Loop-Free* routes: OSPF-calculated routes are always loop-free.
- *Scalability*: With OSPF, an AS can be subdivided into contiguous groups of networks called areas. Routes within areas can be summarized to minimize route table entries. Areas can be configured with a default route summarizing all routes outside the AS or outside the area.

  Each *area* is self-contained; the topology of an area is hidden from the rest of the Autonomous System (AS) and from other *areas* too. As a result, OSPF can scale to large and very large internetworks. In contrast, RIP for IP internetworks cannot be subdivided and no route summarization is done beyond the summarizing for all subnets of a network ID.

OSPF Basic Principle

If every   router knows how to reach its directly connected neighbours, one can *distribute* the local knowledge of each router to all other routers so that every router can construct a weighted graph. With this knowledge, a node can always determine the shortest path to any other router.

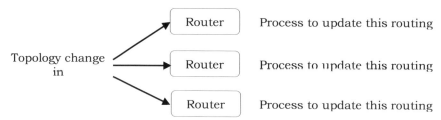

OSPF Basic Operation

OSPF is a very complex routing protocol but its fundamental operation is quite simple. The steps of operation might be pictured as follows:

1. Each router sends so called *hello packets* out of all OSPF-enabled interfaces. This way, the OSPF-enabled router discovers directly connected routers which also run OSPF. If certain parameters in the hello packets match between the neighboring routers, they form the relationship called *he adjacency*.
2. Then, each router exchanges packets called *Link State Advertisements* (LSAs) with its neighbors (adjacent routers). In OSPF terminology the word link is the

same as the interface. LSAs contain details such as: addresses/network masks configured on the links (interfaces running OSPF of course), the metric, the state of the link (which is its relation to the rest of the network), and list of neighbors connected to the link.

3. Each router stores the LSAs in its Link State Database (LSDB). These LSAs are then flooded (advertised) to all OSPF neighbors. As a result of the LSA flooding, all routers in the area have identical LSDBs. An analogy would be having the same road map of a given country which all drivers use. Their journey's starting point is different but the map is still the same.

4. Each router runs *Dijkstra's* algorithm to select the best path from this topological database (LSDB). This way, each router creates loop free graph indicating the shortest (best) path to each network/subnet advertised. The best paths end up in the routing table.

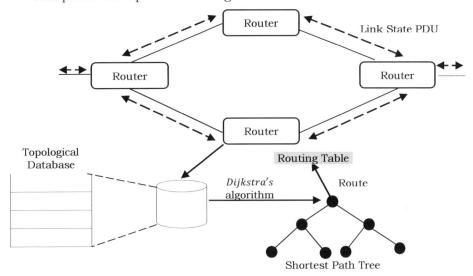

SPF Algorithm

The SPF routing algorithm is the basis for OSPF operations. When an SPF router is powered up, it initializes its routing protocol data structures and then waits for indications from lower-layer protocols that its interfaces are functional.

Once a router is assured that its interfaces are functioning, it uses the OSPFHello protocol to acquire neighbors. Neighbors are routers with interfaces to a common network. The router sends hello packets to its neighbors and receives their hello packets. In addition to helping acquire neighbors, hello packets also act as keep alive to let routers know that other routers are still functional.

On multi-access networks (networks supporting more than two routers), the Hello protocol elects a designated router and a backup designated router. The designated router is responsible, among other things, for generating LSAs for the entire multi-access network. Designated routers allow a reduction in network traffic and in the size of the topological database.

When the link state databases of two neighboring routers are synchronized, the routers are said to be adjacent. On multi-access networks, the designated router determines which routers should become adjacent. Topological databases are synchronized between pairs of adjacent routers. Adjacencies control the distribution of routing protocol packets. These packets are sent and received only on adjacencies.

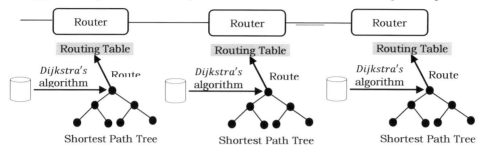

Each router periodically sends an LSA. LSAs are also sent when a router's state changes. LSAs include information on a router's adjacencies. By comparing established adjacencies to link states, failed routers can be quickly detected and the network's topology altered appropriately. From the topological database generated from LSAs, each router calculates a shortest-path tree, with itself as root. The shortest-path tree, in turn, gives a routing table.

Routing Hierarchy in OSPF

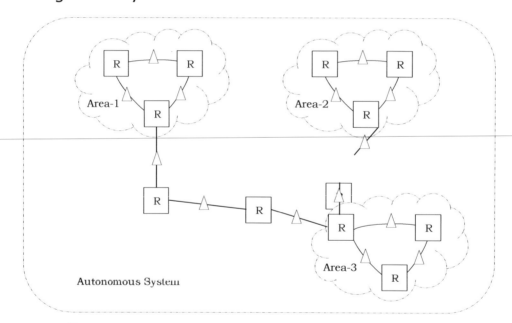

OSPF (unlike RIP) can operate within a hierarchy. The largest entity within the hierarchy is the autonomous system (AS). An AS is a collection of networks under a common administration, sharing a common routing strategy. OSPF is an intra-AS (interior gateway) routing protocol, although it is capable of receiving routes from and sending routes to other ASs.

An AS can be divided into a number of areas. An area is a group of contiguous networks and attached hosts. Routers with multiple interfaces can participate in multiple areas. These routers, which are called area border routers, maintain separate topological databases for each area. A topological database is essentially an overall picture of networks in relationship to routers. The topological database contains the collection of LSAs received from all routers in the same area. Because routers within the same area share the same information, they have identical topological databases.

The term domain is sometimes used to describe a portion of the network in which all routers have identical topological databases. Domain is frequently used interchangeably with AS. An area's topology is invisible to entities outside the area. By keeping area topologies separate, OSPF passes less routing traffic than it would if the AS were not partitioned.

Area partitioning creates two different types of OSPF routing, depending on whether the source and destination are in the same or different areas. Intra-area routing occurs when the source and destination are in the same area; inter-area routing occurs when they are in different areas. An OSPF backbone is responsible for distributing routing information between areas. It consists of all area border routers, networks not wholly contained in any area, and their attached routers.

8.9.2 OSPF Neighbour State Machine

There are 8 OSPF neighbour states in total. They are:

8.9.2.1 Down

In this state, a router has not heard a hello packet from any OSPF neighbour yet.

8.9.2.2 Attempt

This state is valid only for manually configured neighbours in NBMA environment. The neighbours are not discovered dynamically but must be configured manually.

8.9.2.3 Init

This state indicates that the router has received a hello packet from its neighbour, but the receiving router's ID was not included in the hello packet. It simply means that the router did received hello messages from a neighbour, but they don't have the Router ID of the receiving router, as a known neighbour.

8.9.2.4 2-Way

It means that router did receive hello message from neighbour and that hello message includes its Router ID. This means the both routers are able to see each other Hello Messages, which also means that now they have 2-way communication going on. A router has seen its own Router ID in the hello packet from the neighbour(s).

8.9.2.5 ExStart

In this state the master/slave relationship is established necessary to exchange Database Description Packets. Since all the packets have their sequence number allowing routers to detect more recent information, initial numbers are negotiated in this state. The router with the highest Router ID becomes the master.

8.9.2.6 Exchange

In this OSPF neighbour state, DBD packets are exchanged. These packets only contain the LSA header information. This information will be used by routers to see what LSA's they have and what LSA's they don't have.

The routers will send Database Description packets (description of the LDSB). Link State Request packets to request more recent LSAs are also sent in this state.

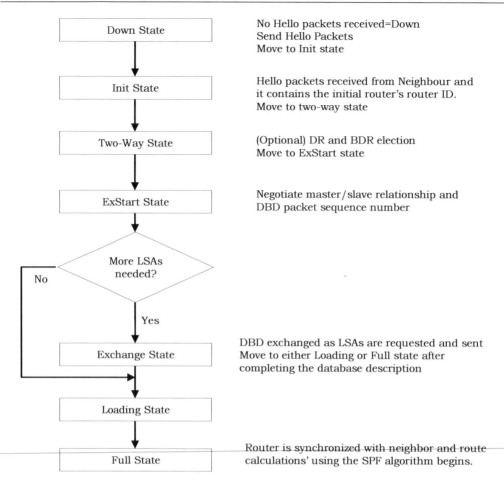

8.9.2.7 Loading

This is where the actual exchange of OSPF Database information happens. On basis of the information gathered in the above stage, Link State Requests (LSR's) are generated to request for missing LSA's and the requests are fulfilled by Link State Update (LSU's) packets.

The LSR packets are sent to neighbours in the loading state. They request more recent LSAs discovered in the Exchange state. Link State Updates are sent in response to LSRs.

8.9.2.8 Full

Once both routers have a synchronized database after the LSR/LSU exchange process, they exchange LSA Ack's with each other in order to confirm & then move on to Full state. OSPF neighbours are fully adjacent. All information about networks/subnets have been exchanged and acknowledged.

8.9.3 OSPF Network Types

A neighbour relationship is required for OSPF routers to share routing information. A router will try to become adjacent, or neighbour, to at least one other router on each IP network to which it is connected. Some routers may try to become adjacent to all their neighbour routers. Other routers may try to become adjacent to only one or two neighbour routers.

OSPF routers determine which routers to become adjacent based on the type of network they are connected to. Once an adjacency is formed between neighbours, link-state information is exchanged. OSPF interfaces recognize three types of networks:

1. Point-to-point networks
2. Broadcast multi-access, such as Ethernet
3. Non-broadcast multi-access (NBMA)

8.9.3.1 Point-to-point networks

A point-to-point network is a link between exactly two routers. A packet sent from one of the routers will always have exactly one recipient on the local link.

8.9.3.2 Broadcast multi-access

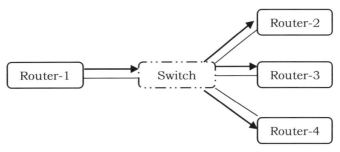

Point-to-point links don't scale well. A much more efficient manner of connecting a large number of devices is to implement a multi-access segment. Multi-access segment is a segment which can be accessed by multiple end points. An *Ethernet* segment is an example of such a network.

Ethernet networks support broadcasts; a single packet transmitted by a device can be multiplied by the medium (in this case an Ethernet switch) so that every other end point receives a copy. This is advantageous not only in bandwidth savings, but also in facilitating automatic neighbour discovery.

In the example above, Router-1 can multicast (a broadcast intended only for certain recipients) an OSPF hello message to the link, knowing that all other OSPF routers connected to the link will receive it and reply with their own multicast message. Consequently, neighbours can quickly identify each other and form adjacencies without knowing addresses beforehand.

OSPF routers on a multi-access segment will elect a designated router (DR) and backup designated router (BDR) with which all non-designated routers will form an adjacency. This is to ensure that the number of adjacencies maintained does not grow too large.

8.9.3.3 Non-broadcast multi-access (NBMA)

Unfortunately, not all multi-access technologies support broadcast transmissions. Frame relay and ATM are probably the most common examples of non-broadcast transport, requiring individual permanent virtual circuits (PVCs) to be configured between end points.

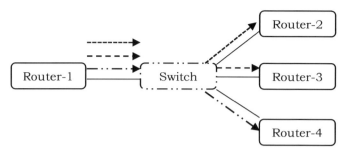

In the figure, note that Router-1 must transmit an individual packet for every destination. Also, this is inefficient with regard to bandwidth and requires the router to know the addresses of his neighbours before it can communicate to them.

8.9.4 Link State Advertisements

The Link State Database of a router contains Link State Advertisements (LSA's). There are five different types of LSA's.

8.9.4.1 Type 1 LSA

It is a Router Link Advertisement (RLA). This type of advertisement is between routers in the same area. It contains the status of the router's link to the area it is connected to.

8.9.4.2 Type 2 LSA

It is a Network Link Advertisement (NLA) generated by the Designated Routers (DRs). The DR uses type 2 LSAs to send out info on the state of other routers which are part of the same network. Type 2 LSA is only sent to routers that are in the area containing the specific network.

8.9.4.3, .4 Type 3 and 4 LSA

A Summary Link Advertisement (SLA) generated by area border routers. They advertise intra-area routes to area 0 and both intra-area and inter-area routes to non-backbone areas.

8.9.4.4 Type 5 LSA

It is an Autonomous System External Link Advertisement usually sent by Autonomous System Boundary Routers (ASBRs). These are used to advertise routes that are external to the OSPF autonomous system.

8.9.5 OSPF Area Types

Area types are used to reduce router cpu overhead.

8.9.5.1 Stub Area

Stub area does not receive Type 5 LSAs. Uses default routes instead.

8.9.5.2 Totally Stubby Area

Totally Stubby area does not receive Type 5 LSAs or Summary (Type 3 and 4 LSAs). This is a Cisco Specific feature.

8.9.5.3 Not-so-Stubby area (NSSA)

Not-so-Stubby area does not receive type 5 LSAs but must utilize external routes on a limited basis. In this case the NSSA imports type 7 LSAs and converts them to type 5 LSAs.

8.9.6 Dijkstra's Shortest Path Algorithm

A famous solution for shortest path problem was given by *Dijkstra*. Let us understand how the algorithm works. Here, we use the distance table. The algorithm works by keeping the shortest distance of vertex v (*aka router*) from the source s in *Distance* table.

The value *Distance*[v] holds the distance from s to v. The shortest distance of the source to itself is zero. *Distance* table for all other vertices is set to -1 to indicate that those vertices are not already processed.

Vertex	Distance[v]	Previous vertex which gave Distance[v]
A	-1	-
B	-1	-
C	0	-
D	-1	-
E	-1	-
F	-1	-
G	-1	-

After the algorithm finishes *Distance table* will have the shortest distance from source s to each other vertex v. To simplify the understanding of *Dijkstra's* algorithm, let us assume that the given vertices are maintained in two sets. Initially the first set contains only the source element and the second set contains all the remaining elements.

After the kth iteration, the first set contains k vertices which are closest to the source. These k vertices are the ones for which we have already computed shortest distances from source.

The algorithm can be better understood through an example, which will explain each step that is taken and how *Distance* is calculated. The weighted graph below has 5 vertices from $A - E$.

The value between the two vertices is known as the edge cost between two vertices. For example, the edge cost between A and C is 1. Dijkstra's algorithm can be used to find shortest path from source A to the remaining vertices in the graph.

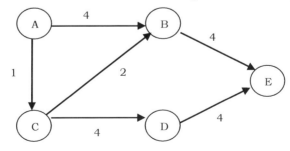

Initially the *Distance* table is:

Vertex	Distance[v]	Previous vertex which gave Distance[v]
A	0	-
B	-1	-
C	-1	-
D	-1	-
E	-1	-

After the first step, from vertex A, we can reach B and C. So, in the *Distance* table we update the reachability of B and C with their costs and same is shown below.

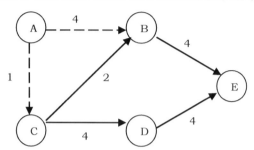

Shortest path from B, C from A

Now, let us select the minimum distance among all. The minimum distance vertex is C. That means, we have to reach other vertices from these two vertices (A and C). For example B can be reached from A and also from C. In this case we have to select the one which gives low cost.

Since reaching B through C is giving minimum cost $(1 + 2)$, we update the *Distance* table for vertex B with cost 3 and the vertex from which we got this cost as C.

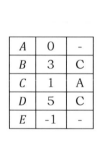
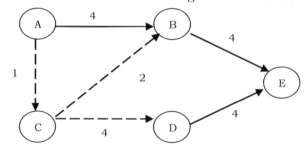

Shortest path to B, D using C as intermediate vertex

The only vertex remaining is E. To reach E, we have to see all the paths through which we can reach E and select the one which gives minimum cost. We can see that if we use B as intermediate vertex through C then we get the minimum cost.

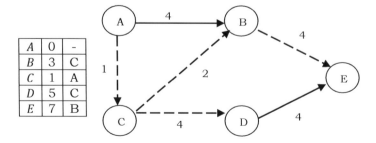

The final minimum cost tree which *Dijkstra's* algorithm generates is:

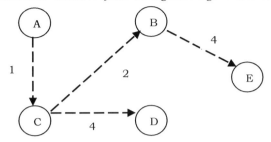

8.9.6.1 Disadvantages of Dijkstra's Algorithm

- As discussed above, the major disadvantage of the algorithm is that it does a blind search thereby wasting time and necessary resources.
- Another disadvantage is that it cannot handle negative edges. This leads to acyclic graphs and most often cannot obtain the right shortest path.

8.9.6.2 Relatives of Dijkstra's Algorithm

- The *Bellman–Ford* algorithm computes single-source shortest paths in a weighted digraph. It uses the same concept as that of *Dijkstra's* algorithm but can handle negative edges as well. It has more running time than *Dijkstra's* algorithm.
- *Prim's* algorithm finds a minimum spanning tree for a connected weighted graph. It implies that a subset of edges that form a tree where the total weight of all the edges in the tree is minimized.

8.9.7 OSPF Packet Types

OSPF sends packets to neighbours to establish and maintain adjacencies, send and receive requests, ensure reliable delivery of Link-state advertisements (LSAs) between neighbours, and to describe link-state databases. Link-state databases are generated from all the LSAs that an area router sends and receives.

OSPF runs directly over the IP network layer:

IP Header
OSPF Header
Packet Header

All OSPF packets share a common OSPF Header of 24-bytes. This header allows the receiving router to validate and process the packets. The format of common OSPF header is:

00 To 07	08 To 15	16 To 31
Version	Type	Packet Length
Router ID		
Area ID		
Checksum	Authentication Type	
Authentication Data		
Authentication Data		

Version   : The values of 2 and 3 indicate OSPF versions 2 and 3 respectively.

Type: Differentiates the 5 types of OSPF packets.

Packet Length: The length of an OSPF packet, including LSA header and contents, in bytes.

Router ID: Uniquely identifies the source or originating OSPF router of an OSPF packet. It is not necessary to be reachable or exist in the routing table.

Area ID   : Identifies the area from which an OSPF packet is originated and allows the receiving router to associate the packet to the proper level of OSPF hierarchy and ensure that OSPF hierarchy is configured consistently. The neighbouring router interfaces must reside on the same subnet and area to form adjacencies. The Area ID for an OSPF packet sent over a virtual link is 0.0.0.0 (the backbone's Area ID), as virtual links are considered part of the backbone.

Checksum: Specifies a standard IP checksum of the entire packet including the header.

Authentication Type: The values of 0, 1, and 2 indicate Null (no authentication), Simple Password (plain text), and Message Digest 5 (MD5).

There are *five* types of OSPF packets:
1. Hello packet
2. Database Description packet
3. Link State Request packet
4. Link State Update packet
5. Link State Acknowledgment packet

8.9.7.1 Hello packet

The hello packets are sent over a period of time on all interfaces for the purpose of establishing and maintaining neighbour relationships. Hello packets are multicast on the networks having multicast capability, which enables discovery of neighbouring routers dynamically.

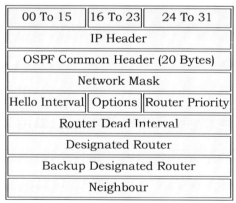

Network Mask [4-bytes]: Subnet mask of the advertising OSPF interface. For unnumbered point-to-point interfaces and virtual-links, it is set to 0.0.0.0.

Hello Interval: Interval at which Hello packets are advertised. By default, 10 seconds for point-to-point link and 30 seconds for NBMA/Broadcast links.

Options: The local router advertises its capabilities in this field.

Router Priority: The Priority of the local router. It is used for DR/BDR election. If set to 0, the router is ineligible for the election.

Router Dead Interval: The Dead Interval as requested by the advertising router. By default, 40 seconds for point-to-point link and 120 seconds for NBMA/Broadcast links.

Designated Router [4-bytes]: The IP address of the current DR. Set to 0.0.0.0 if no DR is elected yet.

Backup Designated Router [4-bytes]: The IP address of the current BDR. Set to 0.0.0.0 if no BDR is elected yet.

Neighbour [4-bytes]: The Router IDs of all OSPF routers from whom a valid Hello packet have been seen on the network.

8.9.7.2 Database Description packet

At the time of adjacency is being initialized, these packets are exchanged. These packets describe topological database contents. The database may be described by using multiple packets. A poll-response procedure is used for the description of multiple packets usage.

Among the routers, one is designated to be master, and the other a slave. The Database Description packets are sent by the slave after sending the Database Description packets by the master.

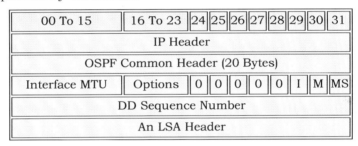

00 To 15	16 To 23	24	25	26	27	28	29	30	31
IP Header									
OSPF Common Header (20 Bytes)									
Interface MTU	Options	0	0	0	0	0	I	M	MS
DD Sequence Number									
An LSA Header									

Interface MTU [2-bytes]: Contains the MTU value of the outgoing interface. For virtual-links, this field is set to 0x0000.

Options [1-byte]: Same as Options field in a Hello packet.

I — Initial Bit: Indicates this is the first in the series of DBD packets.

M — More bit: Indicates whether the DBD packet is the last in the series of packets. Last packet has a value of 0, while all previous packets have a value of 1.

MS — Master/Slave bit: Master=1, Slave=0.

DBD Sequence Number: Used to sequence the collection of DBD packets. The initial value should be unique. The sequence number then increments by 1 until the complete database description has been sent.

LSA Header [Variable length]: This field contains the LSA headers describing the local router's database.

Note: During the DBD packet exchange, a Master/Slave relationship is established between the neighbours. The router with the highest Router ID becomes the Master and initiates DBD packet exchange. The Interface MTU should match on neighbours otherwise FULL adjacency is not reached.

8.9.7.3 Link State Request packet

A router may find the parts of its topological database are out of date, after database description package exchange with a neighbouring router. The *Link State Request* packet is utilized for requesting the pieces of the neighbour's database which are more up to date. There may be a need to utilize multiple Link State Request packets.

00 To 31
IP Header
OSPF Common Header (20 Bytes)
Link State Type
Link State ID
Advertising Router
...

Link State Type [4-bytes]: Type of LSA requested.

Link State ID [4-bytes]: Depends upon the type of LSA.

Advertising Router [4-bytes]: Router ID of the requesting router.

8.9.7.4 Link State Update packet

The flooding of link state advertisements is implemented by these packets. A collection of link state advertisements are carried by each *Link State Update* packet, one hop further from its origin. A packed may be included by several link state advertisements.

00 To 31
IP Header
OSPF Common Header (20 Bytes)
LSAs
LSAs
....

 # LSAs [4-bytes]: Number of LSAs within an LSU packet.

LSAs: The complete LSA is encoded within this field. The LSU may contain single or multiple LSAs.

8.9.7.5 Link State Acknowledgment packet

The reliability of flooding link state advertisement is made by acknowledging flooded advertisements. The accomplishment of this acknowledgement is done through the sending and receiving of *Link Sate Acknowledgement* packets. A single Link State Acknowledgement packet is used to acknowledge the multiple link state advertisements.

00 To 31
IP Header
OSPF Common Header (20 Bytes)
An LSA Header

LSA Header: List of LSA Headers being acknowledged.

8.10 Border Gateway Protocol [BGP]

The Border Gateway Protocol (BGP) is the routing protocol used to exchange routing information across the Internet. It makes it possible for ISPs to connect to each other and for end-users to connect to more than one ISP. BGP is the only protocol that is designed to deal with a network of the Internet's size, and the only protocol that can deal well with having multiple connections to unrelated routing domains.

BGP first became an Internet standard in 1989. The current version, BGP4 was adopted in 1995.

8.10.1 What is BGP?

The Border Gateway Protocol is an inter-Autonomous System routing protocol. BGP is a standardized exterior gateway protocol (EGP), as opposed to RIP, OSPF, and EIGRP which are interior gateway protocols. BGP Version 4 (BGPv4) is the current standard deployment.

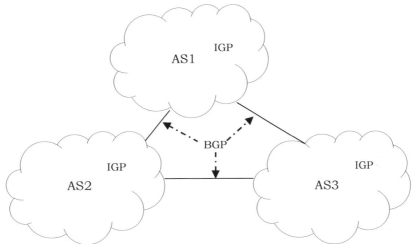

BGP is an example of *Path Vector* routing protocols. BGP was not built to route within an Autonomous System (AS), but rather to route between AS's. BGP maintains a separate routing table based on shortest AS Path and various other attributes, as opposed to IGP metrics like distance or cost. BGP is the routing protocol of choice on the Internet. Essentially, the Internet is a collection of interconnected Autonomous Systems.

BGP Autonomous Systems are assigned an Autonomous System Number (ASN), which is a 16-bit number ranging from 1 – 65535. A specific subset of this range, 64512 – 65535, has been reserved for private (or internal) use.

BGP utilizes TCP for reliable transfer of its packets, on port 179.

8.10.2 Internal and External BGP

An intra-AS routing protocol (that is, Interior Gateway Protocol (IGP), examples of which are Routing Information Protocol (RIP), Open Shortest Path First (OSPF), etc.) provides the routing within an autonomous system.

In some cases, BGP is used to exchange routes within an AS. In those cases, it is called *Internal* BGP (I-BGP), as opposed to *External* BGP (E-BGP) when used between ASs.

A BGP router can communicate with other BGP routers in its own AS or in other ASs. Both the I-BGP and E-BGP implement the BGP protocol with a few different rules. All I-BGP speaking routers within the same AS must peer with each other in a fully connected mesh.

They are not required to be physical neighbours, just to keep a TCP connection as a reliable transport mechanism. Since there is no loop detection mechanism in I-BGP, all I-BGP speaking routers must not forward any 3rd −party routing information to their peers. In contrast, E-BGP routers are able to advertise 3rd −party information to their EBGP peers, by default.

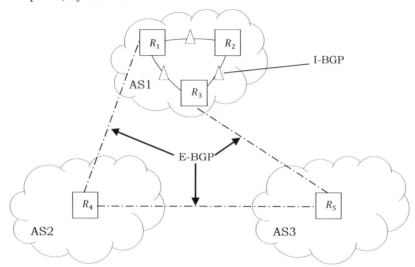

Figure shows routers R_1, R_2, and R_3 using I-BGP to exchange routing information within the same AS, and router pairs R_4-R_1, R_3-R_5, and R_4-R_5 using E-BGP to exchange routing information between ASs.

8.10.3 BGP Speakers and Peers

Routers that run a BGP routing process are often called *BGP speakers*. A pair of BGP-speaking routers that form a TCP connection to exchange routing information between them are called BGP *neighbours* or *peers*.

When a connection is established, all possible BGP routes are exchanged. After this, incremental updates are sent as the network information changes.

A single router can participate in many peering sessions at any given time. Each BGP session takes place exactly between two nodes, where two routers exchange routing information dynamically, over TCP port 179.

8.10.4 BGP Routing and Forwarding Tables

For any two BGP peers in a network to be able to send and receive traffic with each other, all intermediate BGP routers have to forward traffic such that the packets get closer to the destination. Because there can be multiple paths to a given target, BGP routers use a routing table to store all known topology information about the network.

Based on its *routing table*, each BGP router selects the best route to use for every known network destination. That information is stored in a *forwarding table* together with the outgoing interface for the selected best path.

8.10.5 BGP Message Types

There are *four* possible message types used with BGP:

1. *OPEN*: It is the first message to open a BGP session, transmitted when a link to a BGP neighbour comes up. It contains AS number (ASN) and IP address of the router who has sent the message.
2. *UPDATE*: Message contains routing information, including path attributes. It contains Network Layer Reachability Information (NLRI), listing IP addresses of new usable routes as well as routes that are no longer active or viable and including both the lengths and attributes of the corresponding paths.
3. *NOTIFICATION*: It is the final message transmitted on a link to a BGP neighbour before disconnecting. It usually describes atypical conditions prior to terminating the TCP connection, and provides a mechanism to gracefully close a connection between BGP peers.
4. *KEEP − ALIVE*: It is a periodic message between BGP peers to inform neighbour that the connection is still viable by guaranteeing that the transmitter is still alive. It is an application type of message that is independent of the TCP keep-alive option.

8.10.6 BGP Operation

AS numbers are managed by the Internet Corporation and as of May 2007, the Internet included more than 25,000 advertised ASs. Requesting a Web page makes the packets passed from one autonomous system to another until they reach their destination. BGP's task is to maintain lists of efficient paths between ASs. The paths must be as short as possible, and must be loop-free. BGP routers store tables of reachability data. This data are lists of AS numbers that can be used to reach a particular destination network.

The reachability information sent between AS is used by each AS to construct graphs of Internet paths that are loop-free and as short as practical. Each AS will have many routers for internal communication, and one or more routers for communications outside the local network. Internal routers use internal BGP (I-BGP) to communicate with each other and external routers use external BGP (E-BGP).

BGP is a path vector protocol used to carry routing information between autonomous systems. The term path vector comes from the fact that BGP routing information contains a sequence of AS numbers that identifies the path of ASs that a network prefix has traversed. The path information associated with the prefix is used to enable loop prevention.

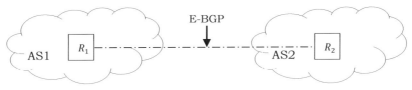

The BGP protocol has four main stages.

8.10.6.1 Opening and Confirming a BGP Connection with a Neighbour Router

After two BGP peers establish a TCP connection, each one sends an OPEN message to the other.

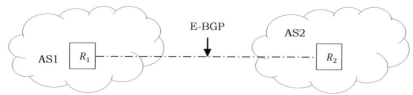

Establish a TCP connection on TCP port 179

When the TCP connection is established, BGP peers immediately identify themselves to each other by simultaneously sending open messages, and move into the *OpenSent* state. The open messages let the peers agree on various protocol parameters, such as timers, and negotiate shared capabilities.

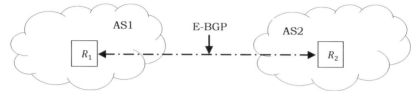

BGP OPEN Message sent simultaneously by both routers

R_1now in OPENSent state R_2now in OPENSent state

When each switch receives an open message, it checks all the fields. If it *disagrees* with the contents of the open message, it sends a notification message, closes the connection and goes into the *Idle* state. If it finds no errors, it moves into the *OpenConfirm* state and sends back a keep-alive message.

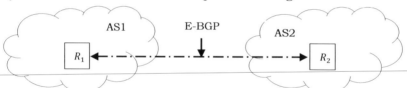

BGP Open Message received by both routers

R_1now in OPENConfirm state R_2now in OPENConfirm state

When both switches have received a keep-alive message, they move into the Established state. The BGP session is now open. BGP sessions typically stay in the Established state most of the time. They only leave the Established state if an error occurs, or the hold time expires with no contact from the far end.

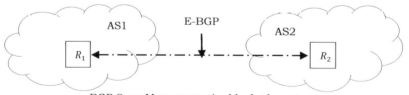

BGP Open Message received by both routers

R_1now in OPENConfirm state R_2now in OPENConfirm state

If a router *disagrees* with the contents of the OPEN message, it sends a notification message, closes the connection and moves into the *Idle* state.

If both nodes accept the OPEN message they send each other a Keep-alive message, move into the *Established* state and start sending Update messages to each other.

8.10.6.2 Maintaining the BGP Connection

A BGP router can detect a link or BGP peer host failure through the exchange of periodic keep-alive messages with the peer router. An error is assumed when no messages have been exchanged for the hold timer period. The hold timer period is calculated the smaller of its configured hold time setting and the hold time value received in the OPEN message.

BGP utilizes periodic keep-alive messages to ensure that the connection between neighbours does not time out. Keep-alive packets are small header-only BGP packets without any routing data.

8.10.6.3 Sending Reachability Information

Routing information is advertised between a pair of BGP neighbours in update messages. Each update message may simultaneously advertise a single feasible route to a neighbour and indicate withdrawal of several infeasible routes from service.

Update messages contain NLRI with a list of $< length, prefix >$ tuples designating reachable destinations, and path attributes, including degree of preference for each particular route, and the list of ASs that the route has traversed.

8.10.6.4 Notifying Error Conditions

Notification messages are sent to a neighbour router when error conditions (incompatibility, configuration, etc.) are detected. Notification messages consist of a main error code and a more detailed sub-code. Through the notification mechanism, a graceful close guarantees the delivery of all outstanding messages prior to closing the underlying TCP session.

8.10.7 BGP Attributes

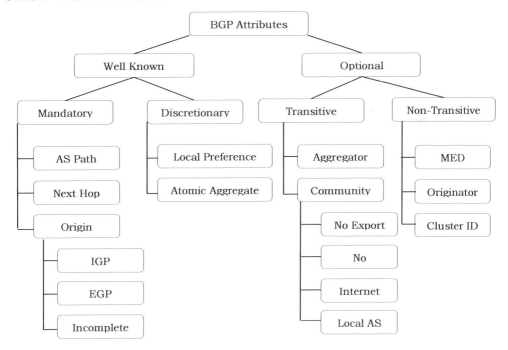

BGP attributes are *metrics* that define characteristics of routed prefixes in a BGP path. They are used to shape routing policy. For example, some of the attributes can be used in combination to equalize the distribution of inbound and outbound traffic among available multiple paths for load balancing.

The attribute information is forwarded when BGP peers advertise routes using UPDATE messages. There are several types of BGP attributes:

1. Well-known Mandatory
2. Well-known Discretionary
3. Optional (or partial) Transitive
4. Optional (or partial) Non-transitive

Optional attributes may not be supported by all BGP implementations. A *mandatory* attribute is one that must show in the description of a route. A *discretionary* attribute is one that does not have to appear. A *transitive* attribute is an optional attribute can be passed unmodified by a BGP speaker that does not have an implementation for it.

After a *transitive* attribute has been passed, it is marked as a *partial* attribute. A BGP speaker that does not have an implementation for a *non-transitive* attribute must delete it, not passing it to other BGP peers.

8.10.7.1 Weight Attribute

Weight is a *Cisco proprietary* attribute that is local to a router. The weight attribute is not advertised to neighbouring routers. If the router learns about more than one route to the same destination, the route with the highest weight will be preferred.

8.10.7.2 Local Preference Attribute

The local preference attribute is used to prefer an exit point from the local autonomous system (AS). The local preference attribute is propagated throughout the local AS.

If there are multiple exit points from the AS, the local preference attribute is used to select the exit point for a specific route. Higher local preference is preferred.

8.10.7.3 Multi Exit Discriminator Attribute [MED]

Multi Exit Discriminator is an optional non-transitive attribute. It is used to suggest an entry point into your AS. If you have two connections with single service provider so you can suggest the entry point into your AS. Lower is better.

8.10.7.4 Origin Attribute

The origin attribute indicates how BGP learned about a particular route.

8.10.7.5 IGP

Route is interior to the originating AS or advertised via network command.

8.10.7.6 EGP

Route is learned via the Exterior Border Gateway Protocol (EBGP).

8.10.7.7 Incomplete (?)

Incomplete occurs when a route is redistributed into BGP.

8.10.7.8 AS-Path Attribute

When a route advertisement travels through an autonomous system, the AS number is added to an ordered list of AS numbers that the route advertisement has travelled. This attribute is mandatory attribute and it is used to avoid loop.

8.10.7.9 Next-Hop Attribute

The EBGP next-hop attribute is the IP address that is used to reach the advertising router, which advertises the routes. Typically the IP address of the advertising routers. If receiving routers is on same subnet, next hop remains the same and in IBGP also.

8.10.7.10 Atomic Aggregate Attribute

Atomic Aggregate is a well-known discretionary attribute that has not to be in every single routing update been summarized. It is an attribute that allows BGP peers to inform each other about decisions they have made about overlapping routes.

8.10.7.11 Aggregator Attribute

Aggregator is an optional transitive attribute which tells who summarized that route. What router or what is the IP add of that router who summarized that route. It is an attribute that can be attached to an aggregated prefix to specify the AS and IP address of the switch that performed the aggregation.

8.10.7.12 Community Attribute

The community attribute provides a way of tagging of routes, called *communities*, to which routing decisions (such as acceptance, preference, and redistribution) can be applied. Route maps are used to set the community attribute. Predefined community properties are No-Advertise, No-export, Internet, and Local-AS.

8.10.8 BGP Route Selection

The route selection process involves selecting the best route towards a prefix from all the routes that exist in the BGP RIB. BGP can select from all the routes that it has learned and accepted except for any routes that are unreachable, such as routes that are withdrawn or damped.

When BGP selects a route as the best for a particular prefix, it adds this route into the IP routing table, and advertises the route to all appropriate neighbouring peers.

When there is only one route toward a particular prefix, that route is selected as the best route. When there are multiple routes toward a particular prefix, then BGP uses the rules in the following table to decide which one to select. If a rule results in selection of a single route, the switch uses this route. If multiple routes match a rule, the switch goes to the next rule.

The path selection process is:
1. If the path specifies a next hop that is inaccessible, drop the update.
2. Prefer the path with the largest weight.
3. If the weights are the same, prefer the path with the highest local preference.
4. If the local preferences are the same, prefer the path that was originated by BGP running on this router.
5. If no route was originated, prefer the route that has the shortest AS-path.

6. If all paths have the same AS-path length, prefer the path with the lowest origin type (where IGP is lower than EGP and EGP is lower than incomplete).
7. If the origin codes are the same, prefer the path with the lowest MED attribute.
8. If the paths have the same MED, prefer the external path over the internal path.
9. If the paths are still the same, prefer the path through the closest IGP neighbour.
10. Prefer the path with the lowest IP address, as specified by the BGP router ID.

8.10.9 BGP Multi-Homing

An AS may have multiple EBGP speakers connected to different ASs. This is known as BGP multi-homing. Multi-homing improves reliability of the AS connection to the Internet, and improves network performance because the network's bandwidth is the sum of all the circuits' bandwidth.

Network performance increases when more than one connection is used at a time; otherwise, maximum performance is the bandwidth being used by one connection at a given time. An even split of traffic across multiple connections is called load balancing.

Sites can be multi-homed in the following ways:
- To a single Internet Service Provider (ISP)
- To more than one ISP

The following figure illustrates the most reliable multi-homing topology to a single ISP involving different routers in the ISP and different routers in the customer network.

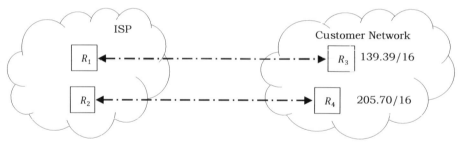

This example is the most reliable because no equipment is shared between the two links. If the traffic between the two networks is equal, the approach to load balancing would be to use the link between R_1 and R_3 for traffic going to 139.39/16 and use the link between R_2 and R_4 for traffic going to 205.70/16.

Multi-homing to more than one provider is shown in figure. The customer is multi-homed to ISP1 and ISP2; ISP1, ISP2, and ISP3 connect to each other. The customer has to decide how to use address space, as this is critical for load balancing from the ISPs to the customer, whether it delegates it by ISP1, ISP2, both, or independently.

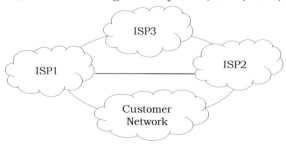

When the customer uses the address space delegated to it by ISP1, the customer uses a more specific prefix out of ISP1's aggregate and ISP1 can announce only the aggregate to ISP2. When the customer gets as much traffic from ISP1 as it gets from both ISP2 and ISP3, load balancing can be good.

When ISP2 and ISP3 together send substantially more traffic than ISP1, load balancing can be poor. When the customer uses the address space delegated to it by ISP2, it does the same although ISP1 is the ISP to announce the more specific route and attract traffic to it.

Load balancing may be quite good if ISP1's address space is used, but not very good if ISP2's space is used.

When the customer uses the address space delegated to it by both ISP1 and ISP2, the degree of load balancing from ISP1 and ISP2 to the customer depends on the amount of traffic destined for the two ISPs. If the amount of traffic for the two is about the same, load balancing towards the customer can be quite good, if not, load balancing can be poor.

8.10.10 BGP Route Filtering

A number of different filter methods allow us to control the send and receive of BGP updates. We can filter BGP updates with route information as a basis, or with path information or communities as a basis.

All methods achieve the same results. The choice of one method over another method depends on the specific network configuration.

In order to restrict the routing information that the router learns or advertises, we can filter BGP based on routing updates to or from a particular neighbour. To achieve this, an access-list is defined and applied to the updates to or from a neighbour.

8.10.11 Triggers

The trigger facility automatically runs specific command scripts when particular triggers are activated. When an event activates a trigger, parameters specific to the event are passed to the script that is run.

8.10.12 BGP Packet Types

8.10.12.1 BGP Packet Common Header

Each BGP message has a fixed-size common header. There may or may not be a data portion following the header, depending on the message type. The layout of these fields is shown below:

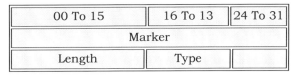

00 To 15	16 To 13	24 To 31
Marker		
Length	Type	

Marker: This is a 16-byte field is included for compatibility; it must be set to all ones.

Length: This 2-byte unsigned integer indicates the total length of the message, including the header in bytes. Thus, it allows one to locate the (Marker field of the) next message in the TCP stream. The value of the *Length* field must always be at least 19 and no greater than 4096, and may be further constrained, depending on the message type.

Padding of extra data after the message is not allowed. Therefore, the *Length* field must have the smallest value required, given the rest of the message.

Type: This 1-byte unsigned integer indicates the type code of the message. This document defines the following type codes:

      1 – OPEN
      2 – UPDATE
      3 – NOTIFICATION
      4 – KEEPALIVE

8.10.12.2 BGP OPEN Message Format

After a TCP connection is established, the first message sent by each side is an OPEN message. If the OPEN message is acceptable, a KEEPALIVE message confirming the OPEN is sent back. In addition to the fixed-size BGP header, the OPEN message contains the following fields:

00 To 07	07 To 15	16 To 23	24 To 31
Marker			
Length		Type	Version
My AS		Hold Time	
BGP ID			
Optional Length		Optional	
Optional			

Version: This 1-byte unsigned integer indicates the protocol version number of the message. The current BGP version number is 4.

My Autonomous System: This 2-byte unsigned integer indicates the Autonomous System number of the sender.

Hold Time: This 2-byte unsigned integer indicates the number of seconds the sender proposes for the value of the Hold Timer. Upon receipt of an OPEN message, a BGP speaker *must* calculate the value of the Hold Timer by using the smaller of its configured *Hold Time* and the *Hold Time* received in the OPEN message.

The Hold Time *must* be either zero or at least three seconds. An implementation MAY reject connections on the basis of the Hold Time. The calculated value indicates the maximum number of seconds that may elapse between the receipt of successive KEEPALIVE and/or UPDATE messages from the sender.

BGP Identifier: This 4-byte unsigned integer indicates the BGP Identifier of the sender. A given BGP speaker sets the value of its BGP Identifier to an IP address that is assigned to that BGP speaker. The value of the BGP Identifier is determined upon start-up and is the same for every local interface and BGP peer.

Optional Parameters Length: This 1-byte unsigned integer indicates the total length of the Optional Parameters field in octets. If the value of this field is zero, no Optional Parameters are present.

Optional Parameters: This field contains a list of optional parameters, in which each parameter is encoded as a *<Parameter Type, Parameter Length, Parameter Value>* triplet.

8.10.12.3 BGP UPDATE Message Format

UPDATE messages are used to transfer routing information between BGP peers. The information in the UPDATE message can be used to construct a graph that describes the relationships of the various Autonomous Systems. By applying rules to be discussed, routing information loops and some other anomalies may be detected and removed from inter-AS routing.

An UPDATE message is used to advertise feasible routes that share common path attributes to a peer. The UPDATE message always includes the fixed-size BGP header, and also includes the other fields, as shown below (note, some of the shown fields may not be present in every UPDATE message):

BGP Common Header
Withdrawn Routes Length (2 bytes)
Withdrawn Routes (variable)
Total Path Attribute Length (2 bytes)
Path Attributes (variable)
Network Layer Reachability Information (variable)

Withdrawn Routes Length: This 2-byte unsigned integer indicates the total length of the Withdrawn Routes field in bytes. Its value allows the length of the Network Layer Reachability Information field to be determined, as specified below. A value of 0 indicates that no routes are being withdrawn from service, and that the WITHDRAWN ROUTES field is not present in this UPDATE message.

Withdrawn Routes: This is a variable-length field that contains a list of IP address prefixes for the routes that are being withdrawn from service.

Total Path Attribute Length: This 2-byte unsigned integer indicates the total length of the Path Attributes field in octets.

Path Attributes: A variable-length sequence of path attributes is present in every UPDATE message, except for an UPDATE message that carries only the withdrawn routes. Each path attribute is a triple <attribute type, attribute length, attribute value> of variable length.

Network Layer Reachability Information: This variable length field contains a list of IP address prefixes. The length, in octets, of the Network Layer Reachability Information is not encoded explicitly, but can be calculated as:

UPDATE message Length − 23 − Total Path Attributes Length − Withdrawn Routes Length

where UPDATE message Length is the value encoded in the fixed-size BGP header, Total Path Attribute Length, and Withdrawn Routes Length are the values encoded in the variable part of the UPDATE message, and 23 is a combined length of the fixed-size BGP header, the Total Path Attribute Length field, and the Withdrawn Routes Length field.

8.10.12.4 BGP KEEPALIVE Message Format

BGP does not use any TCP-based, keep-alive mechanism to determine if peers are reachable. Instead, KEEPALIVE messages are exchanged between peers often enough not to cause the Hold Timer to expire.

A reasonable maximum time between KEEPALIVE messages would be one third of the Hold Time interval.

KEEPALIVE messages *must not* be sent more frequently than one per second. An implementation MAY adjust the rate at which it sends KEEPALIVE messages as a function of the Hold Time interval.

If the negotiated Hold Time interval is zero, then periodic KEEPALIVE messages *must not* be sent. A KEEPALIVE message consists of only the message header and has a length of 19 bytes.

8.10.12.5 BGP NOTIFICATION Message Format

A NOTIFICATION message is sent when an error condition is detected. The BGP connection is closed immediately after it is sent. In addition to the fixed-size BGP common header, the NOTIFICATION message contains the following fields:

00 To 07	07 To 15	16 To 23	24 To 31
Marker			
Length		Type	Error Code
Error Subcode		Data (Variable)	

Error Code: This is a 1-byte unsigned integer indicates the type of NOTIFICATION. The following Error Codes have been defined:

Error Code	Symbolic Name
1	Message Header Error
2	OPEN Message Error
3	UPDATE Message Error
4	Hold Timer Expired
5	Finite State Machine Error
6	Cease

Error Subcode: This 1-byte unsigned integer provides more specific information about the nature of the reported error. Each *Error Code* may have one or more Error Subcodes associated with it. If no appropriate *Error Subcode* is defined, then a zero (Unspecific) value is used for the Error Subcode field.

Problems and Question with Answers

Question 1: For the network below (and ignore the line weights), suppose flooding is used for the routing algorithm. If a packet is sent from node C to F, with a maximum hop count of 3, list all the routes it will take. How many packets are sent in this flooding?

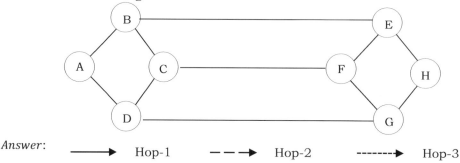

Answer:

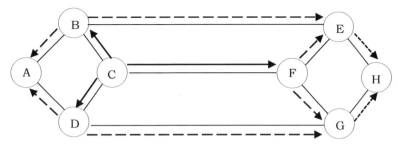

11 packets are sent in this flooding.

Question 2: Give two examples of non-adaptive routing algorithms and three examples of adaptive routing algorithms.

Answer: Non-adaptive routing algorithms are algorithms that don't update routing table entries based on changes in network topology or network traffic. Examples of non-adaptive routing algorithms include: flooding, simple shortest path routing.

Adaptive routing algorithms respond to changes in network topology, link state and/or network traffic. Examples of adaptive routing algorithms include: distance vector, link state routing, hot potato routing, backward learning.

Question 3: Name one way in which distance vector routing is better than link state routing, and name one in which link state routing is better than distance vector routing.

Answer: *Advantage* of *distance vector* routing: Unlike link state routing, which must flood link state update packets to all other routers in the network, distance vectors are only exchanged between adjacent routers. This limits the number of routing packets that are transmitted in the network, thereby saving bandwidth for other data packets in the network.

Advantage of *link state* routing: Because they rely on the flooding of link state update packets, link state routing algorithms propagate routing information to routers more rapidly than distance vector algorithms. Furthermore, link state routing doesn't suffer from the count-to-infinity problem, which plagues the distance vector algorithm.

Question 4: If delays are recorded as 16-bit numbers in a 50-router network, and delay vectors are exchanged twice per second, how much bandwidth per (full-duplex) link is chewed up by the distance vector routing algorithm? Assume that each router is connected to 3 other routers.

Answer: There is actually some extraneous information in this problem that we didn't need. We didn't need to know that each router is connected to 3 other routers in order to solve this problem.

To solve this problem, we need to understand how the distance vector algorithm works. First, we must know which routers a given router sends distance vector packets to. In a distance vector algorithm, a router exchanges distance vector packets only with its adjacent routers.

So, for the link between two routers A and B, there is a distance vector sent from A to B and a distance vector sent from B to A. Distance vector packets from other routers are never sent on this link.

Second, we must know what and how much information is contained in each distance vector packet. Each distance vector packet contains a single distance metric for every router in the network. In this problem, we are told to use 16-bit delays as distance metrics. Since there are 50 routers, each distance vector carries 50 16-bit distance values. The size of a distance vector packet is therefore equal to $50 \times 16 = 800$ bits.

Finally, we must know how often these distance vector packets are exchanged. The problem tells us that routers exchange 2 distance vector packets every second.

Therefore, on a single link, we exchange two 800 bit packets every second in each direction. Thus, we are sending 1600 bits per second in each direction. If we consider the total bandwidth used in both directions, we are using a combined total of twice this amount of bandwidth to send distance vector packets. So the answer is 3200 bits per second.

Question 5: Assume that source S and destination D are connected through two intermediate routers labeled R. Determine how many times each packet has to visit the network layer and the data link layer during a transmission from S to D.

A) Network layer – 4 times and Data link layer – 4 times
B) Network layer – 4 times and Data link layer – 3 times
C) Network layer – 4 times and Data link layer – 6 times
D) Network layer – 2 times and Data link layer – 6 times

Answer: C.

Question 6: In an OSPF autonomous system with n areas, how many areas are connected to the backbone area?
A) 1   B) $n-1$ C) n D) $n+1$

Answer: B.

Question 7: Forwarding tables for routers typically only include network addresses (i.e. 142.36.0.0/24) of destinations and not actual hosts they may route to. Why do routers just include network addresses and not hosts?

Answer: Because this is the primary function of routers - to route to networks. Once the network layer has determined the final network where the destination host resides, the work of the network layer is done (well almost.) It is then up to the local area network (for example, Ethernet or 802.11) to deliver the packet to the destination host.

Question 8: Assume there are two routers - R1 and R2. The network interfaces connecting R1 and R2 are 150.1.4.1 and 150.1.4.2 respectively. Router R1 connects a subnet with the address 150.1.1.0/24. Router R2 connects two subnets: 150.1.2.0/24 and 150.1.3.0/24.

On network 150.1.3.0/24, there are three hosts: a printer with the address 150.1.3.10, a workstation with 150.1.3.20, and a laptop with 150.1.3.30. These three hosts exchange information regularly and thus have the IP addresses for the other hosts in their subnet within their routing tables. Graphically, this network appears as follows:

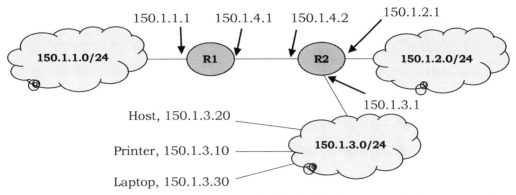

Forwarding tables in routers contain (1) destination network, (2) gateway (next router), and (3) outgoing interface. For example, the forwarding table in router R1 is:

Destination Network	Next Router	Outgoing Interface
150.1.1.0/24	-	150.1.1.1
150.1.2.0/24	150.1.4.2	150.1.4.1
150.1.3.0/24	150.1.4.2	150.1.4.1

Fill in the values of the forwarding table for router R2.

Answer:

Destination Network	Next Router	Outgoing Interface
150.1.1.0/24	150.1.4.1	150.1.4.2
150.1.2.0/24	-	150.1.2.1
150.1.3.0/24	-	150.1.3.1

Question 9: For the previous problem, fill in the values of the forwarding table for printer.

Answer:

Destination Network	Next Router	Outgoing Interface
150.1.1.0/24	150.1.3.1	150.1.3.10
150.1.2.0/24	150.1.3.1	150.1.3.10
150.1.3.0/24	-	150.1.3.10

Question 10: When the router runs out of buffer space, this is called __.
A. Source Quench   B. Redirect
C. Information Request   D. Low Memory

Answer: A. Source quench is the process where the destination router, or end internetworking device will *quench* the date from the *source*, or the source router. This usually happens when the destination router runs out of buffer space to process packets.

Question 11: An autonomous system can only exist if all routers in that system meet which criteria?
A) Interconnected   B) Run the same routing protocol
C) Assigned same autonomous system number
D) Run IGRP only   E) Run RIP only

Answer A,B, and C. An autonomous system is a set of routers and networks under the same administration. Each router must be interconnected, run the same routing protocol, and assigned the same autonomous system number. The network Information Center (NIC) assigns a unique autonomous system number to enterprises.

Question 12: A default route is analogous to a __
    A) Default gateway   B) Static route
    C) Dynamic route   D) One-way route

Answer: A. A default route is analogous to a default gateway. It is used to reduce the length of routing tables and to provide complete routing capabilities when a router might not know the routes to all other networks.

Question 13: Why do bridges have to build a spanning tree whereas routers do not?

Answer: Bridges have to build a spanning tree because they forward packets according to MAC addresses which are not structured and they do not detect frames that loop. Routers do not have to build a spanning tree since they forward packets according to IP addresses which are structured and eventually discard packets that loop.

Question 14: What happens to packets if there is a routing loop with bridges? with routers?

Answer: Packets loop indefinitely if there is a routing loop with bridges. Packets will eventually be discarded if there is a routing loop with routers because of the TTL field.

Question 15: Is it possible for a link-state algorithm to use the Bellman-Ford algorithm? Why or why not?

Answer: The link-state algorithm can use the Bellman-Ford algorithm (static version) for computing the shortest path to all other nodes since the Bellman-Ford algorithm requires only a partial view of the network and the link-state algorithm provides a complete topology view of the network.

Question 16: A router has the following CIDR entries in its routing table:

Address/mask	Next hop
135.46.56.0/22	Interface 0
135.46.60.0/22	Interface 1
192.53.40.0/23	Router 1
default	Router 2

For each of the following IP addresses, what does the router do if a packet with 135.46.63.10 address arrives?

Answer: Taking the first 22 bits of 135.46.63.10 as network address, we have 135.46.60.0. It matches the network address of the 2nd row. The packet will be forwarded to Interface 1.

Question 17: For the Question 16, what if the address is 135.46.57.14?

Answer: Taking the first 22 bits of the above IP address as network address, we have 135.45.56.0. It matches the network address of the first row. The packet will be forwarded to Interface 0.

Question 18: For the Question 16, what if the address is 135.46.52.2?

Answer: Taking the first 22 bits of the above IP address as network address, we have 135.45.52.0. It does not match the network addresses of the first three rows. The packet will be forwarded to default gateway which is Router 2.

Question 19: For the Question 16, what if the address is 192.53.40.7?

Answer: Taking the first 23 bits of the above IP address as network address, we have 192.53.40.0. It matches the network address of the third row. The packet will be forwarded to Router 1.

Question 20: For the Question 16, what if the address is 192.53.56.7?

Answer: Taking the first 23 bits of the above IP address as network address, we have 192.53.56.0. It does not match the network addresses of the first three rows. The packet will be forwarded to default gateway which is Router 2.

Question 21: Which of the following describe router functions?
   A) Packet switching   B) Packet filtering
   C) Internetwork communication   D) Path selection   E) All of the above

Answer: E. Routers provide packet switching, packet filtering, internetwork communication, and path selection.

Question 22: Which of the following statements is false about Internet Protocol (IP)?
   A) It is possible for a computer to have multiple IP addresses
   B) IP packets from the same source to the same destination can take different routes in the network
   C) IP ensures that a packet is forwarded if it is unable to reach its destination within a given number of hopes
   D) The packet source cannot set the route of an outgoing packets; the route is determined only by the routing tables in the routers on the way.

Answer: D. Internet protocol ensures that a packet is forwarded if it is unable to reach its destination within a given no. of hops. One computer can have multiple IP addresses also packets having same source & destination can take different routes. Source doesn't decide where to route the packet, but it is decided by the routing tables at intermediate routers.

CHAPTER
9

TCP and UDP

9.1 Introduction

In the earlier chapters, we have discussed the delivery of data in the following two ways:

1. *Node-to-node delivery*: At the *data-link* level, delivery of frames take place between two nodes connected by a point-to-point link or a LAN, by using the data-link layers address, say MAC address.
2. *Host-to-host delivery*: At the *network* level, delivery of datagrams can take place between two hosts by using IP address.

From user's point of view, the TCP/IP-based Internet can be considered as a set of application programs that use the Internet to carry out useful communication tasks. Most popular internet applications include Electronic mail (E-mail), File transfer, and Remote login. IP routing allows transfer of IP datagrams among a number of stations or hosts, where the datagram is routed through the Internet based on the IP address of the destination.

But, in this case, several application programs (*processes*) running simultaneously on a source host has to communicate with the corresponding processes running on a remote destination host through the Internet. This requires an additional mechanism called *process-to-process* delivery, which is implemented with the help of a *transport-level* protocol.

The transport level protocol will require an additional address, called port number, to select a particular process among multiple processes running on the destination host. So, there is a requirement of the following third type of delivery system.

3. Process-to-process delivery: At the transport level, communication can take place between processes or application programs by using port addresses

Basic communication mechanism is shown in figure. The additional mechanism needed to facilitate multiple application programs in different stations to communicate with each other simultaneously can be provided by a transport level protocol such as UDP or TCP, which is the topic of this chapter.

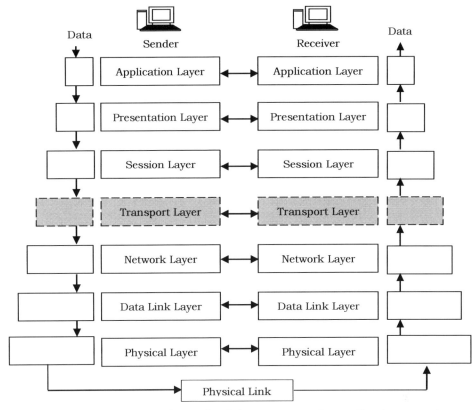

Process-to-process delivery is the task of the transport layer. Getting a packet to the destination system is not quite the same thing as determining which process should receive the packet's content. A system can be running fi le transfer, email, and other network processes all at the same time, and all over a single physical interface. Naturally, the destination process has to know on which process the sender originated the bits inside the packet in order to reply. Also, systems cannot simply transfer a huge file all in one packet. Many data units exceed the maximum allowable size of a packet.

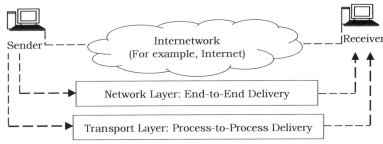

This process of dividing message content into packets is called *segmentation*. The network layer forwards each and every packet independently, and does not recognize any relationship between the packets. (Is this a file transfer or email packet? The network layer does not care.) The transport layer, in contrast, can make sure the whole message, often strung out in a sequence of packets, arrives in order (packets can be delivered out of sequence) and intact (there are no errors in the entire message). This function of the transport layer involves some method of flow control and error control (error detection and error correction) at the transport layer, functions which are absent at the network layer. The transport-layer protocol that performs all of these functions is TCP.

9.2 TCP and UDP

There are two very popular protocol packages at the transport layer:

- *TCP*: This is a connection-oriented, *reliable* service that provides ordered delivery of packet contents.
- *UDP*: This is a connectionless, *unreliable* service that does not provide ordered delivery of packet contents.

Computers running on the Internet communicate to each other using either the Transmission Control Protocol (TCP) or the User Datagram Protocol (UDP).

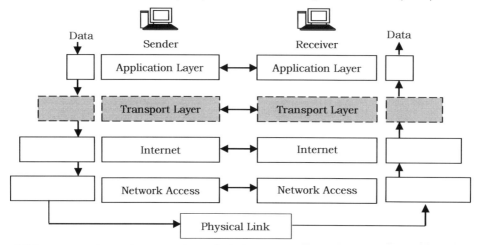

In addition to UDP and TCP, there are other transport-layer protocols that can be used in TCP/IP, all of which differ in terms of how they handle transport-layer tasks. Developers are not limited to the standard choices for applications. If neither TCP nor UDP nor any other defined transport-layer service is appropriate for your application, you can write your own transport-layer protocols and get others to adapt it (or use your application package exclusively).

9.3 TCP/IP Terminology

It is helpful to get familiar with the following terms as they are used in relation to TCP/IP.

Client	It is a computer or process that accesses the data, services, or resources of another computer or process on the network.
Host	A computer that is attached to an Internet network and can communicate with other Internet hosts. The local host for a particular user is the computer at which that user is working. A foreign host is any other host name on the network.
	From the point of view of the communications network, hosts are both the source and destination of packets. Any host can be a client, a server, or both.
Network	The combination of two or more hosts and the connecting links between them. A physical network is the hardware that makes up the network. A logical network is the abstract organization overlaid on all or part of one or more

	physical networks. The Internet network is an example of a logical network. The interface program handles translation of logical network operations into physical network operations.
Packet	Packet is the block of control information and data for one transaction between a host and its network. Packets are the exchange medium used by processes to send and receive data through Internet networks. A packet is sent from a source to a destination.
Port	It is a logical connecting point for a process. Data is transmitted between processes through ports (or sockets). Each port provides queues for sending and receiving data. In an interface program network, each port has an Internet port number based on how it is being used. A particular port is identified with an Internet socket address, which is the combination of an Internet host address and a port number.
Process	A process is a *program* that is *running*. A process is the active element in a computer. Terminals, files, and other I/O devices communicate with each other through processes. Thus, network communications is inter-process communications (that is, communication between processes).
Protocol	A protocol is a set of rules for governing communications at the physical or logical level. Protocols often use other protocols to provide services. For example, a connection-level protocol uses a transport-level protocol to transport packets that maintain a connection between two hosts.
Server	Server is a computer or process that provides data, services, or resources that can be accessed by other computers or processes on the network.

9.4 Ports and Sockets

This section introduces the concepts of *ports* and *sockets*, which are needed to determine which local process at a given host actually communicates with which process, at which remote host, using which protocol. If this sounds confusing, consider the following:

- An application process is assigned a process identifier number (process ID), which is likely to be different each time that process is started.
- Process IDs differ between operating system platforms, hence they are not uniform.
- A server process can have multiple connections to multiple clients at a time; hence simple connection identifiers would not be unique.

The concept of ports and sockets provides a way to uniquely identify connections, programs and hosts that are taken part in communication, irrespective of process IDs.

9.4.1 Ports

Generally speaking, a computer has a single physical connection to the network. All data destined for a particular computer arrives through that connection. However, the data may be intended for different applications running on the computer. So, how does the computer know to which application to forward the data? The answer is through the use of ports.

Data transmitted over the Internet is accompanied by addressing information that identifies the computer and the port for which it is destined. The computer is identified by its 32-bit IP address, which IP uses to deliver data to the right computer on the network. Ports are identified by a 16-bit number, which TCP and UDP use to deliver the data to the right application.

Definition: The TCP and UDP protocols use ports to map incoming data to a particular process running on a computer.

Each process that wants to communicate with another process identifies itself one or more ports. A port is a 16-bit number, used by the host-to-host protocol to identify to which higher level protocol or application program (process) it must deliver incoming messages. The TCP and UDP protocols use ports to map incoming data to a particular process running on a computer.

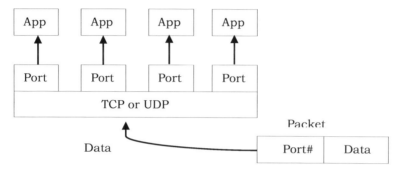

There are two types of ports: *Well-known* ports and *Ephemeral* ports.

9.4.1.1 Well-known Ports

Some ports have been reserved to support common/well known services:

FTP [File Transfer Protocol]	21/TCP
Telnet [Telnet Protocol]	23/TCP
SMTP [Simple Mail Transfer Protocol]	25/TCP
Login [Login Protocol]	513/TCP
HTTP [Hypertext Transfer Protocol]	80/TCP,UDP
HTTPS [Secure Hypertext Transfer Protocol]	443/TCP,UDP

The well-known ports are controlled and assigned by the Internet Assigned Number Authority (IANA). These ports on most systems can only be used by system processes or by programs executed by privileged users (say, *root* or *admin* users). The reason for well-known ports is to allow clients to be able to find servers without configuration information.

Some ports are reserved in both TCP and UDP, although applications might not be written to support them. Port numbers have the following assigned ranges:

- Numbers below 255 are for public applications.
- Numbers from 255-1023 are assigned to companies for marketable applications.
- Numbers above 1023 are unregulated.
- End systems use port numbers to select proper applications. Originating source port numbers are dynamically assigned by the source host; usually, it is a number larger than 1023.

9.4.1.2 Ephemeral Ports

Clients (user level processes) do not need well-known port numbers because they initiate communication with servers and the port number they are using is contained in the UDP datagrams (or TCP packets) sent to the server. Each client process is allocated a port number for as long as it needs it by the host it is running on. Ephemeral port numbers have values greater than 1023, normally in the range 1024 to 65535.

An ephemeral port is a short-lived (temporary) transport protocol port for Internet Protocol (IP) communications allocated automatically from a predefined range by the IP software. Unless a client program explicitly requests a specific port number, the port number used is an ephemeral port number.

Ephemeral ports are temporary ports assigned by a machine's IP stack, and are assigned from a designated range of ports for this purpose. When the connection terminates, the ephemeral port is available for reuse, although most IP stacks won't reuse that port number until the entire pool of ephemeral ports have been used. So, if the client program reconnects, it will be assigned a different ephemeral port number for its side of the new connection.

9.4.2 Sockets

A socket is a *communications connection point* (endpoint) that we can name and address in a network. The processes that use a socket can reside on the same system or on different systems on different networks. Sockets are useful for both stand-alone and network applications.

Sockets commonly are used for client/server interaction. Usually, a typical system configuration places the server on one machine, with the clients on other machines. The clients connect to the server, exchange information, and then disconnect.

9.4.2.1 Socket Characteristics

Sockets share the following characteristics:

- A socket is represented by an integer. That integer is called a *socket descriptor*.
- A socket exists as long as the process maintains an open link to the socket.
- We can name a socket and use it to communicate with other sockets in a communication domain.
- Sockets perform the communication when the server accepts connections from them, or when it exchanges messages with them.
- We can create sockets in pairs.

9.4.2.2 Socket Operations

Sockets can perform a variety of operations. They include:

- Establish a connection to a remote host
- Send data to a remote host
- Receive data from a remote host
- Close a connection

In addition, there is a special type of socket that provides a service that will bind to a specific port number. This type of socket is normally used only in servers, and can perform the following operations:

- Bind to a local port

- Accept incoming connections from remote hosts
- Unbind from a local port

These two sockets are grouped into different categories, and are used by either a client or a server (since some clients may also be acting as servers and some servers as clients). But, it is normal practice for the role of client and server to be separate.

9.4.2.3 Socket Connection Types

The connection that a socket provides can be *connection-oriented* or *connectionless*.

Connection-oriented communication implies that a connection is established, and a communication between the programs will follow. The program that provides the service (*server program*) establishes the connection. It assigns itself a name that identifies where to obtain that service. The client of the service (*client program*) must request the service of the server program.

The client does this by connecting to the distinct name that the server program has indicated. It is similar to dialing a telephone number (an identifier) and making a connection with another party that is offering a service (for example, a plumber). When the receiver of the call (the server) answers the telephone, the connection is established.

Connectionless communication implies that no connection is established over which a dialog or data transfer can take place. Instead, the server program designates a name that identifies where to reach it (much like a post office box). By sending a letter to a post office box, we cannot be absolutely sure the letter is received. We may have to send another letter to reestablish communication.

9.5 User Datagram Protocol [UDP]

The magic word for UDP is *simple*. UDP allows two (or more) processes running on different hosts to communicate (TCP also allows). UDP is a connectionless service. That means there is no initial handshaking phase during which a *pipe* is established between the two processes. Because UDP doesn't have a *pipe*, when a process wants to send a batch of bytes to another process, the sending process must exclude attach the destination process's address to the batch of bytes.

This must be done for each batch of bytes the sending process sends. Thus UDP is similar to a taxi service: each time a group of people get in a taxi, the group has to inform the driver of the destination address. As with TCP, the destination address is a *tuple* consisting of the IP address of the destination host and the port number of the destination process. We shall refer to the batch of information bytes along with the IP destination address and port number as the *packet*.

After creating a packet, the sending process puts the packet into the network through a socket. Continuing with our taxi analogy, at the other side of the socket, there is a taxi waiting for the packet. The taxi then drives the packet in the direction of the packet's destination address. However, the taxi does not guarantee that it will eventually get the datagram to its ultimate destination; the taxi could break down. In other terms, UDP provides an *unreliable* transport service to its processes. It means UDP makes no guarantee that a datagram will reach its destination.

9.5.1 What is UDP?

UDP provides a connectionless datagram service that offers *best-effort* delivery, which means that UDP does not guarantee delivery or verify sequencing for any datagrams. A source host that needs reliable communication must use either TCP or a program that provides its own sequencing and acknowledgment services.

UDP [User Datagram Protocol] is a protocol that provides a mechanism for application programs to send messages to other programs with a minimum of protocol mechanism (overhead). The protocol is transaction oriented; delivery and duplicate protection are not guaranteed. Applications requiring ordered reliable delivery of streams of data should use the Transmission Control Protocol [TCP].

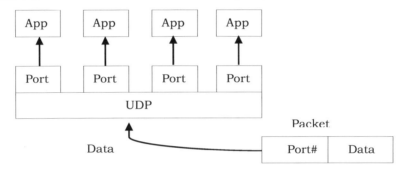

UDP is one of the core protocols of the Internet protocol suite. Using UDP, programs on networked computers can send short messages sometimes called *datagrams* to one another. It was designed by *P. Reed* in 1980.

UDP does not guarantee reliability or ordering in the way that TCP does. Datagrams may arrive *out of order*, may appear *duplicated*, or *go missing without notice*. Avoiding the overhead of checking whether every packet actually arrived makes UDP faster and more efficient, at least for applications that do not need guaranteed delivery.

Time-sensitive applications generally use UDP because dropped packets are preferable to delayed packets. UDP's stateless nature is also useful for servers that *answer small queries* from huge numbers of clients. Unlike TCP, UDP is compatible with packet broadcast (sending to all on local network) and multicasting (send to all subscribers).

UDP is basically an application interface to IP. It adds no reliability, flow-control, or error recovery to IP. It simply serves as a *multiplexer/demultiplexer* for sending and receiving datagrams, using ports to direct the datagrams, as shown in figure. UDP provides a mechanism for one application to send a datagram to another. The UDP layer can be regarded as being extremely thin and consequently has low overheads, but it requires the application to take responsibility for error recovery and so on.

9.5.2 Characteristics of UDP

Following are the characteristics of UDP:

- Connectionless
- Unreliable
- Transmit messages (called user *datagrams*)
- Provides no software checking for message delivery (*unreliable*)

- Does not reassemble incoming messages
- Uses no acknowledgments
- Provides no flow control

Note that applications using UDP must handle all problems to ensure reliable transfer. They must deal with:

- Duplicate messages
- Lost messages
- Delayed and Out-of-Order delivery

9.5.3 How it works? [Communication B/W Applications Using Ports]

It is clear that there are significant differences between TCP and UDP, but there is also an important similarity between these two protocols. Both share the concept of a *communications port*, which distinguishes one application from another.

Many services and clients run on the same port, and it would be impossible to sort out which one was which without distributing them by port number. When a TCP socket establishes a connection to another machine, it requires two very important pieces of information to connect to the remote end—the IP address of the machine and the port number. In addition, a local IP address and port number will be bound to it, so that the remote machine can identify which application established the connection. After all, we wouldn't want our e-mail to be accessible by another user running software on the same system.

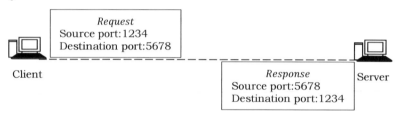

The figure shows a typical usage of the UDP port numbers. The client process uses port number 1234 while the server process uses port number 5678. When the client sends a *request*, it is identified as originating from port number 1234 on the client host and destined to port number 5678 on the server host. When the server process replies to this request, the server's UDP implementation will send the reply as originating from port 5678 on the server host and destined to port 1234 on the client host.

9.5.3.1 What UDP Does?

UDP's only real task is to take data from higher layer protocols and place it in UDP messages which are then passed down to IP for transmission. The basic steps for transmission using UDP are as follows:

1. *Higher Layer Data Transfer*: An application sends a message to the UDP software.
2. *UDP Message Encapsulation*: The higher layer message is encapsulated into the Data field of a UDP message. The headers of the UDP message are filled in, including the Source Port field of the application that send the data to UDP and the Destination Port field of the intended recipient. The checksum value may also be calculated.
3. *Transfer Message* to *IP*: The UDP message is passed to IP for transmission.

On the destination side, the process is *reversed*.

9.5.3.2 What UDP Does Not Do?

UDP is so simple that its operation is often described in terms of what it does not do, instead of what it does. As a transport protocol, UDP does not do the following.

- Establish connections before sending data. It just packages the data and sends it off.
- Provide any guarantees that its messages will arrive.
- Detect lost messages and retransmit them.
- Ensure that data is received in the same order that it was sent.
- Provide any mechanism to handle congestion or manage the flow of data between applications.

9.5.4 UDP Encapsulation

The application packages the data to be sent, and each subsequent layer adds a *header* that is used to describe the protocol and also identify the packet's source and destination (where it originates from, and where it is going, respectively).

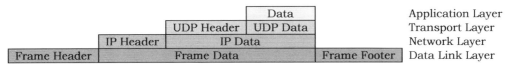

	Application Layer
UDP Header / UDP Data	Transport Layer
IP Header / IP Data	Network Layer
Frame Header / Frame Data / Frame Footer	Data Link Layer

Figure shows the encapsulation of a UDP datagram as an IP datagram. A good analogy for how encapsulation works is a comparison to sending a letter enclosed in an envelope. You might write a letter and put it in a white envelope with a name and address, but if you gave it to a courier for overnight delivery, they would take that envelope and put it in a larger delivery envelope.

Data is passed to IP typically from one of the two main transport layer protocols: TCP or UDP. This data is already in the form of a TCP or UDP message with TCP or UDP headers. This is then encapsulated into the body of an IP message, usually called an IP datagram or IP packet. Encapsulation and formatting of an IP datagram is also sometimes called *packaging*—again, the implied comparison to an envelope is obvious.

9.5.5 UDP Multiplexing and Demultiplexing

A typical UDP/IP (applicable for TCP as well) host has multiple processes each needing to send and receive datagrams. All of them must be sent using the same interface to the internetwork, using the IP layer. This means that the data from all applications (with some possible exceptions) is funnelled down, initially to the transport layer, where it is handled by either TCP or UDP.

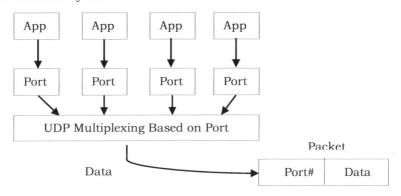

UDP datagrams are received from multiple application programs. A single sequence of UDP datagrams is passed to the IP layer. From there, messages pass to the device's IP layer, where they are packaged in IP datagrams and sent out over the internetwork to different destinations. The technical term for this is *multiplexing* (simply means *combining*).

An opposite mechanism is responsible for receipt of *datagrams*. Each UDP datagram received is passed to appropriate application program. The IP layer must take this stream of unrelated datagrams, and eventually pass them to the correct process (through the transport layer protocol above it). This is the reverse of multiplexing: *demultiplexing*.

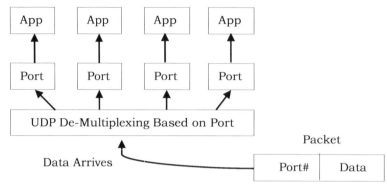

9.5.6 Applications of UDP

Common applications that use UDP include:

- Trivial File Transfer Protocol (TFTP)
- Domain Name System (DNS)
- Remote Procedure Call (RPC), used by the Network File System (NFS)
- Simple Network Management Protocol (SNMP)
- Lightweight Directory Access Protocol (LDAP)
- Streaming media applications such as IPTV
- Voice over IP (VoIP)

9.5.7 UDP Message Format

Each UDP message is called a UDP datagram (just like an IP datagram). Each UDP datagram is sent within a single IP datagram. The IP datagram may be fragmented during transmission; the receiving IP implementation will reassemble it before presenting it to the UDP layer.

Each UDP datagram has two parts: a UDP header and a UDP data area. The header is divided into the following four 16 bit fields.

00 To 15	16 To 31
Source Port	Destination Port
Length	Checksum
Application Data	

Source Port [16-bits]: Indicates the port of the sending process. It is the port to which replies should be addressed.

Destination Port [16-bits]: Specifies the port of the destination process on the destination host.

Length [16-bits]: The length (in bytes) of this user datagram, including the header.

Checksum [16-bits]: An optional 16-bit one's complement of the one's complement sum of a *pseudo*-IP header, the UDP header, and the UDP data. The pseudo-IP header contains the source and destination IP addresses, the protocol, and the UDP length.

Pseudo header is added to the UDP datagram at the time of checksum calculation (at transmitter and at receiver). The pseudo header is not transmitted. It is used to verify the correctness of the IP address.

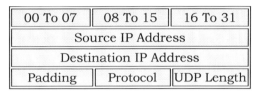

00 To 07	08 To 15	16 To 31
Source IP Address		
Destination IP Address		
Padding	Protocol	UDP Length

Application Data [*Variable size*]: The encapsulated higher-layer message to be sent.

9.5.8 UDP Checksum Calculation

Checksum is an error detection method used by the higher-layer protocol. The LRC (Longitudinal Redundancy Check), CRC (Cyclic Redundancy Check), VRC (Vertical Redundancy Check) are used in lower OSI layer for error detection. But, only the Checksum is used for error detection in the upper layer.

The UDP checksum provides for error detection. UDP at the sender side performs the one's complement of the sum of all the 16-bit words in the segment. This result is put in the checksum field of the UDP segment.

When the segment arrives (if it arrives!) at the receiving host, all 16-bit words are added together, including the checksum. If this sum equals 1111111111111111, then the segment has no detected errors. If one of the bits is a zero, then we know that errors have been introduced into the segment.

Here we give a simple example of the checksum calculation. As an example, suppose that we have the following three 16-bit words:

$$0110\ 0110\ 0110\ 0110$$
$$0101\ 0101\ 0101\ 0101$$
$$0000\ 1111\ 0000\ 1111$$

9.5.8.1 The sum of first of two 16-bit words

0110 0110 0110 0110	
0101 0101 0101 0101	
1011 1011 1011 1011	Sum of first two 16-bit words

9.5.8.2 Adding the third word to the above sum

1011 1011 1011 1011	Sum of first two 16-bit words
0000 1111 0000 1111	Third 16-bit word
1100 1010 1100 1010	Sum of all three 16-bit words

9.5.8.3 Taking 1's complement of the final sum

The 1's complement is obtained by converting all the 0s to 1s and converting all the 1s to 0s. The 1's complement of the sum 1100 1010 1100 1010 is 0011 0101 0011 0101, which becomes the checksum. The 1's complement of final sum is called the checksum in UDP.

1100 1010 1100 1010	Sum of all three 16-bit words
0011 0101 0011 0101	1's complement of final sum

At the receiver, all four 16-bit words are added, including the checksum. If no errors are introduced into the segment, then clearly the sum at the receiver will be 1111 1111 1111 1111. If one of the bits is a zero, then we know that errors have been introduced into the segment.

Sample code which performs the checksum is given below.

```
int checkSum(int * buf, int count) {
    int sum = 0;
    while (count--) {
        sum+= *buf++;
        if (sum & 0xFFFF0000) {
            sum &= 0xFFFF;
            sum++;
        }
    }
    return ~(sum & 0xFFFF);
}
```

9.6 Transmission Control Protocol [TCP]

When two applications want to communicate to each other *reliably*, they establish a connection and send data back and forth over that connection. This is similar to making a *telephone* call. If we want to speak to a person who is in another country, a connection is established when we dial the phone number and the other party answers.

We send data back and forth over the connection by speaking to one another over the phone lines. Like the phone company, TCP guarantees that data sent from one end of the connection actually gets to the other end and in the same order it was sent. Otherwise, an error is reported.

9.6.1 What is TCP?

TCP provides a point-to-point channel for applications that require reliable communications. The Hypertext Transfer Protocol (HTTP), File Transfer Protocol (FTP), and Telnet are all examples of applications that require a reliable communication.

The order in which the data is sent and received over the network is *critical* to the success of these applications. When HTTP is used to read from a URL, the data must be received in the order in which it was sent. Otherwise, we end up with a jumbled HTML file, a corrupt zip file, or some other invalid information.

Application Layer	HTTP, FTP, Telnet, SMTP,...
Transport Layer	TCP, UDP,...

Network Layer	IP,...
Link Layer	Device driver,...

Definition: TCP is a connection-based protocol that provides a reliable flow of data between two computers.

Transport protocols are used to deliver information from one port to another and thereby enable *communication between* application *programs*. They use either a connection-oriented or connectionless method of communication. TCP is a connection-oriented protocol and UDP is a connectionless transport protocol.

The reliability of the communication between the source and destination programs is ensured through error-detection and error-correction mechanisms that are implemented within TCP. TCP implements the connection as a stream of bytes from source to destination.

9.6.2 TCP Steam Delivery

TCP allows the sending proces to deliver data as a stream of bytes and receiving process to get data as a stream of bytes. TCP creates an environment in which two processes are connected by an imaginary pipe that carries their data across the Internet.

9.6.3 TCP Segments

The IP layer sends data as packets not as a stream of bytes. At the transport layer, TCP groups a number of bytes together into a packet called a *segment*. TCP adds a header to each segment and delivers it to the IP layer for transmission.

9.6.3.1 Virtual Circuits

TCP is a *connection-oriented end-to-end* protocol, meaning that some sort of connection must be established between the end-points. Applications establish a connection between end points, use the connection for sending data and then finally close the connection. Having such a connection means that end-points can acknowledge receipt of TCP packets, called *segments*.

These connections between end-points are called *virtual circuits*. This is because the circuit is really just the illusion of a connection; recall that the IP layer is connectionless. A virtual circuit is established when two end-points become associated. In TCP, each end-point is defined by the IP address of the end-point, together with a port number. A port is simply a connection that exists between the TCP layer and the application layer. Each running application will have its own port. This combination of IP address and port number is called a *socket*.

9.6.4 TCP Sending and Receiving Buffers

TCP needs buffers for storing data, because the sending and receiving processes may not at same speed. There are two buffers needed for each direction: *sending buffer* and *receiving buffer*.

9.6.5 TCP/IP

TCP/IP stands for *Transmission Control Protocol/Internet Protocol*. It was developed in 1978 and driven by *Bob Kahn* and *Vinton Cerf*. Today, TCP/IP is a language governing communications among all computers on the Internet.

TCP/IP is two separate protocols, *TCP* and *IP*, which are used together. The Internet Protocol standard controls how packets of information are sent out over networks. IP has a packet-addressing method that lets any computer on the Internet forward a packet to another computer that is a step (or more) closer to the packet's recipient.

The TCP ensures the reliability of data transmission across Internet connected networks. TCP checks packets for errors and submits requests for re-transmissions if errors are found; it also will return the multiple packets of a message into a proper, original sequence when the message reaches its destination.

9.6.6 Characteristics of TCP

Following are the characteristics of TCP:

- Connection-oriented
- Reliable
- Divides outgoing messages into segments
- Reassembles messages at the destination station
- Re-sends anything not received
- Reassembles messages from incoming segments

9.6.7 The Concept of a Transport Protocol

TCP provides an interface to network communications that is different from the User Datagram Protocol (UDP). The properties of TCP make it highly attractive to network programmers, as it simplifies network communication by solving many of the problems of UDP, such as ordering of packets and packet loss.

While UDP is concerned with the transmission of packets of data, TCP focuses instead on establishing a network connection, through which a stream of bytes may be sent and received. The diagram below is the simplest way to show the concept of a *transport* protocol.

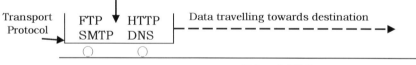

9.6.8 TCP Connection Establishment: Three-Way Handshake

Internet Protocol (IP) handles the delivery of messages (called *packets*) from one computer to another over a network. Transmission Control Protocol (TCP) abstracts the details of IP and makes sure these packets are properly constructed on one end and also make sense on the other end. TCP uses some metadata headers to describe what travels in each packet.

SYN and ACK are types of metadata that comes with the packets. SYN (*sequence number*) is used to identify packets so they can be reassembled, because the network is a strange place with traffic jams and sometimes packets may arrive out of order, if at all. ACK means "Acknowledged" and is a way for one of the computes to say "OK, got that" to the other.

To understand the TCP connection process, let us look at this simple example.

1. The Firefox browser sends a SYN, which is a new sequence ID
2. The server acknowledges with an ACK and also sends a SYN
3. The Firefox browser acknowledges with ACK and at this point the two have been properly introduced and are ready to start talking

These handshake packets are small and regardless of the available bandwidth, they travel at the same speed. A user may have a fast connection, but at this stage it will not be used.

Once a connection is established, then the actual transfer of a file (say, an image) can start. The file is usually sent in several packets, depending on its size. The server sends one packet and waits for acknowledgement ACK from the browser.

The application data is broken into what TCP considers the best sized chunks to send. This is totally different from UDP, where each write by the application generates a UDP datagram of that size. The unit of information passed by TCP to IP is called a *segment*.

What this basically means is that a *connection is established* between the two nodes before any data is transferred. When the term *connection is established* is used; this means that both nodes know about each other and have agreed on the exchange of data. The following diagram explains the procedure of the 3-way handshake:

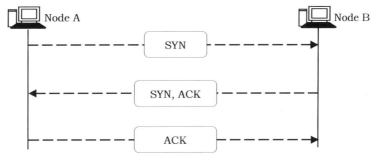

STEP − 1: Node A sends the initial packet to Node B. This packet has the *SYN* bit enabled. Node B receives the packet and sees the *SYN* bit which has a value of "1" (in binary, this means ON) so it knows that Node A is trying to establish a connection with it.

STEP − 2: Assuming Node B has enough resources, it sends a packet back to Node A and with the *SYN and ACK* bits enabled. The SYN that Node B sends, at this step, means 'I want to synchronise with you' and the ACK means 'I acknowledge your previous SYN request'.

STEP − 3: Node A sends another packet to Node B and with the *ACK* bit set (with binary 1); it effectively tells Node B 'Yes, I acknowledge your previous request'.

Once the 3-way handshake is complete, the connection is established (virtual circuit) and the data transfer begins.

9.6.9 Understanding TCP Sequence and Acknowledgment Numbers

To help us understand how these newly introduced fields are used to track a connection's packets, an example is given below.

Before we proceed, we should note that you will come across the terms *ACK flag* or *SYN flag*; these terms should not be confused with the *Sequence* and *Acknowledgment* numbers as they are different fields within the TCP header.

Let understand this by showing two nodes that want to send data to each other in a reliable way. Node A wants to send data to Node B in a reliable way, so we are going to use TCP to accomplish this.

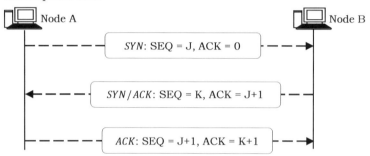

Step − 1: First our Node A will send a TCP SYN, telling Node B that it wants to setup a connection. There's also a sequence number and to keep things simple we picked number J.

Step − 2: Node B will respond to Node A by sending a SYN, ACK message back. We can see it picks its own sequence number K (some random number) and it sends ACK=J+1. ACK= J+1 means that it acknowledges that it has received the TCP SYN from Node A which had sequence number J and that it is ready for the next message with sequence number J+1.

Step − 3: The last step is that Node A will send an acknowledgement towards Node B in response of the SYN that Node B sent towards Node A. We can see it sends ACK=K+1 which means it acknowledges the SEQ=K from Node B. Since Node B sent a ACK=J+1 towards Node A, Node A now knows it can send the next message with sequence number J+1.

9.6.10 Closing a TCP connection

While it takes three packets (segments) to establish a connection, it takes *four* packets (segments) to terminate a connection. This is caused by TCP's *half-close*. Since a TCP connection is full-duplex (that is, data can be flowing in each direction independently of the other direction), each direction must be shut down independently.

The rule is that either end can send a FIN when it is done sending data. When a TCP receives a FIN, it must notify the application that the other end has terminated that direction of data flow. The sending of a FIN is normally the result of the application issuing a *close*.

While it's possible for an application to take advantage of the half-close feature, in practice few TCP applications use it.

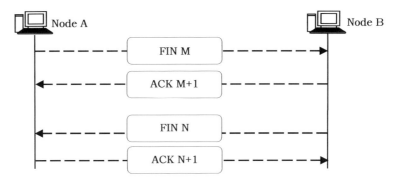

Step-1: One application calls *close* first, and we say that this end (Node A) performs the *active close*. This end's TCP sends a FIN segment, which means it is finished sending data.

Step-2: The other end that receives the FIN performs the *passive close*. The received FIN is acknowledged by TCP. The receipt of the FIN is also passed to the application as an end-of-file (after any data that may have already been queued for the application to receive), since the receipt of the FIN means the application will not receive any additional data on the connection.

Step-3: Sometime later, the application that received the end-of-file will close its socket. This causes its TCP to send a FIN.

Step-4: The TCP on the system that receives this final FIN (the end that did the active close) acknowledges the FIN.

Since a FIN and an ACK are required in each direction, four segments are normally required. We use the qualifier *normally* because in some scenarios, the FIN in Step 1 is sent with data. Also, the segments in Steps 2 and 3 are both from the end performing the passive close and could be combined into one segment.

9.6.10.1 Two-Army Problem

Unfortunately, this protocol does not always work. There is a famous problem that illustrates this issue. It is called the two-army problem. Imagine that a white army is encamped in a valley, as shown in figure.

On both of the surrounding hillsides are blue armies.

The white army is larger than either of the blue armies alone, but together the blue armies are larger than the white army. If either blue army attacks by itself, it will be defeated, but if the two blue armies attack simultaneously, they will be victorious.

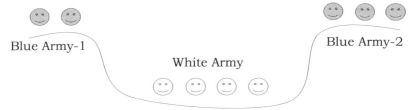

The blue armies want to synchronize their attacks. However, their only communication medium is to send messengers on foot down into the valley, where they might be captured and the message lost (i.e., they have to use an unreliable communication channel). The question is: Does a protocol exist that allows the blue armies to win?

Suppose that the commander of blue army #1 sends a message reading: "I propose we attack at dawn on October 31. How about it?" Now suppose that the message arrives, the commander of blue army #2 agrees, and his reply gets safely back to blue army #1. Will the attack happen? Probably not, because commander #2 does not know if his reply got through. If it did not, blue army #1 will not attack, so it would be foolish for him to charge into battle.

Now let us improve the protocol by making it a *three − way handshake*. The initiator of the original proposal must acknowledge the response. Assuming no messages are lost, blue army #2 will get the acknowledgement, but the commander of blue army #1 will now hesitate. After all, he does not know if his acknowledgement got through, and if it did not, he knows that blue army #2 will not attack. We could now make a four-way handshake protocol, but that does not help either.

In fact, it can be proven that no protocol exists that works. Suppose that some protocol did exist. Either the last message of the protocol is essential or it is not. If it is not, remove it (and any other unessential messages) until we are left with a protocol in which every message is essential.

What happens if the final message does not get through? We just said that it was essential, so if it is lost, the attack does not take place. Since the sender of the final message can never be sure of its arrival, he will not risk attacking. Worse yet, the other blue army know this, so it will not attack either.

To see the relevance of the two-army problem to releasing connections, just substitute "disconnect" for "attack." If neither side is prepared to disconnect until it is convinced that the other side is prepared to disconnect too, the disconnection will never happen.

In practice, one is usually prepared to take more risks when releasing connections than when attacking white armies, so the situation is not entirely hopeless. Figure shows four scenarios of releasing using a three-way handshake. While this protocol is not infallible, it is usually adequate.

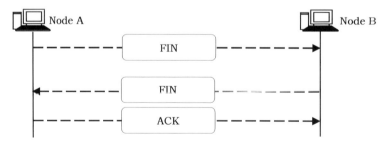

In figure, we see the normal case in which one of the users sends a FIN (Finish) segment to initiate the connection release. When it arrives, the receiver sends back a FIN segment, too, and starts a timer, just in case its FIN is lost. When this FIN arrives, the original sender sends back an ACK segment and releases the connection.

Finally, when the ACK segment arrives, the receiver also releases the connection. Releasing a connection means that the transport entity removes the information about the connection from its table of currently open connections and signals the connection's owner (the transport user) somehow. This action is different from a transport user issuing a DISCONNECT primitive.

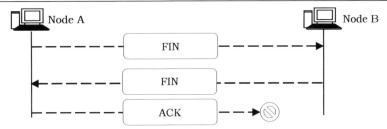

If the final ACK segment is lost, as shown in above figure, the situation is saved by the timer. When the timer expires, the connection is released anyway.

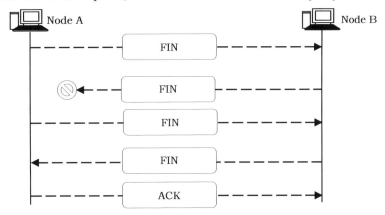

Now consider the case of the second FIN being lost. The user initiating the disconnection will not receive the expected response, will time out, and will start all over again. In above figure we see how this works, assuming that the second time no segments are lost and all segments are delivered correctly and on time.

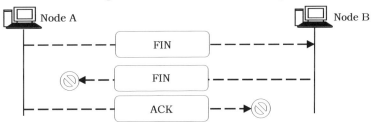

Our last scenario, figure above, is the same as previous case except that now we assume all the repeated attempts to retransmit the FIN also fail due to lost segments. After N retries, the sender just gives up and releases the connection. Meanwhile, the receiver times out and also exits.

While this protocol usually suffices, in theory it can fail if the initial FIN and N retransmissions are all lost. The sender will give up and release the connection, while the other side knows nothing at all about the attempts to disconnect and is still fully active. This situation results in a half-open connection.

We could have avoided this problem by not allowing the sender to give up after N retries but forcing it to go on forever until it gets a response. However, if the other side is allowed to time out, then the sender will indeed go on forever, because no response will ever be forthcoming. If we do not allow the receiving side to time out, then the protocol hangs.

One way to kill off half-open connections is to have a rule saying that if no segments have arrived for a certain number of seconds, the connection is then automatically disconnected. That way, if one side ever disconnects, the other side will detect the lack of activity and also disconnect.

Of course, if this rule is introduced, it is necessary for each transport entity to have a timer that is stopped and then restarted whenever a segment is sent. If this timer expires, a dummy segment is transmitted, just to keep the other side from disconnecting. On the other hand, if the automatic disconnect rule is used and too many dummy segments in a row are lost on an otherwise idle connection, first one side, then the other side will automatically disconnect.

We will not belabour this point any more, but by now it should be clear that releasing a connection without data loss is not nearly as simple as it at first appears.

9.6.11 TCP Reliability

When data is ready to be transmitted via TCP, it is passed from the upper-layer protocol to TCP, where it becomes encapsulated into segments. The IP layer then encapsulates these segments into datagrams and handles the point-to-point transmission of the data.

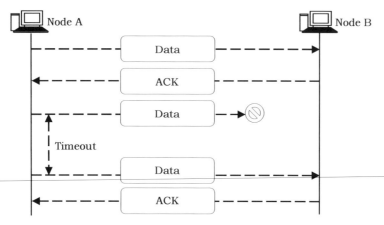

At the other end, the receiving station acknowledges receipt of the segment at the TCP layer by sending back an ACK message. If the original sender does not receive the ACK within a certain time period, then it retransmits the original segment. This is called Positive Acknowledgment Retransmission or PAR.

Of course, it's possible that the original message may just arrive late. In this case, the receiving station will eventually receive two identical segments. The duplicate segment is simply discarded.

How long should the timeout period be? I.e. how long should Node A wait for a response from Node B before it resends the packet? Clearly, within a LAN, Node A would expect packets to be acknowledged within just a few milliseconds. However, if Node A and B are on different sides of the globe, then a much longer timeout period is required.

If the timeout is set too long, unnecessary delays will be introduced into the network. If the timeout is set too short, then premature retransmission will result in packet duplications, leading to network congestion and eventually to a state of collapse. For this reason, TCP uses algorithms to dynamically adjust the timeout period to suit the state of the network.

9.6.12 TCP Flow Control

TCP provides a way for the receiver to control the amount of data sent by the sender. Nodes that send and receive TCP data segments can operate at different data rates because of differences in CPU and network bandwidth. As a result, it is possible for sender to send data at a faster rate than the receiver can handle.

TCP implements a flow control mechanism that controls the amount of data send by the sender. This is achieved by using a *sliding window mechanism*. The receiver TCP module sends back to the sender an acknowledgment that indicates a range of acceptable sequence numbers beyond the last successfully received segment. This range of acceptable sequence numbers is called a *window*.

9.6.12.1 TCP Sliding Window

One of TCP's primary functions is to *properly match* the *transmission rate* of the sender to that of the receiver and the network. It is important for the transmission to be at a high enough rates to ensure good performance, but also to protect against overwhelming traffic at the network or receiving host.

TCP's 16-bit window field is used by the receiver to tell the sender how many bytes of data the receiver is willing to accept. Since the window field is limited to a maximum of 16 bits, this provides for a maximum window size of 65,535 bytes.

The window size advertised by the receiver (called *advertised window*) tells the sender how much data, starting from the current position in the TCP data byte stream can be sent without waiting for further acknowledgements. As data is sent by the sender and then acknowledged by the receiver, the window slides forward to cover more data in the byte stream. This concept is called *sliding window* and is shown in figure.

Window

As shown above, data within the window boundary is eligible to be sent by the sender.

Bytes sent and got ACK's

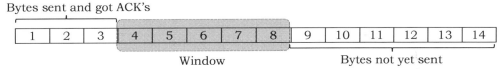

Window   Bytes not yet sent

Those bytes in the stream prior to the window have already been sent and acknowledged. Bytes ahead of the window have not been sent and must wait for the window to *slide* forward before they can be transmitted by the sender. A receiver can adjust the window size each time it sends acknowledgements to the sender.

Window

The maximum transmission rate is ultimately bound by the receiver's ability to accept and process data. However, this technique implies an implicit trust arrangement between the TCP sender and receiver.

The window size reflects the amount of buffer space available for new data at the receiver. If this buffer space size shrinks because the receiver is being overrun, the receiver will send back a smaller window size.

In the extreme case the windows size will decrease to very small or one octet. This is called the *silly window syndrome*. Most TCP implementations take special measure to avoid it.

The goal of the sliding window mechanism is to keep the channel full of data and to reduce the delays for waiting acknowledgements.

Note: For more details refer *TCP Flow Control* chapter.

9.6.13 TCP Error Control

Refer *TCP Error Control* chapter.

9.6.14 TCP Congestion Control

Refer *TCP Congestion Control* chapter.

9.6.15 TCP Checksum Calculation

Refer *TCP Error Control* chapter.

9.6.16 TCP Timer Management

To keep track of lost or discarded segments and to perform the operations smoothly, the following four timers are used by TCP:

1. *Retransmission Timer*: It is dynamically decided by the round trip delay time.
2. *Persistence Timer*: This is used to deal with window size advertisement.
3. *Keep-alive Timer*: Commonly used in situations where there is long idle connection between two processes
4. *Time-waited Timer*: It is used during connection terminations.

9.6.17 TCP Multiplexing and Demultiplexing

A typical TCP/IP (same as UDP) host has multiple processes each needing to send and receive datagrams. All of them must be sent using the same interface to the internetwork, using the IP layer.

This means that the data from all applications (with some possible exceptions) is funnelled down, initially to the transport layer, where it is handled by either TCP or UDP.

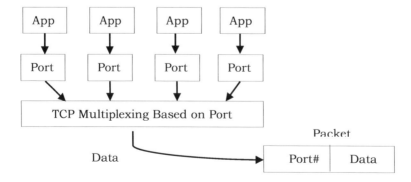

TCP segments are received from multiple application programs. . A single sequence of UDP datagrams is passed to the IP layer. From there, messages pass to the device's IP layer, where they are packaged in IP datagrams and sent out over the internetwork to different destinations. The technical term for this is *multiplexing* (simply means *combining*).

An opposite mechanism is responsible for receipt of *segments*. Each TCP segment received is passed to appropriate application program. The IP layer must take this stream of unrelated segments, and eventually pass them to the correct process (through the transport layer protocol above it). This is the reverse of multiplexing: *demultiplexing*.

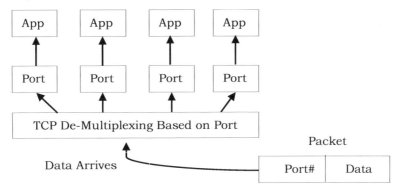

9.6.18 TCP Encapsulation

TCP encapsulation is also pretty much similar to UDP. The application packages the data to be sent, and each subsequent layer adds a *header* that is used to describe the protocol and also identify the packet's source and destination (where it originates from, and where it is going, respectively).

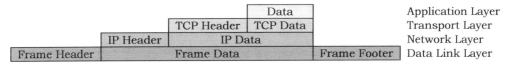

Figure shows the encapsulation of a TCP data as an IP datagram. A good analogy for how encapsulation works is a comparison to sending a letter enclosed in an envelope.

You might write a letter and put it in a white envelope with a name and address, but if you gave it to a courier for overnight delivery, they would take that envelope and put it in a larger delivery envelope.

Data is passed to IP typically from one of the two main transport layer protocols: TCP or UDP. This data is already in the form of a TCP or UDP message with TCP or UDP headers.

This is then encapsulated into the body of an IP message, usually called an IP datagram or IP packet. Encapsulation and formatting of an IP datagram is also sometimes called *packaging*—again, the implied comparison to an envelope is obvious.

9.6.19 TCP State Transition Diagram

A TCP connection goes through a series of states during its lifetime. The eleven states are: LISTEN, SYN-SENT, SYN-RECEIVED, ESTABLISHED, FIN-WAIT-1, FIN-WAIT-2, CLOSE-WAIT, CLOSING, LAST-ACK, TIME-WAIT, and the fictional state CLOSED.

CLOSED is fictional because it represents the state when the connection is terminated.

⟶   Normal transitions for client

---➤   Normal transitions for server

appl: State transitions taken when application issues

recv: State transitions taken when segment received

send: What is sent for this transition

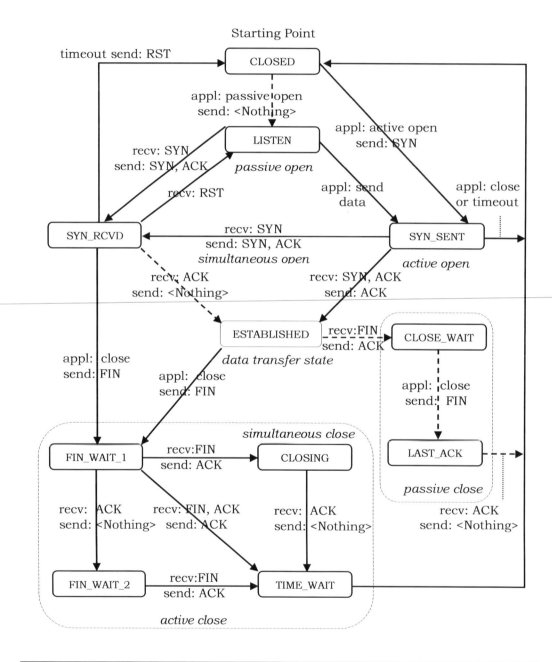

Briefly the meanings of the states are:

LISTEN: LISTEN state indicates waiting for a connection request from any TCP client.

SYN − SENT: SYN-SENT state indicates waiting for a matching connection request after having sent a connection request.

SYN − RECEIVED: This is the state which indicates waiting for a confirming connection request acknowledgment after having both received and sent a connection request.

ESTABLISHED: An open connection, data can be sent in both directions. This is the normal state for the data transfer phase of the connection.

FIN − WAIT − 1: FIN_WAIT_1 state which indicates waiting for a connection termination request from the remote TCP, or an acknowledgment of the connection termination request previously sent.

FIN − WAIT − 2: FIN_WAIT_2 state indicates waiting for a connection termination request from the remote TCP.

CLOSE − WAIT: This is the state which indicates waiting for a connection termination request from the local user.

CLOSING: CLOSING state indicates waiting for a connection termination request acknowledgment from the remote TCP.

LAST − ACK: LAST_ACK state indicates Waiting for an acknowledgment of the connection termination request previously sent to the remote TCP.

TIME_WAIT: This is the state which indicates Waiting for enough time before transitioning to a closed state to ensure the remote TCP received its last ACK.

The two transitions leading to the ESTABLISHED state correspond to the opening of a connection, and the two transitions leading from the ESTABLISHED state are for the termination of a connection. The ESTABLISHED state is where data transfer can occur between the two ends in both the directions.

If a connection is in the LISTEN state and a SYN segment arrives, the connection makes a transition to the SYN_RCVD state and takes the action of replying with an ACK+SYN segment. The client does an active open which causes its end of the connection to send a SYN segment to the server and to move to the SYN_SENT state.

The arrival of the SYN+ACK segment causes the client to move to the ESTABLISHED state and to send an ACK back to the server. When this ACK arrives the server finally moves to the ESTABLISHED state. In other words, we have just traced the THREE-WAY HANDSHAKE.

In the process of terminating a connection, the important thing to keep in mind is that the application process on both sides of the connection must independently close its half of the connection. Thus, on any one side there are three combinations of transition that get a connection from the ESTABLISHED state to the CLOSED state:

This side closes first:

ESTABLISHED → FIN_WAIT_1 → FIN_WAIT_2 → TIME_WAIT → CLOSED

The other side closes first:

ESTABLISHED → CLOSE_WAIT → LAST_ACK → CLOSED

Both sides close at the same time:

ESTABLISHED → FIN_WAIT_1 → CLOSING → TIME_WAIT → CLOSED

The main thing to recognize about connection teardown is that a connection in the TIME_WAIT state cannot move to the CLOSED state until it has waited for two times the maximum amount of time an IP datagram might live in the Inter net. The reason for this is that while the local side of the connection has sent an ACK in response to the other side's FIN segment, it does not know that the ACK was successfully delivered.

As a consequence this other side might re transmit its FIN segment, and this second FIN segment might be delayed in the network. If the connection were allowed to move directly to the CLOSED state, then another pair of application processes might come along and open the same connection, and the delayed FIN segment from the earlier incarnation of the connection would immediately initiate the termination of the later incarnation of that connection.

9.6.20 TCP Header

TCP data is encapsulated in an IP datagram. The figure shows the format of the TCP header. Its normal size is 20 bytes unless options are present. Each of the fields is discussed below.

00 To 15								16 To 31
Source Port Number								Destination Port Number
Sequence Number								
Acknowledgment Number								
4-bit Header Length	Reserved (6-bits)	URG	ACK	PSH	RST	SYN	FIN	Window Size
Checksum								Urgent Pointer
Options (if any)								
Data (if any)								

Source Port [16-bit]: This is the source port of the packet. The source port was originally bound directly to a process on the sending system.

Destination Port [16-bit]: This is the destination port of the TCP packet. Just as with the source port, this was originally bound directly to a process on the receiving system. Today, a hash is used instead, which allows us to have more open connections at the same time.

Sequence Number [32-bit]: The sequence number field is used to set a number on each TCP packet so that the TCP stream can be properly sequenced (e.g., the packets winds up in the correct order).

Acknowledgment Number [32-bit]: This field is used when we acknowledge a specific packet a host has received. For example, we receive a packet with one Sequence number set, and if everything is okay with the packet, we reply with an ACK packet with the Acknowledgment number set to the same as the original Sequence number.

Data Offset [4-bit]: This field indicates how long the TCP header is, and where the Data part of the packet actually starts. It is set with 4 bits, and measures the TCP header in 32 bit words.

Reserved [6-bits]: These bits are reserved for future usage.

URG [1-bit]: This field tells us if we should use the Urgent Pointer field or not. If set to 0, do not use Urgent Pointer, if set to 1, do use Urgent pointer.

ACK [1-bit]: This bit is set to a packet to indicate that this is in reply to another packet that we received, and that contained data. An Acknowledgment packet is always sent to indicate that we have actually received a packet, and that it contained no errors. If this bit is set, the original data sender will check the Acknowledgment Number to see which packet is actually acknowledged, and then dump it from the buffers.

PSH [1-bit]: The PUSH flag is used to tell the TCP protocol on any intermediate hosts to send the data on to the actual user, including the TCP implementation on the receiving host. This will push all data through, unregardless of where or how much of the TCP Window that has been pushed through yet.

RST [1-bit]: The RESET flag is set to tell the other end to tear down the TCP connection. This is done in a couple of different scenarios, the main reasons being that the connection has crashed for some reason, if the connection does not exist, or if the packet is wrong in some way.

SYN [1-bit]: The SYN (or Synchronize sequence numbers) is used during the initial establishment of a connection. It is set in two instances of the connection, the initial packet that opens the connection, and the reply SYN/ACK packet. It should never be used outside of those instances.

FIN [1-bit]: The FIN bit indicates that the host that sent the FIN bit has no more data to send. When the other end sees the FIN bit, it will reply with a FIN/ACK. Once this is done, the host that originally sent the FIN bit can no longer send any data. However, the other end can continue to send data until it is finished, and will then send a FIN packet back, and wait for the final FIN/ACK, after which the connection is sent to a CLOSED state.

Window Size [16-bit]: The Window size field is used by the receiving host to tell the sender how much data the receiver permits at the moment. This is done by sending an ACK back, which contains the Sequence number that we want to acknowledge, and the Window field then contains the maximum accepted sequence numbers that the sending host can use before he receives the next ACK packet. The next ACK packet will update accepted Window which the sender may use.

Checksum [16-bit]: This field contains the checksum of the whole TCP header. It is a one's complement of the one's complement sum of each 16 bit word in the header. If the header does not end on a 16 bit boundary, the additional bits are set to zero. While the checksum is calculated, the checksum field is set to zero. The checksum also covers a 96 bit *pseudo − header* containing the Destination-, Source-address, protocol, and TCP length. This is for extra security.

00 To 07	08 To 15	16 To 31
Source IP Address		
Destination IP Address		
Reserved	Protocol	TCP Header Length

Urgent Pointer [16-bit]: This is a pointer that points to the end of the data which is considered urgent. If the connection has important data that should be processed as soon as possible by the receiving end, the sender can set the URG flag and set the Urgent pointer to indicate where the urgent data ends.

Options [*Variable Size*]. The Options field is a variable length field and contains optional headers that we may want to use. Basically, this field contains 3 subfields at all times. An initial field tells us the length of the Options field, a second field tells us which options are used, and then we have the actual options.

9.7 Comparison of TCP and UDP

The two protocols TCP and UDP have different strengths and weaknesses that need to be considered within the *context* of the application.

TCP is *focused* around *reliable data transmission*. TCP is most *appropriate* where data integrity is critical. That means, lost packets must be retried and recovered 100% of the time, regardless of any resultant delay. The TCP protocol includes provisions for connection creation, packet verification, packet ordering and re-transmission in the event of failure. TCP communications also can intentionally slow themselves down if losses exceed a certain threshold, to prevent congestion collapse.

Property	TCP	UDP
General Description	TCP is connection-oriented protocol.	UDP is connectionless protocol.
Reliability	When a file or message send it will get delivered unless connections fails. If connection lost, the server will request the lost part. There is no corruption while transferring a message.	When we a send a data or message, we don't know if it'll get there, it could get lost on the way. There may be corruption while transferring a message.
Ordered	If we send two messages along a connection, one after the other, we know the first message will get there first. We don't have to worry about data arriving in the wrong order.	If we send two messages out, we don't know what order they'll arrive in i.e. not ordered.
Overhead	When the low level parts of the TCP *stream* arrive in the wrong order, resend requests have to be sent, and all the out of sequence parts have to be put back together, so requires a bit of work to piece together	No ordering of messages, no tracking connections, etc. It's just fire and forget! This means it's faster.
Transmission	Data is read as a *stream*, with nothing distinguishing where one packet ends and another begins. There may be multiple packets per read call.	Packets are sent individually and are guaranteed to be whole if they arrive. One packet per one read call.
Transmission Speed	Less than UDP.	High
Features for managing data flow	TCP provides these features with Sliding Windows, Error Control, and Congestion Control Algorithms.	None
Examples	World Wide Web (TCP port 80), E-Mail (SMTP TCP port 25), File Transfer Protocol (FTP port 21) and Secure Shell (OpenSSH port 22) etc.	Domain Name System (UDP port 53), Streaming applications such as IPTV or movies, Voice over IP (VoIP), Trivial File Transfer Protocol (TFTP) etc.

UDP is a simpler message-based connectionless protocol, with no dedicated end-to-end connection. Communication is achieved by transmitting information in one direction from source to destination without verifying the readiness or state of the receiver.

Because of the lack of reliability, applications using UDP must be tolerant of data loss, errors, or duplication, or be able to assume correct transmission. Such applications generally do not include reliability mechanisms and may even be hindered by them. In these cases, UDP is a much simpler protocol than TCP and can transfer the same amount of data with far less overhead, and can achieve much greater throughput.

UDP is often preferable for real-time systems, since data delay might be more detrimental than occasional packet loss. Streaming media, real-time multiplayer games and voice-over-IP (VoIP) services are examples of applications that often use UDP. In these particular applications, loss of packets is not usually a fatal problem, since the human eye and ear cannot detect most occasional imperfections in a continuous stream of images or sounds.

To achieve higher performance, the protocol allows individual packets to be dropped with no retries and UDP packets to be received in a different order than they were sent as dictated by the application. Real-time video and audio streaming protocols are designed to handle occasional lost packets, so only slight degradation in quality occurs, rather than large delays, which would occur if lost packets were retransmitted. Another environment in which UDP might be preferred over TCP is within a closed network. UDP might be a more efficient and equally reliable protocol in such situations. UDP's stateless nature is also useful for servers answering small queries from huge numbers of clients, such as DNS, SNMP and so on.

Both TCP and UDP are widely used IP transfer layer protocols. For applications requiring reliable transfers, *TCP* is generally preferred, while applications that value throughput more than reliability are best served using UDP.

Most TCP/IP stacks provide both protocols, so the application can use whichever transfer protocol is more appropriate, even changing from one to the other as desired. Rather than rely solely on TCP, the network system developer might want to investigate the trade-offs related to use of UDP.

9.8 Why Some TCP/IP Applications Use UDP?

So what applications use UDP then? UDP's limitation is that because it doesn't provide *reliability* features, an application that uses UDP is responsible for those functions. In general, if an application needs the features that TCP provides but not the ones that UDP provides, it's inefficient to allow the application to implement those features. If the application needs what TCP provides, it should just use TCP!

Applications might use UDP for the following reasons:

- Data Where *Performance* Is More Important Than *Completeness*
- Data Exchanges That Are *Short* and *Sweet*

9.8.1 Data Where *Performance* Is More Important Than *Completeness*

The classic example of this category is a *multimedia* application. For streaming a video clip over the Internet, the most important feature is that the stream starts flowing quickly and keeps flowing. Human beings notice only significant disruption, the flow of this type of information, so a few bytes of data missing due to a lost datagram is not a big problem.

Also, even if someone used TCP for something like this and noticed and retransmitted a lost datagram, it would be useless, because the lost datagram would belong to a part of the clip that is long past-and the time spent in that retransmission might make the current part of the clip arrive late. Clearly, UDP is best for this situation.

9.8.2 Data Exchanges That Are Short and Sweet

There are many TCP/IP applications in which the underlying protocol consists of only a very simple request/reply exchange. A client sends a short request message to a server, and a short reply message goes back from the server to the client. In this situation, there is no real need to set tip a connection the way that TCP does.

Also, if a client sends only one short message, a single IP datagram can carry the message. This means that there is no need to worry about data arriving out of order, flow control between the devices, and so forth.

How about the loss of the request or the reply? These can be handled simply at the application level using timers. If a client sends a request and the server don't get it, the server won't reply, and the client will eventually send a replacement request. The same logic applies if the server sends a response that never arrives.

Problems and Question with Answers

Question 1: The transport layer protocols used for real time multimedia, file transfer, DNS and email respectively are
A) TCP, UDP,UDP and TCP
B) UDP TCP,TCP and UDP
C) UDP, TCP,UDP and TCP
D)TCP, UDP,TCP and UDP

Answer : C. TCP is connection oriented and UDP is connectionless, this makes TCP more reliable than UDP. But UDP is stateless (less overhead), that makes UDP is suitable for purposes where error checking and correction is less important than speed. For real time multimedia and DNS, speed is more important than correctness. For these applications UDP is suitable. For file transfer and Email, reliability is necessary. Hence TCP is suitable.

Question 2: An end system sends 50 packets per second using the User Datagram Protocol (UDP) over a full duplex 100 Mbps Ethernet LAN connection. Each packet consists 1500B of Ethernet frame payload data. What is the throughput, when measured at the UDP layer?

Answer:

Frame Size = 1500B
Packet has the following headers:
IP header (20B)
UDP header (8B)
Total header in each packet = 28B
Total UDP payload data is therefore 1500−28 = 1472B.
Total bits sent per second = 1472 × 8 × 50 = 588800 bps or 588 kbps

Question 3: A client program sends one UDP packet with 100 B of data each second to a server and receives a corresponding reply also with 60 B of data. The client and server are connected by an Ethernet LAN. Calculate the total number of bits sent via the Ethernet network by this program in each second. From the number of bits per second calculate the utilization, given that Ethernet typically operates at 10 Mbps.

Answer: 1 UDP message sent per second, with 1 reply received per second. Each message contains:

MAC-Preamble (8 bytes) + MAC Header (14 bytes) +
IP Header (20 bytes) + UDP (8 bytes) +
UDP Payload (60 bytes) + CRC-32 (4 bytes)

Total sent per second = $(8 + 14 + 20 + 8 + 60 + 4) \times 8 \times 2 = 912 \times 2$ bps = 1824 bps
Total per second= 1824 bits /sec.
Assume 10 Mbps Ethernet operation.
Utilization = $\frac{\text{Total bits per sec}}{\text{clock rate}} \times 100 = (\frac{1824}{10} \times 106) \times 100 = 0.018$ %
Hence, utilization = 0.018 %.

Question 4:   A TCP session sends 10 packets per second over an Ethernet Local Area Network (LAN). Each packet has a total size of 1480 B (excluding the preamble and cyclic redundancy check (CRC)). Calculate the size of the headers, and hence the TCP payload data. What is the TCP throughput of the session?

Answer: First we determine the protocol headers which contribute to the PDU size:

MAC Header (14 bytes) + IP Header (20 bytes) +
TCP(20 bytes) + TCP Payload (?) bytes)

Next determine the size of the payload:
Payload = 1480 - (14 + 20 + 20) = 1426 B
Throughput = Number of useful (data) bits transferred by a layer using the services of the layer below = $1426 \times 8 \times 10 = 114$ kbps.

Question 5:   A small Local Area Network (LAN) has four machines A, B, C and D connected in the following topology:

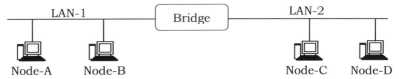

A) The node A sends a graphics file of size 10 MB simultaneously to nodes B, C, and D using Unicast packets constructed by the Universal Datagram Protocol (UDP). Calculate the utilization of LAN 1, given that each frame carries 1024 B of UDP payload data, and transmission is at 50 packets per second to each destination.

B) What is the utilization on LAN 2?

Answer:

A) All packets travel on LAN 1.

Each packet has the following protocol headers (PCI):

MAC-Preamble (8 bytes) + MAC Header (14 bytes) + IP Header (20 bytes) +
UDP(8bytes) + UDP Payload (1024 bytes) + CRC-32 (4 bytes)

Note: The inter-frame gap may also be considered as overhead, which will yield a slightly higher answer.

Total size = $(8 + 14 + 20 + 8 + 1024 + 4) \times 8 = 8624$ bits.

50 UDP message sent per second to 3 computers = 150 UDP messages/second

Assume 10 Mbps Ethernet operation.

Total utilization = $8624 \times 150 / (10 \times 1000\,000 \times 100) = 13\%$.

B) This is different, since this is unicast transmission, the bridge will not forward packets from A to B. It will however forward packets from A to B and C. The utilization on LAN 2 is therefore: 2/3 of 13%, i.e. 9%.

Question 6: Most connection establishment protocols rely on a three-way handshake. Why is a three-way handshake protocol better than a two-way handshake?

Answer: A three-way handshake is better than a two-way handshake because it allows the communicating parties to detect and recover from duplicate connection establishment packets.

Question 7: A TCP sender transmits a 2K-byte packet to the receiver with a sequence number of 0. The receiver has 16K-bytes of buffer space available just before the packet arrives. Assuming the packet remains in the receiver buffer when the receiver generates an acknowledgement, what will the acknowledgement sequence number be? What will the window size be? If the maximum segment size is 2K-bytes, how many more packets can the sender transmit without first waiting for an acknowledgement?

Answer: The TCP acknowledgement sequence number is the sequence number of the byte next expected by the receiver. Since the first data packet from the sender contained bytes with sequences numbers 0 through 2047, the acknowledgement sequence number is number 2048.

The window size is 16K-2K (or 14K) because there is one packet in the receiver-side buffer when the acknowledgement is generated. Since the window size is 14K, the sender can send up to 7 2K packets before waiting for another acknowledgement.

Question 8: Suppose we wanted to do a transaction from a remote client to a server as fast as possible. Would we use UDP or TCP?

Answer: UDP. UDP is faster than TCP.

Question 9: Suppose host A sends two TCP segments back to back to host B over a TCP connection. The first segment has sequence number 190; the second has sequence number 210.
A) How much data is in the first segment?
B) Suppose the first segment is lost but the second segment arrives at B. In the acknowledgment that host B sends to host A, what will be the acknowledgment number?

Answer:

A) The first segment contains $210 - 190 = 20$ bytes of data.

B) TCP acknowledgments are cumulative and hence host B will acknowledge that it has received everything up to and excluding sequence number 190.

Question 10: Which transport layer protocol provides connection-oriented, reliable transport?
A) TFTP   B) UDP   C) Ethernet   D) TCP   E) Secure Shell

Answer: D.

Question 11: Assume two end-hosts communicate using the sliding window protocol. Assume the receiver window is always smaller than the sender's window and the size of the receiver window is w bits. Let C be the link capacity between the two end-hosts in bps, and RTT be the round-trip time between the two end hosts in sec. What is the maximum throughput achieved by the two end-hosts? Assume every bit is acknowledged.

Answer: There are two cases (see figure below)

Case 1: RTT > $\frac{w}{C}$, throughput = $\frac{w}{RTT}$
Case 2: RTT ≤ $\frac{w}{C}$, throughput = C

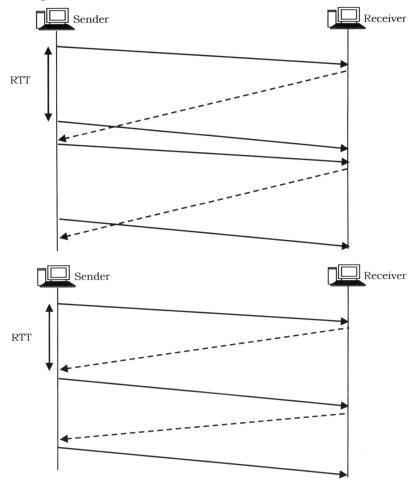

Question 12: Suppose Host A is sending a large file to Host B over a TCP connection. If the sequence number for a segment of this connection is m, then the sequence number for the subsequent segment will necessarily be $m + 1$. Is it true of false?

Answer: False

Question 13: Host A is sending Host B a large file over a TCP connection. Assume Host B has no data to send Host A. Host B will not send acknowledgements to Host A because Host B cannot piggyback the acknowledgements on data.

Answer: False

Question 14: Suppose that the last SampleRTT in a TCP connection is equal to 1 sec. The current value of TimeoutInterval for the connection will necessarily be = 1 sec.

Answer: False

Question 15: Suppose Host A is sending Host B a large file over a TCP connection. The number of unacknowledged bytes that A sends cannot exceed the size of the receive buffer.

Answer: True

Question 16: The size of the TCP RcvWindow never changes throughout the duration of the connection.

Answer: False

Question 17: The TCP segment has a field in its header for RcvWindow.

Answer: True

Question 18: Suppose Host A sends one segment with sequence number 38 and 4 bytes of data over a TCP connection to Host B. In this same segment the acknowledgement number is necessarily 42.

Answer: False

Question 19: Suppose Host A sends two TCP segments back to back to Host B aver a TCP connection. The first segment has sequence number 90; the second has sequence number 110.
A) Suppose that the first segment is lost but the second segment arrives at B. In the acknowledgement that Host B to Host A, what will be the acknowledgement number?
B) How much data is in the first segment?

Answer:
A) Ack number = 90
B) 20 bytes

Question 20: Suppose Client A initiates a Telnet session with Server S. At about the same time, Client B also initiates a Telnet session with Server S. Provide possible source and destination port numbers for
A) The segments sent from A to S.
B) The segments sent from B to S.
C) The segments sent from S to A.
D) The segments sent from S to B.
E) If A and B are different hosts, is it possible that the source port number in the segments from A to S is the same as that from B to S?
F) How about if they are the same host?

Answer:

	Source Port	Destination Port
A) A→S	467	23
B) B→S	513	23
C) S→A	23	467
D) S→B	23	513

E) True.
F) False.

Question 21: UDP and TCP use 1s complement for their checksums. Suppose you have the following three 8-bit bytes: 01010101 01110000 01001100. What is the 1s complement of the sum of these 8-bit bytes? Show all work. With the 1s complement scheme, how does the receiver detect errors? Is it possible that a 1-bit error will go undetected? How about a 2-bit error?

Answer: Note, wrap around if overflow.

$$0\ 1\ 0\ 1\ 0\ 1\ 0\ 1$$
$$\underline{0\ 1\ 1\ 1\ 0\ 0\ 0\ 0}$$
$$1\ 1\ 0\ 0\ 0\ 1\ 0\ 1$$

$$1\ 1\ 0\ 0\ 0\ 1\ 0\ 1$$
$$\underline{0\ 1\ 0\ 0\ 1\ 1\ 0\ 0}$$
$$0\ 0\ 0\ 1\ 0\ 0\ 1\ 0$$

One's complement = 1 1 1 0 1 1 0 1

To detect errors, the receiver adds the four words (the three original words and the checksum). If the sum contains a zero, the receiver knows there has been an error. All one-bit errors will be detected, but two-bit errors can be undetected (e.g., if the last digit of the first word is converted to a 0 and the last digit of the second word is converted to a 1).

Question 22: Suppose we have the following 2 bytes: 00110100 and 01101001. What is the 1s complement of these 2 bytes?

Answer:

$$0\ 0\ 1\ 1\ 0\ 1\ 0\ 0$$
$$\underline{0\ 1\ 1\ 0\ 1\ 0\ 0\ 1}$$
$$1\ 0\ 0\ 1\ 1\ 1\ 0\ 1$$

One's complement =   0 1 1 0 0 0 1 0

Question 23: For the bytes in Question 22:, give an example where one bit is flipped in each of the 2 bytes and yet the 1s complement doesn't change.

Answer:

Suppose First Byte is:	0 0 1 1 0 1 0 1
Suppose Second Byte is:	0 1 1 0 1 0 0 0

If a 0 is changed to 1 in the first byte and a 1 is changed to 0 in the second byte in the same bit position, 1's complement doesn't change and the error goes undetected.

Question 24: Suppose you have the following 2 bytes: 11110101 and 00101001. What is the 1s complement of these 2 bytes?

Answer:

$$1\ 1\ 1\ 1\ 0\ 1\ 0\ 1$$
$$\underline{0\ 0\ 1\ 0\ 1\ 0\ 0\ 1}$$
$$0\ 0\ 0\ 1\ 1\ 1\ 1\ 1$$

One's complement =   1 1 1 0 0 0 0 0

Question 25: The web server www.CareerMonk.com has IP address 76.12.23.240. A client at address 74.208.207.41 downloads a file from the Career Monk web site. Assuming the client has an arbitrary port number > 1024, what is a possible socket pair comprising this connection?

Answer: There are numerous possible answers to this question, however all require the server listening on port 80. If we assume the client is assigned the socket 2500, the socket pair is [76.12.23.240:80] / [74.208.207.41:2500].

Question 26: Protocols in the network stack may be either reliable or unreliable. In the Internet, reliability occurs at the transport layer and TCP offers reliability, UDP is unreliable. Assume a developer prefers to use UDP, however the application they are designing requires reliability. Explain how it is possible to design a reliable protocol stack, yet use UDP at the transport layer.

Answer: Any layer that is considered reliable provides that reliability to the layer(s) above it. In the network protocol stack, if TCP is used at the transport layer, it then provides reliability to the application layer. If TCP is not in use, the application layer has no reliability unless it provides the reliability itself.

Therefore, if reliability is required by an application and UDP is in use at the transport layer, reliability must then be provided by the application. We saw in class how to build a reliable protocol with sequencing and acknowledgements when we broke up into separate groups and each group constructed a reliable protocol. Ideas similar to this can also be put to use at the application layer.

Question 27: The server CareerMonk.com (70.42.23.161) provides an ftp server for downloading software. A client (at address 116.35.22.9) wants to download a file from the ftp server using an active ftp connection. Other than the well-known port numbers for the data and control channels, arbitrary port numbers are > 1024. What is a possible socket pair comprising this active connection?

Answer: For an active ftp connection, let's assume the client is assigned the port numbers 5000 and 5001. The control channel will consist of the socket pair [70.42.23.161:21 / 116.35.22.9:5000]. Once this control channel is established, the data channel would comprise the socket pair [70.42.23.240:20 / 116.35.22.9:5001].

Question 28: Repeat the previous question, except that the connection uses passive FTP.

Answer: For a passive FTP connection, let's assume the client is assigned the port numbers 6000 and 6001. The control channel will consist of the socket pair [70.42.23.161:21 / 116.35.22.9:6000]. Once this is established, the server will listen to an arbitrary port (which it informs the client of.) Assuming the arbitrary port is 7500, the data channel will consist of the socket pair [70.42.23.161:7500 / 116.35.22.9:6001].

Question 29: Assume *CareerMonk*.com hosts a web page named Album.html containing 9 different images. Explain how this web page is downloaded using a non-persistent HTTP connection. Now explain how the same resource is downloaded using a persistent HTTP connection.

Answer: The web page and the 9 images it references means a total of 10 separate resources will be requested from the server. For a non-persistent connection, 10 separate TCP connections will be established, one for each separate resource. These may be downloaded serially or in parallel, depending upon whether pipelining is being used or not.

For a persistent connection, fewer connections will be established as an individual connection may be used to deliver more than one resource. It is possible than one connection may service all 10 resources, but it is more likely that several (although probably less than 10) will be used.

Question 30: The protocols IP, TCP, and UDP all discard a packet that arrives with a checksum error and do not attempt to notify the source. Why?

Answer: In the case of IP and UDP, these are unreliable protocols that do not guarantee delivery, so they do not notify the source. TCP does guarantee delivery. However, the technique that is used is a timeout. If the source does not receive an acknowledgment to data within a given period of time, the source retransmits.

Question 31: Why does the TCP header have a header length field while the UDP header does not?

Answer: The header in TCP is of variable length and UDP has a fixed-sized header.

Question 32: Suppose an application layer entity wants to send an L-byte message to its peer process, using an existing TCP connection. The TCP segment consists of the message plus 20 bytes of header. The segment is encapsulated into an IP packet that has an additional 20 bytes of header. The IP packet in turn goes inside an Ethernet frame that has 18 bytes of header and trailer. What percentage of the transmitted bits in the physical layer correspond to message information, if L = 100 bytes, 500 bytes, 1000 bytes?

Answer: TCP/IP over Ethernet allows data frames with a payload size up to 1460 bytes. Therefore, L = 100, 500 and 1000 bytes are within this limit.

The message overhead includes:
  TCP: 20 bytes of header
  IP: 20 bytes of header
  Ethernet: Total 18 bytes of header and trailer.

Therefore
  L = 100 bytes, 100/158 = 63% efficiency.
  L = 500 bytes, 500/558 = 90% efficiency.
  L = 1000 bytes, 1000/1058 = 95% efficiency.

Question 33: Which information is found in both the TCP and UDP header information?
  A) sequencing   B) flow control
  C) acknowledgments   D) source and destination port

Answer: D

Question 34: Which three features allow TCP to reliably and accurately track the transmission of data from source to destination?
  A) encapsulation   B) flow control   C) connectionless services
  D) session establishment   E) numbering and sequencing
  F) best effort delivery

Answer: B, D, and E

Question 35: Which is an important characteristic of UDP?
  A) acknowledgement of data delivery   B) minimal delays in data delivery
  C) high reliability of data delivery   D) same order data delivery

Answer: B

Question 36: After a web browser makes a request to a web server that is listening to the standard port, what will be the source port number in the TCP header of the response from the server?
  A) 13   B) 53   C) 80   E) 1024   F) 1728

Answer: C

Question 37: Which event occurs during the transport layer three-way handshake?
  A) The two applications exchange data.
  B) TCP initializes the sequence numbers for the sessions.
  C) UDP establishes the maximum number of bytes to be sent.
  E) The server acknowledges the bytes of data received from the client.

Answer: B

Question 38: Why is flow control used for TCP data transfer?
  A) to synchronize equipment speed for sent data

B) to synchronize and order sequence numbers so data is sent in complete numerical order

C) to prevent the receiver from being overwhelmed by incoming data

D) to synchronize window size on the server

E) to simplify data transfer to multiple hosts

Answer: C

Question 39: Which transport layer protocol provides low overhead and would be used for applications which do not require reliable data delivery?

A) TCP   B) IP   C) UDP   D) HTTP   E) DNS

Answer: C

Question 40: During a TCP communication session, if the packets arrive to the destination out of order, what will happen to the original message?

A) The packets will not be delivered.

B) The packets will be retransmitted from the source.

C) The packets will be delivered and reassembled at the destination.

E) The packets will be delivered and not reassembled at the destination.

Answer: C

Question 41: What mechanism is used by TCP to provide flow control as segments travel from source to destination?

A) sequence numbers   B) session establishment

C) window size   D) acknowledgments

Answer: C

Question 42: What is dynamically selected by the source host when forwarding data?

A) destination logical address   B) source physical address

C) default gateway address   D) source port

Answer: D

Question 43: Which OSI model layer is responsible for regulating the flow of information from source to destination, reliably and accurately?

A) application   B) presentation   C) session

D) transport   E) network

Answer: D

Question 44: Packets of the same session may be routed through different paths in

A) TCP, but not UDP   B) TCP and UDP

C) UDP but not TCP   D) Neither TCP, nor UDP

Answer: B. Selection of any path during routing of a packet is done at Network layer not at transport layer, So TCP and UDP both have nothing to do with this.

Question 45: What is the maximum size of data that the application layer can pass on to the TCP layer below?

A) Any size B) 216 bytes-size of TCP header

C) 216 bytes D) 1500 bytes

Answer: B. Application layer pass data to TCP layer. The length is of 16 bits. So total length 2^{16} bytes. But this is not complete payload, it has header also. So actual data. = 2^{16} bytes - Size of TCP header.

CHAPTER

TCP Error Control | 10

10.1 Introduction

TCP is a reliable transport layer protocol. It allows the processes to deliver a stream of data (bytes) in order, without error, and without any part lost or duplicated. It provides mechanisms for detecting errors in:

- Duplicate segments
- Out-of-Order segments
- Lost or Missing segments
- Corrupted segments

Also, TCP provides a mechanism for error correction. In TCP, error detection and correction in TCP is achieved by:

4. Checksum
5. Acknowledgement
6. Timeout and retransmission

10.2 TCP Reliability and Acknowledgement

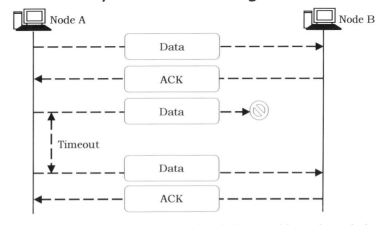

In the figure, the arrows represent transmitted data and/or acknowledgements, and time is represented by the vertical line. An acknowledgement can be *positive* or *negative*. A positive acknowledgement implies that the receiving host recovered the data and that it passed the integrity check. A negative acknowledgement implies that the failed data segment needs to be retransmitted. It can be caused by failures such as data corruption or loss.

When data is ready to be transmitted via TCP, it is passed from the upper-layer protocol to TCP, where it becomes encapsulated into segments. The IP layer then encapsulates these segments into datagrams and handles the point-to-point transmission of the data.

At the other end, the receiving station acknowledges receipt of the segment at the TCP layer by sending back an ACK message. If the original sender does not receive the ACK within a certain time period, then it retransmits the original segment. This is called *Positive Acknowledgment Retransmission* or *PAR*.

Of course, it's possible that the original message may just arrive late. In this case, the receiving station will eventually receive two identical segments. The duplicate segment is simply discarded.

How long should the timeout period be? I.e. how long should Node A wait for a response from Node B before it resends the packet? Clearly, within a LAN, Node A would expect packets to be acknowledged within just a few milliseconds. However, if Node A and B are on different sides of the globe, then a much longer timeout period is required.

If the timeout is set too long, unnecessary delays will be introduced into the network. If the timeout is set too short, then premature retransmission will result in packet duplications, leading to network congestion and eventually to a state of collapse. For this reason, TCP uses algorithms to dynamically adjust the timeout period to suit the state of the network.

10.3 Round Trip Time and Timeout

In TCP, when a host sends a segment into a TCP connection, it starts a timer. If the timer expires before the host receives an acknowledgment for the data in the segment, the host retransmits the segment. The time from when the timer is started until when it expires is called the *timeout* of the timer.

What should be the ideal *timeout* be? Clearly, the timeout should be larger than the connection's round-trip time, i.e., the time from when a segment is sent until it is acknowledged.

Otherwise, unnecessary retransmissions would be sent. But the timeout should not be much larger than the *round-trip time*; otherwise, when a segment is lost, TCP would not quickly retransmit the segment, thereby introducing significant data transfer delays into the application. Before discussing the timeout interval in more detail, let us take a closer look at the round-trip time (*RTT*).

The round trip time calculation algorithm is used to calculate the average time for data to be acknowledged. When a data packet is sent, the elapsed time for the acknowledgment to arrive is measured and the *Van Jacobean* mean deviation algorithm is applied. This time is used to determine the interval to retransmit data.

10.3.1 Estimating the Average Round Trip Time

The sample RTT, denoted *SampleRTT*, for a segment is the time from when the segment is sent (i.e., passed to IP) until an acknowledgment for the segment is received. Each segment sent will have its own associated *SampleRTT*.

Obviously, the *SampleRTT* values will change from segment to segment due to congestion in the routers and to the varying load on the end systems. Because of this fluctuation, any given *SampleRTT* value may be atypical. In order to estimate a typical *RTT*, it is therefore natural to take some sort of average of the *SampleRTT* values.

TCP maintains an average of *SampleRTT* values, denoted with called *EstimatedRTT*. Upon receiving an acknowledgment and obtaining a new *SampleRTT*, TCP updates *EstimatedRTT* according to the following formula:

$$EstimatedRTT = (1-\alpha) * EstimatedRTT + \alpha * SampleRTT$$

The above formula is written in the form of a programming language statement - the new value of *EstimatedRTT* is a weighted combination of the previous value of *EstimatedRTT* and the new value for *SampleRTT*. A typical value of α is $\alpha = .1$, in which case the above formula becomes:

$$EstimatedRTT = .9 \; EstimatedRTT + .1 \; SampleRTT$$

Note that *EstimatedRTT* is a weighted average of the *SampleRTT* values. This weighted average puts more weight on recent samples than on old samples. This is natural, as the more recent samples better reflect the current congestion in the network. In statistics, such an average is called an *exponential weighted moving average (EWMA)*. The word *exponential* appears in EWMA because the weight of a given *SampleRTT* decays exponentially fast as the updates proceed.

10.3.2 Setting the Timeout

The timeout should be set so that a timer expires early (i.e., before the delayed arrival of a segment's ACK) only on rare occasions. It is therefore natural to set the timeout equal to the *EstimatedRTT* plus some margin. The margin should be large when there is a lot of fluctuation in the *SampleRTT* values; it should be small when there is little fluctuation. TCP uses the following formula:

$$Timeout = EstimatedRTT + 4*Deviation,$$

where *Deviation* is an estimate of how much *SampleRTT* typically deviates from *EstimatedRTT*:

$$Deviation = (1-\alpha) \; Deviation + \alpha \; | \; SampleRTT - EstimatedRTT \; |$$

Note that the *Deviation* is an *exponential weighted moving average (EWMA)* of how much *SampleRTT* deviates from *EstimatedRTT*. If the *SampleRTT* values have little fluctuation, then *Deviation* is small and *Timeout* is hardly more than *EstimatedRTT*; on the other hand, if there is a lot of fluctuation, *Deviation* will be large and *Timeout* will be much larger than *EstimatedRTT*.

10.3.3 Karn's/Partridge Algorithm

The first original algorithm, after several years of implementation in the Internet, was found to be inadequate. Problems arose when there was retransmission.

As per the discussions, we have seen TCP adjusts the timeouts in agreement with the Round-Trip-Time (RTT) estimation for the current end-to-end path. RTT estimation is obtained by averaging the measured RTT for the packets sent so far.

A problem arises from the way samples are taken for the calculation of the average: TCP is unable to distinguish two separate acknowledgements for the same sequence number. Therefore, we have the following problem:

When a packet was retransmitted and then an ACK was received, it was impossible to know whether this ACK was associated with the original transmission or the retransmission.

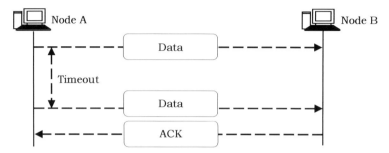

In the above figure, the first two segments indicate the same data packets. First segment represents original transmission and the second one represents retransmission (after timeout). The final segment represents the ACK. If it was assumed that the ACK was for the original transmission, but it was actually for the retransmission as shown in figure, then the calculated Sample RTT would be too large.

Proposed is the following modification to TCP:

1. Do not take into account the RTT sampled from packets that have been retransmitted. This means that, TCP calculated *SampleRTT* only for packets that were sent once, and did not calculate *SampleRTT* for packets that were sent twice, that is, for packets that were retransmitted.
2. On successive retransmissions, set each timeout to twice the previous one. Whenever there was retransmission, TCP used the following formula to calculate:

$$Timeout = Previous\,Timeout \times 2$$

10.3.4 Jacobson/Karels Algorithm

The *Karn/Partridge* algorithm was introduced at a time when the Internet was suffering from high levels of network congestion. That Karn/Partridge algorithm was designed to fix some of the causes of that congestion. It cannot eliminate the congestion. In the year 1988, *Jacobson* and *Karels* proposed a new algorithm TCP for congestion.

It is clear that timeout mechanism is related to congestion. If we time out too soon, we may unnecessarily retransmit a segment, which only adds to the load on the network.

The main problem with the original computation is that it does not take the variance of the sample RTTs into account. Intuitively, if the variation among samples is small, then the *EstimatedRTT* can be better trusted and there is no reason for multiplying this estimate by 2 to compute the timeout. On the other hand, a large variance in the samples suggests that the timeout value should not be too tightly coupled to the *EstimatedRTT*.

In the new approach, the sender measures a new *SampleRTT* as before. It then folds this new sample into the timeout calculation as follows:

$$RTTDifference = SampleRTT\text{-}EstimatedRTT$$
$$EstimatedRTT = EstimatedRTT + (\delta \times RTTDifference)$$
$$Deviation = Deviation + \delta(|RTTDifference| - Deviation)$$

Where δ is a fraction between 0 and 1.

That is, we calculate both the mean RTT and the variation in that mean. TCP then computes the timeout value as a function of both EstimatedRTT and Deviation as follows:

$$TimeOut = \mu \times EstimatedRTT + \theta \times Deviation$$

Where based on experience, μ is typically set to 1 and θ is set to 4.

Thus, when the variance is small, *TimeOut* is close to *EstimatedRTT*; a large variance causes the *Deviation* term to dominate the calculation.

10.4 Duplicate Segments

Suppose that an *old duplicate segment*, e.g., a duplicate data segment that was delayed in Internet queues, was delivered to the receiver at the wrong moment so that its sequence numbers fell somewhere within the current window. There would be no checksum failure to warn of the error, and the result could be an undetected corruption of the data.

The duplicate of segments actually does occur with TCP mechanism. This happens when, for example, a receiver detects that it missed some segment. Then it requests the sender to resend that segment by sending reject. But, then the missing initially sent segment arrives. After this, the second segment that was resent arrives. Then a receiver either just *drops* already received segment or overwrites the data in its buffers with most recent version.

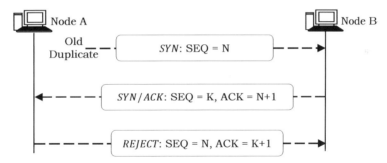

Conceptually, perhaps the most serious threat facing the integrity of TCP data is external old duplicates, that is, from a previous instance of the connection. Suppose a TCP connection is opened between A and B. One segment from A to B is duplicated and unduly delayed, with sequence number N. The connection is closed, and then another instance is reopened, that is, a connection is created using the same ports.

At some point in the second connection, when an arriving packet with SEQ=N would be acceptable at B, the old duplicate shows up. Later, of course, B is likely to receive a SEQ=N packet from the new instance of the connection, but that packet will be seen by B as a duplicate (even though the data does not match), and (we will assume) ignored.

Reception of an old duplicate ACK segment at the sender could be only slightly less serious: it is likely to lock up the connection so that no further progress can be made and a *RST* is required to resynchronize the two ends.

Duplication of sequence numbers might happen in either of two ways:

1. Sequence number wrap-around on the current connection

A TCP sequence number contains 32 bits. At a high enough transfer rate, the 32-bit sequence space may be *wrapped* (*cycled*) within the time that a segment may be delayed in queues.

2.   Segment from an earlier connection

Suppose a connection terminates, either by a proper close sequence or due to a host crash, and the same connection (i.e., using the same pair of sockets) is immediately reopened. A delayed segment from the terminated connection could fall within the current window for the new incarnation and be accepted as valid.

TCP reliability depends upon the existence of a bound on the lifetime of a segment: the *Maximum Segment Lifetime* or MSL. An MSL is generally required by any reliable transport protocol, since every sequence number field must be finite, and therefore any sequence number may eventually be reused. In the Internet protocol suite, the MSL bound is enforced by an IP-layer mechanism, the *Time − to − Live* or TTL field.

10.5 Out-of-Order Segments

TCP assigns a sequence number to each byte transmitted, and expects a positive acknowledgment (ACK) from the receiving TCP. If the ACK is not received within a timeout interval, the data is retransmitted. The receiving TCP uses the sequence numbers to rearrange the segments when they arrive out of order, and to eliminate duplicate segments.

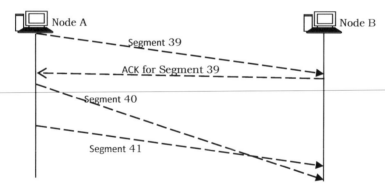

Out-of-order segments can be *detected* using the *sequence number*. Out-of-order segments are not discarded. Instead the receiver maintains a sliding window that temporally *buffers* the out-of-order segments until the missing segment arrives. Out-of-order segments will not be delivered to the process.

10.6 Lost or Missing Segments

When data is ready to be transmitted via TCP, it is passed from the upper-layer protocol to TCP, where it becomes encapsulated into segments. The IP layer then encapsulates these segments into datagrams and handles the point-to-point transmission of the data.

At the other end, the receiving station acknowledges receipt of the segment at the TCP layer by sending back an ACK message. If the original sender does not receive the ACK within a certain time period, then it retransmits the original segment. This is called Positive Acknowledgment Retransmission or PAR.

Of course, it's possible that the original message may just arrive late. In this case, the receiving station will eventually receive two identical segments. The duplicate segment is simply discarded.

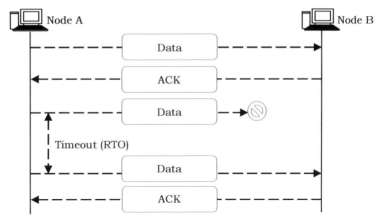

How long should the timeout period be? If the timeout is set too long, unnecessary delays will be introduced into the network. If the timeout is set too short, then premature retransmission will result in packet duplications, leading to network congestion and eventually to a state of collapse.

For this reason, TCP uses algorithms to dynamically adjust the timeout period to suit the state of the network. The sender sets the Retransmission time-out (RTO) timer when sending a segment. If the sender does not receive the corresponding acknowledgement; it assumes the segment is lost and *retransmits* the segment.

10.7 Corrupted Segments

A lost segment and a corrupted segment are treated in the same way by the receiver. Both are considered lost. The checksum is used by the receiver to check for corrupted data. If a segment contains corrupted data, it is discarded. TCP uses source sequence and acknowledgment numbers to confirm reception of uncorrupted segments. If a segment contains corrupted data, the receiver will not send any acknowledgment to sender.

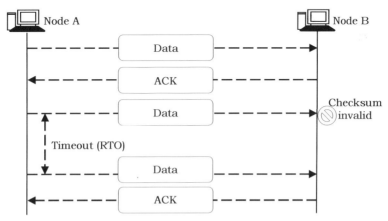

How long should the sender wait? The sender sets the Retransmission time-out (RTO) timer when sending a segment. If the sender does not receive the corresponding acknowledgement; it assumes the segment is lost and *retransmits* the segment.

10.8 ARQ Retransmission Techniques

The receiver can control the pace of incoming segments by carefully timing acknowledgments. But, what happens if a segment is received in error? Of course some set of procedures must be defined so that errors can be dealt with.

Three types of error control are discussed in your text. All are collectively called automatic repeat request, or ARQ. The three types of error control are:

1. Stop and Wait ARQ
2. Go Back N ARQ
3. Selective Reject ARQ

Don't confuse Stop and Wait Flow Control with Stop and Wait ARQ. These are different concepts that are part of a stop and wait transmission protocol.

10.8.1 Stop and Wait ARQ

In a stop and wait system, if a segment arrives and an error check indicates that somewhere in the segment there is an error, the segment is discarded and a message is sent to notify the transmitter. The message sent is a negative acknowledgment, also called a *reject message* (NAK or REJ).

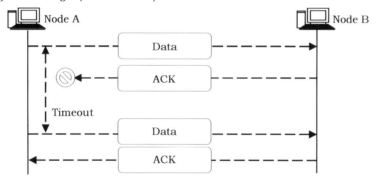

What happens if a segment, an ACK or a NAK are lost in transit? This could be a problem, so when a segment is sent, the transmitter starts a timer. If the timer counts down to zero before an ACK or NAK is received the transmitter resends the segment.

This condition is called a *timeout*. Note the following:

- If a segment is lost, after the transmitter times out, the segment is resent and the receiver accepts it without any knowledge of the lost segment.

- If a NAK is lost, the transmitter times out and resends the segments. The receiver accepts the retransmitted segment as if the NAK had been received normally. There is no requirement to send a NAK. The transmitter will resend the segment anyway. Sending the NAK forces the transmitter to resend immediately, rather than waiting for a time out to occur.

- If an ACK is lost, the transmitter times out and resends the segment. The receiver already has this segment, so it discards the duplicate and resends the ACK.

10.8.2 Go Back N ARQ

The Go-Back-N ARQ error control method is used in combination with sliding window flow control. When the receiver finds a segment in error, it tells the transmitter to go back, resend that segment and all succeeding segments. After the erred segment, some succeeding segments will arrive. The receiver discards these knowing that the erred segment will arrive and the succeeding segments will also follow.

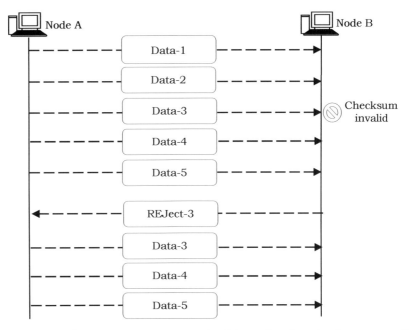

This feature guarantees that segments are received in order, but it also means that some good segments may have to be resent.

In the above figure, note how the transmitter begins by resending the segment that was in error and then continues by sending succeeding segments until its window is exhausted.

10.8.3 Selective Reject ARQ

For a system with ample memory space, Selective Reject Request ARQ may provide improved performance when compared to Go-Back-N ARQ. This error control scheme allows the receiver to selectively reject segments.

The receiver, upon finding and erred segment, will request that segment be resent and only that segment is resent. The receiver has to keep track of what segments are coming in and what sequence they belong in.

Reordering the segments may be required. The receiver cannot deliver segment contents to layer three until the segments have been put in order and no segments are missing in the sequence.

The transmitter also has to keep careful track of which segments have been sent, which have been acknowledged and which are available to be sent. Selective Reject ARQ works in combination with sliding window flow control.

Selective Reject ARQ is not common at the data link layer. It requires much more processing and buffer space to implement. The marginal improvement in capacity is not easy to justify in the hardware used at the data link layer. We will see Selective Reject ARQ later when we study TCP, however.

10.8.4 Comparison of ARQ Retransmission Techniques

Method	Advantages	Disadvantages
Stop and Wait ARQ	Easy to implement Low processor burden Low buffer requirement	Doesn't allow Sliding Window flow control
Go-Back-N ARQ	Easy to implement Permits use of Sliding Window Flow control	May have to retransmit good segments
Selective Reject ARQ	Permits Sliding Window Flow control, only retransmit lost or erred segments	Requires more powerful processing and more buffer space

10.9 Selective Acknowledgments (SACK)

The diagram below illustrates a TCP connection taking place between a sender (client) and a receiver (server) separated by a network. Time progresses vertically from top to bottom as segments are sent.

The sender sends some request to the server, and the server formulates a response broken into four TCP segments (segments). The server sends all four segments in response to the request. However, the second response segment is dropped somewhere on the network and never reaches the host. Let's walk through what happens.

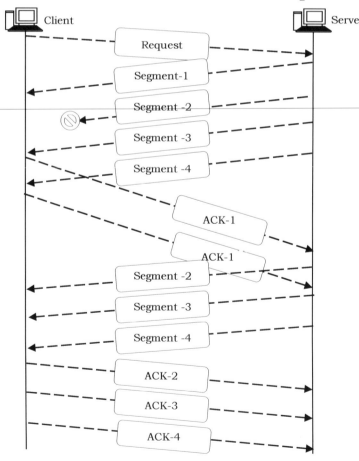

Step 1: Response segment #2 is lost.

Step 2: The client receives segment #3. Upon examining the segment's sequence number, the client realizes this segment is out of order; there is data missing between the last segment received and this one. The client transmits a duplicate acknowledgment for segment #1 to alert the server that it has not received any (reliable) data beyond segment #1.

Step 3: As the server is not yet aware that anything is wrong (because it has not yet received the client's duplicate acknowledgment), it continues by sending segment #4. The client realizes that it is still missing data, and repeats its behavior in step three by sending another duplicate acknowledgment for segment #1.

Step 4: The server receives the client's first duplicate acknowledgment for segment #1. Because the client has only confirmed receipt of the first of the four segments, the server must retransmit all three remaining segments in the response.

The second duplicate acknowledgment received from the client is ignored.

Step 5: The client successfully receives and acknowledges the three remaining segments.

10.9.1 Enter Selective Acknowledgments

You've probably noticed that this design is inefficient: although only segment #2 was lost, the server was required to retransmit segments #3 and #4 as well, because the client had no way to confirm that it had received those segments.

This problem can be addressed by introducing the selective acknowledgment (SACK) TCP option. SACKs work by appending to a duplicate acknowledgment segment a TCP option containing a range of noncontiguous data received. In other words, it allows the client to say "I only have up to segment #1 in order, but I also have received segments #3 and #4". This allows the server to retransmit only the segment(s) that were not received by the client.

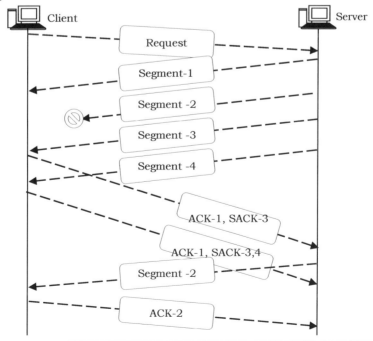

Support for SACK is negotiated at the beginning of a TCP connection; if both hosts support it, it may be used. Let's look at how our earlier example plays out with SACK enabled:

Step 1: Response segment #2 is lost.

Step 2: The client realizes it is missing a segment between segments #1 and #3. It sends a duplicate acknowledgment for segment #1, and attaches a SACK option indicating that it has received segment #3.

Step 3: The client receives segment #4 and sends another duplicate acknowledgment for segment #1, but this time expands the SACK option to show that it has received segments #3 through #4.

Step 4: The server receives the client's duplicate ACK for segment #1 and SACK for segment #3 (both in the same TCP segment). From this, the server deduces that the client is missing segment #2, so segment #2 is retransmitted. The next SACK received by the server indicates that the client has also received segment #4 successfully, so no more segments need to be transmitted.

Step 5: The client receives segment #2 and sends an acknowledgment to indicate that it has received all data up to including segment #4.

10.10 TCP Checksum Calculation

When data is about to travel across the Internet it is first divided into smaller pieces called packets. Those packets along with the regular data contain some additional information which is stored in the packet header. Such as addresses, port numbers and other control arguments. One of those arguments is the Header Checksum.

The checksum is a numerical value which is used for error detection on a packet transmission. How? Before a packet goes on the transmission medium, the checksum is calculated at the source. This process is repeated at the receiving end and the recalculated checksum is *compared* with the original checksum. If they match, the transmission went just fine, if not then it is possible that some data got lost or corrupted.

10.10.1 The IP Header Checksum

Now it's time to take a look at the contents of a packet header. We will first start with the IP Header.

00 To 03	04 To 07	08	09	10	11	12	13	14	15	16	17	18	19 To 31
Version	IHL	ToS		D	T	R	M	R0	Total Length				
IP Identification (IPID)									R0	DF	MF	Fragment Offset	
Time-To-Live (TTL)	Protocol								Header Checksum				
Source IP Address													
Destination IP Address													
Options & padding (variable, usually none)													

For details on this refer *IP Addressing* chapter. For now, we just need to know the following information:

Version	4 bits
IHL	4 bits
ToS	8 bits

Total Length	16 bits
Identification	16 bits
Flags	8 bits
Fragment Offset	8 bits
Time-to-Live	8 bits
Protocol	8 bits
Checksum	16 bits
Source IP	32 bits
Destination IP	32 bits
Total	160 bits = 20 bytes

Let us construct IP Header and add values to these variables. Starting with the *version* we will give it the value 4 (assuming IPv4 is being used). Using a decimal-to-binary convertor we see that the number 4 in binary format is 0100. We will write it down as it is, since it already is 4 bits long.

Internet Header Length (IHL): IHL specifies the length of the IP header, in 32-bit words. This includes the length of any options fields and padding. The normal value of this field when no options are used is 5 (5 32-bit words = 5*4 = 20 bytes). Contrast to the longer *Total Length* field. We will stay with the 5 since it is the most wide spread value and also the smallest possible value. The number 5 in binary is 0101.

Type of Service (ToS) field: It is used carry information to provide quality of service (QoS) features, such as prioritized delivery, for IP datagrams. These parameters are to be used to guide the selection of the actual service parameters when transmitting a datagram through a particular network. We will set this field to 0. This field takes up 8 bits. So, we will have 0000 0000.

Total Length: This is the TCP header length, which has a minimum value of 160 bits, plus the *IP Header Length* (*only* if no data is contained in the packet). We will continue our calculations as if the *TCP Header Length* has a size of 160 bits. So we have *TCP Header Length* + *IP Header Length* = 160 + 160 = 320 bits. But because the *Total Header Length* is measured in bytes we will rewrite the 320 bits in 40 bytes (40 bytes = 320 bits). So again with the help of our binary convertor we can see that 40 in binary is 00101000, but because we want to have 16 bits will add 8 more zeros to this result. So we get: 00000000 00101000.

Identification: Since this is our first constructed packet; we will set the *Identification* field to 1 (we can use whatever value we want). So because we have a 16 bit field we will have: 0000000000000001.

Flags: Which we will set to 0. Again because this is a 8 bit field we will have: 00000000.

Fragmentation Offset: The same goes for the *Fragmentation Offset* field. We will have: 00000000.

Time to Live: This field can get a maximum value off 255. This is measured in seconds but because this value gets reduced at every host it passes, we can say that this is the number of hops a packet can travel through the internet before it gets discarded. We will set it to 127. Were 127 in binary is 01111111.

Protocol: Since we are using TCP as our next level protocol, and because the TCP Protocol's ID number is 6 we will set this to 6. And 6 in binary is 00000110.

Checksum: We will set this to 0, since we haven't completed our calculations. So we get this: 00000000 00000000.

Source IP Address: The source address we are sending the packet from has an IP address of 192.68.43.1. Let us write each number in binary format.

192	11000000
68	01000100
43	00101011
1	00000001

We will write this without the dots as: 11000000 01000100 00101011 00000001.

Destination IP Address: Let us say, we want to send the packet to 10.176.2.34 and its binary representation is 00001010 10110000 00000010 00100010.

We will have a flashback to our binary-format values:

IP Header
0100
0101
00000000
00000000 00101000
00000000 00000001
00000000
00000000
01111111
00000110
00000000 00000000
11000000 01000100 00101011 00000001
00001010 10110000 00000010 00100010

Next, we will divide this stuff into 16 bit words. Then, add them together. We can either use a binary calculator or convert each 16 bit word to decimal and then add it.

16 bit Words	In decimal
01000101 00000000	17664
00000000 00101000	40
00000000 00000001	1
00000000 00000000	0
01111111 00000110	32518
00000000 00000000	0
11000000 01000100	49220
00101011 00000001	11009
00001010 10110000	2736
00000010 00100010	546
Total	113734

We next need to convert this into *Hexadecimal* format: $1BC46$, But something doesn't look so fine. We said that the checksum field is 16 bit long, and what we have here seems to be longer than 16 bits. In-fact it is 20 bits long. Don't worry. In this case we remove the first digit of 1BC46 (which is 1) and we add it to the remaining 4 digits, that is BC46, so we have BC46 + 1 = BC47.

Now the last step that we need to take is to subtract the result from FFFF. FFFF-BC47 = 43B8 (or 65535 - 48199 = 17336, in decimal) which is our final checksum that we will put into the checksum field.

10.10.2 TCP Header Checksum

The contents of a TCP Header:

00 To 15		16 To 31
Source Port Number		Destination Port Number
Sequence Number		
Acknowledgment Number		
4-bit Header Length / Reserved (6-bits) / URG ACK PSH RST SYN FIN		Window Size
Checksum		Urgent Pointer
Options (if any)		
Data (if any)		

As in the IP Header, we have some fields that need to get filled:

Source Port	16 bits
Destination Port	16 bits
Sequence Number	32 bits
Acknowledgment Number	32 bits
Data offset	4 bits
Reserved	6 bits
Flags	6 bits
Window	16 bits
Header Checksum	16 bits
Urgent Pointer	16 bits

Calculating the TCP Header checksum is similar to calculating the IP Header checksum with addition that the TCP Header Checksum also includes a Pseudo Header. This pseudo header has some information that is also found in the IP Header, such as Source IP address, Destination IP address and the Protocol number. It also includes the TCP Header length.

00 To 07	08 To 15	16 To 31
Source IP Address		
Destination IP Address		
Reserved	Protocol	TCP Header Length

Those fields have a total size of 96 bits.

Source IP	32 bits
Destination IP	32 bits
Reserved	8 bits
Protocol	8 bits
TCP Header Length	16 bits

Source Port: We will first start with the TCP Header. What we have here is the *Source Port* number, which we will set to 1645. Just like in the IP Header we will convert this value into binary format. So we get: 0110 0110 1101, but because we have a 16 bit field we end up with 00000110 01101101.

Destination Port: Similarly, for the *Destination Port* we set to 80: 0000 0000 0101 0000.

Sequence Number: As an example, we set to 1 and the result is 00000000 00000000 00000000 00000001.

Acknowledgment Number: For this field also, we set it to 1 and the result is 00000000 00000000 00000000 00000001.

Data Offset: This field is similar to the IHL field in the IP Header. Here we specify the length of the TCP Header and by knowing how long the TCP Header is we know were the data begins. This field, just like the IHL is measured in 32 bit multiples and has a minimum value of 5 (160 bits). So we will use 5: 0101

Reserved: *Reserved* field should be zero. So we have 000000 (6 bits).

Flags: Flags field or Control bits specify the purpose of the packet (URG, ACK, PSH, RTS, SYN, FIN). Here, we have 6 flags and 6 bits so we have one bit for each flag. Example:

FIN	000001
SYN	000010
RST	000100
PSH	001000
ACK	010000
URG	100000

We will send a SYN packet, so we will have 000010.

Window: This we will set to 128. So we get 0000000010000000 in binary.

Checksum: The *Checksum* field will be set to zero (0000000000000000).

Now since we are sending a SYN packet we will set the *Urgent Pointer* field to 00000000 00000000.

Remember when we said that the TCP Header checksum contains a Pseudo Header? Well there is no problem. Since the Pseudo Header fields are IP Header values we already have our binaries.

We have:

Source IP Address(192.68.43.1)	11000000010001000010101100000001
Destination IP Address(10.176.2.34)	00001010101100000000001000100010
Reserved set to 0	00000000
Protocol(6 for TCP)	00000110
TCP Header Length	(Since we have no data the length is 160 bits, the minimum remember?) but because it is measured in bytes we will set it to 20, so we have 20 in binary: 0000000000010100

To finish our calculation we will again rewrite our binary values nice and clean:

TCP Header
0000011001101101
0000000001010000
00000000000000000000000000000001
00000000000000000000000000000001
0101
000000
000010
0000000010000000
0000000000000000
0000000000000000
Pseudo Header
11000000010001000010101100000001
00001010101100000000001000100010
00000000

00000110
0000000000010100

Let us buildup the 16 bit words to add them together.

16 bit Words	In decimal
00000110 01101101	1645
00000000 01010000	80
00000000 00000000	0
00000000 00000001	1
00000000 00000000	0
00000000 00000001	1
01010000 00000010	20482
00000000 10000000	128
00000000 00000000	0
00000000 00000000	0
11000000 01000100	49220
00101011 00000001	11009
00001010 10110000	2736
00000010 00100010	546
00000000 00000110	6
00000000 00010100	20
Total	85874 [14F72 in Hexadecimal]

Notice that again we have 20 bits instead of 16. So, we remove the 1 and add it to 4F72, 4F72 + 1 = 4F73. Then subtract it from FFFF. $FFFF - 4F73 = B08C$ (65535 − 20339 = 45196 in decimal). B08C is our TCP Header checksum!

Problems and Question with Answers

Question 1: Calculate the total time required to transfer a 1.5 MB file in the following cases, assuming RTT of 80 ms, a packet size of 1 KB and an initial 2×RTT of *handshaking* before it is sent.

A) The bandwidth is 10 Mbps, and the data packets can be sent continuously.

B) The bandwidth is 10 Mbps, but after we finish sending each data packet, we must wait one RTT before sending the next

C) The link allows infinitely fast transmits, but limits bandwidth such that only 20 packets can be sent per RTT. Assume zero transmit time.

D) As in (C), but during the first RTT, we can send one packet; during the second RTT we can send two packets; during the third RTT we can send $4 = 2^{3-1}$ and so on.

Answer: We will count the transfer as completed when the last data bit arrives at its destination

A) 1.5 MB = 12,582,912 bits,

2 initial RTTs (160 ms) + $\frac{(12,582,912)}{(10,000,000)}$ bps (transmit) + $\frac{RTT}{2}$ (propagation)=1.458 secs

B) To the above, we add the time for 1499 RTTs for a total of 1.46 + 119.92 = 121.38 secs

C) This is 74.5 RTTs, plus the two initial RTTs, for 6.12 secs.

D) Right after the handshaking is done, we send one packet. One RTT after handshaking, we send 2 packets.

At n RTTs past the handshaking, we have sent $1+2+4+... + 2^n = 2^{n+1} - 1$. At $n = 10$, we have thus been able to send all 1500 packets, the last batch arrives 0.5 RTT later. ∴ Total time is 2 + 10.5 RTTs or 1 sec.

Question 2: Suppose we want to devise a single-bit error-correcting Hamming code for a 16-bit data string. How many parity bits are needed? How about for a 32-bit data string.

Answer: The number of bits actually transmitted is the number of data bits plus the number of parity bits. If we have 16 data bits and only use 4 parity bits, then we would have to transmit 20 bits. Since there are only 16 combinations that can be constructed using 4 parity bits, this is not enough. With 5 parity bits, we must transmit 21 bits. Since there are 32 combinations that can be constructed using 5 parity bits, there will be enough combinations to represent all single-bit errors.

With 32 data bits, using 5 parity bits will not be enough since we would have to transmit 37 data bits and 5 parity bits only allows 32 combinations. With 6 parity bits, we have to transmit 38 data bits. Since 6 parity bits gives 64 combinations, there will be enough combinations to represent all single-bit errors.

Question 3: According to end-to-end argument reliability must be implemented at networking layer. Is it true or false?

Answer: False. Since reliability at the networking layer cannot ensure the application end-to-end reliability, and since it may hurt the latency of applications that do not require reliability (e.g., voice over IP), according to the end-to-end argument the networking layer shouldn't provide reliability.

Question 4: Consider a reliable data transfer protocol that uses only negative acknowledgements. Suppose the sender only sends data infrequently. Would the negative-acknowledgment-only protocol be preferable to a protocol the uses both positive and negative acknowledgements? Explain.

Now consider the scenario where the sender has a lot of data to transmit and the connection experiences very few packet losses. In this scenario, would a negative-acknowledgment-only protocol be preferable to a protocol the uses both positive and negative acknowledgements? Explain.

Answer: If the data is sent infrequently, you could argue that sending both positive (ACK) and negative (NAK) acknowledgements would suffice as generally few acknowledgements would be sent as there is relatively little data to acknowledge.

In the situation where there is a lot of data being transmitted, yet there are very few packet losses, NAKs may work better than both ACK/NAK as there will be fewer negative acknowledgements being generated.

Question 5: Assume host A sends four TCP segments to a receiver B. B will send an ACK to A after correct receipt of a single segment (i.e. it sends an ACK for each segment it receives.) The First and fourth segments arrive, however the second segment is dropped by a router. How will B acknowledge receipt of the segments it has received so far?

Answer: It will ACK 1 both times (or, said differently, it would ACK 2 both times as it is expecting to receive 2.)

Question 6: For the previous question, B then receives the third segment. How will it acknowledge receipt of it?

Answer: Again, it will ACK the segment it is expecting to receive next, which in this case is 2.

Question 7: For the previous question, in terms of acknowledgements, how will B ultimately handle the second (missed) segment?

Answer: A will ultimately timeout and resend it. When B receives the segment, it will send a cumulative acknowledgements for all four segments it has received.

Question 8:   Suppose a TCP message that contains 2048 bytes of data and 20 bytes of TCP header is passed to IP for delivery across two networks of the Internet. The first network uses 14 byte headers and has a MTU of 1024 bytes; the second uses 8-byte headers with an MTU of 512 bytes. Each network's MTU gives the size of the largest IP datagram that can be carried in a link-layer frame. Give the *sizes* and *offsets* of the sequence of fragments delivered to the network layer at the destination host. Assume all IP headers are 20 bytes. Note, the IP requires that fragmentation should always happen on 8-byte boundaries.

Answer: Consider the first network. Packets have room for 1024 - 20 = 1004 bytes of IP-level data; because 1004 is not a multiple of 8 each fragment can contain at most 8× floor((1004/8)) = 1000 bytes. We need to transfer 2048 + 20 = 2068 bytes of such data. This would be fragmented into fragments of size 1000, 1000, and 68.

Fragment	Size	Offset
1	1000	0
2	1000	1000
3	68	2000

Over the second network, the 68-byte packet would be unfragmented but the 1000-data-byte packet would be fragmented as follows. The IP header is 20 bytes, leaving 512-20 = 492 bytes for IP-level data. Again rounding down to the nearest multiple of 8, each fragment could contain 488 bytes of IP-level data. 1000 bytes of such data would become fragments with data sizes 488, 488, and 24.

Fragment	Size	Offset
1	488	0
2	488	488
3	24	976
4	488	1000
5	488	1488
6	24	1976
7	68	2000

Question 9:   Consider the TCP round-trip time and timeout estimation algorithm:

EstimatedRTT = (0.875 × EstimatedRTT) + (0.125 × SampleRTT)
DevRTT = (0.75 × DevRTT) + (0.25 × |SampleRTT - EstimatedRTT|)
Timeout = EstimatedRTT + 4 × DevRTT

Suppose that a TCP connection currently has the values of EstimatedRTT = 24 ms and DevRTT = 8 ms. The next segment transmitted over the TCP connection experiences a timeout and the acknowledgment for that segment arrives 40 ms after the retransmission. The SampleRTT for the segment transmitted next over the TCP connection is measured as 16 ms. Calculate the last value of the Timeout obtained for this TCP connection.

Answer:

EstimatedRTT = (0.875 × 24) + (0.125 × 16) = 23 ms.
DevRTT = (0.75 × 8) + (0.25 × |16 - 23|) = 7.75 ms.
Timeout = 23 + 4 × 7.75 = 54 ms.

Question 10: In a sliding window Go-Back-N ARQ system, A sends packets 0,1,2,3,4,5 and 6. Packet 3 arrives at B corrupted. What do A and B send to each other next?
A) B sends REJ-3 , A then sends packets 3,4,5,6,7,0 and 1
B) B sends REJ-2, A then sends packets 3,4,5,6,7,0 and 1

C) B sends REJ-3, A then sends just packet 3
D) B sends REJ-2, A then sends just packet 3

Answer: A

Question 11: Which of the following are true statements about TCP.
A) The slow-start algorithm increases a source's rate of transmission faster than the additive-increase.
B) Setting RTO (retransmission timeout value) to a value less than the measured RTT may lead to unnecessary retransmissions.
C) TCP segments can only be lost when router queues overflow.
D) TCP connection termination procedure is called two-way handshaking.

Answer: A and B.

Question 12: Consider a TCP connection between two machines (A and B) in an environment with 0% packet loss. Assume the round trip time (RTT) between the two machines is 4 [seconds], and the segment size is 3 [Kbytes]. The bandwidth of the connection is 500 [kbps]. What is the smallest TCP window size for which there will be no stalling? (We say a TCP connection experiences no stalling if the acknowledgments arrive back to the sending machine before the sliding window over the send buffer close to zero. I.e., TCP packets are continuously, back-to-back, sent out of the sending machine.)

Answer: There will be no stalling if

> Time to send entire window ≤ Time for the first ACK to arrive back

That is:

$$\frac{W \times S}{R} \leq RTT + \frac{S}{R} \rightarrow W \leq \frac{RTT \times R}{S} + 1$$

In this particular case: $W \leq \frac{4 \sec \times 500 \text{ kbps}}{24 \text{ kbits}} + 1 \leq 83.3 + 1 \leq 84.3$. That is: $W \leq 84$.

Question 13: A receiving host has failed to receive all of the segments that it should acknowledge. What can the host do to improve the reliability of this communication session?
A) Send a different source port number
B) Restart the virtual circuit
C) Decrease the sequence number
D) Decrease the window size

Answer: D. A TCP window the amount of outstanding (unacknowledged by the recipient) data a sender can send on a particular connection before it gets an acknowledgment back from the receiver that it has gotten some of it. For example if a pair of hosts are talking over a TCP connection that has a TCP window size of 64 KB (kilobytes), the sender can only send 64 KB of data and then it must stop and wait for an acknowledgment from the receiver that some or all of the data has been received.

If the receiver acknowledges that all the data has been received then the sender is free to send another 64 KB. One way to improve the reliability of the TCP connection is to reduce the window size that the receiver needs to receive before sending an acknowledgement. However, this will reduce throughput as more segments and acknowledgements will need to be sent in order to transfer the same amount of data.

Question 14: The maximum window size for data transmission using the selective reject protocol with n-bit frame sequence numbers is
A) 2^n B) 2^{n-1} C) $2^n - 1$ D) 2^{n-2}

Answer: B. n bit frame sequence numbers are used. So possible sequence numbers are 2^n. But sending and receiving window work together; so $\frac{2^n}{2} = 2^{n-1}$.

CHAPTER

TCP Flow Control | 11

11.1 Introduction

TCP provides a way for the receiver to control the amount of data sent by the sender. Nodes that send and receive TCP data segments can operate at different data rates because of differences in CPU and network bandwidth. As a result, it is possible for sender to send data at a faster rate than the receiver can handle.

If the receiver is slower than the sender, bytes will have to be dropped from the receiver's sliding window buffer. TCP deals with this issue using what is known as *flow control*.

11.2 What is Flow Control?

As an example, consider a conversation with your friend. One of you listens while the other speaks. You might nod your head as you listen or you might interrupting the flow with a "Whoa, slow down, you are talking too fast!" This is actually flow control. Some of us are better at it than others, but we all do it to some degree.

You nod to indicate you understood and are ready for the next statement of information or you tell your friend when they are going too fast. That's *flow control*.

11.3 Flow Control and Error Control

Network is responsible for transmission of data from one device to another device. *Flow control* is one of the important design issue for the transport layer that controls the flow of data between *sender* and *receiver*. When Sender sends data to receiver than there can be problem in below case:

Sender sends data at higher rate and receive is too sluggish to support that data rate. To solve the above problem, *flow control* is used in transport layer.

It also works on other layers. The main concept of flow control is to introduce efficiency in computer networks.

The end to end transfer of data from a transmitting application to a receiving application involves many steps, each subject to error. With the *error control* process, we can be confident that the transmitted and received data are identical. Data can be corrupted during transmission. For reliable communication, error must be detected and corrected.

Error control is the *process* of detecting and correcting both the bit level and packet level errors. Error control is the process of detecting and correcting both the bit level and packet level errors.

11.3.1 Types of Errors

- Single Bit Error: The term single bit error means that only one bit of the data unit was changed from 1 to 0 and 0 to 1.
- Burst Error: In term burst error means that two or more bits in the data unit were changed. Burst error is also called packet level error, where errors like packet loss, duplication, reordering.

Also, note that error control, error detection and error correction are slightly different concepts.

1. *Error detection* is the process finding erred segments
2. *Error correction* is the process of finding and correcting erred segments
3. *Error control* is the methodology of dealing with erred segments

Flow control is a way to describe techniques that *prevent* the transmitter from sending frames faster than the receiver can handle them. The receiver has limited buffer space which could fill up, leaving no place to store an incoming frame.

Error control describes procedures used to handle frames that have errors, including how to check a frame for errors, what to do when errors are discovered.

11.4 TCP and Flow Control

TCP implements a flow control mechanism that controls the amount of data send by the sender. This is achieved by using a *sliding window mechanism*. The receiver TCP module sends back to the sender an acknowledgment that indicates a range of acceptable sequence numbers beyond the last successfully received segment. This range of acceptable sequence numbers is called a window.

The window size reflects the amount of buffer space available for new data at the receiver. If this buffer space size shrinks because the receiver is being overrun, the receiver will send back a smaller window size. In the extreme case the windows size will decrease to very small or one octet. This is called the *silly window syndrome*. Most TCP implementations take special measure to avoid it.

The goal of the sliding window mechanism is to keep the channel full of data and to reduce the delays for waiting acknowledgements.

11.5 Stop and Wait Flow Control

The simplest form of flow control is called "Stop and Wait Flow Control." This is very simple. The transmitter sends one segment. Then the transmitter stops and waits for the receiver to confirm that the segment arrived without error. The receiver will confirm that the segment arrived by sending a message back to acknowledge the segment. This message is referred to as an ACK (*acknowledgment*) or RR (*receiver ready*).

Once the transmitter gets the acknowledgment it can send the next segment. In other words, segments are sent one at a time and each must be confirmed before the next one can be sent.

Take a look at the following diagram. The sender is on the left and the receiver is on the right. They are separated by some distance. The vertical scale represents time, with time zero at the top. A segment is transmitted and it takes some time to travel to the receiver. The black arrows crossing the diagram show the leading edge and trailing edge of the segment as it travels to the receiver.

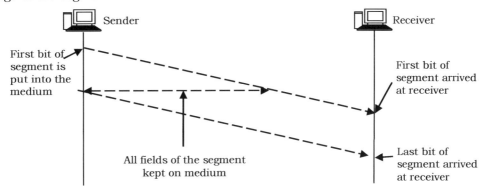

Take a look at Stop and Wait Flow Control in the next diagram. Notice that much of the time, the receiver and the transmitter are doing nothing but waiting.

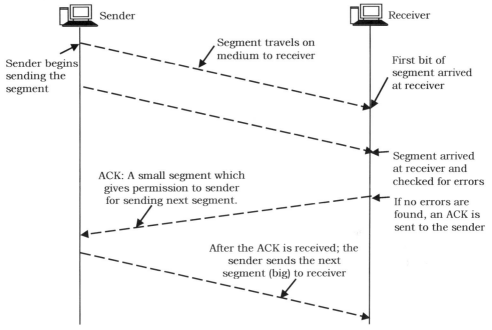

Segments are usually numbered to keep track of them. Acknowledgments are also numbered. Stop and Wait Flow Control need only number the segments as segment 0 and segment 1. The acknowledgments are numbered ACK 0 and ACK 1.

Look how much time the transmitter is doing nothing in the above diagram. When a segment is small, much of the time is spent waiting for it to travel across the network and for the ACK to return.

One solution to this problem of poor efficiency is to send larger segments. When segments are larger, more time is spent sending data. Larger segments are more efficient as long as there are few errors. If there is an error the entire segment has to be resent. The larger the segment the more likely there will be an error in it, so there is a point where no benefits are found by increasing the segment size. When there are frequent errors very small segments might be appropriate.

11.6 Positive Acknowledgment and Retransmission (PAR)

A simple transport protocol can implement a *reliability* and *flow-control technique* where the source sends one packet, starts a timer, and waits for an acknowledgment before sending a new packet. If the acknowledgment is not received before the timer expires, the source retransmits the packet. Such a technique is called *positive acknowledgment and retransmission* (PAR).

By assigning each packet a sequence number, PAR enables nodes to track lost or *duplicate* packets caused by network delays that result in *premature retransmission*. The sequence numbers are sent back in the acknowledgments so that the acknowledgments can be tracked.

PAR is an *inefficient* use of *bandwidth*, however, because a host must wait for an acknowledgment before sending a new packet, and only one packet can be sent at a time.

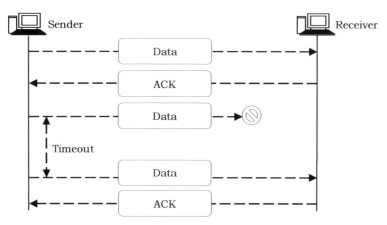

11.7 Sliding Window Mechanism in Data Transmission

Sliding window is a *flow control technique* which belongs to the *Data Link layer* of the OSI model. It solves the problem of missing frames during data transmission between two upper layers, so that they can send and receive frames in order.

11.7.1 Two Acknowledgement Schemes

In sliding window mechanism, receiver sends out acknowledgement to sender to notify of receiving or missing of frames. There are *two* acknowledgement methods.

1. ACK (*acknowledgement*) scheme is used on a noisy link, in which receiver sends an ACK for every frame received (note that when the receiver sends an acknowledgment for frame s, this is understood to mean that all frames up to and including s have been received).

2. NAK (*negative acknowledgement*) is used on a reliable link on which message loss is *not frequent*. In this scheme receiver only sends an ACK for a lost frame.

11.7.2 Sliding Window Mechanism in TCP

TCP is a sliding window protocol. A TCP sliding window provides more efficient use of network bandwidth than PAR because it enables nodes to send multiple bytes or packets before waiting for an acknowledgment.

In TCP, the receiver *specifies* the current window size in every packet. Because TCP provides a byte-stream connection, window sizes are expressed in bytes. This means that a window is the number of data bytes that the sender is allowed to send before waiting for an acknowledgment. Initial window sizes are indicated at connection setup, but might vary throughout the data transfer to provide flow control. A window size of zero, for instance, means *Send no data*.

The window size in sliding window protocols specifies the amount of data that can be sent before the sender has to pause and wait for the receiver to acknowledge them. This limit accomplishes several things.

First, it is a form of flow control, preventing the sending side from overrunning the receive buffer on the receiving side.

Second, it is a form of speed matching, allowing the sending side to keep sending at its own pace without having to stall and wait for the receiving side to acknowledge the sent bytes. The window size specifies how far the sender can get ahead of the receiver. Finally, as we will see below, it is a performance mechanism to take best advantage of the characteristics of the underlying network.

TCP's 16-bit window field is used by the receiver to tell the sender how many bytes of data the receiver is willing to accept. Since the window field is limited to a maximum of 16 bits, this provides for a maximum window size of 65,535 bytes.

The window size advertised by the receiver (called *advertised window*) tells the sender how much data, starting from the current position in the TCP data byte stream can be sent without waiting for further acknowledgements. As data is sent by the sender and then acknowledged by the receiver, the window slides forward to cover more data in the byte stream. This concept is called *sliding window* and is shown in figure.

As shown above, data within the window boundary is eligible to be sent by the sender.

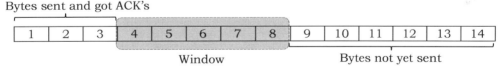

Those bytes in the stream prior to the window have already been sent and acknowledged. Bytes ahead of the window have not been sent and must wait for the window to *slide* forward before they can be transmitted by the sender. A receiver can adjust the window size each time it sends acknowledgements to the sender.

11.7.2.1 An Example

In a TCP sliding-window operation, for example, the sender might have a sequence of bytes to send (numbered 1 to 10) to a receiver who has a window size of four. The sender then would place a window around the first four bytes and transmit them together. It would then wait for an acknowledgment.

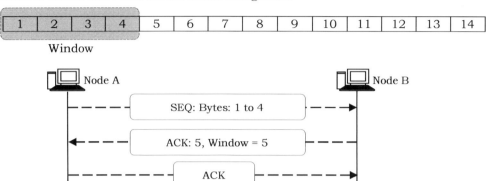

The receiver would respond with an ACK = 5, indicating that it has received bytes 1 to 4 and is expecting byte 5 next. In the same packet, the receiver would indicate that its window size is 5. The sender then would move the sliding window five bytes to the right and transmit bytes 5 to 9.

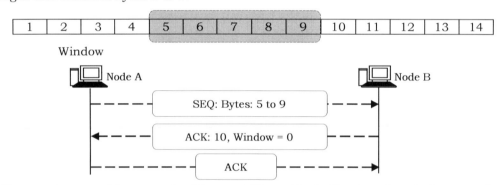

The receiver would respond with an ACK = 10, indicating that it is expecting sequenced byte 10 next. In this packet, the receiver might indicate that its window size is 0 (because, for example, its internal buffers are full). At this point, the sender cannot send any more bytes until the receiver sends another packet with a window size greater than 0.

11.7.3 Buffer Sizes

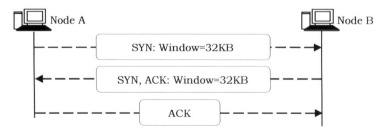

The number of bytes that may be sent at any time before the sender must pause and wait for acknowledgement is limited by *two* factors:

1. The *size* of the *'s buffer*: The size of the receiver's buffer matters because the sender cannot send more bytes than the receiver has room to buffer; otherwise data is lost.
2. The *size* of the *sender's buffer*: The size of the sender's buffer matters because the sender cannot recycle its own buffer space until the receiver has acknowledged the bytes in the send buffer, in case the network loses the data and the bytes must be resent.

The sender knows the receiver's remaining buffer size because the receiver *advertises* this value as the TCP window size in each acknowledgement replied to the sender. The sender always knows its *own* send buffer size.

But the effective window size used by the sender is actually the minimum of the TCP window size advertised by the receiver, based on the unused space in its *receive buffer*, and the sender's own send buffer size. To change the effective window size for best performance, both buffer sizes, one at either end of the connection, must be tuned.

11.7.4 Window Sizes

The TCP window size specifies the number of unacknowledged bytes that may be outstanding from the sender to the receiver. The window size field in the TCP header is an unsigned sixteen-bit value. This provides for a maximum TCP window size of 0xFFFF or 65535 bytes, although as will be explained below, this can be circumvented. A socket will have *two* window sizes, one in each direction. They can be different sizes.

The receiver node advertises its window size in each acknowledgement replied to the sender node. *Acknowledgements* may be standalone segments, called *pure acknowledgements*, or they may be piggy backed on data segments being sent in the other direction. The advertised window size is the space remaining in the receiver's buffer. This is the flow control aspect of the sliding window.

The window size is also the largest number of bytes that may be sent before the sender has to wait for the receiver to reply with an acknowledgement. Sent bytes must be buffered by the sender until they are acknowledged by the receiver, in case the sender must resend them. This is the reliability aspect of TCP. The sender can run at its own rate until the receiver advertises a window size of zero. This is the speed matching aspect of TCP.

The initial TCP window size advertised by the receiver is based on the receive buffer size.

11.8 Flow Control with Advertised Window

With TCP, a slow receiver can limit how much data a sender can transmit. This is integrated within the sliding window algorithm, so the receiver can control how large the sender's window can be. The receiver advertises a window size in bytes to the sender through a 16 bit number in the TCP header (the advertised window field). Upon receipt of a TCP segment from the receiver, the sender adjusts its window size accordingly.

11.8.1 Advertised Window

TCP provides flow control by having the sender maintain a variable called the *receive window* (also called *advertised window*). The advertised window is used to give the sender an idea about how much free buffer space is available at the receiver. In a full-duplex connection, the sender at each side of the connection maintains a different advertised window.

The advertised window is dynamic, i.e., it changes throughout a connection's lifetime. Let's investigate the advertised window in the context of a file transfer. Suppose that source is sending a large file to destination over a TCP connection. Destination allocates a receive buffer to this connection; denote its size by *MaxRcvBuffer*. From time to time, the application process in destination reads from the buffer.

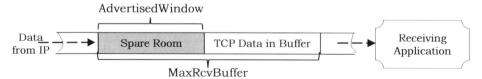

11.8.2 TCP Sending and Receiving Buffers

Sender Buffer :

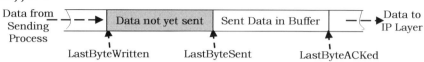

Receiver Buffer:

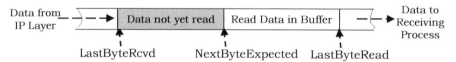

To understand the communication between sending and receiving processes, we need to get clarity on their buffers. In TCP, both the sending and receiving processes maintains buffers. On sending side, this buffer is used to store data that has been sent but not yet acknowledged, as well as data that has been written by the sending application, but not transmitted. On the receiving side, this buffer holds data that arrives that the application process has not yet read.

Let us define the following variables:

LastByteWritten = The number of the last byte in the data stream written to the buffer by the application process in source machine.

LastByteSent = The number of the last byte in the data stream sent to the destination by the application process in source machine. Application process in source machine waits for the ACK for these bytes.

LastByteACKed = The number of the last byte in the data stream for which the ACK was sent by destination and received by the application process in source machine.

LastByteRead = The number of the next byte in the data stream which the application process in destination machine expects.

LastByteRead = The number of the last byte in the data stream read from the buffer by the application process in destination machine.

LastByteRcvd = The number of the last byte in the data stream that has arrived from the network and has been placed in the receive buffer at destination.

Since the receiver cannot have acknowledged a byte that has not yet been sent:

$$LastByteAcked \leq LastByteSent$$

Since TCP cannot send a byte that the application process has not yet written:

$$LastByteSent \leq LastByteWritten$$

The inequalities are a little less intuitive, however, because of the problem of out-of-order delivery. The below relationship is true because a byte cannot be read by the application until it is received and all preceding bytes have also been received.

$$LastByteRead < NextByteExpected$$

NextByteExpected points to the byte immediately after the latest byte to meet this criterion. Also, if data has arrived in order, *NextByteExpected* points to the byte after *LastByteRcvd*, whereas if data has arrived out of order, *NextByteExpected* points to the start of the first gap in the data.

$$NextByteExpected \leq LastByteRcvd+1$$

Note that bytes to the left of *LastByteRead* need not be buffered because they have already been read by the local application process, and bytes to the right of *LastByteRcvd* need not be buffered because they have not yet arrived.

Because TCP is not permitted to overflow the allocated buffer, we must have:

$$LastByteRcvd - LastByteRead \leq MaxRcvBuffer$$

The receive window is denoted *AdvertisedW* and is set to the amount of spare room in the buffer:

$$AdvertisedW = MaxRcvBuffer - [(NextByteExpected - 1) - LastByteRead]$$

Because the spare room changes with time, *AdvertisedW* is dynamic.

How does the connection use the variable *AdvertisedW* to provide the flow control service? Destination informs the source of how much spare room it has in the connection buffer by placing its current value of *AdvertisedW* in the window field of every segment it sends to source. Initially destination sets *AdvertisedW* = *MaxRcvBuffer*. Note that to pull this off, destination must keep track of several connection-specific variables.

Source in turn keeps track of two variables, *LastByteSent* and *LastByteAcked*, which have obvious meanings. Note that the difference between these two variables (*LastByteSent* and *LastByteAcked*) is the amount of unacknowledged data that source has sent into the connection.

By keeping the amount of unacknowledged data less than the value of *AdvertisedW*, source is assured that it is not overflowing the receive buffer at destination. Thus source makes sure throughout the connection's life that

$$LastByteSent - LastByteAcked \leq AdvertisedW$$

There is one *minor* technical problem with this scheme. To see this, suppose destination's receive buffer becomes full so that *AdvertisedW* = 0. After advertising *AdvertisedW* = 0 to source, also suppose that destination has nothing to send to source.

Finally, the sender computes an effective window that limits how much data it can send:

$$EffectiveWindow = AdvertisedW-(LastByteSent-LastByteAcked)$$

As the application process at destination empties the buffer, TCP does not send new segments with new *AdvertisedW* to source. TCP will only send a segment to source if it has data to send or if it has an acknowledgment to send.

Therefore source is never informed that some space has opened up in destination's *receive* buffer: source is blocked and can transmit no more data! To solve this problem, the TCP specification requires source to continue to send segments with one data byte when destination's *advertised window* is zero. These segments will be acknowledged by the receiver. Eventually the buffer will begin to empty and the acknowledgements will contain *non-zero AdvertisedW*. This technique is called *probing*.

Having described TCP's flow control service, we briefly mention here that UDP does*not* provide flow control. To understand the issue here, consider sending a series of UDP segments from a process on source to a process on destination.

For a typical UDP implementation, UDP will append the segments (more precisely, the data in the segments) in a finite-size queue that *precedes* the corresponding socket (i.e., the door to the process). The process reads one entire segment at a time from the queue. If the process does not read the segments fast enough from the queue, the queue will overflow and segments will get lost.

11.9 Segmentation and Nagling

Since TCP is a byte oriented protocol, every byte has its own *sequence number*. However, TCP sends bytes in segments. A related issue to flow control is how TCP decides when to send.

Ideally, TCP uses a *Maximum Segment Size* (*MSS*) for its segments imposed by the *Maximum Transmission Unit* (*MTU*) allowed by the underlying network. Therefore, $MSS < MTU$, which prevents additional segmentation at the network level.

But should TCP wait to accumulate enough bytes to fill an MSS-sized segment? Or should it send data immediately in a smaller segment of few bytes? The latter case implies inefficient use of bandwidth by sending high overhead *tinygrams* with the TCP (and IP) headers consuming most of the bytes. However, this issue is not relevant unless TCP actually has few bytes to send. But why would that be the case? The answer to this lies in three similar yet different problems:

1. *Small Ack Problem*: A receiver's application program with no response to the sender causes the receiver to send empty TCP segments (acks) to ack.
2. *Silly Window Syndrome* (SWS): A receiver's slow application program causes the receiver to advertise a small window size.
3. *Small Segment Problem*: A sender's slow application program provides the sender with only few bytes per second.

11.9.1 Small Ack Problem

To solve the small ack problem, the TCP specification says that TCP should implement a *delayed ack* strategy.

To cut back on network traffic, a host will not send an acknowledgment right away, possibly allowing more than one TCP data package to be acknowledged in one reply packet or an acknowledgment of the packet to be sent along with data to be sent to the remote host.

This means is that TCP should delay the *ack* until the receiver has a response to the sender, and piggybacks the *ack* on the response segment. Such a response may not be available, so the delay must be less than 0.5 seconds, typically 200 ms. Moreover, in a stream of MSS-sized segments there should be an *ack* for at least every second segment.

11.9.2 Silly Window Syndrome (SWS)

Silly window syndrome is a problem that can degrade TCP performance. It can be caused by either end:

- The receiver can advertise small windows (instead of waiting until a larger window could be advertised) and
- The sender can transmit small amounts of data (instead of waiting for additional data, to send a larger segment)

That means, this problem occurs when data are passed to the sending TCP entity in large blocks, but an interactive application on the receiving side reads data 1 byte at a time.

If the slowness of the sender's application causes Silly Window Syndrome, *Nagle's algorithm* is the solution. The prescription is as follows:

1. Sender sends the first segment even if it is a small one.
2. Next, the sender waits until an ACK is received, or a maximum-size segment is accumulated.
3. Step 2 is repeated for the rest of the transmission.

If the slowness of the receiver's application causes Silly Window Syndrome, two solutions are advised:

1. Clark's solution: Send an ACK as soon as the data arrives, and close the wind ow until another segment can be received or buffer is ½ empty.
2. Delayed ACK: Delay sending the ACK, at most 500 ms; this causes the sender stop transmitting, but it does not change its window size.

Clark's solution is to prevent the receiver from sending a window update for 1 byte. Instead it is forced to wait until it has a decent amount of space available and advertise that instead. Specifically, the receiver should not send a window update until it can handle the maximum segment size it advertised when the connection was established or until its buffer is half empty, whichever is smaller. The sender can also help by not sending tiny segments. Instead, it should wait until it has accumulated enough space in the window to send a full segment or at least one containing half of the receiver's buffer size.

Nagle's algorithm and *Clark's* solution to the silly window syndrome are *complementary*. *Nagle's* algorithm tries to solve the problem caused by the *sending* application delivering data to TCP a byte at a time. Clark's solution tries to solve the problem of the receiving application sucking the data up from TCP a byte at a time. Both solutions can work together. The goal is for the sender not to send small segments and the receiver not to ask for them.

11.9.3 Small segment problem

Unlike the previous two problems, a solution to the small segment problem must be placed at the *sender*, but the solution is more complicated as described by the following example.

A user on a SSH application types 25 characters; one character every 200 ms.

If TCP sends data immediately, then each byte of data (character) will generate 20 bytes of TCP header and 20 bytes of IP header (we will see this when we study the IP packet format), resulting in a 40 to 1 overhead (a total of 1000 bytes). While this is acceptable on a LAN like Ethernet, it is not acceptable on highly congested WANs.

If on the other hand, TCP waits to fill an MSS-sized segment, the question is then how long should the wait be? This will affect the responsiveness of the application. For instance, imagine the user hits return and nothing happens because TCP is waiting for more characters!

An engineering solution would be to wait for a predetermined amount of time before sending a small segment (less than MSS bytes). Therefore, TCP can use a timer that fires, say, every 500 ms. When the timer fires, TCP fills the largest possible segment and sends it. Unfortunately, this approach is not satisfactory on most networks.

11.9.3.1 Example 1: LAN with RTT = 50 ms

The user gets a response every 2 or 3 characters. The overhead is 16 to 1 (a total of 400 bytes). This is not a good solution.

11.9.3.2 Example 2: WAN with 5 sec RTT = 5 sec

In this case, the responsiveness is not that bad since the user has to wait 5 sec for the first response anyway. But the overhead is still high; we still have too many segments injected into the WAN (10 segments). What this means is that TCP should have waited longer before sending each segment. But this will only make it worse for the LAN situation of Example 1.

11.9.3.3 Nagle's Algorithm

What we conclude from the above two examples is that we need a timer that is adaptive to the network, e.g. fast for LAN and slow for WAN. John Nagle suggested a self-clocking algorithm for the sender that uses the ack as the firing of a timer. The sender delays a segment until all outstanding data has been acknowledged (stop and wait) or until TCP has an MSS-sized segment.

```
while more data{
    if both available data and the window ≥ MSS
        Send a full segment
    else{
        // stop and wait
        if there is unACKed data in transit
            Buffer the new data
        else
            Send data in a small segment
    }
}
```

Therefore, on fast LANs, Nagle's algorithm behaves like *stop and wait* for small segments, but has high overhead. On slow WANs, Nagle's algorithm implies more wait but is more efficient. Let's revisit the two examples above.

For the LAN example with a 50 ms RTT, every character will see no data in transit (50 ms < 200 ms) and, therefore, is sent immediately. The response is fast, but the overhead is 40 to 1 again (a total of 1000 bytes for 25 characters). This is appropriate for a LAN.

For the WAN example with a 5 sec RTT, the first character will see no data in transit and, therefore, will be sent immediately. The rest of the characters will wait for the ack (5 sec = 25£200 ms). When the *ack* arrives, the 24 remaining characters are sent in one segment. The overhead is 3.2 to 1 (a total of 80 bytes). Only two segments are injected into the WAN. This is appropriate for a WAN.

Problems and Questions with Answers

Question 1: If flow control and error control are performed at the data link layer, then why is it also necessary to perform flow and error control at the transport layer?

Answer: The transport layer is the first end-to-end layer, whereas the data link layer only connects two adjacent nodes. Providing flow and error control is sufficient to prevent packets from being lost or corrupted on a single link, but it doesn't prevent packets from being discarded or corrupted at a higher layer (namely the network layer). A good example is network layer congestion.

If a router discards a packet because one of its buffers overflowed, it doesn't matter that the packet was transmitted reliably by the data link layer – the packet was still discarded at the network layer. In order to recover this packet, we need an error control mechanism at an even higher layer – namely, the transport layer.

Question 2: Sender S communicates with receiver R using a flow control protocol with a window of 3 packets. This means that S can send at most 3 unacknowledged packets at a time. Each packet has a sequence number starting from 1. R always acknowledges a packet by sending back to A the sequence number of that packet (i.e., when R receives a packet with sequence number 2 it sends an acknowledgement (ack) containing 2 to S.)

Ignore packet transmission times, and assume that neither the packets nor the ack are reordered in the network.

Let RTT denote the round-trip time between S and R. S uses two mechanisms to retransmit a packet:

- *timeout*: S retransmits a packet if it has not received an ack for it within T seconds after sending the packet, where T > RTT.
- *out − of − order* ack: S retransmits an unacknowledged packet p when it receives an ack with a sequence number higher than p. For example, if packet 3 hasn't been acknowledged, and S receives ack 4, then S assumes that R hasn't received packet 3 and retransmits it immediately.

Assume S wants to transfer a file that spawns exactly 8 packets to R as fast as possible. During the transfer at most one packet (or ack) is lost. For all questions below express your answer in terms of T and RTT.

A) What is the minimum time it could take to transfer the file? The file transfer time is the time between the moment S sends the first packet and the moment it receives the last ack.

B) What is the maximum possible file transfer time assuming S uses only the *timeout* retransmission mechanism? Please give a scenario which achieves the maximum transfer time. This scenario should indicate which packet (or ack) is dropped, if any.

C) Repeat question (B) but now assume that S uses both the *timeout* and *out-of-order* ack retransmission mechanisms.

Answer:

A) $3 \times RTT$: No packet or ack is lost.

B) $3 \times RTT + T$: A packet in the last window is lost.

C) Same as (B), if the last packet is lost.

Question 3: Flow control is a key function that is typically performed by a protocol. Is it true or false?

Answer: True

Question 4: Consider an error-free 1024-kbps channel used to send 512B data frames in one direction, with very short acknowledgements coming back the other way. Assume a propagation delay of 50 msec. What is the maximum throughput for a window size of 1, 7, 15, 127, and 255?

Answer: A 512B frame (4096 bits) occupies the channel for 4096/1,024,000 sec or 4 msec. The round trip and propagation time is 104 msec, so we need a window of 104/4 or 26 frames to keep the channel busy. With a window size of 1, we can send 4096 bits per 104 msec for a throughput of 39.39 Kbps. For a window of 7 frames, it is 7 times higher, or 275.69 Kbps, etc. 1024 is the upper bound.

Question 5: For the Question ,at what minimum window size can the protocol run at the full rate of the channel?

Answer: For windows above 26 (= 1024/39.39) frames, the full 1,024 kbps is used.

Note: since the problem description was not clear about ignoring ACKs, we will also accept the answer: since ACKs are required to acknowledge the data, the protocol can never run at the full rate.

Question 6: Consider the Go-Back-N protocol with a send window size of 10 and a sequence number range of 1024. Suppose that at time t, the next in-order packet that the receiver is expecting has a sequence number of k. Assume that the medium does not reorder messages. What are the possible sets of sequence number inside the sender's window at time t?

Answer: Here we have a window size of $N = 10$. Suppose the receiver has received packet $k - 1$, and has ACKed that and all other preceding packets. If all of these ACK's have been received by the sender, then the sender's window is $[k, k + N - 1]$. Suppose next that none of the ACKs have been received at the sender.

In this second case, the sender's window contains $k - 1$ and the N packets up to and including $k - 1$. The sender's window is thus $[k - N, k - 1]$. By these arguments, the senders window is of size 10 and begins somewhere in the range $[k - N, k]$.

Question 7: What are all possible values of the ACK field in the message currently propagating back to the sender at time t?

Answer: If the receiver is waiting for packet k, then it has received (and ACKed) packet $k - 1$ and the $N - 1$ packets before that. If none of those N ACKs have been yet received by the sender, then ACK messages with values of $[k - N, k - 1]$ may still be propagating back. Because the sender has sent packets $[k - N, k - 1]$, it must be the case that the sender has already received an ACK for $k - N - 1$. Once the receiver has sent an ACK for $k - N - 1$ it will never send an ACK that is less that $k - N - 1$. Thus the range of in-flight ACK values can range from $k - N$ to $k - 1$.

Question 8: With the Go-Back-N protocol, is it possible for the sender to receive an ACK for a packet that falls outside of its current window?

Answer: Yes. Suppose the sender has a window size of 3 and sends packets 1, 2, 3 at t_0. At t_1 ($t_1 > t_0$) the receiver ACKS 1, 2, 3. At t_2 ($t_2 > t_1$) the sender times out and resends 1, 2, 3.

At t_3 the receiver receives the duplicates and re-acknowledges 1, 2, 3. At t_4 the sender receives the ACKs that the receiver sent at t_1 and advances its window to 4, 5, 6. At t_5 the sender receives the ACKs 1, 2, 3 the receiver sent at t_2. These ACKs are outside its window.

Question 9: Suppose host A is sending to a multicast group. The destinations are leaf nodes of a tree rooted at A with depth N and with each non-leaf node having k children, so there are k^N destinations. Ignore counting the ACK's for this question. How many individual link transmissions are involved if A sends a multicast message to all destinations?

Answer: One multicast transmission involves all $k + k^2 + \ldots + k^N = \frac{k^{N+1} - k}{k-1}$ links.

Question 10: How many individual link transmissions are involved if A sends a unicast message to each destination?

Answer: One unicast retransmission involves N links; sending to everyone would require $N \times k^N$ links.

Question 11: Suppose A sends a multicast message to all destinations, but a fraction f of the destinations fail to receive the message. Option (i) is to send a separate unicast transmission to each of those destinations. Option (ii) is to send a single multicast transmission to all destinations. Which option requires more individual link transmissions? (Your answer should depend on the values of N, k, and f).

Answer: The additional unicast transmission to x fraction of the recipients uses $x \times N \times k^N$ links. Equating this to the answer in Question 9, we get

$$x = \frac{k^{N+1} - k}{(k - 1) \times N \times k^N}$$

Question 12: Host A is sending data to host B over a full duplex link. A and B are using the sliding window protocol for flow control. The send and receive window sizes are 5 packets each. Data packets (sent only from A to B) are all 1000 bytes long and the transmission time for such a packet is 50 µs. Acknowledgment packets (sent only from B to A), are very small and require negligible transmission time. The propagation delay over the link is 200 µs . What is the maximum achievable throughput in this communication?
A) 7.69×10^6 bps   B) 11.11×10^6 bps
C) 12.33×10^6 bps   D) 15.00×10^6 bps

Answer: B.

Data packet size	=	1000 bytes
Number of packets	=	5
Total data	=	5000 bytes
Propagation delay	=	200 µs
Transmission time	=	50 µs per packet
Time to 5 packets	=	5×50 µs = 200 µs
Total time for 5 packets	=	250 + 200 = 450 µs
Rate	=	$\frac{Date}{Time} = \frac{5000}{450 \times 10^{-6}} = 11.11 \times 10^6$ bps

TCP Congestion Control

CHAPTER

12

12.1 Introduction

In today's world, the *Transmission Control Protocol* (TCP) carries huge Internet traffic, so performance of the Internet depends to a great extent on how well TCP works. TCP provides a reliable transport service between two processes running on source and destination nodes.

Another important component of TCP is its *congestion control* mechanism. The important strategy of TCP is to send packets into the network and then to react to *observable events* that occur. TCP congestion control was introduced into the Internet in the late 1980s by *Van Jacobson*; roughly eight years after the TCP/IP protocol stack had become operational.

To address these issues, multiple mechanisms were implemented in TCP to govern the rate with which the data can be sent in both directions (*client to server* and *server to client*): *flow control*, *congestion control*, and *congestion avoidance*.

12.2 What is Network Congestion?

With increase in dependence on networks (say, Internet), there is an increase in contention for their *resources*. This contention has affected the performance of networks. While any network performs reasonably well under light load, problems surface when they are used extensively.

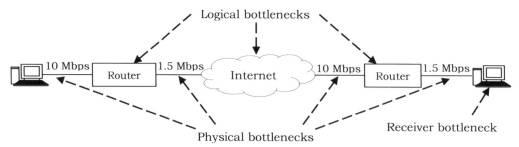

The most notable and common problem that networks are faced with is loss of data. While loss of data in a network can occur due to a variety of reasons, *congestion* in the network is the most common reason. In simple terms, *congestion* refers to the loss of network performance when a network is heavily loaded. This loss of performance can be data loss, large delays in data transmission, which is often unacceptable. Due to this, controlling and avoiding congestion is a critical problem in network management and design.

The most common type of computer network is a packet-switched network, where nodes send data in the form of packets to each other. The most common strategy used to transfer data is *store-and-forward*. Each node waits till it has received a whole packet before forwarding it at a later time to the appropriate output link.

The Internet is an example of a network that is prominently packet-switched. The data route from a source to destination is computed by different methods by routers. When we talk about congestion control we essentially talk about control of data packets in these routers.

Congestion occurs in a router when the aggregate bandwidth of incoming packets, destined for a particular output link, exceeds the link's bandwidth. An example of congestion occurring at a router is shown in figure.

12.3 Types of Congestion

There are two types of congestion: *transient* and *persistent*.

Transient congestion can be managed with a queue of buffer at the router. During to the congestion period the queue will grow and contain the excess packets. When the congestion period ends, the buffered data is forwarded to the appropriate output link.

On the other hand, persistent congestion is said to occur when the data overflows the buffer.

While transient congestion only introduces a delay in data transmission, persistent congestion results in data loss. These problems are tackled in two ways. Either the router detects the queue build up and informs the sources to decrease their transmission rate. Such a strategy is called *congestion avoidance*.

The other method is to use *end-to-end* strategies where the routers do not get directly involved but the hosts use indirect methods to detect congestion. Such a mechanism is called *congestion control*. In TCP/IP, both methods are used to tackle problem related to congestion.

12.4 An Overview of TCP Flow Control

One of TCP's primary functions is to *properly match* the *transmission rate* of the sender to that of the receiver and the network. It is important for the transmission to be at a high enough rates to ensure good performance, but also to protect against overwhelming traffic at the network or receiving host.

TCP's 16-bit window field is used by the receiver to tell the sender how many bytes of data the receiver is willing to accept. Since the window field is limited to a maximum of 16 bits, this provides for a maximum window size of 65,535 bytes.

The window size advertised by the receiver (called *advertised window*) tells the sender how much data, starting from the current position in the TCP data byte stream can be sent without waiting for further acknowledgements. As data is sent by the sender and then acknowledged by the receiver, the window slides forward to cover more data in the byte stream. This concept is called *sliding window* and is shown in figure.

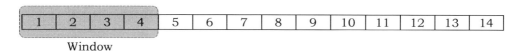

Window

As shown above, data within the window boundary is eligible to be sent by the sender.

Bytes sent and got ACK's

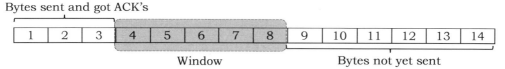

Window   Bytes not yet sent

Those bytes in the stream prior to the window have already been sent and acknowledged. Bytes ahead of the window have not been sent and must wait for the window to *slide* forward before they can be transmitted by the sender. A receiver can adjust the window size each time it sends acknowledgements to the sender.

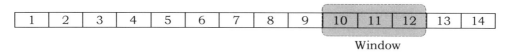

Window

The maximum transmission rate is ultimately bound by the receiver's ability to accept and process data. However, this technique implies an implicit trust arrangement between the TCP sender and receiver. The sender and also the network can play a part in determining the transmission rate of data flow as well.

It is important to consider the *limitation* on the window size of 65,535 bytes. Consider a typical internetwork that may have link speeds of up to 1 Gb/s or more. On a 1 Gb/s network 125,000,000 bytes can be transmitted in one second. This means that if only two TCP stations are communicating on this link, at best 65,535/125,000,000 or only about .0005 of the bandwidth will be used in each direction each second!

Recognizing the need for larger windows on high-speed networks, the Internet Engineering Task Force (IETF) released a standard for a *window scale option*. This standard effectively allows the window to increase from 16 to 32 bits or over 4 billion bytes of data in the window.

12.4.1 Retransmissions, Timeouts & Duplicate Acknowledgements

TCP relies mostly on implicit signals it learns from the network and remote host. That means TCP uses the network and remote host information to *control* the rate of data flow. TCP handles it in a simple way.

A sender's knowledge of network conditions may be achieved through the use of a timer. For each TCP segment sent the sender expects an acknowledgement within some period of time otherwise an error in the form of a timer expiring signals that that something is wrong.

Somewhere in the end-to-end path of a TCP connection a segment can be lost along the way. Often this is due to *congestion* in network routers where excess packets must be dropped. TCP not only must correct for this situation, but it can also learn something about network conditions from it.

Whenever TCP transmits a segment the sender starts a timer which keeps track of how long it takes for an acknowledgment for that segment to return. This timer is known as the *retransmission timer*. If an acknowledgement is returned before the timer expires, the timer is reset with no consequence. The default value of timer is often initialized to 1.5 seconds.

If an acknowledgement for the segment does not return within the timeout period, the sender would *retransmit* the segment and *double* the *retransmission timer* value for each consecutive timeout up to a maximum of about 64 seconds.

If there are serious network problems, segments may take a few minutes to be successfully transmitted before the sender eventually times out and generates an error to the sending application.

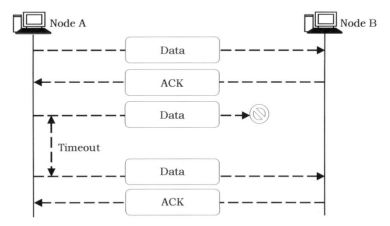

Fundamental to the timeout and retransmission strategy of TCP is the measurement of the *round-trip* time between two communicating TCP hosts. The round-trip time may vary during the TCP connection as network traffic patterns fluctuate and as routes become available or unavailable.

TCP keeps track of when data is sent and at what time acknowledgements covering those sent bytes are returned. TCP uses this information to calculate an estimate of round trip time. As packets are sent and acknowledged, TCP adjusts its round-trip time estimate and uses this information to come up with a reasonable timeout value for packets sent.

If acknowledgements return quickly, the round-trip time is short and the *retransmission timer* is thus set to a *lower value*. This allows TCP to quickly retransmit data when network response time is good, alleviating the need for a long delay between the occasional lost segment. The converse is also true. TCP does not retransmit data too quickly during times when network response time is long.

If a TCP data segment is lost in the network, a receiver will never even know it was once sent. However, the sender is waiting for an acknowledgement for that segment to return. In one case, if an acknowledgement doesn't return, the sender's retransmission timer expires which causes a retransmission of the segment.

If however the sender had sent at least one additional segment after the one that was lost and that later segment is received correctly, the receiver does not send an acknowledgement for the later, out of order segment.

The receiver cannot acknowledgement out of order data; it must acknowledge the last contiguous byte it has received in the byte stream prior to the lost segment. In this case, the receiver will send an acknowledgement indicating the last contiguous byte it has received.

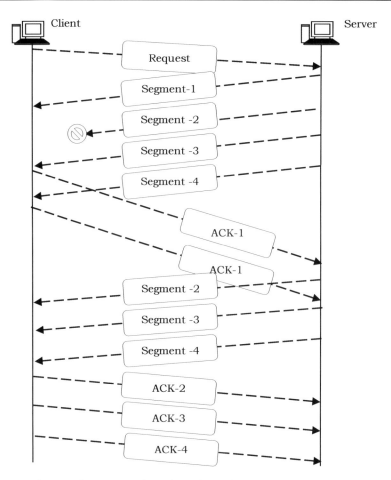

If that last contiguous byte was already acknowledged, we call this a duplicate ACK. The reception of duplicate ACKs can implicitly tell the sender that a segment may have been lost or delayed. The sender knows this because the receiver only generates a duplicate ACK when it receives other, out of order segments.

In fact, the Fast Retransmit algorithm described later uses duplicate ACKs as a way of speeding up the retransmission process.

12.5 Flow Control versus Congestion Control

It is clear that the terms flow control and congestion control are distinct. Flow control is an agreement between a source and a destination to limit the flow of packets without taking into account the load on the network.

The purpose of flow control is to ensure that a packet arriving at a destination will find a buffer there. Congestion control is primarily concerned with controlling the traffic to reduce overload on the network. Flow control solves the problem of the destination resources being the bottleneck while congestion control solves the problem of the routers and links being the bottleneck. Flow control is bipartite agreement.

Congestion control is a *social* (network-wide) law. Different connections on a network can choose different flow control strategies, but nodes on the network should follow the same congestion control strategy, if it is to be useful. The two parties in flow control are generally interested in cooperating whereas the n parties (e.g., different users) in congestion control may be non-cooperative. Fairness is not an issue for the two cooperating parties whereas it is an important issue for n competing parties.

12.6 TCP Self-Clocking

Broadly speaking, the idea of TCP congestion control is for each source to determine how much capacity is available in the network, so that it knows how many packets it can safely have in transit. Once a given source has this many packets in transit, it uses the arrival of an ACK as a signal that one of its packets has left the network and that it is therefore safe to insert a new packet into the network without adding to the level of congestion.

TCP uses an arrival of ACK as a trigger of new packet transmission. Packet arrival interval will change according to the characteristics of the transit networks. TCP adjusts transfer rate to the network capacity automatically and no need for complex mechanism for controlling transfer rate.

Self-clocking is an interesting property of TCP that allows automatic adjustment of the transmission speed to the bandwidth and delay of the path. Therefore, it makes possible for TCP to operate over links with very different speeds. By using ACKs to pace the transmission of packets, TCP is said to be *self-clocking*.

Let us consider that node A uses a window of three segments. It thus sends three back-to-back segments at 10 Mbps and then waits for an acknowledgement. Node A stops sending segments when its window is full. These segments reach the buffers of router R2. The first segment stored in this buffer is sent by router R2 at a rate of 2 Mbps to the destination node.

Upon reception of this segment, the destination sends an acknowledgement. This acknowledgement allows node A to transmit a new segment. This segment is stored in the buffers of router R2 while it is transmitting the second segment that was sent by node A.

Thus, after the transmission of the first window of segments, TCP sends one data segment after the reception of each acknowledgement returned by the destination. In practice, the acknowledgements sent by the destination serve as a kind of *clock* that allows the sending node to adapt its transmission rate to the rate at which segments are received by the destination.

This TCP *self-clocking* is the first mechanism that allows TCP to adapt to heterogeneous networks. It depends on the availability of buffers to store the segments that have been sent by the sender but have not yet been transmitted to the destination.

12.7 Congestion Collapse Problem

However, TCP is not always used in this environment. In the global Internet, TCP is used in networks where a large number of hosts send segments to a large number of receivers. For example, let us consider the network shown below. In this network, we assume that the buffers of the router are infinite to ensure that no packet is lost.

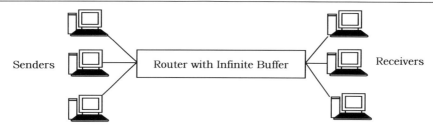

If many TCP senders are attached to the left part of the network above, they all send a window full of segments. These segments are stored in the buffers of the router before being transmitted towards their destination. If there are many senders on the left part of the network, the occupancy of the buffers quickly grows. A consequence of the buffer occupancy is that the round-trip-time, measured by TCP, between the sender and the receiver increases.

The congestion collapse is a problem that all heterogeneous networks face. Different mechanisms have been proposed in the scientific literature to avoid or control network congestion. Some of them have been implemented and deployed in real networks.

To understand this problem in more detail, let us first consider a simple network. Consider a network where 20,000 bits segments are sent. When the buffer is empty, such a segment requires 2 millisecond to be transmitted on the 10 Mbps link and 10 milliseconds to be the transmitted on the 2 Mbps link. Thus, the round-trip-time measured by TCP is roughly 12 milliseconds if we ignore the propagation delay on the links. Most routers manage their buffers as a FIFO queue.

If the buffer contains 100 segments, the round-trip-time becomes $1+100\times10+10$ milliseconds as new segments are only transmitted on the 2 Mbps link once all previous segments have been transmitted.

Unfortunately, TCP uses a retransmission timer and performs go-back-N to recover from transmission errors. If the buffer occupancy is high, TCP assumes that some segments have been lost and retransmits a full window of segments. This increases the occupancy of the buffer and the delay through the buffer. Also, the buffer may store and send on the low bandwidth links several retransmissions of the same segment. This problem is called congestion *collapse*. It occurred several times in the late 1980s.

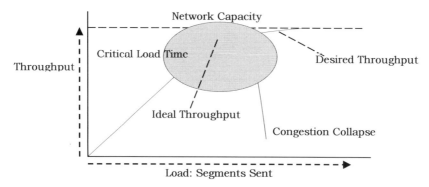

To avoid congestion collapse, the hosts must regulate their transmission rate by using a congestion control mechanism. Such a mechanism can be implemented in the transport layer or in the network layer. In TCP/IP networks, it is implemented in the transport layer, but other technologies such as Asynchronous Transfer Mode (ATM) or Frame Relay include congestion control mechanisms in lower layers.

12.8 Life of a TCP Connection Flow

A typical TCP flow evolves through three phases: connection, transfer and close. Figure gives a high-level view of these phases.

During the connection phase, a source attempts to establish contact with an intended receiver. Inability to establish contact results in a connection failure, which prevents data from flowing between source and receiver; thus, connection establishment procedures provide one form of congestion control implemented by TCP.

During the transfer phase, a source sends data (in the form of segments) on the flow until the required number has been received successfully. A receiver signals receipt of data segments by sending acknowledgments (ACKs) to the source. By sending duplicate acknowledgments, a receiver may also indicate failure to receive specific segments, which the source must then retransmit.

Also, a sender may fail to receive acknowledgments, which requires the sender to raise a timeout and to retransmit unacknowledged data. During the transfer phase, congestion control procedures determine when a source may send data segments to a receiver. The resulting series of segments is known as a flow.

12.8.1 Congestion Windows

TCP flows consist of a series of data segments (or packets) sent from a source to a receiver, along with a corresponding stream of acknowledgment packets flowing in the reverse direction.

Remember that, with the TCP sliding window protocol concept, the window size (*MaxWindow*) is equal to the maximum number of unacknowledged data that a source may send.

Consider a system where the source has infinite data to send. Assume the source uses a FIFO (First In First Out) as a send buffer of size *MaxWindow*. Of the connection, the source immediately fills the buffer which is then dequeued at the rate allowed by the line. Then the buffer can receive new data as old data is acknowledged.

Let T be the average time need to wait for an acknowledgement to come back. This time is counted from the instant the data is put into FIFO. This system is an approximate model of a TCP connection for a source which is infinitely fast and has infinite amount of data to send. In this case, the throughput of the connection can be given as

$$Throughput = \frac{AdvertisedW}{T}$$

The delay T is equal to the propagation and transmission times of the data and acknowledgement, plus the processing time, plus possible delays in sending acknowledgement.

$$T = Propagation\ time + Transmission\ time + Processing\ time + Delays\ in\ sending\ ACK$$

If T is fixed, then controlling *AdvertisedW* is equivalent to controlling the connection rate (*Throughput*). This is the method used in the Internet. But, in general, T also depends on the congestion status of the networks, through queuing delays.

Thus, in the periods of congestions, there is a first automatic congestion control effect: sources reduce their rates whenever the network delay increases. This is because the time to get acknowledgements increase. This has a side effect, which is not essential in the TCP congestion control mechanism.

TCP defines a variable called congestion window (*CongestionW*); the window size *AdvertisedW* is then given as

$$MaxWindow = min(CongestionW, AdvertisedW)$$
$$EffectiveWindow = MaxWindow-(LastByteSent- LastByteAcked)$$

Note that, *MaxWindow* replaces *AdvertisedW* in the calculation of *EffectiveWindow* (refer the formula in *Flow Control with Advertised Window* section of *TCP Flow control* chapter). Thus, a TCP source is allowed to send no faster than the slowest component (the network or the destination host) can accommodate.

12.9 Congestion Avoidance versus Congestion Control

The distinction between congestion control and congestion avoidance is similar to that between deadlock recovery and deadlock avoidance. Congestion control procedures are *cures* and the avoidance procedures are preventive in nature.

A congestion control scheme tries to bring the network back to an operating state, while a congestion avoidance scheme tries to keep the network at an optimal state. Without congestion control a network may cease operating (*zero throughput*) whereas networks have been operating without congestion avoidance for a long time.

The point at which a congestion control scheme is called upon depends on the amount of memory available in the routers, whereas, the point at which a congestion avoidance scheme is invoked is independent of the memory size.

12.10 TCP Congestion Control Techniques

At any given time, a source may send a prescribed number of packets (*CongestionW*) prior to receiving an acknowledgment. Thus, the size of the *CongestionW* controls the rate of packet transmission on a flow.

The problem, of course, is how TCP comes to learn an appropriate value for *CongestionW*. Unlike the *AdvertisedW*, which is sent by the receiving side of the connection, there is no one to send a suitable *CongestionW* to the sending side of TCP. The answer is that the TCP source sets the *CongestionW* based on the level of congestion it perceives to exist in the network.

12.10.1 Additive Increase/Multiplicative Decrease [AIMD]

AIMD works as follows. Every time the source successfully sends a *CongestionW's* worth of packets it adds the equivalent of 1 packet to *CongestionW*. That means, for each packet sent out during the last RTT has been ACKed; *CongestionW* is incremented by 1. And, if a packet loss is detected, *CongestionW* is set to half.

For example, suppose the *CongestionW* is currently set to 8 packets. If a packet loss is detected, *CongestionW* is set to 4. Normally, a loss is detected when a timeout occurs. Additional losses cause *CongestionW* to be reduced to 4, then 2, and finally to 1 packet. *CongestionW* is not allowed to fall below the size of a single packet (that is, maximum segment size (MSS)).

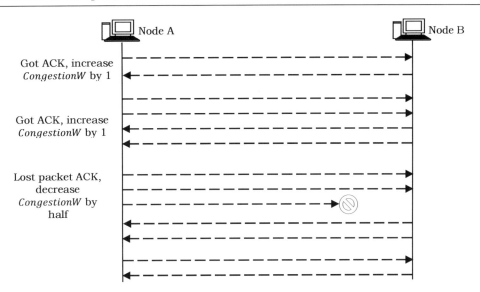

Increments *CongestionW* by a little for each ACK that arrives:

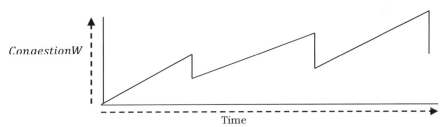

$$IncrementalValue = \text{MSS} \times (\text{MSS}/CongestionW)$$
$$CongestionW = CongestionW + IncrementalValue$$

That is, rather than incrementing *CongestionW* by an entire MSS bytes each RTT, we increment it by a fraction of MSS every time an ACK is received. Assuming that each ACK acknowledges the receipt of MSS bytes, then that fraction is MSS/ *CongestionW*.

This pattern of continually increasing and decreasing the congestion window continues throughout the lifetime of the connection. In fact, if we plot the current value of *CongestionW* as a function of time, we get a *sawtooth* pattern.

The important concept to understand about AIMD is that the source is willing to reduce its congestion window at a much faster rate than it is willing to increase its congestion window. This is in contrast to an additive increase/additive decrease strategy in which the window would be increased by 1 packet when an ACK arrives and decreased by 1 when a timeout occurs.

One main reason to decrease the window aggressively and increase it conservatively is that the consequences of having too large a window are much worse than those of it being too small. For example, when the window is too large, packets that are dropped will be retransmitted, making congestion even worse, thus, it is important to get out of this state quickly.

12.10.2 Slow Start

AIMD is too conservative when a session starts up – there may be plenty of bandwidth available. So, the idea is to start the congestion window at 1 packet and double it each time a new ACK arrives, until a packet times out. Whenever a packet loss is detected, congestion window is set to half (same as AIMD strategy in decrement).

Slow-start is a mechanism used by the sender to control the transmission rate. This is accomplished through the return rate of acknowledgements from the receiver. In other words, the rate of acknowledgements returned by the receiver determines the rate at which the sender can transmit data. This is called *slow* because it's the alternative to using the full advertised window immediately – this is slower than that.

When a TCP connection first begins, the slow-start algorithm initializes a congestion window to 1. Slow-start effectively increases the congestion window exponentially, rather than linearly. When acknowledgements are returned by the receiver, the congestion window increases by double for each acknowledgement returned.

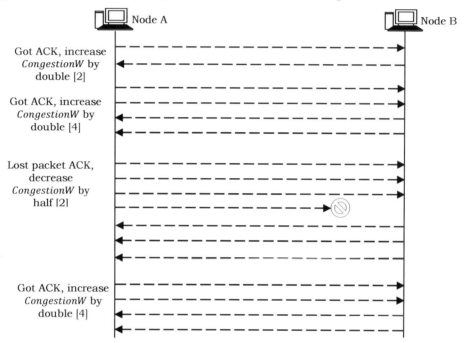

For example, the first successful transmission and acknowledgement of a TCP segment increases the window to two segments. After successful transmission of these two segments and acknowledgements completes, the window is increased to four segments. Then eight segments, then sixteen segments and so on, doubling from there on out up to the maximum window size advertised by the receiver or until congestion finally does occur.

At some point the congestion window may become too large for the network or network conditions may change such that packets may be dropped. Packets lost will trigger a timeout at the sender. When this happens, the sender goes into congestion avoidance mode and congestion window is set to half.

12.10.3 Fast Retransmit and Fast Recovery

The methods discussed so far were part of the original proposal to add congestion control to TCP. The main problem with those techniques is that; TCP timeouts led to long periods of time during which the connection went dead while waiting for a timer to expire.

Because of this, a new mechanism called *fast retransmit* was added to TCP. Fast retransmit is a heuristic that sometimes triggers the retransmission of a dropped packet sooner than the regular timeout mechanism. The fast retransmit mechanism does not replace regular timeouts; it just enhances that facility.

.3.1 Fast Retransmit

When a *duplicate ACK* is received, the sender does not know if it is because a TCP segment was lost or simply that a segment was delayed and received out of order at the receiver. If the receiver can re-order segments, it should not be long before the receiver sends the latest expected acknowledgement.

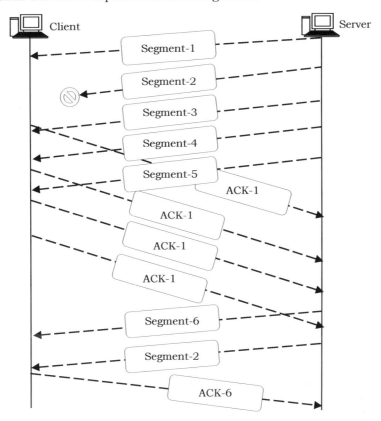

Typically no more than one or two duplicate ACKs should be received when simple out of order conditions exist. If however more than two duplicate ACKs are received by the sender, it is a strong indication that at least one segment has been lost. The TCP sender will assume enough time has lapsed for all segments to be properly re-ordered by the fact that the receiver had enough time to send three duplicate ACKs.

When three or more duplicate ACKs are received, the sender does not even wait for a retransmission timer to expire before retransmitting the segment (as indicated by the position of the duplicate ACK in the byte stream). This process is called the *fast retransmit* algorithm.

.3.2 Fast Recovery

Since the Fast Retransmit algorithm is used when duplicate ACKs are being received, the TCP sender has implicit knowledge that there is data still flowing to the receiver. Why? The reason is because duplicate ACKs can only be generated when a segment is received. This is a strong indication that serious network congestion may not exist and that the lost segment was a rare event. So instead of reducing the flow of data abruptly by going all the way into slow-start, the sender only enters congestion avoidance mode. Rather than start at a window of one segment as in slow-start mode, the sender resumes transmission with a larger window, incrementing as if in congestion avoidance mode. This allows for higher throughput under the condition of only moderate congestion.

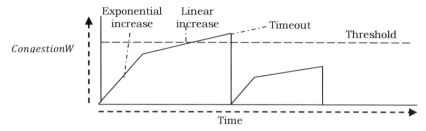

12.11 TCP Congestion Avoidance Techniques

Congestion is said to occur in the network when the resource demands exceed the capacity and packets are lost due to too much queuing in the network. During congestion, the network throughput may drop to zero and the path delay may become very high. A congestion control scheme helps the network to recover from the congestion state.

A congestion avoidance scheme allows a network to operate in the region of low delay and high throughput. Such schemes prevent a network from entering the congested state. Congestion avoidance is a *prevention* mechanism while congestion control is a *recovery* mechanism.

12.11.1 DECbit

DECbit is one of the earlier congestion avoidance methods. DECbit require cooperation of network switches and traffic sources. In the DECbit method, the congested network switches set congestion indication bit in the network layer header of a data packet, where the congestion is indicated by the average queue length greater than or equal to 1. Non-congested switches ignore the congestion indication bit field.

That means, a single congestion bit is added to the packet header. A router sets this bit in a packet if its average queue length is greater than or equal to 1 at the time the packet arrives. This average queue length is measured over a time interval that spans the *last busy* + *idle cycle*, plus the current busy cycle.

At the destination, the bit is copied into the transport header of the acknowledgment packet which is then transmitted to the source. The source updates its window once every two round-trip times, and if at least 50% of the bits examined are set during the interval, the window size is reduced from its current value *CongestionW*, to $\beta \times$ *CongestionW*.

Otherwise it is increased to *CongestionW* $+ \alpha$, where $\beta = 0.875$ and $\alpha = 1$. The scheme uses minimal amount of feedback from the network, with just one bit in the network layer header to indicate congestion. The technique addresses the important issue of fairness and achieves the goal to some extent.

When there is a transient change in the network, *DECbit* is designed to adapt to the change and converge to the efficient operating point.

12.11.2 Random Early Detection (RED)

Random Early Detection (RED) is similar to the DECbit technique in that each router is programmed to monitor its own queue length, and when it detects that congestion is imminent, to notify the source to adjust its congestion window.

RED was invented by *Sally Floyd* and *Van Jacobson* in the early 1990s. It is different from the DECbit scheme in *two* major ways.

The *first* is that rather than explicitly sending a congestion notification message to the source, RED is most commonly implemented such that it implicitly notifies the source of congestion by dropping one of its packets. With this, the source is effectively notified by the subsequent timeout or duplicate ACK.

The *second* difference between RED and DECbit is in the details of how RED decides when to drop a packet and what packet it decides to drop. To understand the basic idea, consider a simple FIFO queue. Rather than wait for the queue to become completely full and then be forced to drop each arriving packet, we could decide to drop each arriving packet with some drop probability whenever the queue length exceeds some drop level. This idea is called early random drop. The RED algorithm defines the details of how to monitor the queue length and when to drop a packet.

RED is designed to be used in conjunction with TCP, which currently detects congestion by means of timeouts (or some other means of detecting packet loss such as duplicate ACKs). The early part of the RED acronym suggests that the router drops the packet earlier than it would have to, so as to notify the source that it should decrease its congestion window sooner than it would normally. That is, the router drops a few packets before it has run out of its buffer space completely so as to cause the source to slow down earlier, with the expectation that it does not have to drop lots of packets later on. Note that RED can easily be adapted to work with an explicit feedback scheme simply by marking a packet instead of dropping it.

The basic idea of how RED decides when to drop a packet and what packet to be dropped can be demonstrated with a simple FIFO queue. Rather than waiting for the queue to become completely full and then being forced to drop each arriving packet, RED drops each arriving packet with some drop probability whenever the queue length exceeds some dropping level.

12.11.3 Source-Based Congestion Avoidance

The earlier two congestion avoidance techniques depend on routers and switches. They were sometimes called Router-based Congestion Avoidance techniques. Source-Based Congestion Avoidance describes a strategy for detecting the incipient stages of congestion (before losses occur) from the end hosts.

Let us take a look at overview of a collection of related mechanisms that use different information to detect the early stages of congestion, and then we describe a specific mechanism in some detail.

In this method, source monitors changes in RTT to detect onset of congestion. The general idea of these techniques is to watch for some sign from the network that some router's queue is building up and that congestion will happen soon if nothing is done about it.

For example, the source might notice that as packet queues build up in the network's routers, there is a measurable increase in the RTT for each successive packet it sends.

One particular algorithm exploits this observation as follows: The congestion window normally increases as in TCP, but every two round-trip delays the second algorithm does something similar. The decision as to whether or not to change the current window size is based on changes to both the RTT and the window size. The window is adjusted once every two round-trip delays based on the product

$$(CurrentWindow-OldWindow) \times (CurrentRTT- OldRTT)$$

If the result is positive, the source decreases the window size by one-eighth; if the result is negative or 0, the source increases the window by one maximum packet size.

12.11.3.1 TCP Vegas

TCP Vegas is a new implementation of TCP proposed by Brakmo. Vegas compares the measured throughput rate with the expected, or ideal, throughput rate.

Vegas use a new retransmission mechanism. This is an improvement over the *Fast Retransmit* mechanism. In the original *Fast Retransmit* mechanism, three duplicate acks indicate the loss of a packet, so a packet can be retransmitted before it times out. Vegas uses a *timestamp* for each packet sent to calculate the round trip time on each ack received.

When a duplicate ack is received Vegas checks to see if the difference between the *timestamp* for that packet and the current time is greater than the *timeout* value. If it is, Vegas retransmit the packet without having to wait for the third duplicate message. This is an improvement over Reno in that in many cases the window may be so small that the source will not receive three duplicate acks, or the acks may be lost in the network.

Upon receiving a non-duplicate ack, if it is the first or second ack since a retransmission, Vegas checks to see if the time interval since the packet was sent is larger than the timeout value and retransmits the packet if so. If there are any packets that have been lost since the retransmission they will be retransmitted without having to wait for duplicate acks.

To avoid congestion, Vegas compares the actual throughput to the expected throughput. The expected throughput is defined as the minimum of all measured throughputs. The actual throughput is the number of bytes transmitted between the time a packet is transmitted and its ack is received divided by the round trip time of that packet.

Vegas then compares the difference of the expected and the actual throughputs to thresholds α and $\exists \beta$. When the difference is smaller than α, the window size is increased linearly and when the difference is greater than bthe window size is decreased linearly.

Reno's Slow-Start mechanism can lead to many losses. Because the window size is doubled every round trip time, when the bottleneck is finally overloaded, the expected losses are half the current window. As network bandwidth increases the number of packets lost in this manner will also increase.

Brakmo propose a modified slow start mechanism where the window size is doubled only every other round trip time. So every other round trip time the window is not changed which allows for an accurate comparison of the expected and actual throughput. The difference is compared to a new threshold called γ at which point the algorithm switches to the linear increase/decrease mode described above.

12.12 Packet Discard Techniques

When network congestion is experienced, the incoming packets at a router consumes the available bandwidth of the link and the router *queues* try to cope with such a situation. As queues are finite memory buffers, they will fill up and, consequently, packet discard is necessary.

Packet discard should not be used as a response for a congestion situation, as any discarded packet has already used a certain amount of network resources up to the point it is discarded. Packets should be discarded in fair way, which means that not only the same source gets its packets discarded but the discarded packets belong to all the present traffic sources. There are four methods for discarding the packet.

1. Tail Drop
2. Early Drop
3. Drop Preference
4. RED

12.12.1 Tail Drop

Tail drop is the simple and common packet discard algorithm and it is commonly used with the FIFO queue discipline. Once the queue gets full, the new incoming packets are dropped. Packets continue to be dropped until new slots are available in the queue. The main disadvantage of this algorithm is its *low fairness*.

A sudden traffic burst from one source may fill up all the available slots of the queue and the new incoming traffic would be discarded. A solution to this problem is placing many service classes within the same queue. Each service class has a maximum amount of slots in the queue. When such a limit is overcome, packets of that service class are discarded.

In this way, there is still space for other service classes even if one of them exceeded its available space. The drawback of this solution is that packet discarding happens even if there is available free memory for accepting new packets in the queue.

12.12.2 Early Drop

Early Drop is a technique meant to give a form of fair resource sharing among different flows. The main idea is to discard bursty flows before the queue overflows, so that there is still space for other flows. According to such a definition, placing many service classes in the same queue (see the previous paragraph about Tail Drop) is one instance of the Early Drop method.

A way of implementing Early Drop consists of monitoring each flow and its traffic characteristics. When the queue length grows up to a certain limit, packets belonging to flows arriving at high rate or bursty flows can be discarded. This is a precise way to achieving Early Drop.

12.12.3 Drop Preference

Another method for choosing which packet to drop consists of using external information for discarding the packet. When congestion arises and the queue length reaches a predefined limit, discarded packets are not the ones in the tail of the queue, but packets marked with a *drop preference* flag (or low priority flag). Such a flag can be set by the source application or by the admission control functions.

In this way, when congestion happens, the first flows to be discarded are the *less important* flows, whereas the most critical traffic is preserved and forwarded. In IP networks, the Drop Preference mechanism is associated with admission control functions. For example, all the packets belonging to a certain service class exceeding the maximum allowed bandwidth for that class are marked so that they are forwarded if bandwidth is available; otherwise they are the first packets to be discarded in case of congestion.

12.12.4 Random Early Drop (RED)

Random Early Drop [RED] is a method for discarding packets to cope with the network congestion problem. The philosophy of RED consists of assist and help congestion responsive protocols, like TCP, to prevent and avoid network congestion. TCP assumes that a packet drop is clear indication of congestion and reduces accordingly its sending rate, going back into slow start or reducing its congestion window size. With other packet discard methods, packets are dropped when congestion is already in act (buffers are full); the idea of RED is to start packet discarding before the queues are full so that congestion is prevented and TCP adjusts its sending rate before congestion happens.

RED uses statistical methods to drop packets before the router queue overflows. It keeps track of the average queue size and discards packets when the average queue size overcomes a certain threshold.

12.13 Traffic Shaping Algorithms

The Internet is based on IP protocol and supports only best effort services. With the exponential growth of Internet during the last years, IP networks are expected to support not only typical services like *ftp* and *email*, but also real-time services and *video streaming* application. The traffic characteristics of these applications require a certain *Quality of Service* (QoS) from the network in terms of bandwidth and delay requirements.

The biggest problems in a network are related to the allocation of network resources (such as buffers and link bandwidth) to different users. A limited amount of resources has to be shared among many different competing traffic flows in an efficient way in order to maximize the performance and the use of the network resources. The behavior of routers in terms of packet handling can be controlled to achieve different kind of services.

There are a number of packet handling mechanisms, which are related to:

- Classification of packets
- Admission Control and Traffic Shaping
- Queuing and scheduling disciplines
- Packet discard techniques

Packet classification indicates the process of categorizing packets into flows in a router. All packets belonging to the same flow or the same class of service are ruled in a predefined manner and are processed in a corresponding way by the router. For example, all packets belonging to a certain application or related to a specific protocol may be defined to form a traffic flow. Packet classification process is needed for those services that require the distinction between different kinds of traffic.

Once packets are classified, *admission control* functions are performed to check whether enough network resources are available according to the packet service classification. If resources are available, packets are handled according to their classification. Traffic shaping functions are used to control the volume of traffic entering in the networks and the rate at which packets are sent. There are two methods for achieving Traffic shaping: leaky bucket and token bucket.

Afterwards, packets are scheduled into *queues* (*buffers*). Queues are managed in a way to ensure each queue gets the level of services required for its class. There are a number of queue disciplines are described: First-In-First-Out (FIFO), Priority Queuing (PQ), etc..

When network congestion is experienced, packets in excess must be *discarded*. Packet discard cannot be avoided but can be controlled. Several techniques for handling packet discard are showed, such as Tail Drop, Early Drop, Drop Preference and RED.

12.13.1 Leaky Bucket Algorithm

Imagine a bucket with a small hole in the bottom. No matter, at what rate water enters the bucket, the outflow is at a constant rate. Also, once the bucket is full, any additional water entering it spills over the sides and is lost. The same idea can be applied to packets.

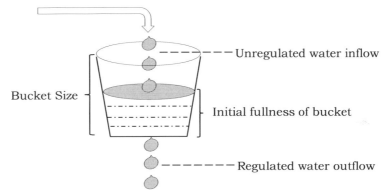

Conceptually, each host is connected to the network by an interface containing a leaky bucket, i.e., a finite internal queue. If a packet arrives at the queue when it is full, it is discarded. In other words, if one or more processes within the host try to send a packet when the maximum number are already queued, the new packet is unceremoniously discarded. This arrangement can be built into the hardware inter face or simulated by the host operating system. It was first proposed by Turner and is called the leaky bucket algorithm.

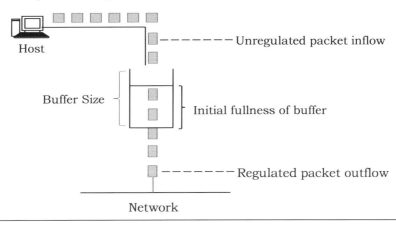

To understand the leaky bucket model, define three parameters of the bucket:

- The capacity (B)
- The rate at which water flows out of the bucket (R)
- The initial fullness of the bucket (F)

Illustration showing a buffer as a bucket, input rate as water entering the bucket, and output rate as water leaving through a hole in the bucket

If water is poured into the bucket at exactly rate R, the bucket will remain at F, because the input rate equals the output rate. If the input rate increases while R remains constant, the bucket accumulates water. If the input rate is larger than R for a sustained period, eventually the bucket overflows. However, the input rate can vary around R without overflowing the bucket, as long as the average input rate does not exceed the capacity of the bucket. The larger the capacity, the more the input rate can vary within a given window of time.

The leaky bucket is defined by *three* parameters:

1. The average bit rate, in bytes per second, which corresponds to the output rate (R)
2. The buffer window, measured in milliseconds, which corresponds to the bucket capacity (B).
3. The initial buffer fullness, which is generally set to zero.

The bit rate measures the average number of bits per second in the encoded stream. The buffer window measures the number of milliseconds of data at that bit rate that can fit in the buffer. The size of the buffer in bits is equal to $R \times (B/1000)$.

12.13.2 Token Bucket Algorithm

The leaky bucket algorithm discussed above, enforces a rigid pattern at the output stream, irrespective of the pattern of the input. For many applications it is better to allow the output to speed up somewhat when a larger burst arrives than to lose the data. *Token bucket* algorithm provides such a solution.

In this algorithm leaky bucket holds token, generated at regular intervals. Main steps of this algorithm can be described as follows: In regular intervals tokens are thrown into the bucket. The bucket has a maximum capacity. If there is a ready packet, a token is removed from the bucket, and the packet is send.

If there is no token in the bucket, the packet cannot be send. However, the limit of burst is restricted by the number of tokens available in the bucket at a particular instant of time. The implementation of basic token bucket algorithm is simple; a variable is used just to count the tokens. This counter is incremented every t seconds and is decremented whenever a packet is sent. Whenever this counter reaches zero, no further packet is sent out.

Token bucket algorithm is a finer way to implement traffic shaping uses a token bucket filter, which allows bursts of packets to be sent every now and then. The tocken bucket filter is a way to implement both admission control and traffic shaping. The philosophy is the same than the leaky bucket's one, however the token bucket allows having permission to send bursts of packets.

Figure shows the token bucket scheme. The algorithm is that every certain period of time – which determines the rate packets are served – a token is saved. Each token can be associated to one packet (blue packets in the figure) or, in general, to a defined quantity of data.

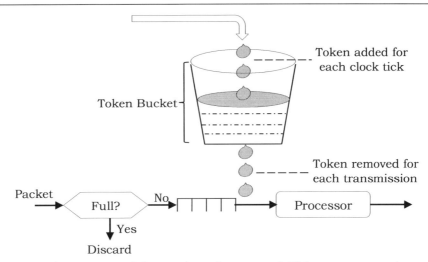

When a packet is sent, one of these tokens is removed. If there are no packets to send, tokens can be retained and used to send new packets later on. In the figure, four tokens are retained in the bucket; hence, a sudden burst of four packets can be served and allowed to go through the network.

The Token bucket algorithm contains three parameters: an average rate, a peak rate, and burst size. Let's look at the meaning of these parameters:

Average rate: The network may wish to limit the long-term average rate at which a flow's packets can be sent into the network. The important point here is the interval of time over which the average rate will be policed.

For example; a flow which has 10000 packets/sec is more flexible than a flow which has 10 packets/msec. Even though both have the same average rate, their behaviors are different. The flow which has 10000 packets/sec can send 100 packets in a one msec long-term, but the flow which has 10 packets/msec cannot sent 100 packets in a one msec long-term. This is one of the important feature we should consider.

Peak rate: Defines the maximum rate at which packets can be sent in short interval time. In above example; even though the flow's long term average rate is 10000 packets/sec peak rate can be limited to 200 packets/msec.

Burst size: Burst size is the maximum number of packets which can be transmitted extremely in a short interval time. In other word, when time interval approaches zero, the burst size limits the number of packets which can be transmitted to the network. when we don't consider time interval as zero, burst size depends on bucket depth b, and maximum speed of output link.

For a token bucket size C bytes, with arrival rate A bytes/sec, and the maximum output rate O bytes/sec, the maximum burst time B can be given as:

$$B = \frac{C}{O - A} \ sec$$

Problems and Questions with Answers

Question 1: Consider a token bucket with token arrival rate of ρ bytes/sec and a token credit capacity of W bytes. The data rate is M bytes/sec. Let S be the duration of the maximum output burst rate from the full token-bucket.
A) Carefully derive an expression for S.

B) What is S if ρ = 16 Mbps and W = 500 KB and if a burst arrives over a channel with data rate 200 Mbps and lasts 40 msec?

C) Complete (B) by indicating what happens after S seconds, assuming bursts arrive every second.

Answer:

A) For a token bucket size W bytes, with arrival rate ρ bytes/sec, and the maximum output rate M bytes/sec, the maximum burst time S can be given as:

$$S = \frac{W}{M - \rho} \; sec$$

B) S = $\frac{500x1024}{(25x106 - 2x106)}$= 22.3 msec. There is a 25 MB/s output burst of 22.3msec after the onset of the incoming burst of data.

C) The maximum burst output of 200 Mbps (25 MBps) lasts only 22.3 msec which means (25×10^6)×(22.3×10^{-3}) = 557.5×10^3 bytes (544.4KB) of data was delivered by the token bucket.

However the incoming burst lasts 40 msec and this means $(200\times 10^6 \times 40\times 10^{-3})$ = 106 bytes of data was delivered to the bucket, that is 442.5×10^3 left after 22.3 msec which then must drain at the token rate of 16 Mbps (2 MBps = 2000 KBps). Thus, there is an additional 16 Mbps burst from the token-bucket after 22.3 msec of (442.5/2000) = 221.25 msec duration. Hence the token-bucket output exhibits the following cyclic behavior: 200 Mbps burst of 22.3 msec duration, 16 Mbps burst of 221.25 msec duration and then 756.45 msec of no output.

Question 2: The standard *packet-counting* implementation of the leaky bucket algorithm allows one packet to be transmitted per token generated, independent of the length of the packet. The byte-counting variation defines a token not as 1 packet but k bytes. Thus if k = 1024, one token can be used to transmit either one 1024-byte packet, or two 512-byte packets (conversely two tokens are needed to transmit one 2048-byte packet). What are the pros and cons of these two approaches for congestion rate control in networks?

Answer: The byte-counting variation achieves a smoother average bit rate than *packet-counting*. However it does not achieve a perfect constant bit rate since tokens will accumulate for large packets which will then be transmitted at full speed. The byte-counting variant also has the following problems:

- The length of the packet needs to be determined, and a count kept, hence a more complex implementation.
- If packets are small the output packet rate will be high and since routers queue and process on a per packet basis this may actually exacerbate end-to-end delays and consequent congestion.

The packet-counting version is simpler to implement and helps control congestion more effectively since the packet rate is constant, but it also has problems:

- A large variance in packet sizes will mean a large variance in bit rate.
- Longer packets will be given an effective higher data rate, which may create congestion problems on networks with smaller MTUs (i.e. packet is segmented as many smaller packets which will then create longer queues and processing delays).

Question 3: A computer on a 6-Mbps network is regulated by a token bucket. The token bucket is filled at the rate of 1 Mbps. It is initially filled to capacity with 8 Mbps. How long the computer transmit at the full 6 Mbps?

Answer: Suppose for time *t*, the computer can transmit at the full 6 Mbps.Then 6t = 8 + t. Hence, t = 1.6 sec.

Question 4:   Suppose that the TCP congestion window is equal to 8K bytes just before a timeout occurs. How big will the congestion window be if the next sixteen packet transmissions are all successfully acknowledged? Assume that the maximum segment size is 1K, all transmitted packets are 1K in length, and the receiver's advertised window is always equal to 64K bytes.

Answer: When a packet transmission times out (i.e., no acknowledgement for the packet arrives within a timeout period determined by the Jacobson-Karels algorithm), then we have to initiate the slow start phase. This means that we set the threshold to half of the current congestion window or half of the current sliding window, whichever is less.

In this case, the congestion window (8K) is less than the sliding window (64K), so the threshold is set to 4K. Since we are using *slow start*, the congestion window is also reduced to 1 maximum segment size – or 1K.

Because the congestion window is now 1K, the TCP sender transmits one packet before stopping to wait for an acknowledgement. (We can only send one congestion window's worth of data, or one sliding window's worth of data, whichever is less.) *During* the *slow start phase*, the congestion window increases by one segment size whenever one segment of data is acknowledged.

Thus, when the packet's acknowledgement arrives at the sender, the sender increases its congestion window from 1K to 2K. Because the window size is now 2K, the sender sends 2 TCP packets without waiting for an acknowledgement first. When the two acknowledgements return, the congestion window at the source increases from 2K to 4K. So far the sender has transmitted 3 packets since the timeout has occurred.

The congestion window has now reached the threshold value (4K), so now we say that the sender is no longer in the slow start phase. Instead, it is in the congestion avoidance (or linear increase) phase. *During* the *congestion avoidance phase*, the congestion window only increases by one segment size whenever a full congestion window's worth of data has been acknowledged. Since the congestion window is currently 4K, the congestion window will not advance to 5K until 4 1K packets have been acknowledged.

So, after sending 4 more packets and receiving their acknowledgements, the sender's congestion window increases to 5K. After sending 5 more packets and receiving their acknowledgements, the congestion window increases to 6K.

Since the timeout, the sender has transmitted 12 packets. In order for the congestion window to increase from 6K to 7K, the sender must receive acknowledgements for an additional 6 packets. However, the problem is only interested in the size of the congestion window after 4 more packets have been transmitted (12+4 = 16). So the answer to this problem is that after sixteen packets have been successfully acknowledged, the size of the congestion window remains at 6K.

Question 5:   A computer on a 16-Mbps network is governed by a token bucket. The token bucket is filled at a rate of 1 Mbps. It is initially filled to capacity with 18 megabits. How long can the computer transmit at the full 6 Mbps?

Answer: Let us suppose that the computer transmits at 16 Mbps for T seconds. After T seconds, the computer transmits at 1 Mbps because the token bucket has been totally drained of token bits. So, how do we solve for T?

To solve this problem, we must first realize that the total number of bits transmitted by the computer into the network during the time period T is equal to the total number of token bits consumed by the computer in the same period of time.

The total number of bits transmitted by the computer in the time period T is equal to 16 Mbits/sec × T. The total numbers of token bits consumed by the computer in the time period T is equal to the initial token bucket occupancy (18 Mbits) plus the number of token bits generated during the time period T (1 Mbits/sec × T). Hence,

16 Mbits/sec × T = 18 Mbits + (1 Mbits/sec × T)

Solving for T, we get T = 1.2 seconds.

Question 6: The Slow-Start algorithm increases a source's rate of transmission faster than additive increase. Is it true or false?

Answer: True

Question 7: A source's retransmission timeout value (RTO) is always set equal to the measured RTT.

Answer: False

Question 8: If the RTO is too small, this might lead to unnecessary retransmissions.

Answer: True

Question 9: A source's retransmission timeout value is set to a value that increases with the variance in measured RTT values.

Answer: True

Question 10: TCP segments can only be lost when router queues overflow.

Answer: False

Question 11: There is no performance benefit to having a window size (measured in seconds) larger than the RTT.

Answer: True

Question 12: A receiver reduces the advertised window size in response to congestion at routers along the path.

Answer: False

Question 13: RED is tolerant of bursts because it never drops consecutive packets from the same flow.

Answer: False

Question 14: RED always drops packets, with probability 1, when the router's average queue length is greater than the maximum threshold value.

Answer: True

Question 15: If two flows, one TCP and one UDP, share a "RED" router, the RED algorithm will ensure that both flows receive an identical share of the outgoing link.

Answer: False

Question 16: Consider an instance of TCP's Additive Increase Multiplicative Decrease (AIMD) algorithm where the window size at the start of the slow start phase is 2 MSS and the threshold at the start of the first transmission is 8 MSS. Assume that a timeout occurs during the fifth transmission. Find the congestion window size at the end of the tenth transmission.

A) 8 MSS   B) 14 MSS   C) 7 MSS   D) 12 MSS

Answer: C. Given threshold = 8

1. Time = 1, during first transmission, window size = 2 (slow start phase)
2. Time = 2, congestion window size = 4 (double the no. of acknowledgments)
3. Time = 3, congestion window size is = 8
4. Time = 4, congestion window size = 9, after threshold (increase by one addictive increase)
5. Time = 5, transmits 10 MSS, but time out occurs congestion window size = 10
6. Hence threshold = $\frac{\text{congestion window size}}{2} = \frac{10}{2} = 5$
7. Time = 6, transmits 2
8. Time = 7, transmits 4
9. Time = 8, transmits 5(threshold is 5)
10. Time = 9, transmits 6
11. Time = 10, transmits 7
12. During 10th transmission, it transmits 7 segments hence at the end of the 10th transmission the size of congestion window is 7 MSS.

Question 17: The following figure shows the TCP congestion window size as a function of time. Assume that the TCP implementation supports fast retransmit / fast recovery. Answer the following questions:

A. Identify the intervals of time when TCP slow start is operating.
B. Identify the intervals of time when TCP congestion avoidance is operating.
C. After the round 16, is segment loss detected by duplicate ACKs or by a timeout?
D. After the round 22, is segment loss detected by duplicate ACKs or by a timeout?
E. What is the initial threshold for the first transmission round?
F. What is the threshold at the 18th transmission round?
G. What is the threshold at the 24th transmission round?
H. During what transmission round is the 70th segment sent?

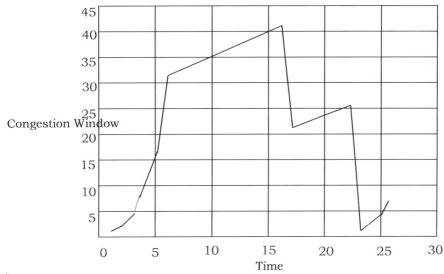

Answer:

A. [1,6] and [23,26] because the window is increasing exponentially.

B. [6,16] and [17,22] because the window increases additively.

C. Segment loss is recognized by duplicate ACKs. If there was a timeout, the congestion window size would have dropped to 1.

D. Segment loss is detected due to timeout, and hence the congestion window size is set to 1.

E. The threshold is initially 32, since it is at this window size that slow start stops and congestion avoidance begins. (Note that the threshold does not have to be precisely 32.)

F. The threshold is set to half the value of the congestion window when packet loss is detected. When loss is detected during transmission round 16, the congestion windows size is 42. Hence the threshold is 21 during the 18th transmission round.

G. The threshold is set to half the value of the congestion window when packet loss is detected. When loss is detected during transmission round 24, the congestion windows size is 26. Hence the threshold is 13 during the 24th transmission round.

H. During the 1st transmission round, packet 1 is sent; packet 2-3 are sent in the 2nd transmission round; packets 4-7 are sent in the 3rd transmission round; packets 8-15 are sent in the 4th transmission round; packets 16-31 are sent in the 5th transmission round; packets 32-63 are sent in the 6th transmission round; packets 64-96 are sent in the 7th transmission round. Thus packet 70 is sent in the 7th transmission round.

Question 18: Suppose a network uses a token bucket scheme for traffic shaping. If a new token is put into the bucket every 10 μsec, and is good for one 64 K Byte packet, what is the maximum sustainable data rate?

Answer:

$$20 \text{ μsec} = 48 \times 8 \times 10^3 \text{ bits}$$
$$1 \text{ sec} = \frac{48 \times 8 \times 10^3}{20 \times 10^{-6}}$$
$$1 \text{ sec} = 19.2 \times 10^9$$

The maximum sustainable data rate is 19.2 Gbps.

Question 19: Consider sending a large file of F bits from node A to node B. There are three links (and two switches) between A and B, and the links are uncongested (that is, no queuing delays). Node A segments the file into segments of S bits each and adds 80 bits of header to each segment, forming packets of L = 80 + S bits. Each link has a transmission rate of R bps. Find the value of S that minimizes the delay of moving the file from node A to node B. Ignore the propagation delay.

Answer: Time at which the first packet is received at the destination = $\frac{S+80}{R} \times 3$ sec.

After this, one packet is received at destination every $\frac{S+80}{R}$ sec.

Thus delay in sending the whole file $(delay) = \frac{S+80}{R} \times 3 + \left(\frac{F}{S} - 1\right) \times \frac{S+80}{R} = \frac{S+80}{R} \times \left(\frac{F}{S} + 2\right)$.

To calculate the value of S which leads to the minimum delay,

$$\frac{d}{dS}(delay) = 0 \text{ implies S} = \sqrt{F}.$$

Question 20: Calculate the token bucket parameters rate r and bucket depth b for a flow with the following traffic requirements: the maximum rate is R = 20 Mbps, the maximum rate can only be used up to 4 seconds, and in the first 10 seconds up to 140 Mb can be transmitted.

Answer: The data sent in the first 4 seconds at the rate R is 80 Mb. Then, in the next 6 s another 60 Mb need to be sent at the rate r. This means r = 10 Mbps.

To compute the value for b, we have $\frac{b}{R-r}$ = 4 s (i.e. b is depleted at the rate $R - r$ up to its exhaustion), thus b = 40 Mb.

Question 21: A static table is more flexible than a dynamic table in responding to both error and congestion conditions. Is it true or false?

Answer: False

Question 22: A static table is more flexible than a dynamic table in responding to both error and congestion conditions. Is it true or false?

Answer: False

Question 23: The diagram at right shows two TCP senders at left and the corresponding receivers at right. Both senders use TCP Tahoe and are sending large files. Assume that the MSS is 1 KB, that the one-way propagation delay for both connections is 50 ms and that the link joining the two routers has a bandwidth of 8 Mb/s.

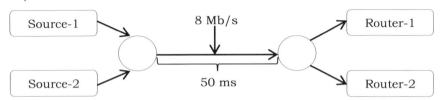

Let *cwnd*1 and *cwnd*2 be the values of the senders' congestion windows. What is the smallest value of *cwnd*1 + *cwnd*2 for which the link joining the two routers could stay busy all the time?

Answer: RTT=0.1, so 0.1×8 Mb=100 KB is enough to keep the link busy.

Question 24: For the previous Question-23, assume that the link buffer overflows whenever *cwnd*1 + *cwnd*2=150 KB and that at time 0, cwnd1=120 KB and cwnd2=30 KB. Approximately, what are the values of cwnd1 and cwnd2 one RTT later?

Answer: Since we're using Tahoe, cwnd1=cwnd2=1 KB

Question 25: For the previous Question-23, approximately how many more RTTs pass before the first sender leaves the slow-start state?

Answer: Since *ssthresh* is set to 60 KB on entering slow-start, it takes about 6 RTTs for *cwnd* to get above the slow-start threshold, triggering the transition out of the slow-start state.

Question 26: Assume that the initial sequence number used by a TCP sender is 2000. TCP sender starts in the Slow Start phase of the congestion control algorithm (assume that ssthresh is initially very large) and transmits a TCP segment with length MSS = 1500 Bytes.

The sender then receives an ACK segment with an acknowledgement number 3500 and a receive window 5000. The sender then sends two segments each with length 1500 Bytes. The next ACK segment the sender receives has an acknowledgement number 5000 and a receive window RW.

If RW = 3000, what is the maximum number of bytes that the sender can transmit further without getting another ACK segment from the receiver?

Answer: Since the initial sequence number is 2000, an ACK is received with sequence number 5000, CongestionW (Congestion Window) becomes 4500 (note that we are at the beginning of slow start where CongestionW = 4500 initially after which it increases to upon the reception of ACK with sequence number 3500 and then to 4500 upon the reception of ACK with sequence number 5000.

> ReceiveW = 3000.
> SendWin = min(CongestionW, ReceiveW) = 3000.
> There are already 1500 unacknowledged bytes.
> Hence number of bytes that sender can send = 3000 – 1500 = 1500 bytes.

Question 27: For the previous question, if RW = 5000, what is the maximum number of bytes that the sender can transmit further without getting another ACK segment from the receiver?

Answer:

> ReceiveW = 5000.
> SendWin = min(CongestionW, ReceiveW) = 4500.
> There are already 1500 unacknowledged bytes.
> Hence number of bytes that sender can send = 4500 – 1500 = 3000 bytes.

Question 28: The ___ (shaping) algorithm allows idle hosts to accumulate credit for the future transmissions.
A) Leaky bucket   B) Token bucket
C) Early random detection   D) None of the above

Answer: B

Question 29: In the slow start phase of TCP congesting control algorithm, the size of the congestion window
A) Does not increase   B) Increases linearly
C) Increases quadratically   D) Increases exponentially

Answer: D. Slow start is one of the algorithm that TCP uses to control congestion inside the network, also known as exponential growth phase, here the TCP congestion window size is increased.

Session Layer

13.1 Introduction

The session layer resides above the transport layer, and provides value added services to the underlying transport layer services. The session layer (along with the presentation layer) adds services to the transport layer that are likely to be of use to applications, so that each application doesn't have to provide its own implementation.

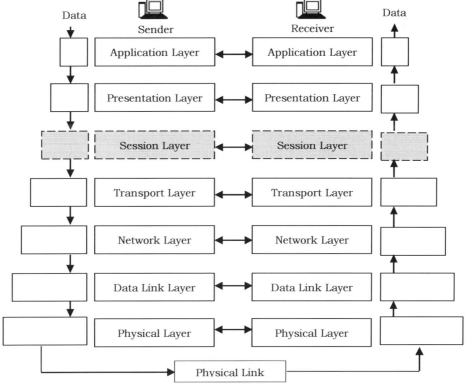

Layer 5 of the OSI reference model is session layer. It does not add many communications features/functionality, and is thus termed a very *thin* layer. On many systems, the Layer 5 features are disabled, but you should nonetheless know what failures can be prevented by a session layer.

Note: The TCP/IP protocols do not include a session layer at all.

13.2 What does Session Layer mean?

The session layer provides the mechanism for opening, closing and managing a session between end-user application processes. Communication sessions consist of requests and responses that occur between applications. Session-layer services are commonly used in application environments that make use of remote procedure calls (RPCs).

This layer allows applications on connecting systems to communicate using a session. It opens, uses, and closes this communication link. It also acts as a dialog control mechanism controlling who is able to transmit. Sessions can allow data to be sent in both directions at the same time or only one direction.

13.3 Session Layer Tasks

The session layer determines who has the ability to transfer at the current time. Another valuable ability is to insert checkpoints during data transfers. During a large file transmission if the system crashes the checkpoints allow the system to start downloading at the last known checkpoint.

An example of this is during either an interactive login or file transfer connection; the session would recognize names in the session and register them into a history. It could then connect and reconnect in case of a system crash at either of the systems.

Following are some of the communication tasks performed at this layer:

- Establishing connections
- Maintaining connections
- Synchronizing communications
- Controlling dialogues
- Terminating connections

13.4 Session Layer Services

The session layer provides the following services:

1. Dialog management
2. Synchronization
3. Activity management
4. Exception handling

13.4.1 Dialog management

Deciding whose turn it is to talk. Some applications operate in half-duplex mode, whereby the two sides alternate between sending and receiving messages, and never send data simultaneously.

Session layer can manage half-duplex communications. In half-duplex communication, data can go in either direction, but transmission must alternate. A session service closely related to this is *dialog management*. In the ISO protocols, dialog management is implemented through the use of a data token. The token is sent back and forth, and a user may transmit only when it possesses the token.

Only the user with the token can send data. After establishing the session, only one user initially gets the token. The user who holds the token is the sender and the other is receiver.

If the receiver wants to send the data, he can request for the token. The sender decides when to give up on acquiring the token, receiver becomes sender.

13.4.2 Synchronization

The *transport* layer handles only *communication errors*, *synchronization* deals with *upper* layer *errors*. For example, in a file transfer, the transport layer might deliver data correctly, but the application layer might be unable to write the file because the file system is full.

Users can split the data stream into pages, inserting *synchronization points* between each page. When an error occurs, the receiver can resynchronize the state of the session to a previous synchronization point. This requires that the sender hold data as long as may be needed.

Synchronization refers to one of *two* distinct but related concepts: *synchronization* of *processes*, and *synchronization* of *data*.

Process synchronization refers to the idea that multiple processes are to join up or handshake at a certain point, so as to reach an agreement or commit to a certain sequence of action. *Data* synchronization refers to the idea of keeping multiple copies of a dataset in coherence with one another, or to maintain data.

In computer networking, *synchronization* is achieved through the use of sequence numbers. The ISO protocols provide both major and minor synchronization points. When *resynchronizing*, one can only go back as far as the previous major synchronization point. In addition, major synchronization points are acknowledged through explicit messages (making their use expensive). In contrast, minor synchronization points are just *markers*.

Let us consider another example. Say we are transferring a database file from one end machine to another. A packet (also called *segment*) gets to the destination transport layer, and an acknowledgement is send back. Unfortunately, this can happen before the destination application has written the received data to disk. If the destination transport layer reboots, it will receive a restart request from the source, but since the source thinks it knows how much data has been received at the destination it will not bother to resend it. Unfortunately, one packet will be lost as it was caught in RAM as the destination computer failed.

The problem is that the two end applications do not hand shake that the data sent got *completely* handled by the destination application. This is call *synchronization*.

13.4.3 Activity Management

With the preceding services, the application can start and stop conversations and alternate speakers. It is also necessary to identify where data starts and ends as it flows between the nodes participating in a conversation.

For example, for a file transfer application, if several files are being transferred, the receiving node must be told somehow where one file ends and the next starts. Delimiters could be inserted into the data stream by the sender, but then the recipient has to scan the stream for them, which requires computing cycles. Data that look like delimiters can also cause problems.

Activity management solves these problems. It divides the data stream into *activities*. For the file transfer example, each file becomes an activity. The Session Layer inserts control information to mark activities in the header and signals the start and end of activities to the application. Session layer allows the user to delimit data into logical units called *activities*. Each activity is independent of activities that come before and after it, and an activity can be processed on its own.

For example, a bank transaction may consist of locking a record, updating a value, and then unlocking the record. If an application processed the first operation, but never received the remaining operations (due to client or network failures), the record would remain locked forever. Activity management addresses this problem.

13.4.4 Exception Handling

It is a general purpose mechanism for reporting errors.

13.5 Remote Procedure Call (RPC) Protocol

Remote procedure calls try to give a programmer the illusion that a program on one machine can call a procedure located on another machine. This requires that the calling program packetize the parameters to send to the destination, and indicates which procedure is to be called at the destination machine. Generally, there is a layer 4 well-known port number (transport layer) monitored by a server which handles incoming procedure calls.

The server cannot normally start up an application containing the destination procedure, and call the procedure in that program (as that program is already running). Thus the destination procedure is usually in a dynamic link library that the RPC server can dynamically link to and call. RPC does not fit into the OSI reference model very well, as it is designed to be fast and is not multilayered.

An RPC can be thought of as a short session. If implemented as a session, normally a connectionless session layer protocol is used. When a client calls a remote procedure, the call is actually made to a local stub (*procedure* or a *function*). The stub marshals parameters together by value into a message, and transmits a request message to the server.

13.5.1 The Ten Steps of a Remote Procedure Call

Let us examine how *local* procedure calls are implemented. This differs among *compilers* and *architectures*, so we will generalize. Every processor provides us with some form of call instruction, which pushes the address of the next instruction on the stack and transfers control to the address specified by the call. When the called procedure is done, it issues a return instruction, which pops the address from the top of the stack and transfers control there. That's just the basic processor mechanism that makes it easy to implement procedure calls.

The actual details of identifying the parameters, placing them on the stack, executing a call instruction are up to the compiler. In the called function, the compiler is responsible for ensuring any registers that may be clobbered are saved, allocating stack space for local variables, and then restoring the registers and stack prior to a return.

None of this will work to call a procedure that is loaded on a *remote machine* or a *distant* machine. This means that the compiler has to do something different to provide the illusion of calling a remote procedure. This makes remote procedure calls a language-level construct as opposed to sockets, which are an operating system level construct. We will have to simulate remote procedure calls with the tools that we do have, namely local procedure calls and sockets for network communication.

The entire trick in making remote procedure calls work is in the creation of stub functions that make it appear to the user that the call is really local. On the client, a stub function looks like the function that the user intends to call but really contains code for sending and receiving messages over a network. The sequence of operations that takes place is shown in figure.

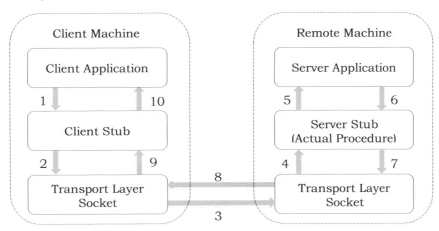

The client calls a local procedure, called the *client stub*. To the client process, this appears to be the actual procedure, because it is a regular local procedure. It just does something different since the real procedure is on the server. The client stub packages the parameters to the remote procedure (this may involve converting them to a standard format) and builds one or more network messages. The packaging of arguments into a network message is called *marshaling* and requires serializing all the data elements into a flat array-of-bytes format.

1. Network messages are sent by the client stub to the remote system (via a system call to the local kernel using transport layer sockets interfaces).
2. Network messages are transferred by the kernel to the remote system via some protocol (either connectionless or connection-oriented: TCP or UDP).
3. A server stub, sometimes called the *skeleton*, receives the messages on the server. It unmarshals the arguments from the messages and, if necessary, converts them from a standard network format into a machine-specific form.
4. The server stub calls the server function (which, to the client, is the remote procedure), passing it the arguments that it received from the client.
5. When the server function is finished, it returns to the server stub with its return values.
6. The server stub converts the return values, if necessary, and marshals them into one or more network messages to send to the client stub.
7. Messages get sent back across the network to the client stub.
8. The client stub reads the messages from the local kernel.
9. The client stub then returns the results to the client function, converting them from the network representation to a local one if necessary.
10. The client code then continues its execution.

The major benefits of RPC are twofold. First, the programmer can now use procedure call semantics to invoke remote functions and get responses. Secondly, writing distributed applications is simplified because RPC hides all of the network code into stub functions. Application programs don't have to worry about details such as sockets, port numbers, and data conversion and parsing. On the OSI reference model, RPC spans both the session and presentation layers (layers five and six).

13.5.2 Implementing Remote Procedure Calls

Several issues arise when we think about implementing remote procedure calls.

13.2.1 How to pass parameters?

With RPC, *passing by value* is simple: just copy the value into the network message. *Passing by reference* is hard. It makes no sense to pass an address to a remote machine since that memory location likely point to something completely different on the remote system.

If we want to support passing by reference, we will have to send a copy of the arguments over, place them in memory on the remote system, pass a pointer to them to the server function, and then send the object back to the client, copying it over the reference.

If remote procedure calls have to support references to complex structures, such as trees and linked lists, they will have to copy the structure into a pointer less representation (e.g., a flattened tree), transmit it, and reconstruct the data structure on the remote side.

13.5.2.2 How to represent data?

On a local system there are no data incompatibility problems; the data format is always the same. With RPC, a remote machine may have different byte ordering, different sizes of integers, and a different floating point representation.

The problem was dealt with in the IP protocol suite by forcing everyone to use *big endian* byte ordering for all 16 and 32 bit fields in headers (hence the use of htons and htonl functions). For RPC, we need to come up with a standard encoding for all data types that can be passed as parameters if we are to communicate with heterogeneous systems.

Big endian representation stores the most significant bytes of a multi-byte integer in low memory. Little endian representation stores the most significant bytes of an integer in high memory. Machines such as Sun SPARCs and the old Motorola 680x0s used big endian storage. Most Intel systems have used little endian storage. Many other architectures use a bi-endian format, where the processor can be configured at boot time to operate in either little endian or big endian mode. Examples of these processors are ARM, MIPS, PowerPC, SPARC v9, and Intel IA-64 (Itanium).

13.5.2.3 What machine and port should we bind to?

We need to locate a remote host and the proper process (*port* or *transport address*) on that host. One solution is to maintain a centralized database that can locate a host that provides a type of service. This is the approach that was proposed by Birell and Nelson in their 1984 paper introducing RPC.

A server sends a message to a central authority stating its willingness to accept certain remote procedure calls. Clients then contact this central authority when they need to locate a service. Another solution, less elegant but easier to administer, is to require the client to know which host it needs to contact. A name server on that host maintains a database of locally provided services.

13.5.2.4 What transport protocol should be used?

Some implementations allow only one to be used (e.g. TCP). Most RPC implementations support several and allow the user to choose.

13.5.2.5 What happens when things go wrong?

There are more opportunities for errors now. A server can generate an error, there might be problems in the network, the server can crash, or the client can disappear while the server is running code for it.

The transparency of remote procedure calls breaks here since local procedure calls have no concept of the failure of the procedure call. Because of this, programs using remote procedure calls have to be prepared to either test for the failure of a remote procedure call or catch an exception.

13.5.2.6 What are the semantics of remote calls?

The semantics of calling a regular procedure are simple: a procedure is executed exactly once when we call it. With a remote procedure, the exactly once aspect is quite difficult to achieve. A remote procedure may be executed:

- 0 times if the server crashed or process died before running the server code.
- Once if everything works fine.
- Once or more if the server crashed after returning to the server stub but before sending the response. The client won't get the return response and may decide to try again, thus executing the function more than once. If it doesn't try again, the function is executed once.
- More than once if the client times out and retransmits. It is possible that the original request may have been delayed. Both may get executed (or not).

RPC systems will generally offer either at least once or at most once semantics or a choice between them. One needs to understand the nature of the application and function of the remote procedures to determine whether it is safe to possibly call a function more than once.

If a function may be run any number of times without harm, it is idempotent (e.g., time of day, math functions, read static data). Otherwise, it is a nonidempotent function (e.g., append or modify a file).

13.5.2.7 What about performance?

A regular procedure call is fast: typically only a few instruction cycles. What about a remote procedure call? Think of the extra steps involved. Just calling the client stub function and getting a return from it incurs the overhead of a procedure call.

On top of that, we need to execute the code to marshal parameters, call the network routines in the OS (incurring a mode switch and a context switch), deal with network latency, have the server receive the message and switch to the server process, unmarshal parameters, call the server function, and do it all over again on the return trip. Without a doubt, a remote procedure call will be much slower.

We can easily expect the overhead of making the remove call to be thousands of times slower than a local one. However, that should not deter us from using remote procedure calls since there are usually strong reasons for moving functions to the server.

13.5.2.8 What about security?

This is definitely something we need to worry about. With local procedures, all function calls are within the confines of one process and we expect the operating system to apply adequate memory protection through per-process memory maps so that other processes are not privy to manipulating or examining function calls.

With RPC, we have to be concerned about various security issues:

- Is the client sending messages to the correct remote process or is the process an impostor?
- Is the client sending messages to the correct remote machine or is the remote machine an impostor?
- Is the server accepting messages only from legitimate clients? Can the server identify the user at the client side?
- Can the message be sniffed by other processes while it traverses the network?
- Can the message be intercepted and modified by other processes while it traverses the network from client to server or server to client?
- Is the protocol subject to replay attacks? That is, can a malicious host capture a message an retransmit it at a later time?
- Has the message been accidentally corrupted or truncated while on the network?

13.5.3 Advantages of RPC

We don't have to worry about getting a unique transport address (picking a unique port number for a socket on a machine). The server can bind to any available port and then register that port with an RPC name server. The client will contact this name server to find the port number that corresponds to the program it needs. All this will be invisible to the programmer.

The system can be independent of transport provider. The automatically-generated server stub can make itself available over every transport provider on a system, both TCP and UDP. The client can choose dynamically and no extra programming is required since the code to send and receive messages is automatically generated.

Applications on the client only need to know one transport address: that of the name server that is responsible for telling the application where to connect for a given set of server functions.

The function-call model can be used instead of the send/receive (read/write) interface provided by sockets. Users don't have to deal with marshaling parameters and then parsing them out on the other side.

13.6 Major Session Layer Protocols

13.6.1 AppleTalk Data Stream Protocol (ADSP)

ADSP is a session-level protocol that provides symmetric, connection-oriented, full-duplex communication between two sockets on the AppleTalk internet. ADSP includes both session and transport services, and it is the most commonly used of the AppleTalk transport protocols. AppleTalk Data Stream Protocol (ADSP) is used to establish a session to exchange data between two network processes or applications in which both parties have equal control over the communication.

13.6.2 AppleTalk Session Protocol (ASP)

The AppleTalk Session Protocol (ASP) manages sessions for higher layer protocols such as AFP. ASP issues a unique session identifier for each logical connection and continuously monitors the status of each connection. It maintains idle sessions by periodically exchanging keep alive frames in order to verify the session status.

13.6.3 Internet Storage Name Service

The Internet Storage Name Service (iSNS) protocol is used for interaction between iSNS servers and iSNS clients. iSNS clients are computers, also called *initiators* that are attempting to discover storage devices, also known as targets, on an Ethernet network. iSNS facilitates automated discovery, management, and configuration of iSCSI and Fibre Channel devices on a TCP/IP network.

13.6.4 Network Basic Input Output (NetBIOS)

NetBIOS (Network Basic Input/Output System) was originally developed by *IBM* and *Sytek* as an Application Programming Interface (API) for client software to access LAN resources.

Since its creation, NetBIOS has become the basis for many other networking applications. In its strictest sense, NetBIOS is an interface specification for accessing networking services.

NetBIOS, a layer of software developed to link a network operating system with specific hardware, was originally designed as THE network controller for IBM's Network LAN. NetBIOS has now been extended to allow programs written using the NetBIOS interface to operate on the IBM token ring architecture.

NetBIOS has since been adopted as an industry standard and now, it is common to refer to NetBIOS-compatible LANs.

13.6.5 Password Authentication Protocol (PAP)

Password Authentication Protocol (PAP) is a simple authentication protocol in which the user name and password is sent to the remote access server in a plaintext (unencrypted) form. Using PAP is strongly discouraged because your passwords are easily readable from the Point-to-Point Protocol (PPP) packets exchanged during the authentication process.

13.6.6 Point-to-Point Tunneling Protocol (PPTP)

Point to Point Tunneling Protocol (PPTP) is a network protocol that enables the secure transfer of data from a remote client to a private enterprise server by creating a VPN (virtual private network) across TCP/IP-based data networks.

13.6.7 Remote Procedure Call Protocol (RPC)

The Remote Procedure Call (RPC) protocol is designed to augment IP in a different way than TCP. While TCP is targeted at the transfer of large data streams (such as a file download), RPC is designed for network programming, allowing a program to make a subroutine call on a remote machine. The most important application of RPC is the NFS file sharing protocol.

13.6.8 Short Message Peer-to-Peer (SMPP)

SMPP is a protocol for sending SMS messages. Commonly referred as *Short Code* or *Express* text messaging, it is technically called *Short Message Peer-to-Peer Protocol* or SMPP. It is designed to provide a flexible data communications interface for transfer of short message data. When you send a text message from your cell to your friend's cell, it's being routed via the SMPP protocol. These messages go through the carriers' cell networks, as compared to the carriers' email network called SMTP.

SMPP is the preferred method as it has priority routing and tends to be delivered at a quicker rate.

13.6.9 Secure Shell (SSH) Protocol

Secure Shell (SSH) Protocol is a protocol for secure network communications designed to be relatively simple and inexpensive to implement. It is used for secure remote login and other secure network services over an insecure network.

Presentation Layer Protocols

CHAPTER

14

14.1 Introduction

The presentation layer is the sixth layer of the OSI model. It responds to service requests from the application layer and issues service request to the session layer. The presentation layer performs certain functions that are requested sufficiently often to finding a general solution for users, rather than letting each user solve the problems. In particular, unlike all the lower layers, which are just interested in moving bits reliably from here to there, the presentation layer is concerned with the syntax and semantics of the information transmitted.

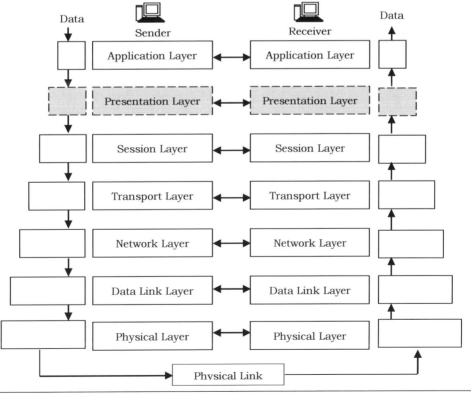

14.2 What does Presentation Layer mean?

The presentation layer sometimes called the *syntax layer* in the OSI is basically used to address and resolve data communication across the 7 layers.

The presentation layer formats the data to be presented to the application layer. It can be viewed as the translator for the network. This layer may translate data from a format used by the application layer into a common format at the sending station, and then translate the common format to a format known to the application layer at the receiving station.

The presentation layer is responsible for presenting data in a form that the receiving device can understand. To better understand the concept, use the analogy of two people speaking different languages. The only way for them to understand each other is to have another person translate. The presentation layer serves as the *translator* for devices that need to communicate over a network.

For example, a sending computer after receiving data from the application layer will need to convert such data from the receiving format (e.g. ASCII) to a format understood and accepted by other layers of the OSI model to ensure smooth file transfer.

14.3 Presentation Layer Tasks

The *Presentation Layer* negotiates appropriate transfer syntaxes which are suitable for conveying the type of user data messages to be exchanged.

This layer also transforms user data from its specified abstract syntax form into the selected transfer syntax form and vice versa. In this way two machines with a different architecture can communicate with each other. So the presentation layer must contain an *encoder/decoder*.

Another important function in this layer is the context management. This function stores for all the synchronization points (see *Session Layer* chapter). Also, the presentation layer provides *data compression* and *data encryption*.

The presentation layer provides:

1. *Data conversion*: Conversion schemes are used to exchange information with systems using different text and data representations (such as EBCDIC and ASCII)
2. *Data representation*: The use of standard image, sound, and video formats (like JPEG, MPEG, and RealAudio) allow the interchange of application data between different types of computer systems.
3. *Data compression*: Reduces the number of bits that need to be transmitted on the network.
4. *Data encryption*: Encrypt data for security purposes. For example, password encryption.

After receiving data from the application layer, the presentation layer performs one, or all, of its functions on the data before it sends it to the session layer. At the receiving station, the presentation layer takes the data from the session layer and performs the required functions before passing it to the application layer.

14.4 Data Conversion

The presentation layer of the Open System Interconnection (OSI) model is responsible for how that data looks or is formatted. When the presentation layer receives data from the application layer, to be sent over the network, it makes sure that the data is in the proper format. If it is not, the presentation layer converts the data to the proper format. On the other side of communication, when the presentation layer receives network data from the session layer, it makes sure that the data is in the proper format and once again converts it if it is not.

To understand how data formatting works, imagine two dissimilar systems. The first system uses Extended Binary Coded Decimal Interchange Code (EBCDIC) to represent characters onscreen. The second system uses American Standard Code for Information Interchange (ASCII) for the same function. (Note: Most personal computers use ASCII, while mainframe computers traditionally use EBCDIC.) Layer 6 provides the translation between these two different types of codes.

The presentation layer provides a variety of coding and conversion functions that are applied to application layer data. These functions ensure that information sent from the application layer of one system would be readable by the application layer of another system. Some examples of presentation layer coding and conversion schemes include common data representation formats, conversion of character representation formats, common data compression schemes, and common data encryption schemes.

Example conversions are:

- Conversion of a Sun .RAS raster graphic to JPG.
- Conversion of ASCII to IBM EBCDIC
- Conversion of .PICT on a MAC to .jpg
- Conversion of .wav to .mp3

14.5 Data Representation

Common data representation formats, or the use of standard image, sound, and video formats, enable the interchange of application data between different types of computer systems. Using different text and data representations, such as EBCDIC and ASCII, uses conversion schemes to exchange information with systems.

Presentation layer implementations are not typically associated with a particular protocol stack. Some well-known standards for video include QuickTime and Motion Picture Experts Group (MPEG).

Presentation Layer standards also determine how graphic images are presented. Three of these standards are as follows:

- PICT: A picture format used to transfer QuickDraw graphics between programs on the MAC operating system.
- TIFF (Tagged Image File Format): A format for high-resolution, bit-mapped images.
- JPEG (Joint Photographic Experts Group): Graphic format used most often to compress still images of complex pictures and photographs.
- GIF (Graphics Interchange Format): GIF is a standard for compressing and coding graphic images.

Other Layer 6 standards guide the presentation of sound and movies. Included in these standards are the following:

- MIDI (Musical Instrument Digital Interface): For digitized music
- MPEG (Motion Picture Experts Group): Standard for the compression and coding of motion video for CDs and digital storage

- QuickTime: A standard that handles audio and video for programs on both MAC and PC operating system. QuickTime is an Apple Computer specification for video and audio, and MPEG is a standard for video compression and coding.

14.5.1 File formats

ASCII and EBCDIC are used to format *text*. ASCII text files contain simple character data, and lack any sophisticated formatting commands, such as boldface or underline. Notepad is an example of an application that uses and creates text files. They usually have the extension .txt.

EBCDIC is very similar to ASCII in that it also does not use any sophisticated formatting. The main difference between the two is that EBCDIC is primarily used on *IBM mainframes* and ASCII is used on personal computers.

Another common file format is the *binary* format. Binary files contain special coded data that can only be read by specific software applications. Programs such as FTP use the binary file type to transfer files. Networks use many different types of files. A previous section briefly touched on graphic file formats.

The Internet uses two binary file formats to display images - Graphic Interchange Format (GIF), and Joint Photographic Experts Group (JPEG). Any computer with a reader for the GIF and JPEG file formats can read these file types, regardless of the type of computer. Readers are software programs designed to display an image of a particular file type. Some programs can read multiple image types as well as convert files from one type to another. Web browsers have the ability to display graphic files in either of these two formats without any additional software.

Another type of file format is markup language. This format acts as a set of directions that tell a Web browser how to display and manage documents. *Hypertext Markup Language* (HTML) is the language of the Internet. HTML directions tell a browser whether to display text, or to hyperlink to another URL. HTML is not a programming language, but is a set of directions for displaying a page.

14.6 Data Compression

Because network operators expect to be paid for their efforts, data compression is performed to reduce the costs for data transfer over networks. Although these costs are not linear with the amount of data sent, it's clear that it can he reduced by compressing the data before sending them.

The existing data compression techniques are based on one of the three approaches:

- The finiteness of the set of symbols
- To be relative frequencies with which the symbols are used
- The context in which a symbol appears

Data compression algorithms fall into two *categories*:

1. *Lossless coding* (sometimes referred to as entropy coding) is used for all types of data, including text, for which exact inversion of the code is required.
2. *Lossy coding* is used for image and audio data, is where exact reproduction is not required and a trade-off between storage and fidelity can be found. The code is irreversible.

14.6.1 Huffman coding algorithm

14.6.1 Definition

Given a set of *n* characters from the alphabet A [each character c ∈ A] and their associated frequency *freq(c),* find a binary code for each character c ∈ A, such that $\sum_{c \in A}$ freq(c)|binarycode(c)| is minimum, where | binarycode*(c)|* represents the length of binary code of character c. That means sum of lengths of all character codes should be minimum [sum of each characters frequency multiplied by number of bits in the representation].

The basic idea behind *Huffman* coding algorithm is to use fewer bits for more frequently occurring characters. Huffman coding algorithm compresses the storage of data using variable length codes. We know that each character takes 8 bits for representation. But in general, we do not use all of them. Also, we use some characters more frequently than others.

When reading a file, generally system reads 8 bits at a time to read a single character. But this coding scheme is inefficient. The reason for this is that some characters are more frequently used than other characters.

Let's say that the character *'e'* is used 10 times more frequently than the character *'q'*. It would then be advantageous for us to use a 7 bit code for e and a 9 bit code for *q* instead because that could reduce our overall message length.

On average, using Huffman coding on standard files can reduce them anywhere from 10% to 30% depending to the character frequencies. The idea behind the character coding is to give longer binary codes for less frequent characters and groups of characters. Also, the character coding is constructed in such a way that no two character codes are prefixes of each other.

14.6.2 An Example

Let's assume that after scanning a file we found the following character frequencies:

Character	Frequency
a	12
b	2
c	7
d	13
e	14
f	85

In this, create a binary tree for each character that also stores the frequency with which it occurs (as shown below).

The algorithm works as follows: Find the two binary trees in the list that store minimum frequencies at their nodes.

Connect these two nodes at a newly created common node that will store no character but will store the sum of the frequencies of all the nodes connected below it. So our picture looks like follows:

Repeat this process until only one tree is left:

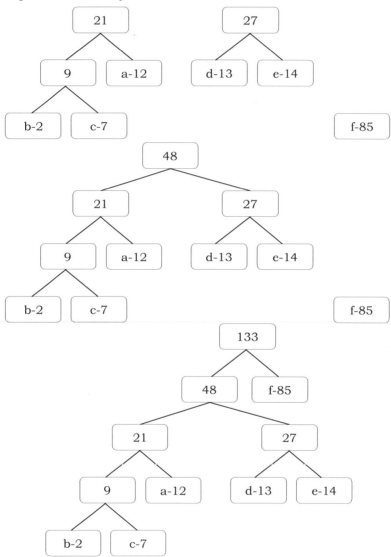

Once the tree is built, each leaf node corresponds to a letter with a code. To determine the code for a particular node, traverse from the root to the leaf node. For each move to the left, append a 0 to the code and for each move right append a 1. As a result for the above generated tree, we get the following codes:

Letter	Code
a	001
b	0000

c	0001
d	010
e	011
f	1

14.6.3 Calculating Bits Saved

Now, let us see how many bits that Huffman coding algorithm is saving. All we need to do for this calculation is see how many bits are originally used to store the data and subtract from that how many bits are used to store the data using the Huffman code.

In the above example, since we have six characters, let's assume each character is stored with a three bit code. Since there are 133 such characters (multiply total frequencies with 3), the total number of bits used is 3 * 133 = 399.

Using the Huffman coding frequencies we can calculate the new total number of bits used:

Letter	Code	Frequency	Total Bits
a	001	12	36
b	0000	2	8
c	0001	7	28
d	010	13	39
e	011	14	42
f	1	85	85
Total			238

Thus, we saved 399 − 238 = 161 bits, or nearly 40% storage space.

14.7 Data Encryption

Another important function of the presentation layer is the encryption of data. Encryption is done to achieve security of data that move between computers.

Without any security an unauthorized person can copy the data for example by wiretap and thereby has a notion of the information of the data. This is an example of a passive threat (violation of security which do not result in modification of any information) and where the system operation is not altered.

Active threats are those which cause system operation to be effected, information to be modified, or services to be interrupted.

In the OSI Reference Model, the need for providing security is well recognized. The ISO defines a basic set of security functions that are believed to be important from the viewpoint of providing secure communication between the peer entities in the OSI Reference Model. Network security concerns with the following objectives:

- Authentication
- Authorization
- Data Integrity
- Confidentiality
- Availability
- Non-Repudiation

14.7.1 Authentication

Authentication is the process of determining whether someone is who it is declared to be. In private and public computer networks, authentication is commonly done through the use of logon passwords. Knowledge of the password is assumed to guarantee that the user is authentic. Each user registers initially, using an assigned or self-declared password.

On each subsequent use, the user must know and use the previously declared password. The weakness in this system for transactions that are significant (such as the exchange of money) is that passwords can often be stolen, accidentally revealed, or forgotten. For this reason, Internet business and many other transactions require a more robust authentication process.

The use of digital certificates issued and verified by a Certificate Authority (CA) as part of a public key infrastructure is the standard way to perform authentication on the Internet.

14.7.2 Authorization

After authentication, a user must gains *authorization* for doing certain tasks. For example, after logging into a system; the user may try to issue commands. The authorization process determines whether the user has the authority to issue such commands.

In other words, authorization is the process of enforcing policies: determining what types or qualities of activities, resources, or services a user is permitted. Usually, authorization occurs within the context of authentication. Once you have authenticated a user, they may be authorized for different types of access or activity.

14.7.3 Data Integrity

Data Integrity is the assurance that data have not been changed inappropriately. There are many ways in which data might be altered: accidentally (through hardware and transmission errors), or because of an intentional attack.

For example, a weakness that allows an administrator to change the permissions on any file on a system would not be security vulnerability because an administrator already has this capability. In contrast, if a weakness allowed an unprivileged user to do the same thing, it would constitute security vulnerability.

14.7.4 Confidentiality

Confidentiality refers to limiting access to information on a resource to authorized people. An attacker that exploits a weakness in a product to access non-public information is compromising the confidentiality of that product.

For example, a weakness in a web site that enables a visitor to read a file that should not be read would constitute security vulnerability. However, a weakness that revealed the physical location of a file would not constitute vulnerability.

14.7.5 Availability

Availability refers to the possibility to access a resource. An attacker that exploits a weakness in a product, denying appropriate user access to it, is compromising the availability of that product.

For example, a weakness that enables an attacker to cause a server to fail would constitute security vulnerability, since the attacker would be able to regulate whether the server provided service or not. However, the fact that an attacker could send a huge number of legitimate requests to a server and monopolize its resources would not constitute security vulnerability, as long as the server operator still could control the computer.

14.7.6 Non-repudiation

To repudiate means to deny. Non-repudiation is the process of ensuring that a transferred message has been sent and received by the parties claiming to have sent and received the message. Nonrepudiation is a way to guarantee that the sender of a message cannot later deny having sent the message and that the recipient cannot deny having received the message.

As an example, someone (say, person A) claims that person B used offensive words and person B attempts to repudiate (deny) the claim. It is easy to prove that he has used offensive words. There is evidence that person B has used offensive words. If person B cannot repudiate the claim about offensive words, the evidence provides non-repudiation.

Non-repudiation is an active attempt to create proofs which may be used against an identified person who is denying that they are the origin of a communication or action. The proofs are identity, authentication of the identity, and something connecting a communication or action to the identity.

In the above example there are legal documents that record the testimony of many witnesses who identified and authenticated person B and witnessed him using offensive words. This is a passive and accidental production of artifacts connecting an action to an identity.

In security we want active purposeful production of proofs that may assist in a non-repudiation argument. In order to do that we must identify an entity, authenticate the identity and connect the identified entity to a specific action or communication.

Some people use public/private key certificates to sign their email. By using their e-mail address they are providing identification. Their use of a private key (to sign the e-mail) provides authentication as long as the private key is known only by the individual.

When they sign an e-mail with their digital signature they are connecting the content of the e-mail to the identity authenticated by the certificate. These proofs may assist in preventing an individual from repudiating the contents of the e-mail; *I never sent that e − mail*.

However, to repudiate the e-mail a sender may claim that their private key was stolen (known by another party) and the thief sent the e-mail.

Note: Although data encryption is commonly mentioned as a typical presentation layer task, almost all OSI layers could perform this task. For more details on security refer Network Security chapter.

Problems and Questions with Answers

Question 1: The __ layer can perform ASCII to non-ASCII character conversions.
   A) Transport   B) Data Link   C) Presentation   D) Application

Answer: C

Question 2:   In the OSI model, which layer performs encryption or data compression?
A) Application   B) Network   C) Data Link   D) Presentation

Answer: D.

Question 3:   Which of the OSI layers concern with the syntax and semantics of the information transmitted?

Answer: Presentation Layer.

CHAPTER

Network Security

15

15.1 What is Network Security?

Network security refers to a set of *activities* and *policies* used by a network administrator to prevent and monitor unauthorized access of a computer network. These activities include protecting the usability, reliability, integrity, and safety of computer network and data.

15.2 Relevant History of Instances

Nothing is more important than securing computer networks for any organization. Network security has become more important for personal computers, organizations, and the military. With Internet, security became a major concern. The internet structure itself allowed for many security threats to occur.

You might have observed that, almost every day, there will be a story in the newspapers about a computer network being attacked by hackers. Below are few such instances:

1. A man arrested for *cyber-attacks* on US military networks: A 28-year-old man from *Suffolk* has been arrested after *network intrusion* against the US Army, military and government. The man and his colleagues attacked the US organizations from October 2012 until October 2013, placing back doors into the networks to let them return and steal more data at a later date. They targeted the US Department of Defense's Missile Defense Agency, NASA and the Environmental Protection Agency.

2. New York Webmaster arrested for Cyber Attack on *former Employer*: A foreign citizen living in New York was recently arrested by the FBI and charged with breaching his former employer, a newspaper publisher, and disabling the company's Web site.

According to the complaint, a *company's* employee contacted the FBI in mid-December, 2012 and stated that an unknown individual had accessed company *FTP* server and changed its *robots*.txt file to remove the site from search results. As a result of the change, company had suffered significant revenue losses from advertising.

The FBI traced the FTP access back to a customer of the ISP Optimum Online, which provided the FBI with subscriber information indicating the user involved in the attack. The FBI also obtained data from Google and Verizon indicating that attacker had more recently been logging into his Gmail address from a Verizon account, having previously logged into the same address via the Optimum Online account that was used to access company FTP server.

Attacker was employed at newspaper publisher from mid-2011 to mid-2012 as a Web administrator and webmaster. According to the employee who contacted the FBI, attacker knew the login user name and password for the company's FTP server, which hadn't been changed after his termination in mid-2012.

3. Computer hackers arrested over *plan* to *steal* millions: A man entered a branch of the *Santander* bank in South East London, where he attempted to install a device that would have allowed hackers to access its network from outside. The device is called keyboard video mouse (KVM), which fit into the back of a machine. It cost as small as £10 and are widely available in computer stores or online.

It records the keyboard activity and also users can send commands to the computer from elsewhere. The gang, which was allegedly operating out of a small office in a shed in West London, was suspected of planning to use Wi-Fi in order to connect to the device and transfer funds electronically.

Had the plan been successful, police believe the hackers could have had access to millions of pounds of customer funds. But the plan was failed following an intelligence led operation by officers from the Metropolitan Police's special E-Crime.

Every year, organizations are spending billions of dollars for network security and it is increasing. Every company should monitor its systems for unauthorized access and attacks.

15.3 Why Do We Need Security?

We all know that today's world is fast changing. It has become a real challenge to keep up with the changes and remain updated. Security is now a basic requirement. As data goes from point A (say, through routers, switches and many other devices) to point B on the Internet, it is giving other users an opportunity to intercept, and even change, it. Even other users on a system may maliciously transform data into something we did not intend.

Unauthorized access to a system may be obtained by intruders. Then, they might use advanced knowledge to impersonate a user, steal information, or even deny access to user's own resources.

15.4 What network security reports say?

There are many organizations which publishes standards and guidelines used by private enterprise to develop safe work environments. One such organization is KMPG and it operates in New Zealand.

In 2012, a survey conducted by KPMG reported that fraud continues to be a growing problem. This latest survey analyses total reported losses from fraud that occurred between 1 February 2010 and January 31 2012 in New Zealand. The KMPG survey received 140 responses (from New Zealand). Also of interest, the survey reported the following [in New Zealand alone]:

- The total amount reported as having been lost to fraud within the survey period was $18.26 million.
- The average loss among those organizations that had experienced at least one incident of fraud was $433,721.
- Just over forty-eight percent (48%) of respondents experienced at least one incident of fraud.
- Of those organizations with more than 500 employees, almost two thirds (62%) experienced at least one incident of fraud. Of those organizations with 1000 or more employees, nearly eighty-six percent (86%) experienced at least one incident of fraud.
- Five respondents each experienced fraud losses exceeding $1 million during the survey period.
- Over sixty percent (60%) of respondents estimated that fifty percent (50%) or less of fraud had been detected in their organization.

We have seen estimates from various sources for the annual financial loss related to computer crime ranging from $5 billion to $45 billion. It seems clear that the annual cost related to computer crime is growing every year.

15.5 History of Network Security

Several key events contributed to the birth and evolution of computer and network security.

The issue of computer security first started in the 1970s as individuals began to break into *telephone* systems. With technology improvements, computer systems became targets for attackers. The Federal Bureau of Investigation (FBI) made one of its first arrests related to computer hacking in the early 1980s.

When computer companies like IBM Corp. and Symantec Corp. began researching ways to detect (and ways to prevent) and remove viruses from computers, virus writers began developing more complicated viruses. By 1991, more than 1,000 viruses had been discovered by computer security experts.

Computer security gaps were exposed by attackers at many major corporations and governmental bodies (including AT&T Corp., NASA, and the Korean Atomic Research Institute) during the early 1990s.

For example, an attack on AT&T's network caused the company's long-distance service to temporarily shut down. During 1995, computers at the U.S. Department of Defense were attacked roughly 250,000 times. A study conducted by the *Computer Security Institute* (CSI) that year determined that one in every five Web sites had been hacked. Also that year, Mitnick was arrested for computer fraud and once again sentenced to serve jail time. His offense that time included stealing *software*, *product plans*, and data from *Motorola* Inc., *Sun Microsystems* Inc., *NEC* Corp., and *Novell* Inc., costing the firms a combined total of almost $80 million.

Later in the 1990s, the Web sites of several federal agencies, including the U.S. Department of Justice, the U.S. Air Force, NASA, and the CIA, were defaced by hackers.

With fast growing Internet, the number of malicious attacks got increased. Hacking in 2000 increased 79% over compared to 1999 numbers. Even leading Web sites such as

Yahoo!, *eBay*, and *Amazon*.com were exposed as vulnerable, costing the firms millions of dollars.

15.6 Four Pillars of Network Security

The four legs of the *network security* are education program, prevention, detection, and correction. These form the foundation for all security policies and measures that an organization develops and deploys.

15.6.1 Education Program

In any organization, security team should educate people and discourage people to break into systems for illegal and malicious reasons

15.6.2 Prevention

The foundation of the network security is prevention. To provide some level of security, it is necessary to implement measures to prevent the exploitation of vulnerabilities.

15.6.3 Detection

Once preventative measures are implemented, procedures need to be put in place to detect potential security problems. This is helpful if the preventative measures fail. It is very important that problems be detected immediately. The sooner a problem is detected the easier it is to correct and cleanup.

15.6.4 Correct

Organizations need to develop a plan that identifies the appropriate correction to a security problem. The plan should be in writing and should identify who is responsible for what actions and the varying corrections and levels of escalation.

15.7 Glossary of Network Security Terms

15.7.1 Vulnerabilities

Vulnerability is a security term that refers to a flaw in a computer system that can leave it open to attack. Vulnerability is a defect in the design, configuration, implementation, or management of a network or system that renders it susceptible to a threat.

15.7.2 Threat

In computer security, a *threat* refers to anything that has the *potential* to cause serious harm to a computer system. A threat is something that *may* or *may not* happen, but has the potential to cause serious damage. Threats can lead to attacks on computer systems, networks and more.

15.7.3 Malware

Malware means *malicious* software. This is a program that is specifically designed to get access and damage a computer without the knowledge of the owner. Malware includes computer viruses, worms, Trojan horses, keyloggers, dialers, spyware, and adware. Majority of active malware threats are usually worms or Trojans rather than viruses.

15.7.4 Computer Virus

A computer virus is a program that is loaded onto a computer without owner's knowledge and runs against their wishes. Viruses can also replicate themselves. All computer viruses are man-made. A simple virus that can make a copy of it *over* and *over* again is relatively easy to produce. Even such a simple virus is dangerous because it will quickly use all available memory and bring the system to a halt.

15.7.5 Worm Virus

Worm Virus is a program that replicates itself over a computer network and performs malicious actions, such as using up the computer's resources and possibly shutting the system down. It is comparable to a computer virus, but able to spread copies of itself from one computer to another without the assistance of users.

15.7.6 Antivirus

Anti-virus software is a program (or a set of programs) that are designed to prevent, search for, detect, and remove software viruses, and other malicious software like worms, Trojans, adware, and more.

These tools are critical for users to have installed and up-to-date because a computer without anti-virus software installed will be infected within minutes of connecting to the internet. The anti-virus companies update their detection tools constantly to deal with the more than 60,000 new pieces of malware created daily.

There are several different companies that offer anti-virus software and what each offers can vary but all perform some basic functions:

- Scan specific files or directories for any malware or known malicious patterns.
- Allow you to schedule a scan.
- Allow you to initiate a scan of a specific file or of your computer, or of a CD or flash drive at any time.
- Remove any malicious code detected –sometimes you will be notified of an infection and asks if you want to clean the file, other programs will automatically do this behind the scenes.
- Show you the *health* of your computer.

15.7.7 Adware

Adware is a program (or software) with advertisements embedded in the application. Adware is an allowed alternative offered to users who do not wish to pay for software. There are many ad-supported programs, games or utilities that are distributed as adware (or freeware). Today we have a growing number of software developers who offer their products as sponsored freeware (adware) until you pay to register. If we are using adware, when we stop running the software, the ads should disappear, and we always have the option of disabling the ads by purchasing a registration key.

15.7.8 Adware Blocker

Adware Blocker is a software program which stops all unwanted pop-up advertisements that disrupts our experience when online. There are many software which stops adware from installing in our PC. Adware are sometimes malicious and hence an Adware Blocker is needed for a PC connected to Internet.

15.7.9 Adware Remover

An adware *remover* is a software program that is used to remove adware from a computer. This functionality is also built into all modern-day antivirus software.

15.7.10 Spyware

Spyware is a program (or software) that gathers user information through the user's Internet connection without his or her knowledge. Spyware is generally used for advertising purposes.

Spyware applications are typically bundled as a hidden component of *freeware* programs that can be downloaded from the Internet. But, it should be noted that the most of the freeware applications do not come with spyware. Once installed, the spyware monitors user activity on the Internet and transmits that information in the background to someone else. Spyware can also gather information about e-mail addresses and even passwords and credit card numbers.

Spyware is mostly classified into four types: *system* monitors, *Trojans*, *adware*, and *tracking cookies*. Spyware is mostly used for the purposes such as; tracking and storing internet users' movements on the web and serving up pop-up ads to users.

15.7.11 Spyware Adware

These are freeware applications which contain adware to track surfing habits in order to serve adverts relevant to the user.

15.7.12 Spyware Blockers

Spyware Blockers are software to block malware that snoops on user's personal information.

15.7.13 Back Door

A *Backdoor* is a program that permits hackers access to other people's computers. This program is complicated to notice and even more difficult to do away with. A back door is a means of access to a computer program that bypasses security mechanisms. A programmer may sometimes install a back door so that the program can be accessed for troubleshooting or other purposes. However, attackers often use back doors that they detect or install themselves, as part of an exploit. It is also called a trapdoor.

15.7.14 Blaster Worm

The Blaster Worm (also known as *Lovsan*, *Lovesan* or *MSBlast*) was a computer worm that spread on computers running the Microsoft operating systems Windows XP and Windows 2000, during August 2003.

The worm's executable contains two messages. The first reads:

> I just want to say LOVE YOU SAN!!soo much

message gave the worm the alternative name of Lovesan. The second reads:

> Billy Gates why do you make this possible ? Stop making money

> **and fix your software!!**

This is a message to Bill Gates, the co-founder of Microsoft and the target of the worm.

The worm also creates the following registry entry so that it is launched every time Windows starts:

> **HKEY_LOCAL_MACHINE\SOFTWARE\Microsoft\Windows\CurrentVersion\Run\windo ws auto update=msblast.exe**

15.7.15 False Positive

A false positive occurs when a virus scanner (say, Nessus) erroneously detects a *virus* that may in fact does not exist. False positives result when the signature used to detect a particular virus is not unique to the virus. That means, the same signature appears in legitimate, non-infected software.

15.7.16 False Negative

A false negative is the opposite of a false positive. A false negative occurs when a virus scanner (say, Nessus) fails to detect a virus that may in fact exist. The antivirus scanner may fail to detect the virus because the virus is new and no signature is yet available, or it may fail to detect because of configuration settings or even faulty signatures.

15.7.17 Firewall

A firewall is a software system designed to prevent unauthorized access to or from a private network. Firewalls can be implemented in both hardware and software, or a combination of both. Firewalls are frequently used to prevent unauthorized Internet users from accessing private networks connected to the Internet, especially intranets. All messages entering or leaving the intranet pass through the firewall, which examines each message and blocks those that do not meet the specified security criteria.

There are several types of firewall techniques:

- *Packet filters*: Looks at each packet entering or leaving the network and accepts or rejects it based on user-defined rules. Packet filtering is fairly effective and transparent to users, but it is difficult to configure. In addition, it is susceptible to IP spoofing.
- *Application gateway*: Applies security mechanisms to specific applications, such as FTP and Telnet servers. This is very effective, but can impose performance degradation.
- *Circuit-level gateway*: Applies security mechanisms when a TCP or UDP connection is established. Once the connection has been made, packets can flow between the hosts without further checking.
- *Proxy server*: Checks all messages entering and leaving the network. The proxy server effectively hides the true network addresses.

15.7.18 Hacker

This is a term for a computer enthusiast. A *hacker* is a person who enjoys learning programming languages and computer systems and can often be considered an expert on the subject. Among professional programmers, depending on how it used, the term can be either complimentary or derogatory, although it is developing an increasingly derogatory connotation.

In positive sense (also called *white hat hacker*), hacker is a person who enjoys exploring the details of computers and how to stretch their capabilities. On the negative side (also called *black hat hacker*), hacker would engage in the above for malicious purposes.

15.7.19 Key Logger Remover

It is a software or program used to remove programs that monitor each keystroke typed on a specific computer's keyboard.

15.7.20 Letter Bomb

Letter bomb is an e-mail containing live data intended to do malicious damage to the recipient's computer.

15.7.21 Logic Bomb

A logic bomb (also called *slag code*) is programming code, inserted intentionally, that is designed to execute under circumstances such as the lapse of a certain amount of time or the failure of a program user to respond to a program command.

A logic bomb is malware that is triggered by a response to an event, such as launching an application or when a specific date/time is reached. Attackers can use logic bombs in a variety of ways. They can embed arbitrary code within a fake application, or Trojan horse, and will be executed whenever you launch the fraudulent software.

Attackers can also use a combination of spyware and logic bombs in an attempt to steal your identity. For example, cyber-criminals use spyware to covertly install a keylogger on your computer. The keylogger can capture your keystrokes, such as usernames and passwords.

The logic bomb is designed to wait until you visit a website that requires you to login with your credentials, such as a banking site or social network. Consequently, this will trigger the logic bomb to execute the *keylogger* and capture *your* credentials and send them to a remote attacker.

15.7.22 Mobile Antivirus

It is a protective software optimized for *mobile platforms* used for identification and removal of computer viruses, as well as other types of malware that target mobile operating systems.

15.7.23 Packet Sniffer

Packet sniffing is a program or software used to monitor packets traveling in a network. Packet sniffing software (also called *network monitoring software*) allows a user to see each byte of information that travels networked computers.

It can be used to detect network problems or intrusions. It can also be used maliciously to try to get access to user names and passwords. There are many software packages available to help you learn how to sniff packets. The selection of that depends on the type and structure of the network and the operating system.

15.7.24 Port Scan

Port scan is a series of messages sent by an intruder to break into a computer. Specific messages are used to determine which computer network services the computer provides. Port scanning gives an idea where to probe for weaknesses.

15.7.25 Spam Filter

Spam filter a software program that *blocks* unsolicited *junk* mail.

15.7.26 Trojan horse

A Trojan horse is full of as much trickery as the mythological Trojan horse it was named after. The Trojan horse, at first glance will appear to be useful software but will actually do damage once installed or run on your computer. Those on the receiving end of a Trojan horse are usually tricked into opening them because they appear to be receiving legitimate software or files from a legitimate source.

When a Trojan is activated on your computer, the results can vary. Some Trojans are designed to be more annoying than malicious (like changing your desktop, adding silly active desktop icons) or they can cause serious damage by deleting files and destroying information on your system.

Trojans are also known to create a backdoor on your computer that gives malicious users access to your system, possibly allowing confidential or personal information to be compromised. Unlike viruses and worms, Trojans do not reproduce by infecting other files nor do they self-replicate.

15.7.27 Wi-Fi

Wi-Fi is the name of a popular wireless networking technology that uses *radio* waves to provide wireless high-speed Internet and network connections. Wi-Fi works with no physical wired connection between sender and receiver by using radio frequency (RF) technology, a frequency within the electromagnetic spectrum associated with radio wave propagation.

When an RF current is supplied to an antenna, an electromagnetic field is created that then is able to propagate through space. The cornerstone of any wireless network is an access point (AP).

The primary job of an access point is to broadcast a wireless signal that computers can detect and tune into. In order to connect to an access point and join a wireless network, computers and devices must have wireless network adapters.

15.8 Network Security Components

Network security concerns with the following objectives:

- Authentication
- Authorization
- Data Integrity
- Confidentiality
- Availability
- Non-Repudiation

15.8.1 Authentication

Authentication is the process of determining whether someone is who it is declared to be. In private and public computer networks, authentication is commonly done through the use of logon passwords. Knowledge of the password is assumed to guarantee that the user is authentic. Each user registers initially, using an assigned or self-declared password.

On each subsequent use, the user must know and use the previously declared password. The weakness in this system for transactions that are significant (such as the exchange of money) is that passwords can often be stolen, accidentally revealed, or forgotten. For this reason, Internet business and many other transactions require a more robust authentication process.

The use of digital certificates issued and verified by a Certificate Authority (CA) as part of a public key infrastructure is the standard way to perform authentication on the Internet.

15.8.2 Authorization

After authentication, a user must gains *authorization* for doing certain tasks. For example, after logging into a system; the user may try to issue commands. The authorization process determines whether the user has the authority to issue such commands.

In other words, authorization is the process of enforcing policies: determining what types or qualities of activities, resources, or services a user is permitted. Usually, authorization occurs within the context of authentication. Once you have authenticated a user, they may be authorized for different types of access or activity.

15.8.3 Data Integrity

Data Integrity is the assurance that data have not been changed inappropriately. There are many ways in which data might be altered: accidentally (through hardware and transmission errors), or because of an intentional attack.

For example, a weakness that allows an administrator to change the permissions on any file on a system would not be security vulnerability because an administrator already has this capability. In contrast, if a weakness allowed an unprivileged user to do the same thing, it would constitute security vulnerability.

15.8.4 Confidentiality

Confidentiality refers to limiting access to information on a resource to authorized people. An attacker that exploits a weakness in a product to access non-public information is compromising the confidentiality of that product.

For example, a weakness in a web site that enables a visitor to read a file that should not be read would constitute security vulnerability. However, a weakness that revealed the physical location of a file would not constitute vulnerability.

15.8.5 Availability

Availability refers to the possibility to access a resource. An attacker that exploits a weakness in a product, denying appropriate user access to it, is compromising the availability of that product.

For example, a weakness that enables an attacker to cause a server to fail would constitute security vulnerability, since the attacker would be able to regulate whether the server provided service or not. However, the fact that an attacker could send a huge number of legitimate requests to a server and monopolize its resources would not constitute security vulnerability, as long as the server operator still could control the computer.

15.8.6 Non-repudiation

To repudiate means to deny. Non-repudiation is the process of ensuring that a transferred message has been sent and received by the parties claiming to have sent and received the message. Nonrepudiation is a way to guarantee that the sender of a message cannot later deny having sent the message and that the recipient cannot deny having received the message.

As an example, someone (say, person A) claims that person B used offensive words and person B attempts to repudiate (deny) the claim. It is easy to prove that he has used offensive words. There is evidence that person B has used offensive words. If person B cannot repudiate the claim about offensive words, the evidence provides non-repudiation.

Non-repudiation is an active attempt to create proofs which may be used against an identified person who is denying that they are the origin of a communication or action. The proofs are identity, authentication of the identity, and something connecting a communication or action to the identity.

In the above example there are legal documents that record the testimony of many witnesses who identified and authenticated person B and witnessed him using offensive words. This is a passive and accidental production of artifacts connecting an action to an identity.

In security we want active purposeful production of proofs that may assist in a non-repudiation argument. In order to do that we must identify an entity, authenticate the identity and connect the identified entity to a specific action or communication.

Some people use public/private key certificates to sign their email. By using their e-mail address they are providing identification. Their use of a private key (to sign the e-mail) provides authentication as long as the private key is known only by the individual.

When they sign an e-mail with their digital signature they are connecting the content of the e-mail to the identity authenticated by the certificate. These proofs may assist in preventing an individual from repudiating the contents of the e-mail; *I never sent that e − mail*. However, to repudiate the e-mail a sender may claim that their private key was stolen (known by another party) and the thief sent the e-mail.

15.9 Types of Attacks

It is very important to understand the types of security attacks what can happen on a network. It is not enough to have focus on security; but, we should also have to be aware of the types of security attacks that can happen on a computer network. Before we go on to discuss about the types of security attacks, an attacker do one of the following:

- *Interruption*: Receiving the messages and stopping the receiver to receive them. The sender will believe that the receiver has received the message but the receiver has not received it. Interruption is an attack on availability.

Interruption attacks' aim is to make resources unavailable. Not too long ago, WordPress.com, a popular Blog Hosting Site was faced with a DOS attack taking down the servers so the service was unavailable to its users.

- *Interception*: Interception is just listening to communication. Interception is an attack to gain unauthorized access to a system. It can be simple eavesdropping on communication.

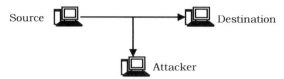

- *Modification*: The middle man receives the message, modifies it and then sends to the actual receiver. Modification is an attack that tampers with a resource. Its aim is to modify information that is being communicated with two or more parties.

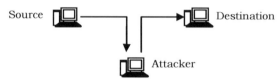

- *Fabrication*: The middle man will just create a new message and will send it to the receiver. The receiver will believe that the message came from the sender. A Fabrication attack is also called counterfeiting. This attack usually inserts new information, or records extra information on a file. It is mainly used to gain access to data or a service.

-

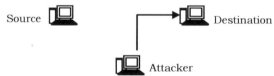

Based on the above discussion, there are two main types of attacks whose aim is to compromise the security of a network.

- Passive attack
- Active attack

15.9.1 Passive Attack

A passive attack can be split into two types. The first type of passive attack is to simply monitor the transmission between two parties and to capture information that is sent and received. The attacker does not intend to interrupt the service, or cause an effect, but to only read the information.

The second type of attack is a traffic analysis. If information is encrypted, it will be more difficult to read the information being sent and received, but the attacker simply observers the information, and tries to make sense out of it; or to simply determine the identity and location of the two communicating parties.

Passive attacks are generally difficult to detect as there is little impact to the information communicated.

15.9.2 Active Attack

An active attack aim is to cause disruption, and it is usually easily recognized. Unlike a passive attack, an active attack modifies information or interrupts a service. There are four types of an active attack:

1. *Masquerade*: To pretend to be someone else. This could be logging in with a different user account to gain extra privileges. For example, a user of a system steals the System Administrators username and password to be able to pretend that they are them
2. *Reply*: To capture information to send it, or a copy it elsewhere
3. *Modification*: To alter the information being sent or received
4. *Denial of service*: To cause a disruption to the network

Even though a passive attack doesn't sound harmful, it is just as bad as an activate attack, if not worse.

15.10 Discussion of known Security Attacks

15.10.1 Denial-of-service

Denial-of-service (DoS) is an attack on a network (or on a machine) that bring the network down (or machine down) by flooding it with useless traffic. Examples of DoS attacks are:

- SYN flooding
- Ping of Death [also called ICMP Flood]

These attacks exploit the limitations in the TCP/IP protocols. DoS attacks do not typically result in the theft or loss of significant information. But, they cost a great deal of time and money to handle.

All known DoS attacks have code fixes that system administrators can install to limit the damage caused by the attacks. But, new DoS attacks are constantly being invented by hackers.

15.10.1.1 SYN flooding

As seen in earlier chapters, when a client makes a TCP connection to a server; the client and server perform a three-way handshake to establish the connection.

- Client sends a SYN message to server.
- Server replies back with SYN/ACK message to client *(synchronize acknowledge)*.
- Client sends ACK message to server *(acknowledge)* and the connection is now established.

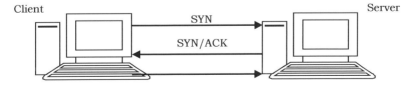

In SYN flood attack, the attacker does not respond to the server with the expected ACK code. The attacker can either simply not send the expected ACK, or uses wrong IP (by spoofing the source IP address) in the SYN. This causes the server to send the SYN/ACK to a wrong IP address (which might not exist at all); which will not send an ACK because it "knows" that it never sent a SYN.

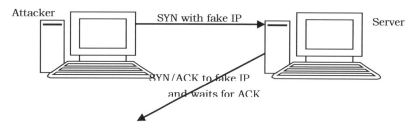

The server will wait for the acknowledgement for some time, but in an attack increasingly large numbers of *half-open connections* will bind resources on the server until no new connections can be made. This results in a denial of service to legitimate traffic. Some systems may also malfunction badly or even crash if other operating system functions are starved of resources in this way.

15.10.1.2 Ping of Death

In late 1996 and early 1997, a flaw in the implementation of networking in some operating systems became well-known and popularized by hackers as a way to crash computers remotely over the Internet.

The maximum allowable IP packet size is 65,535 bytes, including the packet header, which is typically 20 bytes long. An ICMP echo request is an IP packet with a pseudo header, which is 8 bytes long. Therefore, the maximum allowable size of the data area of an ICMP echo request is 65,507 bytes (65,535 - 20 - 8 = 65,507).

While a ping larger than 65,536 bytes is too large to fit in one packet that can be transmitted, TCP/IP allows a packet to be fragmented, essentially splitting the packet into smaller segments that are eventually reassembled. Attacks took advantage of this flaw by fragmenting packets that when received would total more than the allowed number of bytes and would effectively cause a buffer overload on the operating system at the receiving end, crashing the system.

Idea behind the Ping of Death attack is; sending IP packets of a size greater than 65,535 bytes to the target computer. IP packets of this size are illegal, but applications can be built that are capable of creating them. Carefully programmed operating systems could detect and safely handle illegal IP packets, but some failed to do this.

ICMP ping utilities often included large-packet capability and became the namesake of the problem, although UDP and other IP-based protocols also could transport Ping of Death.

15.10.2 Distributed Denial-of-Service (DDoS) attack

In a distributed denial-of-service (DDoS) attack, an attacker may use multiple computers to attack another computer. By taking advantage of security vulnerabilities or weaknesses, an attacker could take control of one computer and then force that computer to send huge amounts of data to a website or send spam to particular email addresses. The attack is distributed because the attacker is using multiple computers, to launch the denial-of-service attack.

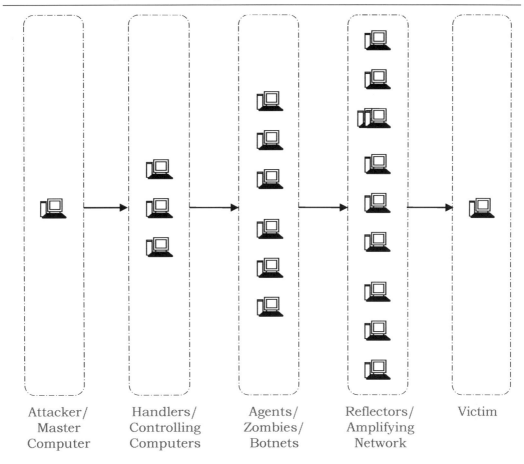

Attacker/	Handlers/	Agents/	Reflectors/	Victim
Master	Controlling	Zombies/	Amplifying	
Computer	Computers	Botnets	Network	

15.10.2.1 How to reduce DoS/DDoS attacks?

Unfortunately, there are no effective ways to prevent being the victim of a DoS or DDoS attack, but there are steps we can take to reduce the possibility that an attacker will use your computer to attack other computers:

- Install and maintain anti-virus software
- Install a firewall, and configure it to restrict traffic coming into and leaving your computer.
- Follow good security practices for distributing your email address. Applying email filters may help you manage unwanted traffic.

15.10.3 Backdoors and Trapdoors

A back door (also called trap door) is a way of giving access to a computer program that bypasses security mechanisms. A programmer may sometimes install a back door so that the program can be accessed for troubleshooting or other purposes. However, attackers often use back doors that they detect or install themselves, as part of an exploit.

Trap doors are snippets of code kept in programs by the programmer(s) to gain access at a later time. Generally, programmers use these techniques during the testing or debugging phase. If a programmer purposely leaves this code in or forgets to remove it, a potential security hole is introduced. Attackers often plant a backdoor on previously compromised systems to gain later access.

15.10.4 Network Sniffing

One of the network's features is that data are transmitted up and down through network pipes, from one piece of equipment to another. That means when you try to send data to another computer, the data go through many network devices. We can use tracert command to help us understand how the packets travel among the devices.

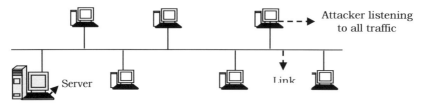

This causes the problem that someone could see your data. It's just like you sending out a mail and the postman can take a peek if he wants too.

Another point we have to make clear that data can be transmitted in Plain text format or encrypted code format. If data encrypted, the attacker only sees a pile of meaningless strings. He can choose to rank his brain to crack them down if he really wants to get the original data from it but it's not easy at all. It's pretty much like what happened in the Second World War. Everybody could receive telegram commands but it took a great effort to crack the code.

15.10.5 Spoofing Attack

15.10.5.1 What is a spoofing attack?

In network security, spoofing is nothing but making data look like it has come from a different source. In spoofing attack, an attacker impersonates another device or user on a network in order to launch attacks against network hosts, steal data, spread malware, or bypass access controls. There are several different types of spoofing attacks that attackers can use to accomplish this. Some of the most common methods include IP address spoofing attacks, ARP spoofing attacks, and DNS server spoofing attacks.

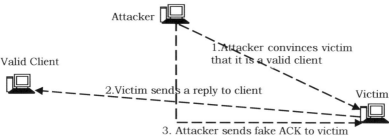

15.10.5.2 IP Address Spoofing

IP address spoofing is one of the most frequently used spoofing attack methods. In an IP address spoofing attack, an attacker sends IP packets from a spoofed source address. Denial-of-service attacks often use IP spoofing to overload networks and devices with packets that appear to be from trusted source IP addresses.

There are two ways that IP spoofing attacks can be used to overload targets with traffic. One method is to simply flood a selected target with packets from multiple spoofed addresses. This method works by directly sending a target more data than it can handle. The other method is to spoof the target's IP address and send packets from that address to many different recipients on the network. When another machine receives a packet, it will automatically transmit a packet to the sender in response. Since the spoofed packets appear to be sent from the target's IP address, all responses to the spoofed packets will be sent to (and flood) the target's IP address.

IP spoofing attacks can also be used to bypass IP address-based authentication. This process can be very difficult and is primarily used when trust relationships are in place between machines on a network and internal systems. Trust relationships use IP addresses (rather than user logins) to verify machines' identities when attempting to access systems. This enables malicious parties to use spoofing attacks to impersonate machines with access permissions and bypass trust-based network security measures.

15.10.5.3 ARP Spoofing

ARP (Address Resolution Protocol), a protocol that is used to resolve IP addresses to MAC (Media Access Control) addresses for transmitting data. In an ARP spoofing attack, an attacker sends spoofed ARP messages across a Local Area Network in order to link the attacker's MAC address with the IP address of a legitimate member of the network.

This type of spoofing attack results in data that is intended for the host's IP address getting sent to the attacker instead. Malicious parties commonly use ARP spoofing to steal information, modify data in-transit, or stop traffic on a LAN. ARP spoofing attacks can also be used to facilitate other types of attacks, including denial-of-service, session hijacking, and man-in-the-middle attacks. ARP spoofing only works on Local Area Networks that use the Address Resolution Protocol.

15.10.5.4 DNS Server Spoofing Attacks

The Domain Name System (DNS) is a system that associates domain names with IP addresses. Devices on the internet depend on the DNS for resolving URLs, email addresses, and other human-readable domain names into their corresponding IP addresses. In a DNS server spoofing attack, an attacker modifies the DNS server in order to reroute a specific domain name to a different IP address. In many cases, the new IP address will be for a server that is actually controlled by the attacker and contains files infected with malware. DNS server spoofing attacks are often used to spread computer worms and viruses.

15.10.5.5 How to reduce Spoofing Attacks?

There are many tools and practices that organizations can use to reduce the spoofing attacks.

- *Packet filtering*: Packet filters inspect packets as they are transmitted across a network. They are useful in IP address spoofing attack prevention because they are capable of filtering out and blocking packets with conflicting source address information (packets from outside the network that show source addresses from inside the network and vice-versa).
- *Avoid trust* relationships: Companies should develop protocols that rely on trust relationships as little as possible. It is easier for attackers to run spoofing attacks when trust relationships are in place because trust relationships only use IP addresses for authentication.
- Use spoofing detection software

- Use *cryptographic network protocols*: Transport Layer Security (TLS), Secure Shell (SSH), HTTP Secure (HTTPS), and other secure communications protocols bolster spoofing attack prevention efforts by encrypting data before it is sent and authenticating data as it is received.

15.10.6 Man in the middle attacks

15.10.6.1 What is a Man-in-the-Middle Attack?

In man-in-the-middle attack, an attacker gets between the sender and receiver of information and sniffs any information being sent. In some cases, users may be sending unencrypted data, which means the man-in-the-middle (MITM) can obtain any unencrypted information. In other cases, an attacker may be able to obtain information, but have to decrypt the information before it can be read. The attacker monitors some or all traffic coming from the computer, collects the data, and then forwards it to the destination the user was originally intending to visit. Man-in-the-Middle attacks are abbreviated with MITM, MitM, MiM, or MIM.

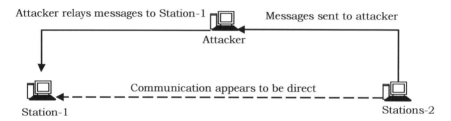

15.10.6.2 Man in the Middle Attack Examples

As an example, suppose *Ram* wishes to communicate with *Mary*. Meanwhile, an attacker wishes to eavesdrop and possibly deliver a false message to *Mary*.

First, *Ram* asks *Mary* for her public key. If *Mary* sends her public key to Ram, but attacker is able to intercept it, a man-in-the-middle attack can begin. Attacker sends a forged message to *Ram* that claims to be from *Mary*, but instead includes attacker's public key.

Ram, believing this public key to be *Mary*'s, encrypts his message with attacker's key and sends the enciphered message back to *Mary*. Attacker again intercepts, deciphers the message using his private key, possibly alters it if he wants, and re-enciphers it using the public key *Mary* originally sent to Ram. When *Mary* receives the newly enciphered message, she believes it came from Ram.

1. *Ram* sends a message to *Mary*, which is intercepted by attacker:

> Ram *"Hi Mary, it's Ram. Give me your key"*-->Mary

2. Attacker relays this message to Mary; Mary cannot tell it is not really from Ram:

> Attacker *"Hi Mary, it's Ram. Give me your key"*-->Mary

3. Mary responds with her encryption key:

> Attacker<--*[Mary's_key]* Mary

4. Attacker replaces Mary's key with his own, and relays this to Ram, claiming that it is Mary's key:

> Ram<--*[Mallory's_key]* Attacker

5. Ram encrypts a message with what he believes to be Mary's key, thinking that only Mary can read it:

> Ram *"Meet me at the bus stop!"[encrypted with Mallory's key]*-->Attacker

6. However, because it was actually encrypted with attacker's key, attacker can decrypt it, read it, modify it (if desired), re-encrypt with Mary's key, and forward it to Mary:

> Attacker *"Meet me at 22nd Ave!"[encrypted with Mary's key]*-->Mary

7. Mary thinks that this message is a secure communication from Ram.

This example shows the need for *Ram* and *Mary* to have some way to ensure that they are truly using each other's public keys, rather than the public key of an attacker. Otherwise, such attacks are generally possible, in principle, against any message sent using public-key technology. Fortunately, there are a variety of techniques that help defend against MITM attacks.

The hacker is impersonating the both sides of the conversation to gain access to funds. This example holds true for a conversation with a client and server as well as person to person conversations. In the example above the attacker intercepts a public key and with that can transpose his own credentials to trick the people on either end into believing they are talking to one another securely.

15.10.7 Replay Attacks

15.10.7.1 What are replay attacks?

Replay attacks are *Man in the middle* attacks that involve eavesdropping data packets and replaying them (resending them) to the receiving server. Replay attacks are the network attacks in which an attacker spies the conversation between the sender and receiver and takes the authenticated information.

15.10.7.2 Examples for Replay Attacks

Suppose in the communication of two stations A and B; A is sharing his key to B to prove his identity but the Attacker C eavesdrop the conversation between them and keeps the information which are needed to prove his identity to B. Later C contacts to B and prove its authenticity.

15.10.8 Phishing Attack

15.10.8.1 What is a phishing attack?

In phishing attack (also called brand spoofing), attacker creates an almost 100 percent perfect replica of a chosen website, then tries to trick the user in to disclosing their personal details – username, password, PIN etc. – via a form on the fake website, allowing the criminal to use the details to obtain money.

Phishers use various techniques to trick users in to accessing the fake website, such as sending emails that pretend to be from a bank. These emails often use legitimate logos, a good business style and often spoof the header of the email to make it look like it came from a legitimate bank.

In general, these letters inform recipients that the bank has changed its IT infrastructure and asks all customers to re-confirm their user information. When the recipient clicks on the link in the email, they are directed to the fake website, where they are prompted to divulge their personal information.

15.10.8.2 Phishing Attack Examples

For example, in 2003 the users received e-mails supposedly from eBay claiming that the user's account was about to be suspended unless he clicked on the provided link and updated the credit card information that the genuine eBay already had.

Because it is relatively simple to make a Web site look like a legitimate organizations site by mimicking the HTML code, the scam counted on people being tricked into thinking they were actually being contacted by eBay and were subsequently going to eBay's site to update their account information.

By spamming large groups of people, the phisher counted on the e-mail being read by a percentage of people who actually had listed credit card numbers with eBay legitimately.

15.10.8.3 How to reduce Phishing Attacks?

Be very wary of any email messages asking for personal information. It's highly unlikely that your bank will request such information by email. If in doubt, call them to check!

Don't complete a form in an email message asking for personal information. Only enter such information using a secure website. Check that the URL starts with *https:/ /*, rather than just *http://*. Look for the lock symbol on the lower right-hand corner of the web browser and double-click it to check the validity of the digital certificate. Or, alternatively, use the telephone to conduct your banking.

- Report anything suspicious to your bank immediately.
- Don't use links in an email message to load a web page. Instead, type the URL into your web browser.
- Check if your anti-virus program blocks phishing sites, or consider installing a web browser tool bar that alerts you to known phishing attacks.
- Check your bank accounts regularly (including debit and credit cards, bank statements, etc.), to make sure that listed transactions are legitimate.
- Make sure that you use the latest version of your web browser and that any security patches have been applied.

15.11 Cryptography

15.11.1 What is Cryptography?

Cryptography is about keeping communications private. Cryptography is the science of information security. The word *cryptography* is derived from Greek. In Greek,*crypto* means *secret* and *graphy* means *writing*.

Cryptography = Crypto + Graphy = Secret + Writing.

It is the art of protecting information by converting it into an unreadable format. Cryptography is an important part of preventing private data from being stolen. Even if the attackers were able intercept our messages they still will not be able to read the data if it is protected by cryptography.

Cryptography is used to fulfill the functions: Authentication, Authorization, Data Integrity, Confidentiality, Availability, and Non-Repudiation (refer *Network Security Components* section).

15.11.2 History of Cryptography

Cryptography has origins 2000 BC, with the Egyptian practice of hieroglyphics. These consisted of complex pictograms, the full meaning of which was only known to experts. A classic work on statecraft (*Arthshashtra*) written by *Kautalya* describes the espionage service in *India* and mentions giving assignments to spies in secret writing.

The ancient *Chinese* used the ideographic nature of their language to hide the meaning of words. Messages were often transformed into ideographs for privacy, but no substantial use in early Chinese military conquests is apparent. Genghis Khan, for example, seems never to have used cryptography.

Little later, the first known use of a modern cipher was by *Julius Caesar* (somewhere between 100 BC and 44 BC). *Caesar* did not trust his messengers when communicating with his governors and officers. For this reason, he created a system in which each character in messages was replaced by a character three positions ahead of it in the Roman alphabet. This substitution cipher is called *Caesar* cipher. This is the most mentioned historic cipher in academic literature.

During the 16th century, Vigenere designed a cipher that was the first cipher which used an encryption key. In one of his ciphers, the encryption key was repeated multiple times spanning the entire message, and then the cipher text was produced by adding the message character with the key character modulo 26.

As with the Caesar cipher, Vigenere's cipher can also easily be broken; however, Vigenere's cipher brought the very idea of introducing encryption keys into the picture, though it was poorly executed. Comparing this to Caesar cipher, the secrecy of the message depends on the secrecy of the encryption key, rather than the secrecy of the system.

In early 19th century, everything became electric. The Enigma machine was invented by *German* engineer *Arthur* at the end of *First* World War. It was heavily used by the *German* forces during the *Second* World War as well. The Enigma machine used 3 or 4 or even more rotors. The rotors rotate at different rates as you type on the keyboard and output appropriate letters of cipher text. In this case the key was the initial setting of the rotors.

The Enigma's cipher was eventually *broken* by Poland. Later, the technology was transferred to the British cryptographers.

15.11.3 Cryptography during Second World War

During Second World War, U.S. had an excellent track record against Japanese codes and ciphers. This experience, combined with other sources of intelligence (especially, *radio interception station* and *decryption center station* HYPO) helped the U.S... They could find that an attack on *Midway* was in the near future.

Japanese *naval codes* were primarily *book* ciphers, while *German* codes are mechanical encipherment (such as, *Enigma* and *Lorenz* machines).

Book ciphers *work* like this: The sender composes his message and then consults the code book. Common words and phrases are replaced with a group of numbers and letters, and any remaining text is encoded character by character. The result is transmitted. The receiver then looks up each group in the corresponding code book and reassembles the message. An additional level of security can be added by enciphering the code groups; this is called *super-enciphering*.

High-grade Japanese naval codes since the 1920s had relied on code books and superencipherment to protect their communications, and the U.S., Great Britain, Australia, and Holland all had had considerable *success* against them. The Japanese navy regularly changed their code books and the superencipherment technique. But, the supherencipherment was generally weak and easily broken (Japanese characters were encoded as *romaji* for transmission, and this made them vulnerable to standard cryptological attacks such as frequency analysis).

The main Japanese code was *JN*25. Finding the contents of the JN25 code book was essentially an exercise in puzzle-solving. Code-breakers at *Station* HYPO used IBM punch-card sorting machines to find messages using specific code groups. The end result was a huge card catalog representing the inferences and deductions of code groups of the JN25 code book.

In early 1942 when the U.S. began detecting signs of an impending attack, the target was encoded as "*AF*." Locations in the JN25 code book were represented by a code group, and AF was not definitively known by the U.S. So the code-breakers at Station HYPO devised an intelligent experiment to confirm the identity of AF. Pearl Harbor and Midway Island were connected by an underwater cable. Station HYPO sent orders to Midway by cable to broadcast a radio message that the *island's desalinization* plant had *broken* down. The radio message was broadcast without encryption to ensure that Japan could read it if it was intercepted.

The radio message was intercepted by Japan and reported by a message encoded in JN25 stating that AF's desalinization plant was out of order. That message was intercepted by Station HYPO. AF was thus confirmed as Midway.

The next question was regarding the timing of attack. Station HYPO said that the attack would come in late May to early June 1942. Station HYPO's intelligence helped U.S. in winning the war with limited resources.

15.11.4 Post Second World War

Up to the Second World War, most of the work on cryptography was for military purposes. However, cryptography attracted commercial attention post war, with businesses trying to secure their data from competitors.

In the early 1970's, IBM got requests from customers for encrypting the data and, so they formed a *crypto group*. They designed a cipher called *Lucifer*.

In 1973, the Nation Bureau of Standards (now called *NIST*) in the US put out a request for proposals for a *block* cipher which would become a national standard. They had obviously realized that they were buying a lot of commercial products without any good crypto support. Lucifer was eventually accepted and was called DES or the Data Encryption Standard.

In 1997, and in the following years, DES was broken by an exhaustive search attack. The main problem with DES was the small size of the encryption key. As computing power increased it became easy to brute force all different combinations of the key to obtain a possible plain text message.

In 1997, NIST again put out a request for proposal for a new block cipher. It received 50 submissions. One of those submissions was in 2000, and named Advanced Encryption Standard (AES).

15.11.5 Cryptanalysis

Cryptanalysis is the art of *breaking* ciphers. That means, retrieving the plaintext without knowing the proper key. *Cryptanalysis* is the study of ciphers, ciphertext, or cryptosystems to finding *weaknesses* in them. In other words, it will allow retrieval of the plaintext *from* the ciphertext, without knowing the key or the algorithm. This is known as breaking the cipher, ciphertext, or cryptosystem.

Breaking is sometimes used interchangeably with weakening. This refers to finding a fault in the design or implementation of the cipher.

15.12 Types of Ciphers

Ciphers can be classified in to two categories: *stream* ciphers or *block* ciphers.

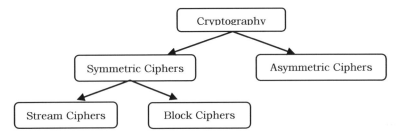

15.12.1 Stream Ciphers

Stream cipher algorithms process plaintext and produces a stream of ciphertext. The cipher inputs the plaintext in a stream and outputs a stream of ciphertext. Figure illustrates the concept of the stream cipher's function. Depending on the cipher, the data may consist of a stream of bits or a stream of bytes.

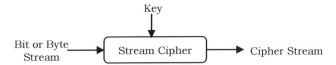

With stream ciphers, patterns in the plaintext can be reflected in the ciphertext. As an example, consider the plaintext "We will discuss one to one" into ciphertext to compare the two patterns:

A	B	C	D	E	F	G	H	I	J	K	L	M	N	O	P	Q	R	S	T	U	V	W	X	Y	Z
1	2	3	4	5	6	A	B	C	D	E	F	G	H	I	J	K	L	M	N	O	P	Q	R	S	T

Plaintext: We will discuss one to one
Ciphertext: Q5 QCFF 4CM3OMM IH5 NI IH5

From the above example, it is clear that words and letters that are repeated in the plaintext are also repeated in the ciphertext. Knowing that certain words repeat makes breaking the code easier. In addition, certain words in the English language appear with predictable regularity. It is not hard for a trained code breaker to break this type of code.

Another problem with stream ciphers is that they can be easily affected to a substitution attack even without breaking the code. This is a type of replay attack where someone can simply copy a section of an old message and insert it into a new message. We don't need to break the code to insert the old section into a new message.

Examples of stream ciphers are:

- *Vernam cipher*
- *Rivest cipher #4* (RC4)
- *One-time pads*

15.12.2 Block Ciphers

Block ciphers differ from stream ciphers in that they encrypt and decrypt information in fixed size blocks instead of each bit or byte individually. A block cipher processes a block of plaintext through its algorithm to generate a block of ciphertext. Ideally, a block cipher should generate ciphertext roughly equivalent in size (in terms of number of blocks) to the plaintext.

Block ciphers encrypt an entire block of plaintext bits at a time with the same key. This means that the encryption of any plaintext bit in a given block depends on every other plaintext bit in the same block.

Typically, blocks consist of 64 bits (8 bytes) or 128 bits (16 bytes) of data (depends on cipher algorithm). Also, note that the *same plaintext* block always encrypts to the *same ciphertext* block.

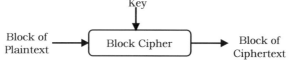

A cipher that generates a block of ciphertext that is significantly larger than the information it is trying to protect is of little practical value. Think about it in terms of network bandwidth: If the ciphertext block was twice the size of the plaintext, the net effect is that your bandwidth would be cut in half. This would also have an impact on files stored in an encrypted format. An unencrypted file 5 MB in size would be 10 MB in size when encrypted.

Examples of block ciphers are:

- Data Encryption Standard (DES)
- International Data Encryption Algorithm (IDEA)
- SKIPJACK

15.13 Encryption and Decryption

15.13.1 Symmetric Key Encryption

15.13.1.1 Introduction

Symmetric encryption is the *oldest* and best-known technique. In this method, a *secret key* is applied to the text of a message to change the content in a particular way. Secret key can be a number, a word, or just a string of random letters. One simple way of applying secret code is shifting each letter by a number of places in the alphabet.

As long as both *sender* and *recipient* know the secret key, they can encrypt and decrypt all messages that use this key. The term *symmetric-key* refers to the *identical private* keys *shared* by users.

Symmetric encryption (also called *conventional encryption* or *single key encryption* was the only type of encryption in use *prior* to the development of public-key encryption in 1976.

15.13.1.2 Components of Symmetric Encryption

Ram has a box with a lock. As usual, the lock has a key that can *lock* and *unlock* the box. So, if Ram wants to protect something, he puts it in the box and locks it. Obviously, only he or someone else with a *copy* of his key can open the box.

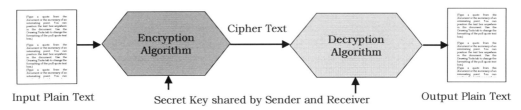

Input Plain Text   Secret Key shared by Sender and Receiver   Output Plain Text

The symmetric encryption scheme has five ingredients:

1. *Plaintext*: This is the original message or data that is fed into the algorithm as input.
2. *Encryption algorithm*: The encryption algorithm performs substitutions and transformations on the plaintext.
3. *Secret key*: The secret key is input to the encryption algorithm. The exact substitutions and transformations performed by the algorithm depend on the key.
4. *Cipher text*: This is the scrambled message produced as output. It depends on the plain text and the secret key. For a given message, two different keys will produce two different cipher texts.
5. *Decryption algorithm*: This is essentially the encryption algorithm run in reverse. It takes the cipher text and the secret key and produces the original plaintext.

15.13.1.3 How it works?

When using symmetric algorithms, both parties share the same key for *encryption* and *decryption*. To provide privacy, this key needs to be *kept secret*. Once somebody else gets to know the key, it is not safe anymore.

15.13.1.4 Requirements for Symmetric Key Cryptosystems

There are two requirements for a symmetric key cryptosystem:

1. It should not be possible to decrypt a message based on the *ciphertext* plus *knowledge* of the encryption/decryption algorithm. That means, we do not need to keep the algorithm secret; we need to keep only the key secret.
2. Sender and the receiver must have obtained copies of the secret key in a secure fashion and must keep the key secure. If someone can *discover* the key and knows the algorithm, all communications using this key is *readable*.

15.13.1.5 Advantages of Symmetric Key Cryptosystems

Advantages of symmetric key cryptosystem are:

- *Simple*: Symmetric key encryption is easy to carry out. All we have to do is specify and share the secret key and then begin to encrypt and decrypt messages.
- Encrypt and decrypt *your own* files: If you use encryption for messages or files which you alone intend to access, there is no need to create different keys. Single-key encryption is best for this.
- *Fast*: Symmetric key encryption is much faster than asymmetric key encryption.
- Uses *less* computer *resources*: Single-key encryption does not require a lot of computer resources compared to public key encryption.
- Prevents widespread message security compromise: A *different* secret key is used for communication with every different party. If a key is *compromised*, only the messages between a particular pair of sender and receiver are affected. Communications with other people are still *secure*.

15.13.1.6 Disadvantages of Symmetric Key Cryptosystems

Disadvantages of symmetric key cryptosystem are:

- Need a *secure channel* for secret key exchange: Sharing the secret key in the beginning is a problem in symmetric key encryption. It has to be exchanged in a way that ensures it remains secret.
- *Too many* keys: A new shared key has to be generated for communication with every different party. This creates a problem with managing and ensuring the security of all these keys.
- *Origin* and *authenticity* of message cannot be guaranteed: Since both sender and receiver use the same key, messages cannot be verified to have come from a particular user. This may be a problem if there is a dispute between the communication parties.

15.13.1.7 Symmetric Key Encryption Algorithms

15.13.1.7.1 Vernam Cipher [One-Time Pads]

Gilbert Vernam invented and patented his cipher in 1917 while he was working at AT&T. Vernam used a bit-wise exclusive ($\oplus$) or of the message stream with a truly random zero-one stream which was shared by sender and recipient. Vernam Cipher is also called the *one-time-pad*.

Example:

Sending		Receiving	
Message:	0 0 1 0 1 1 0 1 0 1 0 1 ...	*Cipher*:	1 0 1 1 1 0 0 1 1 1 1 0 ...
Pad:	1 0 0 1 0 1 0 0 1 0 1 1 ...	*Pad*:	1 0 0 1 1 1 0 0 1 0 1 1 ...
XOR	--------------------------	*XOR*	--------------------------
Cipher:	1 0 1 1 1 0 0 1 1 1 1 0 ...	*Message*:	0 0 1 0 1 1 0 1 0 1 0 1 ...

This cipher is a very strong cipher. The intuition is that any message can be transformed into any cipher (of the same length) by a pad, and all transformations are equally likely. Given a two letter message, there is a pad which adds to the message to give OK, and another pad which adds to the message to give NO. Since either of these pads are equally likely, the message is equally likely to be OK or NO.

15.13.1.7.2 Rivest Cipher #4 (RC4)

Ron Rivest originally designed RC4 in 1987 when he was working for RSA Security. In security industry, people refer *RC* shortcode as *Ron's Code*.

When RC4 was first developed, it was a proprietary algorithm; however, the code was leaked to several locations online and in email starting in September of 1994. Since the algorithm is now known, it is no longer considered to be a secret.

RC4 is an example for *stream* cipher and uses a *variable size* key.

15.13.1.7.4 Data Encryption Standard (DES)

The Data Encryption Standard (DES) is a block cipher that uses shared secret encryption. DES originated at IBM in 1977 and was adopted by the U.S. Department of Defense.

DES is now considered to be insecure for many applications. This is mainly due to the 56-bit key size being too small. In January, 1999, distributed.net and the Electronic Frontier Foundation collaborated to publicly break a DES key in 22 hours and 15 minutes.

The algorithm is believed to be practically secure in the form of *DES*, *although* there are theoretical attacks. In recent years, the cipher has been superseded by the *Advanced Encryption Standard* (AES). Also, DES has been withdrawn as a standard by the National Institute of Standards and Technology (NIST).

15.13.1.7.5 International Data Encryption Algorithm (IDEA)

IDEA (International Data Encryption Algorithm) is an encryption algorithm developed in Zurich, Switzerland. It uses a block cipher with a 128-bit key.

It is generally considered to be very secure and best publicly known algorithms. In the several years that it has been in use, no practical attacks on it have been published despite of a number of attempts to find some.

It is more efficient to implement in software than DES and triple DES. Since it was not developed in the United States, it is not subject to U.S. export restrictions.

15.13.1.7.6 SKIPJACK

Skipjack is an example for block cipher developed by the U.S. National Security Agency (NSA). *Skipjack* supports a 64-bit *block* size and a 80-bit key. The block is internally divided into *four* 16-bit words.

15.13.2 Asymmetric Key Encryption [Public-Key Encryption]

15.13.2.1 Introduction

Asymmetric key encryption is called as *public key* encryption. This method of encrypting messages makes use of *two* keys:

- Public key and
- Private key

The keys' names describe their function. One key is kept private, and the other key is made public. Knowing the public key does not reveal the private key. A message encrypted by the private key can only be decrypted by the corresponding public key.

Conversely, a message encrypted by the public key can only be decrypted by the private key.

Any user who wants to send an encrypted message can get the intended recipient's *public* key from a *public* directory. They use this key to encrypt the message, and send it to the recipient. When the recipient gets the message, they decrypt it with their private key, which no one else should have access to.

For centuries, all cryptography was based on the symmetric key cryptosystems. Then in 1976, two computer scientists, *Whitfield Diffe* and *Martin Hellman* of *Stanford University*, introduced the concept of asymmetric cryptography.

15.13.2.2 Components of Asymmetric Key Encryption

In asymmetric-*key* cryptography, the *public* and *private* key pair comprise of two uniquely related keys (basically long random numbers). Below is an example of a public key:

3048 0241 00C9 18FA CF8D EB2D EFD5 FD37 89B9 E069 EA97 FC20 5E35 F577 EE31 C4FB C6E4
4811 7D86 BC8F BAFA 362F 922B F01B 2F40 C744 2654 C0DD 2881 D673 CA2B 4003 C266 E2CD
CB02 0301 0001

The *public* key is what its name suggests - *public*. It is made available to everyone. Whereas, the *private key* must remain confidential to its respective owner.

Because the key pair is mathematically related, whatever is encrypted with a *public* key may only be decrypted by its corresponding *private* key and vice versa.

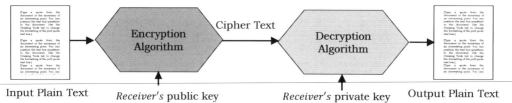

Input Plain Text   *Receiver's* public key   *Receiver's* private key   Output Plain Text

The symmetric encryption scheme has five ingredients:

1. *Plaintext*: This is the original message or data that is fed into the algorithm as input.
2. *Encryption algorithm*: The encryption algorithm performs substitutions and transformations on the plaintext.
3. *Public* and *private keys*: *Public* key is what its name suggests - *public*. It is available to everyone. Whereas, the *private key* must remain *confidential* to its *respective* owner. The exact substitutions and transformations performed by the algorithm depend on the key.
4. *Cipher text*: This is the scrambled message produced as output. It depends on the plain text and the secret key. For a given message, two different keys will produce two different cipher texts.
5. *Decryption algorithm*: This is essentially the encryption algorithm run in reverse. It takes the cipher text and the secret key and produces the original plaintext.

15.13.2.3 How it works?

Authentication: Anyone may encrypt a message using the public key, but only the owner of the private key is able to read it. In this way, *Ram* may send private messages to the owner of a key-pair (*Alice*) by encrypting it using *Alice's* public key. Only the *Alice* can decrypt it.

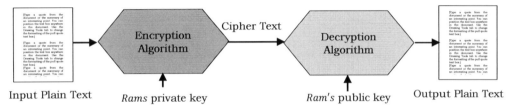

Input Plain Text   *Rams* private key   *Ram's* public key   Output Plain Text

Confidentiality: For example, if *Ram* wants to send sensitive data to *Mary*, and wants to be sure that only *Mary* may be able to read it, he will encrypt the data with *Mary's public* key. Only *Mary* has access to her corresponding private key and as a result is the only person with the capability of decrypting the encrypted data back into its original form.

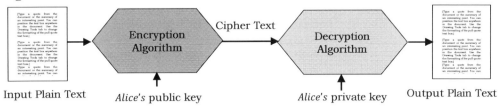

Input Plain Text   *Alice's* public key   *Alice's* private key   Output Plain Text

As only *Mary* has access to her *private* key, it is possible that only *Ram* can decrypt the encrypted data. Even if someone else gains access to the encrypted data, it will remain confidential as they should not have access to *Mary's private* key. Public key cryptography can therefore achieve Confidentiality.

15.13.2.4 Requirements of Asymmetric Key Encryption

Requirements for public-key cryptography are:

1. It should be computationally *easy* for a communication partner (either *sender* or *receiver*) to generate a pair (public key , private key).
2. It should be computationally *easy* for a sender, knowing the public key of *receiver* and the *message* to generate a *ciphertext*.
3. It should be computationally *easy* for the *receiver* to decrypt the resulting ciphertext using his/her private key.
4. It should be computationally *difficult* for anyone, knowing the public key, to determine the private key.
5. Either of the two related keys can be used for encryption, with the *other* used for *decryption*.

15.13.2.5 Advantages of Asymmetric Key Encryption

Advantages of asymmetric key cryptosystem are:

- *Convenience*: It solves the problem of distributing the key for encryption. Everyone publishes their public keys and private keys are kept secret.
- Provides for message *authentication*: Public key encryption allows the use of digital signatures which enables the recipient of a message to verify that the message is truly from a particular sender.
- *Detection* of *tampering*: The use of digital signatures in public key encryption allows the receiver to detect if the message was altered in transit. A digitally signed message cannot be modified without invalidating the signature.
- Provides *non-repudiation*: Digitally signing a message is akin to physically signing a document. It is an acknowledgement of the message and thus, the sender cannot deny it.

15.13.2.6 Disadvantages of Asymmetric Key Encryption

Disadvantages of asymmetric key cryptosystem are:

- *Public* keys must be *authenticated*: No one can be absolutely sure that a public key belongs to the person it specifies and so everyone must verify that their public keys belong to them.
- *Slow*: Public key encryption is slow compared to symmetric encryption. Not feasible for use in decrypting bulk messages.
- Uses *more* computer *resources*: It requires a lot more computer supplies compared to single-key encryption.
- Widespread security *compromise* is *possible*: If an attacker determines a person's private key, his or her entire messages can be read.
- Loss of private key may be *impossible* to *repair*: The loss of a private key means that all received messages cannot be decrypted.

15.13.2.7 Asymmetric Key Encryption Algorithms

15.13.2.7.1 Diffie-Hellman

Diffie–Hellman key exchange (D–H) is a specific method of exchanging keys. It is one of the earliest *practical* examples of key exchange implemented within the field of cryptography.

The Diffie–Hellman key exchange method allows two parties that have no prior knowledge of each other to jointly establish a shared secret key over an insecure communications channel. This key can then be used to encrypt subsequent communications using a symmetric key cipher.

The scheme was first invented by *Whitfield Diffie* and *Martin Hellman* in 1976. In 2002, *Hellman* suggested the algorithm be called *Diffie–Hellman–Merkle* key exchange in recognition of *Ralph Merkle's* contribution to the invention of public-key cryptography.

15.13.2.7.2 RSA

The RSA is a public key algorithm developed by Ron Rivest, Adi Shamir, and Len Adelman at Massachusetts Institute of Technology (MIT). To generate keys, RSA algorithm multiplies large prime numbers.

Its strength lies in the fact that it is extremely difficult to factor the product of large prime numbers. This algorithm is one of the most well-known public key encryption algorithms. The RSA also provides digital signature capabilities.

15.13.2.7.3 Digital Signature Algorithm (DSA)

DSA was developed as part of the Digital Signature Standard (DSS). Unlike the *Diffie-Hellman* and RSA algorithms, DSA is not used for encryption but for digital signatures. Refer *Digital Signatures* section for more details.

15.14 Hashing: Message Integrity

In cryptography, a hash function is a function that takes an arbitrary size data (plain text) and returns a *fixed-size* bit string called *message digest*. Any change to the data will change the *digest*. The closest real-life example we can think is *a tamper – evident seal on a software package*: if we open the box (change the file), it's detected.

Input Plain Text

15.14.1 Examples of Cryptographic Hash Functions

There are a large number of cryptographic hash algorithms and it's not always obvious which one should be used. In 1990, *Rivest* invented the hash function MD4. In 1992, he improved on MD4 and developed another hash function: MD5. In 1993, the National Security Agency (NSA) published a hash function very similar to MD5, called the Secure Hash Algorithm (SHA). Then in 1995, the NSA made a change to SHA. The new algorithm was called SHA-1. Today, the most popular hash function is SHA-1, with MD5 still being used in older applications.

Breaking a hash function means showing that two messages getting same hash code (same message digests for two different messages). On other words, getting a collision for two different input plain texts is nothing but breaking a hash function.

Security researches announced some pretty impressive cryptographic results against MD5 and SHA-1. Collisions have been demonstrated in MD5 and SHA-1. It's time for us all to migrate away from SHA-1. Luckily, there are alternatives which are harder-to-break hash functions: SHA-224, SHA-256, SHA-384 and SHA-512.

15.14.2 Examples of Hashes at Work

Let's first see some examples of hashes at work. Many Unix and Linux systems provide the *md5sum* program, which reads a stream of data and produces a fixed, 128-bit number that summarizes that stream using the popular *MD5* method. Here, the *streams of data* are *files* (two of which we see directly, plus one that's too large to display).

```
$ cat smallTestFile
This is a very small file with a few characters
```

```
$ cat bigTestFile
This is a larger file that contains more characters. This demonstrates that no matter how big the input stream is, the generated hash is the same size (but
of course, not the same value). If two files have a different hash, they surely contain different data.
```

```
$ ls -l smallTestFile bigTestFile
-rw-rw-r--   1 monk     monk        48 2013-08-20 08:48 smallTestfile
-rw-rw-r--   1 monk     monk       260 2013-08-20 08:48 bigTestFile
```

```
$ md5sum smallTestfile bigTestFile
75cdbfeb70a06d42210938da88c42991  smallTestfile
6e0b7a1676ec0279139b3f39bd65e41a  bigTestFile
```

This shows that all input streams gives hashes of the *same* length, and to experiment, try changing just one character of a small test file.

15.14.3 Avalanche Effect

Also, we will find that even a very small change to the input gives big changes in the value of the hash, and this is known as the *avalanche effect*. The avalanche effect can be best seen by hashing two files with nearly identical content. We've changed the first character of a file from T to t, and when looking at the binary values for these ASCII characters, we see that they differ by just one bit:

```
T -> 0x54 -> 0 1 0 1  0 1 0 0
t -> 0x74 -> 0 1 1 1  0 1 0 0
```

This single bit of change in the input produces a very large change in the output:

```
$ cat file1
This is a very small file with a few characters
```

```
$ cat file2
this is a very small file with a few characters
```

```
$ md5sum file1 file2
75cdbfeb70a06d42210938da88c42991  file1
6fbe37f1eea0f802bd792ea885cd03e2  file2
```

15.14.4 Requirements for Cryptographic Hash Function

An ideal cryptographic hash function has four main properties:

- It should be easy to compute the hash value for any given message
- It should be infeasible to generate a message that has a given hash
- It should be infeasible to modify a message without changing the hash
- It should be infeasible to find two different messages with the same hash

15.14.5 Hashes are not Encryption

This is a common confusion, especially because all these words are in the category of cryptography, but it's important to understand the difference. Encryption transforms data from a *plain input text* to *cipher text* and back (given the right keys), and the two texts should roughly correspond to each other in size: *big plain* text gives *big cipher* text, and so on.

Encryption is a two-way operation. That means, the *original* message can be determined from its *cipher* text form using decryption algorithm.

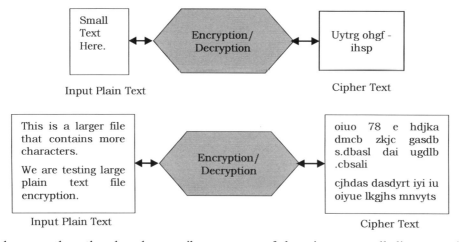

Hashes, on the other hand, compile a stream of data into a small digest, and it's strictly a one way operation. All hashes of the same type - this example show the MD5 variety - have the *same* size no matter how big the inputs are.

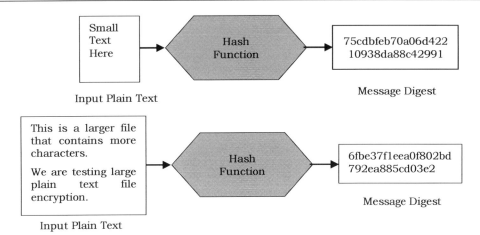

15.14.6 How they work?

The same hash function is used by both sender and receiver to verify the message. For example, the sending computer uses a hash function and *shared* key to compute the checksum for the message, including it with the packet. The receiving computer performs the *same* hash function on the received message and shared key and compare it to the original (included in the packet from the sender). If the message has changed in transmission, the hash values are *different* and the packet is *rejected*.

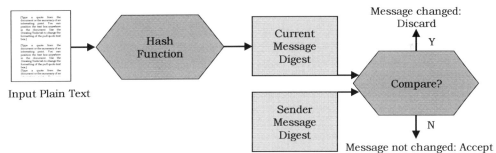

15.14.6.1 MD4

MD4 was developed by Ron Rivest when he was working at RSA. MD4 is an example for one-way hash function. It takes a message of variable length and produces a 128-bit message digest. MD4 has been proven to have weaknesses.

15.14.6.2 MD5

MD5 was also created by Ron Rivest as an improvement on MD4. Like MD4, MD5 creates a unique 128-bit message digest derived from the message. This value, which is a fingerprint of the message, is used to verify the integrity of the message.

If a message or file is modified in any way, even a single bit, the MD5 cryptographic checksum for the message or file will be different. It is considered very difficult to alter a message or file in a way that will cause MD5 to generate the same result as was obtained for the original file.

While MD5 is more secure than MD4, it too has been found to have some weaknesses.

15.14.6.3 SHA-1

SHA-1 is a one-way hash algorithm used to create digital signatures. SHA-1 is derived from SHA, which was developed in 1994 by the NIST. SHA-1 is similar to the MD4 and MD5 algorithms developed by Ron Rivest. SHA-1 is slightly slower than MD4 and MD5, but it is reported to be more secure.

The SHA-1 hash function produces a 160-bit hash value or message digest. I am aware of no known cryptographic attacks against SHA-1 that have been successful. Since it produces a 160-bit message digest it is more resistant to brute force attacks than MD4 and MD5, which produce a 128-bit message digest.

15.15 Digital Signatures

15.15.1 Introduction

The major objective of digital signatures was to *simulate* the handwritten signatures we are seeing every day. Singing the documents normally indicates that the signer has read and agreed with all of the statements made on the paper. Signatures are such a *daily* circumstance observed in our lives. We rarely take for granted that they are used in transferring money through checks and credit cards; acting as identification on driver's licenses; or even acting as *proof* that a document has been read, understood and agreed to.

To minimize operational costs and provide enhanced services; applications such as banking, and stock trading are enabling the customers to go with electronic transactions. This has led to heavy increase in the amounts of electronic documents that are generated, processed, and stored in computers and transmitted over networks. The electronic information in these applications is *valuable* and *sensitive* and must be protected against attackers.

Traditionally, paper documents are validated and certified by written signatures, which work fairly well to provide authenticity. For electronic documents, a similar mechanism is needed. *Digital signatures*, which are nothing but a string of *ones* and *zeroes* generated by using a digital signature algorithm, serve the purpose of validation and authentication of electronic documents.

Validation refers to the process of certifying the contents of the document, and *authentication* refers to the process of certifying the sender of the document. In this article, the terms document and message are used interchangeably.

15.15.2 Characteristics of Conventional and Digital Signatures

A conventional signature has the following salient characteristics:

- Relative ease of establishing that the signature is authentic,
- Difficulty of forging a signature,
- Non-transferability of the signature,
- Difficulty of altering the signature, and
- Nonrepudiation of signature to ensure that the signer cannot later deny signing.

A digital signature should have *all* the above *features* of a conventional signature *plus* a few more as digital signatures are being used in practical, but sensitive, applications such as secure e-mail and credit card transactions over the Internet.

Since a digital signature is just a sequence of zeroes and ones, it is desirable for it to have the following properties:

- Signature must be a bit pattern that depends on the message being signed (so, for the same originator, the digital signature is different for different documents).
- Signature must use some information that is unique to the sender (*signer*) to prevent forgery and denial.
- It must be relatively easy to produce.
- It must be relatively easy to recognize and verify the authenticity of digital signature.
- It must be computationally infeasible to forge a digital signature *either* by constructing a new message for an existing digital signature *or* constructing a fraudulent digital signature for a given message.

To verify that the received document is from the *claimed* sender and that the contents have not been modified; several procedures have been developed, and they are called *authentication* techniques.

However, message authentication techniques cannot be directly used as digital signatures due to *inadequacies* of authentication techniques. For example, although message authentication protects the two parties exchanging messages from a third party, it does not protect the two communication parties against each other.

In addition, basic authentication techniques produce signatures that are as long as the message themselves.

15.15.3 Basic Idea and Terminology

The *idea* behind digital signature is the same as the handwritten signature. A digital signature doesn't involve signing something with a pen and paper then sending to the receiver. But like a paper signature, it attaches the identity of the signer to a transaction.

Digital signatures are computed based on the documents (*message/information*) that need to be signed and on some private information held only by the *sender* (*signer*).

A hash function is applied to the whole message to obtain the *message digest*. Instead of using part of the message, hash function is applied to the whole message. A hash function takes an arbitrary-sized message as input and produces a fixed-size *message digest* as output.

Among the commonly used hash functions in practice are:

1. MD-5 (message digest 5): MD5 is a message digest algorithm designed by *Professor Ronald Rivest* of MIT in 1992. In December 2008, a group of researchers used this technique to fake SSL certificate validity and says that MD5 should be considered *cryptographically broken* and unsuitable for further use.
2. SHA (secure hash algorithm): The Secure Hash Algorithm is a family of cryptographic hash functions designed by the National Institute of Standards and Technology (NIST).

As of now, *secure hash algorithms* are fairly sophisticated and ensure that it is highly improbable for two different messages to be mapped to the same hash value.

There are *two* broad techniques used in digital signature computation—symmetric key cryptosystem and public-key cryptosystem.

Symmetric key system: In the symmetric key system, a secret key known only to the sender and the legitimate receiver is used. However, there must be a unique key between any two pairs of users. Thus, as the number of user pairs increases, it becomes difficult to generate, distribute, and keep track of the secret keys.

Public (Symmetric) key cryptosystem: A public key cryptosystem uses a pair of keys: a *private* key, known only to its owner, and a public key, known to everyone who wants to communicate with the owner.

- For *confidentiality* of the message to be sent to the owner (for sending messages to owner), it would be encrypted with the owner's public key. That could only be decrypted by the owner (since, only owner has the private key).
- For purposes of *authentication*, a message would be encrypted with the private key of the sender. This message could be decrypted by anyone using the public key of sender. If this gives the proper message, then it is evident that the message was indeed encrypted by the private key of sender, and thus only sender could have sent it.

A digital signature looks like a random series of numbers and alphabetical characters. Each signature is unique because it uses the content of the electronic document to create the character string. An example of a digital signature is:

--------- BEGIN SIGNATURE ---------

idkflkmejsdaoiB441klklk08+kadlkdflioe993+1alkfdlasd4ksrlk41ksafj81kadfkl61ardlfj+kd akljfl61adfldfjl+adfsdfddf+

--------- END SIGNATURE---------

15.15.4 Creating a Digital Signature

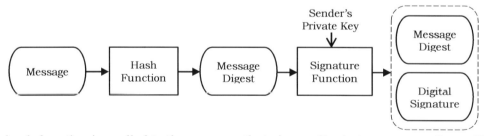

A hash function is applied to the message that gives a *fixed-size* message *digest*. The *signature* function uses the message digest and the *sender's* private key to generate the *digital signature*. The message and the signature can now be sent to the recipient. The message is unencrypted and can be read by anyone. However, the signature ensures authenticity of the sender (something similar to a circular sent by a proper authority to be read by many people, with the signature *attesting* to the authenticity of the message).

15.15.5 Verifying a Digital Signature

At the receiver, the inverse signature function is applied to the digital signature to recover the *original message* digest. The received message is subjected to the same hash function to which the original message was subjected. The resulting message digest is *compared* with the one recovered from the digital signature. If they match, then it ensures that the message has been sent by the (*claimed*) *sender* and that it has not been modified.

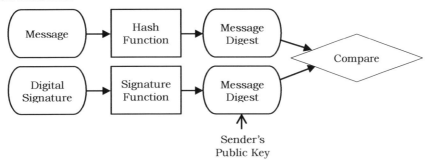

15.15.6 Creating a Digital Envelope

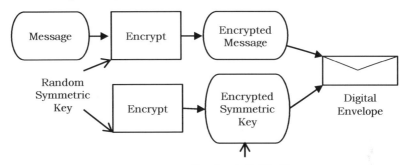

A digital envelope is the equivalent of a sealed envelope containing an unsigned letter. The outline of creating a digital envelope is shown in figure. The message is encrypted by the sender using a randomly generated symmetric key.

The symmetric key itself is encrypted using the intended recipient's public key. The combination of the encrypted message and the encrypted symmetric key is the digital envelope.

15.15.7 Opening a Digital Envelope

The process of opening the digital envelope and recovering the contents is shown in figure. First, the encrypted symmetric key is recovered by a decryption using the recipient's private key. Subsequently, the encrypted message is decrypted using the symmetric key.

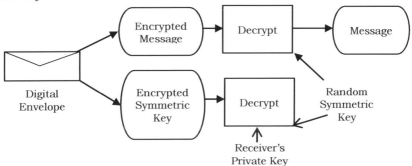

15.15.8 Creating Digital Envelopes Carrying Signed Messages

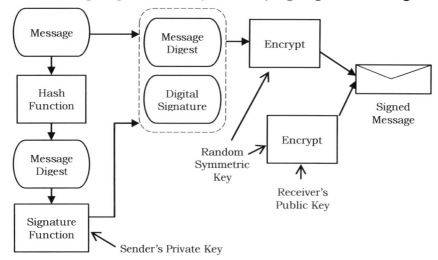

The process of creating a digital envelope containing a signed message is shown in figure. A digital signature is created by the signature function using the message digest of the message and the sender's private key.

The original message and the digital signature are then encrypted by the sender using a randomly generated key and a symmetric-key algorithm.

The symmetric key itself is encrypted using the recipient's public key. The combination of encrypted message and signature, together with the encrypted symmetric key, form the digital envelope containing the signed message.

15.15.9 Opening Digital Envelopes Carrying Signed Messages

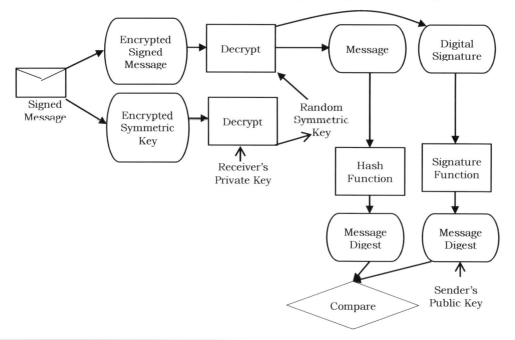

Figure shows the process of opening a digital envelope, recovering the message, and verifying the signature. First, the symmetric key is recovered using the recipient's private key. This is then used to decrypt and recover the message and the digital signature. The digital signature is then verified as described earlier.

15.15.10 Direct and Arbitrated Digital Signature

A variety of modes have been proposed for digital signatures that fall into two basic categories: *direct* and *arbitrated*.

The direct digital signature involves only the communication parties, sender and receiver. This is the simplest type of digital signature. It is assumed that the recipient knows the public key of the sender. In a simple scheme, a digital signature may be formed by encrypting the entire message or the hash code of the message with the sender's private key. Confidentiality can be provided by further encrypting the entire message plus signature with either the receiver's public key encryption or the shared secret key, which is conventional encryption.

A sender may later deny sending a particular message by claiming that the private key was lost or stolen and that someone else forged his signature. One way to overcome this is to include a time stamp with every message and requiring notification of loss of key to the proper authority. In case of dispute, a trusted third party may view the message and its signature to arbitrate the dispute.

In the *arbitrated* signature scheme, there is a trusted third party called the *arbiter*. Every signed message from a *sender* A to a *receiver* B goes first to an *arbiter* T, who subjects the message and its signature to a number of tests to check its origin and content. The message is then dated and sent to B with an indication that it has been verified to the satisfaction of the arbiter.

The presence of T solves the problem faced by direct signature schemes, namely that A might deny sending a message. The arbiter plays a sensitive and crucial role in this scheme, and all parties must trust that the arbitration mechanism is working properly. There are many variations of arbitrated digital-signature schemes. Some schemes allow the arbiter to see the messages, while others don't.

The particular scheme employed depends on the needs of the applications. Generally, an arbitrated digital-signature scheme has advantages over a direct digital-signature scheme such as the trust in communications between the parties provided by the trusted arbiter and in the arbitration of later disputes, if any.

15.15.11 A Public versus a Private Approach to Digital Signatures

Another way of classifying digital signature schemes is based on whether a private-key system or a public-key system is used. The public-key system based digital signatures have several advantages over the private-key system based digital signatures.

The two most popular and commonly used public-key system based digital signature schemes are the *RSA* (named after *Rivest*, *Shamir*, and *Aldeman*, the inventors of the RSA public-key encryption scheme) and the digital signature algorithm (*DSA*) approaches. The DSA is incorporated into the Digital Signature Standard (DSS), which was published by the National Institute of Standards and Technology.

RSA is a commonly used scheme for digital signatures. In RSA approach, the message to be signed is input to a hash function that produces a secure hash code of fixed length. This hash code is then encrypted using the sender's private key to form the signature. Both the signature and the message are then concatenated and transmitted.

The recipient takes the message and produces a hash code. The recipient also decrypts the signature using the sender's public key. If the calculated hash code matches the decrypted signature, the signature is accepted as valid.

This is because only the sender knows the private key, and thus only the sender could have produced a valid signature. The signature generation and verification using RSA is identical to the schemes discussed earlier.

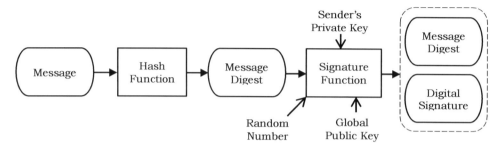

The signing process in DSS (using DSA) is shown in figure. The DSA approach also makes use of a hash function. The hash code is provided as input to a signature function together with a random number generated for this particular signature.

The signature function also uses the sender's private key and a set of parameters known to a group of communicating parties, referred to as global public key. The output signature consists of two components.

The signature verification process is shown in figure. At the receiving end, the hash code of the incoming message is generated and input to a verification function, together with the two components of the signature. The verification function uses the global public key as well as sender's public key and recreates (one of the two components of) the original digital signature. A *match* between the recreated and the original signature indicates the authenticity of the signature. The signature function is such that it assures the recipient that only the sender, with the knowledge of the private key, could have produced the valid signature.

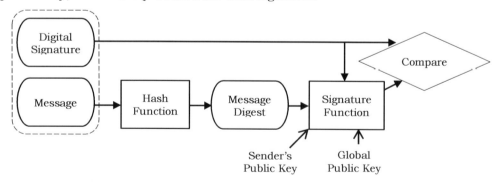

The basis of the RSA scheme is the difficulty of factoring of large prime numbers. That of the DSA scheme is the difficulty of computing discrete logarithms. The DSA provides only the signature function whereas the RSA scheme could additionally provide encryption and key exchange. The signature verification using the RSA scheme is about 100 times faster than a DSA scheme. The signature generation is slightly faster in the DSA scheme.

Work is underway for several extensions of the basic digital signature scheme such as enabling signatures by multiple parties (group digital signatures), signatures by a hierarchy of signatories, and protocols for simultaneous signing of contracts electronically by two or more signatories, separated by wide distances.

15.15.12 Digital Signatures in Real Applications

Increasingly, digital signatures are being used in secure e-mail and credit card transactions over the Internet. The two most common secure e-mail systems using digital signatures are Pretty Good Privacy and Secure/Multipurpose Internet Mail Extension. Both of these systems support the RSA as well as the DSS-based signatures. The most widely used system for the credit card transactions over the Internet is Secure Electronic Transaction (SET). It consists of a set of security protocols and formats to enable prior existing credit card payment infrastructure to work on the Internet. The digital signature scheme used in SET is similar to the RSA scheme.

15.16 Kerberos Authentication System

15.16.1 Introduction

Kerberos is an authentication protocol. The protocol gets its name from the three-headed dog (*Kerberos*) that guarded the gates of *Hades* in Greek mythology. It is an open source protocol, typically used as network security system in a client-server environment.

Kerberos was developed by *Project Athena*. It is a joint project between the Massachusetts Institute of Technology (MIT), Digital Equipment Corporation and IBM. The first public release of the protocol was Kerberos version 4. Following wide industry review of the protocol, its authors developed and released Kerberos version 5 with solutions to the problems that Kerberos version 4 has.

15.16.2 What is Kerberos?

The basic concept of Kerberos is *very simple*: If a secret is known by only two people, then either person can verify the identity of the other by confirming that the other person knows the secret.

As an example, let's suppose that Ram often sends messages to Mary and that Mary needs to be sure that a message from Ram really has come from Ram before she acts on its information. Also, assume that they have decided to solve their problem by selecting a password, and they agreed not to share this secret with anyone else. If Ram's messages can somehow demonstrate that the sender knows the password, Mary will know that the sender is Ram.

The only question left for Ram and Mary to resolve is how Ram will show that he knows the password. He could simply include it somewhere in his messages (say, a signature block at the end—*Ram, OurSecretCode*). This would be simple and efficient and might even work if Ram and Mary can be sure that no one else is reading their mail. Unfortunately, that is not the case. Their messages pass over a network used by attacker, who has a network analyzer and a hobby of scanning traffic in hope that one day he might find a password. So it is out of the question for Ram to prove that he knows the secret simply by saying it. To keep the password secret, he must show that he knows it without revealing it.

The Kerberos protocol solves this problem with *secret* key cryptography. Rather than sharing a password, they share a cryptographic *key*, and they use knowledge of this key to verify one another's identity. For the technique to work, the shared key must be symmetric—a single key must be capable of both encryption and decryption. One party proves knowledge of the key by encrypting a piece of information, the other by decrypting it.

Kerberos is an authentication protocol for *trusted hosts* on *untrusted networks*. Kerberos is a network protocol that uses *secret-key* cryptography (*symmetric* key cryptography) to authenticate client-server applications. The user's password does not have to pass through the network. It works by assigning a unique key (called a *ticket*) to each user that logs on to the network. The ticket is then embedded in messages to identify the sender of the message.

15.16.3 Aims of Kerberos

Before discussing the components of Kerberos, some of the aims of this are listed below:
- The user's password must not travel over the network.
- The user's password must not be stored in any form on the client machine: it must be immediately removed after being used.
- The user's password should never be stored (*not even* in an unencrypted form) in the authentication server database.
- The user is asked to enter a password only once per work session. Therefore users can transparently access all the services they are authorized for without having to re-enter the password during this session. This characteristic is called *Single Sign-On*.
- Authentication information resides on the authentication server. The application servers must not contain the authentication information for their users. This is essential for obtaining the following results.
  - The administrator can disable the account of any user by acting in a single location without having to act on the several application servers providing the various services.
  - When a user changes its password, it is changed for all services at the same time.
  - There is no redundancy of authentication information which would otherwise have to be safeguarded in various places.
- Not only do the users have to demonstrate that they are who they say, but, when requested, the application servers must prove their authenticity to the client as well. This property is called *mutual authentication*.

15.16.4 Components and Terms used in Kerberos

This section provides the definition of the objects and terms, knowledge of which is essential for the subsequent description of the Kerberos protocol.

15.16.4.1 Boundaries of Kerberos Authenticity: Realm

In English literature, realms indicates a community or territory over which a ruler rules. In Kerberos, the term *realm* (sometimes called *domain*) indicates an authentication administrative domain. A realm creates the boundaries within which an authentication server has the authority to authenticate a user, host or service.

Basically, a user/service belongs to a realm if and only if he/it shares a secret (password/key) with the authentication server of that realm.

While configuring the realm, remember that the name of a realm is case sensitive. That means, there is a difference between upper and lower case letters, but normally realms always appear in upper case letters. For example, if an organization belongs to the DNS domain *CareerMonk*.com, it is a practice to use the related Kerberos realm as CAREERMONK.COM.

15.16.4.2 Entries in Database: Principals

A principal is associated with each user, host or service of a given realm (domain). A principal is the name used to refer to the entries in the authentication server database. A principal in Kerberos 5 is of the following type:

component1/component2/.../componentN@REALM

However, in practice a maximum of two components are used. For an entry referring to a user the principal is the following type:

Name[/Instance]@REALM

The instance is optional and is used to tell the type of user. For example administrator users normally have the admin instance. The following are examples of principals referred to users:

info@CAREERMONK.COM
admin/admin@CAREERMONK.COM
hr/admin@CAREERMONK.COM

If the entries are services, then the principals will use the following form:

Service/Hostname@REALM

The first component is the name of the service (say, *ftp*). The second component is the complete hostname (FQDN: Fully Qualified Domain Name) of the machine providing the requested service. It is important that this component exactly matches (in lower case letters) the DNS reverse resolution of the application server's IP address. The following are valid examples of principals referring to services:

imap/mbox.careermonk.com@CAREERMONK.COM
host/server.careermonk.com@CAREERMONK.COM
afs/careermonk.com@CAREERMONK.COM

Finally, there are principals which do not refer to users or services but play a role in the operation of the authentication system. An overall example is *krbtgt/REALM@REALM* with its associated key is used to encrypt the Ticket Granting Ticket.

In Kerberos 4 there can never be more than two components and they are separated by the character "." instead of "/" while the hostname in the principals referring to services is the short one, i.e. not the FQDN. The following are valid examples:

info@CAREERMONK.COM
monk.admin@CAREERMONK.COM
imap.mbox@CAREERMONK.COM

15.16.4.3 Ticket

It is a record that helps a client to authenticate itself with a server. It contains the client's identity; a session key, a timestamp, and other needed information. This information is encrypted using server's secret key.

In other words, a ticket is a record that a client machine sends to an application server for its authenticity. Tickets are issued by the authentication server and are encrypted using the secret key of the service. Since this key is a secret shared only between the authentication server and the server providing the service, not even the client which requested the ticket can know it or change its contents. The main information contained in a ticket includes:

- The requesting user's principal (generally the username)
- The principal of the service it is intended for
- The IP address of the client machine from which the ticket can be used. In Kerberos 5 this field is optional and may also be multiple in order to be able to run clients under NAT
- The date and time (timestamp) when the tickets validity commences
- The ticket's maximum lifetime
- The session key

Each ticket has expiration (generally 10 hours). This is needed because the authentication server no longer has any control over an already issued ticket. Even though the realm administrator can prevent the issuing of new tickets for a certain user at any time, it cannot prevent users from using the tickets they already possess. Tickets contain a lot of other information and flags which characterize their behavior, but we won't go into that here.

15.16.4.4 Encryption

As you can see Kerberos often needs to encrypt and decrypt the messages (tickets and authenticators) passing between the various participants in the authentication. It is important to note that Kerberos uses only symmetrical key encryption (in other words the same key is used to encrypt and decrypt).

15.16.4.4.1 Encryption type

Kerberos 4 implements a single type of encryption which is DES at 56 bits. The weakness of this encryption algorithm has made Kerberos 4 obsolete. Kerberos 5 was developed to address this issue.

15.16.4.5 Authenticator

In secret key authentication, authentication begins when someone is outside a communications door and wants to go in. To gain entry, this person (say, client) presents an authenticator in the form of a piece of information encrypted in the secret key. The information in the authenticator must be different each time the protocol is executed; otherwise an old authenticator could be reused by attackers to overhear the communication.

On receiving an authenticator, the person guarding the door decrypts it. If it was successful, the doorkeeper knows that the person giving the authenticator has the correct key. Only two people have the correct key; the doorkeeper is one of them, so the person who presented the authenticator must be the other.

If the person outside the door wants mutual authentication, the same protocol can be executed in reverse, with a small difference. The doorkeeper can extract part of the information from the original authenticator, encrypt it in a new authenticator, and then give the new authenticator to the person waiting outside the door. The person outside the door can then decrypt the doorkeeper's authenticator and compare the result with the original. If there is a match, the person outside the door will know that the doorkeeper was able to decrypt the original, so he must have the correct key. This is called *mutual authentication*.

It will help if we go through an example. Suppose *Ram* and *Mary* decide that before transferring any information between their computers, each will use knowledge of a shared secret key to verify the identity of the party at the other end of the connection. They agree to follow this protocol:

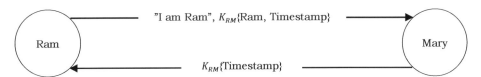

Note: K_{RM}: Secret key of Ram and Mary

1. Ram sends Mary a message containing his name in plaintext and an authenticator encrypted in the secret key he shares with Mary. In this protocol, the *authenticator* is a data structure with two fields. One field contains information about Ram. The second field contains the current time on Ram's machine.

2. Mary receives the message, sees that it is from someone claiming to be Ram, and uses the key she shares with Ram to decrypt the authenticator. She extracts the field that contains the time on Ram's machine, and evaluates the time.

   Mary's task will be easier if her clock is synchronized with Ram's. Assume that both Ram and Mary use a network time service to keep their clocks fairly close. This way, Mary can compare the time from the authenticator with the current time on her clock. If the time is within the allowable skew, it's probable that the authenticator came from Ram, but Mary still does not have proof that the authenticator actually came from him.

   Another person might have been watching network traffic and might now be replaying an earlier attempt by Ram to establish a connection with Mary. However, if Mary has recorded the times of authenticators received from Ram during the past five minutes, she can defeat attempts to replay earlier messages by rejecting any message with a time that is the same as or earlier than the time of the last authenticator. If this authenticator yields a time later than the time of the last authenticator from Ram, then this message must be from Ram.

3. Mary uses the key she shares with Ram to encrypt the time taken from Ram's message and sends the result back to him.

   Note that Mary does not send back all of the information taken from Ram's authenticator, just the time. If she sent back everything, Ram would have no way of knowing whether someone posing as Mary had simply copied the authenticator from his original message and sent it back to him unchanged. She sends just a piece of the information in order to demonstrate that she was able to decrypt the authenticator and manipulate the information inside. She chooses the time because that is the one piece of information that is sure to be unique in Ram's message to her.

4. Ram receives Mary's reply, decrypts it, and compares the result with the time in his original authenticator. If the times match, he can be confident that his authenticator reached someone who knows the secret key needed to decrypt it

and extract the time. He shares that key only with Mary, so it must be Mary who received his message and replied.

15.16.4.6 Key Distribution Center (KDC)

One problem with the simple protocol described in the previous section is that it does not explain how or where Ram and Mary got a secret key to use in sessions with each other. If they are people, Ram and Mary could meet and agree on a secret key. But that method will not work if Ram is a client program that is running on a workstation and Mary is a service that is running on a network server.

There is also the further problem that the client, Ram, will want to talk to many servers and will need keys for each of them. Likewise, the service, Mary, will talk to many clients and will need keys for each of them as well. If each client needs to have a key for every service, and each service needs one for every client, key distribution could quickly become a tough problem to solve. And the need to store and protect so many keys on so many computers would present an enormous security risk.

The *Key Distribution Center* (KDC) is a service that runs on a physically secure server. It maintains a database with account information for all security principals in its realm. Along with other information about each security principal, the KDC stores a cryptographic key known only to the security principal and the KDC. This key is used in exchanges between the security principal and the KDC and is known as a *long-term* key. In most implementations of the protocol, it is derived from a user's *logon password*.

When a client wants to talk to a server, the client sends a request to the KDC, and the KDC distributes a unique, *short-term session key* for the two parties to use when they authenticate each other. The server's copy of the session key is encrypted in the server's *long-term* key. The client's copy of the *session* key is encrypted in the client's *long-term* key.

Since it resides entirely on a single physical server it can be logically considered divided into three parts: *Database*, Authentication Server (AS) and Ticket Granting Server (TGS).

15.16.4.6.1 Session Key

The KDC responds to the client's request to talk to a server by sending both copies of the session key to the client. The client's copy of the session key is encrypted with the key that the KDC shares with the client. The server's copy of the session key is embedded, along with information about the client, in a data structure called a session ticket. The entire structure is then encrypted with the key that the KDC shares with the server. The ticket—with the server's copy of the session key safely inside—becomes the client's responsibility to manage until it contacts the server.

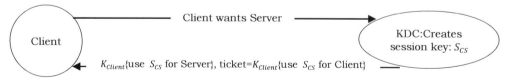

Key Distribution

Note that the KDC is simply providing a ticket-granting service. It does not keep track of its messages to make sure they reach the intended address. No harm will be done if the KDC's messages fall into the wrong hands. Only someone who knows the client's secret key can decrypt the client's copy of the session key. Only someone who knows the server's secret key can read what is inside the ticket.

When the client receives the KDC's reply, it extracts the ticket and the client's copy of the session key, putting both aside in a secure cache (located in volatile memory, not on disk). When the client wants admission to the server, it sends the server a message that consists of the ticket, which is still encrypted with the server's secret key, and an authenticator, which is encrypted with the session key. The ticket and authenticator together are the client's credentials to the server.

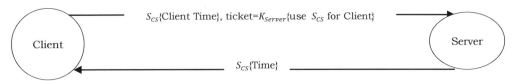

S_{CS}{Client Time}, ticket=K_{Server}{use S_{CS} for Client}

S_{CS}{Time}

Mutual authentication (Client/server)

When the server receives credentials from a client, it decrypts the session ticket with its secret key, extracts the session key, and uses the session key to decrypt the client's authenticator. If everything checks out, the server knows that the client's credentials were issued by a trusted authority, the KDC. If the client has asked for mutual authentication, the server uses its copy of the session key to encrypt the timestamp from the client's authenticator and returns the result to the client as the server's authenticator.

One benefit gained by using session tickets is that the server does not have to store the session key that it uses in communicating with this client. It is the client's responsibility to hold a ticket for the server in its credentials cache and present the ticket each time it wants access to the server. Whenever the server receives a session ticket from a client, it can use its secret key to decrypt the ticket and extract the session key. When the server no longer needs the session key, it can discard it.

Another benefit is that the client does not need to go back to the KDC each time it wants access to this particular server. Session tickets can be reused. As a precaution against the possibility that someone might steal a copy of a ticket, session tickets have an expiration time, specified by the KDC in the ticket's data structure. How long a ticket is valid depends on Kerberos policy for the domain. Typically, tickets are good for no longer than eight hours, about the length of a normal logon session. When the user logs off, the credentials cache is flushed and all session tickets—as well as all session keys—are destroyed.

15.16.4.6.2 Database

The database is the container for entries associated with users and services. We refer to an entry by using the *principal* (i.e. the name of the entry) even if often the term *principal* is used as a *synonym* for *entry*. Each entry contains the following information:

- The principal to which the entry is associated
- The encryption key and related *kvno* (Kerberos version number)
- The maximum validity duration for a ticket associated to the principal;
- The maximum time a ticket associated to the principal may be renewed (only Kerberos 5)
- The attributes or flags characterizing the behavior of the tickets
- The password expiration date

- The expiration date of the principal, after which no tickets will be issued

In order to make it more difficult to steal the keys present in the database, the implementations encrypt the database (including database backups).

15.16.4.6.3 Authentication Server (AS)

The Authentication Server (AS) is the part of the KDC and it replies to the initial authentication request from the client. In response to an authentication request, the AS sends a special ticket known as the *Ticket Granting Ticket* (TGT).

The principal associated with this is *krbtgt*/REALM@REALM. The users can use the TGT to get other *service tickets*, without having to re-enter their password.

15.16.4.6.4 Ticket Granting Server (TGS)

The Ticket Granting Server (TGS) is the KDC component which distributes service tickets to clients with a valid TGT. This guarantees the authenticity of the identity to get the requested resource on the application servers.

The TGS can be considered as an application server which provides the issuing of service tickets as a service. It is important not to confuse the abbreviations TGT and TGS: the *first* indicates a *ticket* and the *second* indicates a service.

15.16.5 Kerberos Operation: How it Works?

Finally, having acquired the concepts described in the preceding sections, it is possible to discuss how Kerberos operates. We'll do this by listing and describing each of the packets which go between the client and KDC and between client and application server during authentication. At this point, it is important to underline that an application server never communicates directly with the Key Distribution Center. The messages we will discuss are listed below (see also the figure below):

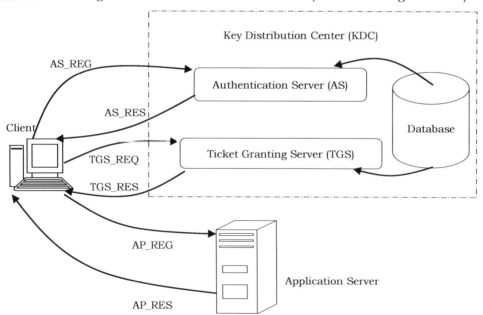

- *AS_REQ* is the initial user authentication request. This message is directed to the KDC component known as Authentication Server (AS);

- *AS_REP* is the reply of the Authentication Server to the previous request. Basically it contains the TGT (encrypted using the TGS secret key) and the session key (encrypted using the secret key of the requesting user);
- *TGS_REQ* is the request from the client to the Ticket Granting Server (TGS) for a service ticket. This packet includes the TGT obtained from the previous message and an authenticator generated by the client and encrypted with the session key;
- *TGS_REP* is the reply of the Ticket Granting Server to the previous request. Located inside is the requested service ticket (encrypted with the secret key of the service) and a service session key generated by TGS and encrypted using the previous session key generated by the AS;
- *AP_REQ* is the request that the client sends to an application server to access a service. The components are the service ticket obtained from TGS with the previous reply and an authenticator again generated by the client, but this time encrypted using the service session key (generated by TGS);
- *AP_REP* is the reply that the application server gives to the client to prove it really is the server the client is expecting. This packet is not always requested. The client requests the server for it only when mutual authentication is necessary.

15.16.6 Kerberos Subprotocols

The Kerberos protocol consists of three subprotocols.

1) *AS Exchange*: KDC gives the client a logon session key and a TGT.
2) *TGS Exchange*: KDC distributes a service session key and a session ticket for the service.
3) *CS Exchange*: Client presents the session ticket for admission to a service.

To see how the three subprotocols work together, let's look at how Ram, a user at a client, gets access to Mary, a service on the network.

15.16.6.1 AS Exchange

Ram begins by logging on to the network. He types his logon name and his password. The Kerberos client on Ram's machine converts his password to an encryption key and saves the result in its credentials cache.

The client then sends the KDC's authentication service a Kerberos Authentication Service Request (AS_REQ). The first part of this message identifies the user, Ram, and the name of the service for which he is requesting credentials, the ticket-granting service. The second part of the message contains *preauthentication* data that proves Ram knows the password. This is usually a timestamp encrypted with Ram's long-term key, although the protocol permits other forms of *preauthentication* data.

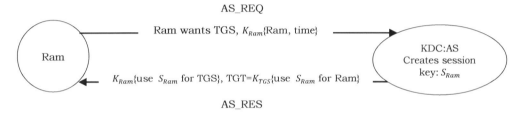

When the KDC receives AS_REQ, it looks up the user Ram in its database, gets his long-term key, decrypts the preauthentication data, and evaluates the timestamp inside. If the timestamp passes the test, the KDC can be assured that the preauthentication data was encrypted with Ram's long-term key and thus that the client is *genuine*.

After it has verified Ram's identity, the KDC creates *credentials* that the Kerberos client on his machine can present to the ticket-granting service. First, the KDC invents a logon session key and encrypts a copy of it with Ram's long-term key. Second, it embeds another copy of the logon session key in a TGT, along with other information about Ram such as his authorization data. The KDC encrypts the TGT with its own long-term key. Finally, it sends both the encrypted logon session key and the TGT back to the client in a Kerberos Authentication Service Reply (AS_REP).

When the client receives the message, it uses the key derived from Ram's password to decrypt his logon session key and stores the key in its credentials cache. Then it extracts the TGT from the message and stores that in its credentials cache as well.

15.16.6.2 TGS Exchange

The Kerberos client on Ram's machine requests credentials for the service Mary by sending the KDC a Kerberos Ticket-Granting Service Request (TGS_REQ). This message includes the user's name, an authenticator encrypted with the user's logon session key, the TGT obtained in the AS Exchange, and the name of the service for which the user wants a ticket.

TGS_REQ

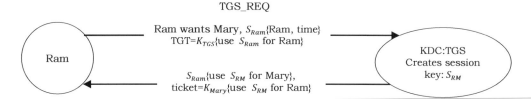

TGS_RES

When the KDC receives TGS_REQ, it decrypts the TGT with its own secret key, extracting Ram's logon session key. It uses the logon session key to decrypt the authenticator and evaluates that. If the authenticator passes the test, the KDC extracts Ram's authorization data from the TGT and invents a session key for the client, Ram, to share with the service, Mary.

The KDC encrypts one copy of this session key with Ram's logon session key. It embeds another copy of the session key in a ticket, along with Ram's authorization data, and encrypts the ticket with Mary's long-term key. The KDC then sends these credentials back to the client in a Kerberos Ticket-Granting Service Reply (TGS_REP).

When the client receives the reply, it uses Ram's logon session key to decrypt the session key to use with the service, and stores the key in its credentials cache. Then it extracts the ticket to the service and stores that in its cache.

15.16.6.3 CS Exchange

The Kerberos client on Ram's machine requests service from Mary by sending Mary a Kerberos Application Request (AP_REQ). This message contains an authenticator encrypted with the session key for the service, the ticket obtained in the TGS Exchange, and a flag indicating whether the client wants mutual authentication. (The setting of this flag is one of the options in configuring Kerberos. The user is never asked.)

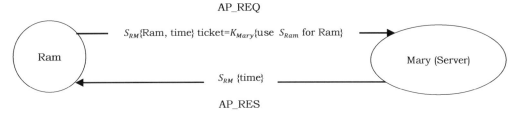

AP_REQ

S_{RM}{Ram, time} ticket=K_{Mary}{use S_{Ram} for Ram}

Ram

Mary (Server)

S_{RM} {time}

AP_RES

The service, Mary, receives AP_REQ, decrypts the ticket, and extracts Ram's authorization data and the session key. Mary uses the session key to decrypt Ram's authenticator and then evaluates the timestamp inside. If the authenticator passes the test, Mary looks for a mutual authentication flag in the client's request. If the flag is set, she uses the session key to encrypt the time from Ram's authenticator and returns the result in a Kerberos Application Reply (AP_REP).

When the client on Ram's machine receives AP_REP, it decrypts Mary's authenticator with the session key it shares with Mary and compares the time returned by the service with the time in the client's original authenticator. If the times match, the client knows that the service is genuine, and the connection proceeds. During the connection, the session key can be used to encrypt application data or the client and server can share another key for this purpose.

15.16.7 Problems with Kerberos

Even though Kerberos is robust, but it has few disadvantages as well.

- The protocol assumes a secure *storage* for the *passwords* in the authentication server, *compromising* them would provide entry to all the services.
- The tickets and the session keys must not be *cached* in the system. This could mean trouble in a multi user system, as wrong permission would enable a user to view his peer's session keys.
- Kerberos relies on *time stamps* in the authenticators to prevent replay attacks. So, it is necessary that the clocks of the machines in the distributed system must be synchronized. If a server can be misled about the correct time, stale ticket could be replayed and entry gained. Kerberos relies implicitly on the underlying formalism in the precision of clocks on the servers.
- Another problem with Kerberos is, if the attackers could *capture* the *login* of the user; then it would give access to all services. A solution to this weakness could be solved with the use of the challenge/response mechanism, where the server would generate the timestamp encrypted using client-key and the client would respond with some function of the timestamp proving its accuracy.
- Kerberos can be improved by *decoupling* the protocol from the encryption *algorithm* used. It is seen that with the faster desktops; the security offered by 56-bit DES algorithms is insufficient. The more sophisticated 128 bit AES algorithms give better security. By making Kerberos independent of the encryption algorithm, the above change would be seamless.

In *conclusion* Kerberos is a robust protocol for authentication and security though with drawbacks, its pros far out weight the cons.

15.16.8 Important Notes on Kerberos

The following are some important points we should remember about the Kerberos Authentication System:

- For the client to communicate with the server *tickets* are issued. The first ticket (initial ticket) is issued by the Kerberos Authentication Server to validate the Ticket Granting Server. All the *remaining tickets* will be issued by the TGS only.
- Tickets are reusable whereas a new authenticator is required every time the client initiates a new connection with the server.
- Every ticket is assigned a *unique session* key.
- The server should maintain a history of previous requests for which the timestamp in the authenticator is still valid. This helps the server to *reject duplicate* requests that could arise from a *stolen* ticket and authenticator.

15.17 Firewalls

15.17.1 Introduction

Firewall is an important aspect of the Internet and network security. Firewall is a familiar word for regular Internet users and for working people. You might have also heard of people saying *firewalls protect their computer from web attacks and hackersor a certain website has been blocked by firewall in their work place*. In this section, we try to understand the background of firewalls in layman's terms.

15.17.2 What is a Firewall?

The term firewall was derived from *civil engineering* and intended to *prevent* the*spread* of fire from one *room* to another. From the computer security perspective, the Internet is an unsafe environment; therefore *firewall* is an excellent metaphor for network security.

A firewall is a system designed to prevent unauthorized access to or from a private network. Firewalls can be implemented in either hardware or software form, or a combination of both. Firewalls prevent unauthorized users from accessing private networks. A firewall sits between the two networks, usually a private network and a public network such as the Internet.

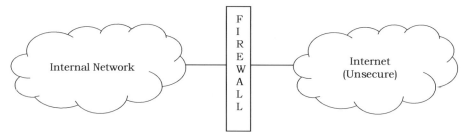

Connecting a computer or a network of computers may become targets for malicious software and hackers. A firewall can offer the security that makes a computer or a network less vulnerable.

The basic requirements of an effective firewall are:

1. All traffic must *pass* through it (both incoming and outgoing). This can be achieved by blocking all access to the LAN except via the firewall.
2. It must allow *only authorized* packets to pass.
3. It must be immune to penetration or compromise. That means, for the firewall we should use a secured operating system.

15.17.3 Advantages of Firewalls

Firewalls discard the unauthorized traffic from entering/leaving the local network. A firewall examines all the packets routed between the two networks to see if it meets certain criteria. If it does, it is routed between the networks, otherwise it is discarded. A firewall filters both incoming and outgoing traffic.

It can be used to log all attempts to enter the private network and trigger alarms when attacker or unauthorized entry is attempted. Firewalls can filter packets based on their source and destination addresses and port numbers. This is known as address filtering. Firewalls can also filter specific types of network traffic. This is also known as protocol filtering because the decision to forward or reject traffic is dependent upon the protocol used, for example *http*, *ftp* or *telnet*. Firewalls can also filter traffic by packet attribute or state.

A firewall can provide NAT for systems or networks that don't have an IP address. Firewalls are effective at maintaining logs of all activity that pass through, connections to, or attempts to connect to the system. These logs can be used to identify abnormal events.

15.17.4 Disadvantages of Firewalls

We all know what happens if we put all *eggs* in a *single box*! Firewalls also have a similar issue as it represents a single point of failure.

Success of firewalls depends on *configuration*. If we make a mistake configuring; it may allow unauthorized access.

If the *firewall* goes *down*; connection to the outside *network* is *down*. That means, DoS attack may take the network down by making firewall down.

Since firewall examines all the traffic going in and out; a firewall tends to degrade network *performance* (network throughput) between the outside network and the inside network.

A firewall by itself does *not* assure a *secure* network. A firewall is only a tool. Firewalls need to be configured properly, and they need to be monitored.

Firewalls cannot monitor internal traffic and hence *cannot* stop *attacks*. Employee misconduct or carelessness cannot be controlled by firewalls. Policies involving the use and misuse of passwords and user accounts must be strictly enforced.

When developing firewall access *policies*, there are two general approaches that can be employed. The first is to deny anything that is not explicitly allowed. The second is to allow that which is not explicitly denied. And, the first approach is the more secure.

15.17.5 How Firewalls Work?

Firewalls basically acts as a guard between a computer (or a *network*) and the Internet (outside unsecure world). A firewall can be simply compared to a security guard who stands at the entrance of house (or an organization) and filters the visitors coming to that place. He may allow some visitors to enter while denying others whom he suspects of being intruders.

Similarly a firewall is a *software program* or a *hardware device* that filters the information (packets) coming through the Internet to your personal computer or a computer network.

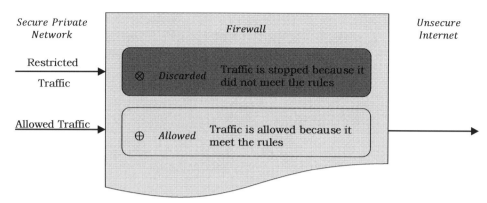

Firewalls may decide to allow or block network traffic between devices based on the rules that are pre-configured or set by the firewall administrator.

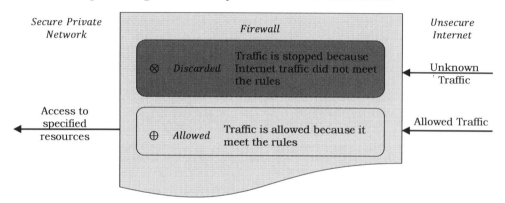

Personal firewalls are easy to install and use and preferred by end-users for use on their personal computers. But, large networks and companies prefer those firewalls that have plenty of options to configure so as to meet their customized needs.

For example, a company may set up different firewall rules for *ftp* servers, *telnet* servers and Web servers. Also, the company can even control how the employees connect to the Internet by blocking access to certain websites or restricting the transfer of files to other networks. In addition to security, a firewall can give the company a tremendous control over how people use the network.

15.17.6 Types of Firewalls

As discussed, firewalls can be implemented in either *hardware* or *software* form. Firewalls can be classified in *several different* ways. Different firewalls operate at different levels. They can be classified by the general approach they employ, or by the layer of the OSI reference model at which they operate, by the technology they implement.

Based on the approaches used by firewalls, we can classify them into two different categories:

1. Filtering firewalls
2. Proxy firewalls

Based on the level of the OSI reference model at which they operate, we can classify them into three different categories:

1. Network level firewalls (packet filtering firewalls)
2. Application level firewalls (proxy server firewalls)
3. Circuit level firewalls (proxy server firewalls)

15.17.6.1 Hardware and Software Firewalls

15.17.6.1.1 Hardware Firewalls

Hardware firewalls provide higher level of security and are *preferred* for *servers* where security has the top most priority.

In general, hardware firewalls come as an in-built unit of a *router* and gives maximum security as it filters each packet in the hardware level itself before it manages to enter your computer.

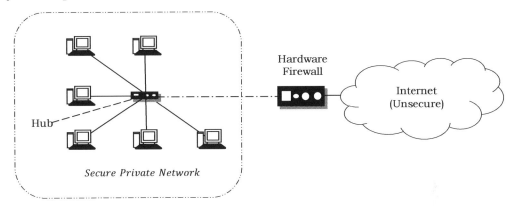

Hardware firewalls are more complex. They also have software components, but run either on a specially engineered network appliance or on an optimized server dedicated to the task of running the firewall. The operating system underlying a hardware firewall is as basic as possible and very difficult to attack. Since no other software runs on these machines, and configuration is little more complicated. These are difficult to compromise and tend to be extremely secure.

A hardware firewall is placed between a local network (such as a corporation), and a less secure area (such as the Internet). There are many different default configurations for these devices - some allow no communications from the outside and must be configured, using rules, others (like those available for the home market) are already configured to block access over risky ports. Rules can be as simple as allowing port 80 traffic to flow through the firewall in both directions, or as complex as only allowing 1433 (SQL server) traffic from a specific IP address outside of the network through the firewall to a single IP address inside the network.

Firewalls are also used for Network Address Translation (NAT). This allows a network to use private IP addresses that are not routed over the Internet. Private IP address schemes allow organizations to limit the number of publicly routed IP addresses they use, reserving public addresses for Web servers and other externally accessed network equipment. NAT allows administrators to use one public IP address for all of their users to access the Internet - the firewall is *smart* enough to send the requests back to the requesting workstation's internal IP. NAT also allows users inside a network to contact a server using a private IP while users outside the network must contact the same server using an external IP.

In addition to port and IP address rules, firewalls can have a wide variety of functionality. They can also act as caching servers, VPNs, routers, and more. Some examples of hardware firewalls are *CheckPoint*, *Cisco PIX*, *SonicWall*, and *Contivity* from *Nortel*.

15.17.6.1.2 Software Firewalls

Software firewalls are less expensive and hence preferred in home computers and laptops. Software firewalls are also called *personal firewalls* because they are installed on individual computers. A software firewall prevents unwanted access to the computer over a network connection by identifying and preventing communication over risky *ports*. Computers communicate over many different recognized ports, and the firewall will tend to permit these without prompting or alerting the user.

For example, computers access Web pages over port 80 (http) and use port 443 for secure Web communications (https). A home computer would expect to receive data over these ports. However, a software firewall would block any access from the Internet over port 421. Software firewalls can also detect *suspicious* activity from the outside.

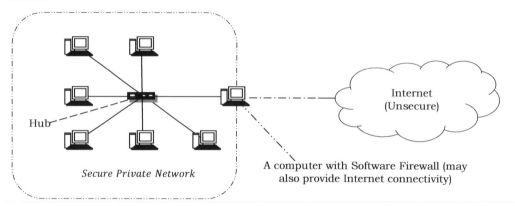

Secure Private Network

A computer with Software Firewall (may also provide Internet connectivity)

A software firewall also allows certain programs on the user's computer to access the Internet, often by express permission of the user. Windows Update, and antivirus software are a few programs that a user might expect to access the Internet.

One drawback to software firewalls is that they are software running on a personal computer operating system. If the underlying operating system is compromised, then the firewall can be compromised as well. Since many other programs also run on a home computer, malicious software could potentially enter the computer through some other application and compromise the firewall.

Software firewalls also rely heavily upon the user making the right decisions. If someone using a software firewall mistakenly gives a keylogger or a Trojan permission to access the Internet, security on that machine is compromised even though there is nothing wrong with the firewall itself.

15.17.6.2 Network Level Firewalls

Network level firewalls operate at the network level of the OSI reference model. In general, network level firewalls monitors all packets and screens (filters) them. Network level firewalls are sub categorized into two different filtering approaches:

1. Static packet filtering
2. Dynamic packet filtering/stateful inspection

15.17.6.2.1 Static Packet Filtering

A static packet filtering firewall (sometimes simply called as packet filtering firewall) uses a process of filtering incoming and outgoing packets to discard or authorize access. Packet filtering firewalls work at the network level of the OSI model (*or* the IP layer of TCP/IP). Generally, they are part of a router firewall. A *router* is a device that receives packets from one network and forwards them to another.

In a packet filtering firewall, each packet is compared to a set of *criteria* (*rules*) before it is forwarded. Depending on the packet and the criteria, the firewall can *drop* the packet, *forward* it, or *send* a message to the originator.

Packet filtering policies may be based upon any of the following:

- Allowing or disallowing packets on the basis of the source IP address
- Allowing or disallowing packets on the basis of their destination port
- Allowing or disallowing packets according to protocol.

The advantage of packet filtering firewalls is their *low cost* and *low* impact on network performance. Most *routers* support *packet* filtering. Even if other firewalls are used, implementing packet filtering at the router level gives an initial degree of security at a low network layer. This type of firewall only works at the network layer, however, and does not support sophisticated rule based models.

Network Address Translation (NAT) routers offer the advantages of packet filtering firewalls but can also hide the IP addresses of computers behind the firewall, and offer a level of circuit-based filtering.

The filtering rules used to determine whether to deny or authorize a packet are non-dynamic. In other words, they don't change. The rules are *static*, hence the name static packet filtering firewall.

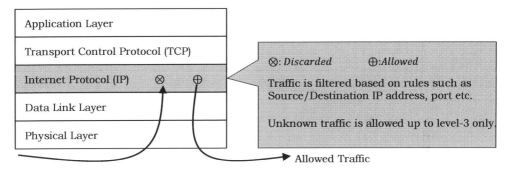

15.17.6.2.2 Dynamic Packet Filtering/Stateful Inspection

Dynamic packet filtering (also called *stateful* inspection) also works at the network level of the OSI model (*or* the IP layer of TCP/IP). A stateful inspection packet filtering firewall also filters packets, but it can modify the rules according to need. The rules are dynamic in that they can change, as conditions require.

For example, a stateful inspection firewall remembers outgoing packets and permits any corresponding incoming packet responses to pass through.

Stateful multilayer inspection firewalls determine whether *session* packets are legitimate and evaluate contents of packets at the application layer. They allow direct connection between client and host, reduces the problem caused by the *lack* of transparency of application level gateways. They depend on algorithms to recognize and process application layer data. These firewalls give high level of security, good performance and transparency to end users.

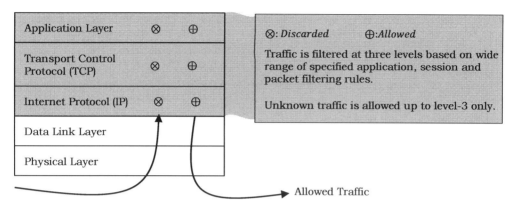

Static packet filtering examines a packet based on the information in its header. Unlike static packet filtering, stateful inspection tracks each connection traversing all interfaces of the firewall and makes sure they are valid. For example, a stateful firewall may examine not just the header information but also the contents of the packet up through the application layer to determine more about the packet than just information about its source and destination.

A stateful inspection firewall also monitors the state of the connection and *compiles* the information in a *state table*. Because of this, filtering decisions are based not only on administrator-defined rules (as in static packet filtering) but also on context that has been established by prior packets that have passed through the firewall.

15.17.6.2.3 How does a Network Firewall Interact with OSI and TCP/IP?

Network firewalls operate at different layers to use different criteria to restrict traffic. The lowest layer at which a firewall can work is layer three. In the OSI model this is the network layer. In TCP/IP it is the Internet Protocol layer. This layer is concerned with routing packets to their destination. At this layer a firewall can determine whether a packet is from a trusted source, but cannot be concerned with what it contains or what other packets it is associated with.

Firewalls that operate at the *transport* layer know a little more about a packet, and are able to grant or deny access depending on more sophisticated criteria. At the application level, firewalls know a great *deal* about what is going on and can be very selective in granting access.

Based on this discussion, it would appear that firewalls functioning at a higher level in the stack must be superior in every respect. But, this is not necessarily the case. The lower in the stack the packet is *intercepted*, the more secure the firewall. If the intruder cannot get past level three, it is impossible to gain control of the operating system.

15.17.6.3 Circuit level Gateway

Circuit level gateways work at the *session* layer of the OSI model (or the TCP layer of TCP/IP). They monitor TCP handshaking between packets to decide whether a requested session is legitimate. Information passed to a remote machine through a circuit level gateway appears to have originated from the gateway. This is useful for hiding information about protected networks.

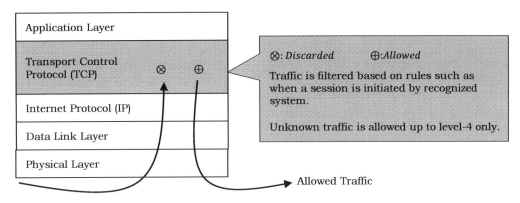

They filter packets based on specified session rules, such as when a session is initiated by a recognized computer.

Circuit level gateways are relatively low cost and they have the advantage of hiding information about the private network they protect. But, they do not filter individual packets.

15.17.6.4 Application level Gateway

Application level gateways (also called proxies) are similar to circuit-level gateways except that they are *application* specific. They can filter packets at the application layer of the OSI model.

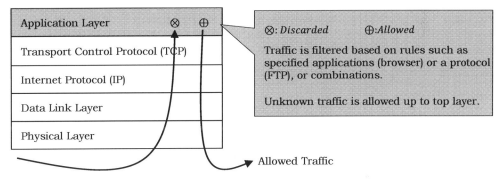

An application level gateway that is configured to be a web proxy (*http*) will not allow any *ftp*, *ssh*, *telnet* or other traffic through. Because they examine packets at application layer, they can filter application specific commands such as http:post and get, etc. This cannot be accomplished with either packet filtering firewalls or circuit level neither of which knows anything about the application level information. Application level gateways can also be used to log user activity and logins.

15.17.7 Firewall Rules

Firewalls rules can be customized as per needs, requirements & security threat levels of organization. We can create or disable firewall filter rules based on conditions such as:

- IP Addresses
- Domain Names
- Protocols
- Port

- Keywords

15.17.7.1 IP Addresses

As seen earlier chapters, each machine on the Internet is assigned a unique address called an *IP address*. IP addresses are 32-bit numbers, normally expressed as four *octets* in a *dotted decimal number*. A typical IP address looks like this: 216.27.61.19. For example, if a certain IP address outside the company is reading too many files from a server, the firewall can block all traffic to or from that IP address.

15.17.7.2 Domain names

Since it is hard to remember the string of numbers that make up an IP address, and because IP addresses sometimes need to change, all servers on the Internet also have human-readable names, called *domain names*.

For example, it is easier for most of us to remember www.*CareerMonk*.com than it is to remember 216.27.61.19. A company might block all access to certain domain names, or allow access only to specific domain names. We can only allow certain specific domain names to access your systems/servers or allow access to only some specified types of domain names or domain name extension like *.edu* or *.org*.

15.17.7.3 Protocols

The protocol is the pre-defined way that someone who wants to use a service talks with that service. The *someone* could be a person, but more often it is a computer program like a Web browser. Protocols are often text, and simply describe how the client and server will have their conversation. A firewall can decide which of the systems can allow or have access to common protocols like IP, SMTP, FTP, UDP, ICMP, Telnet or SNMP. Some common protocols that we can set firewall filters for include:

- IP (Internet Protocol) - the main delivery system for information over the Internet
- TCP (Transmission Control Protocol) - used to break apart and rebuild information that travels over the Internet
- HTTP (Hyper Text Transfer Protocol) - used for Web pages
- FTP (File Transfer Protocol) - used to download and upload files
- UDP (User Datagram Protocol) - used for information that requires no response, such as streaming audio and video
- ICMP (Internet Control Message Protocol) - used by a router to exchange the information with other routers
- SMTP (Simple Mail Transport Protocol) - used to send text-based information (e-mail)
- SNMP (Simple Network Management Protocol) - used to collect system information from a remote computer
- Telnet - used to perform commands on a remote computer

A company might set up only one or two machines to handle a specific protocol and ban that protocol on all other machines.

15.17.7.4 Ports

Any server machine makes its services available to the Internet using numbered ports, one for each service that is available on the. For example, if a server machine is running a Web (http) server and an *ftp* server, the Web server would typically be available on port 80, and the *ftp* server would be available on port 21. A company might block port 21 accesses on all machines but one inside the company. Blocking or disabling ports of servers that are connected to the internet will help maintain the kind of data flow we want to see it used for and also close down possible entry points for hackers or malignant software.

15.17.7.5 Keywords

Firewalls also can search through the data flow for a match of the keywords or phrases to block out offensive or unwanted data from flowing in. This can be anything. For example, we could instruct the firewall to block any packet with the word $X - rated$ in it. The key here is that it has to be an exact match. The $X - rated$ filter would not catch $X \, rated$ (no hyphen). But we can include as many words, phrases and variations of them as we need.

15.17.8 Firewall Architectures

There are many different ways to deploy the components to implement a firewall. There is little difference whether the approach employed uses packet filtering or proxies. Many organizations use a combination of packet filtering and proxies in their firewall configuration. The most widely implemented architectures are listed as follows:

- Screening routers
- Bastion hosts
- Dual-homed hosts
- Screened hosts
- Screened subnets
- Tri-homed hosts

15.17.8.1 Screening Routers

The simplest way to implement a firewall is by placing *packet* filters on the router itself. A screening router performs *packet* filtering as a firewall. The screening router is the simplest approach we can use for firewalling network. If we are connecting a company network to the Internet we will probably need the router anyway. Usually, the router is supplied by ISP.

Routers can provide a cheap and useful level of security by allowing us to filter connections based on the IP address and the protocol. Most router software comes standard with the ability to filter traffic.

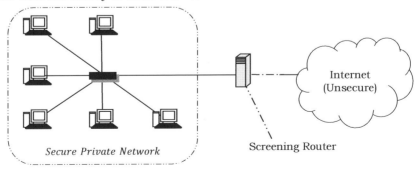

Figure describes the way the screening router functions. Basically, the router monitors each packet as it attempts to pass through. This examination can occur for both incoming and outgoing packets. Based on the rules loaded in the router, it either passes the packet on through or drops it. Screening routers are sometimes referred to as border routers because they sit on the border separating two or more networks.

15.17.8.2 Bastion Hosts

A bastion host represents the private network on the Internet. The host is the point of contact for incoming traffic from the Internet, and as a proxy server allows intranet clients access to external services.

A bastion host runs only a few services, for example, e-mail, FTP, Domain Name System (DNS), or Web services. Internet users must use the bastion host to access a service. A bastion host does not require any authentication or store any company-sensitive data.

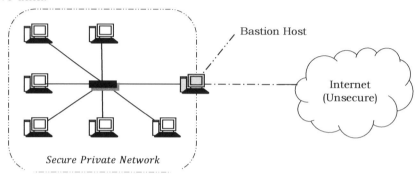

A bastion host is the public face of an internal network. It is one computer or more, depending upon the size of the system. Generally, a network administrator will configure a bastion host to have only a single application, such as a proxy server, on the machine, because it is completely exposed to larger distrusted networks such as the Internet. All other applications, unnecessary services, programs, protocols and network ports are removed or disabled in such a way as to lessen threats to the bastion host.

15.17.8.3 Dual-homed Hosts

A dual-homed host is a firewall that uses two (or more) network interfaces. *One* connection is an internal network and the *second* connection is to the Internet. A dual-homed host works as a simple firewall with no direct IP traffic between the Internet and the internal network.

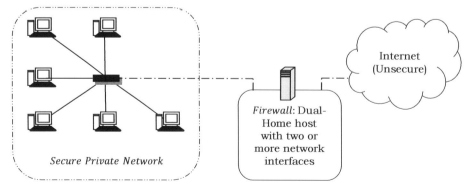

In firewall configurations, a dual homed host is used to block some or all of the traffic trying to pass between the networks. It is a computer that sits between two networks and act as a router between the networks. So, the packets from the Internet are not transferred directly to the internal network. Systems inside the private network can communicate with the dual-homed host, and systems outside the firewall can only communicate with the dual-homed host.

15.17.8.4 Screened Hosts

Screened hosts architecture consists of two host machines:

- Screening router
- Screening host (*Bastion* host)

Screening router is placed between a local network and the Internet. Its purpose is to block all direct communication between two networks. Only traffic that is allowed to pass through is that coming from the host machine and destined for the Internet or coming from the Internet and destined for the host machine.

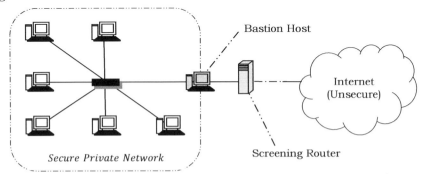

Screened host (Bastion host) is the only machine that can be accessed from the Internet and runs proxy applications for allowed services. Other hosts on the secure private network (*Intranet*) must connect to proxy service on the host machine in order to use the Internet.

A bastion host runs only a few services, for example, e-mail, *ftp*, Domain Name System (DNS), or Web services. Internet users must use the bastion host to access a service. This architecture is more flexible than Dual Homed Host architecture.

15.17.8.5 Screened Subnets

This architecture is an extension of the screened host architecture. A screened subnet adds an additional router, so that it keeps a bastion host between two routers that separate the internal network from the outside network. This establishes a separate subnetwork that acts as a barrier between the internal and external networks.

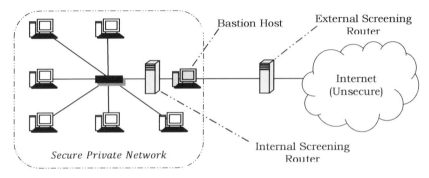

This separate subnet is a buffer that acts as a *demilitarized zone* (DMZ) that provides additional protection for the internal network. In computer networks, a DMZ is a computer host or small network inserted as a *neutral zone* between a company's private network and the outside public network. It prevents outside users from getting direct access to a server that has company data.

With a *screened* subnet, the *external* router communicates only with the outside network and the bastion host on the subnet. The *external* router is *never* allowed to communicate directly with the internal router or the internal network.

The internal router communicates *only* with the internal network and the bastion host. The two routers never directly communicate with each other.

15.17.8.6 Tri-homed Hosts

Tri-homed firewall is a firewall with three network interfaces. Tri-homed firewalls connect three network segments with different network addresses. Typically, these would be protected, DMZ, and unprotected segments.

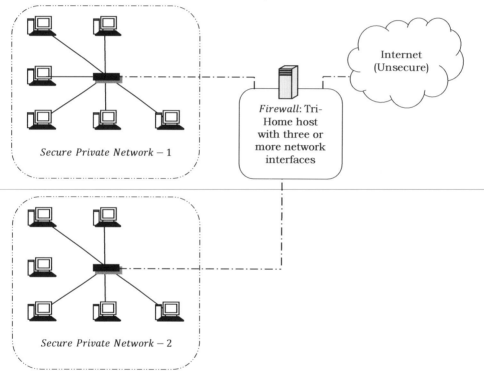

A *tri-homed* firewall may offer some security advantages over firewalls with two interfaces.

Problems and Questions with Answers

Question 1:   Using public key cryptography, X adds a digital signature s to message M, encrypts <M, s>, and sends it to Y, where it is decrypted. Which one of the following sequences of keys is used for the operations?
A) Encryption: X's private key followed by Y's private key; Decryption: X's public key followed by Y's public key

B) Encryption: X's private key followed by Y's public key; Decryption: X's public key followed by Y's private key

C) Encryption: X's public key followed by Y's private key; Decryption: Y's public key followed by X's private key

D) Encryption: X's private key followed by Y's public key; Decryption: Y's private key followed by X's public key

Answer: D.

Question 2: A firewall is typically placed at the edge of a network to protect against attacks and intrusions. It inspects all the packets that enter and leave the network. Argue if firewalls violate or conform to the end-to-end principles and fate sharing. Provide a similar argument for NAT boxes.

Answer: Firewalls do not conform to the *end-to-end* principles because it performs a functionality that can be done at the end hosts (like packet inspection). Also, the performance of the firewall has an effect on the *end-to-end* communication, and its crash might derail the communication (shares the fate, in addition to the end-hosts).

NATs also do not conform to the *end-to-end* principles. By sitting in the critical path, it makes the communication dependent on its health.

Question 3: Each instance of the code-pink worm infects 1 machine in one second. If we start from a single infected machine, how many new machines get infected from second 10 to second 11? How many were infected by second 11?

Answer: From second 0 to 1, 1 machine gets infected. From second 1 to 2, 2 new machines get infected. From second n to n+1, 2^n new machines get infected. From second 10 to 11 we have 2^{10} which is 1024 new machines. The total number of machines infected by second 11 is 2048.

Note: We also gave full credit for solutions which assumed that time starts at 1, instead of 0.

Question 4: Assume you know the public key of entity X, but X has no information about you. Can you design a simple protocol to communicate confidentially with X in both directions (i.e., no one else knows what you and X are sending to each other)? If yes, specify the protocol, otherwise argue why this is not possible.

Answer: Yes. You send messages to X encrypted with X's public key and only X can decrypt them. Also, you send X in the first message your public key or a secret key with each X can encrypt the return communication. Note that this does not imply you are authenticated to X.

Question 5: The principal feature of ____ is that it can encrypt and/or authenticate all traffic at the IP level.

A) IAB   B) VPN   C) IPSec   D) TCP,UDP

Answer: C

Question 6: Consider a block cipher with a block size of 8 bits that is used to encrypt English text, represented by ASCII characters. Assume we augment this with cipher block chaining. So, the first byte is xor-ed with an 8 bit initialization vector before encrypting it and each subsequent byte is xor-ed with the previous ciphertext byte before encrypting it. Explain the purpose of cipher-block chaining.

Answer: Cipher block chaining is intended to prevent an attacker from exploiting statistics to help it break a cipher. Specifically, it keeps different instances of a given plaintext block from having the same ciphertext value. That prevents an intruder from looking for the most commonly occurring ciphertext byte and concluding that it corresponds to the letter 'e', for example.

Question 7: For the previous question, describe how you could break this encryption system. Be specific.

Answer: There are at most 256 different ciphertext blocks. This means that a given ciphertext value will appear repeatedly in a long stream of ciphertext. If we pick one such ciphertext value and find all its occurrences in the ciphertext, all the characters that immediately follow these positions are xor-ed with the same value. So, we can analyze the statistics of the characters in these positions in order to break the code, with respect to the characters in that position. The process can be repeated for other ciphertext values.

Question 8: In a typical SSL session between a client and a remote server, how does the client verify that it is communicating with the desired server, rather than some intruder? Be specific.

Answer: The server sends the client a certificate containing its public key that has been signed by a certificate authority. The client uses its copy of the CA's public key to check that the certificate was signed by the CA. If the signature matches and is not on the CA's revocation list, it accepts it.

Question 9: For the previous question, suppose that an intruder removed a record from an SSL packet sent from the server to the client. How would the client's SSL software detect that something is wrong? Be specific.

Answer: Records in an SSL session are numbered, starting at the beginning of the session. The sequence numbers are included in the MAC calculation used to verify each record, so if a record is removed, the SSL software will detect a mismatch in the MAC.

Question 10: For the previous question, suppose an intruder sent a TCP FIN packet to the server that looked like it came from the client. Would this cause the TCP connection to be closed? If so, how would the SSL software detect that something was wrong. Be specific.

Answer: The connection would be closed. Each SSL record has a type field. The last record of a session has a special type value, so if the connection is closed before the client sends its last record, the SSL software could detect it by just checking the type field of the last record received.

Question 11: A commonly employed encryption method used by businesses to send and receive secure transactions is:
A) Manchester encoding   B) Data Encryption Standard (DES)
C) Pulse Code Modulation   D) Kerberos

Answer: B

Question 12: How many DES keys on average encrypt a particular plaintext block to a particular ciphertext block?

Answer: For a particular 64-bit block of plaintext there are 2^{64} possible blocks of ciphertext. There are only 2^{56} possible DES keys. Each key has a one in 2^{64} chance of transforming the chosen plaintext into a particular ciphertext. If all possible keys are tried the overall probability reduces to one in 2^8.

Question 13: Why can't the initial permutation in DES have any security value?

Answer: If the initial permutation had value than it must be a factor in making DES unbreakable (except by exhaustive key search). If this were the case than removing the permutation should render DES breakable. However, the removal of a known permutation which can easily be reversed cannot enable DES to be broken and therefore it is clear that the permutation has no security value.

Question 14: If the DES mangler function were to transform all 32-bit inputs into the all zero stream regardless of input and stage key what function would DES encryption perform?

Answer: The 28 left side bits would be the new 28 right side bits and vice versa.

Question 15: What value do the 8 parity bits in DES have?

Answer: The 8 parity bits have no security value.

Question 16: A bank which manages 100,000 accounts has correspondent relationships with other banks of comparable size in numbers of accounts managed. For same day value payments messages it allows payments of between $10,000 and $1,000,000 in multiples of $1,000 to be transmitted and appends a 16-bit MAC to each payment message which is created using a key shared with the correspondent bank. If the payment message contains the home account number, the payment figure and the destination account number, how many possible payment messages to a specified correspondent bank will have the same MAC? If the payment clerk is able to run dummy messages through his system to check that a MAC is created, how many messages would he try before he is likely to find two with the same MAC for a specified destination bank?

Answer: The number of possible payments is 990 There are 10^5 possible home account numbers and an equal number of destination account numbers. The number of possible messages is therefore 9.9×10^{12}. The number of possible MACs is just 2^{16} or 65,536.

Therefore the number of payment messages with the same MAC will be on average $9.9 \times 10^{12} / 6.5536 \times 104 = 1.51 \times 108$. From the Birthday Paradox the payment clerk will need to test only $2^8 = 256$ messages before he is likely to find two with the same MAC.

Question 17: Why does SHA-1 require padding of messages that are already a multiple of 512 bits?

Answer: SHA-1 requires a field which gives the actual length in bits. This will cause the message to require additional padding to satisfy the requirement to be an exact multiple of 512 bits.

Question 18: What are the minimal and maximal amounts of padding required in SHA-1?

Answer: 1 and 512 bits.

Question 19: What properties should a good message digest function have? The following schemes are proposed as efficient Message Digest functions. Determine whether they would make good message digest functions.
1) In order to compress a message prior to computing an RSA signature it is proposed by sign the message *mod n*.
2) In order to improve on the performance of MD5 which provides a 128-bit MD is proposed to divide the message into 128-bit chunks and + all the chunks together to get a 128-bit result on which MD5 would be applied.

Answer: A good message digest function has the following properties: if the message digest for a particular message is known, it should not be feasible (from that information alone) to find the message digest for another message; and secondly it should not be feasible to find two messages with the same message digest.

1) This fails both the above tests
2) This also fails both tests

Question 20: In Kerberos the KDC database is not encrypted as a unit but each principal's master key is encrypted under the KDC master key. If replicated KDCs received a download from the master (i.e. without any cryptographic integrity check) how could a rogue principal registered on the KDC attack the database in transit and then impersonate another principal on the system. Assume the rogue principal cannot obtain the KDC master key.

Answer: If there is no cryptographic integrity check on the KDC database then an attacker could remove an authorized user's entry and substitute his own. How would then be in a position to impersonate the other party.

Question 21: In Kerberos V5 the idea behind the requirement to renew tickets before they expire is to remove the requirement for a KDC to remember blacklisted tickets indefinitely. Does this apply also to post-dated tickets which may be requested with a start-time arbitrarily far into the future?

Answer: A KDC must remember all blacklisted post-dated tickets.

Question 22: In a PKI why must a CRL be issued periodically even when no new certificates have been revoked?

Answer: If a CRL were not issue periodically then it would be possible to intercept a CRL without causing any alarm.

Question 23: If there is a revocation mechanism why do certificates need an expiration date?

Answer: In order to make the storage of blacklisted certificates manageable.

Application Layer Protocols

16.1 Introduction

The application layer of the OSI model provides the first step of getting data onto the network. Application software is the software programs used by people to communicate over the network. Examples of application software are HTTP, FTP, email, and others.

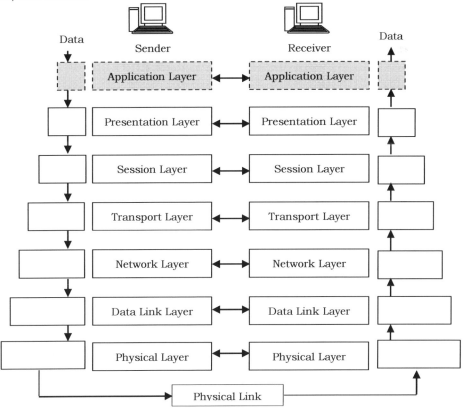

Although the TCP/IP protocol suite was developed prior to the definition of the OSI model, the functionality of the TCP/IP application layer protocols fits into the framework of the top three layers of the OSI model: application, presentation, and session.

In the OSI and TCP/IP models, information is passed from one layer to the next, starting at the application layer on the transmitting host and proceeding down the hierarchy to the physical layer, then passing over the communications channel (physical link) to the destination host, where the information proceeds back up the hierarchy, ending at the application layer.

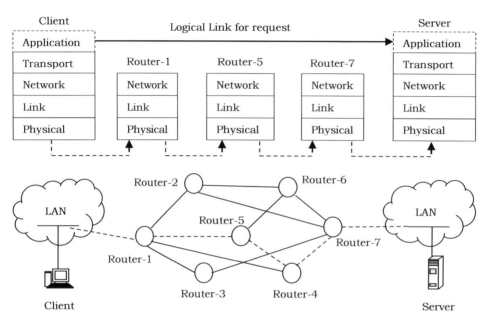

The application layer is built on the transport layer and provides network services to user applications. It provides the interface between the applications we use to communicate and the underlying network over which our messages are transmitted. Application layer protocols are used to exchange data between programs running on the source and destination hosts.

Application	Application Layer protocol	Underlying Transport protocol
E-Mail	SMTP	TCP
Remote terminal access	Telnet	TCP
Web	HTTP	TCP
File transfer	FTP	TCP
Streaming multimedia	HTTP (example: YouTube)	TCP or UDP
Internet telephony	RTP (example: Skype)	Typically UDP
Internet chat	IRC (Internet Relay Chat)	TCP
Host Configurations	DHCP (Dynamic Host Configuration Protocol)	UDP

The application layer is built on the transport layer and provides network services to user applications. It provides the interface between the applications we use to communicate and the underlying network over which our messages are transmitted. Application layer protocols are used to exchange data between programs running on the source and destination hosts.

16.2 Hypertext Transfer Protocol [HTTP]

16.2.1 What is HTTP?

HTTP (Hypertext Transfer Protocol) is the set of rules for transferring files on the World Wide Web. The files can be text files, graphic images, sound, video, or other multimedia files. As soon as a Web user opens their Web browser, the user is indirectly making use of HTTP. HTTP is an application protocol that runs on top of the TCP/IP suite of protocols (the foundation protocols for the Internet).

Hypertext means an electronic document text that is connected (hyperlinked) to the other chunks of text. HTTP concepts include (as the Hypertext part of the name implies) the idea that files can contain references to other files whose selection will need additional transfer requests. Any Web server machine contains, in addition to the Web page files it can serve, an HTTP daemon, a program that is designed to wait for HTTP requests and handle them when they arrive.

Web browser is an HTTP client, sending requests to server machines. When the browser user enters file requests by either "opening" a Web file (typing in a Uniform Resource Locator or URL) or clicking on a hypertext link, the browser builds an HTTP request and sends it to the Internet Protocol address (IP address) indicated by the URL. The HTTP daemon in the destination server machine receives the request and sends back the requested file or files associated with the request. A Web page generally consists of more than one file.

16.2.2 Why HTTP?

When you browse the web the situation is basically this: you sit at your computer and want to see a document somewhere on the web, to which you have the URL.

Since the document you want to read is somewhere else in the world and probably very far away from you some more details are needed to make it available to you. The first detail is your browser. You start it up and type the URL into it (at least you tell the browser somehow where you want to go, perhaps by clicking on a link).

However, the picture is still not complete, as the browser can't read the document directly from the disk where it's stored if that disk is on another continent. So for you to be able to read the document the computer that contains the document must run a web server. A web server is a just a computer program that listens for requests from browsers and then execute them.

The browser will display HTML documents directly, and if there are references to images, video clips etc. in it and the browser has been set up to display these it will request these also from the servers on which they reside. It's worth noting that these will be separate requests, and add additional load to the server and network. When the user follows another link the whole sequence starts anew.

These requests and responses are issued in a special language called HTTP, which is short for Hypertext Transfer Protocol.

It's worth noting that HTTP only defines what the browser and web server say to each other, not how they communicate. The actual work of moving bits and bytes back and forth across the network is done by TCP and IP.

When you continue, note that any software program that does the same as a web browser (ie: retrieve documents from servers) is called a client in network terminology and a user agent in web terminology. Also note that the server is properly the server program, and not the computer on which the server is an application program.

16.2.3 How does HTTP work?

Step 1: Parsing the URL

The first thing the browser has to do is to look at the URL of the new document to find out how to get hold of the new document. Most URLs have this basic form: "protocol://server/request-URI". The protocol part describes how to tell the server which document we want and how to retrieve it.

The server part tells the browser which server to contact, and the request-URI is the name used by the web server to identify the document (term request URI means uniform resource identifier defined by HTTP standard).

Step 2: Sending the request

Usually, the protocol is *http*. To retrieve a document via *http* the browser transmits the following request to the server: "GET /request-URI HTTP/version", where version tells the server which HTTP version is used.

One important point here is that this request string is all the server ever sees. So the server doesn't care if the request came from a browser, a link checker, a validator, a search engine robot (web-crawler) or if we typed it in manually. It just performs the request and returns the result.

Step 3: The server response

When the server receives the HTTP request it locates the appropriate document and returns it. However, an HTTP response is required to have a particular form. It must look like this:

```
HTTP/[VER] [CODE] [TEXT]
Field1: Value1
Field2: Value2

...Web page content here...
```

The first line shows the HTTP version used, followed by a three-digit number (the HTTP status code) and a reason phrase meant for humans. Usually the code is 200 (which mean that all is well) and the phrase *OK*. The first line is followed by some lines called the header, which contains information about the document. The header ends with a blank line, followed by the document content. This is a typical header:

```
HTTP/1.0 200 OK
Server: CareerMonk-Communications/1.1
Date: Tuesday, 25-Nov-97 01:22:04 GMT
Last-modified: Thursday, 20-Nov-97 10:44:53 GMT
Content-length: 6372
Content-type: text/html

<!DOCTYPE HTML PUBLIC "-//W3C//DTD HTML 3.2 Final//EN">
<HTML>
...followed by document content...
```

We see from the first line that the request was successful. The second line is optional and tells us that the server runs the CareerMonk Communications web server, version 1.1. We then get what the server thinks is the current date and when the document was modified last, followed by the size of the document in bytes and the most important field: $Content - type$.

The content-type field is used by the browser to tell which format the document it receives is in. HTML is identified with $text/html$, ordinary text with $text/plain$, a GIF is $image/gif$ and so on. The advantage of this is that the URL can have any ending and the browser will still get it right.

An important concept here is that to the browser, the server works as a black box. The browser requests a specific document and the document is either returned or an error message is returned. How the server produces the document remains unknown to the browser. This means that the server can read it from a file, run a program to generate it, or compile it by parsing some kind of command file. It is decided by the server administrator.

What the server does

While setting up the server, it is usually configured to use a directory somewhere on disk as its root directory and that there be a default file name (say, $index.html$) for each directory. This means that if we ask the server for the file "/" (as in $http://www.CareerMonk.com$) we'll get the file $index.html$ in the server root directory.

Usually, asking for $/foo/bar.html$ will give us the $bar.html$ file from the foo directory directly beneath the server root. The server can be set up to map $/foo/$ into some other directory elsewhere on disk or even to use server-side programs to answer all requests that ask for that directory.

16.2.4 What is HTTPS?

Hyper Text Transfer Protocol Secure (https or HTTPS) is a secure version of the http. https allows secure ecommerce transactions, such as online banking.

Web browsers such as Google Chrome, Internet Explorer, and Firefox display a padlock icon to indicate that the website is secure, as it also displays https:// in the address bar. When a user connects to a website via https, the website encrypts the session with a Digital Certificate. A user can tell if they are connected to a secure website if the website URL begins with https:// instead of http://.

16.3 Simple Mail Transfer Protocol [SNMP]

16.3.1 What is SMTP?

SMTP stands for Simple Mail Transfer Protocol and is a TCP/IP protocol used in sending and receiving e-mail. It's a set of communication rules that allow software to send email over the Internet. Most email software is designed to use SMTP for communication for sending email, and it only works for outgoing messages.

16.3.2 Why SMTP?

Email is very similar to sending a letter in the mail. We have a mailbox, and a number of post offices. The SMTP servers act like post offices that handle the routing of the messages. When we put a letter in our mailbox the post office picks it up then routes it to the appropriate post office for delivery. Email is the same way. When we send an email to SMTP server; it is routed to the appropriate receiving server for delivery.

16.3.3 How does SMTP work?

SMTP provides a set of codes that simplify the communication of email messages between servers. It is a kind of shorthand that allows a server to break up different parts of a message into categories the other server can understand.

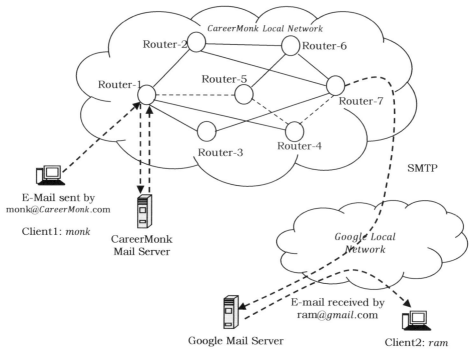

Any email message has a sender, a recipient (sometimes multiple recipients), a message body, and usually a title heading (subject). From users perspective, when they write an email message, they see the graphical user interface of their email software (for example, Outlook), but once that message goes out on the Internet, everything is converted into strings of text. This text is separated by code words or numbers that identify the purpose of each section. SMTP provides those codes, and email server software is designed to understand what they mean. The most common commands are:

Command	Description
HELO	Introduce yourself
EHLO	Introduce yourself and request extended mode
MAIL ROM	Specify the sender
RCPT TO	Specify the recipient
DATA	Specify the body of the message (To, From and Subject should be the first three lines)
RSET	Reset
QUIT	Quit the session
HELP	Get help on commands
VRFY	Verify an address
EXPN	Expand an address
VERB	Verbose

The other purpose of SMTP is to set up communication rules between servers. For example, servers have a way of identifying themselves and announcing what kind of communication they are trying to perform. There are also ways to handle errors, including common things like incorrect email addresses.

In a typical SMTP transaction, a server will identify itself, and announce the kind of operation it is trying to perform. The other server will authorize the operation, and the message will be sent. If the recipient address is wrong, or if there is some other problem, the receiving server may reply with an error message of some kind.

16.3.4 POP3 and IMAP

Post Office Protocol 3 (POP3) and Interactive Mail Access Protocol (IMAP) are two different protocols used to access email. POP3 and IMAP function very differently and each has its own advantages. POP3 is useful in checking emails from a computer that is in a specific location. IMAP is the better option when we need to check our emails from multiple locations, such as at work, from home, or on the road, using different computers.

Advantages of POP3

- We can use only one computer to check our email
- Mails are stored on the computer that you use
- Outgoing email is stored locally on our PC
- Email is available when we are offline
- Email is not stored on the server, so disk usage on the server is less

Advantages of IMAP

- We can use multiple computers (or any email client) to check our email
- Mails are stored on the server
- Outgoing email is filtered to a mailbox on the server for accessibility from another machine.
- Email is stored on the server, so our email cannot be deleted/destroyed even if our computer crash, stolen, or destroyed.
- If we read a message on one computer, it is read on any other computer we use to access our mail. If we reply to an email on one computer, that reply is available on any computer we use.

16.4 File Transfer Protocol [FTP]

16.4.1 What is FTP?

FTP is particularly useful for transferring *larger* files. FTP is a more robust and more capable protocol than the HTTP. Since no special browser is required, FTP is also more universal than HTTP. All major operating systems, including Mac OS, Windows and Linux allow FTP file transfers directly from the command line.

File Transfer Protocol (FTP) is an Internet protocol for transferring files between nodes on the Internet. FTP is used for connecting to a remote machine; send or fetch an arbitrary file. Like HTTP (which transfers displayable Web pages and related files), and the SMTP (transfers e-mail), FTP is an application protocol that uses the Internet's TCP/IP protocols. It is also commonly used to download programs and other files to a computer from other servers.

16.4.2 Why FTP?

If we want to copy files between two computers that are on the same local network (LAN), we can simply share a drive or folder, and copy the files the same way we would copy files from one place to another on our own PC.

What if we want to copy files from one computer to another that is far away (around the world)? One possibility could be, using Internet connection and sharing folders over the Internet. But, this way of transferring the files is not secure. To address this *issue*, FTP was invented. File transfers over the Internet use special technique called FTP.

16.4.3 How does FTP work?

In order to transfer a file from a client to a server (or to download a file from a server to a computer), a user must authenticate to an FTP server. By authenticating, the user creates a session on the server during which he can transfer or modify as many files as necessary. The authentication process also allows remote hosts to set proper file permissions, keeping users from viewing files or directories to which they do not have access, and allowing an individual user to set read, write, and execute permissions on his own files or subdirectories.

When the user session is complete, the user simply disconnects from the server and the session is closed. Some FTP servers also allow anonymous connections, where members of the public can connect anonymously to the FTP server and initiate file transfers; these settings are generally used when publicly available information--like program files released for free--needs to be available for download by knowledgeable users.

As a user, we can use FTP with a simple command line interface or with a commercial program (for example, FileZilla) that offers a graphical user interface. Web browser can also make FTP requests to download programs we select from a Web page. Using FTP, we can also update (delete, rename, move, and copy) files on a server. We need to logon to an FTP server. However, publicly available files are easily accessed using anonymous FTP.

16.4.4 FTP uses multiple ports

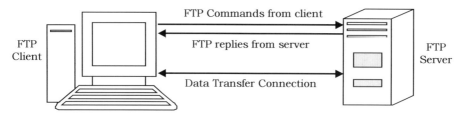

FTP uses one connection (port) for commands and the other for sending and receiving data. FTP has a standard port number on which the FTP server *listens* for connections. A port is a *logical connection point* for communicating using the Internet Protocol (IP). The standard port number used by FTP servers is 21 and is used only for sending commands. Since port 21 is used exclusively for sending commands, this port is referred to as a command port. For example, to get a list of folders and files present on the FTP server, the FTP Client issues a *list* command. The FTP server then sends a list of all folders and files back to the FTP Client.

So what about the internet connection used to send and receive data? The port that is used for transferring data is called *data port*. The number of the data port will vary depending on the mode of the connection.

16.4.5 Active and Passive Connection Modes of FTP

The FTP server may support Active or Passive connections, or both. In an Active FTP connection, the client opens a port and listens and the server actively connects to it. In a Passive FTP connection, the server opens a port and listens (passively) and the client connects to it.

Most FTP client programs select passive connection mode by default because server administrators prefer it as a safety measure. Firewalls generally block connections that are *initiated* from the outside. Using passive mode, the FTP client is *reaching out* to the server to make the connection. The firewall will allow these outgoing connections, meaning that no special adjustments to firewall settings are required.

FTP Active Connections

If you are connecting to the FTP server using Active mode of connection you must set your firewall to accept connections to the port that your FTP client will open. However, many Internet service providers block incoming connections to all ports above 1024. Active FTP servers generally use port 20 as their data port.

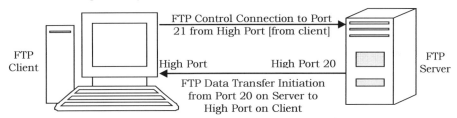

The sequence of events for an active FTP connection goes like this:

- FTP *client*: Opens random response ports in the high number range (for example, we will assume ports TCP 6000 and TCP 6001).
- FTP *client*: Sends a request to open a command channel from its TCP port 6000 to the FTP server's TCP port 21.
- FTP *server*: Sends an *OK* from its TCP port 21 to the FTP client's TCP port 6000 (the command channel link). The command channel is established at this point.
- FTP *client*: Sends a data request (PORT command) to the FTP server. The FTP client includes in the PORT command the data port number it opened to receive data. In this example, the FTP client has opened TCP port 6001 to receive the data.
- FTP *server*: The FTP server opens a new inbound connection to the FTP client on the port indicated by the FTP client in the PORT command. The FTP server source port is TCP port 20. In this example, the FTP server sends data from its own TCP port 20 to the FTP client's TCP port 6001.

FTP Passive Connections

It's a good idea to use Passive mode to connect to an FTP server. Most FTP servers support the Passive mode. For Passive FTP connection to succeed, the FTP server administrator must set his / her firewall to accept all connections to any ports that the FTP server may open. However, this is the server administrator's problem (and standard practice for servers). We can go ahead, make and use FTP connections.

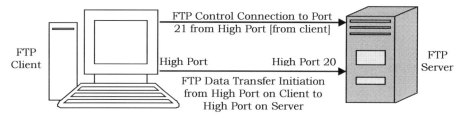

A passive FTP connection will have the following sequence of events:

- FTP *client*: This opens random response ports in the high number range (for example, we'll assume ports TCP 6000 and TCP 6001).
- FTP *client*: This sends a request to open a command channel from its TCP port 6000 to the FTP server's TCP port 21.
- FTP *server*: This sends an OK from its TCP port 21 to the FTP client's TCP port 6000. The command channel is now established.
- FTP *client*: This sends a PASV command requesting that the FTP server open a port number that the FTP client can connect to establish the data channel.
- FTP *server*: This sends over the command channel the TCP port number that the FTP client can initiate a connection to establish the data channel. In this example, the FTP server opens port 7000.
- FTP *client*: This opens a new connection from its own response port TCP 6001 to the FTP server's data channel 7000. Data transfer takes place through this channel.

16.5 Domain Name Server [DNS]

16.5.1 What is DNS?

Domain name server (DNS) is a protocol with a set of standards for how computers exchange data on the Internet and it is an application protocol that runs on top of the TCP/IP suite of protocols.

A domain name locates an organization or other entity on the Internet. For example, the domain name

www.CareerMonk.com

locates an Internet address for *CareerMonk.com* at IP address199.5.10.2 and a particular host server named *www*. The *com* part of the domain name reflects the purpose of the organization or entity (in this example, *commercial*) and is called the top-level domain name.

The *CareerMonk* part of the domain name defines the organization and together with the top-level is called the *second-level* domain name. The second-level domain name maps to and can be thought of as the *readable* version of the Internet address (IP address).

A third level can be defined to identify a particular host server at the Internet address. In our example, *www* is the name of the server which handles Internet requests (a second server might be called *www*2.) A third level of domain name is not required. For example, the fully-qualified domain name (FQDN) could have been *CareerMonk.com* and the server assumed.

Subdomain levels can also be used for modularity and ease of maintenance. For example, we could have *www.TechnicalServer.CareerMonk.com*. Together, *www.CareerMonk.com* constitutes a fully-qualified domain name.

Second-level domain names must be unique on the Internet and registered for the *com*, *net*, and *org* top-level domains. Where appropriate, a top-level domain name can be geographic. Currently, most non-U.S. domain names use a top-level domain name based on the country the server is in (for example, India uses *.in*).

On the Web, the domain name is that part of the Uniform Resource Locator (URL) that tells a domain name server using the domain name system (DNS) whether and where to forward a request for a Web page. The domain name is mapped to an IP address.

More than one domain name can be mapped to the same Internet address. This allows multiple individuals, businesses, and organizations to have separate Internet identities while sharing the same Internet server.

16.5.2 Hierarchy of domain names

Domain Names are hierarchical and each part of a domain name is referred to as the root, top level, and second level or as a sub-domain. To allow computers to properly recognize a fully qualified domain name, dots are placed between each part of the name. All resolvers treat dots as separators between the parts of the domain name.

The fully qualified domain name is split into pieces at the dots and the tree is searched starting from the root of the hierarchical tree structure. All resolvers start their lookups at the root; therefore the root is represented by a dot and is often assumed to be there, even when not shown.

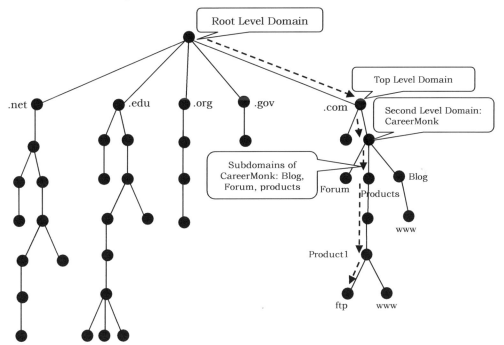

The resolver navigates its way down the tree until it gets to the last, left-most part of the domain name and then looks within that location for the information it needs. Information about a host such as its name, its IP address and occasionally even its function are stored in one or more zone files which together compose a larger zone often referred to as a domain.

- Top Level Domains (TLD's)
- Second Level Domains
- Sub-Domains
- Host Name (a resource record)

Within the hierarchy, we will start resolution at the top level domain, work our way down to the second-level domain, then through zero, one or more sub-domains until we get to the actual host name we want to resolve into an IP address. It is traditional to use different DNS servers for each level of the DNS hierarchy.

A domain is a label of the DNS tree. Each node on the DNS tree represents a domain. Domains under the top-level domains represent individual organizations or entities. These domains can be further divided into subdomains to ease administration of an organization's host computers.

For example, company *CareerMonk* creates a domain called *CareerMonk.com* under the .com top-level domain. *CareerMonk* has separate LANs for its *Forum*, *Blog*, and *Products*. Therefore, the network administrator for *CareerMonk* decides to create a separate subdomain for each division, as shown in figure. Any domain in a subtree is considered part of all domains above it. Therefore, *Forum.CareerMonk.com* is part of the *CareerMonk*.com domain, and both are part of the *.com* domain.

16.5.3 Understanding zones

DNS data is divided into manageable sets of data called *zones*. Zones contain name and IP address information about one or more parts of a DNS domain. A server that contains all of the information for a zone is the authoritative server for the domain. Sometimes it may make sense to *delegate* the authority for answering DNS queries for a particular subdomain to another DNS server. In this case, the DNS server for the domain can be configured to refer the *subdomain* queries to the appropriate server.

For *backup* and *redundancy*, zone data is often stored on servers other than the authoritative DNS server. These other servers are called *secondary* servers, which load zone data from the authoritative server.

Configuring secondary servers allows us to balance the demand on servers and also provides a backup in case the primary server goes down.

Secondary servers obtain zone data by doing zone transfers from the authoritative server. When a secondary server is initialized, it loads a complete copy of the zone data from the primary server. The secondary server also reloads zone data from the primary server or from other secondary's for that domain when zone data changes.

16.5.3 Why DNS is needed?

Computers and other network devices on the Internet use an IP address to route our request to the site we are trying to reach. This is similar to dialling a mobile number to connect to the person we are trying to call. DNS makes our life easy. We don't have to keep our own address book of IP addresses. Instead, we just connect through a domain name server, also called a DNS server or name server, which manages a massive database that maps domain names to IP addresses.

16.5.4 How does DNS work?

A DNS program works like this - every time a domain name is typed in a browser it is automatically passed on to a DNS server, which translates the name into its corresponding IP address. When we visit a domain such as *CareerMonk.com*, our computer follows a series of steps to turn the human-readable web address into a machine-readable IP address. This happens every time we use a domain name, whether we are viewing websites or sending email.

For example, the name specified could be the FQDN for a computer, such as *development.CareerMonk.com*, and the query type specified to look for an address (A) resource record by that name. Think of a DNS query as a client asking a server a two-part question, such as "Do you have any address (A) resource records for a computer named *development.CareerMonk.com*? When the client receives an answer from the server, it reads and interprets the answered A resource record, learning the IP address for the computer it asked for by name.

DNS queries resolve in a number of different ways. Client can sometimes answer a query locally using cached information obtained from a previous query. The DNS server can use its own cache of resource record information to answer a query. A DNS server can also query or contact other DNS servers on behalf of the requesting client to fully resolve the name, and then send an answer back to the client. This process is known as *recursion*.

Also, the client itself can attempt to contact additional DNS servers to resolve a name. When a client does so, it uses separate and additional non-recursive queries based on referral answers from servers. This process is known as *iteration*.

In general, the DNS query process occurs in two parts:

- A name query begins at a client computer and is passed to a resolver, the DNS Client service, for resolution.
- When the query cannot be resolved locally, DNS servers can be queried as needed to resolve the name.

Both of these processes are explained in more detail in the following sections.

Part 1: The local resolver

The following figure shows an overview of the complete DNS query process.

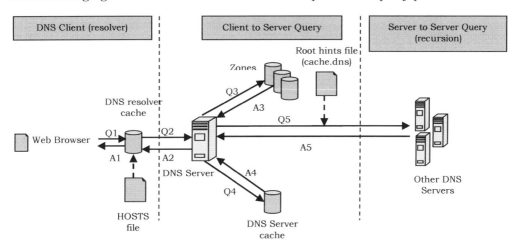

As shown in the initial steps of the query process, a DNS domain name is used in a program on the local computer. The request is then passed to the DNS Client service for resolution using locally cached information. If the queried name can be resolved, the query is answered and the process is completed.

The local resolver cache can include name information obtained from two possible sources:

- If a Hosts file is configured locally, any host name-to-address mappings from that file are preloaded into the cache when the DNS Client service is started.
- Resource records obtained in answered responses from previous DNS queries are added to the cache and kept for a period of time.

If the query does not match an entry in the cache, the resolution process continues with the client querying a DNS server to resolve the name.

Part 2: Querying a DNS server

As indicated in the previous figure, the client queries a preferred DNS server. The actual server used during the initial client/server query part of the process is selected from a global list. For more information about how this global list is compiled and updated.

When the DNS server receives a query, it first checks to see if it can answer the query authoritatively based on resource record information contained in a locally configured zone on the server. If the queried name matches a corresponding resource record in local zone information, the server answers authoritatively, using this information to resolve the queried name.

If no zone information exists for the queried name, the server then checks to see if it can resolve the name using locally cached information from previous queries. If a match is found here, the server answers with this information. Again, if the preferred server can answer with a positive matched response from its cache to the requesting client, the query is completed.

If the queried name does not find a matched answer at its preferred server -- either from its cache or zone information -- the query process can continue, using recursion to fully resolve the name. This involves assistance from other DNS servers to help resolve the name. By default, the DNS Client service asks the server to use a process of recursion to fully resolve names on behalf of the client before returning an answer. In most cases, the DNS server is configured, by default, to support the recursion process as shown in the following figure.

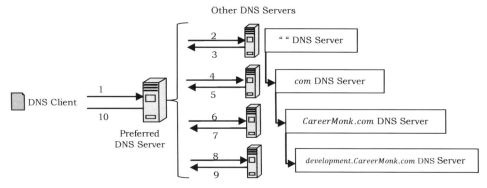

In order for the DNS server to do recursion properly, it first needs some helpful contact information about other DNS servers in the DNS domain namespace. This information is provided in the form of *root hints*, a list of preliminary resource records that can be used by the DNS service to locate other DNS servers that are authoritative for the root of the DNS domain namespace tree. Root servers are authoritative for the domain root and top-level domains in the DNS domain namespace tree.

By using root hints to find root servers, a DNS server is able to complete the use of recursion. In theory, this process enables any DNS server to locate the servers that are authoritative for any other DNS domain name used at any level in the namespace tree.

For example, consider the use of the recursion process to locate the name *development.CareerMonk*.com when the client queries a single DNS server. The process occurs when a DNS server and client are first started and have no locally cached information available to help resolve a name query. It assumes that the name queried by the client is for a domain name of which the server has no local knowledge, based on its configured zones.

First, the preferred server parses the full name and determines that it needs the location of the server that is authoritative for the top-level domain, *com*. It then uses an iterative (that is, a nonrecursive) query to the *com* DNS server to obtain a referral to the *CareerMonk*.com server. Next, a referral answer comes from the *CareerMonk.com* server to the DNS server for *development.CareerMonk.com*.

Finally, the *development.CareerMonk.com* server is contacted. Because this server contains the queried name as part of its configured zones, it responds authoritatively back to the original server that initiated recursion. When the original server receives the response indicating that an authoritative answer was obtained to the requested query, it forwards this answer back to the requesting client and the recursive query process is completed.

Although the recursive query process can be resource-intensive when performed as described above, it has some performance advantages for the DNS server. For example, during the recursion process, the DNS server performing the recursive lookup obtains information about the DNS domain namespace.

This information is cached by the server and can be used again to help speed the answering of subsequent queries that use or match it. Over time, this cached information can grow to occupy a significant portion of server memory resources, although it is cleared whenever the DNS service is cycled on and off.

16.6 Trivial File Transfer Protocol [TFTP]

FTP is an Application layer protocol for transferring files using the TCP protocol on the Transport layer. Trivial File Transfer Protocol (TFTP) is a protocol for the same kind of application (transferring files) but based on UDP protocol on the Transport layer.

The difference between TCP and UDP is that while TCP checks whether each data packet arrived correctly at destination, UDP does not. Another difference is that TCP reorder packets that may have arrived out-of-order, while UDP doesn't.

On the other hand, because it does not use this acknowledge system nor any reordering system, UDP packets are smaller (since UDP header is smaller than TCP header) and also require less computational power to be processed (as reordering and acknowledging aren't necessary). It will be the application (not the protocol) that will be in charge of these functions.

An example application of TFTP is diskless remote boot (also known as RIPL, Remote Initial Program Loading).

We can have a computer with no hard disk drive or any other storage media and configure it to boot from the network, i.e., load the operating system and programs from a server. The program for loading the operating system remotely needs to be stored on a very small ROM memory located on the network card from the diskless computer.

As it will need a protocol for transferring files, TFTP suits better than FTP, as TFTP clients are far smaller than FTP clients, fitting the network card ROM memory – for you to have an idea, the size of the largest ROM chips used for remote booting is only 64 KB (yes, kilobytes).

In summary, TFTP is an Application layer protocol using UDP protocol (using port 69) on the Transport layer.

16.7 Dynamic Host Configuration Protocol [DHCP]

DHCP protocol was introduced in 1993. The standard supports a mix of static and dynamic IP addressing.

The Dynamic Host Configuration Protocol (DHCP) provides a method for passing configuration information to hosts on a TCP/IP network. DHCP is based on its predecessor Bootstrap Protocol (BOOTP), but adds automatic allocation of reusable network addresses and additional configuration options.

16.7.1 What is DHCP?

Dynamic Host Configuration Protocol (DHCP) is a protocol for *automatically* assigning IP addresses to devices throughout a network, and of re-assigning those addresses as they are no longer needed by the device that used them. It provides an effective alternative to manually assigning IP addresses to every client, server, and printer.

Apart from *eliminating* the manual effort of creating and maintaining a list of IP address assignments for network devices, DHCP also provides a measure of *protection* against the *mistakes* that can arise when the process of IP addressing is manual.

For example, when two devices are mistakenly given duplicate IP addresses, only one of them—the first to boot—will be able to communicate on the network at any given time. Finally, DHCP makes it unnecessary to manually re-assign IP addresses when a computer is moved from one subnet to another.

16.7.2 History of DHCP

Historically, the assignment of Internet addresses to host machines required administrators to manually configure each machine and manually keep track of IP address assignments. While this is sufficient for small networks with a few systems, the overhead of manually managing a site's address name space becomes prohibitively expensive as the number of hosts increases.

DHCP was developed from an earlier protocol called *Bootstrap Protocol* (BOOTP), which was used to pass information during initial booting to client systems. The BOOTP standard was originally released in 1985 based on work by *John Gilmore* of Sun Microsystems and *Bill Croft* of Stanford University. It allowed diskless clients (systems without any disk) to store configuration data in a centralized server.

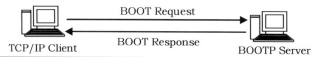

TCP/IP Client   BOOT Request   BOOT Response   BOOTP Server

The BOOTP standard was designed to store and update static information for clients, including IP addresses. The BOOTP server always issued the same IP address to the same client. As a result, while BOOTP addressed the need for central management, it did not address the problem of managing IP addresses as a dynamic resource.

To address the need to manage dynamic configuration information in general, and dynamic IP addresses specifically, the IETF standardized a new extension to BOOTP called Dynamic Host Configuration Protocol, or DHCP. DHCP servers utilize BOOTP packets, with DHCP-specific flags and data, to convey information to the DHCP clients.

To standardize the DHCP environment, the IETF issued a series of RFCs focused on DHCP extensions to the BOOTP technology in 1997. DHCP is still an area of active development and it is reasonable to assume that there will be additional RFCs related to the DHCP environment. Sun is working with other vendors to ensure that DHCP continues to be a standard supported by a large number of vendors.

16.7.3 Why DHCP Is Important?

For enterprise clients, the best way to reduce the cost of distributed computing is to move the administration of their client systems to centralized management servers.

DHCP can reduce the cost of ownership for large organizations by shifting the job of managing network configuration information from client systems to remote management by a small pool of system and network managers. It is difficult for organizations to acquire additional Internet addresses.

Corporations must often justify the requirement for these additional addresses through a long and sometimes difficult process of needs definition. DHCP helps reduce the impact of the increasing scarcity of available IP addresses in two ways.

First, DHCP can be used to manage the limited number of standard, routable IP addresses that are available to an organization. It does this by issuing the addresses to clients on an as needed basis and reclaiming them when the addresses are no longer required.

When a client needs an IP address, the DHCP server will issue an available address, along with a lease period during which the client may use the address. When the client is done with the address (or when the lease on the address expires), the address is put back in a pool and is available for the next client seeking an address.

Second, DHCP can be used in conjunction with Network Address Translation (NAT) to issue private network addresses to connect clients (through a NAT system) to the Internet. The DHCP server will issue an address to the client that will not route, such as 192.169.*.* or 10.*.*.*4. The client will use a NAT system as the gateway machine, which packages up the request with the permanent address of the NAT system.

When the response comes back from the Internet, the NAT server will forward the packet back to the client. DHCP enables this to be done without taking up valuable routable addresses and makes certain that all clients use consistent parameters, such as subnet masks, routers, and DNS servers.

16.7.4 Where DHCP Is Useful?

The most common usage of DHCP is to move the management of IP addresses away from the distributed client systems and onto one or more centrally managed servers. These central servers maintain databases of parameter information (addresses, netmasks, etc.), eliminating the need for clients to store static network information on their machines. This specifically obviates the need to configure TCP/IP parameters into client machines.

Since most client systems now ship from the factory with dynamically assigned IP addresses as the default configuration, the user need only boot the machine to be up and running with the TCP/IP protocol. This approach saves time configuring or debugging the network environment, thereby reducing the cost of ownership for client systems.

DHCP is particularly useful in the following environments:

- Sites that have many more TCP/IP clients than network administrators. By using DHCP, managers can more effectively manage a large community of client systems.
- Sites where laptops commonly move among networks within the site. By using DHCP, laptop users can plug into the network at any location and use a local DHCP-assigned IP address to communicate with the local systems.
- Sites that have fewer available TCP/IP addresses than they have clients that need them. Typically, this occurs in dial-up situations, such as an Internet service provider (ISP) environment, where there is a large community of potential users, but only a small percentage of them are online at any given time.

   Here, DHCP is used to issue the IP address to a client machine at the connection time, allowing the DHCP server to reuse the same address once the current client has logged off. Most ISPs have moved to this approach to reduce their need for scarce Internet addresses.
- Sites that frequently need to move the location of services from host to host. Since DHCP delivers the location of services, moving services from one machine to another and changing the appropriate DHCP configuration information means that any DHCP client will automatically pick up the change (without the administrator having to make a trip to the user's machine).
- Sites that support diskless clients. More details on this use of DHCP are provided in the Client Implementation section.
- Any combination of the above.

16.7.5 How does DHCP work?

DHCP is essentially, as its name suggests, a protocol that enables client stations joining a network to obtain an IP address from a DHCP server. DHCP servers lease IP addresses from a pool of IP addresses they are authorized to dispense (the DHCP server's scope), and are themselves configured with static addresses—a DHCP server cannot itself be a client.

DHCP clients do not need to know the IP address of the DHCP server itself to communicate with DHCP servers on their subnet, as DHCP uses UDP network broadcasts to initiate connection between a DHCP client and a DHCP server.

The request from DHCP client to a server involves a *four-way handshake*. First, the client broadcasts a "DHCPDISCOVER" message to the local subnet asking for configuration information. In this message, the client fills in the *'xid'* field with a unique identifier (usually a randomly generated number). It also fills in the *'chaddr'* filed with its hardware, or MAC, address. It may request additional information as described above. The client then collects one or more "DHCPOFFER" messages from one or more DHCP servers with matching values in the *'xid'* field. The client chooses one to accept based upon the offered configuration parameters.

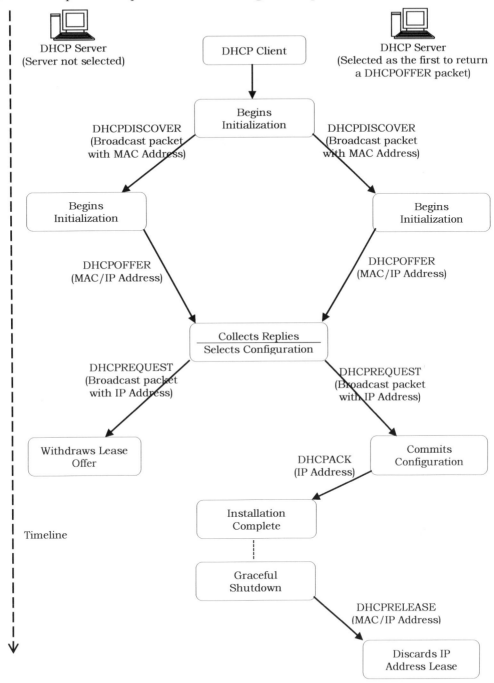

The client then sends a "DHCPREQUEST" message specifying its selected server. Servers not selected use this message as notification that the client has declined their offer. The selected server then responds with a "DHCPACK" message if the requested parameters are acceptable or a "DHCPNAC" message if they are not. The timeline for this four-way handshake is outlined below in figure.

When a DHCP client boots, the following basic steps occur:

1. The DHCP client loads a minimal version of TCP.

2. It then broadcasts an *IP address lease request* packet (a "DHCPDISCOVER" packet). This packet includes the MAC address of the DHCP client, and may contain other configuration information as well. The DHCPDISCOVER packet is sent to a specific TCP port number that is recognized as that used by DHCP servers. The packet causes all DHCP servers receiving it to offer an IP address that the client can use, with a "DHCPOFFER" packet.

3. The DHCP client then selects the first offer it receives and broadcasts another packet (a "DHCPPREQUEST" packet) requesting that it can keep the IP address it has on offer. DHCP clients can also arbitrate between offers from numerous DHCP servers in a number of other ways that are outside the scope of this discussion.

4. The DHCP server that offered the selected IP address then starts the client's IP address lease. It also broadcasts an acknowledgement to the client, sending a "DHCPACK" packet. Other DHCP servers with outstanding lease offers for that client will also receive the acknowledgement packet and withdraw their offers at this point.

    If the IP address on offer becomes unavailable in the interval between a server's offer of an IP address (marked by the DHCPOFFER packet) and the client's request to accept the offer (marked by the DHCPPREQUEST packet), the DHCP server offering the IP address will instead send a negative acknowledgement to the client (a "DHCPNACK" packet). The process of negotiating an IP address must then begin again, with the client issuing a new DHCPDISCOVER packet.

5. When a DHCP client is finished with its IP address, it can release that address to let it be made available again to the pool of IP addresses in the DHCP servers' scope. This is done with a "DHCPRELEASE" packet. Alternatively, the address may be retained and re-established the next time that device re-joins the network.

By default, each time it boots, a DHCP client will attempt to renew its IP address lease. If the client cannot communicate with a DHCP server, it will continue to use the IP address it has on lease until that lease expires. Clients also will attempt to renew their leases halfway through the lease period (by default in Windows, after four days).

16.7.6 DHCP Across Subnets

Imagine a situation with multiple subnets joined by routers, and no DHCP server on the same subnet as a DHCP client needing an IP address. This scenario needs a mechanism for DHCP clients to communicate with the DHCP server so broadcasts with DHCPDISCOVER packets can reach outside the subnet, making direct contact with the DHCP server possible.

Three solutions are usual and discussed below.

16.7.6.1 Routers can be configured with BOOTP support

With this solution, BOOTP (the bootstrap protocol) can enable routers to forward IP address lease requests issued by DHCP clients. DHCP is designed to work with BOOTP conventions. Some additional network traffic will result with this solution, as DHCP communications will be forwarded to other subnets.

16.7.6.2 DHCP servers can be installed on each subnet

This solution may be expensive, particularly if DHCP servers for each subnet are not already available. On the other hand, the drawback of added network traffic discussed above does not exist.

16.7.6.3 A DHCP relay agent can be configured

A DHCP relay agent is essentially a gateway that resides on a DHCP subnet and listens for DHCP lease requests from clients on its subnet. It is configured with the IP address of a DHCP server on a subnet different from the one it resides on, and forwards broadcast lease requests to that DHCP server.

The DHCP server makes its lease offer back to the DHCP relay agent. In turn, the DHCP relay agent broadcasts that lease offer to the subnet, where it can be collected by the DHCP client that initiated the process in the beginning.

Advantages of DHCP relay agents are that they can be inexpensively configured on client computers sitting in a given subnet, yet limit the subnet-to-subnet traffic caused by DHCP communications.

16.7.7 DHCP State Transition Diagram

Dynamic address allocation is probably the most important new capability introduced by DHCP. The DHCP standard uses an FSM to describe the lease life cycle from the perspective of a DHCP client. The client begins in an initial INIT state where it has no lease, and then transitions through various states as it acquires, renews, rebinds and/or releases its IP address. The FSM also indicates what message exchanges occurs between the server and client at various stages.

Initializing: This is the initialization state, where a client begins the process of acquiring a lease. It also returns here when a lease ends, or when a lease negotiation fails. ISCOVER: The client creates a DHCPDISCOVER message and broadcasts it to try to find a DHCP server. It transitions to the SELECTING state.

Selecting: The client is waiting to receive DHCPOFFER messages from one or more DHCP servers, so it can choose one. The client chooses one of the offers it has been sent, and broadcasts a DHCPREQUEST message to tell DHCP servers what its choice was. It transitions to the REQUESTING state.

Requesting: The client is waiting to hear back from the server to which it sent its request. The client remains in the requesting state until it receives a DHCPACK message from the server that creates the binding between the client physical address and its IP address. After receipt of the DHCPACK, the client goes to the bound state.

Bound: In this state, the client can use the IP address until the lease expires. When 50 percent of the lease period is reached, the client sends another DHCPREQUEST to ask for renewal. It then goes to the renewing state. When in the bound state, the client can also cancel the lease and go to the initializing state.

Renewing: The client remains in the renewing state until one of two events happens. It can receive a DHCPACK, which renews the lease agreement. In this case, the client resets its timer and goes back to the bound state. Or, if a DHCPACK is not received, and 87.5 percent of the lease time expires, the client goes to the rebinding state.

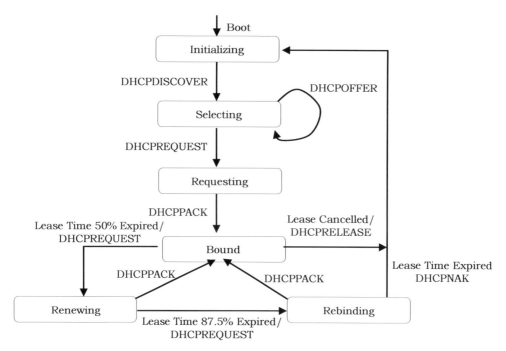

Rebinding: The client remains in the rebinding state until one of three events happens. If the client receives a DHCPNACK or the lease expires, it goes back to the initializing state and tries to get another IP address. If the client receives a DHCPACK, it goes to the bound state and resets the timer.

Problems and Questions with Answers

Question 1:   The transport layer protocols used for real time multimedia, file transfer, DNS and email respectively are
A) TCP, UDP,UDP and TCP   B) UDP TCP,TCP and UDP
C) UDP, TCP,UDP and TCP   D)TCP, UDP,TCP and UDP

Answer : C

Question 2:   Which of the following transport layer protocols is used to support electronic mail?
A) SMTP   B) IP   C) TCP   D) UDP

Answer: C. E-mail uses SMTP in application layer to transfer mail and SMTP uses TCP to transfer data in transport layer.

Question 3:   The protocol data unit (PDU) for the application layer in the Internet stack is
A) Segment   B) Datagram   C) Message   D) Frame

Answer: C.

Layer	Protocol Data Unit (PDU)
Application layer	Message
Transport layer	Segment
Network layer	Datagram
Data Link layer	Frame

Question 4: Why do HTTP, FTP, SMTP, and POP3 run on top of TCP rather than on UDP?

Answer: The applications associated with those protocols require that all application data be received in the correct order and without gaps. TCP provides this service whereas UDP does not.

Question 5: Can SMTP transfer multiple email messages be over a single TCP connection?

Answer: Yes. SMTP has a state machine that returns into the initial state after successful delivery of a message. There is in addition an abort command which resets the state machine into the initiate state. Hence, it is possible to send multiple email messages over a single TCP connection.

Question 6: Which DNS records are relevant for forwarding email messages?

Answer: The MX record specifies a list of SMTP server accepting email for a given domain name. To obtain the IP addresses of the SMTP servers, a lookup using A or AAAA records must be done.

Question 7: What is a whois database?

Answer: For a given input of domain name (such as CareerMonk.com), IP address or network administrator name, whois database can be used to locate the corresponding registrar, whois server, dns server, etc.

Question 8: Agent MonkPerson of the FBI agent walks into Cafe, which has wireless Internet and runs its own local DNS server. The agent wants to figure out whether anyone in the cafe has recently accessed www. *CareerMonk*.com, before Agent MonkPerson arrived. How can the agent do this using standard computer networking tools, and without breaking into any computers or servers?

Answer: Bellow are three possible solutions. All solutions use the fact that if the site has been accessed recently, it will be in the local DNS server's cache. Here are three ways to determine whether the name is in the cache.

1. Time nslookup www.*CareerMonk*.com. If it's in the cache, this will complete faster than if it isn't.
2. Use dig to query www. *CareerMonk*.com at the local DNS server. If the returned TTL is large (about equal to the value when querying the domain from a DNS server which doesn't have it cached), then it wasn't cached. If the returned TTL is smaller, then it was cached.
3. Use dig, with recursion explicitly turned off, to query www. *CareerMonk*.com at the local DNS server. If the server returns a mapping to an IP address (Type A record for www. *CareerMonk*.com), then it was in the cache. Otherwise, it wasn't.

Question 9: Suppose that a Web server runs in Host C on port 80. Suppose this Web server uses persistent connections and is currently receiving requests from two different Hosts, A and B. Are all of the requests being sent through the same socket at Host C? If they are being passed through different sockets, do both of the sockets have port 80? Discuss and explain.

Answer: For each persistent connection, the Web server creates a separate *connection socket*. Each connection socket is identified with a four-tuple: (source IP address, source port number, destination IP address, destination port number). When Host C receives an IP datagram, it examines these four fields in the datagram/segment to determine to which socket it should pass the payload of the TCP segment.

Thus, the requests from A and B pass through different sockets. The identifier for both of these sockets has 80 for the destination port; however, the identifiers for these sockets have different values for source IP addresses. Unlike UDP, when the transport layer passes a TCP segment's payload to the application process, it does not specify the source IP address, as this is implicitly specified by the socket identifier.

Question 10: Is it possible for an application to enjoy reliable data transfer even when the application runs over UDP? If so, how?

Answer: Yes. The application developer can put reliable data transfer into the application layer protocol. This would require a significant amount of work and debugging, however.

Question 11: Consider a network with four hosts A, B, C, D and two routers X and Y with IP addresses 1.2.3.31, 1.2.3.23. Which of these is the IGMP querier?

Answer: Y is the querier

Question 12: For the previous Question-11, assume that A is configured to receive packets sent to 229.1.1.1 and 231.1.1.1, B is configured to receive packets sent to 237.1.1.1, C is configured to receive packets sent to 231.1.1.1 and D is configured to receive packets sent to 231.1.1.1 and 237.1.1.1. If the querier sends out an IGMP general query packet, how many IGMP membership reports will be sent by the hosts, assuming that the switches in the network do not implement IGMP snooping?

Answer: One report is sent for each multicast address for which there is a subscriber. So three reports will be sent.

Question 13: For the Question-11, how many membership reports will be sent by the hosts if the switches do implement IGMP snooping?

Answer: In this case, every host sends a report for each of the multicast addresses it is subscribed to, so six reports will be sent.

Question 14: The protocol that allows dynamic assignment of IP Addresses to workstations is known as:
A) ICMP   B) DHCP   C) SMTP   D) SNMP

Answer: B

Question 15: Which one of these following is an error reporting protocol?
A) ARP   B) ICMP   C) TCP   D) UDP

Answer: B. ICMP is an error reporting protocol.

Question 16: What are two forms of application layer software? (Choose two.)
A) applications   B) dialogs   C) requests   E) services   F) syntax

Answer: A and E.

Question 17: What is the purpose of resource records in DNS?
A) temporarily holds resolved entries
B) used by the server to resolve names
C) sent by the client to during a query
D) passes authentication information between the server and client

Answer: B.

Question 18: What three protocols operate at the Application layer of the OSI model? (Choose three.)
A) ARP   B) DNS   C) PPP   D) SMTP   E) POP   F) ICMP

Answer: B, D, and E.

Question 19: Which application layer protocols correctly match a corresponding function? (Choose two.)
    A) DNS dynamically allocates IP addresses to hosts
    B) HTTP transfers data from a web server to a client
    C) POP delivers email from the client to the server email server
    D) SMTP supports file sharing
    E) Telnet provides a virtual connection for remote access

Answer: B and E.

Question 20: As compared to SSH, what is the primary disadvantage of telnet?
    A) not widely available
    B) does not support encryption
    C) consumes more network bandwidth
    D) does not support authentication

Answer: B.

Question 21: What are three properties of peer-to-peer applications? (Choose three.)
    A) acts as both a client and server within the same communication
    B) requires centralized account administration
    C) hybrid mode includes a centralized directory of files
    D) can be used in client-server networks
    E) requires a direct physical connection between devices
    F) centralized authentication is required

Answer: A, C and D.

Question 22: Which email components are used to forward mail between servers? (Choose two.)
    A) MDA   B) IMAP   C) MTA   D) POP   E) SMTP   F) MUA

Answer: C and E.

Question 23: What application layer protocol describes the services that are used for file sharing in Microsoft networks?
    A) DHCP   B) DNS   C) SMB   D) SMTP   E) Telnet

Answer: C.

Question 24: Which statements are correct concerning the role of the MTA in handling email? (Choose three.)
    A) routes email to the MDA on other servers
    B) receives email from the client's MUA
    C) receives email via the POP3 protocol
    D) passes email to the MDA for final delivery
    E) uses SMTP to route email between servers
    F) delivers email to clients via the POP3 protocol

Answer: B, D, and E.

Question 25: How does the application layer on a server usually process multiple client request for services?
    A) ceases all connections to the service
    B) denies multiple connections to a single daemon
    C) suspends the current connection to allow the new connection

D) uses support from lower layer functions to distinguish between connections to the service

Answer: D.

Question 26: Which layer of the OSI model supplies services that allow user to interface with the network?

A) physical   B) session   C) network
D) presentation   E) application   F) transport

Answer: E.

Question 27: What is the automated service that matches resource names with the required IP address?

A) HTTP   B) SSH   C) FQDN   D) DNS   E) Telnet   F) SMTP

Answer: D.

Question 28: Which two protocols are used to control the transfer of web resources from a web server to a client browser? (Choose two.)

A) ASP   B) FTP   C) HTML   D) HTTP   E) HTTPS   F) IP

Answer: D and E.

Question 29: A layer-4 firewall (a device that can look at all protocol headers up to the transport layer) CANNOT

A) block HTTP traffic during 9:00PM and 5:00AM
B) block all ICMP traffic
C) stop incoming traffic from a specific IP address but allow outgoing traffic to same IP
D) block TCP traffic from a specific user on a specific IP address on multi-user system during 9:00PM and 5:00AM

Answer: A. HTTP is an application layer protocol. Since the given firewall is at layer 4, it cannot block HTTP data.

Question 30: Consider different activities related to email.

m1: Send an email from a mail client to a mail server
m2: Download an email from mailbox server to a mail client
m3: Checking email in a web browser

Which is the application level protocol used in each activity?

A) m1: HTTP   m2: SMTP   m3: POP
B) m1: SMTP   m2: FTP   m3: HTTP
C) m1: SMTP   m2: POP   m3: HTTP
D) m1: POP   m2: SMTP   m3: IMAP

Answer: C. Post Office Protocol (POP) is used by clients for receiving mails. Simple Mail Transfer Protocol (SMTP) is typically used by user clients for sending mails. Checking mails in web browser is a simple HTTP process.

Question 31: Which one of the following uses UDP as the transport protocol?

A) HTTP   B) Telnet   C) DNS   D) SMTP

Answer: C. HTTP and SMTP uses TCP to make calls. DNS which is used for mapping names to IP addresses uses UDP to make function calls.

Question 32: Match the following:

P. SMTP	1. Application layer
Q. BGP	2. Transport layer

R. TCP	3. Data link layer
S. PPP	4. Network layer
	5. Physical layer

A) P-2,Q-1,R-3,S-5   B) P-1,Q-4,R-2,S-3

C) P-1,Q-4,R-2,S-5   D) P-2,Q-4,R-1,S-3

Answer: B. SMTP (Simple mail transfer Protocol) is application layer based. BGP is network layer based. TCP (Transport Control Protocol) is transport layer based. PPP (Point to Point protocol).

Question 33: Why is it that an ICMP packet does not have source and destination port numbers?

Answer: The ICMP packet does not have source and destination port numbers because it was designed to communicate network-layer information between hosts and routers, not between application layer processes. Each ICMP packet has a "Type" and a "Code". The Type/Code combination identifies the specific message being received. Since the network software itself interprets all ICMP messages, no port numbers are needed to direct the ICMP message to an application layer process.

Question 34: Which layer in the Internet model is the user support layer?

Answer: Application layer

CHAPTER

Miscellaneous Concepts

17

17.1 How traceroute (or tracert) works?

Tracert (and ping) are both command line utilities that are built into Windows (traceroute and ping for Linux operating systems) computer systems. The basic tracert command syntax is "tracert hostname". For example, "tracert CareerMonk.com" and the output might look like:

```
1 51 ms 59 ms 49 ms 10.176.119.1
2 66 ms 50 ms 38 ms 172.31.242.57
3 54 ms 69 ms 60 ms 172.31.78.130
```

Discover the path: Tracert sends an ICMP echo packet, but it takes advantage of the fact that most Internet routers will send back an ICMP *'TTL expired in transit'* message if the TTL field is ever decremented to zero by a router. Using this knowledge, we can discover the path taken by IP Packets.

How tracert works: Tracert sends out an ICMP echo packet to the named host, but with a TTL of 1; then with a TTL of 2; then with a TTL of 3 and so on. Tracert will then get *'TTL expired in transit'* message back from routers until the destination host computer finally is reached and it responds with the standard ICMP *'echo reply'* packet.

Round Trip Times: Each millisecond (ms) time in the table is the round-trip time that it took (to send the ICMP packet and to get the ICMP reply packet). The faster (smaller) the times the better. *ms* times of 0 mean that the reply was faster than the computers timer of 10 milliseconds, so the time is actually somewhere between 0 and 10 milliseconds.

Packet Loss: Packet loss kills throughput. So, having no packet loss is critical to having a connection to the Internet that responds well. A slower connection with zero packet loss can easily outperform a faster connection with some packet loss. Also, packet loss on the last hop, the destination, is what is most important. Sometimes routers in-between will not send ICMP *'TTL expired in transit'* messages, causing what looks to be high packet loss at a particular hop, but all it means is that the particular router is not responding to ICMP echo.

17.2 How ping works?

The basic ping command syntax is *"ping hostname"*. For example, "ping visualroute.com" and the output might look like:

> Pinging careermonk.com [182.50.143.69] with 32 bytes of data:
> Reply from 182.50.143.69: bytes=32 time=130ms TTL=116
> Reply from 182.50.143.69: bytes=32 time=130ms TTL=116
> Reply from 182.50.143.69: bytes=32 time=137ms TTL=116

1. The source host generates an ICMP protocol data unit.
2. The ICMP PDU is encapsulated in an IP datagram, with the source and destination IP addresses in the IP header. At this point the datagram is most properly referred to as an ICMP ECHO datagram, but we will call it an IP datagram from here on since that's what it looks like to the networks it is sent over.
3. The source host notes the local time on its clock as it transmits the IP datagram towards the destination. Each host that receives the IP datagram checks the destination address to see if it matches their own address or is the all hosts address (all 1's in the host field of the IP address).
4. If the destination IP address in the IP datagram does not match the local host's address, the IP datagram is forwarded to the network where the IP address resides.
5. The destination host receives the IP datagram, finds a match between itself and the destination address in the IP datagram.
6. The destination host notes the ICMP ECHO information in the IP datagram performs any necessary work then destroys the original IP/ICMP ECHO datagram.
7. The destination host creates an ICMP ECHO REPLY, encapsulates it in an IP datagram placing its own IP address in the source IP address field, and the original sender's IP address in the destination field of the IP datagram.
8. The new IP datagram is routed back to the originator of the PING. The host receives it, notes the time on the clock and finally prints PING output information, including the elapsed time
9. The process above is repeated until all requested ICMP ECHO packets have been sent and their responses have been received or the default 2-second timeout expired. The default 2-second timeout is local to the host initiating the PING and is NOT the Time-To-Live value in the datagram.

17.3 What is QoS?

QoS (Quality of Service) refers to a broad collection of networking technologies and techniques. The goal of QoS is to provide guarantees on the ability of a network to deliver predictable results. Elements of network performance within the scope of QoS generally includes availability (uptime), bandwidth (throughput), latency (delay), and error rate.

QoS involves prioritization of network traffic. QoS can be targeted at a network interface, toward a given server or router's performance, or in terms of specific applications. A network monitoring system must typically be deployed as part of QoS, to insure that networks are performing at the desired level.

QoS is especially important for the new generation of Internet applications such as VoIP, video-on-demand and other consumer services. Some core networking technologies like Ethernet were not designed to support prioritized traffic or guaranteed performance levels, making it much more difficult to implement QoS solutions across the Internet.

17.4 Wireless Networking

17.4.1 What Is a Wireless Network?

A wireless local-area network (LAN) uses radio waves to connect devices such as laptops to the Internet and to your business network and its applications. When we connect a laptop to a WiFi hotspot at a cafe, hotel, airport lounge, or other public place, we are connecting to that business's wireless network.

17.4.2 Wireless Network versus Wired Network

A wired network connects devices to the Internet or other network using cables. The most common wired networks use cables connected to Ethernet ports on the network router on one end and to a computer or other device on the cable's opposite end.

In the past, some believed wired networks were faster and more secure than wireless networks. But continual enhancements to wireless networking standards and technologies have eroded those speed and security differences.

17.4.3 Advantages of Wireless Network

Wireless LANs offer the following productivity, convenience, and cost advantages over wired networks:

- *Mobility*: Wireless LAN systems can provide LAN users with access to real-time information anywhere in their organization. This mobility supports productivity and service opportunities not possible with wired networks.
  There are now thousands of universities, hotels and public places with public wireless connection. These free you from having to be at home or at work to access the Internet.
- *Installation Speed* and *Simplicity*: Installing a wireless LAN system can be fast and easy and can eliminate the need to pull cable through walls and ceilings.
- *Reduced Cost-of-Ownership*: While the initial investment required for wireless LAN hardware can be higher than the cost of wired LAN hardware, overall installation expenses and life-cycle costs can be significantly lower. Long-term cost benefits are greatest in dynamic environments requiring frequent moves and changes.
- *Scalability*: Wireless LAN systems can be configured in a variety of topologies to meet the needs of specific applications and installations. Configurations are easily changed and range from peer-to-peer networks suitable for a small number of users to full infrastructure networks of thousands of users that enable roaming over a broad area.

17.4.4 Disadvantages of Wireless Network

Despite these benefits, the wireless network is not without some problems, perhaps the most important:

- *Compatibility issues*: Products made by different companies may not be able to communicate with each other or we may need to extra effort to overcome these problems.
- Traditionally, the wireless networks are often slower than networks.
- Wireless networks the weakest in terms of privacy protection as any person within the scope of coverage of a wireless network can attempt to penetrate this network In order to solve this problem, there are several programs provide protection for wireless networks such as Equivalent Privacy wired networks Wired Equivalent Private (WAP), which did not provide adequate protection for wireless networks and the Wi-Fi Protected Access (WPA), which showed greater success in preventing breaches of its predecessor.

Problems and Questions with Answers

Question 1: Which one of the following is not a client-server application ?
    A) Internet chat   B) Web browsing   C) E-mail   D) Ping

Answer: D. Internet- Chat is maintained by chat servers, web browsing is sustained by web servers, E-mails are stored at mail servers, but ping is an utility which is used to identify connection between any two computer. One can be client, other can be client or server anything but aim is to identify whether connection exists or not between the two.

Question 2: What is the port number used by Ping command?

Answer: The answer is none. No ports required for Ping as it uses ICMP packets. The ICMP packet does not have source and destination port numbers because it was designed to communicate network-layer information between hosts and routers, not between application layer processes. Each ICMP packet has a "Type" and a "Code". The Type/Code combination identifies the specific message being received. Since the network software itself interprets all ICMP messages, no port numbers are needed to direct the ICMP message to an application layer process.

References

[1] W. Stallings. Local and Metropolitan Area Networks. Prentice Hall, Upper Saddle River, NJ, sixth edition, 2000.

[2] W. Stallings. Cryptography and Network Security. Prentice Hall, Upper Saddle River, NJ, third edition, 2003.

[3] W. Stallings. Data and Computer Communications. Prentice Hall, Upper Saddle River, NJ, eighth edition, 2007.

[4] A. S. Tanenbaum. Modern Operating Systems. Prentice Hall, Upper Saddle River, NJ, second edition, 2001.

[5] A. S. Tanenbaum. Computer Networks. Prentice Hall, Upper Saddle River, NJ, fourth edition, 2003.

[6] csee.usf.edu

[7] T. V. Lakshman and D. Stiliadis. "High-Speed Policy-Based Packet Forwarding Using Efficient Multidimensional Range Matching." Proceedings of the SIGCOMM '98 Symposium, pp. 203–214, September 1998.

[8] W. Leland, M. Taqqu, W. Willinger, and D. Wilson. "On the Self-Similar Nature of Ethernet Traffic." IEEE/ACM Transactions on Networking, 2:1–15, February 1994.

[9] J. Mashey. "RISC, MIPS, and the Motion of Complexity." UniForum 1986 Conference Proceedings, pp. 116–124, 1986.

[10] J.Mogul and S. Deering. "Path MTU Discovery." Request for Comments 1191, November 1990.

[11] cse.ohio-state.edu

[12] ee.ryerson.ca

[13] National Research Council, Computer Science and Telecommunications Board. Realizing the Information Future: The Internet and Beyond. National Academy Press, Washington, DC, 1994.

[14] National Research Council. Looking Over the Fence at Networks. National Academy Press, Washington DC, 2001.

[15] T. R. N. Rao and E. Fujiwara. Error-Control Coding for Computer Systems. Prentice Hall, Englewood Cliffs, NJ, 1989.

[16] K. Ramakrishnan, S. Floyd, and D. Black. "The Addition of Explicit Congestion Notification (ECN) to IP." Request for Comments 3168, September 2001.

[17] R. Rejaie, M.Handley, and D. Estrin. "RAP: An End-to-End Rate-Based Congestion ControlMechanism for Realtime Streams in the Internet." INFOCOM (3), pp. 1337–1345, 1999.

[18] D. Ritchie. "A Stream Input-Output System." AT&T Bell Laboratories Technical Journal, 63(8):311–324, October 1984.

[19] Y. Rekhter, T. Li, and S. Hares. "A Border Gateway Protocol 4 (BGP-4)." Request for Comments 4271, January 2006.

[20] T. G. Robertazzi, editor. Performance Evaluation of High-Speed Switching Fabrics and Networks: ATM, Broadband ISDN, and MAN Technology. IEEE Press, Piscataway, NJ, 1993.

Printed in Great Britain
by Amazon.co.uk, Ltd.,
Marston Gate.

0096b9214